David C. Cook
Bible Lesson
Commentary

The Essential Study Companion *for* Every Disciple

David C. Cook
Bible Lesson
Commentary

NIV

David C Cook®
transforming lives together

DAVID C. COOK NIV BIBLE LESSON COMMENTARY 2015–2016
Published by David C Cook
4050 Lee Vance View
Colorado Springs, CO 80918 U.S.A.

David C Cook Distribution Canada
55 Woodslee Avenue, Paris, Ontario, Canada N3L 3E5

David C Cook U.K., Kingsway Communications
Eastbourne, East Sussex BN23 6NT, England

The graphic circle C logo
is a registered trademark of David C Cook.

Lessons based on *International Sunday School Lessons: The International Bible Lessons for
Christian Teaching*, © 2012 by the Committee on the Uniform Series.

ISBN 978-1-4347-0870-0

© 2015 David C Cook

Researched, written, and edited by Dan Lioy, PhD
The Team: Catherine DeVries, Doug Schmidt, Amy Konyndyk, Channing Brooks,
Karen Athen
Cover Design: Nick Lee
Cover Photo: Shutterstock

Printed in the United States of America
First Edition 2015

1 2 3 4 5 6 7 8 9 10

030515

The Christian Community Comes Alive

Unit I: Seeds of New Growth

Unit II: A Bold Testimony

Unit III: Expansion of the Gospel

The Special Occasions

Unit I: What We Bring to God

Unit II: What We Encounter with God

Unit III: What We Commemorate with God

The Gift of Faith

The Journey to a New Way of Life

Index of Printed Scripture Texts

A Word to the Teacher

When I took my car to a gas station near the school where I teach, I was hoping that the mechanic could patch the leak in my tire for a few dollars. Later, however, he informed me that the tire could not be patched and I should replace it, since the tire could blow out on me while I was driving.

The mechanic promised that he could get an inexpensive new tire for me. After I briefly considered the hazards of the coming winter weather, I told the mechanic to go ahead and replace the tire. A few days later, I discovered I would have paid half as much had I purchased a new tire at most other places.

Too many people in our society do not put much value on their promises. Then, when promises get broken, people get hurt. In contrast, God takes the promises He has made in Scripture quite seriously. When He pledges something, we can be sure that He will do it.

A number of years ago, bestselling Christian author Elizabeth Sherrill received a handmade birthday card from a photographer friend. The card featured a color photo of the sun sending a crimson trail across a wave-swept beach. The flaming sunrise reminded Sherrill of God's faithfulness and promises. The sunrise pointed to the dawning of a new day. To Sherrill, God's salvation, peace, and righteousness send their beams of light across the whole earth.

Admittedly, not everyone can fall back on a dramatic experience of God's faithfulness. Nonetheless, all of us can take courage from accounts recorded in Scripture of how the Lord faithfully dealt with His people. For example, God promised Abraham that he would have innumerable descendants (see Gen. 13:16), and to this day God continues to faithfully fulfill that promise. The Gospels and Acts reveal that the Father has carried out His pledge through His Son, the Lord Jesus.

As we begin our journey through a new season of Sunday school teaching, we will learn that God keeps His promises to His people. The Lord's faithfulness takes a variety of forms, and all of them are designed to strengthen us in our daily walk with Him.

Sometimes what God has pledged to do is not necessarily what we want, but proves to be what we need. On other occasions, God's promises are what we have wanted for a long time. Regardless of the situation, we discover that God, according to His eternal plan, brings to pass what He has pledged to do.

May God richly bless you as you share the riches of His truth and grace with your students!

Your fellow learner at the feet of the Master Teacher,
Dan Lioy

Using the *David C. Cook NIV Bible Lesson Commentary* with Materials from Other Publishers

Sunday school materials from the following denominations and publishers follow International Sunday School Lesson outlines (sometimes known as Uniform Series). Because the *David C. Cook NIV Bible Lesson Commentary* (formerly *Peloubet's*) follows the same outlines, you can use the *Commentary* as an excellent teacher resource to supplement the materials from these publishing houses.

NONDENOMINATIONAL:

    Standard Publishing: *Adult*

    Urban Ministries

    Echoes Teacher's Commentary (David C Cook): *Adult*

DENOMINATIONAL:

    Advent Christian General Conference: *Adult*

    American Baptist (Judson Press): *Adult*

    United Holy Church of America: *Adult*

    Church of God in Christ (Church of God in Christ Publishing House): *Adult*

    Church of Christ Holiness: *Adult*

    Church of God (Warner Press): *Adult*

    Church of God by Faith: *Adult*

    National Baptist Convention of America (Boyd): *All ages*

    National Primitive Baptist Convention: *Adult*

    Progressive National Baptist Convention: *Adult*

    Presbyterian Church (U.S.A.) (Bible Discovery Series, Presbyterian Publishing House or P.R.E.M.): *Adult*

    Union Gospel Press: *All ages*

    United Holy Church of America: *Adult*

    United Methodist (Cokesbury): *All ages*

Praying for One Another

Scripture

Background Scripture: *Acts 4:1–31*

Scripture Lesson: *Acts 4:23–31*

Key Verse: After [the believers] prayed, the place where they were meeting was shaken. And they were all filled with the Holy Spirit and spoke the word of God boldly. *Acts 4:31*

Scripture Lesson for Children: *Acts 4:23–31*

Key Verse for Children: [The believers] were all filled with the Holy Spirit and spoke the word of God boldly. *Acts 4:31*

Lesson Aim

To rely upon the Spirit for courage in telling others about the Savior.

Lesson Setting

Time: A.D. *30*

Place: Jerusalem

Lesson Outline

Praying for One Another

I. Affirming God's Supreme Authority: Acts 4:23–28
  A. *Recounting What Happened: vs. 23*
  B. *Recognizing God's Sovereignty: vss. 24–28*

II. Asking God for Courage in Witnessing to Others: Acts 4:29–31
  A. *The Believers' Prayer for Boldness: vss. 29–30*
  B. *The Spirit's Provision of Boldness: vs. 31*

Introduction for Adults

Topic: *Be Bold*

Peter once had been terrified to be named as Jesus' companion. But after Pentecost, Peter and John boldly responded to the religious leaders by saying the two were Jesus' followers. The apostles also courageously proclaimed Jesus to be the Messiah whom God resurrected.

At the first International Congress on World Evangelization held in Lausanne, Switzerland, an evangelistic rally took place in a local stadium. Speakers from around the world told how Jesus Christ had changed their lives.

An Indian neurosurgeon of Hindu background recounted how the Lord had freed him from depression and guilt and given him joy in serving others. A Japanese evangelist, raised as a Buddhist, described the brokenness of his boyhood home and the emptiness of his life until he was a student in high school when he met a missionary who led him to Christ. An African bishop, born into a home where tribal gods were worshiped, declared how the forgiveness of Jesus had liberated him from the disease of hatred.

These are just a few examples of how Christians were bold in their witness and how the Lord used the sharing of the truth to powerfully change lives.

Introduction for Youth

Topic: *Help to Be Strong*

God used Peter and John to heal a crippled beggar at the Jerusalem temple. Then the Spirit enabled the apostles to proclaim the Gospel. Even when the temple authorities arrested Peter and John and interrogated them before the Sanhedrin, the apostles remained determined to tell others about Jesus.

It is not easy for many saved teens to tell their peers about the Lord. Believing adolescents run the risk of being rejected, shunned, or ostracized. These dire prospects can easily squelch the enthusiasm youth have for the things of Christ.

Praying with the teens in your class is one way to address this problem. Another way is to invite them to share their perspective on the challenges they face in witnessing for Christ. Finally, you can remind your students about the presence and power of the Spirit to work through them to impact their peers for the Savior.

Concepts for Children

Topic: *Shout out!*

1. God used Peter and John to heal a man.
2. Some religious leaders were mean to Peter and John for what they had done.
3. God gave Peter and John the courage to tell others about Jesus.
4. Peter, John, and their friends gave thanks to God.
5. We can praise God for the wonderful ways He works in our lives.

Lesson Commentary

I. Affirming God's Supreme Authority: Acts 4:23–28

A. Recounting What Happened: vs. 23

On their release, Peter and John went back to their own people and reported all that the chief priests and elders had said to them.

The Book of Acts picks up where the Gospels leave off by telling about the early days of the Christian church. Moreover, Acts bridges the gap between the Gospel accounts and the letters of instruction that compose most of the rest of the New Testament. In Acts we learn that, after Jesus returned to heaven, the church experienced significant growth. We also discover that Jesus did not leave His followers unprepared for the task at hand. He gave them the gift of the Holy Spirit, who filled them with supernatural power to do God's work.

A case in point would be the episode narrated in chapter 3 involving Peter and John at the Jerusalem temple. One day, the two apostles went to the sanctuary at three in the afternoon, which was the time of the evening sacrifice offered at the sanctuary. It may be that Peter and John were merely going to the temple to meet with other believers. However, Luke's description of them going to the sanctuary at a recognized prayer time is also confirmation of the apostles' continued adherence to the rituals and practices of Judaism. At this point in the life of the early church, Jesus' followers were not breaking away from or disassociating themselves from their Jewish faith.

As Peter and John entered the temple courts, they met a crippled man begging at the Beautiful Gate. This may have been the Gate of Nicanor, which led from the Court of the Gentiles into the Court of Women. This entrance was constructed of fine Corinthian brass and was adorned with much richer and thicker plates of gold than the other gates of the sanctuary. As the two apostles approached the crippled beggar, he asked them for money. Doing so was in keeping with what he had done over the course of his 40-year life (see 4:22).

When the lame man saw that he had gained the attention of the pair, he looked at them, expecting to receive a handout. Much to the beggar's surprise, however, Peter told him to walk (see 3:6). By mentioning the Lord's name, Peter clearly identified the divine source of power for the healing. In Hebrew thought, a person's name expressed the nature of one's being. The crippled man responded in faith by allowing Peter to help him up to his feet. At that moment, the beggar's feet and ankles gained strength and immediately he was able to walk. Not only did the Savior restore power to the beggar's legs, but also, in the same instant, Jesus provided the beggar with an innate understanding of how to walk.

The man responded by walking and leaping throughout the temple courts, all the while giving thanks to God (see vs. 8). This activity amazed onlookers, who were used to the familiar sight of the man begging at the Beautiful Gate. The former cripple also attracted a crowd. Peter took the opportunity to proclaim Jesus as the source of the miraculous healing and identify Him as the long-awaited Jewish Messiah. The apostle also called on the listeners to repent and put their faith in Jesus. Peter declared that Jesus was the ultimate fulfillment of the covenant God had established with Abraham. The apostle explained that even though the leaders had crucified Jesus, the Father stood ready to accept believing Jews as heirs to His promises in the new covenant He had established in His Son (see vss. 11–26).

Chapter 4 indicates that the healing of the lame man and subsequent preaching of Peter led to many new converts. According to verse 4, the total of those who believed grew to "about five thousand." Because this total only included men, the entire number of believers in Jerusalem was actually much higher than that by now. When women and children were included, the full number of believers was probably closer to 20,000. Against this backdrop, it is not surprising that the ensuing commotion caught the attention of the temple authorities, who intervened in the middle of Peter's message.

The Sadducees, who controlled the captain of the sanctuary police force, had political and theological reasons for intervening with Peter's preaching. The popularity of the apostles threatened the Sadducees' position and power. Also, they were annoyed with the apostles' preaching, for the leaders regarded any claim that someone had risen from the dead to be fraudulent (see 23:8). Even though the Sadducees had no legitimate grievance against Peter and John, the authorities still had them arrested and imprisoned until their case could be heard in the morning.

The temple gates closed at four in the afternoon. Also, established legal procedure required that court decisions involving life and death had to begin and conclude on the same day. Since it was already too close to evening, the apostles' case could not be adequately litigated before nightfall. For this reason, the Sanhedrin (the Jewish supreme court) would hear the case on the following day. When the council met, they questioned Peter about the source of power for the miracle. By this time, many people knew about the miracle. Furthermore, the members of the council could not deny what had happened, for the healed beggar was standing in their presence.

The Spirit empowered Peter to speak. He pointed to Jesus, the person whom the leaders had crucified and God raised from the dead, as the healer of the crippled beggar (see 4:5–12, 14, 16). The Sanhedrin regarded Peter and John as laypersons with no special training in the Scriptures (see vs. 13). For this reason, the members of the council were startled by the way in which the two apostles confidently and courageously held their ground, especially as the religious leaders interrogated them about their actions and claims concerning Jesus. The Sanhedrin noted that Peter and John had been with Jesus. The religious leaders may have recalled that even though Jesus did not receive any formal education, He also could not be matched in His handling of the Old Testament (see John 7:14–15).

The members of the council concluded that the only action they could take in this situation was to warn Peter and John not to speak or teach anymore in the name of Jesus. Of course, the two apostles realized that it was impossible for them to remain faithful in telling others about the Savior and heed the religious leaders' directive. Not surprisingly, Peter and John resolved that they would continue to proclaim what they had seen and heard (see Acts 4:18–20).

For the time being, the widespread knowledge and rejoicing over the healing of the crippled beggar kept the Sanhedrin from punishing the two apostles. To do otherwise risked starting a riot (see vs. 21). Once Peter and John were released, they rejoined their fellow believers. Undoubtedly, the disciples were overjoyed to see the two apostles. At some point, Peter and John reported every-thing that the high priests and elders had said to them (see vs. 23). The ensuing response of Jesus' followers was characterized by praise, song, and prayer.

B. Recognizing God's Sovereignty: vss. 24–28

When they heard this, they raised their voices together in prayer to God. "Sovereign Lord," they said, "you made the heaven and the earth and the sea, and everything in them. You spoke by the Holy Spirit through the mouth of your servant, our father David: 'Why do the nations rage and the peoples plot in vain? The kings of the earth take their stand and the rulers gather together against the Lord and against his Anointed One.' Indeed Herod and Pontius Pilate met together with the Gentiles and the people of Israel in this city to conspire against your holy servant Jesus, whom you anointed. They did what your power and will had decided beforehand should happen."

The believers were united in mind and heart as they lifted up their voices in prayer (see Acts 4:24). They acknowledged God to be the "sovereign Lord," that is, the all-powerful Ruler of the cosmos. Jesus' followers also affirmed God to be the Creator of the universe and everything it contains (see Exod. 20:11; Neh. 9:6; Ps. 146:6; Isa. 42:5). Psalm 104 affirms this truth by producing a magnifi-cent poetic and musical commentary on the creation. Even the structure of the psalm draws praise in that it is modeled quite closely on the day-by-day creation events recorded in Genesis 1. Indeed, as the psalmist described in grandiose detail the daily acts of creation, he seemed to preach in glowing terms that what God created on each day is reason enough to praise Him.

It's clear that the psalmist used the various stages of creation as his starting points for praise. Yet as he developed each creation-day theme, there is a con-stant anticipation for more, especially for the later days of the creation. For instance, as the poet sang of the glory of the Lord's creation, he exclaimed at "how many are [God's] works" (vs. 24). Whether it is the lights in the sky, the heavens and the waters, the land and vegetation, the sun, moon, and stars, the fish and birds, or the animals, people, and food to sustain them, the Lord in

His wisdom made them all. This sentiment reflects the mind-set of the Hebrew wisdom writers. They looked at the world with reverence because it reflected the glory of its Creator.

Jesus' disciples also affirmed the Creator as being in control of time and eternity. For instance, in Acts 4:25–26 they quoted the Septuagint version (or ancient Greek translation) of Psalm 2:1–2. The believers stated that long ago the Holy Spirit enabled King David, the ancestor of the Jews, to articulate truths having messianic importance. The poem seems to have been composed for a coronation ceremony for a monarch. Verses 1–3 set the scene against a backdrop of danger. The passage says that the rulers of nations under Israel's control were on the verge of rebelling against God and the king whom He placed over His people.

The preceding monarch is called the Lord's "anointed" (vs. 2; literally, "Messiah"), because anointing with olive oil was part of the enthronement ceremony. On the one hand, it's possible that a situation of danger actually existed at the coronation of one of Israel's kings. On the other hand, it may be that the psalmist was describing a hypothetical threat as a means of heightening the rhetorical impact his poem would have on his readers. In any case, Peter and John interpreted the passage in light of Jesus' life, death, and resurrection. Indeed, His followers made this passage a part of their prayer to God. They voiced the truth that the opposition they experienced from the religious establishment mirrored what they found in this psalm and anticipated its full and final fulfillment in the end times.

Under the Spirit's inspiration, David revealed that the unsaved people of the earth wasted their time concocting futile plans against God and His chosen Ruler. The most futile of all would be the adversaries' brazen attempt in the last days to assemble together in battle against the Father and His Son. Likewise, the early church recognized that the opposition they and their Savior experienced from the religious leaders of their day was a harbinger of more sinister times to come at the end of the age.

In particular, Jesus' followers noted how, in Jerusalem, Herod Antipas, Pontius Pilate, and the people of Israel united together against Jesus, God's holy Servant (see Luke 23:7–12; Acts 3:13). It was the Father's will to anoint His Son, whom He set apart to accomplish His redemptive purposes (see Acts 4:27). From a legal perspective, the crucifixion of the Messiah was a travesty of justice. Yet all the reprehensible acts the civil and religious leaders committed against Jesus were in accordance with the eternal will and plan of God (see Acts 4:28). In a sense, the Father had sovereignly determined beforehand that His Son would die on a cross and be raised from the dead.

II. Asking God for Courage in Witnessing to Others: Acts 4:29–31

A. The Believers' Prayer for Boldness: vss. 29–30

"Now, Lord, consider their threats and enable your servants to speak your word with great boldness. Stretch out your hand to heal and perform miraculous signs and wonders through the name of your holy servant Jesus."

Because Jesus' disciples recognized God's control over the unfolding chain of events, they shunned the temptation to seek relief from their trials or revenge on their antagonists. Instead, these believers asked the Lord to take notice of the threats their enemies made and give His bondservants the courage to proclaim His good news of redemption with boldness (see Acts 4:29). The early church also petitioned the Creator to complement their verbal witness with works of power.

In particular, Jesus' followers asked the Lord to extend His hand to heal as well as to bring about amazing "signs and wonders" (vs. 30). These were to be done in the name of Jesus, God's "holy servant." This last point indicates that the miracles were not to be performed as ends in themselves. Also, they were not to draw attention to the believers. Instead, the miracles were to spotlight the Messiah and the good news of His power to save the lost. In short, the early church asked God to use episodes of persecution to bring glory to Himself.

Once Jesus brings about real and lasting change in His followers, their lives will invariably run contrary to the direction of the world. Admittedly, when conflict arises, many believers are tempted to avoid it, especially by taking the path of least resistance. Yet, as verses 29 and 30 suggest, a changed life will eventually clash with the value system and priorities of Satan's kingdom. Persecution is inevitable in the lives of those who choose to follow the path of godliness (see John 15:20; Acts 14:22; 2 Tim. 3:12). After all, those who threaten the Devil's domain will gain his attention.

B. The Spirit's Provision of Boldness: vs. 31

After they prayed, the place where they were meeting was shaken. And they were all filled with the Holy Spirit and spoke the word of God boldly.

The petition made by Jesus' followers met with God's approval. This is evident from the divine response. The building where the disciples had gathered was shaken, perhaps due to a supernaturally caused, localized earthquake (see Acts 4:31). This phenomenon was a clear sign that the Lord was present and active among His people (see Exod. 19:18; Ps. 114:7; Isa. 6:4; Acts 16:26). In addition to this, Acts 4:31 says the believers were all filled with the Holy Spirit. This means He empowered them for effective service, and they in turn yielded fully to His control. For instance, they began to herald the divine message of salvation with boldness and courage. From this we see that the prayer uttered by the early church was answered immediately.

In Ephesians 5:18, Paul set up an interesting contrast to drunkenness. Instead of putting ourselves under the control of alcohol, we should put ourselves under the control of the Spirit. After all, only He can quench the needs that so many try to drown in alcohol. At salvation, we received the Spirit, and at different times in our Christian lives we can yield anew to the Spirit's control. People dependent on alcohol or drugs need to know about the superiority of spiritual filling over any artificial "high." Moreover, those who are filled with the Spirit desire to worship God and in this way bring glory to His name (see vss. 19–20).

Discussion Questions

1. Why had the religious authorities placed Peter and John under arrest?
2. What prompted Jesus' disciples to affirm God's supreme authority over creation?
3. What does it mean to be a bondservant of Jesus (see Acts 4:29)?
4. Why did the believers ask God to give them courage in witnessing to others?
5. How is it possible to offer praise to God in the midst of difficult circumstances?

Contemporary Application

One of the clearest evidences of the Spirit's work was the change in Jesus' disciples after His resurrection. Consider Peter. Because of his denial of Jesus before His crucifixion, we would hardly expect Peter to witness boldly in Jerusalem for the Savior. Yet, when challenged by the authorities, Peter unflinchingly stood tall for the Savior.

In addition to being courageous, the apostles resisted the temptation to take credit for the miraculous healing of the crippled man. Instead, Peter and John focused the people's attention on the Messiah and His power through the Spirit to bring about healing and wholeness to people.

The Spirit's power still changes lives. At times the power is evident in health situations where medical science has no explanation for the apparent healing. The Spirit's power also brings changes in behavior, turning around those who once lived selfishly, so that their lives now courageously focus on others.

Although many worldly forces are intent on removing the Savior from people's lives, they are feeble when they encounter His all-sufficient power. So we can rejoice, not only because His power is far greater than any earthly power, but also because His power enables us to be bold in our witness to others.

Sharing with One Another

Scripture

Background Scripture: *Acts 4:32—5:11*
Scripture Lesson: *Acts 4:34—5:10*
Key Verse: There were no needy persons among them. For from time to time those who owned lands or houses sold them, brought the money from the sales. *Acts 4:34*
Scripture Lesson for Children: *Acts 4:32–37*
Key Verse for Children: There were no needy persons among them. *Acts 4:34*

Lesson Aim

To develop a lifestyle of being generous to others.

Lesson Setting

Time: A.D. *30*
Place: Jerusalem

Lesson Outline

Sharing with One Another

   I. Believers Sharing Their Possessions: Acts 4:34–37
      A. *A Remarkable Display of Generosity: vss. 34–35*
      B. *An Exemplary Role Model: vss. 36–37*
  II. God's Judgment on Ananias and Sapphira: Acts 5:1–10
      A. *Peter Confronts Ananias: vss. 1–4*
      B. *God Caused Ananias to Die: vss. 5–6*
      C. *Peter Confronts Sapphira: vss. 7–9*
      D. *God Caused Sapphira to Die: vs. 10*

Introduction for Adults

Topic: *Being Generous*

Since the coming of the Holy Spirit at Pentecost, the Spirit indwells each believer. The Spirit's presence in the lives of the early Christians was demonstrated as they proclaimed the Gospel to the lost and shared their wealth with the needy.

Urban ministry can be pictured as a pot of steaming stew. If it is made of healthy, compatible ingredients, the supper served will be nutritious and palatable. If not, it can leave a bitter aftertaste—or worse, its foul smell can turn away the hungry.

The large city I live near has a program in which churches cooperate with one another to meet needs in the community. Some run soup kitchens. Others arrange housing for those who cannot find or afford it. Some concentrate their efforts on job training. Others offer child care programs. Some have ministries that target alcoholics, drug abusers, and prostitutes. The list runs on because the needs run on. With a concerted effort, help is consistently offered in the name of Christ.

Introduction for Youth

Topic: *Free to Share*

The early believers in Jerusalem worked hard at getting along. They chose to share what they had with others and make sure that the needs of the impoverished among them were met.

Saved young people are at a time in their lives when it can be difficult for them to think beyond themselves. And their self-focused concerns can distract them from noticing the concerns and needs of their fellow Christians. Believing teens also might not realize at times that they and other members of the church belong together in one united fellowship.

Imagine adolescents within a congregation working together with other church members to help people in need. Yet in order for this to happen, saved teens must set aside what they crave. By saying *yes* to the Spirit of God, young people have a wonderful opportunity to glorify the Lord and be a powerful witness to the lost.

Concepts for Children

Topic: *Let's Share*

1. In the early days of the church, believers got along with each other.
2. Believers also shared everything they had.
3. Barnabas is one believer who shared what he had with others.
4. Believers also told others about Jesus.
5. God can help us to share with others.

Lesson Commentary

I. BELIEVERS SHARING THEIR POSSESSIONS: ACTS 4:34–37

A. A Remarkable Display of Generosity: vss. 34–35

There were no needy persons among them. For from time to time those who owned lands or houses sold them, brought the money from the sales and put it at the apostles' feet, and it was distributed to anyone as he had need.

Last week, we learned that temple officials, in reaction to the public preaching of Peter and John, arrested them. During the trial, Peter boldly witnessed about Jesus' resurrection and the salvation He offers. The officials released the two apostles with a warning not to preach in Jesus' name anymore. After Peter and John rejoined the rest of Jesus' disciples, the group prayed in such a way as to express their trust in God's will, even when it included persecution. They asked God to give them boldness in preaching, and the attendees received a powerful new filling of the Holy Spirit (see Acts 4:1–31).

At this time, all those who trusted in the Lord Jesus were united in spirit and focused on the same goals. They desired to glorify the Lord by proclaiming the Gospel and encouraging one another in the faith. To that end, nobody claimed that their possessions were their own. Instead, Jesus' disciples shared everything they had with each other (see vs. 32). The sharing was strictly voluntary, and the believers were under no obligation to participate, as long as they were honest about their giving (see 5:1–10).

We also learn that the apostles gave powerful witness to the Son's resurrection (see 4:33). On the day of Pentecost, Peter proclaimed to a crowd of people that Jesus was risen from the dead, and the Lord used the apostle's testimony to bring many to a knowledge of the truth (see 2:14–41). That witness to the resurrection continued in the weeks and months that followed. In fact, the truth of the resurrection quickly became a central doctrine of the early church (see 1 Cor. 15:3–8). On the downside, the destitution of some believers in the church may have resulted from them being harassed and marginalized by those who were antagonistic to the preaching of the Gospel.

The grace and generosity of God was evident among Jesus' followers. No one went in need of anything, for those who owned property—whether plots of land or houses—sold it and brought the money to the apostles (see Acts 4:34). The leaders, in turn, distributed the money to those who needed it (see vs. 35). The mutual generosity of the believers ensured that those who were in need of essentials had those needs fully met (see 2:44–45). Jesus' followers recognized that one of their responsibilities was to help the impoverished in whatever way possible. By doing this, Christians gave evidence of the Spirit's presence in their lives and showed how He had transformed them from selfish individuals into members of a caring faith community.

Here we see that the first believers talked, prayed, and focused on all they had in union with the Savior. Later, Christians began drawing lines, by insisting that others agree on every fine point of their doctrine and shutting out those who would not see things their way. Once these relational walls went up and communication ceased, believers began to lose touch with one another. They allowed themselves to forget the important biblical truths and divine blessings they had in common. Today, believers can work to reverse that wall-building. We can open lines of communication, prayer, faith, and love, lay down our differences, and take up our commonalities in Jesus' name.

B.   An Exemplary Role Model: vss. 36–37

Joseph, a Levite from Cyprus, whom the apostles called Barnabas (which means Son of Encouragement), sold a field he owned and brought the money and put it at the apostles' feet.

"Joseph" (Acts 4:36) was especially known for his generosity. He was a Levite who came from Cyprus, a large island in the northeast corner of the Mediterranean. The apostles called him "Barnabas," which means "son of encouragement." As other portions of Acts reveal, he possessed exceptional spiritual qualities. For instance, the Spirit was in control of his life, and Barnabas had an unshakable confidence in God. Barnabas also had the understanding and affirming nature to build up others who were struggling in their Christian walk.

Barnabas was a Jew of the Dispersion (those scattered out of Israel's promised land). Most likely, Barnabas knew Greek and was familiar with both Hellenistic Judaism (practiced by Jews who spoke Greek and observed Greek culture) and Gentile life. His heritage as a Levite also meant he knew the Mosaic law. Though Levites traditionally lived off the temple system (see Num. 18:20; Deut. 10:9), Barnabas had real estate (possibly a farm). But on coming into the faith, he sold the property and donated the proceeds from the sale to the apostles for the care of the poor (see Acts 4:37). Later, Barnabas joined with Paul in refusing to make a living from the ministry of the Gospel (see 1 Cor. 9:6). Barnabas served as a good example of a Christian who freely gave to the needs of others.

People of the world struggle with selfishness and greed. When they see Christians sharing with one another and providing for those in need, it is a powerful testimony. It is also a strong indication that the Spirit is at work in our lives when we care enough to help one another. God can use such a positive witness—as exemplified in the life of an early believer such as Barnabas—to draw people to the saving message of the Gospel and faith in the Lord Jesus.

Some have wondered whether Barnabas' extraordinary display of generosity was some form of socialism. There are several reasons, though, why it was not. First, Jesus' disciples were not establishing an economic system, but rather simply responding to one another with gracious, Christlike compassion. Second, Scripture never mandated an equal distribution of goods, nor did it call for the elimination of property or ownership. Acts 4:32–37, along with 2:44–45, is a historical account, not a philosophical treatise. Expressed differently, these passages document the work of God in establishing and strengthening His blossoming church.

II. GOD'S JUDGMENT ON ANANIAS AND SAPPHIRA: ACTS 5:1–10

A. Peter Confronts Ananias: vss. 1–4

Now a man named Ananias, together with his wife Sapphira, also sold a piece of property. With his wife's full knowledge he kept back part of the money for himself, but brought the rest and put it at the apostles' feet. Then Peter said, "Ananias, how is it that Satan has so filled your heart that you have lied to the Holy Spirit and have kept for yourself some of the money you received for the land? Didn't it belong to you before it was sold? And after it was sold, wasn't the money at your disposal? What made you think of doing such a thing? You have not lied to men but to God."

Acts 5:1–10 contrasts the honest and heartfelt generosity demonstrated by Barnabas with the dishonest and self-serving actions of a married couple named Ananias (which means "the Lord is gracious") and Sapphira (which means "beautiful"). They lived in Jerusalem and were part of the congregation of believers in the city. This couple wanted others to think they were as generous and self-sacrificing as Barnabas.

Together, Ananias and Sapphira devised a plan in which they sold a parcel of their land and kept some of the proceeds for their private use. Even as they donated the remainder of the money to the apostles, they claimed their gift was the full amount of the sale price. Because they gave the false impression of being unsparingly generous, they were guilty of hypocrisy and financial fraud. In contrast, it was impossible for their Creator to act deceitfully (see Num. 23:19; Prov. 30:5; Titus 1:2; Heb. 6:18). The couple's transgressions threatened to dishonor the Savior and convey to unbelievers that His church did good works without regard for the truth of the Gospel and the needs of others.

Undoubtedly, the Spirit gave Peter (perhaps as the spokesperson for the rest of the apostles) the insight he needed to recognize what was taking place (see Acts 5:3). Peter's rhetorical questions implied that Ananias had allowed Satan to exercise control over his thoughts and actions. Ananias failed to recognize that the Devil was characterized by dishonesty (see John 8:44), sought to undermine the faith of believers (see Eph. 6:11), and preyed on unsuspecting Christians like a ravenous beast (see 1 Pet. 5:8).

Peter noted that when Ananias decided to withhold some of the proceeds he obtained from the sale of his property, he was not just lying to Jesus' followers, but also to the Holy Spirit (see Acts 5:3). The apostle clarified that Ananias maintained full control over the parcel before he sold it, and afterward he could have chosen to give away all the money he received from the transaction. Peter declared that Ananias allowed a Satan-inspired evil deed to arise in his heart, with the result that he lied more to the Creator than to anyone else (see vs. 4).

B. God Caused Ananias to Die: vss. 5–6

When Ananias heard this, he fell down and died. And great fear seized all who heard what had happened. Then the young men came forward, wrapped up his body, and carried him out and buried him.

The instant Peter's declaration reached the ears of Ananias, he collapsed and died (perhaps nearby a pile of donated silver or gold coins that had become the basis for his premeditated sin; Acts 5:5). Peter directed some younger believers in the church to wrap up the corpse in a sheet of cloth and remove it from the site. Then, despite the crime Ananias had committed, that same day he was given a decent burial in a tomb (see vs. 6). This action, which was in keeping with the Jewish custom in the first century A.D. (see Deut. 21:23), eliminated the disrepute of Ananias' crime from the church. Meanwhile, all who heard the sobering report of what had happened were overcome with fear. Acts 5:11 suggests this response was felt by both believers and unbelievers, perhaps resulting in the name of the Lord Jesus being respected and extolled (see 19:17). The implication is that the Savior was to be revered.

C. Peter Confronts Sapphira: vss. 7–9

About three hours later his wife came in, not knowing what had happened. Peter asked her, "Tell me, is this the price you and Ananias got for the land?" "Yes," she said, "that is the price." Peter said to her, "How could you agree to test the Spirit of the Lord? Look! The feet of the men who buried your husband are at the door, and they will carry you out also."

We learn in Acts 5:7 that for whatever reason, Sapphira was not present with Ananias when Peter confronted him. Also, Sapphira did not know that God had already taken Ananias' life in judgment for his transgression. Three hours later, Sapphira met with Peter. This was an opportunity for Sapphira to tell the truth to Peter and to distance herself from her husband's trespass. Yet, when Peter asked Sapphira to confirm the amount Ananias claimed the couple received for the sale of their property, Sapphira was unequivocal in affirming the alleged proceeds (see vs. 8). In doing so, she showed she was complicit with Ananias in trying to deceive the apostles and lying to the Holy Spirit.

Peter's rhetorical question challenged Sapphira's decision to join her husband in putting the Spirit to the "test" (see vs. 9). The underlying Greek verb means to "evaluate" or "examine." Its usage here implies the couple had flouted the Lord's authority and questioned His resolve to preserve the integrity and honor of the church. Tragically, Ananias and Sapphira had deceived themselves into thinking they could somehow outsmart the all-powerful and all-knowing Creator of the universe. Ultimately, though, their gamble proved to be fatal, for just as the Spirit took the life of Ananias, so too, He caused Sapphira to die on the spot. The same believers who had removed and buried Ananias' corpse were about to do the same thing with Sapphira's body.

Psalm 95:7–11 discloses the grim consequences an entire generation of Israelites experienced for putting God to the test during their long sojourn in the wilderness. Because they hardened their hearts, tried to put themselves above the Lord, and repeatedly defied His will, He prevented them from entering Canaan by consigning them to die in the Sinai desert. Likewise, Hebrews 3:7—4:13 reveals that rebelling against the leading of our Shepherd brings frustration, dissatisfaction, and sadness into our lives.

The deity of the Holy Spirit and the doctrine of the Trinity are both affirmed in Acts 5:1–9. For example, Peter declared to Ananias that he had lied to the Spirit (see vs. 3) and to God (see vs. 4). The apostle then told Sapphira that she had tested the "Spirit of the Lord" (vs. 9). From this we see that lying to the Spirit is the same as lying to triune God, for the Spirit is the third person of the Trinity. Moreover, the Gospels reveal that Jesus sent the Spirit to live in us and give us the ability to do God's will. Without the Spirit, we would have to fight Satan and resist temptation in our own strength—which would be impossible for us to do (see Eph. 6:12). Only the Spirit can give us the ability to do what is right and avoid doing what is wrong.

D. God Caused Sapphira to Die: vs. 10

At that moment she fell down at his feet and died. Then the young men came in and, finding her dead, carried her out and buried her beside her husband.

Just as the Spirit had declared through Peter, Sapphira immediately collapsed in front of the apostle and died. Next, Peter summoned the same group of younger believers to enter the premises. In turn, they found Sapphira's corpse, lifted it up, removed it, and placed it in the tomb where her husband's body lay (see Acts 5:10). In both instances, God showed His impartiality in dealing justly and forthrightly with sin among His people. As noted earlier, the somber news of what happened to this greedy couple filled the entire congregation in Jerusalem with "great fear" (vs. 11). Even those outside the church, when they heard what had happened, were filled with alarm. In this way, the name of the Lord was honored and the integrity of His church was affirmed.

Proverbs 1:7 reveals that a reverent fear of God is the starting point of all biblical wisdom. This respect for the Lord is what sets apart prudence of Scripture from all its worldly counterparts. This foundational truth is repeated throughout the wisdom literature of the Bible (see Job 28:28; Ps. 111:10; Prov. 9:10; 15:33; Eccl. 12:13). It is clarifying to note that on the one hand, fearing God is not an irrational feeling of dread or impending doom. Yet, on the other hand, it is more than courteous reverence. Scripture teaches that fearing God is characterized by a deep awareness of His sovereignty and power. The Lord is to be revered in awe and obeyed unconditionally.

Discussion Questions

1. What does it mean for believers today to be united in heart and mind?
2. What are some ways that believers can strive to be as encouraging and unselfish as was Barnabas?
3. Why do you think Ananias and Sapphira thought they could get away with their fraudulent decision?
4. What does it mean to fear the Lord?
5. How can believers avoid putting God to the test?

Contemporary Application

The presence of the Spirit in the lives of the early Christians was demonstrated as they preached the Gospel to the lost and shared their wealth with the needy. Barnabas was a premier example of such generosity. Oppositely, Ananias and Sapphira proved to be the epitome of selfishness and greed.

At the moment of our conversion, God's Spirit takes up residence within us and empowers us to obey the Savior. This truth is important to remember, for we face a daily struggle with sinful habits and ungodly temptations. When we yield our lives to the Spirit's control, we are transformed from being self-centered to showing a genuine concern for others around us.

In order to meet the needs of others, we must say *no* to some of our desires. This is often difficult to do in a materialistic, self-centered culture. If we succumb to the temptation to try to be powerful, wealthy, or famous, we will think more of ourselves than we do of others, and we will miss the many opportunities that exist in our lives to minister to others in the Spirit's power.

Each of us, as a believer, has received at least one special ability, which the Spirit has graciously given us so that we can serve one another (see 1 Pet. 4:10). We should never forget that what the Spirit gives us, He intends for us to use. In fact, the Spirit displays His power in us when we minister, through our God-given gifts, to one another.

There are countless ways the Spirit enables us to help others. For example, if someone needs a word of encouragement, the Spirit will give us the wisdom to know how to say it. If people are in financial difficulty, the Spirit will give us the desire to help them in whatever way we can.

As members of God's family, we have a responsibility to reach out to others who are struggling. We may be tempted to think only of ourselves, but we must look beyond our own lives to the circumstances of others. When the Spirit is powerfully at work in our lives, we will be able to do far more for others than we ever imagined possible.

Witnessing to God's Truth

Scripture

Background Scripture: *Acts 5:12–42*

Scripture Lesson: *Acts 5:27–29, 33–42*

Key Verse: Peter and the other apostles replied: "We must obey God rather than men!" *Acts 5:29*

Scripture Lesson for Children: *Acts 5:27–29, 33–42*

Key Verse for Children: [The apostles] never stopped teaching and proclaiming the good news that Jesus is the Christ. *Acts 5:42*

Lesson Aim

To remain obedient to God regardless of the pressure to compromise one's faith.

Lesson Setting

Time: A.D. *30*
Place: Jerusalem

Lesson Outline

Witnessing to God's Truth

    I. The Resolve of the Apostles: Acts 5:27–29
        A. *The Pressure to Compromise: vss. 27–28*
        B. *The Decision to Obey God: vs. 29*
    II. The Tenacity of the Apostles: Acts 5:33–42
        A. *The Advice Offered by Gamaliel: vss. 33–39*
        B. *The Joy and Devotion of the Apostles: vss. 40–43*

Introduction for Adults

Topic: *Speak Out*

The apostles knew they had a choice, but they did not hesitate to make the right decision. They chose to obey God's command to tell others about Jesus (see Acts 5:29).

Adults in your class probably consider themselves law-abiding citizens. It would be extremely difficult for them not to conform to the laws and regulations of society. They may fudge here and there, such as driving five miles over the speed limit, but they wouldn't flagrantly disregard the laws of the land, such as driving through red lights.

At times, however, your students are faced with situations in which they must obey God or submit to an authority that challenges their commitment to Christ. When that occurs, they need to understand that they should set aside their desire to be "good" citizens, "good" employees, "good" adult children, or even "good" spouses if they are to be obedient children of God. This is neither easy nor pleasant, but with the Spirit's help it can be done.

Introduction for Youth

Topic: *Empowered to Speak*

Occasionally the Christian young people in your class will feel pressured to please others as much as they can. But there are times when doing this means disobeying the Lord. It's in those moments when they have to say to their peers (for example), "I must obey God above all other human authority." (This is similar to what Peter declared in Acts 5:29.)

These are powerful words! Admittedly, they are difficult for your students to say in the moment of testing, for they have learned not to upset others. Nevertheless, part of growing in faith is gaining courage to say clearly what they believe about Jesus and behaving in the way He expects.

When Christian young people must explain why they don't engage in sinful practices, the Spirit can give them wisdom and courage. Retreat doesn't have to be an option, for Jesus said, "Take heart! I have overcome the world" (John 16:33).

Concepts for Children

Topic: *Don't Stop Now!*

1. Jesus' followers were telling others about Him.
2. A group of angry leaders told Jesus' followers to stop what they were doing.
3. The leaders punished Jesus' followers.
4. Jesus' followers knew God wanted them to continue what they were doing.
5. God also wants us to tell others about Jesus.

Lesson Commentary

I. THE RESOLVE OF THE APOSTLES: ACTS 5:27–29

A. The Pressure to Compromise: vss. 27–28

Having brought the apostles, they made them appear before the Sanhedrin to be questioned by the high priest. "We gave you strict orders not to teach in this name," he said. "Yet you have filled Jerusalem with your teaching and are determined to make us guilty of this man's blood."

There is little doubt the Spirit empowered the early church to be faithful and effective in proclaiming Jesus as the promised Messiah. Despite intensified opposition from those who were antagonistic to the Gospel, Jesus' disciples remained undaunted in heralding His death as the sacrifice for sins and His resurrection as proof He is the Son of God. Even though some rejected the Good News, many others were convinced. As the apostles spoke with authority, God backed up their message with powerful miracles (including healings and exorcisms), which were signs pointing people to trust in Jesus (see Acts 5:12).

Verse 13 indicates that there was an outer circle of unresponsive people who kept their distance from the believers. Possibly some individuals were fearful due to what had happened to Ananias and Sapphira. Or perhaps this group was afraid of what the religious leaders in Jerusalem might do to those who became Jesus' followers. Admittedly, conditions were not ideal for church growth. For instance, the authorities had already shown hostility toward the apostles. None of these developments, though, prevented increasing numbers of men and women from trusting in the Savior (see vs. 14). These new converts were convinced that Jesus is Lord, and their commitment to Him was resolute.

So the authorities' threats could not stop people from believing. Indeed, the influence of the church in Jerusalem continued to grow daily. As more and more believed and shared the truth of the Gospel, even the residents of the surrounding towns of Judea heard the Good News. In turn, people flocked to Jerusalem, bringing the sick to be healed. Verses 15 and 16 indicate that the streets Peter traveled became filled with people who hoped at least to have his shadow fall on them so they could be cured of their maladies (see Mark 6:56; Acts 19:12). Those tormented by evil spirits (or demons) were set free by God's power.

The high priest and his Sadducean officials, who dominated the Sanhedrin, became alarmed by what they heard was taking place (see Acts 5:17). In their view, the Christian movement was becoming difficult to contain and control. The religious leaders believed the apostles were turning the people against the Sadducees as their rightful leaders. Also, with each new addition to the church, the Sadducees felt their own influence weakening. For them, more than theological issues were at stake. While messianic claims and talk of resurrection were serious matters, equally important to these officials was politics, especially in connection with the Roman government, which granted the high priest his position.

Consequently, the religious leaders arrested the apostles and put them in a public jail, with the intent of holding a hearing the next day (see vs. 18). However, God had a plan of His own. During the night, He sent an angel, who freed them from their ropes or chains, opened the doors of the prison, and released the apostles (see vs. 19). The angel also directed the apostles to continue to proclaim the Good News about Jesus, even in the temple courts (see vs. 20). The implication is that despite the pressure the apostles felt to compromise their faith, they were to remain obedient to God. So at dawn, when worshipers typically gathered at the temple courts for morning sacrifices, the apostles reentered the area and resumed their teaching (see vs. 21).

Meanwhile, the high priest assembled a meeting of the entire Sanhedrin. This judicial body was composed of religious leaders, mostly upper class Sadducees. Following Moses' pattern in choosing (see Num. 11:16), the Sanhedrin had 70 members, or 71 with the presiding high priest. When the group convened, the members sat in a semicircle with two clerks, one to record votes for condemnation of the person on trial and one to record votes for acquittal. Also seated in the chamber were disciples of the learned rabbis on the court. A simple majority was needed for acquittals, but condemnation took at least a two-thirds majority. Understandably, it could be quite frightening to be on trial before these powerful officials.

That day, when the council members sent for their prisoners, the apostles were missing (see Acts 5:22–24). Then came news from the temple courts that the apostles not only had somehow escaped but also had returned to the scene of the crime (as the members of the Sanhedrin perceived it; see vs. 25). The apostles continued to teach about Jesus, even though they knew their actions would cause trouble. The commander of the Jewish soldiers guarding the temple took his officers and retrieved the prisoners, taking care to keep the situation as calm as possible (see vs. 26). The crowds were solidly behind the apostles, which created a dangerous situation for the religious leaders. Nonetheless, the apostles willingly cooperated by returning with the officers to appear before the Sanhedrin.

Caiaphas, with the whole Sanhedrin behind him, interrogated the apostles (see vs. 27). The high priest, undoubtedly filled with indignation, reminded the apostles of the council's previous warning not to teach in Jesus' name (see vs. 28; 4:18). The words of Caiaphas indicated that neither he nor the rest of the Sanhedrin had any interest in determining the truth of the apostles' message. The religious leaders only wanted to protect their authority and maintain their control over the people. In fact, the apostles had been so zealous in their preaching that it was as if all of Jerusalem, like a basin, had been inundated with talk about Jesus. In short, the good news about the Messiah was getting out.

The members of the Sanhedrin were particularly upset that the apostles had accused them of being responsible for "this man's blood" (5:28). The latter was a Jewish idiom that meant the religious leaders were culpable for Jesus' death on the cross (see Matt. 23:35; 27:25). Evidently, the high priest did not even want to say Jesus' name. Previously, it had been Jesus who had upset the members of the council with His accusations. Now the situation had grown worse for the members of the Jewish Supreme Court, because the apostles had publicly denounced them for unjustly crucifying Jesus.

B. The Decision to Obey God: vs. 29

Peter and the other apostles replied: "We must obey God rather than men!"

Peter and the rest of the apostles did not hold back in their response. In fact, it appeared from their reply that they were the prosecutors and the Sanhedrin was on trial. To some, the apostles' boldness might seem unwise, but from God's perspective it indicated great valor. To appreciate the bravery of the apostles, we have to consider the situation facing them. They stood before a hostile, self-serving court that was hardly concerned about justice. Also, the apostles faced stiff cross-examination without the benefit of legal counsel or protection from a Bill of Rights.

The apostles knew what was at stake. The Sanhedrin could demand that Jesus' followers be executed, just as they had ruled that Jesus be crucified. Be that as it may, the apostles recognized that something even greater was at stake. As God's stewards, they had been entrusted with the divine message that the Father, through the Son, was reconciling the world to Himself (see 2 Cor. 5:19). For this reason, the apostles considered their lives secondary in importance to their message. Accordingly, they dared to stand before the stern judges and proclaim that in this matter it was a moral necessity for them to "obey God" (Acts 5:29), rather than people. The council may have had some influence and authority, but the Creator, who had commissioned the apostles, had supreme authority over the universe.

The apostles mustered the courage to face opposition because the Spirit's power was active within them. The Spirit enabled them to recognize and accept the truth about Jesus of Nazareth. In particular, Peter presented the heart of the apostolic message, contrasting Jesus' harsh treatment by the council with His exaltation to the place of highest honor at God's right hand (see vss. 30–31). Contrary to the words of the high priest (see vs. 28), the Sanhedrin did have a role in bringing shame and disgrace upon the Messiah (see vs. 30; Deut. 21:22–23). More generally, the apostles could not help but continue proclaiming their message. They had witnessed Jesus' life, teaching, death, and resurrection. Also, the Spirit prompted them, by bearing witness inside them, to teach that Jesus was indeed the Jewish Messiah and Savior of the world (see Acts 5:31–32).

II. THE TENACITY OF THE APOSTLES: ACTS 5:33–42

A. The Advice Offered by Gamaliel: vss. 33–39

When they heard this, they were furious and wanted to put them to death. But a Pharisee named Gamaliel, a teacher of the law, who was honored by all the people, stood up in the Sanhedrin and ordered that the men be put outside for a little while. Then he addressed them: "Men of Israel, consider carefully what you intend to do to these men. Some time ago Theudas appeared, claiming to be somebody, and about four hundred men rallied to him. He was killed, all his followers were dispersed, and it all came to nothing. After him, Judas the Galilean appeared in the days of the census and led a band of people in revolt. He too was killed, and all his followers were scattered. Therefore, in the present case I advise you: Leave these men alone! Let them go! For if their purpose or activity is of human origin, it will fail. But if it is from God, you will not be able to stop these men; you will only find yourselves fighting against God."

Peter's bold accusations left the members of the Sanhedrin "furious" (Acts 5:33). The underlying Greek verb literally means "to be cut to the heart." In essence, the effect of the apostles' accusation, as voiced by Peter, was like a chain saw on a pile of wood. Indeed, the religious leaders were so enraged that they demanded the apostles be executed (possibly by stoning; see 7:54–60) for what the officials regarded as an outrageous contempt for the Jewish Supreme Court. The apostles would have received the death sentence if it had not been for one moderate voice, namely, that of a respected scribe and Pharisee of the time named Gamaliel (see 5:34).

Gamaliel is reported to have been the grandson of the renowned Jewish rabbi, Hillel, who was the founder of a liberal school of interpretation. Theologically, Gamaliel followed in his grandfather's footsteps. Gamaliel was well known for his learning and piety. He was the first of seven rabbis to be given the title Rabban (see John 20:16), which means "our rabbi." History's record of Gamaliel's cautious, tolerant character fits perfectly with Luke's description of him in Acts. Paul stated that he studied under Gamaliel (see Acts 22:3). Even though Paul later rejected Gamaliel's belief in salvation through the performance of good works, the apostle benefitted from Gamaliel's teaching.

During the meeting of the Sanhedrin involving the apostles, Gamaliel stood up and requested that the accused be removed from the chamber so he could speak openly before his peers (see Acts 5:34). He warned them not to do anything rash (see vs. 35). He expressed the general teaching of the Pharisees that God was in control and did not need help from them to fulfill His purpose in the matter involving the apostles. He reminded the council of other insurrectionist movements that had enjoyed popularity for a short time and then died out after the death of their respective leaders.

Gamaliel referred to two uprisings, namely, those of Theudas and Judas the Galilean (see vss. 36–37). The first example probably occurred about 4 B.C., while the second took place in A.D. 6. Theudas alleged to be someone of importance (that is, a messianic figure) and convinced 400 men to join him in guerrilla warfare. But then the Romans executed Theudas, scattered his freedom fighters, and caused the movement he led to implode. Later, Judas the Galilean claimed to be the anointed leader of the Jewish nation and convinced a group of people to rise up against Roman rule. (The census mentioned here was different from the registration taken around the time of Jesus' birth; see Luke 2:1.) Yet again, the Romans killed Judas the Galilean and put his supporters to flight.

Gamaliel implied that, like these rebel causes, the aspirations and undertakings of the one associated with Jesus of Nazareth would probably be overthrown soon and then die out. After all, its leader perished at the hands of the Romans (see Acts 5:38). Gamaliel also noted there was a remote possibility that God had ordained this movement. If that was the case, nothing could stop it. Worse, the Sanhedrin would find itself in the awkward position of opposing God (see vs. 39).

B. The Joy and Devotion of the Apostles: vss. 40–43

His speech persuaded them. They called the apostles in and had them flogged. Then they ordered them not to speak in the name of Jesus, and let them go. The apostles left the Sanhedrin, rejoicing because they had been counted worthy of suffering disgrace for the Name. Day after day, in the temple courts and from house to house, they never stopped teaching and proclaiming the good news that Jesus is the Christ.

Thankfully, Gamaliel's advice convinced the members of the Sanhedrin to take a moderated approach. Instead of executing the apostles, the council decided to have them "flogged" (Acts 5:40). This was often carried out in front of the judges themselves, who had pronounced the sentence. Given the severity of the apostles' crime, the flogging the Sanhedrin ordered could have been the 40 lashes specified in the Mosaic law (see Deut. 25:1–3). The Pharisees on the council were probably the first to go along with the advice of their esteemed colleague. The Sadducees, though not a majority on the Jewish Supreme Court, could not proceed without the support of the Pharisees, who enjoyed the popular support of the people.

Even though the law specified 40 lashes, for lesser crimes the rabbis reduced the number to 39. This decision was to prevent someone from accidentally exceeding the limit and thereby breaking the law (see 2 Cor. 11:24). Also, while the Jewish regulations were more humane than those enacted by the Romans, people did sometimes die from 39 lashes with a three-stranded whip (especially when the leather cords were embedded with pieces of metal or bone to tear away skin). The victim received a series of alternating blows—two delivered to the back, followed by one to the chest—until the cycle was completed. Even a healthy person could be left in agony for days. While this was a lesser penalty than the Sadducees originally demanded, it was still a severe punishment.

Despite being brutally beaten, the apostles were overjoyed because God considered them worthy to suffer for the sake of the Messiah (see Acts 5:41). This is because the apostles regarded themselves as suffering for Jesus in the same way that He had suffered (see Mark 15:15). Before His crucifixion, Jesus told His followers to expect suffering, and now His words were being fulfilled (see Matt. 10:17–22; Mark 13:9–13; Luke 12:11–12; 21:12–19; John 15:18–25; 16:1–3, 33). In short, the apostles considered the trauma they endured as a badge of honor, rather than a sign of disgrace.

It seems a paradox to say that someone is "worthy" (Acts 5:41) of dishonor, as well as to find joy in pain. Yet Jesus' disciples were living paradoxes. That being so, after the warnings and the beatings, the apostles continued to proclaim the Gospel. They boldly told others about Jesus, regardless of whether the people they encountered were in the courts of the Jerusalem temple or in their private homes (see vss. 42–43). In this regard, the apostles demonstrated their firm conviction that they needed to heed the Lord rather than the Sanhedrin. According to Acts 6:1, the apostles' obedience led to further growth in the church.

Discussion Questions

1. From the high priest's remarks, what do we learn about his attitude toward the apostles?
2. What was the nature of Gamaliel's advice to the Sanhedrin?
3. Why did the apostles insist on telling others about Jesus?
4. What challenges do you face in choosing to remain obedient to God?
5. What advice would you give to other believers who feel pressured to compromise their faith?

Contemporary Application

The apostles' bold stand in the presence of the Sanhedrin can serve as a model for us when we are opposed by evil. There can be no compromise. If following certain people prevents us from serving the Lord, we must obey Him rather than those people.

The issue goes far beyond mere legal matters. Many "laws" are unwritten—cultural expectations, prevailing attitudes in society, pressure from peers, the influence of traditions, and so on. All of these weigh heavily upon believers, who must choose between the ways of people and the ways of God. When the ways of people are morally neutral, there's no problem. But when they violate God's principles, a choice is required.

To choose for God in the face of popular opinion requires great courage. Like the apostles, this is why we need the indwelling power of the Spirit. This is also why we, like the apostles, need to be absolutely convinced about the reality of the resurrection. This includes affirming that Jesus is alive and lives in us.

We may never stand before a legal body like the Sanhedrin. But every day we face other kinds of challenges to our faith. And every day we need the same courage and conviction that motivated the apostles.

Recalling God's Fidelity

Scripture

Background Scripture: *Acts 7:1–53*
Scripture Lesson: *Acts 7:2–4, 8–10, 17, 33–34, 45–47, 53*
Key Verse: Stephen, full of the Holy Spirit, looked up to heaven and saw the glory of God, and Jesus standing at the right hand of God. *Acts 7:55*
Scripture Lesson for Children: *Acts 7:2–4, 8–10, 17, 33–34, 45–47, 53*
Key Verse for Children: "You who have received the law that was put into effect through angels but have not obeyed it." *Acts 7:53*

Lesson Aim

To recognize that the world still opposes Spirit-filled believers.

Lesson Setting

Time: A.D. *30*
Place: Jerusalem

Lesson Outline

Recalling God's Fidelity

  I. Abraham and Joseph: Acts 7:2–4, 8–10
    A. *God's Appearance to Abraham: vss. 2–4*
    B. *God's Presence with Joseph: vss. 8–10*
  II. Moses, the Tabernacle, and the Temple:
    Acts 7:17, 33–34, 45–47, 53
    A. *The Increase in the Israelite Population: vs. 17*
    B. *The Lord's Announcement to Moses: vss. 33–34*
    C. *The Lord's Abiding Presence Among His People:*
      vss. 45–47
    D. *The Israelites' Disobedience: vs. 53*

Introduction for Adults

Topic: *Stand Firm*

Organizations in the West can be very competitive. This is evident from the sports teams that dominate athletics and the fierce rivalry that exists among businesses. Even the entertainment industry is marked by ruthless self-interest.

Individuals are also competitive. Students try to outdo their peers in terms of grades. Employees do whatever they can to climb to the top of their professions. Many people want to drive a better car and own a nicer home than their neighbors.

Being a faithful servant is a revolutionary concept to adults who are highly competitive. When you put the interests of others first, as Stephen did, you're not thinking about eliminating them to get to the top. Instead, you're cultivating relationships and showing love, even if it demands personal sacrifice. Isn't this what being a Christian is really all about?

Introduction for Youth

Topic: *Stand and Speak Up*

For hundreds of years, the Auca Indians had brutally attacked all strangers who ventured into their forests. Yet this knowledge didn't dissuade five young missionaries from penetrating the Ecuadorian jungles with the Gospel. On Sunday, January 8, 1956, Nate Saint, Jim Elliot, Pete Fleming, Roger Youderian, and Ed McCully died at the hands of the Auca Indians.

As with the stoning of Stephen in A.D. 35 (see Acts 7:60), could God have intervened to save these missionaries? Although in either case the Lord could have, He chose not to do so. In Stephen's case, God used his death to bring about the spread of the Gospel (see 8:1). The same holds true for the martyrdom of the five young missionaries.

In the aftermath of the preceding tragedy, God opened the way for Betty Elliot and her daughter and Nate Saint's sister, Rachel, to live among the same Indians who had killed their loved ones. Nate Saint's brother, Phil, later joined his sister in her efforts to evangelize the Auca Indians. By 1972, 75 Aucas had put their faith in the Lord Jesus!

Concepts for Children

Topic: *Stephen Faces Death*

1. Stephen told some leaders he was serving Jesus.
2. Stephen said the leaders were wrong for not believing in Jesus.
3. The leaders were angry when they heard what Stephen said.
4. Jesus helped Stephen accept a hard situation.
5. Jesus is always with us, no matter what we are going through.

Lesson Commentary

I. ABRAHAM AND JOSEPH: ACTS 7:2–4, 8–10

A. God's Appearance to Abraham: vss. 2–4

To this he replied: "Brothers and fathers, listen to me! The God of glory appeared to our father Abraham while he was still in Mesopotamia, before he lived in Haran. 'Leave your country and your people,' God said, 'and go to the land I will show you.' So he left the land of the Chaldeans and settled in Haran. After the death of his father, God sent him to this land where you are now living."

Through God's grace and power, Stephen became an acclaimed miracle worker (see Acts 6:8), evangelist (see vs. 10), and the first believer recorded in Acts to give his life for the cause of Christ (see 7:60). One group of freed Jewish slaves told the Sanhedrin that Stephen was preaching against the authority of the Mosaic law, the sacredness of the promised land, and the supremacy of the Jerusalem temple (see 6:8–11). This led to Stephen's arrest and appearance before the Sanhedrin to answer the charges brought against him (see vss. 12–15). In his formal response, Stephen followed Hebrew custom by surveying the history of Israel. He did so to emphasize that Jesus of Nazareth was Israel's promised Messiah and Redeemer.

As Stephen stood in the presence of the Sanhedrin, his countenance seemed like that of an angel (namely, a heavenly-sent messenger). One can only imagine how Caiaphas, the high priest, felt as he directed Stephen to respond to the accusations made against him (see 7:1). Ironically, even though Stephen was on trial, his appraisal of Israel's history showed that it was the religious leaders who were guilty of disobeying God and deserving of His condemnation.

Out of respect for his audience, Stephen addressed the council members as "brothers and fathers" (vs. 2) and urged them to listen attentively to his speech. In referring to the Lord as the "God of glory," Stephen emphasized the Creator's supreme holiness and majesty. Even though He is transcendent, He manifested His presence to Abraham, the revered ancestor of the Jews, while the patriarch was in Mesopotamia and prior to him settling in Haran. At the time, he was 75 years old (see Gen. 12:4). God commanded Abraham to leave his homeland and settle in Haran (see Acts 7:3). Then, after the death of the patriarch's father, God directed him to relocate to Canaan, which became the promised land of Abraham's descendants, the Jews (see vs. 4).

B. God's Presence with Joseph: vss. 8–10

"Then he gave Abraham the covenant of circumcision. And Abraham became the father of Isaac and circumcised him eight days after his birth. Later Isaac became the father of Jacob, and Jacob became the father of the twelve patriarchs. Because the patriarchs were jealous of Joseph, they sold him as a slave into Egypt. But God was with him and rescued him from all his troubles. He gave Joseph wisdom and enabled him to gain the goodwill of Pharaoh king of Egypt; so he made him ruler over Egypt and all his palace."

In Acts 7:5, Stephen explained that God did not actually give Abraham one square foot of Canaan as an inheritance. Also, even though the patriarch and his wife did not yet have a child, God promised that Abraham's descendants would one day possess the land (see Heb. 11:8–12). The patriarch learned that for over four centuries, his descendants would be oppressed as noncitizens and slaves in a foreign country, namely, Egypt (see Acts 7:6; Gen. 15:13; Exod. 12:40). Then, at the divinely appointed moment, the Lord would judge the taskmasters and free His chosen people. Subsequently, He would enable them to conquer Canaan and worship Him there (see Acts 7:7; Gen. 15:14).

Stephen disclosed that God commanded Abraham and his descendants to observe the "covenant of circumcision" (Acts 7:8; see Gen. 17:1–14 and the corresponding commentary in lesson 8). At the time, the patriarch was 99 years old (see Gen. 17:1). One year later, when Abraham was 100 (see 21:5), God fulfilled His promise by enabling Sarah to become pregnant and give birth to Isaac (see vss. 1–3). Then, when the baby was eight days old, Abraham had him circumcised (see vs. 4). Stephen stated that the practice of circumcision was also observed by Isaac, his son, Jacob, and his 12 sons (see Acts 7:8).

Genesis reveals that Joseph, one of Jacob's sons, was pivotal in the history of God's chosen people. Stephen explained that because the siblings resented their father's preferential treatment of Joseph, they sent him off to Egypt as a slave (see Acts 7:9). Yet, despite that seemingly tragic turn of events, God remained actively present in Joseph's life and delivered him from the hardships he faced. Furthermore, God made Joseph so wise that he impressed Egypt's pharaoh, who appointed Joseph as the viceroy over the entire nation (see vs. 10).

When a famine eventually engulfed much of the Fertile Crescent, people living in both Egypt and Canaan, including the Israelites, struggled to survive (see vs. 11). So, when Jacob learned that there was grain available for purchase in Egypt, he sent his sons there for the first time (see vs. 12). God used the unfolding series of events to bring Jacob's entire family to a safe place in Egypt, where he and they eventually died (see vss. 13–15).

In mentioning Joseph, Stephen demonstrated that even in antiquity, the people of God raised their hand in defiance against a servant of the Lord. Throughout Stephen's message, he explained that this rebellious tendency continually existed in Israel and reached its height in the nation's rejection of the Messiah. Just as Joseph was spurned by his brothers and yet he later rescued them, so too, the people of Israel disdained Jesus, the One through whom they would find salvation.

After Jacob's death, his bones were moved to Shechem and placed in a tomb that he previously purchased from the sons of a local resident named Hamor (see vs. 16; Gen. 23:9; 33:18–19; 49:29–32; Josh. 24:32). In mentioning the patriarchs buried in Shechem, Stephen wanted to remind his audience that God had done momentous things in the lives of His people apart from Jerusalem and its temple. Put differently, these two significant pieces of real estate were not always central to God's redemptive plan.

II. MOSES, THE TABERNACLE, AND THE TEMPLE: ACTS 7:17, 33–34, 45–47, 53

A. The Increase in the Israelite Population: vs. 17

"As the time drew near for God to fulfill his promise to Abraham, the number of our people in Egypt greatly increased."

Stephen pointed out that in accordance with God's promise to Abraham (see Acts 7:6), the population of the Israelites in Egypt grew dramatically (see vs. 17). Exodus 1:1–7 reveals that they were so numerous that it seemed as if they filled the entire land. Verse 8 notes that a new pharaoh, who knew nothing about Joseph, reigned over Egypt (see Acts 7:18). He was merciless in exploiting God's chosen people, and even tried to force the parents of newborns to abandon them so that they would die (see vs. 19; Exod. 1:9–22).

Despite these hardships, God ensured the survival of the Israelites, including their future leader, Moses. The Lord oversaw human events so that Pharaoh's daughter adopted Moses and brought him up as her own son (see Acts 7:20–21; Exod. 2:1–10). She had Moses educated in all the wisdom of the Egyptians, and he became a powerful orator and a person of action (see Acts 7:22). Then, at the age of 40, because he murdered an Egyptian, Moses fled to the land of Midian, where he spent the next 40 years (see vss. 23–29; Exod. 2:11–22; Heb. 11:24–25). During Moses' period of exile, he learned to do God's work in His way, according to His timetable, and for His reasons.

B. The Lord's Announcement to Moses: vss. 33–34

"Then the Lord said to him, 'Take off your sandals; the place where you are standing is holy ground. I have indeed seen the oppression of my people in Egypt. I have heard their groaning and have come down to set them free. Now come, I will send you back to Egypt.'"

Stephen commented that when Moses was 80 years old, he was tending his father-in-law's flock in the Sinai desert when the Lord's angel appeared to Moses as a flame of fire from within a thorny bush (see Acts 7:30). Being intrigued by the sight, Moses went over to investigate it (see vs. 31). He was startled to hear the Lord's voice declare from the bush that He was the God of the patriarchs, Moses' ancestors (see vs. 32). The Lord, through His heavenly emissary, directed Moses to remove his sandals, for the ground beneath his feet was sacred, due to God's holy presence being there (see vs. 33; Exod. 3:1–6).

Moses learned that the Lord was aware of the Egyptians' mistreatment of His chosen people and that He would set them free from their taskmasters. In turn, Moses found out that God would send him back to Egypt to confront the Egyptians and deliver the Israelites from their plight (see Acts 7:34; Exod. 3:7–10). In mentioning this incident, Stephen wanted the Sanhedrin to note that at Mount Sinai, not Jerusalem or its temple, the Lord revealed Himself to Moses. It was also at Mount Sinai that God later made His most important address to His people (see Exod. 19).

In Acts 7:35, Stephen observed that Moses was the person whom the ancestors of the religious leaders had rejected. He was the same person whom God had chosen to perform amazing miracles as a prelude to the Israelites' rescue from Egypt (see vs. 36). In Stephen's day, it was the Sanhedrin who were guilty of spurning Jesus, another person whom God had chosen to be the supreme Ruler and Savior of His people (see vs. 37; Deut. 18:15). In mentioning "Mount Sinai" (Acts 7:38), Stephen wanted the Council to remember that this sacred spot was nowhere near Jerusalem and the temple.

Stephen's opponents had accused him of slandering Moses, the law, the temple, and God. In verses 39–43, Stephen argued before the Sanhedrin that throughout Israel's history, the chosen people had opposed Moses and the prophets. The people had also lived contrary to the letter and spirit of the law that Moses had received at Mount Sinai. For instance, instead of worshiping God in the tabernacle and temple, they offered pagan sacrifices and venerated foreign deities. Also, rather than give their allegiance to the Messiah, about whom Moses and the rest of the Old Testament prophets spoke (see John 5:45–47), the descendants of the patriarchs were guilty of betraying and murdering the Savior.

C. The Lord's Abiding Presence Among His People: vss. 45–47

Having received the tabernacle, our fathers under Joshua brought it with them when they took the land from the nations God drove out before them. It remained in the land until the time of David, who enjoyed God's favor and asked that he might provide a dwelling place for the God of Jacob. But it was Solomon who built the house for him."

In Acts 7:44, Stephen drew attention to the tabernacle that the Israelites had in the desert and that Moses built according to God's exacting specifications. The Israelites carried around this portable, tent-like structure on their wilderness wanderings. It was a visible testimony to the loving nature of the invisible God and of the just demands He had placed upon His people. The tabernacle also showed forth the judgment and mercy of the Lord, as exemplified in the offering of sacrifices.

The Israelites under Joshua's command brought the tabernacle with them when God enabled them to drive the Canaanites out of the promised land. Moreover, the tabernacle remained with God's chosen people until the time of King David (see vs. 45). While he found "favor" (vs. 46) with God, the Creator worked through Solomon, David's successor as king, to build the temple in Jerusalem (see vs. 47). The Lord wanted His people to understand that He was not confined to one particular location (for example, Jerusalem) and that they should not overly identify His presence with one particular place (namely, the temple; see 2 Sam. 7:5–7).

As Stephen emphasized in Acts 7:48–50 (quoting Isaiah 66:1–2), though God manifested His glorious presence in the temple, He did not live there. Also, because the Creator is present everywhere at the same time, He cannot be confined by anything He has made (see 1 Kings 8:27–30). Earlier, Stephen's detractors had accused him of speaking against the temple (see 6:13). Yet before the building of the sanctuary in Jerusalem, the tabernacle had been the focus of Israel's national worship. By mentioning the latter, Stephen reminded the Sanhedrin that regardless of where God's chosen people lived, the testimony of His presence was constantly with them in the tabernacle.

D. The Israelites' Disobedience: vs. 53

"You who have received the law that was put into effect through angels but have not obeyed it."

Stephen used harsh language in calling the members of the Sanhedrin "stiff-necked" (Acts 7:51) and "uncircumcised." These Hebrew idioms mean the religious leaders, like their ancestors, were stubborn and calloused to the truth of Scripture and the Spirit's ministry (see Exod. 33:3, 5; 34:9; Lev. 26:41; Deut. 9:6, 13; Jer. 4:4; 6:10; 9:26). Stephen pointed out that the ancestors of the council persecuted God's true prophets (see Matt. 23:34–36; Luke 11:47–51; 13:34), the same individuals whom His Spirit empowered to foretell the advent of the "Righteous One" (Acts 7:52; see Isa. 53:11; Jer. 23:5; Acts 3:14–15). This is the Messiah, whom the Sanhedrin had rejected and advocated being crucified. Stephen also charged the religious leaders of hypocrisy, for in renouncing the Savior, they transgressed the Mosaic law, which God mediated through "angels" (7:53; see Acts 7:38; Gal. 3:19; Heb. 2:2).

In brief, it was the religious leaders, not Stephen, who were guilty of rebelling against God. Even though Stephen faced imminent death, he demonstrated before his antagonists what it truly meant to honor and worship the Lord. Stephen's desire was not to perpetuate a dead institution and its lifeless traditions. Rather, he sought to please God, regardless of the circumstances or the cost to himself. Throughout his speech (the longest discourse in Acts), Stephen wanted the members of the council to repent of their arrogance and unbelief. Tragically, the Sanhedrin became enraged by Stephen's withering indictment (see vs. 54).

Even though there were legal "witnesses" to Stephen's crime, as required by the Mosaic law (Deut. 17:5–7), it was a virtual lynch mob that pounced on Stephen, dragged him outside the city, and stoned him to death (see Acts 7:57–60). A young Pharisee named Saul (who later became the apostle Paul) suddenly appears in the narrative. (He was around 30 years of age at this time.) By standing with the clothing of the executioners, Saul did not show mere passive approval of the execution. Some have suggested that this act meant Saul was in charge of it. In any case, 8:1 portrays him actively and wholeheartedly condoning the stoning of Stephen.

As Stephen died, he prayed much as Jesus Himself did when He was crucified (see Luke 23:34, 46). Stephen asked that God would receive his spirit and forgive his executioners (see Acts 7:60). Until Stephen's death, Christian converts were content to remain in Jerusalem. But on the day of Stephen's martyrdom, a "great persecution" (8:1) erupted against Jesus' followers. A second-century church leader named Tertullian wrote that the "blood of the martyrs is the seed of the church." Here we see that God providentially used this persecution to scatter believers everywhere, especially to Judea and Samaria. The apostles, however, remained in Jerusalem to provide leadership there.

Discussion Questions

1. Why were the religious leaders so calloused to the truth about Jesus?
2. In what ways were the religious leaders like their ancestors?
3. How was it possible for Stephen to remain gracious in his witness while being mistreated by the Sanhedrin?
4. Describe a time when you were courageous in speaking about the Lord. What resulted from it?
5. How would an active, consistent prayer life strengthen a believer who is facing opposition?

Contemporary Application

Acts 7:2–53 records the speech that Stephen gave to the Sanhedrin. Following Hebrew custom, he surveyed the history of Israel, concluding with an accusation that the members of the council had murdered God's Righteous Servant, Jesus. When the religious leaders heard this, they became enraged. Yet, despite their anger, Stephen remained in the Spirit's control.

For many of us, the thought of telling others about our faith brings on sweaty palms and a suddenly vacant mind. We fear embarrassment, ridicule, and rejection. We also fear violating the rules of etiquette that religion should never be discussed in polite society. Perhaps we are ultimately afraid of failing, and the possibility of losing face as well as a soul for the kingdom of God. Stephen's testimony before the people and leaders of the Jews provides us with an excellent example of how to courageously witness of God's grace. Stephen spoke his mind straightforwardly and authoritatively, even when he encountered opposition.

Maintaining a courageous witness does not mean we are disrespectful, obnoxious, or overly aggressive. We are not trying to pick a fight with others or alienate them from the Lord Jesus and His Gospel. Our desire is to be persistent and make the truth known in a way that is biblically accurate and relevant. We can do so, especially as we lean on the Spirit for inner strength and clarity of mind to say the right words at the right time.

Freely Receiving the Spirit

DEVOTIONAL READING

Ephesians 1:3–10

DAILY BIBLE READINGS

Monday September 28
  Psalm 15 Never Moved

Tuesday September 29
  Hebrews 13:5–10 Be Content

Wednesday September 30
  Ephesians 6:14–18 Stand Firm

Thursday October 1
  Acts 13:52—14:3 Stand Boldly

Friday October 2
  Acts 8:1–8 Stand Regardless

Saturday October 3
  Acts 8:9–24 God's Gift of the Spirit

Sunday October 4
  Acts 8:26–40 Stand Ready

Scripture

Background Scripture: *Acts 8:9–25*
Scripture Lesson: *Acts 8:9–24*
Key Verse: [Peter declared], "Repent of this wickedness and pray to the Lord. Perhaps he will forgive you for having such a thought in your heart." *Acts 8:22*
Scripture Lesson for Children: *Acts 8:9–24*
Key Verse for Children: [Peter declared], "You have no part or share in this ministry, because your heart is not right before God." *Acts 8:21*

Lesson Aim

To emphasize that God provides many opportunities for us to share the Gospel.

Lesson Setting

Time: Around A.D. 35
Place: Samaria

Lesson Outline

Freely Receiving the Spirit

  I. The Conversion of Simon the Sorcerer: Acts 8:9–13
    A. *The Sorcery of Simon: vss. 9–10*
    B. *The Decision of Simon to Believe: vss. 11–13*
  II. The Confrontation with Simon the Sorcerer: Acts 8:14–24
    A. *The Dispatching of Peter and John: vss. 14–17*
    B. *Simon's Offer of Money: vss. 18–19*
    C. *Peter's Rebuke of Simon: vss. 20–23*
    D. *Simon's Repentant Response: vs. 24*

Introduction for Adults

Topic: *The True Source of Power*

In his book *Cultural Anthropology*, Paul G. Hiebert defines a social culture as an "integrated system of learned patterns of behavior, ideas and products, characteristic of a society." The social setting that we come from usually defines who we are as a person. Most people are comfortable living and working around those with whom they are most familiar and with whom they share a social culture.

When Jesus comes into our lives, He begins to replace our fear of other people with a love for them. Instead of fearing how they might harm or reject us, we are more able to think of their need for the Lord and, therefore, we will want them to experience God's forgiveness and love.

We see this perspective at work in Philip's evangelistic outreach in Samaria. He could have been put off by Simon the sorcerer, who acted as if he were the great power broker of God (so to speak). Despite Simon's swagger, Philip remained committed to sharing the Gospel with him. And the Lord used Philip to bring Simon to the place where he, too, "believed and was baptized" (Acts 8:13).

Introduction for Youth

Topic: *Where Is Your Heart?*

The formation of cliques remains a prevalent phenomenon among teens. And with the existence of such groups can come the notion that people in one clique are unwelcome in another clique.

This adversarial mentality runs counter to the truth of the Gospel. Jesus wants saved teens to share the Good News even with those they might feel are their enemies. To be sure, this can be difficult. But it's amazing how the power of Christ can break down barriers between people.

The mission field of believing young people may begin with their families, then extend into their schools or neighborhood, and finally into the larger society. Regardless of whom the Lord brings into the lives of your students, they should be alert to the opportunities to tell others how much Jesus means to them. And as Peter emphasized to Simon, God's grace is offered freely to the lost and cannot be purchased at any price.

Concepts for Children

Topic: *Get It Right!*

1. Philip went to Samaria to tell people about Jesus.
2. In Samaria, Philip did many amazing things.
3. God used Philip to encourage a famous person named Simon to believe in Jesus.
4. The church in Jerusalem sent Peter and John to help Christians in Samaria.
5. God wants us to help others around us.

Lesson Commentary

I. THE CONVERSION OF SIMON THE SORCERER: ACTS 8:9–13

A. The Sorcery of Simon: vss. 9–10

Now for some time a man named Simon had practiced sorcery in the city and amazed all the people of Samaria. He boasted that he was someone great, and all the people, both high and low, gave him their attention and exclaimed, "This man is the divine power known as the Great Power."

The church, being no more than a few years old at the beginning of Acts 8, faced its first real persecution. Amazingly, God used the adversity to provide believers with opportunities to share the Gospel with those outside the Jewish community. For instance, we learn in verse 4 that the believers who had fled Jerusalem went wherever they could to spread the Good News. The unsaved discovered that Jesus is the promised Messiah of the Old Testament and that, despite His death on the cross, He rose from the dead. Furthermore, the message being heralded included an emphasis on repentance and faith.

Among the believers scattered by the persecution was Philip (see vs. 5). He was one of the persons previously selected along with Stephen to look after the Greek-speaking widows (see 6:5). Philip, like Stephen, illustrates how a person faithful in one ministry was given a wider sphere of service. His works recorded in this chapter were only the beginning of a long, fruitful span of ministry (see 21:8). At some point, Philip decided to travel "down" (8:5; or downhill) from Jerusalem to the principal "city in Samaria" (which was about two or three days away). Samaria was a region in central Palestine first occupied by the tribe of Ephraim and part of the tribe of Manasseh.

One of the region's most prominent centers, the ancient town of Shechem (also near Mount Gerizim, Samaria's highest peak), became the capital of the northern kingdom of Israel under Jeroboam (931–910 B.C.; see 1 Kings 12:25). Later, a city named Samaria (established by Omri around 880 B.C.) became the capital of the northern kingdom, and remained so through several kings until it fell to the Assyrians in 722 B.C. When the northern kingdom collapsed, most of its prominent citizens were deported to Assyria, Aram (Syria), and Babylon. The depleted Israelite population was then replaced with foreigners from Babylon and elsewhere (see 2 Kings 17:24). Through the intermarriage between the newcomers and the Israelites left in the land, the resulting people later known as Samaritans were formed.

Because of their mixed Jewish-Gentile blood, early pagan worship (1 Kings 12:28–29), and later religious ceremonies that centered on Mount Gerizim rather than the temple in Jerusalem (see John 4:20–22), the Samaritans were generally despised by the Jews throughout their history. This certainly remained true in New Testament times. In fact, the Jews of Philip's day regarded the Samaritans to be racially impure. The Jews also saw Samaritans as religious half-breeds since Samaritans rejected much of the Scriptures, accepting only the first five books. Moreover, despite their common ancestry, their equal regard for the Mosaic law, and their shared hope for a prophet like Moses (see Deut. 18:15, 18; Acts 3:22), Jews and Samaritans usually refused to have anything to do with each other (see Luke 9:51–56; John 4:9).

There is some doubt about the exact identity of the city where Philip took up temporary residence (see Acts 8:5). Some conjecture it was the region's capital, which also happened to be called Samaria. Regardless of which particular city Philip visited, it was there that he proclaimed the truth about the Messiah to the residents. It is somewhat surprising that the Samaritans listened to Philip, for he was a Jew (see vs. 6). It may have helped that he was a Hellenistic Jew (see 6:1), that is, a Jew who spoke Greek and was influenced by Greek culture. It also may have helped that Philip had recently endured Jewish persecution. Perhaps the Samaritans had heard about and approved of disputes about the temple that Christians such as Stephen had carried on with the religious leaders in Jerusalem (see vss. 13–14).

At any rate, when the Samaritans heard Philip's message and saw the miracles he performed, they listened intently to what he proclaimed (see 8:6; for example, that Jesus was crucified, resurrected, and exalted to God's right hand). The Samaritans knew something unusual was happening among them. They watched wide-eyed as those with evil spirits (or demons) were set free and as paralytics and cripples walked (see vs. 7). Philip's record of miracles reads like a list of the same sorts of signs Jesus performed during His earthly ministry. The Savior's deeds were extraordinary expressions of God's power.

As Philip brought about various signs, God used these miracles to give evidence of His presence and truth to a previously despised, neglected people. It is no wonder "there was great joy in that city" (vs. 8). From this information, we see that supernatural power was impressive to the Samaritans. In turn, this explains why many Samaritans followed Simon, a sorcerer (see vs. 9). In the ancient world, the kind of magic he practiced flourished. Luke recorded three incidents related to magic: the episode involving Simon (see vss. 9–24), the account concerning Elymas (see 13:4–12), and the incident dealing with seven Jewish exorcists (see 19:13–20).

The Greco-Roman magic practiced by Simon tended to be practical. On behalf of their clients, sorcerers tried to prevent or avert harm, to hurt enemies with curses, to inspire love or submission in others, and to gain revelations from the spirit world. Simon's own involvement with magic extended back a number of years. He beguiled people with his antics and claimed that he was someone important (see 8:9). He was able to convince the Samaritans—from the least to the most prominent—that he was the great power of the divine (see vs. 10). The idea probably is that Simon either claimed to be God or alleged to be God's chief representative.

B. The Decision of Simon to Believe: vss. 11–13

They followed him because he had amazed them for a long time with his magic. But when they believed Philip as he preached the good news of the kingdom of God and the name of Jesus Christ, they were baptized, both men and women. Simon himself believed and was baptized. And he followed Philip everywhere, astonished by the great signs and miracles he saw.

It was because of the magic Simon performed that he held such sway over the people of Samaria (see Acts 8:11). But the arrival of Philip changed all that. He announced the "good news" (vs. 12) about the divine kingdom, especially as it centered on Jesus the Messiah. As a result of Philip's evangelistic activities, many put their trust in the Messiah. They also gave evidence of their decision to believe by being baptized.

We learn in Scripture that the divine kingdom embraces all who walk in fellowship with the Lord and do His will. The kingdom is governed by God's laws, which are summed up in our duty to love the Lord supremely and love others as ourselves. Moreover, this kingdom, which was foretold by the prophets and introduced by Jesus, will one day displace all the kingdoms of this world, following the return of the Redeemer.

Simon decided to put his faith in the Messiah and get baptized. Simon did so because the amazing things God did through Philip enthralled Simon. The missionary's works of power were so superior to Simon's conjuring that the former sorcerer stayed close to Philip wherever he went (see vs. 13). On the one hand, Simon marveled at the miracles he saw Philip perform. On the other hand, the evangelist's intent was not to make a name for himself. Instead, his goal was to confirm the truth he proclaimed, especially Jesus' ability to rescue people from their life of sin. It was the grace of God that enabled the Samaritans and Simon to give up their sinful attitudes and believe in the Lord Jesus.

II. THE CONFRONTATION WITH SIMON THE SORCERER: ACTS 8:14–24

A. The Dispatching of Peter and John: vss. 14–17

When the apostles in Jerusalem heard that Samaria had accepted the word of God, they sent Peter and John to them. When they arrived, they prayed for them that they might receive the Holy Spirit, because the Holy Spirit had not yet come upon any of them; they had simply been baptized into the name of the Lord Jesus. Then Peter and John placed their hands on them, and they received the Holy Spirit.

In the persecution following Stephen's stoning, the apostles bravely maintained the church's presence at its original center, Jerusalem. There news of Philip's successes in evangelizing the lost of Samaria reached the apostles. Peter and John, as representatives of the apostles, went to see for themselves what was happening in Samaria (see Acts 8:14). Peter and John arrived at a city that had been transformed by the power of God. The two were able to build on the foundation laid by Philip. This included the apostles strengthening and developing the faith of the new believers. Accordingly, the first action

Peter and John took was to pray that the new converts might be given the Holy Spirit (see vs. 15).

Luke explained that the Spirit had not yet fallen on any of the converts. The reason is that the Samaritan believers had only undergone water baptism in Jesus' name (see vs. 16). This statement raises an intriguing question. How was it possible for the Spirit not to be received by those who had believed the truth about "the kingdom of God and the name of Jesus Christ" (vs. 12)? Specialists differ in their answers to this question. Problematic is the notion that Peter's and John's ministry conveyed a second, separate blessing of grace—a work of the Spirit beyond His initial indwelling. Some view the apostles' work as a sort of confirmation with the goal of bringing intellectual faith up to a higher level. The most likely explanation is that this was a unique occurrence in which God used Peter and John to communicate the Spirit in such a way that the Jerusalem believers would accept the Samaritans.

Peter and John clearly expected something more to happen in the Samaritans' lives. So the apostles showed their affirmation, solidarity, and support for the new converts by laying their hands on them. When the apostles did so, God blessed the Samaritan converts with the gift of the Spirit (see vs. 17). The laying on of hands was a common practice among Jews for blessing people or putting them into a ministry or service. Luke did not detail everything that followed the praying and laying on of hands, other than that the Spirit indwelt the Samaritan believers. Luke had earlier described in greater detail signs that accompanied fillings of the Spirit (see 2:2–4; 4:31). Though we are not told exactly what happened when the Spirit came upon the Samaritans, we know that some demonstration of God's power appeared. Those who looked on recognized this manifestation as a supernatural event.

B. Simon's Offer of Money: vss. 18–19

When Simon saw that the Spirit was given at the laying on of the apostles' hands, he offered them money and said, "Give me also this ability so that everyone on whom I lay my hands may receive the Holy Spirit."

Simon, the former sorcerer, was one of the observers to the apostles' laying on of hands. (The text gives no suggestion that Simon was a participant.) When he saw the demonstration of God's power that came when the apostles ministered to the Samaritan converts and prayed, something of Simon's former ways stirred within him. What he witnessed was a supernatural ability like nothing he'd ever seen, an influence and control over people far better than any scheme he'd ever used. Simon, being unable to hide his eagerness, "offered . . . money" (Acts 8:18) to Peter and John. Perhaps Simon crassly reasoned that if he could manipulate the mysterious power to give others the Spirit by laying hands on them, he could then recapture his lost fame and influence (see vs. 19).

C. Peter's Rebuke of Simon: vss. 20–23

Peter answered: "May your money perish with you, because you thought you could buy the gift of God with money! You have no part or share in this ministry, because your heart is not right before God. Repent of this wickedness and pray to the Lord. Perhaps he will forgive you for having such a thought in your heart. For I see that you are full of bitterness and captive to sin."

Peter saw through Simon's request. The apostle told Simon in no uncertain terms that since he tried to use money to acquire the "gift of God" (Acts 8:20), both he and his precious silver could eternally "perish." If such language seems too harsh, it is precisely what Peter intended. In telling Simon he might languish in hell, Peter used the same Greek noun appearing in Jesus' statement, "Broad is the road that leads to *destruction*" (Matt. 7:13, emphasis added).

Next, Peter firmly told Simon that he could not have any "part or share" (Acts 8:21) in the evangelistic work, for he tried to bargain with the Lord and bribe His ambassadors. Peter urged Simon to abandon his evil plan and turn away from his sinful motives. If he did so, God could forgive him for his warped thinking (see vs. 22). Peter described Simon's spiritual condition as being consumed by envy, resentment, and greed. Moreover, the apostle said that Simon remained in bondage to wickedness (see vs. 23).

On one level, Simon desired a good thing, that is, to be able to impart the Holy Spirit to others. But on another level, Simon asked for the wrong reasons. In particular, he was more interested in serving himself than in serving the Lord or others. Whenever we desire to do something good in service to God, we must take care that our motives are pure. It's easy to put selfish ambition into good works when sacrifice and commitment are needed instead.

D. Simon's Repentant Response: vs. 24

Then Simon answered, "Pray to the Lord for me so that nothing you have said may happen to me."

Even though Peter's words were blunt, they remained appropriate and effective. Acts 8:24 reveals that Simon displayed a change of heart. He asked that Peter would petition the Lord, so that none of what the apostle said would take place in Simon's life. After this episode, Peter and John spent a little more time solemnly proclaiming the truth of God to the local residents. Then, as the two apostles journeyed back to Jerusalem, they declared the Good News in numerous villages in Samaria (see vs. 25).

There is a lingering question whether Simon was a genuine believer. While verse 13 seems to indicate that he was, verses 20–23 seem to suggest that he was not. There are several possible answers to this query. Some say Simon only appeared to believe when he saw and experienced Philip's power. Others say Peter used exaggerated terms, meaning only that Simon had sinned badly, not that he was an unbeliever. A third group maintains that Simon abandoned his faith when he tried to buy divine power.

In the early centuries of the church, believers used the name Simon Magus to refer to the Simon of Acts 8. (Magus means "magician.") Furthermore, they placed on him the status of arch-heretic. An early Christian philosopher named Justin Martyr (who died about A.D. 165) said Simon was a Samaritan from the village of Gitta who practiced magic for a time in Rome and taught false theology. The apocryphal Acts of Peter (from the late second century A.D.) describes spiritual conflicts between Peter and Simon, resulting in Simon's death.

The Pseudo-Clementine writings (also from the second century A.D.) tell of Simon's using magic to take over control of a group of John the Baptizer's disciples. Eventually, Simon Magus came to be identified in Christian belief as the source of Gnosticism, a heretical belief system that infected the church in its early centuries. It is impossible to know whether any of these Christian traditions about Simon rest on a foundation of truth. But if so, they would indicate that Simon's public "conversion" under the ministry of Philip was only a show.

Discussion Questions

1. How did Simon the sorcerer make a name for himself in Samaria?
2. What astonished Simon the most about Philip?
3. What did Peter and John do when they arrived in the Samaritan city?
4. What is the purpose of miracles in promoting the Gospel?
5. What can we do to let go of our own ways so that God can show us His ways?

Contemporary Application

Despite Jesus' command to witness to the ends of the earth, the church might have stayed comfortably in Jerusalem if the early Christians had not been persecuted (see Acts 8:1–3). Thankfully, under God's direction, Philip was willing to be used to proclaim the Gospel to the Samaritans. The evangelist was not put off by their despised status in the Jewish society of the day.

We function better within our comfort zone, where people are familiar and circumstances are easy. Often, though, God sends us into unfamiliar or scary places because He has work for us there. A sign in a church that people see as they leave says, "You are now going out into the mission field." Where might God be sending you to share the Gospel?

You may say, "I do not speak very well." Instead, you could smile and say "God loves you" to a very tired store clerk; or you could tell a peer at work or school that you are a Christian; or you could help a person carry heavy packages as a prelude to sharing your faith.

God may place you in an unusual situation. If so, submit to Him in the power of His Spirit. The Lord may want you to talk to a handicapped person. You could feed a child who comes to the local soup kitchen or join with others in your church to resettle a refugee family. Any of these contacts might open a door to share the Gospel.

Obtaining Credibility

Scripture

Background Scripture: *Acts 9:19–31*
Scripture Lesson: *Acts 9:19–31*
Key Verse: At once [Saul] began to preach in the synagogues that Jesus is the Son of God. *Acts 9:20*
Scripture Lesson for Children: *Acts 9:19–31*
Key Verse for Children: Saul stayed with [the apostles] and moved about freely in Jerusalem, speaking boldly in the name of the Lord. *Acts 9:28*

Lesson Aim

To affirm that the risen Lord still changes lives.

Lesson Setting

Time: Around A.D. 35, 38
Place: Damascus, Jerusalem, Caesarea, and Tarsus

Lesson Outline

Obtaining Credibility

I. Saul in Damascus: Acts 9:19–25
   A. *Saul's Conversion: vs. 19*
   B. *Saul's Proclamation of the Gospel: vss. 20–22*
   C. *Saul's Departure from Damascus: vss. 23–25*

II. Saul in Jerusalem: Acts 9:26–31
   A. *The Disciples' Apprehension: vs. 26*
   B. *The Endorsement Offered by Barnabas: vs. 27*
   C. *The Departure from Jerusalem: vss. 28–30*
   D. *The Period of Peace: vs. 31*

Introduction for Adults

Topic: *An About–Face*

Many adults in America today would say they believe in Jesus. That sounds pretty impressive until we realize that demons assert the same thing (see Jas. 2:19). So, what makes a disciple is the issue most adults resist: commitment. Interestingly, the word *disciple* has its root in the concept of discipline, and spiritual discipline is what we need if we are to be genuinely committed to the Savior.

Most, if not all, adults in church would probably say without hesitation that they believe in Jesus. But to what extent have they committed their lives to Him? Certainly they may be committed enough to go to church, but how much further does their discipleship go? How often do they pray? How much time is spent studying God's Word? How frequently do they share the Gospel with others?

Some have said the true disciple is one who not only acknowledges Jesus as Savior, but also has truly made Him Lord of their life. This was true for Saul (Paul) after his dramatic conversion. The Spirit can use the account of Saul's encounter with Jesus to make a difference in the lives of your students.

Introduction for Youth

Topic: *From Adversary to Advocate*

The account of Saul's conversion is one of the most pivotal moments in early church history. At one point, this influential religious leader was poised to bring a crippling blow on the fledgling group of Jesus' followers living in Damascus. But then Saul encountered the risen Savior and Saul's life was forever changed.

Teens need to know that Jesus still transforms lives. We come to Him first for our salvation, an act dependent on His power and grace alone. Then, as the Holy Spirit works through our obedience and submission, day by day, the exalted Messiah is changing us into His image (see Rom. 12:1–2).

As we study God's Word, the Spirit helps us recognize the life changes that we need to make. Our Lord is very gentle. He never forces Himself on anyone. Little by little, however, Jesus transforms the areas of our lives that we surrender to Him.

Concepts for Children

Topic: *Tell It Like It Is*

1. Saul once was mean to Jesus' followers.
2. After Saul met Jesus, Saul became one of Jesus' followers.
3. Saul told others that Jesus rose from the dead.
4. Even though others tried to hurt Saul, he continued to share the Good News.
5. God wants us to let others know that Jesus loves them.

Lesson Commentary

I. SAUL IN DAMASCUS: ACTS 9:19–25

A. Saul's Conversion: vs. 19

And after taking some food, he regained his strength. Saul spent several days with the disciples in Damascus.

After persecuting the believers in Jerusalem, Saul decided to go after those Christians who had fled the city, to bring them back to face trial before the Sanhedrin and possible execution (see Acts 9:1–2; 22:4–5; 26:9–11). On the road near Damascus (see 9:3), about noon one day (see 22:6), a light far brighter than the sun (see 26:13) blazed around Saul and his companions, who all fell to the ground (see vs. 14). Saul heard the voice of Jesus repeat his name and ask why he was maltreating the Savior (see 9:4). Saul's traveling companions were witnesses that something had happened. But even though they could hear the sound of Jesus' voice and see the light of His presence, they did not comprehend what was happening (see vs. 7; 22:9).

Since the message was not directed to these men, it makes sense why only Saul understood the words. He recognized this voice as coming from God. Saul, presuming he was bringing God's enemies to justice, asked, "Who are you, Lord?" (9:5). The reply came back that it was Jesus, whom Saul had been oppressing. Saul learned that Jesus was not a dead blasphemer but the risen, living Lord. This would require a complete change of Saul's beliefs—and indeed, of his life. Saul must have been in shock, with a dawning sense of horror at what he had done. Hope also emerged, for Jesus told Saul to arise and go into Damascus, where he would receive instructions (see vs. 6).

During the short conversation, Saul kept his eyes shut against the bright light. When he opened them afterward, he could not see. And so the proud Pharisee had to be led by the hand like a child into Damascus (see vs. 8). For three days Saul touched no food or water. This blinded man just looked inward (see vs. 9). During this time, a disciple named Ananias, who was living in the city, experienced a vision (see vs. 10). In it, the Lord directed Ananias to go to the house of a man named Judas, whose home was located on the street named "Straight" (vs. 11). This was a mile-long boulevard from one end of Damascus to the other.

The Lord told Ananias to inquire about a man from Tarsus named Saul. Jesus revealed to Ananias that Saul experienced a vision. The blind Pharisee had seen Ananias restoring his eyesight through the laying on of hands. This is the reason Saul was immersed in prayer (see vs. 12). Ananias hesitated, for he felt unsure whether helping Saul was a good idea. Ananias told the Lord that he had heard many reports from others about the Pharisee. In particular, Ananias was aware of how much harm Saul had done to the believers living in Jerusalem (see vs. 13).

Saul's tirade against Jesus' followers did not stop there. Ananias knew the Pharisee's mission was to terrorize the believers in Damascus. The chief priests had authorized him to imprison everyone who called on Jesus' name in saving faith (see vs. 14). If Saul's purpose in coming to the city was ever meant to be covert, the secret was out, for word had preceded him. The Lord did not let Ananias' protests continue any further. He was to obey the Savior without hesitation. Jesus revealed that Saul would be His chosen instrument (or tool) to herald His name to Gentile monarchs and their subjects, as well as to the people of Israel (see vs. 15). Here we discover that this once proud Pharisee would minister to all nations, including Israel (see Rom. 1:16–17).

Before his encounter with the risen Lord, Saul had vigorously persecuted the church. Now, as a follower of Jesus, Saul would learn from personal experience what it meant to suffer for the sake of the Savior's name (see Acts 9:16). Indeed, the Lord's reply to Ananias foretold a dramatic and complete turnaround for Saul. Jesus' former enemy was to become a chief ally—not just a neutral observer in the spiritual war. The staunch defender of the Mosaic law and the Jewish nation would take the message of grace to all sorts of people. Instead of having influence with the authorities, he would suffer at their hands for the name of Jesus.

In obedience, Ananias departed, went to the house of Judas, and Ananias placed his hands on Saul. Next, Ananias gave this remarkable greeting: "Brother Saul" (vs. 17). Ananias accepted Saul for what he had become, not rejected him for what he had been. Saul, now a Christian brother, needed to be healed and filled with the Spirit. Saul and Ananias were colleagues because both had come to know the Messiah in a convincing way. Ananias made sure Saul knew that Jesus had sent him, implying that it was Jesus who would bring about the miracle Ananias was about to perform.

By mentioning Saul's encounter with Jesus on the Damascus road, Ananias may have been letting Saul know that he had supernatural knowledge of the event. Of course, rumors of Saul's conversion may have reached Ananias, just as rumors of Saul's persecution mission had reached him. In any case, several actions followed in swift succession. A crusty covering like scales peeled away from Saul's eyes and he could see again (see vs. 18). Moreover, after receiving the Spirit, Saul got up from where he had been resting and praying. Then he was baptized and given something to eat. For several more days, Saul remained with Jesus' followers in Damascus (see vs. 19).

B. Saul's Proclamation of the Gospel: vss. 20–22

At once he began to preach in the synagogues that Jesus is the Son of God. All those who heard him were astonished and asked, "Isn't he the man who raised havoc in Jerusalem among those who call on this name? And hasn't he come here to take them as prisoners to the chief priests?" Yet Saul grew more and more powerful and baffled the Jews living in Damascus by proving that Jesus is the Christ.

Our knowledge of Saul's early years is sketchy. Yet what we do know shows that God was quietly preparing a person with considerable insight into the Mosaic law and who felt at home in the Greco-Roman world. Most likely, Saul was born around A.D. 5 in his family's hometown of Tarsus. Though Roman citizens, the members of Saul's family were also devout Jews of the tribe of Benjamin. Saul, while still a child or adolescent, moved to Jerusalem, where he had relatives, to obtain a religious education. As noted in lesson 3, Saul studied under Gamaliel, the leading scribe and Pharisee of the day. Saul eventually joined the Pharisees, a Jewish sect that emphasized strict obedience to the Mosaic law, along with the teachings of their own leaders.

Saul had come to Damascus to defend the law and Jewish traditions. He had also come to prove that Jesus was an impostor, arrest His followers, and bring them bound in chains to the chief priests in Jerusalem (see Acts 9:21). Instead, Saul was now going from synagogue to synagogue in Damascus and proclaiming that Jesus is "the Son of God" (vs. 20). By this Saul meant that Jesus is God incarnate, whom the Father commissioned for the special work of redeeming the lost through the Son's atoning sacrifice on the cross (see John 1:1, 14, 18, 49). Later, preaching the Gospel first in Jewish synagogues became part of the missionary strategy that Saul (Paul) used as he took the Good News to the rest of the Roman world (see Acts 13:5; 17:1–2; 18:19).

Imagine Saul's excitement as he went back to look at the Hebrew Scriptures with new eyes. The man who would become perhaps the greatest Christian expositor of Scripture in the early church was learning his first lessons. Without delay, Saul shared his new insights with his fellow Jews. Though still a spiritual newborn, he quickly grew adept at debating with religious experts, arguing persuasively that Jesus is the Messiah (see 9:21). Saul presented irrefutable proof that Jesus fulfilled the prophecies of Scripture in ways the specialists could never have anticipated. Those who heard and contended with Saul were completely "baffled" (vs. 22) by his claims and behavior. They also were unable to adequately refute Saul's claims concerning Jesus.

C. Saul's Departure from Damascus: vss. 23–25

After many days had gone by, the Jews conspired to kill him, but Saul learned of their plan. Day and night they kept close watch on the city gates in order to kill him. But his followers took him by night and lowered him in a basket through an opening in the wall.

Since Saul's opponents could not defeat him in debate, they resorted to other means. Specifically, after "many days" (Acts 9:23) had elapsed, they plotted against Saul's life. According to Galatians 1:13–18, it was at least three years after Saul's conversion when he traveled from Damascus to Jerusalem and attempted to affiliate with Jesus' followers (see Acts 9:26). Possibly during those three years, Saul journeyed to Arabia to proclaim the Gospel and spend private moments with the Lord before later returning to Damascus.

In any case, Saul's opponents kept constant watch at the city gates so that they would know when he left Damascus (see vs. 24). Then, apparently, they planned to follow him and murder him in a secluded spot. According to 2 Corinthians 11:32, the governor of the region had ordered Saul's arrest because of his preaching in the synagogues. Perhaps Saul's antagonists convinced the governor to go along with them in their efforts to get rid of Saul. However, he became aware of the threats on his life. In response, a group of believers lowered him in a basket from a window or other opening in the city wall (see vs. 25). Saul, who had proudly left Jerusalem to defend the Jewish traditions, was now forced to escape from Damascus in a large woven container normally used to store food, a fugitive from his own people (see Acts 9:25). Already, he was beginning to suffer for Jesus' name (see vs. 16).

Because of its location, Damascus was a major trade center during the first century A.D. As the capital of Syria, the city had close economic ties with Israel. Two major highways passed through Damascus: the Via Maris, which extended from Mesopotamia to the Mediterranean coast; and the King's Highway, which headed south all the way to Arabia. The city was considered an oasis in the middle of the desert because of its abundant water supplies from the Abana and Pharpar rivers. A long list of conquerors ruled Damascus: the Assyrians, Babylonians, Persians, Greeks, Ptolemies, Seleucids, and finally the Romans. The city grew even larger in area and importance after Pompey, a Roman general, made Syria into a province of the Roman Empire in A.D. 64. Once the Romans occupied the city, many Jews migrated there and established synagogues.

II. SAUL IN JERUSALEM: ACTS 9:26–31

A. The Disciples' Apprehension: vs. 26

When he came to Jerusalem, he tried to join the disciples, but they were all afraid of him, not believing that he really was a disciple.

The tense of the Greek verb rendered "tried" (Acts 9:26) indicates that Saul made repeated efforts to associate with Jesus' disciples in Jerusalem. Yet, despite Saul's attempts, the fledgling Christian community remained wary. Given Saul's notoriety in persecuting believers, it is understandable that followers of the Savior couldn't accept the fact that Saul had been truly converted. In fact, they suspected he was trying to infiltrate the church so he could betray its members.

B. The Endorsement Offered by Barnabas: vs. 27

But Barnabas took him and brought him to the apostles. He told them how Saul on his journey had seen the Lord and that the Lord had spoken to him, and how in Damascus he had preached fearlessly in the name of Jesus.

We shouldn't blame the believers for their suspicions. After all, Saul's reputation had been built on cruelty toward the church. Jesus' followers could not easily dismiss what Saul had done. Caution, therefore, seemed the sensible course.

Yet, in this case, someone was needed who could show that wariness should give way to acceptance. That person was Barnabas. As we learned in lesson 2, he was also known as Joseph, a Levite who had earned the nickname "Barnabas" (Acts 4:36), which means "son of encouragement."

Barnabas encouraged Saul by staking his own reputation on the authenticity of Saul's conversion. Regardless of whether Barnabas had met Saul before he came to Jerusalem or was simply a believer with keen powers of discernment, Barnabas somehow knew that Saul's conversion was genuine. That is why Barnabas introduced Saul to the apostles. This included explaining how Saul had encountered the risen Lord, how Jesus had made His will known to Saul, and how the new convert risked his own life to proclaim with boldness the good news about Jesus (see 9:27).

C. The Departure from Jerusalem: vss. 28–30

So Saul stayed with them and moved about freely in Jerusalem, speaking boldly in the name of the Lord. He talked and debated with the Grecian Jews, but they tried to kill him. When the brothers learned of this, they took him down to Caesarea and sent him off to Tarsus.

At the time, the apostles in residence in Jerusalem were Peter and James (Jesus' half-brother; see Gal. 1:18–19). Either the rest of the church leaders were preaching the Gospel in other areas or they were too afraid to meet with Saul. Evidently, the strength of Barnabas' character and his vouching for Saul's integrity convinced the apostles that he was indeed one of them. As a result, this once-violent persecutor of the church was able to associate freely with Jesus' disciples and courageously proclaim the Good News to the unsaved (see Acts 9:28). Saul began a new assault on the views held by the Hellenistic Jews of Jerusalem. He debated with them, arguing that Jesus is the Messiah. In turn, this prepared Saul for his upcoming evangelistic ministry to the Gentiles.

Previously, Saul had guarded the religious leaders' tunics while they stoned Stephen. After Saul's conversion, he argued Stephen's point of view. Earlier, Saul had helped his peers hound and arrest Jesus' followers. Now, in the view of the Jerusalem authorities, Saul had betrayed them, the law, and Moses. When we recall that it was Hellenistic Jews who had carried out Stephen's trial and execution, we can see that Saul must have been empowered by the Holy Spirit. Like the antagonistic Jews in Damascus, the Hellenistic Jews of Jerusalem were outraged and made plans over a period of time to murder Saul (see vs. 29). The Lord revealed the plot to Saul while he was praying at the temple (see 22:17–21). In response, Jesus' followers managed to get Saul out of Jerusalem and take him down to the Mediterranean port of Caesarea. From there he sailed to his hometown of Tarsus, which proved to be a safe haven for him (see Acts 9:30).

D. The Period of Peace: vs. 31

Then the church throughout Judea, Galilee and Samaria enjoyed a time of peace. It was strengthened; and encouraged by the Holy Spirit, it grew in numbers, living in the fear of the Lord.

Luke provided a marvelous summary of the outcome of the church's witness to the Savior. After the initial flare-up of persecution, things seemed to subside for a while. The disciples throughout Judea, Galilee, and Samaria worshiped the risen Lord and enjoyed a "time of peace" (Acts 9:31). This circumstance enabled them to live in wholehearted agreement, be gracious to one another, and cooperate with each other in preaching the Gospel.

Moreover, the Spirit refreshed, invigorated, and built up Jesus' followers. Perhaps the Spirit did this by abiding His presence and power in their lives. The church also grew numerically because Christians lived in the "fear of the Lord." This means Jesus' followers honored, trusted, and obeyed Him (see also the corresponding commentary in lesson 2). They saw His good hand in bringing them through severe persecution. Indeed, despite the prospect of maltreatment, they remained resolute in their proclamation of Jesus' resurrection from the dead.

Discussion Questions

1. What brought about Saul's dramatic conversion?
2. How was it possible for Saul to grow more capable in his ability to proclaim the Gospel?
3. Why did Saul's antagonists plot to kill him?
4. How much of a change should trusting in Jesus as the Savior make in a person's life?
5. How can believers help others experience the power of the risen Lord?

Contemporary Application

Acts 9 records one of the greatest turning points in human history. Saul of Tarsus was an accomplice to the stoning of Stephen and the driving force behind the first noteworthy persecution of the church. Yet, while Saul was traveling on the road to Damascus, he encountered the risen Savior and was transformed from persecutor to apostle.

Quickly, Saul became Exhibit A of Jesus' ability to change lives. For instance, after Saul met the Messiah, Saul became a powerful preacher. Despite the prospect of death, Saul was willing to affirm to others the reality of the Son's resurrection.

As Jesus' followers, we need to recognize the importance of affirming that His resurrection actually took place. But how do we do it? We do so by cultivating a personal relationship with the Lord in our daily life. This should then prompt us to share the Gospel with others.

Expression may take the form of evangelism, but also it may take the form of song or prayer. In fact, there are many ways we can express our faith in Jesus' resurrection. But regardless of the approach we take, the Father is pleased when we show our trust and hope in the Son.

Taking a Risk

Scripture

Background Scripture: *Acts 10:1–44*
Scripture Lesson: *Acts 10:24–38*
Key Verse: "I now realize how true it is that God does not show favoritism but accepts men from every nation who fear him and do what is right." *Acts 10:34–35*
Scripture Lesson for Children: *Acts 10:24–38*
Key Verse for Children: "I now realize how true it is that God does not show favoritism." *Acts 10:34*

Lesson Aim

To keep the proclamation of the Gospel free from unbiblical concepts.

Lesson Setting

Time: Around A.D. *40*
Place: Caesarea

Lesson Outline

Taking a Risk

I. Peter's Arrival in Caesarea: Acts 10:24–29
   A. *Meeting Cornelius: vss. 24–26*
   B. *Providing Clarification: vss. 27–29*
II. Peter's Proclamation of the Gospel: Acts 10:30–38
   A. *The Explanation Offered by Cornelius: vss. 30–33*
   B. *The Good News Offered by Peter: vss. 34–38*

Introduction for Adults

Topic: *Follow God's Lead*

The relay race was one event of the Isthmian Games in ancient Greece. The competitors lined up side by side at the starting line, each bearing a torch. In the distance waited lines of other athletes. At the signal, the participants started to run, bearing their lighted torches. When an athlete reached his partner in the next line, he would pass on his light, and so on to the finish line. Accordingly, the Greeks coined the phrase, "Let those who have the light pass it on."

The same could be said of our opportunities to evangelize. God has given us the light of the Gospel to share with others. A key part of doing so is ensuring that what we share is free from unbiblical concepts. As Peter's experience with the household of Cornelius shows, our effort includes eliminating any prejudicial thoughts we may have about who supposedly is worthy or unworthy to receive the good news about the Savior.

Introduction for Youth

Topic: *Remove the Fences*

Even though Peter was an apostle, he held unbiblical views about Gentiles that prevented him from sharing the Gospel with them. God revealed to Peter that his insular attitude was standing in the way of him reaching those who needed to hear the Good News.

We sometimes mistakenly imagine a great hardwood sending down roots deep into the soil. But naturalists point out that a healthy tree is one whose roots go sideways, not deep down. And the roots don't just protect that one tree, but rather are woven together with the roots of different trees in order to hold up the entire forest.

Like a healthy growth of trees in a forest, Jesus' followers do not consider merely looking out for their own personal interests. They realize that the loneliness, meaninglessness, and alienation in the world stem from the refusal of people from various backgrounds to relate to God and to one another—often due to cultural bias. Indulging in self-interest and self-preservation produces an unstable person who, like a poorly rooted tree, will be weak and easily toppled. If believers are going to be strong and effective in evangelizing, they must let go of unscriptural concepts and be rooted together in Christ.

Concepts for Children

Topic: *Taking a Risk*

1. A soldier named Cornelius wanted to know God better.
2. God sent Peter to tell Cornelius about Jesus.
3. Peter learned that everyone needs to hear about Jesus.
4. God showed Peter that he should not be afraid to speak about Jesus.
5. God helps us share the Good News about Jesus with others.

Lesson Commentary

I. PETER'S ARRIVAL IN CAESAREA: ACTS 10:24–29

A. Meeting Cornelius: vss. 24–26

The following day he arrived in Caesarea. Cornelius was expecting them and had called together his relatives and close friends. As Peter entered the house, Cornelius met him and fell at his feet in reverence. But Peter made him get up. "Stand up," he said, "I am only a man myself."

Acts 10 describes how God used Peter to open the doors of the church to the Gentiles. While there was a rift between the Samaritans and Jews, a practically unbridgeable chasm existed between Jews and Gentiles. For example, when devout Jews came back from traveling in Gentile territories, they would shake off the dust from their clothes and feet because they did not want to carry contaminated soil into Judea. Also, a Jew was not permitted to enter the house of a Gentile or eat a meal that had been prepared by Gentile hands. Some Jews would not even buy meat that had been cut by Gentiles' knives.

The Lord targeted Peter to move the church to reach out to unsaved Gentiles with the Gospel. This involved two visions from God about who should be included in His kingdom. One came to a Roman centurion named Cornelius (see vss. 3–6). Another related vision came to Peter in Joppa, while he was on the housetop of Simon the tanner (see vss. 9–18, which are covered in more detail in next week's lesson). The two visions came together as Peter obeyed God and unhesitatingly went to Caesarea to see Cornelius when the centurion's men asked the apostle to go with them (see vss. 19–24).

Verse 1 indicates that Cornelius was stationed at Caesarea. The city was located on the coast of Palestine south of Mount Carmel (not Caesarea Philippi) and about 65 miles northwest of Jerusalem. A Roman historian named Tacitus called Caesarea the capital for the province of Judea. Caesarea, being largely Gentile in population, was a center of Roman administration and the location of many of Herod the Great's building projects. Caesarea contained the residences for the Roman governor of Judea as well as a regular Roman garrison.

We also learn that Cornelius was a noncommissioned officer in the Italian Regiment of the Roman army. In New Testament times, a Roman legion numbered about 6,000 men. Each legion had about 10 regiments (or cohorts) of about 600 men each. In the auxiliary territories, such as Judea, a regiment might have as many as 1,000 men. Along with the Italian Regiment, there was also the Imperial, or Augustan, Regiment (see 27:1). The regiments were divided into centuries of a hundred men, and a centurion—who was roughly equivalent to a modern army sergeant—commanded each century. In fact, centurion was the highest rank that an ordinary enlisted soldier could attain.

The position of centurions was prestigious and they were generally paid quite well, their salaries being up to five times the pay an ordinary soldier received. If his superiors thought highly of him, a centurion could serve throughout the Roman Empire. Army service for males typically began around age 17, and only about half of the enlisted men who would survive the required 20 years of service would then be handsomely rewarded. Also, if a soldier reached the level of centurion, he generally stayed in that position for life. Promotion to this position was dependent upon battle experience and military savvy. Since centurions were given a great deal of autonomy on the battlefield, they had to think well on their feet.

Knowing these facts, we might expect Cornelius to have been a hardened military man, committed to might and duty above all. But his piety and generosity leave a different impression. For instance, he gave to the poor and prayed regularly to God (see 10:2). What had made the difference? Cornelius, apparently an Italian, had adopted the religion of his new land. Like a number of other Gentiles, he had converted to Judaism. He had turned away from the polytheism of his culture so that he could worship the one true God.

Attracted by Judaism's higher ethical standards and disillusioned with the parade of pagan deities, many Gentiles seriously considered converting. Ancient inscriptions indicate that numerous soldiers like Cornelius were interested in foreign religions like Judaism. However, more women than men converted to Judaism, since they needed to fulfill only two of the three requirements: (1) be circumcised, (2) be baptized, and (3) offer a sacrifice. Those who had not met all the requirements, but were close, were called "God-fearers." They could worship in the synagogues. Cornelius, the centurion, was a God-fearer.

Verse 3 more literally reads, "the ninth hour of the day." This would have been the customary time for prayer in Judea in the first century A.D. By our reckoning, it would have been three o'clock in the afternoon when Cornelius had a vision. It began with an angel of God appearing and calling the centurion's name. Staring at the angel in fear, Cornelius somehow managed to reply, "What is it, Lord?" (vs. 4). The soldier naturally wondered why the angel had come to him.

The heavenly visitor explained that God had chosen Cornelius to be an instrument of His grace. Cornelius' good works (and the true faith and piety behind them) had not gone unnoticed. The angel compared the centurion's prayers and charitable gifts to a memorial offering to God. This was a portion of the grain offering burned on the altar (see Lev. 2:2, 9, 16). It was pleasing to God.

The angel, having assured Cornelius of God's approval, gave the centurion his instructions. Cornelius was to send for a man named Simon Peter. He could be found staying at the home of a tanner, also named Simon, who lived near the sea in Joppa (see Acts 10:5–6). This city was 31 miles south of Caesarea. A tanner made his living by turning the hides of animals into leather goods.

Peter's host, the tanner named Simon, may have made his home by the sea for convenience. Sea salt was sometimes used for curing leather before tanning. Handling carcasses was distasteful for Jews because it left a person ritually unclean (see Lev. 11:8, 39–40). For a tanner such as Simon, purification would have been quite difficult. His daily contact with dead animals left him almost perpetually unclean. Peter showed his openness toward unclean people, which included Gentiles, by staying at the home of a tanner.

As a soldier, Cornelius was familiar with obeying orders as well as giving them. So, while he probably felt overwhelmed by the vision, he nevertheless hurried to do as he had been commanded. He told two of his servants and a devout soldier (who was one of his personal attendants) what had happened and then sent them on to bring back Peter from Joppa (see Acts 10:7–8). Cornelius' household probably consisted of relatives and servants. Since Roman custom expected members of the household to follow the religion of the head of the family unit, it was natural for Cornelius to have spread his faith to his entire household.

As noted earlier, God used a vision to direct Peter to accompany Cornelius' men from Joppa to Caesarea (see vss. 19–20). First, though, Peter invited the three Gentile men to be his guests for the remainder of the day—something no strict Jew would have done (see vs. 23). The next day, Peter, along with six Jewish believers from Joppa (see 11:12), traveled to Caesarea with the visitors. After lodging somewhere for the night, the group used part of the following day to finish their journey. Meanwhile, Cornelius and a houseful of guests had assembled in anticipation of Peter's arrival (see 10:24).

When the apostle entered Cornelius' home, the centurion greeted Peter, fell prostrate at his feet, and worshiped him (see vs. 25). This was the way in which the Roman soldier, in his ignorance, demonstrated his piety and showed respect for Peter. Nonetheless, the apostle did not want even a hint of misplaced honor. So, after helping Cornelius get up, Peter stated that he was neither an angel nor a god, but rather a mere mortal (see vs. 26).

B. Providing Clarification: vss. 27–29

Talking with him, Peter went inside and found a large gathering of people. He said to them: "You are well aware that it is against our law for a Jew to associate with a Gentile or visit him. But God has shown me that I should not call any man impure or unclean. So when I was sent for, I came without raising any objection. May I ask why you sent for me?"

In the first century A.D., wealthier families of Palestine lived in homes with one or more courtyards. A courtyard in the home of Cornelius may have been where Peter addressed a crowd the centurion had gathered (see Acts 10:27). Evidently, the apostle passed through the gate room and on into the courtyard full of curious Gentiles. Upon seeing them, Peter explained the laws of his nation prohibited Jews from fraternizing with or approaching a non-Jew (see vs. 28).

There was no specific Old Testament law that forbade Jews from fraternizing with Gentiles. Nonetheless, the purity regulations curtailed many forms of socializing. Jewish oral and written traditions banned having any dealings with foreigners. Later Jewish laws actually provided Jewish-Gentile partnerships. Jews could even bathe in the same bathhouses with Gentiles.

The problem was that such encounters always left Jews ceremonially unclean. Yet, as Peter explained to his audience, God used a vision to reveal to the apostle that he must not label any person as either ritually sullied or impure. This is the reason Peter, upon learning that Cornelius had sent for the apostle, came without lodging a protest. Now that Peter was at Cornelius' home, the apostle politely asked why the centurion wanted Peter to come (see vs. 29).

II. PETER'S PROCLAMATION OF THE GOSPEL: ACTS 10:30–38

A. The Explanation Offered by Cornelius: vss. 30–33

Cornelius answered: "Four days ago I was in my house praying at this hour, at three in the afternoon. Suddenly a man in shining clothes stood before me and said, 'Cornelius, God has heard your prayer and remembered your gifts to the poor. Send to Joppa for Simon who is called Peter. He is a guest in the home of Simon the tanner, who lives by the sea.' So I sent for you immediately, and it was good of you to come. Now we are all here in the presence of God to listen to everything the Lord has commanded you to tell us."

In response to Peter's question, Cornelius explained that four days earlier (namely, the day before the apostle experienced his vision; see Acts 10:3, 9), the centurion was praying around three o'clock in the afternoon. Then he saw an angel wearing dazzling garments standing in front of him (see vs. 30). The heaven-sent messenger stated that God had not only heard Cornelius' prayer but also took note of his charitable acts to the impoverished (see vs. 31; vs. 4).

Verse 32 reiterates what appears in verse 3—namely, that Cornelius was to request Peter to come to the centurion's home in Caesarea. Cornelius clarified that he acted promptly, and then expressed his appreciation for Peter's willingness to make the trip on short notice. As the apostle could see, an entire group of people had assembled to listen attentively to whatever the Spirit had placed on Peter's heart to share. From the centurion's perspective, God was actively present in the gathering to convey His message through His chosen spokesperson (see vs. 33).

B. The Good News Offered by Peter: vss. 34–38

Then Peter began to speak: "I now realize how true it is that God does not show favoritism but accepts men from every nation who fear him and do what is right. You know the message God sent to the people of Israel, telling the good news of peace through Jesus Christ, who is Lord of all. You know what has happened throughout Judea, beginning in Galilee after the baptism that John preached—how God anointed Jesus of Nazareth with the Holy Spirit and power, and how he went around doing good and healing all who were under the power of the devil, because God was with him."

The desire shared by Cornelius and his household was to know God better. Put differently, the centurion and his family had a teachable attitude and eagerly desired to learn what the Lord's representative had to say. For his part, Peter recognized that he could not allow his traditions and previously held prejudices to stand in the way of a work that God wanted to do. In the presence of Gentile listeners, the apostle acknowledged a new understanding of the way God works.

Peter admitted that God is interested in non-Jews, as well as Jews, and that He does not show partiality in dealing with people (see Acts 10:34). Rather than exclude people from all over the world due to their ethnicity or cultural background, the Creator welcomes them into His spiritual family (see Matt. 28:18–20; Luke 24:47; Acts 1:8). These are individuals of faith who revered God and sought to live virtuously (see Acts 10:35). The latter included treating others with justice, mercy, and compassion (see Mic. 6:8).

Having made these points, Peter shifted the focus to the Gospel. Its message was straightforward—namely, that Jesus, the Messiah, came to the "people of Israel" (Acts 10:36) to bring them "peace" (namely, reconciliation with God; Rom. 5:1, 9–11; 2 Cor. 5:18–21; Eph. 2:17). On the eve of His crucifixion, Jesus told His followers He would not only leave them the Spirit and the Savior's teachings but also His peace (see John 14:27).

Peter declared that because Jesus is "Lord of all" (Acts 10:36; see Dan. 7:13–14; Rom. 10:12; Eph. 1:22; Col. 1:15–20), the Good News was meant for everyone. The apostle summarized the Messiah's three-year ministry (from A.D. 26–30) by noting that after the baptism performed by John, Jesus traveled throughout Galilee and Judea (among other places; see Acts 3:37). After growing up and spending His early adult years in Nazareth, Jesus ventured forth with the Father's anointing and the Spirit's enabling presence (see Matt. 3:16–17; Mark 1:10–11; Luke 1:32–34, 3:21–22). As the Savior, Jesus performed works of healing and was victorious over Satan (see Acts 10:38; Luke 10:18; John 12:31; Col. 2:15).

Peter emphasized that he and the rest of the apostles were privileged to be eyewitnesses of what Jesus taught and performed, whether in Judea or Jerusalem (see Acts 10:39; 1 John 1:1–3). Peter also noted that the civil and religious authorities unjustly crucified Jesus (see Deut. 21:22–23; Isa. 53:5; Zech. 12:10; Acts 5:30; Gal. 3:13). Yet, despite this travesty, the Father raised His Son from the dead on the third day and enabled Him to become visible to a select group (see Acts 10:40). These were not members of the general public, but Jesus' followers. They "ate and drank" (vs. 41) with Him during the period between His resurrection and ascension into heaven (see Luke 24:35–49; Acts 1:1–3).

Peter related that God had commissioned the apostles to proclaim Jesus as the Judge of all humankind, both "the living and the dead" (Acts 10:42; see John 5:22; Acts 17:31; Rom. 14:9; 2 Cor. 5:10; 2 Tim. 4:1; 1 Pet. 4:5). Furthermore, Jesus is the person about whom all the Old Testament prophets testified (see Luke 24:44–47; John 5:46; Rom. 1:2). Their central message was that by believing in the Savior, people could have their sins forgiven (see Acts 10:43). This truth applied to those listening to Peter. The Father wanted them to hear the Good News and receive the Son by faith (see Luke 24:47; Acts 13:38; 26:18).

Before Peter could finish, the Spirit fell upon Cornelius and the rest of his household (see Acts 10:44). Their tongues-speaking was a sign that the gift of the Spirit poured out on the saved Gentiles was in every respect equivalent to what the believing Jews experienced at Pentecost (see vs. 45; 2:1–4). Also, the tongues-speaking incident at Caesarea emphasized that God authorized believers to proclaim the Gospel to all people, regardless of their station in life, their nationality, or their material possessions (see 10:46).

In light of what had occurred, it was clear to Peter that it was God's will for the Gentile converts to be baptized, especially now that they, along with their saved Jewish peers, were indwelt by the Spirit (see vs. 47; 2:33; 11:15–18). Peter accepted the request of his hosts to stay with them a few more days, evidently to teach them further about their faith in the Messiah (see vs. 48). The apostle undoubtedly rejoiced in what God had done in bringing non-Jews to salvation.

Discussion Questions

1. Why did Peter travel from Joppa to Caesarea?
2. Why is it important for us to remain open to the Spirit's leading in our lives?
3. Why did Cornelius assemble his entire household to listen to Peter?
4. With whom does God want us to share the Gospel?
5. Why did Peter emphasize Jesus' healing ministry during His time on earth?

Contemporary Application

God used Peter to bring the Gospel to the household of Cornelius. Yet, before that could happen, the Lord needed to free Peter of unbiblical concepts. This included the incorrect notion that God did not want the apostle to affiliate with Gentiles. Peter also learned that when it comes to the need for salvation, God treats all people alike. So it was wrong for the apostle to regard others as being unfit, especially in terms of hearing the Good News.

Sometimes we can entertain unbiblical concepts when we proclaim the Gospel. This can happen when we allow our understanding of the Good News to be distorted by the perspective of our culture and life experiences. It can also occur when we filter scriptural truths through the narrow prism of our own ideas about who should or should not be allowed to become part of God's spiritual family.

As this week's lesson shows, God is most honored when our proclamation of the Gospel remains untainted by prejudice and narrow-mindedness. In Romans 10, Paul stated that since Jesus is "Lord of all" (vs. 12), everyone is invited to trust in Him for eternal life (see vs. 13). Yet, as the apostle asked, how is it possible for the lost to believe in Jesus apart from hearing the proclamation of the Gospel (see vs. 14)? This is where Jesus can use us, as His faithful followers, to share the Good News with the unsaved (see vs. 15). A key part of that endeavor is ensuring that when we tell others about the Messiah, we do not let biblically inaccurate ideas distort our message.

Trusting the Spirit

Scripture

Background Scripture: *Acts 11:1–18*
Scripture Lesson: *Acts 11:1–18*
Key Verse: "If God gave them the same gift as he gave us, who believed in the Lord Jesus Christ, who was I to think that I could oppose God?" *Acts 11:17*
Scripture Lesson for Children: *Acts 11:1–18*
Key Verse for Children: "Who was I to think that I could oppose God?" *Acts 11:17*

Lesson Aim

To build bridges of faith to people from different ethnic and cultural backgrounds.

Lesson Setting

Time: Around A.D. 40
Place: Caesarea and Joppa

Lesson Outline

Trusting the Spirit

    I. An Explanation Demanded: Acts 11:1–3
       A. *Evangelizing Gentiles: vs. 1*
       B. *Confronting Peter: vss. 2–3*
    II. An Explanation Offered: Acts 11:4–18
       A. *The Vision Peter Experienced: vss. 4–10*
       B. *The Spirit's Directive to Peter: vss. 11–14*
       C. *The Spirit's Indwelling Gentile Converts: vss. 15–18*

Introduction for Adults

Topic: *The Welcoming Committee*

In George Orwell's book titled *Animal Farm*, the statement is made that all creatures are equal, but some are more equal than others. Tragically, that's the way things often work in congregational gatherings. Some members seem to be more important and valuable than others. When this attitude prevails, it drives people away from Jesus.

Peter had to swallow his pride and set aside his religious traditions when he went to visit a Gentile named Cornelius. Likewise, there are times when the adults in your class will have to do the same, especially when new people show up at church activities. Let your students know that God plays no favorites, not even within the church.

Because God wants all people to be saved, believers should work hard to make everyone in the church feel accepted, welcomed, and loved. Yes, this is an act of faith on the part of your students. Let them know they can trust the Lord to help them overcome their reservations.

Introduction for Youth

Topic: *Heresy Trial!*

Most teens struggle with some form of prejudice in their lives. Such intolerance among Christians is like a disease that threatens to harm and destroy the church. Taking a close look at our attitudes toward others is the first step in eliminating prejudice. It means we are willing to admit that when it comes to salvation, everyone is God's favorite.

In this regard, saved teens can take some pointers from the first Christians, who were Jews. Regrettably, they had been taught to hate and fear Gentiles. This week's lesson will help your students to examine Peter's visit to Cornelius, to learn how the Holy Spirit helped the apostle triumph over his prejudice, and to find out how the Spirit used him to convince his friends in Jerusalem to do the same.

Concepts for Children

Topic: *Make Room for Others*

1. Some of Peter's friends were angry because he talked to outsiders.
2. Peter said that God wanted these people to put their faith in Jesus.
3. Peter noted that God helped him to share the Gospel with the outsiders.
4. Peter explained that God wanted all sorts of people to join the church.
5. God can use us to welcome others who visit our church.

Lesson Commentary

I. AN EXPLANATION DEMANDED: ACTS 11:1–3

A. Evangelizing Gentiles: vs. 1

The apostles and the brothers throughout Judea heard that the Gentiles also had received the word of God.

From our study last week of Acts 10, we learned about Cornelius, a Roman centurion who revered God. While Cornelius was praying, he experienced a vision in which an angel told him to send for Peter. At that time, the apostle was staying at the house of a tanner named Simon, who lived in Joppa. After Peter arrived, he told Cornelius and his household that the Lord had convinced the apostle to place no restrictions on the proclamation of the Gospel. This is because God accepts everyone who honors and follows Him. Indeed, Peter acknowledged that he personally had witnessed Jesus, during His earthly ministry, spreading the Good News throughout Galilee, Judea, and Jerusalem.

Peter's sermon to his Gentile listeners was an immediate success. When the apostle spoke about Jesus being empowered by the Holy Spirit, that same Spirit began to fill the non-Jews who had gathered at the house of Cornelius to hear Peter's proclamation. In short, the Spirit gave the centurion and his guests the same power that had fallen upon the Jewish believers in the upper room on the day of Pentecost. From God's perspective, there was no difference in the spiritual status of believing Jews and Gentiles, for they all belonged to the body of Christ as equals and partners in the faith (see Gal. 3:26–29; Eph. 2:14–15). Peter recognized that this incident was God's way of confirming His acceptance of not only Cornelius but also any Gentiles who would believe the Good News. It is for this reason that the apostle baptized the Gentiles who heard his message that day and put their faith in the Savior.

Acts 10:45 draws attention to the Jews who accompanied Peter from Joppa to Caesarea. Peter was prudent in bringing six Jewish believers with him (see 10:23; 11:12). Indeed, they would serve as confirming witnesses that the Spirit had been poured out upon Gentiles. At the moment it occurred, Peter's colleagues became "astonished" (10:45). The underlying Greek verb refers to people feeling overwhelmed by a shocking experience. As Acts 11 reveals, the early Jewish Christians initially did not realize that God had meant the Gospel for Gentiles as well as Jews. They could accept the possibility that God would seek Gentiles. But the Jewish followers of the Savior thought that it was something entirely different for God not to require believing Gentiles to become ceremonially clean as full converts before He baptized them with the Spirit.

It did not take long for the Jewish believers back in Jerusalem, as well as those residing in Judea, to learn that as a result of Peter's preaching, Gentiles (whom the Jews viewed as uncircumcised pagans) had accepted the saving message about Jesus (see vs. 1). God was using this event to teach the young church an important lesson. It was not circumcision or any other action that opened the way for the provision of the Spirit. Rather, it was God's grace alone that touched hearts through faith (see Eph. 2:8–9). Also, God's unmerited favor, which was revealed through the cross of Christ, transformed unregenerate sinners into God's holy people.

B. Confronting Peter: vss. 2–3

So when Peter went up to Jerusalem, the circumcised believers criticized him and said, "You went into the house of uncircumcised men and ate with them."

After arriving in Jerusalem, Peter experienced a strong response from his Jewish peers. Acts 11:2, in referring to them as "circumcised believers," drew attention to their scrupulous observance of the Mosaic law. The Greek verb translated "criticized" refers to expressing sharp disapproval concerning what someone has done. The tense of the verb indicates that those who found fault with Peter did so repeatedly. Their deeply ingrained assumptions prevented them from comprehending the extraordinary work God had done among the Gentiles. For this reason, the Lord had to intervene in a dramatic way to ensure that the early church fully accepted believing Gentiles and sponsored evangelistic efforts to reach non-Jews with the Gospel.

Circumcision had been practiced for thousands of years by many peoples around the world, especially those living in the ancient Near East. As noted in lesson 4, God chose this practice as a sign to mark those males who were in covenant with Him. Hebrew circumcision began with Abraham and was formalized in the law of Moses (see Gen. 17:10–14; Lev. 12:3). Over time, some Jews began to see circumcision, not as a *sign* of relationship with God, but as the *means* to a relationship with Him. For a while, the early church held on to this overvaluation of circumcision. Eventually, church leaders recognized that even though believing Jews were free to decide whether to circumcise themselves and their sons, no one should force saved Gentiles to be circumcised.

Years later, Paul would encounter a similar level of opposition from religious legalists in Galatia (see Gal. 2:11–21). During a period in which Paul was absent from the Gentile believers there, some Jews who professed to be Christians had come among the Galatians and begun calling into question the apostle's authority and spreading false doctrine. Today these false teachers are called Judaizers. The legalists apparently taught that faith in Christ was not adequate for acceptance by God. Obedience to the Mosaic law, or at least to parts of it (for example, dealing with circumcision, the sabbath, and dietary restrictions), was also necessary. Consequently, the antagonists were trying to enforce the law on the Gentile believers in Galatia.

The Judaizers' teaching drew a fierce reaction from Paul. In the apostle's mind, to make the law mandatory for salvation was, in effect, to nullify the Gospel. Salvation was by grace through faith in the Son alone, apart from the works of the law. Believers were not bound by the law, but were freed from its condemnation due to their union with the Messiah. For the time being, Paul could not go to Galatia to straighten out the churches in person. So he wrote to them, defending his teachings and his status as an apostle (chaps. 1—2), explaining Christian freedom from the law (chaps. 3—4), and encouraging the Galatians to live out their freedom in Christ (chaps. 5—6).

II. AN EXPLANATION OFFERED: ACTS 11:4–18

A. The Vision Peter Experienced: vss. 4–10

Peter began and explained everything to them precisely as it had happened: "I was in the city of Joppa praying, and in a trance I saw a vision. I saw something like a large sheet being let down from heaven by its four corners, and it came down to where I was. I looked into it and saw four-footed animals of the earth, wild beasts, reptiles, and birds of the air. Then I heard a voice telling me, 'Get up, Peter. Kill and eat.' I replied, 'Surely not, Lord! Nothing impure or unclean has ever entered my mouth.' The voice spoke from heaven a second time, 'Do not call anything impure that God has made clean.' This happened three times, and then it was all pulled up to heaven again."

The summary in Acts 11:4–10 of the vision Peter experienced mirrors what is recorded in 10:9–16. God used this incident to teach the revolutionary truth that believing Gentiles can become a part of the church. Peter, realizing this, told his Jewish colleagues exactly what occurred, and he was careful to do so point by point (see 11:4). Peter's vision took place on the flat root of Simon's house in Joppa (see 10:9; 11:5). Roofs in that era were used something like suburban decks are used today. Most likely, Peter used an outside stairway to access the rooftop at about noon for prayer. It must have been a pleasant place to pray, with the Mediterranean sparkling in the distance and the call of seabirds in the air.

Eventually, Peter became hungry and asked for lunch. While waiting to eat, Peter fell into a trance and saw a vision (see 10:10; 11:5). Like dreams, visions were experiences through which supernatural insight or awareness was bestowed by divine revelation. While dreams occurred only during sleep, visions could happen while a person was awake (see Dan. 10:7).

In Peter's case, he was filled with a heightened awareness of God's will regarding Cornelius. The apostle stared at what looked like a huge linen sheet being lowered by its corners from heaven (see Acts 10:11; 11:5). The sheet contained many kinds of tame and wild mammals, reptiles, and birds (see 10:12; 11:6). As a devout Jew, Peter immediately recognized that the sheet included both clean and unclean creatures. Among the clean animals may have been cows, sheep, and fish. Among the unclean animals may have been pigs, lizards, and vultures. Since the animals were all mixed together, by Jewish thinking even the clean animals were now unclean.

Old Testament law made a distinction between clean and unclean animals (see Lev. 11). Jews were permitted to eat clean animals, but not unclean ones.

The distinction between clean and unclean creatures did not necessarily have anything to do with the actual dirtiness of the animals. The differentiation itself was what was important. It symbolized the distinction between God's covenant people—the Jews—and all others (see lesson 2 of the December quarter for more information). As noted earlier, under the new covenant established by Jesus, believing Jews and Gentiles are equals within the church. So the distinction symbolized by uncleanness no longer exists. This was a key emphasis in Peter's vision (see Acts 10:34–35; 11:17).

The incredible sight unfolding before Peter was accompanied by a voice commanding the apostle to slaughter and eat the creatures on the large sheet (see 10:13; 11:7). Though he was hungry, the apostle protested that he had never consumed anything unclean (see 10:14; 11:8). Jesus had already taught that the dietary laws were obsolete and discontinued (see Matt. 15:11–20; Mark 7:14–23), but apparently Peter had not yet learned the lesson. He thought God could not seriously want him to eat unclean meat. For each of us, learning what God expects is a lifelong process. God forgives us when we repent. But He wants us to move along in our understanding of His wishes and our obedience to them as fast as we are able.

As Peter's vision continued, the voice sounded again, this time forbidding Peter (and all Christians) from calling anything common or unclean (and thus unacceptable) that God had called clean (and thus acceptable; see Acts 10:15; 11:9). By telling Peter to eat the animals on the sheet, God had declared the animals clean. Symbolically, the Lord had done away with the distinction between clean and unclean animals. But, as previously stated, the vision was not mainly about food. God reinforced the impact of the vision by showing it to Peter three times. Then the vision ended with the linen sheet suddenly being pulled back to heaven (see 10:16; 11:10).

B. The Spirit's Directive to Peter: vss. 11–14

"Right then three men who had been sent to me from Caesarea stopped at the house where I was staying. The Spirit told me to have no hesitation about going with them. These six brothers also went with me, and we entered the man's house. He told us how he had seen an angel appear in his house and say, 'Send to Joppa for Simon who is called Peter. He will bring you a message through which you and all your household will be saved.'"

Acts 11:11–14 restates some of the same information appearing in 10:17–20, while adding a few more details. As Peter contemplated the meaning of the vision, the men Cornelius had dispatched discovered the location of Simon the tanner's house. The men approached the gate and asked whether this was the place where Peter was lodging. Meanwhile, as the apostle puzzled over the vision, the Spirit disclosed that three men were looking for him.

Peter was directed to get up, go downstairs (that is, by using an exterior stairway), and accompany the visitors without hesitation. The apostle could travel with these Gentiles without any misgivings, for the Lord ultimately was responsible for sending them. Peter noted that six believing Jews also came along with him, and it was the entire group that entered the centurion's house. After doing so, Cornelius explained to the apostle that an angel directed the centurion to request that Peter travel to Caesarea. The angel also told the centurion that the apostle would deliver a word from God concerning how Cornelius and his entire household would be saved.

C. The Spirit's Indwelling Gentile Converts: vss. 15–18

"As I began to speak, the Holy Spirit came on them as he had come on us at the beginning. Then I remembered what the Lord had said: 'John baptized with water, but you will be baptized with the Holy Spirit.' So if God gave them the same gift as he gave us, who believed in the Lord Jesus Christ, who was I to think that I could oppose God?" When they heard this, they had no further objections and praised God, saying, "So then, God has granted even the Gentiles repentance unto life."

Acts 11:15 summarizes corresponding information appearing in 10:44. Peter remembered that the Holy Spirit fell upon the Gentiles listening to the apostle just as He did on Jesus' Jewish disciples on the day of Pentecost (see 2:1–4). Peter recalled the statement Jesus made sometime during the 40-day period between His resurrection and ascension (see 11:16; Luke 3:16; Acts 1:1–5). Specifically, Jesus drew a contrast between the baptism performed by John and that provided by the Spirit. The first was physical in nature ("with water"; Acts 11:16) while the second was supernatural in nature ("with the Holy Spirit"). The passive tense of the Greek verb rendered "will be baptized" (Acts 1:5) indicates that this act did not depend on the efforts of Jesus' followers to bring it about, but rather on the work of the Lord. Through the ministry of the Spirit, Jesus' disciples would be placed into spiritual union with one another in the body of Christ, the church (see 1 Cor. 12:12–13).

The Lord's teaching during this 40-day period included a command that the apostles were to wait in Jerusalem until they had received the gift of the Holy Spirit (see Acts 1:4). What was Jesus' purpose for having the disciples wait until the Spirit came? One reason may have been so that the fulfillment of the promise might coincide with the day of Pentecost and mark the beginning of a new phase in the development of God's plan. From a practical perspective, the waiting period possibly impressed the disciples with the important role the Spirit would serve in the fulfillment of their mission. As crucial as that mission was, it could not begin until the Spirit had been given.

Moreover, it was the same Spirit who came upon the Gentiles while Peter was speaking at the home of Cornelius. The apostle reasoned that the Father graciously bestowed upon them the "gift" (11:17) of the Spirit, just as God had done for Jesus' Jewish followers on the day of Pentecost. Both Jews and Gentiles, having repented of their sin and put their faith in the Messiah, were spiritually regenerated. In the New Testament, the Greek noun translated "repentance" conveys the idea of changing one's mind. In a religious sense, it signifies a turnabout in attitude toward God and life's priorities. Repentance is part of the conversion process. Through the working of the Spirit, sinners come to the point at which they are ready to turn away from sin and place their trust in Jesus for salvation.

In light of what Peter witnessed taking place among Cornelius and the members of his household, Peter saw no reason to hinder the work of God. The implication was that neither should the apostle's Jewish peers in Jerusalem stand in the way of God's will. Thankfully, they agreed, for they discontinued raising any further objections to what Peter had done. Instead, they began praising the Father for enabling Gentiles to abandon their sins, turn to Jesus in faith, and receive eternal life (see vs. 18).

Discussion Questions

1. Why did the believers in Jerusalem criticize Peter for what he had done in Caesarea?
2. Why did Peter initially recoil from the thought of eating anything that was ceremonially unclean?
3. What convinced Peter's Jewish peers that God had opened the door of the church to believing Gentiles?
4. Why would it be wrong to exclude certain groups of people from hearing the Gospel?
5. What sorts of challenges does your church face in reaching out to those who are from another culture?

Contemporary Application

Peter's audience knew that at one time he would not have associated with Gentiles. The fact that he was now meeting with Cornelius and his household was undeniable proof that God could change someone from being prejudiced to being equitable and loving. Peter's personal testimony powerfully influenced his peers in Jerusalem to sponsor reaching out to all people with the Gospel.

At first we may not be in the mood to change the way we think about others. In these situations we should choose to obey God regardless of how we feel. This is an act of faith on our part. We trust the Lord to help us overcome our prejudices. We know that He will not let us down. In time we will change our feelings to match the way we are acting.

Like Peter, we may continue to struggle with prejudices that tend to prevent or weaken our outreach to certain people (see Gal. 2:11–14). We can overcome our irrational attitudes by including all types of people, rather than excluding certain ones, as we tell them the good news about Jesus.

Experiencing God's Rescue

Scripture

Background Scripture: *Acts 12:1–24*
Scripture Lesson: *Acts 12:1–11*
Key Verse: Peter was kept in prison, but the church was earnestly praying to God for him. *Acts 12:5*
Scripture Lesson for Children: *Acts 12:1–11*
Key Verse for Children: Peter came to himself and said, "Now I know without a doubt that the Lord sent his angel and rescued me." *Acts 12:11*

Lesson Aim

To appreciate the power of prayer in difficult situations.

Lesson Setting

Time: Around A.D. *43*
Place: Jerusalem

Lesson Outline

Experiencing God's Rescue

    I. Peter's Arrest: Acts 12:1–4
        A. *The Execution of James: vss. 1–2*
        B. *The Imprisonment of Peter: vss. 3–4*
    II. Peter's Miraculous Escape: Acts 12:5–11
        A. *The Believers' Earnest Prayer: vs. 5*
        B. *The Angel's Appearance: vss. 6–7*
        C. *The Angel's Intervention: vss. 8–10*
        D. *The Realization of What Happened: vs. 11*

Introduction for Adults

Topic: *Who Will Come to the Rescue?*

The beheading of James and the arrest of Peter must have been occasions for deep introspection among Jesus' followers in the Jerusalem congregation. Perhaps unconfessed sins were acknowledged and recommitments made to wholeheartedly follow the Savior.

Even when we go through the painful process of repentance, we must never forget that God shows mercy and bestows blessings upon us because it pleases Him to do so, not because we deserve it. Many people, believers and unbelievers alike, act as if God is somehow obligated to grant any and all requests made of Him. But since sin placed all humanity under a death sentence, it would be unwise indeed to demand that a just and holy God give us what we deserve.

The wonderful truth arising from this week's lesson is that God still answers the prayers of His children today, whether for themselves or for others in crisis. But there is a condition. He expects us to be walking in obedience to His will when we come to Him with our requests (see John 15:7). If there is unconfessed sin in our lives, the first prayer the Lord wants to hear from us is one of confession and repentance. Then the way is clear for prayers of petition and intercession.

Introduction for Youth

Topic: *Miraculous Prison Break!*

When new offices or shopping centers are built today, they can be "instantly" landscaped with bushes, rolls of sod, and even large trees. That kind of portable landscaping is not what the prophet Jeremiah described when he told his audience to "plant" themselves in God (Jer. 17:7–8). Like firmly rooted trees, Jesus' followers in the Jerusalem congregation could remain faithful to Him, and do so regardless of their harsh circumstances.

Always standing for what is right challenges our faith. It is tempting to follow the crowd instead. Yet just as a tree embeds itself in the soil to brace itself against the wind and rain, so we believers can anchor ourselves in the Lord Jesus to withstand attacks against us. In this week's lesson, we see how the early church stood against the wrath of King Herod. Just as the Lord was with them, so He will be with us, especially as we honor Him in all that we say and do.

Concepts for Children

Topic: *Rescued!*

1. Herod was an evil ruler.
2. Herod wanted to kill a church leader named Peter.
3. Jesus' followers asked God to protect Peter.
4. God answered the prayers of Jesus' followers.
5. God listens to our prayers, regardless of what is going on in our lives.

Lesson Commentary

I. PETER'S ARREST: ACTS 12:1–4

A. The Execution of James: vss. 1–2

It was about this time that King Herod arrested some who belonged to the church, intending to persecute them. He had James, the brother of John, put to death with the sword.

As noted in lesson 4, after Stephen's stoning (see Acts 7:59–60), many from Jerusalem fled for their lives (see 8:2–4). Some were Greek-speaking Jews, and they were telling the Gospel to Jews in Phoenicia (a coastal area north of Palestine), Cyprus (an island in the northwest corner of the Mediterranean), and the city of Antioch (the capital of the province of Syria, with a population of about half of a million; 11:19). Some unnamed believers from Cyprus and Cyrene (a city in North Africa) began preaching to the Greeks in Antioch (whether God-fearing Gentiles or pagans), and many of them put their faith in Jesus (see vss. 20–21).

We can imagine the leaders of the Jerusalem congregation vigorously discussing how the Gentiles in Antioch had come to faith in the Savior and deciding whom they should send to look into the matter. They wisely chose Barnabas (see vs. 22). As he investigated the situation (possibly around A.D. 38), he was convinced that the new converts were the recipients of God's saving grace (see vs. 23). Barnabas was aware of the challenges that lay ahead for them, so he urged them to remain devoted to the Lord with a steadfast heart. Barnabas lived in a way that was consistent with his words. Verse 24 says the Spirit was in complete control of Barnabas' life, and he had an unshakable confidence in God.

There were other reasons why Barnabas was an exceptional choice. First, since he was from Cyprus, he may have known some of the believers from the island who had preached to the Greeks in Antioch. Second, Barnabas—who was nicknamed "son of encouragement" (4:36; see the corresponding commentary in lesson 2)—was gracious to others. Third, Barnabas was wise, for he recognized that he could not nourish the growing congregation alone. So, perhaps around A.D. 39, he brought Saul (or Paul) from Tarsus to help him disciple the young believers for the next year (see 11:25–26).

Saul had been out of the limelight for about three years. During this time, as he operated out of Tarsus, he may have concentrated on personal growth. Undoubtedly, he also shared the Gospel with his family and friends. Luke noted that Jesus' followers at Antioch were the first to be called Christians (namely, "those of the household of Christ"). Some think opponents of the church sarcastically referred to believers as Christians. Others think the disciples adopted the name to draw attention to their allegiance to the Messiah. Either way, the moniker distinguished Jesus' followers from other religious and political groups (see Acts 26:28; 1 Pet. 4:16).

The Jerusalem congregation sent not only Barnabas, but also "prophets" (Acts 11:27) to help the church in Antioch. These believers had the ability to proclaim revelations from God, including predictions of future events. For instance, a prophet named Agabus foretold, perhaps in an assembly of believers, that a severe famine was imminent. By this he did not mean a global famine, but a chronic lack of food due to successive years of inadequate harvests in various regions of the Roman Empire (see vs. 28). Luke noted that this incident occurred during the reign of Claudius Caesar (A.D. 41–54).

At this time, the believers living in Judea were hit especially hard by a severe food shortage. Previously, the Jerusalem congregation had given spiritual resources (including leaders) to the believers in Antioch. Now the latter group returned the favor by collecting relief for their fellow Christians, which was then given to Barnabas and Saul to take to the elders of the Jerusalem church (see vss. 29–30). Next, these monies were distributed in an appropriate manner to the believers in need of help. Even though one congregation was primarily Jewish and the other mainly Gentile, both groups of Christians strove for unity by helping the other any way they could.

"About this time" (12:1) would have been A.D. 43, when another wave of persecution came against the church. "King Herod" was Herod Agrippa I, who ruled from A.D. 37 to 44. He was born in 10 B.C. to Aristobulus and Bernice. Aristobulus was the son Herod the Great, while Bernice was the daughter of Herod's sister, Salome. This information indicates that Agrippa was an Edomite, not a Jew. During Agrippa's youth, he attended school in Rome, and after his mother's death, he lived in an irresponsible, lavish manner. In the ensuing years, Agrippa incurred more debts and was imprisoned by the Emperor Tiberius for a subversive comment Agrippa made.

Six months later, in A.D. 37 when Tiberius died, Agrippa's friend Caligula became emperor. He not only freed Agrippa from prison but also installed him as king over portions of northern and eastern Palestine. Caligula was murdered in A.D. 41 and succeeded by Agrippa's childhood friend Claudius. He both reaffirmed Agrippa's kingship and made him ruler over Judea and Samaria. This meant Agrippa exercised control over approximately the same amount of territory once ruled by his grandfather, Herod the Great. Agrippa presided over this reunited domain until his sudden death in A.D. 44 at the age of 54. That event, which took place in Caesarea, is detailed in both Acts 12:20–23 and the writings of Josephus (a first-century Jewish scholar and historian).

Even though Agrippa was a benefactor of Rome, he was shrewd enough to recognize that he had to deal diplomatically with his Jewish subjects. In an attempt to win their favor, Agrippa began interrogating and beating members of the Jerusalem congregation (see vs. 1). Along with arresting some believers, Agrippa had James beheaded with a "sword" (vs. 2; a common form of Roman execution). Though we may not understand why, it was God's will to allow James to be executed.

James was the son of Zebedee and brother of John (see Luke 5:10; 6:14), and is not to be confused with James, the half-brother of Jesus. The beheading of James marks the first known martyr among the apostles (see Acts 1:13). During Jesus' earthly ministry, He foretold the suffering John and James would experience (see Matt. 20:23; Mark 10:39). The action Agrippa took against James ended the brief period of peace enjoyed by Jesus' disciples in Jerusalem and Judea (see Acts 9:31). Yet, as the narrative in chapter 12 reveals, not even a powerful Gentile ruler could thwart God's supreme power in advancing the proclamation of the Gospel.

B. The Imprisonment of Peter: vss. 3–4

When he saw that this pleased the Jews, he proceeded to seize Peter also. This happened during the Feast of Unleavened Bread. After arresting him, he put him in prison, handing him over to be guarded by four squads of four soldiers each. Herod intended to bring him out for public trial after the Passover.

In Galatians 2:8, Paul's reference to Peter indicates that he was in a lead role among the apostles. Moreover, verse 9 refers to Peter, along with James (the half-brother of Jesus) and John, as esteemed "pillars" of the Jerusalem congregation. Like columns supporting the temple, these three believers had a reputation of upholding the church. Put differently, they were the chief leaders of the Jerusalem congregation at this time. This may explain why Agrippa targeted Peter, knowing that the decision to behead James (the son of Zebedee) met with the approval of the religious leaders.

Acts 12:3 states that Peter's arrest occurred during the Festival of Unleavened Bread. This weeklong observance is first mentioned in Exodus 12:17 in conjunction with the Passover on the eve of Israel's departure from Egypt (see vs. 11). The Festival of Unleavened Bread involved eating bread made without yeast, holding several assemblies, and making designated offerings. It was designed to commemorate how the Lord rescued the Israelites out of Egypt with rapid speed. Because there were so many pilgrims in Jerusalem to observe the holy convocation, it was an opportune time for Agrippa to execute another prominent Christian leader.

After Peter was apprehended, Agrippa had the apostle taken to a prison, a place that most likely was crowded and filthy. The detention center may have been the Tower of Antonia, which was located on the northwest corner of the temple complex. In that day, a battalion of Roman soldiers was stationed at the fortress. Four squads of four Roman soldiers (that is, one detachment for each of the three-hour-long nighttime watches) stood guard over Peter.

Given the miraculous escape of the apostles from prison in A.D. 30 (see Acts 5:17–20 and the commentary in lesson 3), Agrippa did not want to take any chances of a similar episode occurring with Peter. The king's intent was that after the Passover festival, he would stage a "public trial" (12:4), in which Peter's conviction and execution were an assured outcome. Yet the Savior explicitly stated that Peter would lose his life only when he was old (see John 21:18–19). So, in the wave of persecution over the church instigated by Agrippa, the time for Peter to die had not yet come.

II. PETER'S MIRACULOUS ESCAPE: ACTS 12:5–11

A. The Believers' Earnest Prayer: vs. 5

So Peter was kept in prison, but the church was earnestly praying to God for him.

While Peter was in a secure prison, the rest of Jesus' followers in Jerusalem turned to the Lord in prayer (see Acts 12:5). The Greek adverb rendered "earnestly" implies that the believers' petitions were constant and intense, especially given the real danger Peter faced. James 5:16 reveals that when God's holy people enter into prayer, He enables their petitions to result in amazing outcomes. This certainly would be the case in the harrowing situation involving Peter.

In every case, whether public or private, one truth is clear—namely, that prayer is a powerful and effective means of accomplishing God's will. The Lord especially uses the earnest prayer of righteous believers (those who are characterized by virtue and integrity) to produce wonderful results in the lives of His people. Verse 17 offers a clarifying illustration. Elijah was an Old Testament prophet with the same human frailties that we have. This man, who was just like us, prayed earnestly that no rain would fall, and none fell for three and a half years (see Luke 4:25). Then, when he prayed again, rain fell from the skies and made the crops grow (see Jas. 5:18; 1 Kings 17:1; 18:41–46).

B. The Angel's Appearance: vss. 6–7

The night before Herod was to bring him to trial, Peter was sleeping between two soldiers, bound with two chains, and sentries stood guard at the entrance. Suddenly an angel of the Lord appeared and a light shone in the cell. He struck Peter on the side and woke him up. "Quick, get up!" he said, and the chains fell off Peter's wrists.

Acts 12:6 notes that during the night before Peter was to be tried publicly, God miraculously intervened. At this time, each of the apostle's wrists was shackled to chains, and he sat between two soldiers. Also, while Peter slept, several more soldiers were closely watching the entrance to the prison gate. It may be that the apostle was resigned to the inevitability of being executed within a short period of time.

Agrippa wanted to ensure that Peter could not break free and get away. Yet, despite the king's authority and power, he could not thwart God's will for the apostle and the Jerusalem congregation. We learn from verse 7 that all at once, a light flooded the cell and an angel sent by the Lord stood over the apostle. The heavenly emissary nudged Peter on his side in order to awaken him. The angel also directed the apostle to stand up at once, and enabled him to do so by causing the chains to drop from his wrists.

C. The Angel's Intervention: vss. 8–10

Then the angel said to him, "Put on your clothes and sandals." And Peter did so. "Wrap your cloak around you and follow me," the angel told him. Peter followed him out of the prison, but he had no idea that what the angel was doing was really happening; he thought he was seeing a vision. They passed the first and second guards and came to the iron gate leading to the city. It opened for them by itself, and they went through it. When they had walked the length of one street, suddenly the angel left him.

Once Peter was freed from his restraints, the angel directed the apostle to don his belt (or sash) and sandals. After Peter did so, the angel told the apostle to wrap himself with his outer garment (or cloak; Acts 12:8). Once Peter finished dressing (and even though he seemed groggy and confused), he accompanied the angel out of the prison. At this point the apostle did not realize what was happening, for he imagined he was seeing a vision (see vs. 9).

The angel led Peter past the first guard post and then the second. At last, the two came to an iron gate that led to a city street. The gate opened without anyone touching it and enabled the pair to leave. Then, as the angel and Peter started to walk down a side alley, the heavenly emissary all at once disappeared (see vs. 10). There may be a degree of irony to the timing of this escape. The Passover commemorated God's setting free His chosen people from bondage to Egypt. Similarly, God freed Peter from the shackles Herod imposed on the apostle in prison.

D. The Realization of What Happened: vs. 11

Then Peter came to himself and said, "Now I know without a doubt that the Lord sent his angel and rescued me from Herod's clutches and from everything the Jewish people were anticipating."

It did not take long for Peter to realize he was not experiencing a dream. He could see for himself that God had dispatched an angel to set the apostle free from the murderous clutches of Herod and the religious leaders (see Acts 12:11). Next, Peter walked to the home of Mary (who was possibly a wealthy widow), where some of Jesus' disciples had gathered to pray (see vs. 12). Mary was the mother of John Mark, who was the cousin of Barnabas (see Col. 4:10), an occasional traveling companion of Barnabas, Paul, and Peter (see Acts 12:25; 15:37; 1 Pet. 5:13), and the author of the second Synoptic Gospel.

After Peter arrived at the courtyard entrance, he knocked on the door. A female slave named Rhoda came to see who it was (see Acts 12:13). When she recognized the apostle's voice, Rhoda became so excited that she forgot to let him in. While Peter stood in the street, Rhoda ran back inside the house and told the group that the apostle was at the gate (see vs. 14). At first, though, no one believed her, even when she repeatedly said that Peter was outside. Supposedly, Rhoda had encountered the apostle's attending angel (see vs. 15; Gen. 48:16; Ps. 34:7; Matt. 18:10; Heb. 1:14). During this exchange, Peter continued knocking on the door, though without attracting the attention of nearby soldiers. Finally, when someone from the group opened the door, they were amazed to see the apostle standing there to greet them (see Acts 12:16).

Perhaps there was quite a bit of commotion, for Peter signaled with his hand that his fellow believers remain quiet. Next, the apostle briefly summarized how God's angel had led Peter out of the prison. He asked the disciples to let James (the half-brother of Jesus) and the rest of the believers with him (at another location) know what had happened. Then Peter went into hiding (see vs. 17). The chain of events summarized in verses 18 and 19 indicates the precarious nature of the situation. When it was early morning, the soldiers became distressed upon discovering that Peter was gone. After being told about the apostle's escape, Agrippa ordered that a search be made, which proved unsuccessful. Then, once the king had interrogated the sentries (perhaps involving torture), they were beheaded for their dereliction of duty.

Discussion Questions

1. Who was Herod?
2. Why did Herod decide to arrest Peter?
3. How did Jesus' disciples respond to the news of Peter's imprisonment?
4. What incentive do believers have to pray as a group?
5. What are some extraordinary ways God has intervened in your life?

Contemporary Application

The Jerusalem congregation faced a new wave of persecution, this time from Herod Agrippa. First, he had James beheaded. Second, he ordered Peter's arrest. His beheading would have been a foregone conclusion had Jesus' followers not prayed earnestly and God not miraculously intervened to deliver Peter.

From this episode we learn that prayer works. Anyone who prays regularly would agree. It is our strongest communication link with the God who created us. It is a powerful means for giving voice to our faith. Most important of all, God can use our prayers to change our world.

Hands, feet, back, and pocketbook—these are some of the means that come to mind when we think of helping our fellow Christians. They enable us to comfort, carry, accompany, and contribute. They are solid, tangible reminders that our petitions matter.

Prayer can also be power-producing and effective in more ways than we might realize at first. On the one hand, while prayer may not change our circumstances, it can indeed alter our response to those situations. On the other hand, prayer very well may change our circumstances. As we pray, our lives will reflect our prayerful hearts. We will find ourselves more in tune with the needs of others and better able to meet them because of our deeper walk with God. Our spiritual maturity will enrich our own lives even as it extends to those to whom we minister, bearing fruit in many ways as it touches many lives.

Affirming God's Impartiality

Scripture

Background Scripture: *Acts 15:1–35*

Scripture Lesson: *Acts 15:1–12*

Key Verses: "God, who knows the heart, showed that he accepted them by giving the Holy Spirit to them, just as he did to us. He made no distinction between us and them, for he purified their hearts by faith." *Acts 15:8–9*

Scripture Lesson for Children: *Acts 15:1–12*

Key Verse for Children: "[God] made no distinction between us and them." *Acts 15:9*

Lesson Aim

To affirm that we are saved by God's grace through faith.

Lesson Setting

Time: Around A.D. 49 or 50

Place: Jerusalem

Lesson Outline

Affirming God's Impartiality

    I. The Dispute: Acts 15:1–4

        A. *An Argument Erupts: vss. 1–2*

        B. *A Delegation Is Sent: vss. 3–4*

    II. The Deliberation: Acts 15:5–12

        A. *The Assertion Made by Some Pharisees: vs. 5*

        B. *The Testimony Offered by Peter: vss. 6–11*

        C. *The Testimony Offered by Barnabas and Paul: vs. 12*

Introduction for Adults

Topic: *Only in Jesus*

When the Jerusalem Council met, they affirmed that Jesus freely offers salvation without any preconditions. Yet, because this truth seems too simplistic or too available to everyone, some people today have attempted to place other prerequisites on becoming a part of God's family. For example, attending church regularly, being more good than bad, and having upstanding parents have been cited as a means of earning our way into heaven. Such heresy can quickly move into the church.

Most of your students probably have encountered people who have asserted these sorts of false teachings about salvation. Whether students have heard it from a member of a cult or discussed it with a neighbor or coworker, they probably all wished that they had been better prepared to reply to the other person's incorrect comments. This week's lesson will give class members the help they need to respond appropriately the next time.

Introduction for Youth

Topic: *Saved by Grace*

An anesthesiologist was administering a controlled mixture of oxygen and gas to a patient in a New York hospital. When one of the tanks was empty, the physician began using a new one clearly marked "Oxygen." Almost immediately the patient died. The coroner's autopsy revealed carbon dioxide poisoning. Upon investigation the second tank was found to contain pure carbon dioxide and to have been mislabeled.

Thankfully, such errors are rare. But in the spiritual realm they occur all the time. Regarding salvation, many younger and older people say, "As long as I sincerely try to be a good person, I'll come out all right in the end." Yet, no matter how correct such notions may seem, they are tragically wrong. As the leaders at the Jerusalem conference declared, the only way a person can be saved is by trusting in Jesus for eternal life.

Concepts for Children

Topic: *Faith in Jesus*

1. Long ago, some people said faith in Jesus alone does not save us.
2. These people said we had to follow a long list of rules.
3. Some church leaders talked about what they believed.
4. These church leaders said only faith in Jesus saves us.
5. When we trust in Jesus, God forgives our sins.

Lesson Commentary

I. THE DISPUTE: ACTS 15:1–4

A. An Argument Erupts: vss. 1–2

Some men came down from Judea to Antioch and were teaching the brothers: "Unless you are circumcised, according to the custom taught by Moses, you cannot be saved." This brought Paul and Barnabas into sharp dispute and debate with them. So Paul and Barnabas were appointed, along with some other believers, to go up to Jerusalem to see the apostles and elders about this question.

Despite the episodes of persecution Jesus' followers experienced, they continued to proclaim the Gospel, resulting in many more converts to the faith (see Acts 12:24). We learn in 13:1–3 that during a time of corporate worship, the Spirit told Jesus' followers at Syrian Antioch to set apart Barnabas and Saul for a special task. Once this was done, the church sent the two out on a journey to Gentile areas. Chapters 13 and 14 chronicle the first recorded missionary journey involving Barnabas and Saul (A.D. 46–48). They began by sailing from the port of Seleucia to the island of Cyprus. While there, God used Saul to display His power over a Jewish sorcerer, and as a result, the proconsul (or governor) in the city of Paphos believed (see 13:4–12).

Starting in 13:9, the narrative begins using Saul's Roman and Hellenistic name, Paul. This was appropriate since the apostle launched his career as a missionary to the Gentiles. Also, in verse 13, the account made a subtle shift by referring to "Paul and his companions," apparently indicating that from then on the apostle would take the lead role in the evangelistic outreach. So after Paul and Barnabas left Paphos, they first journeyed to the coast of Asia Minor and then traveled inland eight miles to the city of Perga. With them was John Mark, who, the passage says, decided to leave and return to Jerusalem. No reason is given for his departure, though 15:37–39 notes Paul's annoyance with John Mark for deserting the missionary team. Even without his help and despite the occurrence of opposition from antagonists to the Gospel, Paul and Barnabas witnessed many people put their trust in the Savior.

Upon their return to Antioch in Syria, the missionaries assembled the church and rehearsed how the Lord worked powerfully through them (see 14:26–27). This especially included how God had thrown the "door of faith" wide open to the Gentiles. Then, for the next year, Paul and Barnabas remained in the city to proclaim the Gospel (see vs. 28). Previously, when Gentiles such as Cornelius and his household became Christians, it left some Jewish believers feeling uneasy. This discomfort became more acute when they heard that many Gentiles in Asia Minor had come to faith through the ministry of Paul and Barnabas.

In A.D. 49 or 50, some of the dissatisfied Jewish believers decided to take action. They traveled about 300 miles from Judea to Antioch in Syria—the epicenter of Gentile converts to Christianity—and began teaching that these non-Jews had to be "circumcised" (15:1), as well as obey the other laws of Moses, in order to be saved. The message that faith was not enough for salvation ignited a firestorm of debate, in which Paul and Barnabas vigorously argued that people are saved by God's grace through faith (see vs. 2). The two missionaries had witnessed God at work among uncircumcised Gentiles, and had seen their lives changed in ways the Mosaic law could never achieve. The sharp disagreement eventually came to Jerusalem, where Paul, Barnabas, and some other believers were appointed to argue before the apostles and elders against imposing any additional requirements for salvation.

Acts 15 is sometimes called the "Continental Divide" of the New Testament. Indeed, the events recorded here have affected the flow of church history ever since. The narrative records how God moved the church from the dangers of rigid legalism to spiritual freedom, and from rules that coddle the sinful nature to dependence on the Spirit to transform one's heart. Perhaps some of the religious legalists, who may have been Pharisees (see vs. 5), later affiliated with the Judaizers (see also the corresponding information in lesson 8). In any case, the apostles and elders who assembled to confront the antagonists became what is commonly called the Jerusalem Council. The participants' mandate was not to determine the message of the Gospel, since that was never in doubt. Instead, they met to counteract the serious ethnic tensions between Jews and Gentiles that threatened to tear apart the delicate unity of the early church.

Later in Paul's ministry, he wrote about this point of contention in the early church experience (see Rom. 3:29–30; 4:9–12; Gal. 5:11–12; 6:12–13; Phil. 3:2; Col. 2:11; 3:11). The apostle declared that to mandate circumcision for Gentiles undermined the all-sufficient work of the Savior (see Gal. 2:21; 5:2–6). While there was nothing inherently objectionable about circumcision, Paul argued that it was wrong to make this religious rite conditional to salvation (see Rom. 3:20–29). The reason is that physical circumcision was no longer the sign of the covenant for Jews and Gentiles who put their faith in the Messiah (see Eph. 2:8–9; Gal. 2:15–16). In New Testament times, circumcision and uncircumcision were used as metaphors for the spiritual condition of the heart. A heart that was desensitized to the things of God was called uncircumcised, whereas a heart that was fully devoted to the Lord was called circumcised.

B. A Delegation Is Sent: vss. 3–4

The church sent them on their way, and as they traveled through Phoenicia and Samaria, they told how the Gentiles had been converted. This news made all the brothers very glad. When they came to Jerusalem, they were welcomed by the church and the apostles and elders, to whom they reported everything God had done through them.

Along the way to Jerusalem (a journey taking three to four weeks), the delegation told Christians about the conversion of Gentiles in Antioch as well as in places Paul and Barnabas had evangelized. Believers in these regions rejoiced at the news that non-Jews turned to the Savior in faith (see Acts 15:3). Undoubtedly, the missionaries' travelogue through "Phoenicia and Samaria" enabled them to refine their talking points, especially how God brought about the conversion of many Gentiles. It also may have helped build support for the grace-oriented position Paul and Barnabas sought to champion. Upon their arrival in Jerusalem, the believers there, including the "apostles and elders" (vs. 4), welcomed the visitors from Antioch.

Jesus' followers in the early church recognized that the Jerusalem conference provided the opportunity for a pivotal issue to be decided at the highest levels of leadership. Indeed, the majority of these Christians would regard the way the council resolved the matter as establishing an official and permanent precedent. Some think that in Galatians 2:1–10, Paul was discussing this meeting. A more likely option is that this passage refers to private discussions Paul had with James, Peter, and John during the closing portion of the famine relief visit Barnabas and Paul made to Jerusalem about a decade earlier (see Acts 11:27–30).

II. THE DELIBERATION: ACTS 15:5–12

A. The Assertion Made by Some Pharisees: vs. 5

Then some of the believers who belonged to the party of the Pharisees stood up and said, "The Gentiles must be circumcised and required to obey the law of Moses."

After Paul, Barnabas, and their colleagues summarized what God had done through them, some of the believing Pharisees argued that God required Gentiles to be circumcised and keep the entire Mosaic law (including regulations about acceptable foods, the sabbath, and major Jewish festivals; Acts 15:5). Otherwise, their conversion experience was deemed illegitimate. This was a serious matter that threatened to divide the unity of believing Jews and Gentiles. From these verses we see that Paul wasn't the only Pharisee to convert to the Christian faith (see Acts 23:6; Phil. 3:4–6). But unlike Paul, some of the Pharisees at the council had not made a clean break with their past. They had been taught that a right standing with God came through obedience to the law, and they still believed it. They continued to look down on people who didn't observe the customs and rites of their religious tradition.

B. The Testimony Offered by Peter: vss. 6–11

The apostles and elders met to consider this question. After much discussion, Peter got up and addressed them: "Brothers, you know that some time ago God made a choice among you that the Gentiles might hear from my lips the message of the gospel and believe. God, who knows the heart, showed that he accepted them by giving the Holy Spirit to them, just as he did to us. He made no distinction between us and them, for he purified their hearts by faith. Now then, why do you try to test God by putting on the necks of the disciples a yoke that neither we nor our fathers have been able to bear? No! We believe it is through the grace of our Lord Jesus that we are saved, just as they are."

Since the apostles and elders had no written New Testament to consult, they hammered out doctrine on the anvil of practical experience, guided by the Old Testament, the teachings of Jesus, and the illuminating ministry of the Spirit. The participants discussed the issue openly and at length, as all churches should do when debating a controversial matter (see Acts 15:6). Peter delivered the decisive speech, which was in keeping with the leading role he occupied among the apostles in the early church. He began by reminding those present how God used him to bring about the conversion of Cornelius and his household (see vs. 7). Specifically, in response to the Lord's command, Peter proclaimed the Gospel and those gathered in the centurion's home believed the message. God responded by pouring out His Spirit on them before the apostle had even finished speaking (see vs. 8).

Even though most of the attendees knew the details of what had happened, Peter's retelling of the event demonstrated that God had settled the controversy about the inclusion of Gentiles. To make this truth explicit, the apostle drew four conclusions from what God had done at that time. First, the real test of salvation should be the condition of a person's heart, which God alone knows. Second, God proved that He accepted believing Gentiles by giving them the Holy Spirit. Third, God did not distinguish between those who were circumcised and those who were uncircumcised. Fourth, God did not lower His standards. He gave His Spirit to all those He had made pure through faith in the Savior (see vs. 9). Peter had a reputation for observing the laws of Moses and for being a personal disciple of the risen Lord. So the apostle was a credible and convincing witness to his peers. If Peter claimed that Jews and Gentiles were saved by God's grace, the Christian leaders could accept what he said as true.

Peter knew that he was not redeemed because of anything he had done. In fact, he argued that the Mosaic law's demands were like a burdensome yoke too heavy for anyone to bear (see vs. 10). The apostle asked how his legalistic peers could challenge God's authority (see Exod. 17:2; Deut. 6:16) by imposing an oppressive weight on Gentile believers when the agitators couldn't even carry it themselves. Peter concluded by stating that both Jews and Gentiles were saved by the Savior's grace. There was no difference (see Acts 15:11). Likewise, there were to be no divisions between the two groups, for both were redeemed in the same way (see Eph. 2:11–22). During Jesus' earthly ministry, He described Himself as being "gentle and humble in heart" (Matt. 11:29). Also, He would accept the "weary and burdened" (vs. 28) who came to Him. They could trade their load for His "yoke" (vs. 30), which was "easy." Here Jesus was presenting a picture of salvation. In a manner of speaking, He graciously unloads people of their sin.

Years later, Paul taught in his writings that God has a way of providing righteousness, and it is apart from the Mosaic law. Of course, the entire Old Testament bears witness to the fact that being justified in God's eyes cannot occur from keeping the law. God treats everyone alike. He views people as being acceptable in His sight only when they trust in Jesus for salvation. All must come to the Father through the Son, for all have sinned and fallen short of God's glory (see Rom. 3:21–23). The Father unreservedly justifies people by His grace, and His justification is made available through the redemption from sin that the Son purchased at Calvary. The Father offered His Son on the cross as an atoning sacrifice for sins. Jesus shed His blood so that by faith in Him we could come to God. The Lord did this to show that in the past He was right and fair to be patient and not punish people for their sins. Similarly, we see that the Father acts righteously when He declares people to be reconciled to Him on the basis of their faith in the Son (see vss. 24–26).

C. The Testimony Offered by Barnabas and Paul: vs. 12

The whole assembly became silent as they listened to Barnabas and Paul telling about the miraculous signs and wonders God had done among the Gentiles through them.

Barnabas and Paul picked up the thread of Peter's arguments, and the entire assembly listened attentively as the two missionaries spoke. The pair declared that the Father had given them the ability to perform miracles and signs among the Gentiles and to lead many to trust in the Son (see Acts 15:12). This fact proved that what had happened with Cornelius was not a fluke. God was still making it clear that He was giving grace to Gentiles without requiring them to obey the laws of Moses. After another period of discussion among those present at the Jerusalem conference, everyone stopped talking. James, the half-brother of the Lord and the one presiding over the meeting, made a statement to his colleagues (see vs. 13).

James had become a moderator of the church in Jerusalem because of his outstanding character and piety (see Acts 12:17; 21:18; Gal. 1:19). Tradition says that his knees were like those of camels because he had spent so much time kneeling in prayer. He also had a reputation as a rigorous keeper of the Mosaic law, which probably made the legalists confident that he would decide in their favor. James began by referring to Peter's description of how God had taken the initiative in bringing Gentiles into the church. James must have stunned the legalists when he said that God had chosen from among the Gentiles a people to belong to Him (see Acts 15:14). In times past, the physical descendants of Abraham were identified as God's chosen people. But James declared that God had spiritually united saved Jews and Gentiles within His spiritual family under the lordship of Christ.

To drive home his point, James cited the Septuagint (Greek) version of Amos 9:11 and 12 (see Acts 15:15). Amos had foretold that God would one day rebuild and set up the ruined temple. This implied that the Israelites would be restored to a place of prominence. Amos also foretold that one day the rest of humanity would seek the Lord and that Gentiles, as well as Jews, would be among the redeemed (see vss. 16–17). The point James made was clear to his audience. The prophets had foreseen a day when both Jews and Gentiles would be included in the believing community and share in the messianic blessing. From eternity past, God had decided to bring about this tremendous work of grace (see vs. 18). James concluded by stating that the council should not make circumcision a requirement for Gentile converts to be saved (see vs. 19). James also urged the council to ask Gentile believers to abstain from certain practices and foods that would be particularly offensive to Jews (see vs. 20).

Discussion Questions

1. Why were the religious legalists eager for the Gentile converts to observe the Mosaic law?
2. Why did Paul and Barnabas react so strongly to the teaching of the legalists?
3. What do you think was Peter's strongest argument against imposing circumcision on Gentile converts? Why?
4. What are some of the false teachings about salvation that you have heard?
5. Why is Scripture a better test of truth than experience?

Contemporary Application

Troublemakers from Judea told the Gentile believers in Antioch that they had to be circumcised in order to be saved. After Paul and Barnabas argued sharply with the religious legalists, the Antioch church sent representatives (including Paul and Barnabas) to receive instructions on this issue from leaders in the Jerusalem church.

How can Christians today be prepared to reply to current false teachings about salvation? First, we should be immersed in what Scripture has to say about the issue. We should be able to turn to the key passages in the Bible that point to Jesus as the only one who can save us or that teach that salvation is a gift of God (see Acts 4:12; Eph. 2:8–9).

Second, we can study the writings of Christians who are specialists on world religions, cults, and current religious movements. These believers have spent years examining false doctrines about salvation and evangelizing people who are captives of these heretical teachings.

Third, we can go out of our way to talk with people who hold mistaken views about salvation. At first we might want to bring a knowledgeable Christian friend along for encouragement and support. Eventually, we will feel comfortable talking to unsaved people on our own. The more times we do it, the more ready we will be. And more importantly, perhaps some will come to trust in Jesus as their Savior.

Spreading the Good News

Scripture

Background Scripture: *Acts 16:1–15*
Scripture Lesson: *Acts 16:1–5, 8–15*
Key Verse: After Paul had seen the vision, we got ready at once to leave for Macedonia, concluding that God had called us to preach the Gospel to them. *Acts 16:10*
Scripture Lesson for Children: *Acts 16:1–5, 8–15*
Key Verse for Children: God had called us to preach the Gospel to them. *Acts 16:10*

Lesson Aim

To remain undeterred in our evangelistic efforts.

Lesson Setting

Time: A.D. *50*
Place: Philippi

Lesson Outline

Spreading the Good News
    I. Timothy Accompanies Paul and Silas: Acts 16:1–5
        A. *Timothy's Family and Reputation: vss. 1–2*
        B. *Timothy's Ministry: vss. 3–5*
    II. Lydia's Conversion: Acts 16:8–15
        A. *The Vision of the Macedonian Man: vss. 8–10*
        B. *The Missionaries' Arrival at Philippi: vss. 11–12*
        C. *The Bearing of Spiritual Fruit: vss. 13–15*

Introduction for Adults

Topic: *Ready, Set, Go!*

The Spirit empowered Paul and his team to lead Lydia and her household to faith in Christ. Lydia could have insisted that the relationship end there. Thankfully, though, this godly merchant who lived in Philippi opened her heart and home to meet the needs of the missionaries (see Acts 16:13–15).

In China alone it is estimated that 28,000 people are giving their lives to Christ every day. Also, despite political unrest and economic turmoil in countries such as Ukraine, the "wall" continues to come down in other former Soviet block nations in Eastern Europe, opening up regions once closed to the Gospel for decades. Missionary opportunities are springing up in many new places. How can adults in your class offer themselves in support and participate in your church's missionary efforts?

Three ways in which adults can participate in missions are through giving financially, going on short-term missionary trips, and joining the missions committee or the group of individuals that establishes the missions strategy in your church. Stepping out into missions will stretch their faith in the Savior, and that is a great blessing.

Introduction for Youth

Topic: *More than Expected*

The Lord used Paul and his colleagues to proclaim the Gospel to a business-woman named Lydia and her household. In turn, Lydia offered her home as a place for the missionaries to lodge (see Acts 16:13–15).

Jesus encouraged His followers to store up "treasures in heaven" (Matt. 6:20). What better way for teens to do that—and thereby become more gracious converts—than to prayerfully support those taking the Gospel to people who otherwise would not hear it?

Believing young people can participate in missions by encouraging their parents to offer food and lodging for ministers and their families on furlough. Saved teens can attend missions conferences and work to enhance the quality of their church's missionary efforts. Finally, your students can befriend missionaries and offer them encouragement at critical times.

Concepts for Children

Topic: *Spreading the News*

1. A church leader named Paul was traveling with some believers.
2. God wanted Paul to go share the Gospel in a place called Macedonia.
3. Paul and his friends came to Philippi, where they met a group of women.
4. One of these women was named Lydia, and she believed the Good News about Jesus.
5. Hearing the Gospel with an open heart can lead to belief in Jesus.

Lesson Commentary

I. TIMOTHY ACCOMPANIES PAUL AND SILAS: ACTS 16:1–5

A. Timothy's Family and Reputation: vss. 1–2

He came to Derbe and then to Lystra, where a disciple named Timothy lived, whose mother was a Jewess and a believer, but whose father was a Greek. The brothers at Lystra and Iconium spoke well of him.

Sometime after the Jerusalem Council, Paul and Barnabas discussed the possibility of going on another missionary journey. But they sharply disagreed over whether they should take John Mark, who had deserted them on their previous evangelistic undertaking. Because the issue could not be resolved, Barnabas took John Mark with him to Cyprus, while Paul took Silas with him on his journeys through Syria and Cilicia (see Acts 15:36–41). The year was A.D. 50, and this new pair may have visited Paul's birthplace, Tarsus, along the way. Derbe and Lystra were only a short distance west of Tarsus, but to reach them, Paul and Silas had to travel northerly through the Cilician Gates. This was a narrow pass through the Tarsus Mountains and into Commagene, the tiny kingdom ruled by Antiochus.

Lystra, Timothy's hometown, was located about 60 miles northwest of Derbe in the Roman province of Galatia. Timothy was an ardent follower of the Lord Jesus, and Timothy's Jewish mother was also a "believer" (16:1). In contrast, Timothy's father was a pagan Greek. That said, the Christians in Timothy's hometown and in the larger nearby city of Iconium to the north vouched for his virtuous character (see vs. 2). This observation suggests that Paul had seen the advantages of the Barnabas-Paul-Mark trio and had been looking for someone to complete another threesome for the current missionary journey. The apostle may have been impressed by three factors: (1) Timothy's knowledge of Judaism and the Hebrew Scriptures; (2) Timothy's Gentile connections through his Greek father; and (3) Timothy's reputation as a devout Christian.

B. Timothy's Ministry: vss. 3–5

Paul wanted to take him along on the journey, so he circumcised him because of the Jews who lived in that area, for they all knew that his father was a Greek. As they traveled from town to town, they delivered the decisions reached by the apostles and elders in Jerusalem for the people to obey. So the churches were strengthened in the faith and grew daily in numbers.

Timothy grew up in an environment that was ideal for someone who was to be Paul's troubleshooter among the largely Gentile congregations in Greece and Asia Minor. Long before Timothy's family came into contact with Paul, Timothy had become familiar with the Old Testament. His mother, Eunice, and his grandmother, Lois, apparently had read the Hebrew Scriptures to Timothy from the time he was a child (see 2 Tim. 3:15). However, contrary to first-century Jewish law, Timothy's mother had married a Gentile. Because of

Eunice's marriage, Timothy grew up under two worlds of thought, the Jewish and the Greek.

When Paul arrived in the obscure little town of Lystra in Galatia on his first missionary journey (A.D. 46–48), Lois, Eunice, and Timothy all appear to have committed their lives to Jesus as their Messiah. By the time of Paul's second missionary journey (A.D. 50–52), Timothy had developed sufficient leadership potential that the apostle added the young man to the team to help Silas establish the house churches that already peppered Asia Minor.

Timothy's background in Judaism and Hellenistic paganism made him a useful emissary to Thessalonica (see 1 Thess. 3:2) and, a few years later, Corinth (see 1 Cor. 4:17). More of the time, though, Timothy spent with Paul on his preaching excursions (see Rom. 16:21; 2 Cor. 1:19). Timothy also accompanied Paul and several other associates to Jerusalem with the collection (see Acts 20:4), and to Ephesus (see 1 Tim. 1:3). It was there that Timothy handled the problems being experienced by the congregation and where he may have been imprisoned for a time (see Heb. 13:23).

Because Timothy's mother was Jewish, Paul decided early in his second missionary journey to circumcise the young man. This would ensure the Jews could not use the issue against Timothy (see Acts 16:3). The apostle's decision has been a focus of controversy. Earlier, in Galatians 2:3, Paul made an issue how Titus, a Greek, should not be compelled by legalistic Jews to be circumcised. Also, in 5:2, the apostle had written that if the Galatians allowed themselves to be circumcised, Jesus would do them no good at all.

Was Paul now doing with Timothy what he had told others not to do? Part of the answer seems to be that Timothy's mother was Jewish. According to Jewish law, a child was to take the religion of his mother. So the Jews would expect that Timothy would have been raised a Jew and been circumcised. Paul reasoned that if Timothy remained uncircumcised, he would hamper the cause of Christ. The apostle circumcised Timothy so he would be a more effective evangelist, not to secure his salvation.

Another aspect of this issue lies in the timing of Paul's visit. When he traveled to Derbe and Lystra, the controversy discussed in last week's lesson was still alive (despite the apostle's letter to the Galatians). So, to avoid hindering Timothy's acceptance, the apostle had him circumcised. Such an act, Paul hoped, would silence those for whom circumcision was a major issue. What was at stake, after all, was not Timothy's salvation, but a petty controversy. In the case of Titus, some Jews were attempting to make circumcision necessary for his salvation.

With the matter of Timothy's circumcision resolved, he joined the missionary team and began traveling from one town to the next with Paul and Silas (see Acts 16:4). First Timothy 4:14 suggests that the elders at the church in Lystra commissioned and commended Timothy to the ministry before he joined the team. He had come a long way in the year or two since his conversion to Christ.

But Timothy had much more to learn as he left Lystra and Iconium and headed west with Paul and Silas.

As the trio pressed on, they told the followers of the Lord Jesus what the apostles and leaders in Jerusalem had decided at the recent conference (see 15:19–20). The missionaries urged their fellow Christians to follow these instructions conscientiously (see 16:4). As a result of the witness given by Paul, Silas, and Timothy, the churches grew stronger with respect to their faith. Also, as each day passed, more people trusted in Jesus for salvation (see vs. 5).

II. LYDIA'S CONVERSION: ACTS 16:8–15

A. The Vision of the Macedonian Man: vss. 8–10

So they passed by Mysia and went down to Troas. During the night Paul had a vision of a man of Macedonia standing and begging him, "Come over to Macedonia and help us." After Paul had seen the vision, we got ready at once to leave for Macedonia, concluding that God had called us to preach the Gospel to them.

Paul, Silas, and Timothy traveled throughout the Phrygian and Galatian region (see Acts 16:6). These areas were located in south and central Asia Minor. Initially, the missionary team planned to evangelize the Roman province of Asia, which would have taken them in a west by southwest direction. However, the Holy Spirit somehow prevented the trio from proclaiming the Gospel there. So they journeyed in a northwest direction to the province of Mysia. Their intent was to continue in a northeast direction toward the province of Bithynia. Once more, the "Spirit of Jesus" (vs. 7) did not permit the missionaries to do this. This is a corresponding reference to the Holy Spirit, and emphasizes the truth that Jesus is fully divine (see Rom. 8:9; Gal. 4:6; Phil. 1:19; 1 Pet. 1:11).

Perhaps in both instances, the Lord revealed His will through a vision, a prophetic gift, or an explicit turn of events. In any case, it is clear that Paul, Silas, and Timothy faithfully followed the Spirit's guidance. So, after the missionaries traveled through Mysia, they reached the large port city of Troas (see vs. 8). Because of its location on the Aegean coast, Troas was considered the gateway from Asia Minor to Greece. While Paul was in Troas, he had a nighttime dream-vision of a "man of Macedonia" (vs. 9), who summoned the apostle to come and assist in this European region of the Roman Empire. Macedonia was on the northwestern sector of what is now Greece and predominately Gentile in population. The terrain of the region is mountainous and cut by wide rivers and fertile valleys.

For the first time in Acts, we find the word "we" (vs. 10), rather than words like "they" (vs. 7) or "him" (vs. 9), referring to Paul and his traveling companions (see 20:5–15; 21:1–18; 27:1—28:16). The change in pronouns likely means that at this point the author—Luke, the physician (see Col. 4:14)—began to accompany Paul and his associates on their travels. Some have suggested that Luke, after joining Paul at Troas, spoke to the apostle about the spiritual need in Macedonia. If so, God may have used this conversation to prepare the apostle for the vision of the Macedonian man. Paul and his companions took the vision seriously. After concluding that God wanted them to preach the Gospel in Macedonia, the missionaries made preparations to do so (see vs. 10). What might have been out-of-bounds before (Europe) for Paul was now in bounds. Geographic barriers could not confine his proclamation of the Gospel.

B. The Missionaries' Arrival at Philippi: vss. 11–12

From Troas we put out to sea and sailed straight for Samothrace, and the next day on to Neapolis. From there we traveled to Philippi, a Roman colony and the leading city of that district of Macedonia. And we stayed there several days.

Luke briefly described the evangelists' trip to Macedonia, initially by sea and then by Roman highway. Their voyage took them first to Samothrace, a major landmark because of its mountainous location. Then they sailed to Neapolis (one of the two best ports of Macedonia) directly serving Philippi (see Acts 16:11). From Troas to Neapolis was a distance of about 150 miles, and it took Paul and his colleagues only two days to make the journey, most likely due to favorable winds. Later, the trip in the opposite direction would take five days, apparently because of contrary winds (see 20:6). Luke may have been a resident of Philippi, for he apparently stayed there when Paul left and did not rejoin the group again until the apostle revisited the city on his third missionary journey (see vss. 5–15).

Philippi, which lay 10 miles inland from Neapolis, was founded in 356 B.C. by Philip II of Macedonia, the father of Alexander the Great, and named for him. The city became a Roman possession in the second century B.C. In the time of Paul, Philippi was a Roman colony and a predominant city within one of the four judicial districts of Macedonia (see 16:12). This meant Philippi was responsible directly to the government in Rome, not the administration of the province. The city's residents, though living away from Rome, had all the rights of Roman citizenship. Because the architecture and customs of Philippi bore a resemblance to the capital of the Empire, Philippi looked like a "miniature Rome." Philippi was an entirely pagan enclave, including shrines dedicated to an assortment of gods and goddesses, as well as centers devoted to the veneration of the emperor. For Paul the time at Philippi signified a major turning point in his proclamation of the Gospel to recipients who were mainly Gentile.

C. The Bearing of Spiritual Fruit: vss. 13–15

On the Sabbath we went outside the city gate to the river, where we expected to find a place of prayer. We sat down and began to speak to the women who had gathered there. One of those listening was a woman named Lydia, a dealer in purple cloth from the city of Thyatira, who was a worshiper of God. The Lord opened her heart to respond to Paul's message. When she and the members of her household were baptized, she invited us to her home. "If you consider me a believer in the Lord," she said, "come and stay at my house." And she persuaded us.

After arriving in a new city, it was Paul's practice to visit the local synagogue on the sabbath. Jewish tradition required that there be at least 10 men before a synagogue could be established. Apparently, the Jewish population of Philippi was too small to form a synagogue. Consequently, the missionaries searched for a place of prayer, which usually would have been outdoors near a river. Nonrabbinic sources attest the ancient habit of the Jews to recite prayers near rivers or the seashore. Paul and his associates found some women meeting along the banks of the Gangites River (see Acts 16:13). This was a deep and rapid stream about 10 miles from the sea. The women undoubtedly welcomed any visiting Jewish teacher who could help them as they read and studied Scripture.

Though a man had summoned Paul into Europe, the first recorded person to receive the Gospel on the continent was a woman. Her name was Lydia, and she was a "worshiper of God" (vs. 14). This means she was a Gentile who revered the Lord of Israel and heeded the ethical teachings of the Mosaic law. However, Lydia had not become a full proselyte to Judaism. Moreover, she was a businesswoman (perhaps unmarried or widowed) who sold "purple cloth" (including carpets, garments, and blankets). Her native home was 600 miles away in Thyatira. This city was located in the Hellenistic district of Lydia, a region in western Asia Minor. The city had long been a center for the production of expensive purple (or crimson) dyes. These were obtained from the madder plant and the murex shellfish found in the eastern Mediterranean Sea. The resulting products were in high demand because royal purple was used for the official togas in Rome and its colonies.

While Lydia focused her attention on the Good News, the Lord enabled her to understand and believe what Paul was saying. After Lydia confessed her faith in the Messiah, the new convert and the members of her household were baptized. In New Testament times, a household included more than just immediate family members. In Lydia's case, the occupants were likely comprised of servants, dependent relatives, and possibly children (if she was a widow). There are others in the New Testament who came to faith in the Savior with their household: Cornelius (see 10:24, 44), the Philippian jailer (see 16:31–34), Crispus (see 18:8), Aristobulus and Narcissus (see Rom. 16:10–11), and Stephanas (see 1 Cor. 1:16). When these people believed in Jesus, it impacted their entire household.

Lydia placed herself and her house at the disposal of Paul and his associates, who undoubtedly were exhausted from traveling (see Acts 16:15). Lydia's success in sales is indicated by her sizable house in Philippi, which could accommodate not only her household but also four traveling missionaries. Lydia's newfound faith expressed itself in hospitality toward Paul and his party. Indeed, Lydia's generosity extended beyond this first visit (see vs. 40). In addition to Lydia, the New Testament records other believers using their homes to further the work of the Gospel, such as Priscilla and Aquila (see 18:26) and Philemon (see Philem. 1:1–2, 22). Martha kept her home open to Jesus (Luke 10:38). Also, Scripture exhorts believers to practice hospitality (literally, a "love of strangers") as a Christian service (Rom. 12:13; 1 Tim. 3:2; Titus 1:8; Heb. 13:2). Even today, our homes are to be opened to God's work, just as are our hearts.

Lydia is an outstanding example of the fact that God had thrown wide a "door of faith to the Gentiles" (Acts 14:27). Jesus revealed to Paul that he would be the Savior's instrument to "open [Gentile] eyes and turn them from darkness to light" (26:18). Lydia's conversion was a magnificent fulfillment of Jesus' promise.

Discussion Questions

1. Why do you think Paul wanted Timothy to go with him on his missionary travels?
2. Why did Paul and his colleagues go to the river by Philippi on the sabbath?
3. What does it mean that God opened Lydia's heart to the proclamation of the Gospel?
4. What challenges do you face in sharing the Gospel with unsaved loved ones?
5. How may God use the homes of believers to facilitate the evangelization of the lost?

Contemporary Application

As Paul set out with his partners on the second missionary journey, the Holy Spirit prevented them from preaching the Gospel in the province of Asia (see Acts 16:6). Then, when the team tried to enter Bithynia, the Spirit again would not permit them to do so (see vs. 7). It was only after Paul's experience of a nighttime vision that they recognized the Spirit was directing them to proclaim the Gospel in Macedonia and the European continent (see vss. 8–10).

We all encounter situations that could frustrate our efforts to spread the Gospel. Like Paul and his associates, we should not let the problems we face derail us from the supreme goal of telling others about Jesus. God can enable us to triumph over our times of difficulty and to remain undeterred in our efforts to share the Good News with the lost.

What situations could test our resolve to be undeterred? We might encounter rejection from our peers, harassment from local authorities, and even public protests. We could face ridicule from those who consider the Gospel to be a myth or fable. We might encounter jealousy, antipathy, or power struggles within our faith community.

We might face racial, social, and economic challenges when presenting the Gospel in our society. Perhaps one of the toughest issues to deal with is the tendency to stereotype nonbelievers, particularly when we encounter people who come from another geographic location or a different set of circumstances. Thankfully, none of these situations is too big for God to handle.

Differing Responses

Scripture

Background Scripture: *Acts 17:1–32*
Scripture Lesson: *Acts 17:1–4, 10–12, 22–25, 28*
Key Verse: "For as I walked around and looked carefully at your objects of worship, I even found an altar with this inscription: To AN UNKNOWN GOD. Now what you worship as something unknown I am going to proclaim to you." *Acts 17:23*
Scripture Lesson for Children: *Acts 17:1–4, 10–12, 22–25, 28*
Key Verse for Children: "This Jesus I am proclaiming to you is the Christ." *Acts 17:3*

Lesson Aim

To be proactive in sharing the Good News with people from all walks of life.

Lesson Setting

Time: A.D. *50*
Place: Athens

Lesson Outline

Differing Responses

   I. Paul and Silas at Thessalonica: Acts 17:1–4

     A. *Proclaiming the Gospel: vss. 1–3*

     B. *Responding to the Gospel: vs. 4*

  II. Paul and Silas at Berea: Acts 17:10–12

     A. *Confirming the Good News: vss. 10–11*

     B. *Receiving the Good News: vs. 12*

 III. Paul at Athens: 17:22–25, 28

     A. *Ignorance of God: vss. 22–23*

     B. *Dependence on God: vss. 24–25, 28*

Introduction for Adults

Topic: *Making a Difference for Jesus*

On March 9, 2014, a science documentary titled *Cosmos: A Spacetime Odyssey* aired on television. In the opening scene of the first of 13 episodes, the narrator—astrophysicist Neil deGrasse Tyson—intoned that "the Cosmos is all that is, or ever was, and or ever will be." This statement implied that because the universe allegedly is eternal and self-sustaining, there is no need for a Creator.

In the address Paul delivered to the elitists at Athens, he presented an entirely different view of reality. The apostle disclosed that there is a sovereign and eternal Creator who brought into existence everything in "heaven" (Acts 17:24) and on "earth." Moreover, Paul declared that the Creator gave "life" (vs. 25) and "breath" to every creature. The implication is that God alone rules supreme over the universe. For this reason, believers correctly affirm that the starting point for a relationship with the Creator is for people to "believe that he exists" (Heb. 11:6) and "rewards those who earnestly seek him."

Introduction for Youth

Topic: *More than Expected*

Paul and his colleagues met all sorts of people in Thessalonica, Berea, and Athens. Regardless of whether they proved to be receptive or antagonistic to the Gospel, the missionaries let their listeners know that God invites "all people everywhere to repent" (Acts 17:30).

A church in Great Britain grew tired of petty vandalism and harassment by neighborhood teenagers. When a dead fish was hurled through the church door in the middle of worship one Sunday and kids tossed stones at the building, the congregants decided to take action. They received permission to put up razor wire and anti-intruder paint on a fence around the church property to keep the local youths away.

Then there's the congregation on the east coast of the United States who has these words carved in stone over the entrance of the lovely façade of their church building: "Suffer the little children to come unto me." Below the carved inscription is a sign on the locked gates of the entrance. The sign reads, "No ball playing in front of the church!" Is either of these situations welcoming news for intellectually curious and receptive adolescents?

Concepts for Children

Topic: *Sharing What Counts*

1. Paul and his friends visited three different cities.
2. Paul and his friends told people about Jesus.
3. Paul and his friends invited people to believe in Jesus.
4. God used Paul and his friends to bring many people to faith.
5. God can use us to invite our friends to trust in Jesus.

Lesson Commentary

I. PAUL AND SILAS AT THESSALONICA: ACTS 17:1–4

A. Proclaiming the Gospel: vss. 1–3

When they had passed through Amphipolis and Apollonia, they came to Thessalonica, where there was a Jewish synagogue. As his custom was, Paul went into the synagogue, and on three Sabbath days he reasoned with them from the Scriptures, explaining and proving that the Christ had to suffer and rise from the dead. "This Jesus I am proclaiming to you is the Christ," he said.

Last week we learned that during Paul's time in Philippi, he and his colleagues won converts (including a merchant named Lydia) and faced opposition. For instance, after Paul delivered a girl from an evil spirit, he and Silas were imprisoned in the city. Then an earthquake shattered the prison and led to the conversion of the jailer and his family (see Acts 16:16–40).

Upon leaving Philippi, the missionaries traveled east along a major road called the Egnatian Way (see 17:1). This trade route linked Philippi, Amphipolis, Apollonia, and Thessalonica. Amphipolis was a military post about 33 miles southwest of Philippi. Apollonia was 28 miles west of Amphipolis and 38 miles east of Thessalonica. This made the total distance between Philippi and Thessalonica almost 100 miles, and it would have taken about three or four days for the evangelists to travel by foot.

Thessalonica was located on the Thermaikos Gulf below the Hortiates mountains on the northwest corner of the Aegean Sea. Thessalonica was founded in 315 B.C. by Cassander, the king of Macedonia. Cassander named the city in honor of his wife, Thessalonike, the daughter of King Philip II of Macedon and stepsister of Alexander the Great. In 146 B.C., the Romans made Thessalonica the capital of the province of Macedonia and the seat of Roman administration.

As a free city of the empire, Thessalonica enjoyed a number of commercial and civic privileges. This included the right to mint its own coinage and the absence of a Roman garrison within its walls. The city's location along the Egnatian Way made it a major trade route joining Rome and the eastern portions of the empire. This increased Thessalonica's stature as a major hub of communication and mercantile exchange. This vibrant seaport was also the most populous and cosmopolitan town in Macedonia.

Thessalonica was not only a prosperous commercial center but also the capital of one of the four divisions of Macedonia. Also, Thessalonica had an active Jewish community, giving Paul his first occasions for ministry in the city. He preached for three sabbaths in the local synagogue and used the Old Testament to clarify what it had to say about the Messiah (see vs. 2). In particular, the apostle demonstrated that it was necessary for the Anointed One to "suffer and rise from the dead" (vs. 3). Paul noted that Jesus of Nazareth, whom the apostle made known to his audience, was their promised Messiah.

B. Responding to the Gospel: vs. 4

Some of the Jews were persuaded and joined Paul and Silas, as did a large number of God-fearing Greeks and not a few prominent women.

Paul convinced some of his Jewish attendees in the synagogue of Jesus' messiahship. The apostle also influenced the thinking of numerous devout Greeks, along with quite a few aristocratic women living in Thessalonica. All of them agreed to join Paul and Silas (see Acts 17:4). Nonetheless, some hardline legalists seethed with envy due to the missionaries' objectionable claims and the large number of converts they made. So the antagonists gathered some thugs from the marketplace, created a mob, and started a riot in the city. Evidently, the new house church met in the home of a believer named Jason, for the rabble attacked his residence in an effort to find Paul and Silas and coerce them to stand before a public assembly at the Roman forum in the center of the city (see vs. 5).

When the throng could not locate the missionaries, they decided to grab Jason and some other believers, forcing them to appear, as representatives of the new religious movement, before the city magistrates. The antagonists denounced Paul, Silas, and their colleagues for causing an insurrection, not only in Thessalonica, but also in other cities of the Roman Empire (see vs. 6). The mob also accused Jason of showing hospitality to the troublemakers. Supposedly, the missionaries had violated the emperor's decrees and acted treasonously by declaring Jesus to be a rival monarch (see vs. 7).

The false charges the instigators shouted provoked the crowd and alarmed the officials (see vs. 8). They compelled Jason and the believers with him to post bail before they were released from custody (see vs. 9). In paying the required amount of money, they agreed to ensure there would be no more disorderly conduct arising from the evangelistic efforts of Paul and Silas. The implication is that the missionaries had to depart from Thessalonica, especially since their antagonists were determined to cause trouble for Jesus' followers if the missionaries remained in the city.

II. PAUL AND SILAS AT BEREA: ACTS 17:10–12

A. Confirming the Good News: vss. 10–11

As soon as it was night, the brothers sent Paul and Silas away to Berea. On arriving there, they went to the Jewish synagogue. Now the Bereans were of more noble character than the Thessalonians, for they received the message with great eagerness and examined the Scriptures every day to see if what Paul said was true.

Once nighttime fell, the believers in Thessalonica immediately sent off Paul and Silas to a small city in southwest Macedonia named Berea (see Acts 17:10). The town was located on the Astraeus River about 45 miles west of Thessalonica. Despite the long journey by foot, Berea became a temporary place of refuge for Paul and Silas (along with Timothy) from their opponents.

Once the missionaries arrived in Berea, they wasted no time in going to the synagogue and proclaiming the Good News to its attendees. The members of the Jewish community in this city, along with devout Gentiles, proved themselves to be more open-minded, discerning, and receptive to the Gospel. They not only welcomed the missionaries' teaching about Jesus but also were eager to learn as much as they could about Him. For several days, the recipients carefully scrutinized the Old Testament and deliberated with Paul and Silas to verify that the message they heard was accurate and valid (see vs. 11).

B. Receiving the Good News: vs. 12

Many of the Jews believed, as did also a number of prominent Greek women and many Greek men.

The Spirit blessed the efforts of the missionaries to facilitate dialogue and discussion among the Bereans. Consequently, a sizable number of Jews, along with many Greek women and men of high social standing, accepted the truth that Jesus is the Messiah promised in the Old Testament (see Acts 17:12). Despite this encouraging progress, it did not take long for hardline legalists from Thessalonica to reach Berea in an attempt to thwart the effort of Paul and his colleagues to proclaim the Gospel there. The opponents used the same sort of tactics that worked in Thessalonica, namely, to turn a crowd of people against the missionaries (see vs. 13).

The disciples in Berea recognized that Paul was the principal target of the instigators, so the believers decided to send him to the coast (about a 20-mile trek). Meanwhile, Silas and Timothy stayed in Berea to teach and strengthen the new converts in their faith (see vs. 14). Perhaps to ensure Paul's safety, Christians from Berea accompanied him to Athens in the Roman province of Achaia. It would have been a two-day journey by ship at sea. If they took the coastal road, the distance they traveled would have been 222 miles. Once the group reached the city and before Paul's escort returned to Berea, the apostle directed that Silas and Timothy should not delay in rejoining him (see vs. 15).

II. PAUL AT ATHENS: 17:22–25, 28

A. Ignorance of God: vss. 22–23

Paul then stood up in the meeting of the Areopagus and said: "Men of Athens! I see that in every way you are very religious. For as I walked around and looked carefully at your objects of worship, I even found an altar with this inscription: To AN UNKNOWN GOD. Now what you worship as something unknown I am going to proclaim to you.

The city-state of Athens was located five miles inland from the Aegean Sea. In Paul's day, it was a center of Greek learning and culture. Paul had time on his hands, since he was waiting for Silas and Timothy to depart from Berea and rejoin the apostle (see Acts 17:14–15). As Paul progressively made his way through Athens, he focused his attention on the multitude of graven images scattered throughout the pagan shrines in the city (see vs. 16). It did not take long for the apostle to become exasperated by what he saw and to formulate a cogent response to his conversation partners in Athens.

Paul took every opportunity he could get to discourse with a variety of different groups. This included Jews and devout Gentiles, both of whom congregated in the synagogue on the sabbath. Paul also deliberated with the patrons he encountered in the marketplace of Athens from one day to the next (see vs. 17). Verses 18–21 state why Paul's activities eventually led him to give a speech to the members of the Athenian Council. The apostle had caught the attention of some Epicurean and Stoic philosophers, among whom he dialogued and debated the truths of the Gospel.

Some regarded Paul as an ignorant forager of confused and incoherent notions, while others were wary of the foreign spiritual entities he seemed to be hawking. These disparaging attitudes resulted from hearing the apostle proclaim the truth about the Messiah, particularly His rising from the dead (see vs. 18). The intense curiosity of the intellectuals prompted a group of them to take Paul into custody and escort him to the Areopagus. There, in response to their interrogation, he spoke at length about the "new teaching" (vs. 19) the elitists heard him proclaiming. Because the philosophers found the apostle's notions both unfamiliar and startling, they wanted him to explain the meaning and significance of his discourse (see vs. 20). This interest reflected the common practice among resident Athenians and foreigners to the city to idle their time away by exchanging new and novel ideas with one another (see vs. 21).

For the preceding reason, the council assembled to pass judgment on Paul's religious ideas. Ironically, his speech would reveal that it was the elitists who were guilty of adhering to a mishmash of chaotic and jumbled thoughts. The apostle began his oration by collectively referring to his listeners as residents of Athens (see vs. 22). He discerned that in every conceivable way, they were extremely "religious." On the one hand, Paul was complimenting his listeners for their piety. On the other hand, as verse 23 indicates, Paul drew attention to their spiritual ignorance and superstition. The paradox is that even though those assembled at the Areopagus considered themselves to be enlightened and wise, they failed to discern God's true nature. There is also an ironic reversal of roles, in which it was the beliefs of the Athenian elitists, not just that of the apostle, which were under scrutiny.

Earlier, during Paul's excursion through Athens, he looked attentively at the objects representing the idols the people venerated. The apostle found especially noteworthy an elevated platform on which was engraved the epigraph, "To an unknown God" (vs. 23). The implication is that the altar was dedicated to any deity the devout Athenians had failed to consider. The motivation for doing so was their fear of offending some overlooked god or goddess. Paul made this altar an appropriate starting point for his discourse. He said he would disclose what his audience, in their ignorance, tried to revere. Put another way, the apostle would make known to the Epicurean and Stoic philosophers (among other elitists) what they failed to recognize and comprehend. Paul would do so by pointing them to the Messiah.

B. Dependence on God: vss. 24–25, 28

"The God who made the world and everything in it is the Lord of heaven and earth and does not live in temples built by hands. And he is not served by human hands, as if he needed anything, because he himself gives all men life and breath and everything else. . . . 'For in him we live and move and have our being.' As some of your own poets have said, 'We are his offspring.'"

As religious as the Athenians were, they did not know the Creator. For this reason, Paul declared that the Lord is the only true and living God. He is not made by humans, as idols are made, but rather He made everything that exists. Also, He is not confined to temples, as the pagan deities were sometimes thought to be, but instead He is present everywhere throughout the universe (see Acts 17:24). Moreover, He is not greedy for sacrifices, as the gods and goddesses were believed to be, and He does not need anything from humans to sustain His existence (see vs. 25).

Paul declared that the Creator made all people—including the Greeks—from one person (Adam). God marked out the boundaries of the nations' set times (or historical eras) and the borders of their respective territories (see vs. 26). The Creator involved Himself with human beings because He wanted them to seek Him. Paul compared the process to the unsaved feeling around in the dark for clues about God's existence, even though in their fallen state they were unable to alight upon anything informative. The apostle noted that the Creator, though transcendent, was actively involved in human history and not far removed from each human being (see vs. 27).

Paul clarified what he meant by quoting in verse 28 from two fragments of poetry. The first citation comes from *Cretica*, which was written about 600 B.C. by the Cretan poet, Epimenides. The second citation may have come from a work titled *Phaenomena*, which was written by the Cilician poet, Aratus (315–240 B.C.), or from the *Hymn to Zeus*, which was written by Cleanthes (331–233 B.C.). Paul's citation of these pagan sources did not mean he thought they were divinely inspired. Instead, he simply regarded the observations they made to be fitting illustrations of specific eternal truths found in God's Word. The apostle clarified that it was God who gave every person the ability to exist, journey through life, and become productive members of society.

Paul reasoned that it was irrational to suppose the Creator could be compared to anything found on earth. Paradoxically, unsaved artisans leveraged their God-given aptitude and imagination to use "gold or silver or stone" (vs. 29) to make sculpted figures. Paul explained that even though in the past the Creator intentionally disregarded the ignorance of the lost, He now summoned all people in every place to "repent" (vs. 30). God forestalled punishment so that, at the appointed time, He could make His Son the atoning sacrifice for humankind's iniquities (see Acts 14:16; Rom. 3:25–26). With the advent of the Messiah, a new era had dawned for the human race. God extended to people everywhere an opportunity to be reconciled to Him (see Rom. 5:10; 2 Cor. 5:20).

Paul asserted that God had chosen a day known only to Him when He would evaluate all humankind according to the benchmark of His righteous moral standard. This coming judgment was verified by Jesus' resurrection (see Acts 17:31). Once Paul mentioned the resurrection, his listeners cut short his speech. Some sneered at the idea of rising from the dead (see vs. 32). These may have been the Epicureans, who did not believe in life after death. Stoics affirmed the immortality of the soul. But many of Paul's Stoic listeners may have found the idea of bodily resurrection difficult to accept. As the apostle exited from the Areopagus (see vs. 33), a modest number of new believers accompanied him (see vs. 34). Of particular note were such converts as Dionysius, who was a member of the council, along with a woman named Damaris and a few other unnamed individuals.

Discussion Questions

1. Why did Paul choose to reason from the Scriptures with the lost?
2. What brought about Paul's trip to Athens?
3. If the Athenians were so religious, why did Paul bother to preach the Gospel?
4 If you were to make a list of your loyalties in life, where would Jesus be in that list?
5. What aspects of modern culture could you use in presenting the Gospel to unbelievers?

Contemporary Application

At the World's Parliament of Religions in Chicago, some years ago, it was apparent to the thousands of Christians who attended that those of non-Christian religions were aggressively pursuing their agendas of converting people to their views. The parliament was like trying to play a football game with 30 teams on the field at the same time.

Nevertheless, despite calls for tolerance and acceptance of all faiths as equally true, the church cannot back down. Christians must be proactive in asserting, as Paul did, that God commands all people to repent (see Acts 17:30). Judgment is coming (see vs. 31). This is not a matter of intolerance but of dreaded certainty.

God the Creator has not made all religions equally valid. Paul did not tell the Greek philosophers at Athens that their views were as good as his. The apostle risked the sneers of the philosophers, but he did not back down from declaring that Jesus was God's appointed instrument of His righteous judgment. Christians today need the same kind of holy fervor to declare their faith in a pluralistic society. We can respect the individual but still speak the truth of God's Word with zeal.

Teaching God's Word

Scripture

Background Scripture: *Acts 18*
Scripture Lesson: *Acts 18:1–11, 18–21*
Key Verses: One night the Lord spoke to Paul in a vision: "Do not be afraid; keep on speaking, do not be silent. For I am with you, and no one is going to attack and harm you, because I have many people in this city." *Acts 18:9–10*
Scripture Lesson for Children: *Acts 18:1–11, 18–19*
Key Verses for Children: "Do not be afraid; keep on speaking, do not be silent. For I am with you." *Acts 18:9–10*

Lesson Aim

To evaluate the ministries God wants us to undertake.

Lesson Setting

Time: A.D. *51–52*
*Place: Corinth, Ephesus, Caesarea, Jerusalem, and Antioch
(in Syria)*

Lesson Outline

Teaching God's Word

   I. Ministering in Corinth: Acts 18:1–11
     A. *Arriving in Corinth: vs. 1*
     B. *Partnering with Aquila and Priscilla: vss. 2–4*
     C. *Deciding to Evangelize the Gentiles: vss. 5–8*
     D. *Receiving God's Assurance: vss. 9–11*
  II. Departing from Corinth: Acts 18:18–21
     A. *Saying Farewell to the Believers: vs. 18*
     B. *Spending a Short Time in Ephesus: vss. 19–21*

Introduction for Adults

Topic: *Serving Together*

The church was between pastors and called a man to serve in the interim. He was happy to minister in this way and reported to the elders for his instructions. "Are we ever glad to see you," they gushed. "Now we don't have to do the visiting and make the hospital calls anymore!"

These church leaders had no concept of partnering in mission. Their idea was to employ someone with a religious degree to do all the work. They looked forward to having more free time.

In most cases, the demands of ministry are such that congregations employ full-time pastors. But the needs of parishioners also require the work of all believers. No one is exempt, and no pastor can do it alone. God has gifted every Christian to partner in teaching, service, and evangelism, not just locally, but around the world. Blessed is the church that has discovered willing partners and hard workers like Aquila and Priscilla.

Introduction for Youth

Topic: *Keep Serving Jesus*

We sometimes get the impression that ours is a uniquely mobile society. But our country's history shows that people were always on the move. To keep up with them, churches employed itinerant preachers called circuit riders because they traveled on horseback. Their circuits might include half a dozen churches.

Paul, Aquila, and Priscilla were something like that. In the Book of Acts, we can follow their travels around the Roman world. Wherever they went, they talked about Jesus and taught converts in the new house churches.

That same mobility is required of us today. Many teenagers have moved three or four times in their brief lives. Some have gone to seven different schools. But wherever we go, we can take Jesus and the Gospel with us. He does not change, and the good news about Him also remains the same. We can put down deep roots in the Savior, even if we have to move to a new school and make new friends.

Concepts for Children

Topic: *Speak Out!*

1. Paul went to a city called Corinth.
2. Paul met a godly couple named Aquila and Priscilla.
3. Paul stayed with this couple, and they all worked together.
4. Paul told people about Jesus.
5. Like Paul, Aquila, and Priscilla, God wants us to serve Him.

Lesson Commentary

I. MINISTERING IN CORINTH: ACTS 18:1–11

A. Arriving in Corinth: vs. 1

After this, Paul left Athens and went to Corinth.

We learned last week that during Paul's second missionary journey, he stopped at Athens. His conversations with patrons at the local marketplace created an opportunity for him to present his views before the Areopagus, Athens' chief council (see Acts 17:16–21). At the meeting, the apostle proclaimed the true God, who far exceeded the bounds of the Greek's prevailing religious views. Nonetheless, when Paul mentioned Jesus' resurrection and the final judgment, the apostle's listeners began to dispute. Meanwhile, before he left the city, some Athenians were converted to Christianity (see vss. 22–34).

Though Paul could have stayed longer in Athens, he determined that traveling to Corinth was a higher priority. Yet 1 Corinthians 2:1–4 indicates he was weary and distressed as he made the journey. After all, the trouble caused by hardline legalists in Thessalonica and Berea weighed heavily upon the apostle. So did the lackluster response to his evangelistic efforts in Athens. Paul went to Corinth alone and awaited the arrival of Silas and Timothy from Berea.

New Testament Corinth was located on a narrow isthmus of land in southern Greece about 50 miles from Athens, in the Roman province of Achaia (roughly the southern half of ancient Greece). The lower portion of Greece is connected to the rest of the country by this four-mile-wide isthmus, so all traffic between the two areas of the country passed by Corinth. The isthmus was bounded on the east by the Saronic Gulf and on the west by the Gulf of Corinth.

Sea captains could literally have their ships rolled across the isthmus on a stone tramway and avoid a 250-mile trip around southern Greece. This circumstance enabled Corinth to prosper as a major trade center, not only for most of Greece but also for much of the Mediterranean area, including North Africa, Italy, and Asia Minor. Nearby Isthmia hosted the Isthmian games, one of two major athletic events of the day (the other being the Olympic games). This situation created more people-traffic through Corinth and likewise increased potential for business and prosperity.

Besides trade, Corinth was famous for its rampant immorality. Greek philosophy was discussed and wisdom was emphasized, but such considerations in no way bridled the debauchery practiced in the city. In some respects, Corinth's religious makeup helped create this atmosphere of depravity. Though the Jews had established a synagogue near the city's forum, at least 12 temples to various pagan deities existed in Corinth—overshadowing the city's Jewish influence. One of the most famous of these temples was the Temple of Aphrodite (the goddess of love), where at one time more than 1,000 priestess-prostitutes served the shrine's patrons. Despite negative aspects, because Corinth had a population of 80,000 to 100,000, many of its resident Greeks and Jews had an opportunity to hear Paul and his colleagues proclaim the Gospel.

B. Partnering with Aquila and Priscilla: vss. 2–4

There he met a Jew named Aquila, a native of Pontus, who had recently come from Italy with his wife Priscilla, because Claudius had ordered all the Jews to leave Rome. Paul went to see them, and because he was a tentmaker as they were, he stayed and worked with them. Every Sabbath he reasoned in the synagogue, trying to persuade Jews and Greeks.

Paul had come to a wealthy, immoral city to share the Good News. And it was in Corinth that the apostle met a Jewish couple named Aquila and Priscilla. Aquila was originally from Pontus, a Roman province on the southern coast of the Black Sea in Asia Minor. He and his wife had traveled to Corinth from Italy because Claudius had ordered the Jewish people to leave Rome (see Acts 18:2). The emperor issued this edict about A.D. 50 to maintain public order. This was not the first time that the Roman authorities had sought to clean up the city by expelling all Jews who were not Roman citizens.

The Roman writer, Suetonius, stated that the expulsion under Claudius resulted from riots among the Jews instigated by someone named "Chrestus." It is possible that this was a Jewish insurrectionist in Rome at the time, but it is more likely a reference to Christ. The disorder in Rome may have resulted from the introduction of the Christian faith into one of the synagogues in the city. Suetonius, writing about 70 years after the expulsion, may have thought his sources indicated this "Chrestus" was in the city at the time of the riots.

Aquila and Priscilla were most likely Christians when they arrived in Corinth. Luke does not record their conversion, and Paul never refers to them as his converts. We know that the Gospel reached Rome ahead of the apostle, possibly after the day of Pentecost. Evidently, the couple became believers as a result of the early witness in Rome. It seems Paul met Aquila and Priscilla in the local synagogue in Corinth (see vs. 3). It is possible that Jews who practiced the same trade sat together in the synagogue during sabbath worship services. Aquila and Priscilla soon became friends with Paul, due to their common vocation as tentmakers and their Jewish heritage, which dovetailed into their Christian faith. The devout couple evidently were people of considerable generosity and wealth. They not only agreed to let Paul work with them in their tentmaking and leatherworking business, but also invited him to stay in their home.

First Thessalonians 3:1 suggests that Silas and Timothy had been with Paul for a while in Athens, and then he sent them away to minister elsewhere. As he waited for their arrival in Corinth, Aquila and Priscilla provided a refuge for the apostle, who was so unsettled, both emotionally and physically, by recent events. Since Paul ministered in cities where there were no churches to pay him a salary, he had to support himself while preaching the Gospel. During the weekdays, he labored with Aquila and Priscilla as tentmakers, and each night the apostle lodged in their home. Then "every Sabbath" (vs. 4) in the local synagogue Paul spoke and debated with Jews and Greeks in an effort to persuade them about the truth of the Gospel.

C. Deciding to Evangelize the Gentiles: vss. 5–8

When Silas and Timothy came from Macedonia, Paul devoted himself exclusively to preaching, testifying to the Jews that Jesus was the Christ. But when the Jews opposed Paul and became abusive, he shook out his clothes in protest and said to them, "Your blood be on your own heads! I am clear of my responsibility. From now on I will go to the Gentiles." Then Paul left the synagogue and went next door to the house of Titius Justus, a worshiper of God. Crispus, the synagogue ruler, and his entire household believed in the Lord; and many of the Corinthians who heard him believed and were baptized.

Once Silas and Timothy returned from the Roman province of Macedonia, they rejoined Paul at Corinth. The apostle learned that the believers in Thessalonica, despite hardship, were resolute in their faith (see 1 Thess. 3:6–10). Also, Paul received a monetary gift from the Christians in Philippi (see 2 Cor. 11:9; Phil. 4:14–18). This assistance enabled the apostle to focus all his time and attention on proclaiming the Gospel. In particular, he bore witness to the truth that Jesus is the Messiah (see Acts 18:5). Paul's ministry in Corinth followed the pattern he had experienced in Thessalonica and Berea. It was not long before hardline legalists became hostile toward Paul and reviled his message.

In a dramatic move, the apostle shook off every speck of synagogue dust (see Neh. 5:13; Luke 10:11; Acts 13:51). The Hebrew idiom "Your blood be on your own heads" (Acts 18:6) meant his antagonists were responsible for their rejection of the Messiah (see Lev. 20:9; Josh. 2:19; 2 Sam. 1:16; 3:28–29; 1 Kings 2:31–33, 37; Ezek. 33:1–9). In contrast, because Paul had done his duty, he was innocent of failing to shoulder his God-given responsibility to preach the Gospel. From that point on, he decided to shift the focus of his evangelistic ministry to the Gentiles. Despite the opposition the apostle encountered to the Good News, many Corinthians became believers. A Gentile named Titius Justus, who worshiped God, put his faith in the Savior (see vs. 7). This believer's house was adjacent to the synagogue. Even the leader of the synagogue, Crispus, along with all the members of his household, trusted in the Messiah (see vs. 8).

D. Receiving God's Assurance: vss. 9–11

One night the Lord spoke to Paul in a vision: "Do not be afraid; keep on speaking, do not be silent. For I am with you, and no one is going to attack and harm you, because I have many people in this city." So Paul stayed for a year and a half, teaching them the word of God.

Even with the beginnings of a new church, Paul still may have wondered when the next part of his pattern of experience would reoccur in Corinth. He had seen enough opposition to know that he could expect a beating, an imprisonment, or maybe a stoning. Just when the apostle needed it, he received encouragement through a nighttime vision. Jesus directed Paul not to be intimidated or silenced by enemies of the Gospel (see Acts 18:9). Not only was the Messiah with the apostle, but also through his evangelistic outreach, the city would become filled with converts. They would ensure that Paul was neither assaulted nor maltreated (see vs. 10). After having received this assurance from Jesus, the apostle continued his missionary work in Corinth for the next 18 months. He both shared the Good News and discipled new converts in the faith (see vs. 11).

II. DEPARTING FROM CORINTH: ACTS 18:18–21

A. Saying Farewell to the Believers: vs. 18

Paul stayed on in Corinth for some time. Then he left the brothers and sailed for Syria, accompanied by Priscilla and Aquila. Before he sailed, he had his hair cut off at Cenchrea because of a vow he had taken.

After Paul had ministered in Corinth for a while, the hardline legalists tried to get an advantage over him with the new governor in the city (see Acts 18:12). According to an inscription discovered at the temple of Apollo in Delphi (in central Greece), Gallio (the brother of the Stoic philosopher, Seneca) was proconsul of Achaia in A.D. 51 and 52. Paul's antagonists brought him before the judgment seat. This was a large, raised platform in the open air of the Corinthian marketplace, just in front of Gallio's residence. The instigators charged the apostle with undermining the proper worship of God specified in the "law" (vs. 13). It is unclear whether this refers to Jewish religious law or Roman civil law.

Allegedly, Paul proclaimed a religion the Roman Empire did not authorize (in contrast to Judaism, which was authorized). Yet Gallio remained skeptical. Based on the accusations the proconsul heard, the disagreement had all the appearance of an internal religious dispute, not a matter involving any criminal activity (see vs. 14). Paul did not even have to make his defense before Gallio threw the case out of court, insisting that the matter be settled among the litigants (see vss. 15–16). This decision had far-reaching implications. Gallio, in effect, declared Christianity a legitimate form of Judaism, and so extended Judaism's official recognition to include Christianity. With this important legal precedent, believers were able to spread the Gospel in relative freedom for over a decade—that is, until Nero mounted his violent persecution of the church (A.D. 64–68).

Upon the case's dismissal, violence broke out against Sosthenes, the synagogue ruler who had replaced Crispus (see vs. 17). Sosthenes presumably spearheaded the prosecution. If this is the Sosthenes mentioned in 1 Corinthians 1:1, then he later became a Christian, just as his predecessor had. It remains unclear who committed the violence. It may have been observers who were angry with the hardline legalists for bringing such a foolish case before the proconsul. Or it may have been the antagonists themselves who were venting their frustration against their leader for a legal maneuver gone awry. Regardless, Gallio stood by and let the beating go on.

Eventually, Paul determined that he should end his time of ministry at Corinth. After saying farewell to the believers, he began his journey to Syria (his base of operation), accompanied by Priscilla and Aquila (see Acts 18:18). First, though, Paul went to Cenchrea. This was the main harbor of Corinth on the Saronic Gulf about seven miles east of the city. At this nearby seaport, the apostle had his head shaved, which according to Jewish custom signaled the fulfillment of a vow. It is unclear whether this was a private vow to thank God for His protection (see vss. 9–10) or a Nazirite vow of dedication to the Lord (see Num. 6).

The names of "Priscilla and Aquila" (Acts 18:18) are always mentioned together, but not always in the same order (see vs. 2). In four of the six instances in the New Testament, Priscilla's name comes first. This is unusual in first-century writings, where women were not given much importance. Some think her name occurs first because she came from a wealthier or socially higher family, perhaps one with Roman citizenship that Aquila (who could have been a Jewish slave) joined by marriage. However, the fact that Priscilla worked in manual labor along with her husband suggests that she did not outrank him socially or have independent wealth.

Others maintain that Priscilla was more outspoken or enthusiastic in supporting Paul's ministry. If so, the arrangement of the names points to Priscilla's important position of service in the early Christian community. In this case, she could have taken a more prominent role in ministry than Aquila. While Priscilla and her husband both taught Apollos (see vs. 26), risked their lives for Paul (see Rom. 16:4), and hosted two churches (see Rom. 16:5; 2 Tim. 4:19), the mere fact that Priscilla is equally mentioned in these activities points to her special place in ministry.

B. Spending a Short Time in Ephesus: vss. 19–21

They arrived at Ephesus, where Paul left Priscilla and Aquila. He himself went into the synagogue and reasoned with the Jews. When they asked him to spend more time with them, he declined. But as he left, he promised, "I will come back if it is God's will." Then he set sail from Ephesus.

Ephesus was located at the intersection of several major east-west trade routes and became a vital commercial, political, and educational center of the Roman Empire. The size of the city is shown by its theater, which could seat over 24,000 people. The city was perhaps best known for its magnificent temple of Diana, or Artemis, one of the seven wonders of the ancient world. (Diana was the Greek goddess of the moon, forests, wild animals, and women in childbirth.) More important, Ephesus figured prominently and dramatically in early church history, for Paul used the city as a center for his missionary work in that region.

Toward the end of the apostle's second missionary journey, he left Priscilla and Aquila at Ephesus. Before departing, Paul spent a short while deliberating with the Jews in the local synagogue (see Acts 18:19). The attendees not only responded favorably to his message, but also invited him to stay for a longer period. Paul, however, said he was unable to do so (see vs. 20). It may be that the apostle wanted to return to Jerusalem to participate in an upcoming Jewish festival (such as Passover), and he needed to do so before the Mediterranean Sea became unnavigable due to harsh winter weather. In any case, after saying farewell, Paul reassured the members of the synagogue that if God permitted, the apostle would return to Ephesus (see 1 Cor. 4:19; Jas. 4:15). When he departed, he left Priscilla and Aquila to continue his work (see Acts 18: 21, 26). Eventually, Paul reached his home church in Antioch of Syria (see vs. 22).

Discussion Questions

1. What circumstances did God use to bring together Paul and Aquila and Priscilla?
2. Why did Paul decide to discontinue tentmaking?
3. In what way did the Lord reassure Paul?
4. What are some reasons Christians give for not making themselves available for ministry?
5. How can believers determine whether they have taken on the ministries they should?

Contemporary Application

Because most of us lead busy, hectic lives, it is difficult for us to find the time to participate in one or more Christian ministries. No doubt Paul, Aquila, and Priscilla were busy people, too. They were employed in a tentmaking business and did a fair amount of traveling.

Despite their busy schedules, Paul, Aquila, and Priscilla made themselves available for ministry. We do not know all the challenges they faced in managing competing priorities. But we do know they took their God-given abilities and used them for the Lord's glory.

By making ourselves available for ministry, we can significantly impact the lives of others. For example, by teaching a junior Sunday school class, we may lead to Christ a child who might one day become a powerful evangelist. The foreign exchange student we invite into our home might return to his or her country and become a positive witness for Jesus.

Making ourselves available for ministry might mean saying no to some other outlets in our lives. As we prepare to teach juniors on Sunday, we may have to forgo watching a few hours of television during the week. If we hosted a foreign exchange student, we may have to spend extra money on food for a while. Visiting a rescue mission would require a sacrifice of time on our part.

Regardless of the sacrifices and adjustments we make, they are worth it in order to minister to others. Through our willing spirit, God can accomplish much of eternal good. It is impossible to predict how much good even our smallest efforts can make for the kingdom of God.

A Sacred Day

Scripture

Background Scripture: *Exodus 16:23; 20:8–11; 31:12–18; Leviticus 23:3–8; Deuteronomy 5:12–15; Matthew 12:1–14; Acts 13:42*

Scripture Lesson: *Exodus 20:8–11; 31:12–16*

Key Verse: "Remember the sabbath day by keeping it holy." *Exodus 20:8*

Scripture Lesson for Children: *Exodus 20:8–11*

Key Verse for Children: "Remember the sabbath day by keeping it holy." *Exodus 20:8*

Lesson Aim

To recognize that we exist to worship and serve God.

Lesson Setting

Time: 1446 B.C.
Place: Mount Sinai

Lesson Outline

A Sacred Day

I. The Sabbath Injunction Declared: Exodus 20:8–11
   A. *The Command: vs. 8*
   B. *The Details: vss. 9–11*

II. The Sabbath Injunction Restated:
   Exodus 31:12–16
   A. *A Sign of the Covenant: vss. 12–13*
   B. *An Occasion for Holiness: vss. 14–16*

Introduction for Adults

Topic: *Holding On to Principles*

In the exhilaration of their newly granted freedom from Egypt, the Israelites were not prepared for the moral and spiritual dangers that would soon confront them. So God called them to make a monumental covenant or agreement with Him. One sign of that covenant was the sabbath (see Exod. 31:13), and it was the reason why God wanted His people to keep that day "holy" (vs. 14).

Rarely do believing adults think the stakes are so high. And rarely do they put their commitment to the Savior in terms of a solemn agreement based on sacred moral principles. Rarely do they even set aside one day to recall the special relationship they have with the Lord Jesus and His spiritual body, the church.

Encourage your students to think about the fourth commandment, along with the rest of the Ten Commandments, as more than a collection of rules. Explain that these are truths about God in relationship to His people, especially His abiding love and care for them. This includes the members of your class!

Introduction for Youth

Topic: *Serving Together*

The only restrictions on youth used to be the legal age for driving, drinking, and voting. *No more.* The rules now extend to what they can't wear to school, the weapons and drugs they can't carry into school, the hours they can't keep, the music they can't listen to, and the substances they can't abuse. It's no use arguing that the reason for most of these rules is the safety and well-being of adolescents. If a few youths had not started to carry habits of adult lawbreakers into school, the rules would not be necessary.

In somewhat the same way, God saw the moral dangers the Israelites faced. He knew the world was filled with idolaters, murderers, thieves, and adulterers. So His people needed a set of rules called the Ten Commandments. The sabbath regulation especially focused on what holiness means (see Exod. 20:8, 11).

For Christian youth, their allegiance is to the Savior, for He atoned for their sins at Calvary and rescued them from ungodly lifestyles. To get off to a good start, they need to know the importance of remaining devoted to the Lord each day of the week.

Concepts for Children

Topic: *A Special Day*

1. A long time ago, God gave His people ten commands.
2. One of those commands was about a special day called the sabbath.
3. On that day, God wanted His people to stop working.
4. For an entire day, God wanted His people to think about how He loved and cared for them.
5. Even today, God still loves and cares for us.

Lesson Commentary

I. THE SABBATH INJUNCTION DECLARED: EXODUS 20:8–11

A. The Command: vs. 8

"Remember the Sabbath day by keeping it holy."

The Ten Commandments are the ethical directives that God spoke to Moses and that God wrote on stone tablets at Mount Sinai (see Exod. 19). Given the origin and role of these decrees in the life of Israel and the faith of the church, they have been called the Magna Carta of the Mosaic covenant. This distinctive status is seen in 34:28, where the Ten Commandments are literally referred to as the "words of the covenant, the ten words." In Deuteronomy 4:13 and 10:4, they are also literally called "the ten words." The Ten Commandments are also referred to as the Decalogue, which is a transliteration of a Greek noun that means "ten words." The Decalogue first appears in Exodus 20 and is repeated with some variation in Deuteronomy 5.

Like many other ancient political treaties and royal covenants, the Decalogue begins with a preamble in which the great King identified Himself (see Exod. 20:1–2; Deut. 5:6). Yahweh declared that He was the Lord and God of Israel (see lesson 2 for an explanation of the name *Yahweh*). The preamble is followed by a brief historical prologue. In this section, Yahweh summarized the gracious acts He had displayed toward His covenant people. He noted that He had rescued them from Egypt, the land of slavery (see Exod. 20:2; Deut. 5:6). The Lord was not just reviewing Israel's past to give a history lesson. Rather, He recounted the past to instill a sense of gratitude in His people. God also used the epic events of the past to form the foundation for the Israelites' obligations to remain obedient to the stipulations of His covenant with them.

Yahweh next delineated the stipulations of the covenant He was making with His people. The Lord expected His subjects to obey these directives, which were ten in number (see Exod. 20:3–17; Deut. 5:1–3, 7–21). Later, prophets of Israel held God's people accountable for heeding the stipulations recorded in the Decalogue (see Jer. 7:9; 29:23; Ezek. 18:5–18; 22:6–12; Hos. 4:2). The prophets also held the priests accountable for not fulfilling their duty to make the moral demands of the Decalogue known among God's people (see Hos. 4:1–9; Mal. 2:1–9). Yet, unlike other ancient treaties, the Decalogue does not contain any mention of penalties for violating Yahweh's compact with His people. One possible reason is that the Decalogue is not strictly a legal code, as other treaties would have been in ancient times. Instead, the Decalogue is a foundational covenant document. It served as a creed and way of life for the Israelites.

Yahweh took the covenant principles outlined in the Decalogue and expanded them in Exod. 20:22—23:19. The latter contains a set of laws with penalties attached. The severity of the Ten Commandments is such that violation of most of them is elsewhere said to be punishable by death. Moreover, God inscribed the text of the Decalogue on two stone tablets (see Exod. 31:18; 32:16) and He instructed Moses to place them in the ark of the covenant (see Exod. 25:16, 22; Deut. 10:1–5). Consistent with ancient Near Eastern royal treaties, one copy of the Decalogue belonged to each treaty partner and the copies were stored in the respective shrines. Yahweh instructed Moses to place both copies in the ark because it was the focal point of Israel's sanctuary and the special dwelling place of God. Both the Mosaic covenant and its stipulations were to be adopted by the Israelites and used as the basis for their behavior.

Exodus 20:3 (see Deut. 5:7) records the first stipulation of the Decalogue. In short, it is a prohibition against serving false gods. The Hebrew can be rendered "before My face," "against Me," or "in hostility toward Me." The idea is that the Lord had exclusively claimed the Israelites as His own. So He would permit no rivals—whether real or imagined—in His presence. Such would create a hostile dynamic, one that would go against God and His relationship with His people. The second commandment of the Decalogue is a prohibition against venerating idols (see Exod. 20:4–6; Deut. 5:8–10). Whereas the first commandment deals with the issue of who is the true and living God, the second commandment focuses on how He is to be worshiped. Put another way, while the opening injunction discloses the true object of the believers' worship, the subsequent injunction reveals the correct way in which worship is to be undertaken.

The third commandment of the Decalogue is a prohibition against misusing the Lord's name (see Exod. 20:7; Deut. 5:11). In Old Testament times, the names of people were not simply a convenient form of identification, but practically equivalent to the bearer of the title (see 1 Sam. 25:25). Likewise, there is an essential identity between God and His name (see Ps. 18:49; Isa. 25:1; Mal. 3:16). Furthermore, the Lord's name is characterized by sacredness and reflects the fact that He is infinitely exalted as well as set apart from His creation. In addition, He is morally pure and perfect in the most unsurpassed way. The holiness of God dictated that any reference the Israelites made to Him had to be done in a manner that expressed reverence and respect.

The fourth commandment of the Decalogue is an injunction to "remember" (Exod. 20:8) the sabbath by consecrating it (see Deut. 5:12). The Hebrew verb translated "remember" (Exod. 20:8) not only includes the idea of recalling something important but also of proclaiming and commemorating its significance to others (for example, by observing specific ceremonies on a regular basis). This emphasis is brought out in Deuteronomy 5:12, which says the Israelites were to "observe the Sabbath." The noun rendered "Sabbath" denotes a period of time for resting. The meaning of the corresponding verb is "to cease" or "to desist," with the basic idea being "to put a stop to the week's work." The notion of a day of rest was a radical departure from the prevailing customs of the day. In this case, the sabbath was to be kept "holy." The underlying verb refers to something that is set apart as sacred. Keeping the sabbath day special involved celebrating it differently than the other six days of the week.

B. The Details: vss. 9–11

"Six days you shall labor and do all your work, but the seventh day is a Sabbath to the LORD your God. On it you shall not do any work, neither you, nor your son or daughter, nor your manservant or maidservant, nor your animals, nor the alien within your gates. For in six days the LORD made the heavens and the earth, the sea, and all that is in them, but he rested on the seventh day. Therefore the LORD blessed the Sabbath day and made it holy."

Both Exodus 20:9 and 10 relate how the Israelites were to treat the sabbath. Deuteronomy 5:13 and 14 also discuss the issue, but these verses contain some additional information. The different versions of the fourth commandment in these two parts of Scripture should be seen as complementary, rather than contradictory. In each text, God directed His people to commemorate the sabbath as a testimony to His saving activities, both in creation and in deliverance from captivity. When examined together, the verses in Exodus and Deuteronomy reveal that God directed His people to perform their labor during the first six days of the week. However, He prohibited them from doing any labor on the sabbath. Neither they, their family members, their servants, the visitors within their city gates, nor their animals were to do any work. Every creature was to be given the opportunity to rest.

As noted above, Exodus 20:11 gives one reason why the Israelites were to commemorate the sabbath as a sacred day. During the first six days of creation, the Lord brought all things into existence—the heavens with their stars, planets, and moons, and the earth with all its land, seas, fish, animals, birds, and plants. On the seventh day, however, He ceased from His creative activity. In this way, God blessed the seventh day of the week and made it holy. Deuteronomy 5:15 gives an additional reason why the Israelites were to observe the sabbath. The Lord explained that His people had once been slaves in Egypt, then He reached out His mighty arm and rescued them. Just as God gave them rest from their oppressive situation in Egypt, so they were to give themselves, their families, their servants, their foreign residents, and their animals an opportunity to rest from the wearying labors of the first six days of the week.

When taken together, Exodus 20:11 and Deuteronomy 5:15 reveal that the sabbath ordinance is rooted in both the orders of creation and redemption. The implication is that the sabbath looks backward to the good and wonderful creation of God (see Gen. 2:2–3) and forward to the final redemptive sabbath rest for the people of God (see Heb. 4:1–11). In their zeal to obey the fourth commandment and keep the sabbath holy, the Israelites created layer upon layer of regulations that dictated what could and could not be done on that day. In turn, Jesus criticized these restrictions, especially noting that the sabbath was made for people and not people for the sabbath (see Mark 2:27).

Jesus' criticisms of the sabbath regulations, along with the eventual break between Christianity and Judaism, meant that Christians stopped celebrating the sabbath on Saturday. That observation notwithstanding, many believers consider the fourth commandment to be a moral principle that calls people of faith to set aside one day of the week for mental, physical, and spiritual restoration. For this reason, numerous Christians still observe the principle by setting aside their day of the week on Sunday, especially to commemorate Jesus' resurrection. Interestingly, the sabbath injunction is the only one of the Ten Commandments not repeated in the New Testament.

II. THE SABBATH INJUNCTION RESTATED: EXODUS 31:12–16

A. A Sign of the Covenant: vss. 12–13

Then the LORD said to Moses, "Say to the Israelites, 'You must observe my Sabbaths. This will be a sign between me and you for the generations to come, so you may know that I am the LORD, who makes you holy.'"

Exodus chapters 25 through 31 contain instructions for building the tabernacle and making the priestly garments. The Lord concluded His directives by stressing to His people the importance and necessity of keeping the sabbath. Just as circumcision was the sign of the Abrahamic covenant (see Gen. 17:1–14), so the observance of the sabbath became a sign of the Mosaic covenant (see Exod. 31:12–13). As noted earlier, the sabbath reminded the Israelites of God's purposes for them in creation and of their deliverance from slavery in Egypt. So, as they observed this sacred day, they would affirm the truth that it was the supreme, eternal Lord who set them apart and chose them as His own special people. From a New Testament perspective, the sabbath points to Jesus, the Creator and Redeemer of the lost and the one who brings them eternal rest (see Matt. 11:28; Col. 2:16–17).

B. An Occasion for Holiness: vss. 14–16

"'Observe the Sabbath, because it is holy to you. Anyone who desecrates it must be put to death; whoever does any work on that day must be cut off from his people. For six days, work is to be done, but the seventh day is a Sabbath of rest, holy to the LORD. Whoever does any work on the Sabbath day must be put to death. The Israelites are to observe the Sabbath, celebrating it for the generations to come as a lasting covenant.'"

Because of the Israelites' relationship with the Lord, they were morally obligated to observe the sabbath (see Lev. 19:30) and regard it as an inherently sacred day (see Exod. 31:14). The Hebrew verb translated "desecrates" refers to treating what is sacred in a profane and disrespectful manner. God promised to bless those among them who refrained from dishonoring the sabbath (see Isa. 56:2). Also, later prophets considered the keeping of the sabbath a barometer indicating the spiritual condition of God's people (see Jer. 17:19–27; Ezek. 20:12–24).

Exodus 31:14–15 state that working on the sabbath was punishable by "death." Presumably, if a person failed to observe that holy day, he or she was to be "cut off" from the covenant community, and this in itself led to death. People separated from their protective social networks often fell into the hands of violent nomads or starved to death. Also, if the individual refused to be set apart for God by observing the sabbath, then that person was to be forcibly removed from the covenant community.

In verses 16–17, God reiterated to Moses that the sabbath was a "sign" that commemorated His enduring "covenant" with the Israelites. In turn, they were to observe the sabbath perpetually, based on His own resting after six days of creating the universe. Because the people were joining in a covenant relationship with God, they were to do as He had done by resting on the seventh day. Exodus 35:2–3 provide some specific sabbath regulations. God prohibited His people from lighting a fire in any of their dwellings on the holy day. Those who violated the Lord's injunctions had to be put to death. Moreover, Jeremiah 17:21–22 banned the Israelites from carrying any load on the sabbath.

When God had finished speaking with Moses on Mount Sinai, He presented Moses with the two tablets of stone on which He had inscribed the Ten Commandments (see Exod. 31:18). The writer of Exodus said the tablets were "inscribed by the finger of God." Some think God wrote on the tablets using supernatural phenomena. Others say He did so using a natural phenomenon, such as lightning. Still others say the "finger of God" simply represents His might and power. In ancient times, both parties making an agreement usually kept a copy of the covenant. For this reason, many think the two tablets given to Moses were actually duplicates. Just as the ancient Israelites were responsible to obey laws of God inscribed on stone, so we are responsible to obey God's Word as it is recorded in Scripture.

There are numerous New Testament references to the sabbath. For example, in Matthew 12:1–12, Jesus declared that it was lawful to do good on the sabbath. In essence, Jesus was claiming the right to redefine the status of the sabbath. Such authority could only belong to someone who was equal to God. The Savior's remark contradicted the teaching of those who prohibited healing on the sabbath (see Mark 3:1–6; Luke 6:1–11). Later, during one of the pilgrim festivals held in Jerusalem, Jesus went to the holy city and healed an invalid on the sabbath. Although this infuriated some of the religious authorities, Jesus nevertheless stressed the validity of what He had done (see John 5:1–18). The Savior wanted people to know that meeting urgent human needs was more important than their idiosyncratic way of observing the sabbath.

In stepping back from the sabbath regulation, as well as the rest of the Ten Commandments, it is important to recognize that these were not a formula detailing how to be saved. Rather, for God's people in the Old Testament, the Mosaic law signified instruction or teaching. Even more important, the law denoted for them a way of life that was supposed to direct the entire course of their existence. Psalm 19:7 describes the "law of the LORD" as "perfect" and its "statutes" as "trustworthy." Similarly, 119:105 depicts God's Word as a "lamp" for the "feet" of believers and a "light" for their "path." Understandably, in Romans 7:12, Paul referred to the "law" as being "holy, righteous and good."

During Jesus' earthly ministry, He summed up the last six commandments of the Decalogue with the exhortation, "Love your neighbor as yourself" (Matt. 22:39; see Lev. 19:18). As the parable of the Good Samaritan illustrates (see Luke 10:25–37), our neighbor can be anyone who needs us. From this we see that the Decalogue, including the sabbath ordinance, is not simply a list of actions and attitudes to avoid. When taken together in the context of the entire Old Testament, the Ten Commandments summon us to reach out and treat others the way we would like them to treat us.

Discussion Questions

1. What did it mean for the Israelites to keep the sabbath holy?
2. Why did God forbid the Israelites to do work on the sabbath?
3. In what way was the sabbath a sign between God and the Israelites?
4. What does it mean for us, as believers, to "remember the sabbath" (Exod. 20:8)?
5. Why is it important for us to worship God in special ways on a regular basis?

Contemporary Application

God's covenant with Israel was very specific. It is quite different from our modern way of deciding between many options. Ours is a pick-and-choose, take-it-or-leave-it society. For instance, supposedly we can choose to keep whatever parts of Scripture we want and forget the rest.

In this kind of cultural climate, it's often hard for believers to be unequivocal about God's decrees. On the one hand, they don't want to be considered narrow-minded, bigoted, and intolerant. On the other hand, they know the Word of God is best for society as well as for their individual lives.

Therefore, we cannot afford to dismiss the ethical injunctions recorded in the Bible. Neither do we want to moderate them or make exceptions to gain popular approval. So much of society is at risk, and so many people's lives are messed up, that we must insist the only way to improvement lies in following the moral principles laid down in the fourth commandment concerning the sabbath, as well as the rest of the Decalogue.

Admittedly, the sabbath injunction, along with the Decalogue as a whole, doesn't address all of life's complexities. Still, God's Word can help us keep our perspective on track and assist us in arriving at sound conclusions. Our decisions can be based on the bedrock principles about what the Creator desires for us in our relationship with Him and in our relationships with others.

An Acceptable Offering

DEVOTIONAL READING

Hebrews 11:4–16

DAILY BIBLE READINGS

Monday December 7
Psalm 40:1–8 Living Sacrifice

Tuesday December 8
Psalm 51:15–19 Contrite Sacrifice

Wednesday December 9
Mark 12:28–34 Loving Sacrifice

Thursday December 10
Romans 12:1–8 Complete Sacrifice

Friday December 11
Hebrews 11:4–16 Faithful Sacrifice

Saturday December 12
1 John 4:9–16 Perfect Sacrifice

Sunday December 13
Leviticus 22:17–25, 31–33 Acceptable Offerings

Scripture

Background Scripture: *Leviticus 22:17–33, 23:9–14, 31–32; Deuteronomy 22:6–7; Isaiah 1:10–20; Micah 6:6–8; Romans 12:1–2; 1 Corinthians 10:14–22*

Scripture Lesson: *Leviticus 22:17–25, 31–33*

Key Verse: I urge you, brothers, in view of God's mercy, to offer your bodies as living sacrifices, holy and pleasing to God—this is your spiritual act of worship. *Romans 12:1*

Scripture Lesson for Children: *Leviticus 22:17–21, 31–32*

Key Verse for Children: "Keep my commands and follow them. I am the LORD." *Leviticus 22:31*

Lesson Aim

To live in a way that brings honor to God.

Lesson Setting

Time: 1446 B.C.
Place: Mount Sinai

Lesson Outline

An Acceptable Offering

I. Unblemished Offerings: Leviticus 22:17–25
   A. *The Prohibition against Unacceptable Sacrifices: vss. 17–19*
   B. *The List of Disqualifying Characteristics: vss. 20–25*

II. Total Obedience: Leviticus 22:31–33
   A. *Following God's Commands: vs. 31*
   B. *Honoring God: vss. 32–33*

Introduction for Adults

Topic: *Choosing to Honor God*

Living in a sacrificial way means that we not only need the right information but also the right spiritual attributes. In this regard, what we learn from
Leviticus 22 may not be new to us who are seasoned believers. But we have to
admit that we often fail to live up to the divine standard for the unblemished
behavior advocated in God's Word.

For instance, we know that we shouldn't be proud and that we should be
patient in affliction. We also know that we should bless our enemies and not
seek revenge when they wrong us. Regrettably, though, sometimes doing what
is right and avoiding doing what is wrong eludes our grasp.

It's wise, therefore, for us to remain accountable to God and our fellow believers. Accountability to God can be maintained by means of practicing such
spiritual disciplines as prayer and Scripture study. Also, accountability to our
fellow believers can be maintained by corporate worship, one-on-one times of
fellowship, and small groups. Our mutual goal should be to develop proper
attitudes and habits. Through the grace of God, the ministry of the Word, and
the encouragement of other believers, we will be able to honor the Lord.

Introduction for Youth

Topic: *Seeking to Please God*

The act of offering sacrifices was an aspect of religion that Israel shared in
common with other nations in the ancient Near East. We learn from Leviticus
22 that sacrifices constituted a key part of all major Hebrew festivals.

From the New Testament we discover that Jesus sacrificed Himself on the
cross to atone for our sins. In turn, He invites us to live sacrificially for Him. This
includes times of worship on Sunday, along with how we relate to others each
day throughout the week.

Jesus is pleased when we seek to be living sacrifices for Him (see Rom. 12:1).
This includes exercising the courage and faith that is needed to follow His high
standards. Because Jesus lives in us as believers, we can be strong in the face of
adversity and temptation. He enables us to take a stand for truth and goodness.
Perhaps unknown to us, many of our peers will respect us because we have
chosen to honor the Lord, rather than esteem the corrupt ways of the world.

Concepts for Children

Topic: *What Does God Want?*

1. God wants us to give our best.
2. God also wants us to obey Him.
3. God is pleased when we pray to Him.
4. God is pleased when we help others.
5. God is pleased when we tell others about Jesus.

Lesson Commentary

I. UNBLEMISHED OFFERINGS: LEVITICUS 22:17–25

A. The Prohibition against Unacceptable Sacrifices: vss. 17–19

The LORD said to Moses, "Speak to Aaron and his sons and to all the Israelites and say to them: 'If any of you—either an Israelite or an alien living in Israel—presents a gift for a burnt offering to the LORD, either to fulfill a vow or as a freewill offering, you must present a male without defect from the cattle, sheep or goats in order that it may be accepted on your behalf.'"

The beginning of the Israelites' encampment at Mount Sinai is recorded in Exodus 19:2. While they were at Sinai, God gave Moses instructions for building the tabernacle and its furnishings (chaps. 25—31). Once the tabernacle was constructed, the Israelites needed further direction on how to worship and honor God. Leviticus provided this direction. The book was named after the tribe of Levi, who administered the laws as priests among the Hebrew people. The book's focus is on religious regulations, including rituals describing what sinful persons had to do after they broke the law. Instructions on moral laws, ceremonial cleanness, and holy days are described in detail. In essence, the book's purpose was to show God's people what was pleasing and displeasing to the Lord.

In chapters 17 through 27, Moses discussed the ramifications of the Israelites' call to holiness. This included an explanation of how God's people were to consecrate themselves to Him in different areas of their lives (for example, involving sacrifices and food, remaining virtuous, and showing love for God and one's neighbor). Chapter 22 provides instructions for the priests concerning how to properly handle the sacred gifts the Israelites dedicated to the Lord (see vs. 1). Verses 2–16 detail the rules the priests had to follow in handling appropriately the people's holy offerings. Ritual uncleanness could result from contact with skin disease, bodily discharges, or touching a human corpse or animal carcass. If the priests violated God's decrees, they would become guilty of treating the place of worship with disdain and experience an untimely death as a result.

The creation account recorded in Genesis 1 forms part of the theological backdrop of Leviticus. Specifically, the construction of the Hebrews' portable sanctuary (called the Tent of Meeting, or tabernacle), as described in Exodus 40, echoes the seven-day pattern of creation in Genesis. Exodus concludes with a vision of a new creation where God dwells with His redeemed people. Moreover, the opening chapters of Genesis portray the earth as God's cosmic temple and human beings created in His image as His servants to care for the world. In turn, the tabernacle serves as a renewal of creation. God has delivered Israel and now on a small scale begins to renew all creation, with His people as His servants for the sake of the world.

Leviticus develops the preceding emphases further by discussing the priests who were to serve at the tabernacle and detailing the regulations the priests and people were to follow. Underlying the book is the reality of sin. The transgressions of the people ruptured their relationship with God. The Lord revealed the sacrificial system as the means to have the penalty of sin paid and the guilt associated with it removed. This information clarifies the context of 22:17–19, which concerns a member of the covenant community, as well as foreigners living among the Israelites, presenting a "burnt offering" as a "gift" to the Lord. The worshipers might do so either to "fulfill a vow" they had pledged or to make an offering voluntarily. Regardless of the nature of the sacrifice, in order for it to be acceptable to God, the animal (whether from the "cattle, sheep or goats") had to be a "male" and not have any defects (in other words, be free of blemish).

The disqualification for physical imperfections was not based on any moral failure. Instead, the issue was one of ceremonial cleanness or uncleanness (see lesson 8 of quarter 1 for more information). When the officiating priests approached the Creator's sacred presence at the tabernacle, the animal sacrifices they offered needed to be flawless. By acting in the prescribed manner, they honored God's Word, affirmed His holiness, and expressed gratitude for the abundance of His mercy. In this regard, large sections of Leviticus deal with ethical and ritual holiness. The former refers to separation from sin, while the latter concerns separation from various defilements. The first seven chapters of Leviticus provide instructions about the five main types of sacrifices to be offered at the altar. Making sacrifices reminded the Israelites—who were meant to be holy people dedicated to God—that sin has consequences and must be dealt with.

The purpose of the burnt offering was to express total devotion and dedication to the Lord, as well as to atone for general sins. The unique feature of this offering was that the entire animal (whether bull, ram, or male bird) was burned. The intent of the grain offering was to express thankfulness to the Lord for His goodness and care. The flour that was used to make the bread for this offering contained no yeast or honey. The purpose of the fellowship offering was to express the people's desire to enjoy harmony, not only between God and themselves but also among themselves. This offering included a communal meal consisting of the meat of either a lamb or a goat. The intent of the sin offering was to atone for unintentional transgressions, resulting in the cleansing of the participant from spiritual defilement. This offering focused on the confession and forgiveness of trespasses. The purpose of the guilt offering was also to atone for unintentional sins. In this ritual, rams or lambs were sacrificed and restitution was given to anyone injured as a result of the sin.

B. The List of Disqualifying Characteristics: vss. 20–25

"Do not bring anything with a defect, because it will not be accepted on your behalf. When anyone brings from the herd or flock a fellowship offering to the LORD *to fulfill a special vow or as a freewill offering, it must be without defect or blemish to be acceptable. Do not offer to the* LORD *the blind, the injured or the maimed, or anything with warts or festering or running sores. Do not place any of these on the altar as*

an offering made to the LORD by fire. You may, however, present as a freewill offering an ox or a sheep that is deformed or stunted, but it will not be accepted in fulfillment of a vow. You must not offer to the LORD an animal whose testicles are bruised, crushed, torn or cut. You must not do this in your own land, and you must not accept such animals from the hand of a foreigner and offer them as the food of your God. They will not be accepted on your behalf, because they are deformed and have defects.'"

Leviticus 22:20–25 lists the characteristics that disqualified sacrifices from being acceptable to God. This information corresponds to 21:17–23, which deals with physical blemishes that could disqualify priests from approaching the tabernacle to make an offering. If they violated God's decree, they would defile the sanctuary He had sanctified. For the most part, the imperfections listed for animals and priests were visible to the observer. Concerning the priests, the catalog of defects included being "blind," "lame," "disfigured," "deformed," "crippled" (either in one's hands or feet), "hunchbacked," or "dwarfed" (or having a withered limb). It also included the presence of defective eyes, skin diseases (for example, the presence of sores or scabs), and crushed "testicles" (possibly a reference to those who were eunuchs). These physical flaws notwithstanding, the priests having them were still permitted to eat from the sacred offerings presented to the Lord.

The regulations recorded in 22:20–25 are just as emphatic in delineating what was considered acceptable to God. Verse 20 states the general premise that if any animals with physical flaws were offered, the Lord would reject them. Then verses 21–25 put forward specific examples. The first item involved worshipers bringing to the tabernacle a "fellowship offering" (vs. 21) from a "herd" of cattle or a "flock" of sheep. Regardless of whether this was to carry out a "special vow" or make a voluntary offering, the animal had to be free from any mark or imperfection to be pleasing to the Lord. Concerning animals presented as special gifts to be burned on the altar to God, they could neither be "blind" (vs. 22) nor have broken bones or other injuries. Also, they could not have "warts," blistering or bleeding skin, or scabs on their bodies.

Oxen or sheep with limbs that were too long or too short (possibly due to congenital defects) could be presented as "freewill" (vs. 23) offerings (especially in light of the optional nature of these sacrifices). But they were unsuitable in keeping a pledge made to God. Also, it was inadmissible in the promised land to offer to the Lord animals whose "testicles" (vs. 24) were injured in any way (including being "bruised, crushed, torn or cut," possibly due to castration). Moreover, the Israelites could not present animals they bought from a "foreigner" (vs. 25) as a food offering to God. Such animals were considered to have deformities and mutilations and consequently were unacceptable to the Lord. In fact, those attempting to offer such animals would not derive any personal benefit from their sacrilegious action.

These verses form part of the theological backdrop for the emphasis in the New Testament on the Messiah as the believers' perfect, atoning sacrifice. For example, Hebrews 9:14 states that Jesus "offered himself unblemished to God." Similarly, 1 Peter 1:19 reveals that the Son, through His death on the cross, was comparable to a "lamb without blemish or defect." Moreover, these truths provide the incentive for believers to grow in holiness. Ephesians 5:27 depicts the Son as presenting the "church" to Himself, in which His spiritual body is "radiant," "holy," and "blameless," and not having any "stain," "wrinkle," or "blemish."

According to Philippians 2:15, God's children are to become "blameless and pure," as well as irreproachable and innocent, within a society characterized by dishonesty and perversion. Second Peter 2:13 adds that the unsaved are like moral "blots and blemishes" who "carouse in broad daylight" and maltreat the redeemed. Yet, as 3:14 reveals, Jesus will vindicate His followers at His second advent and welcome them, "spotless" and "blameless," into His holy presence. Luke 14:13 and 21 suggest that Jesus' heavenly banquet will include those who were once "poor," "crippled," "lame," and "blind." In fact, those who have been spurned by this world are more likely to accept Jesus' invitation, and there is no indication they will be rejected by the Savior. Even today, the Spirit continues to invite each person to come and partake of the heavenly banquet the Savior makes freely available.

II. TOTAL OBEDIENCE: LEVITICUS 22:31–33

A. Following God's Commands: vs. 31

"Keep my commands and follow them. I am the LORD."

In Leviticus 22:31, God reminded His people about the importance of heeding His "commands." The underlying Hebrew noun refers to a range of ordinances and injunctions recorded in the Pentateuch (the first five books of the Old Testament). In general, the content of the legislation can be summarized under the traditional headings of civil, moral, and ceremonial law. Civil law included marriage and family, inheritance, property, slaves, debt, taxes, and wages. Moral law involved murder, adultery, theft, debased behavior, bearing false witness, assault, and financial obligation. The Israelites organized their ceremonial legislation under four major ideas—namely, sacrifice, purification, the mode or object of worship, and festival observance.

One type of Old Testament legislation was case law, usually cast in a conditional "if ... then" formula. This formula made reference to a specific hypothetical legal situation. A second type of legislation consisted of direct affirmation and negative commands. These set the bounds of appropriate behavior in Hebrew society. A third type of legislation was prohibition or negative command. This referred to hypothetical offenses and stated no fixed penalty. A fourth type of legislation was death law. This was a hybrid of the prohibition that made a distinct legal statement about specific crimes meriting the death penalty. A fifth type of legislation was the curse, which addressed crimes committed in secret.

The curse was designed to protect the faith community from uncleanness due to the violation of covenant stipulations and to bring divine judgment on the perpetrators of the crimes.

One incentive for the Israelites to remain obedient was the reminder that God is the "LORD." The underlying Hebrew noun is *Yahweh* and designated the unique name of the Creator. It was a deeply personal name that carried implications of the covenant relationship between God and His chosen people. Exodus 3:14 is the only place in the Old Testament where the significance of the name is touched on. The assertion "I AM" comes from a Hebrew verb that means "to exist" or "to be." In essence, the name *Yahweh* signifies that God is pure being. Expressed differently, He is the eternal, self-existent one.

When the Creator identified Himself to Moses, He did not say that He "was" the God of Abraham, Isaac, and Jacob, but declared, "I *am* the God of your father" (vs. 6; emphasis added). With this statement, God instructed Moses about eternal life. The ancestors of the Hebrews still lived, even though their bodies had been dead for hundreds of years. Jesus used this passage from Exodus when confronting the Sadducees over their disbelief in the resurrection. Because of God's words to Moses at the burning bush, Jesus argued His antagonists should have believed in the resurrection (see Matt. 22:32). According to Jesus, the message was clear: the patriarchs were alive with God when He spoke to Moses.

B. Honoring God: vss. 32–33

"Do not profane my holy name. I must be acknowledged as holy by the Israelites. I am the LORD, who makes you holy and who brought you out of Egypt to be your God. I am the LORD."

In Leviticus 22:32–33, God reiterated to the Israelites the inherent holiness of His person and name. He was the one who chose them, set them apart for Himself, and redeemed them from slavery in Egypt. Accordingly, He prohibited His people from desecrating His "name." This injunction draws to mind the third commandment of the Decalogue (see Exod. 20:7; Deut. 5:11), which directed the Israelites not to use God's name for mundane, unholy purposes. Speaking the name of the Lord with the proper respect and reverence was not an offense, but careless or abusive use of His name was strictly forbidden. Because His name was absolutely sacred, His people were never to use His name for evil purposes.

Centuries later, Isaiah recorded a vision of God seated on His celestial throne and surrounded by innumerable angels (see Isa. 6:1–3). The prophet did not physically see God's innermost nature with the naked eye. Rather, Isaiah was able to perceive the Lord in appearance with the hem, or fringe, of His robe filling the heavenly temple. This description expresses the overwhelming presence of God as both King and Judge over all creation. Isaiah's lofty view of God gives us a sense of the Lord's greatness, mystery, and power. The Lord used Isaiah's vision to commission him as His messenger to His people.

God Himself was the focus of this cosmic scene. The angels lauded the Creator with the thunderous chorus, "Holy, holy, holy is the Lord Almighty." The threefold repetition was the strongest way in the Hebrew language to stress nothing is as holy as God. As noted in last week's lesson, the basic meaning of "holy" is to be set apart from that which is commonplace. The word also refers to what is special or unique.

Discussion Questions

1. What duties did Aaron and his sons perform?
2. What was the difference between an offering made to fulfill a special vow and a freewill offering?
3. Why was it important for the Israelites to obey God's commands?
4. What sorts of sacrifices can we offer to God that would be acceptable to Him?
5. What does it mean to profane God's name, and how can we avoid doing this?

Contemporary Application

There can be no poorer testimony for a church or for individual believers than for a non-Christian to say, "I did not notice anything different about those people. They were just as unneighborly, uncaring, and self-absorbed as everyone I know. What makes being a Christian so special anyway?"

From our study of Leviticus 22, we would say that the people of God behave in ways that honor Him. This includes continuously living in a sacrificial manner for the Lord. It also involves total obedience to His will.

The preceding approach to life is directly opposite to what the world practices. The world says, "Honor and take care of yourself first"; Christians say, "Honor others above yourself and share freely with them." The world says, "Do not get angry, get even"; the Christian says, "Love your enemies and leave revenge to God." The world says, "Money and social status are important"; the Christian says, "Everyone is equal in God's kingdom."

The principles of God's Word are as active today as when they were written thousands of years ago. We are not to blend into the social landscape around us but challenge it. God wants us to do things the world does not do or understand. This includes finding people to serve instead of always wanting to be served, looking out for others before ourselves, loving those who hate us, blessing people rather than cursing them, looking for the sorrowful and helping them, and sharing what we have instead of keeping it to ourselves. These are conditions of the heart that should characterize our actions and be expressed in sacrificial ways in our daily experiences.

A Declaration of Praise

Scripture

Background Scripture: *Exodus 13:11–16; Leviticus 12;*
Numbers 3:5–13; Luke 2:21–39
Scripture Lesson: *Exodus 13:13–15; Luke 2:22–32*
Key Verse: When the time of their purification
according to the Law of Moses had been completed,
Joseph and Mary took him to Jerusalem to present him
to the Lord. *Luke 2:22*
Scripture Lesson for Children: *Luke 2:22–32*
Key Verse for Children: Simeon took [Jesus] in his
arms and praised God. *Luke 2:28*

Lesson Aim

To follow Simeon's example of faith, hope, and
obedience.

Lesson Setting

Time: 1446 B.C. and 6 or 5 B.C.
Place: Red Sea and Jerusalem

Lesson Outline

A Declaration of Praise

    I. Consecration of the Firstborn: Exodus 13:13–15
        A. *Redeeming the Firstborn: vs. 13*
        B. *Explaining the Meaning of the Ritual: vss. 14–15*
    II. Consecration of Jesus: Luke 2:22–32
        A. *The Presentation of Jesus: vss. 22–24*
        B. *The Prophecy Made by Simeon: vss. 25–32*

Introduction for Adults

Topic: *Having a Servant's Heart*

The story is told of a village whose inhabitants incorrectly thought a vagrant passing through their town was the government inspector. They not only treated him as royalty but also quickly set into motion a plan to cover up years of fraud. Their mistaking the man for someone else cost them dearly.

This fable is a reminder of how important it is to search for hope in the right place—namely, the Savior of the Bible—not some figment of our imagination. Jesus is no longer a newborn baby in a manger. He is also not just a wise and loving person. He is the Lord of life, the King of kings, and the Redeemer of the world.

Simeon was a person who recognized these truths about Jesus. For Simeon, He was light, hope, and salvation. In fact, all who receive Jesus by faith can partake of the forgiveness and grace He now offers. Certainly, this is exciting news we can share with others!

Introduction for Youth

Topic: *Listening to God*

Young people hear many promises during their years of adolescence. For instance, if they do their schoolwork, they are told they will graduate from school. If they pass their driving test, they will be allowed to operate a car. And if they take care of themselves, they will enjoy a long life. How gratifying it is when all such statements come true!

As Christians, we trust the promises that God has made to us in Scripture. We need not doubt His ability or willingness to fulfill His pledges to us, for He is faithful to keep His word. In turn, He calls us from the earliest days of our lives to be faithful to Him.

The advent of Jesus is the fulfillment of one of God's greatest promises. Simeon recognized this. He could see that the Christ child was the Savior. Even today, Jesus saves all who come to Him in faith (including young people). So, when we struggle with doubts and are tempted to question our faith, we should turn our attention to the Lord and believe His promises. They are the only ones fully guaranteed by Him.

Concepts for Children

Topic: *Let's Celebrate!*

1. A long time ago, there was a Jewish hope that God would send the Savior.
2. When Joseph and Mary brought Jesus to the temple, Simeon was happy to see them.
3. Simeon felt good inside when he held Jesus.
4. Simeon gave thanks to God at the sight of Jesus.
5. We can have joy and hope when we trust in Jesus.

Lesson Commentary

I. CONSECRATION OF THE FIRSTBORN: EXODUS 13:13–15

A. Redeeming the Firstborn: vs. 13

"Redeem with a lamb every firstborn donkey, but if you do not redeem it, break its neck. Redeem every firstborn among your sons."

The account of the Israelites' escape from Egypt is recorded in Exodus 5:1 through 14:31. So that Pharaoh would let the Hebrews leave, God brought 10 plagues on Egypt. The waters of the Nile River turned to blood, and then frogs, lice, and flies descended on the land. A pestilence infected Egypt's cattle, and then came hail, locusts, and darkness. Yet, despite all these calamities, Pharaoh's heart remained hardened, and he would not let the Hebrews leave Egypt.

In the last plague, involving the death of all the firstborn of Egypt, the Hebrews' firstborn were passed over. To commemorate this event, God instituted the celebration of the Passover (see vss.12:1–30). Pharaoh let the Hebrews go, but he changed his mind and pursued them until he trapped them between his army and the uncrossable waters of the Red Sea. The account of what the Lord did in Egypt to rescue His people would be told and retold to future generations as proof of two truths: the Lord was greater than all the pagan deities of the people the Hebrews would encounter, and the outcome of the Exodus proved that God cared for His people and watched over them at all times.

In verse 41, Moses stated that Israelites had spent 430 years—"to the very day"—in Egypt when the Lord led them out. Because non-Israelites traveled with Israelites into the wilderness, it became necessary to provide additional Passover regulations. The Lord said non-Israelites who did not identify with the covenant community through circumcision should not be allowed to celebrate Passover. But God said foreigners who were willing to identify themselves with the Israelites by submitting to circumcision should be welcomed into the Passover celebration "like one born in the land" (vs. 48).

During the Israelites' first days in the wilderness, God reminded Moses to be sure the people observed the Passover celebration. Even so, God wanted the Hebrews to remember His deliverance more often than just one week a year. So He instructed Moses to tell the Israelites to set apart for God's purpose the first male born into every human family, flock, or herd (see vss. 13:1–2). In response to the Lord's instructions, Moses reminded the people to mark the day of their departure from Egypt by refraining from eating bread made with yeast. Even when arriving in the promised land, the Israelites were to remember and commemorate the day the Exodus began (see vss. 3–7).

In anticipation of the questions the Hebrew children might ask about the observance, Moses said the parents' explanation should point out how the Lord brought His people out of Egypt by performing miracles. Also, observing the

Passover would serve as a constant reminder for the Israelites to obey the laws the Lord would give them (see vss. 8–10). Next, Moses conveyed to the people what God had said about consecrating their firstborn sons to the Lord. Moses said once the people arrived in their new homeland (see vs. 11), they would be obligated to "give over to the LORD" (vs. 12) their first sons and the firstborn among their livestock.

Because the firstborn among the Israelites had been spared in the tenth plague unleashed on Egypt, the Lord wanted His people to acknowledge that their firstborn belonged to Him. God allowed one exception to this law. Because donkeys were considered unclean and also valuable for carrying the people's goods, the animals could be redeemed by sacrificing lambs in their place. The Hebrew verb translated "redeem" (vs. 13) means to rescue or deliver by paying a price or offering an equivalent substitute. If a firstborn donkey was not redeemed, the owner had to kill the animal by breaking its neck. Firstborn sons were always to be redeemed by sacrificing a lamb. In this way, human beings were to be consecrated to God by their lives instead of by their deaths.

B. Explaining the Meaning of the Ritual: vss. 14–15

"In days to come, when your son asks you, 'What does this mean?' say to him, 'With a mighty hand the LORD brought us out of Egypt, out of the land of slavery. When Pharaoh stubbornly refused to let us go, the LORD killed every firstborn in Egypt, both man and animal. This is why I sacrifice to the LORD the first male offspring of every womb and redeem each of my firstborn sons.'"

Moses anticipated future generations of God's people asking their parents about the significance of the firstborn being consecrated to the Lord. In response, the parents were to recount how God used His mighty power to rescue the Israelites from Egypt—that is, from the land in which they were enslaved (see Exod. 13:14). Because Pharaoh adamantly refused to release the Israelites, the Lord responded by taking the life of all the nation's "firstborn" (vs. 15), whether among the people or animals. Generations yet to be born and those who were not old enough to remember the Exodus would need to learn why firstborn animals were sacrificed and why the firstborn sons of each family were set apart to God and redeemed by the sacrifice of a lamb.

II. CONSECRATION OF JESUS: LUKE 2:22–32

A. The Presentation of Jesus: vss. 22–24

When the time of their purification according to the Law of Moses had been completed, Joseph and Mary took him to Jerusalem to present him to the Lord (as it is written in the Law of the Lord, "Every firstborn male is to be consecrated to the Lord"), and to offer a sacrifice in keeping with what is said in the Law of the Lord: "a pair of doves or two young pigeons."

Over a thousand years after the Exodus, Jesus was born in Bethlehem (see Luke 2:1–20). After that momentous event, Mary and Joseph stayed on for a while in the city. During that time, they traveled at least twice to the temple in nearby Jerusalem to fulfill religious duties. On one occasion, they had Jesus circumcised (see vs. 21). Another time, they presented Him to the Lord (see vs. 22). During the second visit, two elderly people—Simeon and Anna—recognized Jesus' special nature and made pronouncements concerning Him. In a sense, they served as two credible Jewish witnesses (one male and the other female) who affirmed the truthfulness of Jesus' status as the Messiah (see Deut. 19:15).

Mary and Joseph were careful to fulfill the requirements of the Mosaic law. In the case of Jesus, while He was God's Son, He was not born above the law. So it was fitting for Jesus' family to observe its customs. Accordingly, eight days after Jesus' birth, Mary and Joseph had Him circumcised (Lev. 12:3; Luke 2:21). The parents also named their firstborn son "Jesus" (Luke 1:31), in accordance with the directive of the Lord's angel before the Christ child was conceived in Mary's womb. "Jesus" is the Greek form of the Hebrew name "Yehoshua" (or "Joshua"). As Joshua—Moses' successor—had led the Israelites into the promised land, so Jesus—God's Son—would lead many into God's salvation (see Matt. 1:21).

A woman who had given birth to a male child was considered to be ceremonially unclean for seven days (see Lev. 12:2). Then for 33 days more she was not to touch any sacred thing, nor was she to enter the sanctuary (see vs. 4). After 40 days, she was required to go to the Jerusalem temple to be purified in the prescribed manner (see Luke 2:22–24). The woman's purification included the offering of a sacrifice. According to Leviticus 12:6, this offering was to be a year-old lamb for a burnt offering and a young pigeon or a dove for a sin offering. But the law also said that if the woman could not afford a lamb, two pigeons or doves would suffice (see vs. 8). Mary evidently chose the second option due to her modest financial situation (see Luke 2:24).

As noted earlier, the woman's firstborn son was considered holy and so had to be dedicated to the Lord in service (see Exod. 13:2, 11–16; Luke 2:23). This requirement went back to that night in Egypt when the firstborn sons were saved from death by blood applied to the doorposts (see Exod. 12:12–13). But since the entire tribe of Levi was chosen for service, a firstborn son could be released from service by a payment of a ransom (see Num. 3:11–13; 18:15–16). This act of buying back, or redeeming, the child from God was performed during a presentation ceremony at the temple, probably at the same time as the mother's purification ceremony (see Luke 2:22).

A sacrificial offering was the means by which the ransom was paid. In this way, the parents acknowledged that their firstborn belonged to God, who alone had the power to give life. In this special circumstance, however, Jesus was a gift from God to the whole world (see John 3:16). Moreover, in the midst of the fulfillment of legal requirements, God put the stamp of approval on His Son with the unusual but blessed ministries of Simeon and Anna.

B. The Prophecy Made by Simeon: vss. 25–32

Now there was a man in Jerusalem called Simeon, who was righteous and devout. He was waiting for the consolation of Israel, and the Holy Spirit was upon him. It had been revealed to him by the Holy Spirit that he would not die before he had seen the Lord's Christ. Moved by the Spirit, he went into the temple courts. When the parents brought in the child Jesus to do for him what the custom of the Law required, Simeon took him in his arms and praised God, saying: "Sovereign Lord, as you have promised, you now dismiss your servant in peace. For my eyes have seen your salvation, which you have prepared in the sight of all people, a light for revelation to the Gentiles and for glory to your people Israel."

While Mary and Joseph were at the Jerusalem temple with Jesus, they met a man named Simeon, whose name means "God has heard" (Luke 2:25). From verse 26 we get the impression that he was advanced in years. Throughout his adult life, Simeon had distinguished himself as being "righteous and devout" (vs. 25). This means he was morally upright in his behavior and zealous in his observance of the Mosaic law. His faithfulness and sincerity in keeping God's ordinances is especially seen in his "waiting for the consolation of Israel." This phrase refers to Simeon's hope that the Messiah would come and deliver the nation (see Isa. 40:1; 49:13; 51:3). Indeed, Simeon loved God so much that he looked with eager anticipation for the comfort the Redeemer would bring to all people.

Simeon was also filled with the Holy Spirit (see Luke 2:25). This means Simeon had been given special insight by God's Spirit to recognize the Redeemer. Furthermore, the Spirit had disclosed to Simeon that he would not die until he had seen the Lord's Messiah (see vs. 26). So, the Spirit led Simeon into the temple courts on the day Mary and Joseph brought Jesus (see vs. 27). As noted in lesson 8 of quarter 1, the Hebrew prophets entertained a lively hope that a time was coming when the Spirit of God would be given out more broadly (see Isa. 32:15; 59:21; Joel 2:28–29). That hope, which was manifested in upright persons such as Simeon, was fulfilled on the day of Pentecost (see Acts 2:14–21).

Because of the special insight Simeon had been given, he immediately recognized Jesus as the Messiah. The reference in Luke 2:27 is to the larger temple area, not to the most holy place. Simeon was either in the court of the Gentiles or the court of women, since Mary was present. Amazingly, the parents allowed the elderly man to hold their son (see vs. 28). Simeon's words of praise concerning the Christ child occurred at the epicenter of the Jewish religion. This implies that, far from being a foreigner and outcast, Jesus was accepted and worshiped by the most pious individuals in Israel.

Simeon's brief prophetic declaration in verses 29–32 is sometimes called the *Nunc Dimittis*, which comes from the opening phrase in Latin, "now dismiss" (in other words, "now permit to die"). In this short refrain, we see the heart of a humble and godly man. Simeon's hymn is a patchwork of passages and themes found in the Book of Isaiah (see vss. 40:5; 42:6; 46:13; 49:6; 52:9–10). Isaiah's vision of the future included salvation for the Gentiles, along with God's chosen people, Israel. We also find similar strains in the Minor Prophets. Simeon's words were revolutionary and, in some respects, visionary. As a loyal and devout Jew to whom God had given special insight, Simeon recognized that because of the advent of the Messiah, God's redemption would now be available for all people—Jews and Gentiles alike.

Simeon said he was God's "servant" (Luke 2:29), a concept that did not imply a menial, servile existence, but rather privilege and honor in service to the Creator. Moreover, Simeon referred to God as the "Sovereign Lord". The latter phrase renders the Greek noun *despótes*, which means "master" or "absolute ruler," and from which we get our English term "despot." The divine promise to Simeon had been fulfilled, and now he could die in peace. He explained that he had seen God's salvation (see vs. 30). The idea is that to see Jesus, the Messiah, is to see the deliverance of the Lord (see John 14:9). There is some debate whether the final phrase in Luke 2:31 refers to the people of Israel alone or to both Israel and the Gentile nations. Verse 32 makes it clear that Simeon included non-Jews as well as Jews. This is a key thematic emphasis of Luke (see Luke 24:47; Acts 10:34–43).

There is also disagreement over the best way to structure Luke 2:32. The KJV sees "light" and "glory" being parallel ideas; in other words, Jesus is a light to bring revelation to Gentiles and glory to the people of Israel. The NIV sees "light" as a summary statement that refers to the entire verse. In this case, "revelation" and "glory" would be corresponding ideas. In other words, Jesus is a light for all, but is a revelation for the Gentiles and glory for Israel (see Luke 1:78–79; Acts 26:22–23). In either case, the central idea is clear that Jesus makes salvation available to all people. Both Mary and Joseph were amazed at what Simeon had said about their infant son (see Luke 2:33). Simeon's words tell us that in the birth of Jesus, the next stage of redemptive history had begun. Gentiles would experience the same deliverance promised to Jews. Indeed, for all who put their faith in Messiah, God promised to give them eternal life.

After invoking God's blessing upon Joseph and Mary, Simeon prophesied concerning Mary and her son (see Luke 2:34). Here we find the first hint in the third Synoptic Gospel that Jesus' advent would be accompanied with great difficulty. Perhaps God revealed to Simeon that Joseph would not be alive when the sorrows foretold would come to pass. Though the Scriptures do not give an account for the death of Joseph, no mention is made of him after Jesus began His public ministry. It is generally believed that Joseph died before that time.

The phrase "falling and rising" emphasizes that Jesus would bring division in the nation. Some would fall (or be judged) and others would rise (or be blessed) because of how they responded to the Messiah (see Isa. 8:14–15; Mal. 4:2). Furthermore, others see in Simeon's words the fact that Jesus' preaching of repentance would cause many to fall from their self-righteous opinion of themselves to the point where they could recognize their sinfulness and be saved, or exalted, through faith in the Redeemer of the lost.

Simeon related that Jesus would be a sign against whom many would speak (see Luke 2:34). This is based on the fact that God would appoint the Messiah as the provision for salvation from sin. While some (like Simeon) would receive Him with joy, others (like the religious leaders) would reject Him. As a result, the deepest thoughts of many people (namely, their reasonings and motives) would be exposed by the way they responded to the Savior (see vs. 35). Although Jesus came to be the Messiah of His people, the majority would despise Him. Tragically, despite the glory of the salvation He would freely offer, many of His contemporaries would reject Him as the Anointed One.

Discussion Questions

1. What does God's redemption of His people from Egypt tell us about who God is?
2. Why was it necessary for Joseph and Mary to bring the infant Jesus to be presented to the Lord in the temple?
3. How did the spiritual qualities Simeon possessed equip him for a unique opportunity?
4. What prophetic message did Simeon share about Jesus?
5. What can we learn from Simeon's testimony about the importance of trusting God to lead us?

Contemporary Application

What is the Advent season really all about? We enjoy talking about peace, good cheer, exchanging gifts, and so on during this holiday period. Tragically, society has placed so much of an emphasis on these things that the ultimate meaning of Christmas gets forgotten.

The message of hope is that the Father sent His Son to earth as our Savior. The Lord did the impossible by enabling Mary—a young, unmarried virgin—to conceive and bear the Christ child. And God worked through a seemingly unimportant, elderly man named Simeon to make some amazing declarations about what lay ahead for Jesus.

We are given the choice to follow God every day, just as Simeon was. Our response to the Lord will determine how we are used. Ordinary people like us can become extraordinary individuals when we submit, as Simeon did, to God and say, "May it be as You have said." Nothing God wants to do through us is impossible, if we are willing.

God did the impossible when Jesus was born to a young virgin and when the Savior rose from the dead. God did the impossible when He anointed the church with His Spirit. Even today, God does the impossible when He enables people like us to turn to Him with our fears and troubles. When we do, we discover that nothing is too hard for God (see Gen. 18:14).

A Generous Gift

Scripture

Background Scripture: *Matthew 23:1–12; Mark 12:38–44*
Scripture Lesson: *Matthew 23:2–12; Mark 12:38–44*
Key Verse: "Whoever exalts himself will be humbled, and whoever humbles himself will be exalted." *Matthew 23:12*
Scripture Lesson for Children: *Mark 12:41–44*
Key Verse for Children: "This poor widow has put more into the treasury than all the others." *Mark 12:43*

Lesson Aim

To give willingly and generously to the work of God.

Lesson Setting

Time: A.D. *30*
Place: Jerusalem

Lesson Outline

A Generous Gift

    I. Avoiding Hypocrisy: Matthew 23:2–12
      A. *Saying One Thing and Doing Another: vss. 2–4*
      B. *Seeking the Approval of Others: vss. 5–7*
      C. *Seeking the Recognition of Others: vss. 8–12*
    II. Being Generous: Mark 12:38–44
      A. *Desiring Notoriety: vss. 38–40*
      B. *Giving Sacrificially: vss. 41–44*

Introduction for Adults

Topic: *Giving from the Heart*

In his book, *A Dance with Deception*, Charles Colson states that most of the money given to secular charities comes from religious believers. The more religious a person is, the more likely he or she is to be generous. People who attend church frequently are three to four times more generous in their giving than are people who attend church infrequently or not at all. Even more interesting is that poor Christians, such as the impoverished widow Jesus commended, give a larger percentage of their income than do wealthier Christians.

One missions agency reported that by the year 2015, 25 percent of all American career missionaries would be called home from their fields of service due to a lack of financial support. That is frightening! As the older generation grows smaller, and their financial support with them, the younger generation needs to step up to the plate of financial responsibility.

This week's lesson challenges us to give to the Lord's work. In short, hold everything you own with an open hand.

Introduction for Youth

Topic: *Genuine Generosity*

A report from Nehemiah Ministries suggests that in churches of 350 or fewer members, 50 percent of the members give nothing in the offering. As the church membership increases to 500 and larger, those who give nothing increases to 75 percent!

In his book, *Thru the Bible,* J. Vernon McGee writes about a wealthy man he knew who gave generously to the Lord's work, yet remained wealthy. McGee asked how that was possible. In response, the man said, "Well, the Lord shovels it in and I shovel it out, and God has the bigger shovel."

While saved teens can't assume that God will make them rich, they can draw inspiration from the example of the destitute widow. Specifically, as believers give to God, He gives to them. They simply can't outgive the Lord!

Concepts for Children

Topic: *Giving with Sincerity*

1. Jesus told His followers about a woman whose husband had died.
2. This woman was very poor.
3. This woman gave all her money so that God's work could continue.
4. Jesus was pleased with this woman's desire to give so much.
5. Jesus is also pleased with us when we do what we can to help others in need.

Lesson Commentary

I. AVOIDING HYPOCRISY: MATTHEW 23:2–12

A. Saying One Thing and Doing Another: vss. 2–4

"The teachers of the law and the Pharisees sit in Moses' seat. So you must obey them and do everything they tell you. But do not do what they do, for they do not practice what they preach. They tie up heavy loads and put them on men's shoulders, but they themselves are not willing to lift a finger to move them."

In A.D. 30, Jesus began His final trip to Jerusalem (see Luke 17:11). His triumphal entry is recorded in Matthew 21:1–11 (see Mark 11:1–10; Luke 19:29–44; John 12:12–19). As Jesus and His disciples drew near the city, He sent a couple of them ahead to a village to procure a donkey. Then, in fulfillment of Scripture, Jesus chose to enter the capital riding on the animal. The crowds treated Jesus as a king entering the city. They sang praises and carpeted His path with their coats and branches. On Monday, Jesus cursed a fig tree and cleared the temple (see Matt. 21:12–13, 18–19; Mark 11:12–18). Then, on Tuesday, the religious authorities questioned Jesus and He taught in the temple (see Matt. 21:23—23:39; Mark 11:27—12:44; Luke 20:1—21:4).

It was within this context that Jesus made pointed comments to His disciples and to the crowds who gathered in the temple courtyard to listen to Him (see Matt. 23:1; see 24:1). The Savior censured the scribes and the Pharisees for their hypocritical and self-serving behavior (see 23:2). The Pharisees were members of a Jewish sect that had risen to prominence during the two centuries before Jesus' birth. Their goal was to increase the righteousness of society. Pharisees insisted on strict obedience to the law of Moses. However, they considered the traditions of religious experts to be equal in authority with the law.

Some Pharisees were trained in the law and had official status as scribes or "teachers of the law." These specialists were authorities on Old Testament legal code. They believed they had received the spirit of Moses and claimed to know divine will in legal matters. The phrase rendered "sit in Moses' seat" figuratively denoted those who claimed to be the lawgiver's authoritative interpreters and arbitrators, as well as the judges of those who violated his pronouncements.

During the Jews' captivity in Babylon (605–445 B.C.), they underwent a rebirth of interest in the Mosaic law. At that time, an unwritten but highly developed body of teachings and commentary about the law began to grow up among religious teachers, who were called rabbis. The original intention was commendable. The teachers wanted to prevent violations of the law. They tried to do this by setting up regulations for all of life, like a hedge around the law. These regulations grew generation by generation until they were gathered in a written collection, called the Mishnah, two centuries after Jesus' death. Even during His life, the tradition had become overvalued, obscuring the law it was meant to safeguard.

For example, Moses had told the people not to gather manna on the sabbath (see Exod. 16:29). The rabbis said that meant nobody could go more than 2,000 cubits (or about 3,000 feet) from their home on the sabbath. The rabbis not only added to the law, but they also built in loopholes. For instance, they revised their sabbath restriction. If somebody placed two meals at a distance of 2,000 cubits from their home the day before the sabbath, they could define that site as their dwelling. So they could walk that distance on the sabbath, and then go another 2,000 cubits beyond. Over time, the Pharisees and some other religious leaders thought these humanly-devised interpretations (called the oral law) had as much force and authority as the written law. In contrast, Jesus called them— not without some scornful contempt—"traditions" (Mark 7:9).

Theoretically, Pharisees and scribes affirmed the importance of integrity and love. In reality, all too often they practiced legalism and hypocrisy. Perhaps this is why Jesus accused the religious leaders of saying one thing and doing another (see Matt. 23:3). The Savior directed His disciples to hear and heed what the Pharisees and scribes taught, that is, as long as it conformed to the truth of Scripture. In contrast, Jesus urged His disciples not to follow their disingenuous example. A case in point would be the specialists creating onerous religious demands and piling them on others to bear, even when the specialists refused to lift a finger to help ease the burden.

B. Seeking the Approval of Others: vss. 5–7

"Everything they do is done for men to see: They make their phylacteries wide and the tassels on their garments long; they love the place of honor at banquets and the most important seats in the synagogues; they love to be greeted in the marketplaces and to have men call them 'Rabbi.'"

Jesus accused the scribes and Pharisees of seeking the approval of others. For instance, they drew attention to themselves by increasing the width of the leather strap attached to their "phylacteries" (Matt. 23:5) and lengthening the "tassels" on the four corners of their outer garments so that they would be more noticeable to others (see Num. 15:38; Deut. 22:12). Phylacteries were small black leather pouches containing Old Testament verses (see Exod. 13:9, 16; Deut. 6:8; 11:18). During morning prayers, participants wore the cases on their foreheads and left arms. Regrettably, customs originally intended to remind God's people of His commandments were being misused.

Other examples of self-serving behavior included the religious leaders maneuvering to be seated in the most honored spots at feasts. They also sought the most prominent locations at the front of the synagogue where others could see them during worship services (see Matt. 23:6). Furthermore, as they strolled through the "marketplaces" (vs. 7), they yearned for others to greet them with respect. They especially coveted individuals publicly referring to them as "Rabbi," which was a title of honor reserved for those whom the public recognized as distinguished teachers of the Mosaic law. "Rabbi" is a Hebrew word that literally means "my great one" or "my master." In the Gospels, Jesus was often referred to as Rabbi or Teacher (see Matt. 26:25, 49; Mark 9:5; 10:51; 11:21; John 1:49; 3:2; 4:31).

About two decades later, James told his readers that passively listening to God's Word was not enough to promote spiritual growth. It was just as important for them to obediently act upon what it says (see Jas. 1:22). To hear the Good News without implementing its teachings is nothing but self-deception. Indeed, the Devil's primary weapon against Christians is deceit. He often comes disguised as an "angel of light" (2 Cor. 11:14) and tries to lure us away from God with whatever feels good. James 4:4 reminds us that friendship with the world (namely, secular human society and culture under the guidance and control of Satan) is actually enmity, or antagonism, toward God.

At the close of the Sermon on the Mount, Jesus compared those who heeded His Word with wise builders who constructed their houses on firm foundations (see Matt. 7:24–27). He later rebuked the Pharisees and called them hypocrites because even though they honored Him with their lips, their hearts were far from Him (see 15:8). Finally, Paul warned against making a show of being religious, but rejecting the power of the Lord that alone could enable people to become godlier (2 Tim. 3:5). From these verses we see that action always makes our faith authentic and believable.

C. Seeking the Recognition of Others: vss. 8–12

"But you are not to be called 'Rabbi,' for you have only one Master and you are all brothers. And do not call anyone on earth 'father,' for you have one Father, and he is in heaven. Nor are you to be called 'teacher,' for you have one Teacher, the Christ. The greatest among you will be your servant. For whoever exalts himself will be humbled, and whoever humbles himself will be exalted."

Jesus warned His followers not to seek the recognition of others. Because all the disciples were spiritually equal with each other, none of them was to solicit the title of "Rabbi" (Matt. 23:8), especially since Jesus was their supreme Teacher. Likewise, none of the disciples were to yearn for others to address them as "father" (vs. 9). After all, the Creator in heaven was the sole "Father" of believers. Only God reigned over the universe and had foremost authority over Jesus' disciples. Moreover, Christians were not to solicit others to call them "teacher" or "instructor" (vs. 10), for the Messiah alone was their true spiritual Leader and Guide. In these verses, Jesus censured the arrogance that accompanied titles. For this reason, He declared that those among His disciples who humbly served one another were the greatest in the heavenly kingdom (see vss. 20:26–28). Indeed, God would humble those who tried to make themselves great. Oppositely, He would honor those who genuinely humbled themselves (see vs. 23:12).

About three decades later, Peter urged all of his readers to clothe themselves with humility. Instead of responding arrogantly to others, they were to be unpretentious and meek. Peter's command provides an interesting word picture.

The Greek verb rendered "clothe yourselves" (1 Pet. 5:5) was commonly used in reference to a slave tying an apron around his or her waist before serving others. The apostle may have been thinking about the incident described in John 13:1–11 in which Jesus washed His disciples' feet. Jesus willingly performed this lowly act to stress the importance of humility (see vss. 12–17). Peter supported his appeal for humility by citing Proverbs 3:34. This verse teaches that God is against those who are arrogant and insolent. In fact, He thwarts their evil plans. He showers His grace, however, on the humble. They receive His favor and kindness because they trust in Him and genuinely want to serve Him.

The persecuted Christians of Asia Minor to whom Peter wrote were in need of divine help. So, the apostle urged them to be humble in the presence of God's mighty power. In other words, they were to recognize their plight and welcome God's assistance. At the moment, they were distressed and discouraged from all the affliction they had to endure. Peter reminded them that when the right time came, God would send relief. He would honor their faith by one day ending their suffering (see 1 Pet. 5:6). The believers in Asia Minor were filled with anxiety as they endured unjust suffering. The Greek noun rendered "anxiety" (vs. 7) means to be troubled with cares. The term refers to an extreme uneasiness of mind or a brooding fear about some trauma in life. Perhaps intentionally echoing Psalm 55:22, Peter told his readers to cast all their concerns on God.

Note that the apostle did not tell believers to share some of their burdens with the Lord. Every matter was to be given over to His control; nothing was to be held back. Peter's friends could roll all their burdens over onto God because He deeply cared about the matters that distressed them. Others might have been indifferent to their afflictions, but God wasn't. He would console and encourage His people in the most troublesome events of their lives. Peter was not giving his readers empty advice. They were at the mercy of those who mocked their God and despised their faith. The law courts evidently provided little relief. The Christians often did not know what would happen next to them, although martyrdom was always a possibility. They would gladly welcome Peter's teaching on God's care of them.

II. BEING GENEROUS: MARK 12:38–44

A. Desiring Notoriety: vss. 38–40

As he taught, Jesus said, "Watch out for the teachers of the law. They like to walk around in flowing robes and be greeted in the marketplaces, and have the most important seats in the synagogues and the places of honor at banquets. They devour widows' houses and for a show make lengthy prayers. Such men will be punished most severely."

Like Matthew 23:2–12, Mark 12:38–44 narrates events that occurred on Tuesday of Jesus' final week on earth. He directed His disciples to beware of the legal experts and their thirst for notoriety. Despite their claims, they relished sauntering through the "marketplaces" (vs. 38) while wearing long, white linen robes with fringes. These garments set them off from the common people. When the teachers passed by in public, the people would rise respectfully. In the synagogues, the scribes sat on the bench before the ark containing the scrolls of Scripture. Only they enjoyed this privilege in the presence of all the other worshipers. The "places of honor" (vs. 39) at a banquet were located at the head of the table, especially next to the host. When legal experts occupied those esteemed spots, all the other guests could witness their favor with the host.

Tragically, the scribes' deplorable behavior went beyond craving public recognition to include mistreating others. In their hubris, they even cheated impoverished widows out of their property. During certain periods, some scribes were beggars. However, by Jesus' day it had become a mark of piety to support a legal expert. For instance, wealthy people would donate money, and in response, teachers would say "lengthy prayers" (vs. 40) on behalf of their benefactors. The religious leaders' quest for power had undermined their morals until they viewed themselves as above the laws they imposed on others. Jesus, without hesitation, exposed the hypocritical motives behind their behavior. In short, they had made religion a vehicle for self–advancement.

B. Giving Sacrificially: vss. 41–44

Jesus sat down opposite the place where the offerings were put and watched the crowd putting their money into the temple treasury. Many rich people threw in large amounts. But a poor widow came and put in two very small copper coins, worth only a fraction of a penny. Calling his disciples to him, Jesus said, "I tell you the truth, this poor widow has put more into the treasury than all the others. They all gave out of their wealth; but she, out of her poverty, put in everything—all she had to live on."

After condemning the scribes for false piety, Jesus drew His disciples' attention to an example of true piety. Jesus observed people give their offerings to the "temple treasury" (Mark 12:41) in the Court of Women. (Both men and women used this court, but women could not use the courts closer to the Jerusalem temple.) The Court of Women housed 13 trumpet-shaped containers for the offerings that all Jews were expected to give. While Jesus looked on, He saw wealthy people give huge sums of "money" (that is, coins made out of copper). In contrast, a destitute "widow" (vs. 42) gave two minuscule "coins" (also made out of copper), which were worth less than a penny in today's currency. She could have saved one of the coins for herself, but she gave both.

The rich may have been the legal experts who had amassed their wealth by stealing from widows. Perhaps the widow was one of those whose property the scribes had looted to satiate their appetites. In any case, Jesus directed the attention of His followers to this destitute person. On the one hand, the rich placed what they had to spare in the offering box. On the other hand, the poverty-stricken widow gave all she owned, even though it undermined her ability to survive. She was all that the scribes pretended to be but were not. The widow had fulfilled the greatest commandment. By her actions it was clear that she loved God with all her heart, soul, mind, and strength.

To our knowledge, this was Jesus' last appearance in the Jerusalem temple and the end of His public teaching. As He looked ahead to the cross, it must have been discouraging to consider the hostility of the religious leaders, the corruption of the temple system, the insincerity of the masses, and the instability of the Twelve. Yet, in the midst of all this, Jesus found joy in watching one true worshiper.

Discussion Questions

1. Why is it objectionable to preach one thing and do another?
2. How did the scribes and Pharisees try to win the recognition of others?
3. What actions do believers typically associate with being "religious"?
4. How can church leaders avoid the temptation of showing false piety?
5. Why is it often difficult for believers to be sacrificial in their giving?

Contemporary Application

Jesus exposed the hypocritical motives behind the religious leaders' behavior. They had made their piety a vehicle for self-advancement. Jesus contrasted these ambitious individuals, who abused their office, with an impoverished widow. Unlike them, she was a sterling example of a generous and obedient person.

If we desire to give God the devotion He deserves, we should take the widow as our role model. It is appropriate for us to emulate her spirit of total dependence on the Lord. It is then, as we give willingly and generously to the work of God, we can be sure that He notices our smallest act of compassion toward others.

Most of us are not wealthy. Yet, regardless of how much we give, the principle is the same: the more generously and cheerfully we give to God's work, the more blessings He gives us. That does not mean that if we give the Lord four dollars He gives us back eight dollars, but that He eternally blesses us more when we give more. In turn, we can expect a harvest of praise to God from those who are the recipients of our acts of generosity.

Jesus told the Twelve that even though they had given up everything to spread the Gospel, they would be rewarded a hundred times over in this world and receive eternal life (see Mark 10:29–31). We know that the Twelve did not become materially wealthy heralding the Good News. However, as Paul told the Philippians, the Father had amply met all the apostles needs according to His abundant provision in the Son, and in the process had richly blessed the Philippians for their generosity (see Phil. 4:17–19). The Lord wants to do the same for us, too.

An Expression of Love

Scripture

Background Scripture: *Genesis 28—30*
Scripture Lesson: *Genesis 29:15–30*
Key Verse: Jacob lay with Rachel also, and he loved Rachel more than Leah. And he worked for Laban another seven years. *Genesis 29:30*
Scripture Lesson for Children: *Genesis 29:15–30*
Key Verse for Children: Jacob … loved Rachel. … And he worked for Laban another seven years. *Genesis 29:30*

Lesson Aim

To note that deceit can destroy relationships.

Lesson Setting

Time: 1929 B.C.
Place: Haran

Lesson Outline

An Expression of Love
    I. Laban's Agreement: Genesis 29:15–19
        A. *Laban's Offer: vs. 15*
        B. *Jacob's Request: vss. 16–19*
    II. Jacob's Marriages to Leah and Rachel:
        Genesis 29:20–30
        A. *Jacob's Years of Service for Rachel: vs. 20*
        B. *Laban's Trickery: vss. 21–24*
        C. *Laban's Explanation: vss. 25–27*
        D. *Jacob's Additional Years of Service: vss. 28–30*

Introduction for Adults

Topic: *Expression of True Love*

A relative of mine saw a layer of lies created when his daughter was in the third grade. Because she wanted the attention of her classmates, she told them that her mother had been in a serious car accident and that her arm was broken. The child's teacher caught wind of the student's fictional story and instructed the entire class to write get-well cards to the "injured" parent.

The scheme came crashing down on the girl when her mother happened to go into the garbage to search for a bill she had misplaced. The parent discovered those cards and realized that her daughter was tangled in a web of lies. The mother took her daughter to school to confess and apologize to the girl's teacher and classmates. That confession produced a flood of tears.

The mother actually felt more sorry for her daughter than upset with her. It was a painful lesson for the third grader. But she and her peers learned that lies are like flies. They breed quickly and menace both the person who lied and the people they tried to deceive. As Jacob could affirm from his own experience, serial lying results in many dashed hopes and unfulfilled expectations.

Introduction for Youth

Topic: *Bait and Switch*

Brad was given some money by his parents when his family went to the flea market. Walking the aisles, he finally decided on buying a whoopee cushion, convinced of the fun that he would have later with his relatives. The salesman's pitch was persuasive as he promised the 11-year-old the lowest price on Cape Cod. Brad accepted the adult's word and bought the novelty for several dollars.

That evening, while Brad and his mother shopped, Brad saw the same whoopee cushion for sale at the store for less than a dollar. Brad was infuriated, claiming that he had been ripped off. If Brad could feel so cheated at something that cost so little, imagine how Jacob felt when he was tricked by Laban. Jacob's dream of marrying Rachel was foiled, at least for the moment. Jacob would have to give Laban an additional seven years of labor to see the goal of marrying Rachel brought to pass.

Concepts for Children

Topic: *Love and Marriage*

1. Jacob worked for his uncle, Laban.
2. Jacob liked Laban's younger daughter, Rachel, and wanted to marry her.
3. Laban tricked Jacob into marrying the older daughter, Leah.
4. Despite being upset, Jacob worked hard so that he could also marry Rachel.
5. Jacob's love for Rachel reminds us of how much God loves us.

Lesson Commentary

I. LABAN'S AGREEMENT: GENESIS 29:15–19

A. Laban's Offer: vs. 15

Laban said to him, "Just because you are a relative of mine, should you work for me for nothing? Tell me what your wages should be."

After Abraham's death (see Gen. 25:1–11), the focus of the narrative shifts to Isaac. When he was 40, he married Rebekah, and for the next 20 years, the couple remained childless. Eventually, the Lord answered Isaac's prayers by enabling Rebekah to conceive fraternal twins, Esau and Jacob. As in many families, there was sibling rivalry between the two boys, fueled in part by their different personalities and their parents' dissimilar preferences for each child (see vss. 27–28).

In one episode, because Esau was famished, he sold his birthright to Jacob for bread and stew (see vss. 29–34). Decades later, Jacob deceived his father, Isaac, into thinking he, the younger son, was Esau. In this way, Jacob received Isaac's blessing, which should have gone to Esau. Both Isaac and Esau were upset over Jacob's deception. Also, Esau detested Jacob and looked for an ideal time to avenge the loss by murdering him.

To secure Jacob's safety, Rebekah convinced Isaac that Jacob should make the nearly 450-mile journey from Beersheba to her relatives in Haran in northwest Mesopotamia, where Jacob could look for a non-Canaanite wife (see vss. 27:1–46). After leaving and stopping for the night at Bethel, Jacob dreamed of a stairway with God standing above it. He promised to bless Jacob's descendants and always be with him. Jacob built an altar there to commemorate his encounter with God. Jacob also vowed that God would be his Lord and that Jacob would always give a tenth of his wealth to God (see vss. 28:1–22).

The following day, Jacob resumed his journey to the land of the east, which lay between Canaan and Mesopotamia (see vs. 29:1). Jacob came upon three flocks of sheep lying in an open field beside a well and waiting to be watered (see vs. 2). It was the custom for all the flocks to arrive before a well's stone was removed. Then, once all the animals had been watered, the stone was rolled back over the mouth of the well (see vs. 3). Jacob learned from shepherds (an occupation shared by both men and women in that culture) that they lived in Haran and that they knew a man named Laban, who was the grandson of Nahor (see vss. 4–5).

Jacob also found out that Laban was faring well. In fact, one of his daughters, Rachel, was about to arrive with some of Laban's sheep (see vs. 6). Jacob advised the shepherds to water their flocks and allow the animals to graze some more (see vs. 7). But they explained that they were in the habit of waiting for all the flocks to be assembled before the stone was rolled off the mouth of the well so that the sheep could be watered (see vs. 8). While the conversation continued,

Rachel arrived with her father's sheep, for she was tending them (see vs. 9). Jacob, perhaps being energized by the sight of this beautiful woman, used his own hands to remove the large stone covering the well. This demonstrated his strength to Rachel and enabled Jacob to be of service by watering his uncle's sheep (see vs. 10).

The patriarch not only gave his cousin a customary kiss of greeting but also wept aloud for joy (see vs. 11). Clearly, this encounter was an emotional one for Jacob. Next, he explained to Rachel that he was a relative of her father and the son of Rebekah. In response, Rachel ran to tell her father. The young woman seems to have been well out in front of Jacob. When Rachel finally reached Laban, she told him about Jacob (see vs. 12). Upon hearing the news, Laban rushed out to meet Jacob, warmly embraced him, gave him a kiss of greeting, and brought him to his house (see vs. 13).

Jacob took the opportunity to relate his situation to his uncle. Upon hearing his nephew's story, Laban openly acknowledged Jacob as being his own "flesh and blood" (vs. 14). The traveler had found a new home, where he lodged for the next month. But Jacob didn't lounge around in ease. He quickly began to participate in the routines of Laban's family. The uncle raised the issue of Jacob's wages. Until now, Laban had not paid anything to his nephew. Laban realized he could not expect Jacob to work for room and board indefinitely, so the uncle asked his nephew how much he wanted to be paid for his labor (see vs. 15).

B. Jacob's Request: vss. 16–19

Now Laban had two daughters; the name of the older was Leah, and the name of the younger was Rachel. Leah had weak eyes, but Rachel was lovely in form, and beautiful. Jacob was in love with Rachel and said, "I'll work for you seven years in return for your younger daughter Rachel." Laban said, "It's better that I give her to you than to some other man. Stay here with me."

It seems as if Laban viewed his relationship with Jacob primarily in economic terms and treated his nephew as a laborer under contract (see Gen. 31:38–42). Laban also treated his two daughters like animals to be bartered in trade. The older daughter was named Leah (which means "cow"), while the younger one was named Rachel (which means "ewe"; 29:16). Leah lacked the kind of beauty people of that day seemed to prize, but the meaning of the Hebrew in verse 17 is uncertain. Views differ whether Leah's eyes were plain and dull or tender and delicate. While they may have been appealing in some way, she did not have the exceptional beauty of Rachel, who was gorgeous in both form and appearance.

Because Jacob had fallen in love with Rachel, he offered to serve Laban seven years in exchange for the privilege of marrying his younger daughter (see vs. 18). An enterprising person could create a lot of wealth in that time. Perhaps Jacob made such a generous offer because he had no dowry (or bride price) to give for Rachel. Laban was not so foolish as to reject such an offer, so he agreed to Jacob's terms (see vs. 19).

II. JACOB'S MARRIAGES TO LEAH AND RACHEL: GENESIS 29:20–30

A. Jacob's Years of Service for Rachel: vs. 20

So Jacob served seven years to get Rachel, but they seemed like only a few days to him because of his love for her.

In light of Laban's statement, his nephew worked for seven years to acquire Rachel. Also, because Jacob's love for Rachel was so strong, the time seemed like only a few days to him (see Gen. 29:20). Perhaps Jacob felt as if the dowry was rather insignificant in comparison to what he was getting in return—Rachel's hand in marriage. Also, the lengthy engagement gave Jacob and Rachel time to develop their relationship so that they could be as ready as possible for marriage.

B. Laban's Trickery: vss. 21–24

Then Jacob said to Laban, "Give me my wife. My time is completed, and I want to lie with her." So Laban brought together all the people of the place and gave a feast. But when evening came, he took his daughter Leah and gave her to Jacob, and Jacob lay with her. And Laban gave his servant girl Zilpah to his daughter as her maidservant.

At the end of seven years, Jacob told Laban that their contractual agreement had been satisfied. So, Jacob wanted to consummate his marriage to Rachel (see Gen. 29:21). In response, Laban invited all the people in the area to celebrate with Jacob at a wedding feast (see vs. 22). Earlier, in verse 19, Laban had responded ambiguously to Jacob. This was a shrewd decision on Laban's part, for he had not explicitly promised to give Rachel to Jacob in marriage. And to Jacob's chagrin, he was not astute enough to discern the vagueness in his uncle's reply.

When evening came, Laban brought his older, veiled daughter (see vs. 24:65), Leah, to Jacob, and he had marital relations with her (see vs. 29:23). Perhaps the older daughter said little or nothing that night, so that Jacob would not recognize her voice. According to the custom of the time, Laban gave his female servant, Zilpah, to Leah as her maid (see vs. 24). Years earlier, Jacob had capitalized on the blindness of his father, Isaac, in order to deceive him and get the family blessing. Now Laban trumped that feat by using the cover of darkness to pull a fast one over his nephew. In this way, he gave the former trickster a large dose of his own toxic, relational medicine.

We can only guess Rachel's feelings as she found out her father's plan. All her hopes and dreams were being cruelly disrupted by Laban's deceptive scheme. Perhaps he felt compelled to concoct it because he regarded Jacob as a worker who was too valuable to lose. Beyond question, the nephew had enabled Laban's flocks to increase steadily. With respect to Leah, she may have been forced to cooperate reluctantly with her father's plan. Without a doubt, God was using this episode to spiritually prune and mature Jacob.

C. Laban's Explanation: vss. 25–27

When morning came, there was Leah! So Jacob said to Laban, "What is this you have done to me? I served you for Rachel, didn't I? Why have you deceived me?" Laban replied, "It is not our custom here to give the younger daughter in marriage before the older one. Finish this daughter's bridal week; then we will give you the younger one also, in return for another seven years of work."

When Jacob woke up in the morning, he discovered that it was Leah, not Rachel, who was beside him. Understandably, Jacob was incensed by his uncle's shameless act of deception. So the nephew confronted Laban. Jacob thought they had agreed he would work seven years for Rachel, but this did not prevent Laban from disregarding their contractual arrangement (see Gen. 29:25). Interestingly, the Hebrew verb rendered "deceived" is lexically related to the noun translated "came deceitfully" appearing in 27:35. The latter term is used in relation to Jacob's deception of Isaac. In this case, the adage "What goes around, comes around" fits.

Laban deftly avoided the ethical issue of his actions by referring to what his clan routinely did. The uncle claimed that it was the custom for the firstborn daughter to be married off before any younger daughters (see vs. 26). We don't know whether Laban was truly concerned about the local practice of marrying the older daughter first. But even if he was, that did not justify his underhanded tactics. If the uncle wanted, he could have told his nephew about the tradition before the wedding.

In an attempt to mollify Jacob's anger, Laban encouraged his nephew to complete Leah's bridal week. (In those days, a marriage ceremony included an entire week of festivities.) Then the father would give his younger daughter, Rachel, to Jacob in marriage. Of course, Laban expected seven more years of hard work out of Jacob in exchange for the younger daughter (see Gen. 29:27). Throughout the transaction, Laban operated in a cunning and calculating fashion, and there was nothing Jacob could do about it. Because his love for Rachel was real and deep, he did not dare jeopardize his chance to marry to her. So, in this contest of wits, Jacob was forced to comply with Laban's stipulations, which probably turned the nephew's marriage into an occasion for community-wide jesting.

D. Jacob's Additional Years of Service: vss. 28–30

And Jacob did so. He finished the week with Leah, and then Laban gave him his daughter Rachel to be his wife. Laban gave his servant girl Bilhah to his daughter Rachel as her maidservant. Jacob lay with Rachel also, and he loved Rachel more than Leah. And he worked for Laban another seven years.

Jacob agreed to work seven more years and completed Leah's bridal week (see Gen. 29:28). It was only at the end of Jacob's bridal week with Leah that the patriarch was officially married to Rachel. Also, according to the custom of the time, Laban gave his female servant, Bilhah, to Rachel as her maid (see vs. 29). Jacob, by having marital relations with Rachel, consummated his union with her. Also, even though the patriarch had been tricked by his uncle, he willingly put in seven additional years of service as a dowry (of sorts) for Rachel.

Verse 30 says that Jacob loved Rachel more than Leah. The irony is that God allowed Leah to give birth to Judah, from whom the future Messiah of Israel would come. Since the discovery of the clay tablets at Nuzi containing ancient legal records, some have regarded the contractual dealings between Laban and Jacob as the uncle's formal adoption of his nephew. The absence of any mention of Laban's sons in the account of Jacob's arrival may indicate that they were not yet born. Also, if that was the case, then Laban would certainly have been concerned about having a male heir.

According to the Nuzi tablets, one man could adopt another in order to gain him as an heir. One ancient tablet records an instance in which an adopted son received the father's daughter in marriage. According to the slab, if sons were born to the father after the adoption, then the inheritance would change, with some of the laws of the firstborn coming into play. If Laban's sons were born after his agreement with Jacob, that would help to explain the later change in the relationship between the uncle and his nephew (see vss. 31:1–2).

Scripture reveals that God is genuinely concerned with the plight of those who are deprived and disadvantaged. In the case of Leah, the Lord took note of the fact that she was unloved. In the original, the verb rendered "not loved" (vs. 29:31) is more literally translated "hated." In the culture of that day, this circumstance put Leah at a distinct disadvantage with respect to Rachel, who was the primary object of Jacob's affection. God intervened by enabling Leah to become pregnant. Meanwhile, Rachel remained childless. Leah named her firstborn "Reuben" (vs. 32), which means "look, a son." It sounds like the Hebrew for "he has seen my misery." In this case, God had taken pity on Leah's oppressed condition. The mother hoped that the birth of Reuben would incline Jacob to respond to her in love (see vs. 33).

The Lord enabled Leah to become pregnant a second time, and again she gave birth to a son. Perhaps the young mother had cried out to God in prayer and interpreted the births as an indication of His positive response to her unloved status. The name Leah gave to her second-born, "Simeon," is derived from a verb that means "to hear." In turn, the name probably means "one who hears," which emphasizes that the Lord had heard about Leah's forlorn situation and intervened accordingly.

For the third time, the Lord enabled Leah to conceive and give birth to a son. The phrase rendered "my husband will become attached to me" (Gen. 29:34) implies that Leah hoped this most recent childbirth would spur Jacob to bond more closely in affection to Leah. Specialists are uncertain about the exact meaning of the name "Levi," which Leah gave to the third of her three sons. It sounds like the Hebrew verb *lavah*, which means "to join" or "to attach," making the name an appropriate one under the circumstances.

For a fourth time, the Lord enabled Leah to become pregnant and give birth to a son. By this time, she was overjoyed at God's favorable response to her cry for help. Indeed, it was an occasion for her to give praise to the Lord. This is the reason why she named her fourth son "Judah" (Gen. 29:35), which means "he will be praised." It sounds like and may be derived from a Hebrew verb that means "to praise." At this point, Leah stopped having children. Chapter 30 continues the account of the birth of Jacob's sons. By the time of the Exodus, Scripture says the patriarch's extended family had over 600,000 men, not counting women and children (see Exod. 12:37).

Discussion Questions

1. What was the nature of the relationship between Laban and Jacob?
2. If you were Jacob, would you have worked seven years for Laban?
3. In what way did Laban deceive Jacob?
4. After Jacob married Leah, what did Laban say Jacob had to do in order to marry Rachel?
5. What experiences in your life has God used to help you spiritually mature?

Contemporary Application

One of the guiding principles of modern business is this: "Fool me once, shame on you. Fool me twice, shame on me." In other words, it should take only one hard-won lesson to make us forever wary. If we fail to be sufficiently on our guard after that, it is clearly our own fault.

Not surprisingly, that attitude does not lead to mutually satisfying business partnerships. It makes even less sense when it becomes the guiding principle of our personal lives. It turns once loving, trusting relationships into bitter disappointments: "I cannot believe she said that about me. I will never trust her again!" "You swore you would never do that again. How can I ever believe another of your promises?" "He said he would not tell anybody—and he claimed to be my best friend!"

Relationships are built on trust. Once deception enters the picture—a violated confidence, a broken promise, an outright lie—trust is shattered, and the memory of the deceit taints everything that follows. Consider the way Laban treated Jacob regarding the issue of his planned marriage to Rachel. The excuse the uncle gave was offered flatly and without any sense of regret. The toxicity introduced during that early exchange tarnished the family dynamic for years to come.

Far too many Christians are involved in one or more relationships in which they are entangled in a web of deceit. The falsehoods may be small or great, but either way, they don't do the relationships any good. The best course of action is to set these dysfunctional relationships on the right path by dealing honestly and candidly with all forms of pretense and duplicity.

A Beautiful Bride

Scripture

Background Scripture: *Song of Solomon; John 10:1–11*
Scripture Lesson: *Song of Solomon 6:4–12*
Key Verse: My dove, my perfect one, is unique, the only daughter of her mother, the favorite of the one who bore her. *Song of Solomon 6:9*
Scripture Lesson for Children: *Song of Solomon 1:2–8; John 10:11*
Key Verse for Children: I am my lover's and my lover is mine. *Song of Solomon 6:3*

Lesson Aim

To affirm that God-given love is the joy of life.

Lesson Setting

Time: Sometime during the reign of Solomon (about 970–930 B.C.)
Place: Jerusalem

Lesson Outline

A Beautiful Bride

    I. A Declaration of Love: Song of Solomon 6:4–9
       A. *The King's Description of His Bride: vss. 4–7*
       B. *The Bride's Incomparable Beauty: vss. 8–9*
    II. An Affirmation of Love: Song of Solomon 6:10–12
       A. *The Chorus of Praise: vs. 10*
       B. *The King's Anticipation: vss. 11–12*

Introduction for Adults

Topic: *Marital Love*

Nowhere is the joy and wonder of love better described than in the Song of Solomon. The poem's beauty, respect for God's gift of love and physical intimacy in marriage, and its honest descriptions in powerful images stand in sharp contrast to the way contemporary culture talks about such matters.

Sadly, too many marriages grow stale and flounder on the lack of genuine intimacy. We need to renew the wonder and joy of love in our marriage relationships. We need to talk frankly about these matters with our children, especially those who are junior and senior high students.

Song of Solomon opens the door to a wide range of possibilities and applications. This simple, yet dramatic, love ballad can change us for the better and give us a new appreciation for the delights of God's gift of love.

Introduction for Youth

Topic: *God's Gift of Love*

Teens will be especially drawn to the subject matter of the Song of Solomon. Whereas the other poems of Solomon covered a broad range of themes, this ballad is specifically about love. Young people are able to appreciate the song's exquisite expression of human romantic love.

Teens will benefit from learning that the Song of Solomon reveals the romantic feelings of a woman and a man. The ballad also portrays the enduring strength of love. For instance, the couple expressed their security by pointing to their mutual desire and longing for each other. Their shared passion within marriage made them feel assured in their love.

The inclusion of such a book in the Old Testament shows that God, the Creator of intimacy between people, endorses such passion as good when expressed between a husband and wife. There is little doubt that the love described in Solomon's ballad comes from God and that He takes a hand in preserving this picture of romantic love. Through this poem, He shows how human love in all its fullness, between a married couple, was meant to be.

Concepts for Children

Topic: *The Meaning of Love*

1. Solomon was the king of Israel.
2. Solomon was going to marry a beautiful woman.
3. Solomon and his bride were very happy together.
4. Solomon and his bride loved each other very much.
5. This couple's love reminds us how much God cares for us.

Lesson Commentary

I. A DECLARATION OF LOVE: SONG OF SOLOMON 6:4–9

A. The King's Description of His Bride: vss. 4–7

You are beautiful, my darling, as Tirzah, lovely as Jerusalem, majestic as troops with banners. Turn your eyes from me; they overwhelm me. Your hair is like a flock of goats descending from Gilead. Your teeth are like a flock of sheep coming up from the washing. Each has its twin, not one of them is alone. Your temples behind your veil are like the halves of a pomegranate.

According to 1 Kings 4:32, Solomon composed 1,005 songs. Numerous Bible scholars think that the Song of Solomon (sometimes called the Song of Songs) is one of these. Whereas the odes Solomon wrote probably covered a broad range of themes, this poem is specifically about love. It portrays love's subtlety and mystery, its beauty and pleasures, and its captivation and enchantment. It reveals the romantic feelings shared between a woman and a man. The canticle also portrays the power of love, declaring that it rivals the strength of death. So, one of the main lessons to be learned from a study of Solomon's song is that God intends for rock-solid love to be a hallmark of a marital relationship.

It seems most reasonable to accept Solomon as the God-inspired composer, especially since the title refers to him by name (see vs. 1:1). In fact, his name appears throughout the book (see vss. 1:5; 3:7, 9, 11; 8:11–12). There are some who question Solomon's authorship of the poem, arguing that the real author used the monarch's name to give prestige to his work. They follow various lines of reasoning, such as pointing to the presence of some rare Hebrew words. Nonetheless, these arguments are unconvincing to many conservative scholars. Those who are uncertain of Solomon's authorship are likewise divided over when the song was composed. Yet, since it is sensible to accept that Solomon was the author, the date seems just as clear: sometime during his long reign between 970 and 930 B.C.

Both Jewish and Christian theologians have held the Song of Solomon in high esteem, though perhaps no other book of the Old Testament has been subjected to so many different interpretations. There are three basic approaches worth mentioning. The canticle has often been taken as allegorical. In this approach, the lovers are viewed not as historical figures, but as symbolic characters. Jewish interpreters who take the allegorical approach often see the characters as representing God and Israel, while Christian interpreters often see them as representing Jesus and the church. A somewhat related interpretation sees the Song of Solomon as typological. Put another way, the characters in this song are accepted as historical, but their love is taken to also illustrate the love God has for His people. Christians see in the love relationship between the young bride and groom the love that Jesus, the Bridegroom, has for His bride, the church.

When taken at face value, a straightforward interpretation of this song appears to portray an actual case of romantic love. This is the approach adopted in the Lesson Commentary. Of course, a literal interpretation does not preclude the author's use of metaphorical language, in which a word or phrase that ordinarily designates one situation is used to denote another. So, when the author referred to physical appearance, he may also have been focusing on character, personality, and so on. There is no clear plot in the Song of Solomon as there would be in a play or a story. While specialists have suggested a variety of story lines, the Lesson Commentary takes the view that the poem shows the love between Solomon and one of his wives.

Following the title (see vs. 1:1), the ode contains a cluster of five meetings in which the lovers pass through courtship, their wedding, the consummation of their love in marriage, and later occasions in which they renew their love. According to this analysis of the action, there are three sources of the speeches in the poem: the bride, her attendants (the daughters of Jerusalem), and the groom. The bride was identified as a Shulammite (see vs. 6:13), a dark-skinned country girl (see vs. 1:6). She was brought to the palace to become Solomon's wife (see vs. 4). We have no details about their courtship. Their songs begin with her introduction to the court from which she celebrates the bridegroom's love and name. Their songs fit the character and customs of an ancient Middle Eastern wedding. In that day, brides commonly were in their teens.

It will help if we try to catch the spirit of the occasion and contemplate the intimate dialogue between the bride and bridegroom. They described their love in the colorful imagery of King Solomon's time. In anticipation of their union, it was important for her to recall their young love. She celebrated her lover's physical and moral qualities. The bride used many word pictures to depict their relationship (see vss. 12–14). As a point of clarification, women wore small perfume pouches around their necks, and henna blossoms were thought to be the most beautiful flowers. As the two sang to each other, they rejoiced in the beauty that had attracted them to one another (see vss. 15–17).

Whereas the scenes of love in chapters 1 through 4, which occurred before marriage, were blissful and joyous, the first scene after the wedding portrays the anxiety of the bride. This uneasiness is described in what is apparently a dream the young woman experienced. Here we find Solomon endeavoring to be realistic and objective in his presentation. So, after portraying the wedding procession (see vss. 3:6—5:1), the king showed that, like all brides and bridegrooms, this couple brought personal frailties into their marriage. Specifically, in the bride's dream, her husband had gone away because she was too lethargic to answer his knocking and open their door. The bride responded by seeking help from the city watchmen. Yet, much to the woman's dismay, they beat her and stole her cloak. Perhaps these are images of her feelings of guilt and inadequacy in the marriage (see vss. 5:2–8).

The young maidens of the city responded to the bride's cry for help by asking her to describe her husband, and she did so in a beautiful portrait of the man she loved (see vss. 9–16). Next, the daughters of Jerusalem asked the Shulammite where her "beloved" (vs. 6:1) had gone. The maidens, who referred to the bride as being exceptionally "beautiful," stated their desire to help her search for him. The Shulammite noted that the bridegroom was at his "garden" (vs. 2), where "beds of spices" grew. Moreover, he was feeding his flock and gathering "lilies." It's possible to interpret these statements as a reference to a physical garden to which the king went for repose. Another option is to regard the bride's remark as a metaphorical reference to the physical intimacy the couple enjoyed with each other. In either case, the Shulammite affirmed the mutual love she and her husband shared at their home (see vs. 3). Perhaps it was at this point that she awakened and, seeing the bridegroom sleeping next to her, felt reassured.

With his new bride awake and lying beside him in their bed, Solomon offered her a tribute. The first part of it repeats some of what he had already said (compare vss. 4–7 with 4:1–3). For instance, the king declared his dearest to be as lovely as Tirzah and pleasing as Jerusalem (two prominent cities in Israel). Expressed another way, Solomon felt as if the beauty of his new bride was as spectacular as the nation's most renowned cities. Likewise, she was as breathtaking as a phalanx of Israelite warriors entering into battle. Put differently, her allure was as awe-inspiring as a powerful army with its banners flying (see vs. 6:4).

The Shulammite's husband was captivated by her dazzling eyes, so much so that he asked her to turn away (see vs. 5). To the king, his beloved's hair seemed to dance about gracefully. It was comparable to a shimmering "flock" of female "goats" rushing down from the hills of Gilead in a coordinated, flowing movement. Likewise, the Shulammite's aligned, white teeth reminded Solomon of a "flock" (vs. 6) of freshly cleaned "sheep." Not one animal was "missing," and each perfectly matched with another. Furthermore, the bride's crimson cheeks, though behind a "veil" (vs. 7), gleamed through the cover like the split "halves" of pomegranates. The latter was a fruit prized in ancient times for its glossy, red color and juicy, sweet taste.

B. The Bride's Incomparable Beauty: vss. 8–9

Sixty queens there may be, and eighty concubines, and virgins beyond number; but my dove, my perfect one, is unique, the only daughter of her mother, the favorite of the one who bore her. The maidens saw her and called her blessed; the queens and concubines praised her.

In Solomon's estimation, not even 60 "queens" (Song of Sol. 6:8; his primary wives) or 80 "concubines" (his secondary wives) or innumerable young women (female attendants in his royal court) outshone his new bride in terms of her beauty, intelligence, and stamina. It is certainly possible that Israel's monarch was here comparing the Shulammite to the other women in his harem. Regrettably, he would eventually have as many as 1,000 wives and concubines (see 1 Kings 11:3). Even so, in his eyes his darling was flawless and distinctive. It was as if she was the sole girl and best-loved child in her family. Even the young women of the kingdom complimented the king's beloved. Similarly, all the other wives and concubines in Solomon's court lauded the Shulammite for her singular poise and elegance (see Song of Sol. 6:9).

II. An Affirmation of Love: Song of Solomon 6:10–12

A. The Chorus of Praise: vs. 10

Who is this that appears like the dawn, fair as the moon, bright as the sun, majestic as the stars in procession?

Solomon was not the only person to extol the Shulammite's beauty. Her friends, the daughters of Jerusalem, also did. To them she was as majestic as the early morning "dawn" (Song of Sol. 6:10) and as luminous as the "moon." Likewise, the king's bride was as radiant as the "sun" and glorious as the "stars" parading like an army with its unfurled banners through the nighttime sky. Without question, she was the sole focus and center of Solomon's attention.

Even though it is clear that the friends of the young bride called her a "Shulammite" (vs. 13), there is no consensus as to what they meant by this distinction. Following is a list of possible meanings for that term: a reference to the bride's birthplace, which was possibly Shunem in Galilee; her actual name; a feminine form of the name *Solomon*; a reference to a pagan goddess of fertility; and a name derived from a Hebrew word that means "the peaceful one."

B. The King's Anticipation: vss. 11–12

I went down to the grove of nut trees to look at the new growth in the valley, to see if the vines had budded or the pomegranates were in bloom. Before I realized it, my desire set me among the royal chariots of my people.

Sometime after the friends added their praise, Solomon told in his song how he left his house to check on his harvest of walnuts, grapes, and "pomegranates" (Song of Sol. 6:11). The orchard was situated in a nearby "valley." It remains unclear, though, whether this was a physical location (such as the Valley of Jezreel) or a metaphorical reference to the deep love existing between the king and his bride. In either case, Israel's monarch suddenly visualized himself sitting in one of his "royal chariots" (vs. 12) among his "people."

What does the preceding reference mean? To be candid, interpreters remain unsure. Indeed, specialists agree that this passage constitutes one of the most difficult portions in the entire poem to translate. Some suggest that these verses be interpreted as intimate imagery. Others suggest that the spokesperson was not the husband, but the wife. In that case, she was remembering being carried to the king's royal palace garden after being summoned by his guards. Regardless of which rendition is preferred, the friends of the Shulammite bride called on her to return to their midst so that they might enjoy seeing her beauty once more (see vs. 13). As noted earlier, this is the only verse in the entire poem in which the young bride is referred to as a "Shulammite."

Israel's monarch continued to praise his new bride. He did so with a question: "Why would you gaze on the Shulammite as on the dance of Mahanaim?" The identity of the latter reference, though, remains debated. There was a town in the Transjordanian region by that name, so perhaps it was a dance that took place there. Or, since "Mahanaim" literally means "two armies" or "double camp," this dance may have involved two groups of performers or may have been carried out in the presence of two armies. In any case, the expressive lyrics that follow this question provide answers in abundance for why people would look admiringly at the woman.

In 7:1–9, the groom offered his most complete description of his new wife, praising her from foot to head. Also, this time, in addition to using imagery from nature and architecture, Solomon drew upon references from precious tableware, a bountiful harvest, and exquisite tapestry. Evidently, the king's intent was to extol everything about his bride—from her charm and grace to her strength of character and disposition. He said he thought her "feet" (vs. 1) in sandals were lovely, and he noted that her "graceful" thighs were like artistically sculpted "jewels." Furthermore, Israel's monarch exclaimed that the Shulammite's "navel" (vs. 2) was like a round wine-mixing bowl, and her "waist" was similar to a heap of "wheat" hedged about with "lilies."

After Solomon repeated his description of his bride's breasts as two gazelle fawns (see vs. 3; 4:5), he went on to praise her neck, eyes, and nose, comparing them to ivory towers and sparkling pools of water (see vs. 7:4). Next, the king extolled the Shulammite's hair, saying it crowned her stately head like "Mount Carmel" (vs. 5). Then, after comparing the flowing locks of her head to purple "tapestry," Israel's monarch admitted that the beauty of his darling's hair captivated him. As Solomon praised his wife, he could hardly hold back his enthusiasm. He exclaimed, "How beautiful you are and how pleasing, O love, with your delights!" (vs. 6). Then he unashamedly poured out his feelings about their most physically intimate moments since having been married (see vss. 7–9). The words the groom used to describe his wife's breath and mouth might also refer to her pleasing way of speaking and holding conversation. If so, his attraction to her was far more than just physical. He was drawn to her entire personality as well as to her beauty.

These verses show how the couple's understanding of love had matured. Their love was more than the temporal arousal of passion. Its extent superseded even the depth of their physical intimacy. Their affection would endure long after their passion's flames had subsided. Their unquenchable flame "always protects, always trusts, always hopes, always perseveres" (1 Cor. 13:7). Regardless of what we think about the parallel some interpreters make between the lovers of the Song of Solomon and Jesus and the church, we can receive the over-arching message of God's love in our own lives. In the Song of Solomon, the husband and wife called each other to lasting love and contentment. Similarly, in Revelation 22:17, the Spirit and the bride called for anyone who is thirsty to come. We are the thirsty ones, and God summons us to accept His invitation to love Him with all of our heart, mind, and soul. If we respond by running to Him, He will quench our thirst with everlasting life and eternal blessings.

Discussion Questions

1. How did Israel's king describe his bride in Song of Solomon 6:4–5?
2. What indications of mutual affection are evident from the statements recorded in verses 11–12?
3. How strong was the desire of the bride and bridegroom for one another?
4. What can married couples do to keep their love for each other exclusive?
5. How can spouses keep the ardor of their affection vibrant throughout the years of marriage?

Contemporary Application

Few concepts have become as distorted today as that involving love. The worldly tendency is to make too much of romantic love. To listen to many popular songs, one might imagine that love is all that matters. As the Beatles sang, "Love is all you need." Meanwhile, books, television programs, and movies often present brief, superficial liaisons as being entirely acceptable.

Admittedly, many unbelievers think love is mainly about sex and that it is just as good, if not better, when experienced outside of marriage. In contrast, a sterner sort of Christian may claim that we should care only about "spiritual" matters and ignore romantic love entirely. One wonders whether that sort of person even knows what love is!

Romantic love is by no means as important to our eternal well-being as our salvation. Yet, the needs sin promises to fulfill can be met, without guilt, by the provisions God sends (see Jas. 1:17). The Song of Solomon teaches that love is among God's gracious gifts to humanity.

As long as we obey God's basic ethical guidelines (for instance, no sexual relations outside of marriage, no adultery, and so on), there is no reason we cannot enjoy love as much as we want. In fact, God's love for us—self-sacrificial, faithful, and forgiving—provides a model that should make Christians the best examples of affection and compassion. Regardless of what people look like, what their station in life may be, or how old they are, it pleases God to bless them with the gift of love.

An Unfaithful Bride

Scripture

Background Scripture: *Hosea 1—3*
Scripture Lesson: *Hosea 1*
Key Verse: The LORD said to [Hosea], "Go, take to yourself an adulterous wife and children of unfaithfulness, because the land is guilty of the vilest adultery in departing from the LORD." *Hosea 1:2*
Scripture Lesson for Children: *Hosea 1*
Key Verse for Children: The LORD said to [Hosea], "Go, take to yourself [a] wife." … So he married Gomer. *Hosea 1:2–3*

Lesson Aim

To discern that God wants us to remain faithful to Him.

Lesson Setting

Time: 722–721 B.C.
Place: Samaria

Lesson Outline

An Unfaithful Bride

   I. Hosea's Commission: Hosea 1:1
  II. Hosea's Object Lessons: Hosea 1:2–11

     A. *The Marriage of Hosea to Gomer: vss. 2–3*
     B. *The Birth of Jezreel: vss. 4–5*
     C. *The Birth of Lo-Ruhamah: vss. 6–7*
     D. *The Birth of Lo-Ammi: vss. 8–9*
     E. *The Future Time of Restoration: vss. 10–11*

Introduction for Adults

Topic: *Broken Relationships*

A newly elected governor had been in office for just a few months when he proposed a host of tax increases. Reminded of his campaign promise not to raise taxes, he simply said, "I changed my mind." The governor's excuse is typical of how easily we disregard our promises to one another. For instance, it's not unusual for people to say they will show up for a social event, but then fail to appear—with no word of apology.

Too often, it seems, we treat our Christian commitments just as casually. How many of us remember the pledges we made when we joined our church? Or the vows we made when we got married? Or the promises we made to repay our loans? When it comes to our Christian commitments, God holds us accountable to them.

God created a special relationship with Israel that He equated with marriage. Israel promised to love, obey, and serve the Lord. But the Israelites broke their word. God then sent prophets like Hosea to remind Israel—and believers today—that He will not tolerate such disloyalty to Him.

Introduction for Youth

Topic: *Faithful Friendships and Relationships*

A young lawn service worker showed up unexpectedly at the home of an ill church member. He said he would cut the grass for the entire summer. From May until November he kept his word. No one told him to do it. He simply wanted to do it and he did it.

Learning to serve others faithfully builds strong spiritual muscles. Jesus promised even greater responsibilities for those who do minor tasks well (see Matt. 25:21). From this we see that keeping our word is important to God.

The people of Israel said the right things, but they did not keep their word. They followed idols instead of the Lord. Hosea had to remind them that their unfaithfulness would bring God's judgment. When we profess to follow Jesus, He expects us to remain unwavering in our commitment to Him. And when we come to realize how much God hates sin, we will be motivated to remain faithful to Him.

Concepts for Children

Topic: *An Unhappy Family*

1. Hosea told people about God.
2. Hosea married someone who lied to him.
3. Despite this, Hosea chose to love his wife.
4. There are times when we do things that leave God feeling sad.
5. Even then, God still loves and forgive us.

Lesson Commentary

I. HOSEA'S COMMISSION: HOSEA 1:1

The word of the LORD that came to Hosea son of Beeri during the reigns of Uzziah, Jotham, Ahaz and Hezekiah, kings of Judah, and during the reign of Jeroboam son of Jehoash king of Israel.

Hosea 1 begins with the commissioning of the prophet. Verse 1 states his name, along with the names of the kings who reigned during his ministry. Hosea, the son of Beeri, came from the northern kingdom of Israel. His messages were primarily directed at Israel, but in some cases they encompassed Judah as well. Since Uzziah, Ahaz, and Hezekiah were alive during the time of Hosea's ministry, we know that he was a contemporary of Isaiah (see Isa. 1:1).

Some Bible scholars think Hosea's ministry extended from about 755 to 715 B.C., a period of about 40 years. When Hosea preached, Assyria was emerging as a new superpower under the leadership of Tiglath-Pileser III (745–727 B.C.). In fact, the deterioration of Israel's moral resolve under Jeroboam II (793–753 B.C.) paved the way for the fall of the nation in 722 B.C. Some specialists conjecture that after the fall of the northern capital, Samaria, Hosea retired in the southern kingdom of Judah, where he put his prophetic messages into writing (most likely between 722–721 B.C.).

Early in Hosea's ministry, the Lord told the prophet to compare Israel's loyalty to Him with the unfaithfulness of a wife to her husband. The resulting account is a tender, yet tragic, love story. It is tender in that Hosea and God loved their wives with an unfailing affection. The book is tragic in that their wives were habitually unfaithful. For instance, Israel left her true husband (God) to pursue a pagan husband (Baal) and become his prostitute. Heartbroken, God pleaded with Israel to return and be faithful, but the nation stubbornly refused to listen.

Accordingly, sadness is woven throughout the literary fabric of Hosea. The parallel between Gomer's adultery and Israel's betrayal of God graphically teaches the meaning of forgiveness and enduring love in the face of sorrow. Hosea, whose name means "salvation," tried to deliver his wife from prostitution. In like manner, God desired that His people repent of their adultery. Yet that was not to be the case. Hosea described Israel's idolatry and wickedness, resulting in judgment, captivity, and deportation by the Assyrians. God's unchanging love, though, offers hope, for Hosea tells us about the remnant who would be restored to God and their homeland.

II. HOSEA'S OBJECT LESSONS: HOSEA 1:2–11

A. The Marriage of Hosea to Gomer: vss. 2–3

When the LORD began to speak through Hosea, the LORD said to him, "Go, take to yourself an adulterous wife and children of unfaithfulness, because the land is guilty of the vilest adultery in departing from the LORD." So he married Gomer daughter of Diblaim, and she conceived and bore him a son.

As noted earlier, Hosea was God's instrument to warn the Israelites about the hardships He would use to punish them unless they repented and reformed. The Book of Hosea is a mixture of literary genres. Threat and promise, doom and hope, judgment and salvation alternate rapidly with one another in Hosea. Yet the dominant theme is Israel's unfaithfulness. That theme comes out early in the book in the living parable of Hosea's marriage to Gomer.

God commanded the prophet to marry a promiscuous woman. In turn, she would bear "children" (Hos. 1:2), who would prove to be as unfaithful in their behavior as adults as their "adulterous" mother. The divine command is interpreted in different ways. One view is that Hosea was to marry a prostitute and have offspring who would commit sexual sins as adults. A second, comparable theory is that Hosea was to marry a woman who would become a prostitute after Hosea married her and have offspring who would commit sexual sins as adults. A third option is that Hosea was to marry a woman who was spiritually unfaithful to God and have offspring who would be similarly disloyal to Him as adults.

Regardless of which view is favored, the purpose for God's command is clear. The prophet's family members were to be living reminders that the Israelites had committed spiritual adultery. They did this by forsaking their relationship with Him and bowing down before the fertility gods and goddesses of Canaan. Accordingly, Hosea's wife, as a sexually unfaithful woman, would represent Israel, a spiritually unfaithful nation. Hosea, in turn, would represent God.

Hosea picked "Gomer" (vs. 3) to be his wife. Her name possibly means "completion" or "accomplished." Hosea's prompt obedience shows that God had chosen the right person. The biblical text says that Gomer was the daughter of man named Diblaim. We do not know anything more about Diblaim than this. Later Gomer would fulfill her role as an unfaithful spouse. But at least for a while Hosea and Gomer seemed to enjoy a relatively stable family life. Specifically, they remained together several years, long enough to have three children, the first of whom was a son.

In this chapter, Hosea portrayed God's zeal to maintain the affection of His people. The Lord's demand for exclusiveness was a necessary part of a permanent relationship with the Israelites. As in a marital union, this kind of commitment protected and preserved the bond of love between God and the nation. Starting in the first of the Ten Commandments, God prohibited His people from having any other gods before Him (see Exod. 20:5; Deut. 5:7 and the corresponding commentary in lesson 1). Likewise, they were to be just as zealous in remaining faithful to their covenant with Him.

B. The Birth of Jezreel: vss. 4–5

Then the LORD said to Hosea, "Call him Jezreel, because I will soon punish the house of Jehu for the massacre at Jezreel, and I will put an end to the kingdom of Israel. In that day I will break Israel's bow in the Valley of Jezreel."

It's not difficult to imagine the scandal connected with Hosea's domestic life. Perhaps like a tragic melodrama, his troubled marriage to Gomer played out before the audience of Israel. In this case, once Gomer gave birth to a son, Hosea obeyed God's directive to name the infant "Jezreel" (Hos. 1:4). The Hebrew noun means "God sows" or "God scatters," so perhaps the Lord chose this name in part to indicate how He would scatter the Israelites by sending them into exile. The biblical text, however, links the name with events that had happened and would happen in a place called Jezreel.

Jezreel was the name of a city in northern Israel that Jehu, a general who became king of Israel, had once mercilessly attacked. It was there that Jehu had murdered both Joram the king of Israel and Jezebel, a former queen. Jehu had also had Ahaziah the king of Judah murdered as he fled Jezreel. At Jezreel, furthermore, Jehu had received the slaughtered remains of the descendants of King Ahab. Also, there Jehu had had many worshipers of Baal put to death (see 2 Kings 9:14—10:28). Even though it had been about 90 years since these events had come to pass, God still remembered Jehu's bloodiness.

While by Hosea's day Jehu had long been dead, Jehu's dynasty was still in power. On a descendant of Jehu, therefore, would fall the Lord's vengeance for Jehu's bloody acts of violence. This prophecy was fulfilled in a few years when Jehu's descendant, Zechariah, was murdered after ruling only six months in Israel (see 2 Kings 15:8–12). God also promised to break the bow of Israel in the Valley of Jezreel, which was a fertile plain that extended across the north-central part of Palestine (see Hos. 1:5). In ancient times, the bow was a symbol of military strength, and a broken bow represented total defeat. Specifically, in 724 B.C., the Assyrian victory in the Jezreel Valley was the handwriting on the wall foretelling the end of Israel's existence as an independent nation.

C. The Birth of Lo-Ruhamah: vss. 6–7

Gomer conceived again and gave birth to a daughter. Then the LORD said to Hosea, "Call her Lo-Ruhamah, for I will no longer show love to the house of Israel, that I should at all forgive them. Yet I will show love to the house of Judah; and I will save them—not by bow, sword or battle, or by horses and horsemen, but by the LORD their God."

Gomer again became pregnant and gave birth to a daughter. It remains unclear, though, whether Hosea was the actual father of any of the children Gomer bore. Following God's instructions, the prophet named Gomer's daughter "Lo-Ruhamah" (Hos. 1:6), which means "not loved" or "not pitied." This name signified that the Lord was nullifying His covenantal relationship with the northern kingdom of Israel. The Hebrew verb rendered "love" denotes the presence of compassion and mercy, especially from a superior to a subordinate. Here we find that the names of Hosea's second and third children represent increasingly severe warnings.

The underlying Hebrew in the last part of verse 6 is emphatic and could be paraphrased, "I will certainly not take away." The implication is that the Lord refused to pardon (or remove) the guilt incurred by His people for their shameless, adulterous pursuit of pagan deities. As biblical history makes clear, the Israelites remained obstinate and unrepentant in their sin, which included idol worship, child sacrifice, and temple prostitution. Consequently, God expelled them from the promised land. There is a profound theological truth evident from this object lesson. God is merciful and He forgives repentant sinners. However, when people refuse to abandon their wicked ways, they ultimately face God's judgment.

Why was Israel so captivated by idols made out of carved wood and molded metal? One reason was agricultural. When God led His nomadic, desert people to Canaan, the land's fertility and plentiful crops amazed them. Even today, an adequate supply of rainfall in the area is crucial for crops. Thousands of years ago, seasonal rains ensured bountiful harvests, supplying food, trade, prosperity, and sacrifices for festival days. The Canaanites believed all life and the renewal of the earth's fertility depended upon the rains, which allegedly were rewards of their benefactor and weather deity, Baal.

Depending on the context in which it was used, the name "Baal" meant "owner," "master," or "husband." Ancient Baal liturgy from Hosea's time reveals praises made to Baal, including the following: "Baal is my father," "Baal is strong," and "Baal is my answer." Even though God, Israel's loving husband, was an excellent provider, the nation committed harlotries with Baal. Gradually, the Israelites adopted sacrifices to Baal as insurance that the rains—and consequently prosperity—would continue without any disruption.

A second reason for Israel's attraction to idols was Baal's perverse sexual rituals. These were tied in to the annual agricultural cycles. The Canaanites believed that every year, Asherah, Baal's mother and mistress, engaged in sexual union with Baal. So, Baal worshipers engaged in religious prostitution (see 1 Kings 14:23–24). Within a theater-like setting, priests or a man from the Baal-believing community performed immoral acts on pagan altars with a priestess or cult prostitute (perhaps a woman like Gomer). The assumption was that this debased behavior ensured a greater harvest.

Clearly, the people of the northern kingdom were guilty of engaging in vile acts. Just as tragic was their unrelenting refusal to abandon their wicked ways and return to the Lord in faith. Habitual sin without consequence would have encouraged a continuation of destructive, hurtful conduct. So, in an attempt to restore the relationship and dramatically change the moral direction of the entire nation, God rejected the inhabitants of Israel for a time.

Initially, the southern kingdom of Judah would be spared the punishment that awaited its northern neighbor (see Hosea 1:7). Apparently, that was due to the cleansing reforms carried out later by Hezekiah. In particular, he destroyed the pagan shrines in his country and restored the true worship of God in the Jerusalem temple (see 2 Kings 18:3—19:36; 2 Chron. 29—32; Isa. 36—37). Judah's deliverance would come not through military might, with Judah's warriors doing battle with their enemies. Rather, the deliverance would come directly through God's intervention. This prophecy was literally fulfilled in 701 B.C., when God miraculously wiped out an Assyrian invasion force of 185,000 soldiers under Sennacherib's command (see 2 Kings 19:32–36; Isa. 37:33–37). Indeed, Judah remained unconquered for more than a century, undoubtedly the result of godly leadership and nationwide repentance.

D. The Birth of Lo-Ammi: vss. 8–9

After she had weaned Lo-Ruhamah, Gomer had another son. Then the LORD said, "Call him Lo-Ammi, for you are not my people, and I am not your God."

When Gomer had finished weaning Lo-Ruhamah, she became pregnant again and gave birth to a second son (see Hos. 1:8). The name of this child, "Lo-Ammi" (vs. 9), means "not my people." This name points to God's rejection of Israel and, in effect, breaking His covenant relationship with the nation (see Exod. 6:7). The Lord's patience finally came to an end, and He would disown His unfaithful people by means of exile (see Hos. 1:9). The Israelites had always been known as God's chosen people. As such, they were to love, obey, and worship Him. They were also to be a lighthouse of truth and holiness to the surrounding nations. Instead, they fell into idolatry and immorality. The disastrous consequences of their betrayal were spelled out in Leviticus 26:14–39.

E. The Future Time of Restoration: vss. 10–11

"Yet the Israelites will be like the sand on the seashore, which cannot be measured or counted. In the place where it was said to them, 'You are not my people,' they will be called 'sons of the living God.' The people of Judah and the people of Israel will be reunited, and they will appoint one leader and will come up out of the land, for great will be the day of Jezreel."

Hosea 1:10—2:1 reveals that Israel's future was not completely hopeless. One day a future generation of Israelites would experience the fulfillment of God's promises. In faithfulness to His covenant pledges, God would restore His people and bless them. The blessing would involve population growth, a renewed relationship to God, and reunification of the northern and southern kingdoms. Whereas before they were called "not my people," eventually they would be known as the children of the "living God" (Hos. 1:10). These promises were perhaps partly fulfilled when Jews returned to Judah from Babylonian exile beginning about 538 B.C. However, many think the final fulfillment comes later. Some say these promises are fulfilled in the church, while others maintain they are yet to be fulfilled in Jewish history.

Some details of these verses deserve special comment. The promise that the Israelites would be as numerous as the "sand on the seashore" (vs. 10) was a repetition of a pledge originally made to Abraham (see Gen. 22:17). Paul applied the promise of divine adoption (see Hos. 1:10) to the inclusion of Gentiles in the church (see Rom. 9:26). The "one leader" (Hos. 1:11) under whom "the people of Judah and the people of Israel" would be united is probably the Messiah. The prophecy that God's people would come up "out of the land" most likely is a reference to a return from exile.

The names of Hosea and Gomer's three children were used as contrasts to promised blessing. In a future day, the Israelites would once again be God's people and the object of His love (see 2:1). These truths were intended to motivate the Israelites to take responsibility for their disobedience and come to terms with their spiritual adultery. As a first step in turning the nation around, successive generations were summoned to abandon their idolatrous heritage. Sadly the call went unheeded and in response, God stripped Israel of her land and possessions.

Discussion Questions

1. Why did God tell Hosea to marry a promiscuous woman?
2. What does God's name for Hosea's first child tell us about divine justice?
3. How do you feel about God's giving Hosea's children the names He did?
4. What promise does Hosea's account hold for those who fail spiritually or morally?
5. How is God's way of showing love different from that of the world?

Contemporary Application

Both Gomer and Israel needed to learn how to be spiritually and morally pure. They no longer could be unfaithful to their commitments and unchaste in their desires. Both Gomer and Israel needed to exclusively devote themselves in unwavering love to their partners (Hosea and God, respectively).

The same is true for us as God's children. Yes, there are times when we fail spiritually and morally. But just as Hosea and God showed love to those who treated them unlovingly, so too the Lord continually reaches out in love to His most rebellious children. Regardless of our sin, we can be redeemed and forgiven if we are willing to repent. When we turn to God in faith, He will shower us with His love and transform our lives with His redeeming grace.

How does such a loving God expect us to love others? We must do so unconditionally and unselfishly. Though this is impossible for us to do in our own strength, God can enable us to be kind to those who are harsh to us. He also can give us the ability to be patient with those who easily provoke us to anger.

When we love as the world does, we expect something in return, show compassion only to those who supposedly deserve it, and display affection in fickle ways. But when we love as God does, we ask nothing in return, show compassion even to those who treat us unlovingly, and remain faithful in our displays of affection.

An Eventful Wedding

Scripture

Background Scripture: *John 2:1–12*
Scripture Lesson: *John 2:1–12*
Key Verse: "Everyone brings out the choice wine first and then the cheaper wine after the guests have had too much to drink; but you have saved the best till now." *John 2:10*
Scripture Lesson for Children: *John 2:1–12*
Key Verses for Children: A wedding took place at Cana in Galilee. Jesus' mother was there, and Jesus and his disciples had also been invited to the wedding. *John 2:1–2*

Lesson Aim

To learn that Jesus is concerned with our ordinary problems.

Lesson Setting

Time: A.D. 27
Place: Cana of Galilee

Lesson Outline

An Eventful Wedding

I. The Social Dilemma: John 2:1–5
    A. *Jesus at the Wedding: vss. 1–2*
    B. *Mary's Request: vss. 3–4*
    C. *Mary's Faith: vs. 5*

II. The Display of Jesus' Glory: John 2:6–12
    A. *The Savior's Command: vss. 6–8*
    B. *The Head Steward's Discovery: vss. 9–10*
    C. *The Disciples' Faith: vss. 11–12*

Introduction for Adults

Topic: *Saving the Best for Last*

Social embarrassments come in all sizes, shapes, and colors. But rarely do they open doors for discussions about spiritual issues. This is because it's hard for people to make the connection between everyday life and God's will.

Nevertheless, seeing is believing when people observe how Christians handle not just social embarrassments, but also the deeper issues of life. For instance, many people take notice when they see a person of faith finding the strength to endure trials, hardships, and sufferings.

Consider how extraordinary it is to witness Christians refusing to take revenge when others have wronged them (see Prov. 20:22). It's also exceptional when a believer uses a gentle response to defuse a potentially explosive situation (see vs. 15:1). Jesus' followers may not be able to turn water into wine (the miracle recounted in John 2:1–12), but they can lead people to faith in the Son by the way they follow His commands in ordinary situations.

Introduction for Youth

Topic: *An Amazing Outcome*

What does it take to believe in Jesus? Miracles? Visions? Facts? Testimonies of others? Generations raised on believing only hard data find it difficult to accept the reliability of other kinds of facts. In response, believers over the centuries have noted that Christianity appeals to the facts of history, which are clearly recognizable and available to everyone. This observation applies to the miracle of Jesus turning water into wine (the subject of this week's lesson).

Believing in Jesus is not a blind leap of faith into the dark void of ignorance. Rather, it is an intelligent decision that is informed by eyewitness accounts (see 1 Cor. 15:1–8). Jesus' original followers wrote about what He did so that we might trust in Him for eternal life (see John 20:30–31). As Jesus said to Thomas in verse 29, "blessed are those who have not seen and yet have believed."

Concepts for Children

Topic: *Celebrating a Wedding*

1. Jesus, His followers, and His mother went to a wedding at Cana in Galilee.
2. Jesus told the servants to fill six stone jars with water.
3. Then Jesus turned the water into wine.
4. Jesus used this miracle to show His glory.
5. Jesus has the power to meet our every need.

Lesson Commentary

I. THE SOCIAL DILEMMA: JOHN 2:1–5

A. Jesus at the Wedding: vss. 1–2

On the third day a wedding took place at Cana in Galilee. Jesus' mother was there, and Jesus and his disciples had also been invited to the wedding.

The Fourth Gospel presents Jesus as the divine, incarnate Son. In particular, He is portrayed as the realization of all the Mosaic law's types, prophecies, and expectations. John's goal was to convince his readers to trust in Jesus as the Messiah, the Son of God, and consequently find eternal life in union with Him (see vss. 20:30–31). The apostle's inclusion of seven signs (see vs. 2:11), or attesting miracles, in the first 12 chapters of the Fourth Gospel helps to accomplish that overarching purpose. The wondrous deeds persuasively demonstrate the messianic identity, power, and authority of the Lord Jesus. Just as in the period of Moses, the great lawgiver and leader of Israel, God intervened in human history, so now with the coming of the Savior, God involved Himself in a new way to bring about eternal redemption for those who believed (see Deut. 11:2–3; 29:2).

After Jesus' baptism by John, and after spending 40 days in the wilderness, Jesus began calling His disciples (see John 1:29–34). In verses 35–51, we read about the summoning of Andrew, Peter, Philip, Nathanael, and probably John. John never identified himself by name in the Fourth Gospel, but he is most likely the person referred to in the narrative as the "disciple whom Jesus loved" (vss. 13:23; 19:26; 21:7, 20). It is quite possible that John was chosen at this time but not specifically mentioned in the first chapter of the Fourth Gospel. In any case, these individuals accompanied Jesus wherever He went.

Jesus' first miracle took place at a wedding feast, which His disciples and His mother also attended (see vss. 2:1–2). The marriage celebration was a symbolic reminder that the age of the Messiah had dawned and inaugurated the blessings of the future divine kingdom (see Gen. 49:11; Isa. 25:6; Jer. 31:5; Hos. 2:22; Joel 3:18; Amos 9:13). The backdrop of this feast was an array of purification rites described in the Old Testament, all of which found their ultimate fulfillment in the Son. The time reference in John 2:1 suggests the Messiah arrived the third day after He and His followers left the Jordan River area, where John the Baptizer had been headquartered. The presence of Mary at the celebration indicates that the bride or bridegroom (or both) was a close friend of the family, rather than just an acquaintance of Jesus and His disciples. It is unclear why no mention is made of Joseph. He may have been deceased by this time.

The changing of water into wine (fermented grape juice) occurred at Cana in Galilee. This village is only mentioned two other times in the Fourth Gospel (see vss. 4:46; 21:2). The second reference identifies Cana as the home of Nathanael, who had just been chosen to follow Jesus (see vs. 1:47). Since Cana was a small town, more than likely Nathanael would have also known the newly married couple. The exact location of this village remains unknown. Two suggested sites are near Nazareth, where Jesus grew up with His family. One is a group of ruins called Khirbet Kana, about nine miles north of Nazareth. However, many specialists think that the present village of Kafr Kanna, about four miles northeast of Nazareth, is the actual location, with its abundant springs and fig trees. Some of the Crusaders identified this location as Cana, and it fits well with the descriptions of medieval travelers. They described a church in this location allegedly containing at least one of the original water jars from the wedding.

B. Mary's Request: vss. 3–4

When the wine was gone, Jesus' mother said to him, "They have no more wine." "Dear woman, why do you involve me?" Jesus replied. "My time has not yet come."

In Jesus' day, wedding festivals could last up to a week. On such occasions, banquets would be prepared to accommodate many guests. The attendees would spend their time celebrating the new life to be enjoyed by the married couple. Archaeological evidence indicates that entire villages would be invited to a wedding celebration. Also, to refuse such an invitation was considered an insult. The wedding meal itself consisted of bread dipped in wine. Typically, the guests would call for innumerable toasts. After that, more visiting, eating, and drinking would occur (though this was rarely an occasion for drunkenness).

Wine diluted with water was the accepted beverage of the times, and people were accustomed to it. Because of a lack of water purification processes, this mixture was safer to drink than water alone. Careful planning was needed to accommodate all who came. This was imperative, for the strong, unwritten rules of hospitality implied that it was humiliating to be caught in short supply of some necessary item. Even the poorest Jewish parents would scrimp and save enough money to provide plenty of food and wine for their children's weddings. Yet, for some unknown reason, the bridegroom failed to supply enough of the latter for the duration of the festivities (see John 2:3). Perhaps more guests came than he had anticipated, or perhaps they stayed longer than he had planned.

Few details are given of what happened next. Evidently, someone reported the predicament to Mary, who then went to her son. Perhaps Jesus was seated at a table with His disciples and enjoying the festivities. One possibility is that Mary quietly sat down next to Jesus and discretely told Him the wine had run out. It is clear from Jesus' response that Mary's statement implied more than a simple observation of fact. Implicit in her words was a request for Jesus to do something about the situation so that the bridegroom could avoid being socially embarrassed. According to verse 11, Jesus had not yet performed any miracles. So, at this point in the account, we can only speculate as to what Mary had observed in her son that would give her the idea He could somehow resolve the problem.

It is unlikely that Mary expected Jesus to send the people home, for that was not His prerogative. Also, Mary probably did not want Him to send His disciples into town to buy more wine, for most likely they lacked the funds to do so. It is possible Mary had seen her son on other occasions do kind and helpful things for hurting people. Perhaps in the privacy of neighborhood life, Jesus was known as an extraordinary and caring person. Regardless of what Mary may have been thinking, Jesus gave her a startling and provocative answer. He did not say either yes or no. Instead, He asked Mary why she had come to Him for help. Without waiting for her reply, Jesus' words indicate that He was no longer under His mother's parental authority. While Jesus continued to honor Mary, His actions were governed by the mission His Father in heaven had given Him (see vss. 8:28–29). In brief, Jesus' mission was to die on the cross in order to atone for the sins of the world (see vs. 1:29).

Jesus was neither cruel nor harsh in His remarks to His mother. "Woman" (see vs. 2:4) was a common term of address that implied no disrespect (see Matt. 15:28, Luke 13:12; John 4:21; 8:10; 19:26; 20:15). Today one might say, "Dear lady." Such observations notwithstanding, in Jesus' response, He wanted Mary to think of Him not so much as the son whom she had parented, but rather as the Redeemer of Israel. Jesus used a social situation to point to a spiritual reality. In fact, the contrast between the wedding crisis and His mission could not have been more vivid. The Savior's query, "Why do you involve me?" (John 2:4), emphasizes Mary's desire that Jesus do something to help a family avoid social embarrassment. Also, the follow-up statement that His hour had not yet arrived stressed that Jesus' atoning sacrifice at Calvary, resurrection from the dead, and return to the Father in glory constituted a more eternally relevant issue (see vss. 12:23, 27; 13:1; 17:1).

C. Mary's Faith: vs. 5

His mother said to the servants, "Do whatever he tells you."

From what transpired, it is clear that Jesus had not offended Mary. In fact, she seemed to instinctively know that her son would intervene in a constructive manner. At this point, Mary returned to the servants and possibly told the head steward to do whatever Jesus directed (see John 2:5). Although Mary did not know what her son might have in mind, she nevertheless trusted Him to initiate what was prudent. Here we see that despite the awkwardness of the situation, the Lord Jesus conducted Himself impeccably in the social affairs of His community. Though His redemptive mission was lofty, He was not above mingling with people on all levels, so that they might be drawn to Him in saving faith as the fulfillment of the Old Testament prophecies made about Him (see vs. 11). Jesus' response to Mary shows that the Savior knew and controlled His eternal future (see vss. 10:17–18). Mary, in turn, submitted to Jesus' decision about how to handle the situation.

II. THE DISPLAY OF JESUS' GLORY: JOHN 2:6–12

A. The Savior's Command: vss. 6–8

Nearby stood six stone water jars, the kind used by the Jews for ceremonial washing, each holding from twenty to thirty gallons. Jesus said to the servants, "Fill the jars with water"; so they filled them to the brim. Then he told them, "Now draw some out and take it to the master of the banquet." They did so.

The Messiah apparently wasted no time in taking action. After getting up from where He had been sitting, He went to the nearby spot where there were six empty stone jars. Perhaps after praying silently to His heavenly Father, Jesus told the servants to fill the jars with water (see vss. 2:6–7). Mary's faith was honored when Jesus did His first miracle at this humble peasant wedding. Jesus performed the miracle in such a way as to not draw attention to Himself or the shortage of wine at the feast.

The six stone vessels at the wedding feast normally kept the family's water supply fresh and cool. The jars of varying size each could hold about 20 to 30 gallons of water (all total, roughly between 120 and 180 gallons of liquid), which the Jews used to wash their hands and vessels according to the Mosaic law's requirements. Apparently, because of the number of wedding guests, the water in the six jars had been used up, so they needed to be refilled. The servants might have been puzzled by Jesus' unusual sounding command. Why take ordinary water to the master of ceremonies? Despite whatever doubts the servants may have had, they did not complain. Instead, they did exactly what Jesus said (see vs. 8).

B. The Head Steward's Discovery: vss. 9–10

And the master of the banquet tasted the water that had been turned into wine. He did not realize where it had come from, though the servants who had drawn the water knew. Then he called the bridegroom aside and said, "Everyone brings out the choice wine first and then the cheaper wine after the guests have had too much to drink; but you have saved the best till now."

After the servants filled the jars to the top with water, they then dipped some out and took it to the person in charge of the festivities (usually a higher-ranking servant or friend of the bridegroom). When the head steward sampled the water now turned into wine, he was so pleasantly surprised that he commended the bridegroom for his good taste (see John 2:9). The head steward noted that it was customary for the host (such as the bridegroom) to serve the best wine first and then later to bring out the less expensive wines. But the bridegroom was congratulated for the brilliant stroke of keeping the best wine until last (see vs. 10).

C. The Disciples' Faith: vss. 11–12

This, the first of his miraculous signs, Jesus performed at Cana in Galilee. He thus revealed his glory, and his disciples put their faith in him. After this he went down to Capernaum with his mother and brothers and his disciples. There they stayed for a few days.

Jesus' first sign was experienced not so much as a miracle, but rather as a wonderful discovery (see John 2:11). Only the Messiah and the servants initially knew what had happened. Jesus evidently took no unusual action, such as touching the stone jars or commanding the water to turn into wine. Most likely, Jesus' simple prayer brought about the attesting sign. Jesus did not call for a pause in the festivities, and He did not summon everyone's attention. He also did not tell those who were present to gather around and see how He had changed water into wine. Rather, Jesus performed His miracle in a quiet and humble manner.

John 1:3 reveals that the Son is the Creator of all things. In fact, acts of creation and transformation are part of His nature (see 2 Cor. 5;17). For this reason, Jesus' turning water into wine should be understood in terms of what the Old Testament said about the coming Redeemer. In the messianic age, the Lord would host a great feast complete with the best food and overflowing wine, symbolizing great joy (see Isa. 25:6; Joel 2:19, 24; 3:18; Amos 9:13–15). In fact, several Jewish writings from the period describe the messianic age as a time of great fertility, with grapes so large that just one would produce huge quantities of wine (see 2 Baruch 29:5; 1 Enoch 10:19). Wine, however, could also symbolize suffering, since its color suggested blood, and drinking its dregs was a sign of punishment (see Pss. 60:3; 75:8; Jer. 25:15–16). Jesus symbolically linked wine with His blood at the Last Supper, which He celebrated when His hour had indeed come (see John 2:4; 13:1; 18:11).

We do not know how Jesus changed the water into wine at Cana in Galilee, only that He did it instantaneously and without fanfare. Jesus used this miracle to validate His claim to be the promised Messiah foretold in the Old Testament (a truth that would later lead to His crucifixion). All the miracles of Jesus were signs that He performed to demonstrate His power so that people would trust in Him. It is true that Jesus healed and helped people in dire situations, and they were blessed in this way by His miracles. Yet, in the end, Jesus' foremost goal was to relieve the deepest spiritual needs of people. The Messiah's changing the water into wine unveiled His glory (that is, His divine nature, presence, and power; see Exod. 24:15–18; 34:29–35; 40:34–38), and the disciples put their faith in Him (see John 2:11). His glory was seen in two aspects at Cana—His love for the neighborhood people and His control over the elements of nature.

From the opening verses of the Fourth Gospel, John—a devoted follower of Jesus and an eyewitness of His miracles—emphasized as one of the apostle's major themes the Savior's mastery over all creation. John's chief means of doing so was to describe in detail seven signs that Jesus performed. In addition to what was stated above, Jesus' turning water into wine revealed Him as the source of life (see vss. 2:1–12). The healing of the royal official's son showed Jesus to be master over distance (see vss. 4:46–54). The healing of the invalid at the pool of Bethesda revealed Jesus as the master over time (see vss. 5:1–17). The feeding of over 5,000 showed Jesus to be the Bread of Life (see vss. 6:1–14). Jesus' walking on water and stilling the storm revealed Him as master over nature (see vss. 6:15–21). The healing of the man blind from birth showed Jesus to be the Light of the World (see vss. 9:1–41). Finally, the raising of Lazarus from the dead (to be studied in next week's lesson) revealed that Jesus has power over death (see vss. 11:17–45).

After Jesus attended the wedding in Cana, He traveled some 20 miles northeast to Capernaum, where He stayed for a few days with His mother, brothers (see vs. 12; Matt. 12:46; Mark 6:3; Luke 8:19), and disciples (see John 1:35–51). Capernaum, the home of some of Jesus' followers, served as the Lord's headquarters during a large portion of His public ministry (see Matt. 4:13; Mark 1:21; 2:1). It was a fishing village built on the northwest shore of the Sea of Galilee. Capernaum hosted a Roman garrison that maintained peace in the region. Major highways crisscrossed at Capernaum, making it militarily strategic. Because of its fishing and trading industries, the city was a melting pot of Greek, Roman, and Jewish cultures.

Discussion Questions

1. What did Mary do when the supply of wine ran out during the festivities?
2. What was the nature of Jesus' response to Mary's statement?
3. Why do you think Mary submitted to Jesus' will in the matter?
4. Why do believers sometimes wonder whether God cares about their problems?
5. How have you seen Jesus show His care for you in the midst of your everyday trials and concerns?

Contemporary Application

Jesus brought good news to a broken world. He announced that God's kingdom was at hand, and that all people should repent and believe in the Gospel (see Mark 1:15). Jesus did so not from the isolation of a religious ghetto, but rather from the everyday world inhabited by ordinary people.

For instance, a neighborhood wedding in Cana of Galilee provided the ideal setting for Jesus to show His love and power. Suddenly He was no longer just a carpenter from Nazareth (see vs. 6:3). Rather, He was the Messiah of Israel, the one who inspired faith and obedience.

People today also need to see Jesus in this way. He is much more than a famous painting or statuesque religious figure. When we trust in Him, He remains ever present to help us through our ordeals. Also, regardless of the nature of our problems, He is there to watch over and strengthen us.

Clearly, then, our Savior is not confined to the sanctuary. Instead, He is present in every place of life. He wants us to find salvation and peace through faith in Him. Moreover, He calls us, as His followers, to declare the message of His love and care to the lost so that He can fill their empty lives with joy and purpose. What a wonderful gift we have to share with others!

A Return to Life

Scripture

Background Scripture: *John 11:1–44*
Scripture Lesson: *John 11:38–44*
Key Verses: Jesus called in a loud voice, "Lazarus, come out!" The dead man came out. *John 11:43–44*
Scripture Lesson for Children: *John 11:38–44*
Key Verses for Children: Jesus called in a loud voice, "Lazarus, come out!" The dead man came out. *John 11:43–44*

Lesson Aim

To consider the implications of Jesus' claim to be the resurrection and the life.

Lesson Setting

Time: A.D. *30*
Place: Bethany

Lesson Outline

A Return to Life

  I. The Death of Lazarus: John 11:38–40
    A. *Jesus' Arrival: vs. 38*
    B. *Jesus' Explanation: vss. 39–40*
  II. The Restoration of Lazarus to Life: John 11:41–44
    A. *Jesus' Prayer: vss. 41–42*
    B. *Jesus' Summons: vss. 43–44*

Introduction for Adults

Topic: *Matters of Life and Death*

Why does time seem to drag on when we're waiting for something important like a surgeon's report? Waiting often tests our faith in and commitment to God.

Consider Mary and Martha. Their patience was tested through days of waiting for Jesus. When He finally came, it looked as if it was too late, for their dearly loved brother, Lazarus, had already died and was buried. Then the bereaved sisters told Jesus that if He had come earlier, He could have prevented the tragedy from happening.

Like Mary and Martha, how many times have we said "If only" to God? "If only" is the antithesis of trust and obedience. If we live with regrets or harbor resentment against God, we cannot enjoy spiritual wellness.

Scripture tells us that God acts on our behalf according to His will, love, and wisdom (see Rom. 8:28). So, it never pays to criticize or question God's timing. This means Jesus never arrives too late to help us. We can rest assured that He will do what is best for us in His perfect will.

Introduction for Youth

Topic: *Another Chance at Life*

Restoring Lazarus to life was the most powerful miracle of Jesus recorded in the Fourth Gospel (apart from His resurrection and ascension). This close friend of the Savior had truly died. And Jesus, out of His great love for Lazarus, brought him back from the grave.

Perhaps the greatest miracle, however, is being born again. After all, before turning to Jesus in faith, we were spiritually dead and condemned because of our sins. We obeyed Satan rather than God, and followed the passions of our evil nature rather than the desires of the Spirit (see Eph. 2:1–3).

But because the Father is rich in mercy and loves us greatly, He gave us new life when we trusted in the Son. We have been united with Jesus in His death, burial, and resurrection. In fact, the Father sees us as being seated with the Son in the heavenly realms (see vss. 4–6). Now that is what it means to be alive again!

Concepts for Children

Topic: *Celebrating Life*

1. Jesus' friend, Lazarus, died.
2. The sisters of Lazarus, Mary and Martha, along with Jesus, were very sad.
3. Jesus brought Lazarus back to life.
4. Mary and Martha were now very happy.
5. When we trust in Jesus, He forgives our sins and gives us new life.

Lesson Commentary

I. THE DEATH OF LAZARUS: JOHN 11:38–40

A. Jesus' Arrival: vs. 38

Jesus, once more deeply moved, came to the tomb. It was a cave with a stone laid across the entrance.

The short time Jesus had spent in the east and northeast of the Sea of Galilee had already come to an end. As the prospect of suffering and death grew closer, He returned to the area of Jerusalem. According to John 11:1, Lazarus lived in Bethany with his sisters, Mary and Martha. The village was located on the east side of the Mount of Olives, along the road leading toward Jericho. Bethany was also about two miles from Jerusalem—close enough for Jesus and His disciples to be in danger, but sufficiently far away to avoid attracting unwelcome attention.

Somehow Lazarus became ill, and his condition worsened to the point that Mary and Martha turned to Jesus for help (see vs. 3). The sisters undoubtedly had seen Him perform many miracles. They were convinced of Jesus' ability to help Lazarus. The message to the Savior most likely took about a day to reach Him. He, in turn, remained in Bethany two more days (see vs. 6), and it probably took about a day for Jesus and His disciples to reach Bethany. It may be that Lazarus died before the messenger reached Jesus. If so, this explains how Lazarus could have been in the grave for four days (see vs. 17).

If Jesus had been with Lazarus during the final moments of his life and healed him of his sickness, the opportunity for an even greater miracle would have been lost. Jesus intended to use the death of Lazarus as an occasion to demonstrate God's power over death to the disciples and others. This was not a trivial desire on the part of the Savior. He knew that His closest followers needed their faith in Him clarified, matured, and strengthened.

Consider, for example, the dialogue between Martha and Jesus, which is recorded in verses 17–27. Despite Jesus' statement that Lazarus would rise again, Martha failed to grasp what He was saying. Instead, she affirmed a more general theological truth about the resurrection of the righteous. Even when Jesus plainly declared Himself to be "the resurrection and the life" (vs. 25), Martha still could not quite understand what this meant for Lazarus. Though Martha affirmed Jesus' messiahship (see vss. 26–27), she remained unaware of the fact that Jesus would restore Lazarus to life. Furthermore, Martha's sister, Mary, and their friends remained just as oblivious to the truth of what Jesus said He would do for Lazarus (see vss. 28–37).

Martha left Jesus outside her village, went back home, and told Mary that the "Teacher" (vs. 28) wanted to see her. Apparently, Mary was in such a rush to comply—and probably was also anxious to see Jesus—that her Jewish comforters (that is, relatives, friends, and neighbors) took notice and followed her.

They assumed that she was going to continue her mourning at her brother's tomb and thought they would join in her grieving (see vss. 29–31). Although Mary's words are almost identical to her sister's first words to Jesus, her actions departed dramatically from Martha's. Mary fell at the feet of the Lord Jesus in homage to Him and wept as she spoke (see vs. 32). She, too, believed He had the power to heal her brother of his illness, but now it was apparently too late.

The Messiah eventually arrived at the tomb where the body of Lazarus had been placed. Verse 33 says that at the sight of the wailing, Jesus was "deeply moved in spirit and troubled." On one level, the phrase suggests Jesus was touched with sympathy at the sight and perhaps indignant at the sorrow caused by death that sin has brought to the human condition. On another level, though, the Savior seemed agitated by the unbelief of His closest followers. The Messiah had plainly stated that He would restore Lazarus to life. Nonetheless, Martha and Mary, instead of rejoicing over what the Son was about to do, remained filled with despair over their brother's death. This attitude of unbelief and doubt is reflected in the statement made by some of the onlookers (recorded in vs. 37).

So that Jesus could demonstrate His divine power at Lazarus's tomb, He asked where the burial site was located (see vs. 34). As the sisters directed Jesus to the grave, He showed His grief by crying (see vs. 35). The Greek verb used to describe His tears suggests a quiet mourning, not the loud wailing of the other mourners. In response, some bystanders noted how much Jesus loved His friend (see vs. 36), while others wondered why He had not healed Lazarus of his sickness. After all, Jesus was able to restore sight to a blind man several months earlier (see vs. 37; 9:1–7). None of the onlookers, however, were anticipating the awesome display of glory that was about to take place in their presence. One can only imagine the emotions the Son felt as He approached the tomb of Lazarus, a cave with a stone rolled across its entrance (see vs. 11:38). In Jesus' day, people used caves carved in the limestone rock of a hillside as tombs. These graves were large enough for people to walk inside, and a tomb could hold several corpses.

B. Jesus' Explanation: vss. 39–40

"Take away the stone," he said. "But, Lord," said Martha, the sister of the dead man, "by this time there is a bad odor, for he has been there four days." Then Jesus said, "Did I not tell you that if you believed, you would see the glory of God?"

The first mention in the Fourth Gospel of the family of Lazarus, Mary, and Martha is found in John 11:1. The sisters are also mentioned in Luke 10:38–42, and Mary's anointing of Jesus is recorded in John 12:1–8. In fact, in anticipation of the latter event, 11:2 says that Mary was the woman who poured the expensive perfume on the Messiah's feet and wiped them with her hair. The Messiah's friendship with Mary and Martha is well documented in the Gospels and was apparently familiar to the Fourth Gospel's first-century readers. John 11:5 emphasizes that Jesus loved each member of the family.

Lazarus and his sisters were by no means poor. Based on some of the minute descriptions of their home and surroundings, it seems they were quite wealthy compared to most of the people of that day. Some specialists also think Lazarus at times materially supported Jesus in His ministry. Whatever the case, Scripture clearly portrays the love Lazarus had for Jesus and Jesus' love for him. They ate together often and talked together often. They were, indeed, friends.

Jesus' friendship with Mary, Martha, and Lazarus shows the humanity of the Lord. Although He was the divine, incarnate Messiah, whom the Father sent to die for humanity's sins, Jesus still experienced the same needs as people do today. So it should not be surprising that Jesus had close friends who were dear to Him. In fact, it is reasonable to expect that He would want such relationships outside His ministry and work. Mary seemed to have a more emotional and devoted relationship with Jesus, as is shown when she fell down at His feet after coming to Him (see vs. 32). Perhaps the most dramatic example of Mary's devotion to Jesus is found in the record of the dinner party that Martha and Mary prepared for the Savior prior to His final entry into Jerusalem (see vs. 12:1–8).

Verse 39 records Jesus' command for the stone to be removed from the entrance to the tomb. We also learn that Martha did not understand why Jesus would want this action taken. Martha noted that after four days the smell from the decomposing corpse of Lazarus would be terrible (see vs. 39). Unlike the Egyptians, the Jews neither tightly wrapped the body of the deceased nor embalmed it. Instead, they loosely wrapped the body in linen cloth and added spices between the layers and folds. The aromatic spices helped to counteract (but not completely eliminate) the objectionable odors resulting from the decomposition of the corpse. The Messiah, ever patient in the midst of Martha's confusion, stated once again that if she had faith, she would witness the glory of God (for example, in Jesus' restoring Lazarus to life; vs. 40).

II. THE RESTORATION OF LAZARUS TO LIFE: JOHN 11:41–44

A. Jesus' Prayer: vss. 41–42

So they took away the stone. Then Jesus looked up and said, "Father, I thank you that you have heard me. I knew that you always hear me, but I said this for the benefit of the people standing here, that they may believe that you sent me."

One can only imagine the bewilderment and skepticism among the onlookers. Though Jesus' command to remove the stone from the tomb of Lazarus seemed to go against common sense, it was done anyway (see John 11:41). The prayer voiced by the Son, which is recorded in verses 41 and 42, is not so much a petition as it is an expression of thanksgiving to the Father. The Messiah knew in advance that the Father would grant the prayer request, and so the Redeemer gave thanks for this.

Jesus declared in the hearing of the onlookers that the Father always answered the Son's requests. Jesus stated this openly, not for His own benefit, but rather for the sake of the bystanders. It was His desire that in seeing the miracle, they would believe His claim to be the Messiah. In restoring Lazarus to life, Jesus would prove that He is the master of death. Ironically, though, this miracle would set in motion a series of events that would lead directly to His arrest and eventual execution. Yet, even in the Son's crucifixion (along with His resurrection from the dead and ascension to heaven), both He and the Father would be glorified (see vss. 17:1, 5).

B. Jesus' Summons: vss. 43–44

When he had said this, Jesus called in a loud voice, "Lazarus, come out!" The dead man came out, his hands and feet wrapped with strips of linen, and a cloth around his face.

When Jesus had finished praying, He simply and directly commanded Lazarus to exit from the tomb (see John 11:43). In one sense, this served as a preview of the power of the Son that would be fully displayed in the final resurrection when all who have died would hear His voice and live (see vss. 5:25, 28–29). Lazarus, who had been unquestionably dead, came out of the tomb. His hands and feet were still wrapped with strips of burial cloth, and a separate cloth covered his face. Next, Jesus told the people to unwrap the burial clothes and headcloth from Lazarus and let him go (see vs. 11:44). By doing this, they would know that Lazarus was truly alive and that his appearance was not merely a magic trick.

Many of the bystanders, when they saw the miracle, put their faith in Jesus as the Messiah (see vs. 45). In fact, Lazarus became something of a curiosity, for he drew numerous onlookers who wanted to see for themselves the person whom Jesus had brought back to life (see vs. 12:9). As noted in last week's lesson, the Fourth Gospel had already presented six other miracles: turning water into wine (see vss. 2:1–11), healing a royal official's son (see vss. 4:46–54), restoring an invalid (see vss. 5:1–15), multiplying the loaves and fishes (see vss. 6:1–14), walking on the water (see vss. 6:15–21), and curing a man born blind (see vss. 9:1–12). Raising Lazarus was the climactic and most dramatic sign in John's Gospel (apart from Jesus' resurrection and ascension). The miracle proved that Jesus could give eternal life to those who put their trust in Him. The miracle also demonstrated that Jesus indeed had the power to keep His promises and forgive sins. In short, He could save those who came to Him and raise them up again in the last day (see vss. 11:25–26).

Other bystanders responded to the miracle by going to the Pharisees and reporting what Jesus had done (see vs. 11:46). In turn, they and the chief priests convened an informal meeting of the ruling council to explore their options (see vs. 47). None of the religious leaders could deny the miraculous signs Jesus performed. But rather than accept His messianic claims, the authorities feared what would happen if Jesus was allowed to continue unchecked. The worst possibility was that a riot would ensue as a result of so many people believing in Him. In the process of quelling the revolt, the Roman legions would also destroy the Jerusalem temple, the holy city, and the entire nation (see vs. 48). Paradoxically, this happened in A.D. 70 at the hands of Titus, a Roman general and future emperor.

Caiaphas, who was the high priest from A.D. 18–36, lampooned the idea that such a doomsday scenario was inevitable (see vs. 49). He noted that it was politically advantageous to eliminate Jesus in order to keep the entire nation from perishing (see vs. 50). In the providence of God, Caiaphas, as high priest, unwittingly foretold that the Son would die to make redemption possible for the Jewish people (see vs. 51; Isa. 53:8; Mark 10:45; 1 Pet. 1:18–19). The Messiah's atoning sacrifice would also lead to the formation of a worldwide spiritual body of saved Jews and Gentiles (see John 11:52; Isa. 43:5; 49:6; Ezek. 34:12; Matt. 20:18–19; Luke 24:47; John 1:12–13, 29; 3:16; 4:42; 10:16; 17:20–23; Acts 1:8; Gal. 6:16; Jas. 1:1; 1 Pet. 1:1). So, it was after the restoration of Lazarus to life that the religious elite finally determined to put Jesus to death (see John 11:46–53).

Because of the increasing levels of hostility Jesus encountered from the religious authorities in Jerusalem, He decided to stop traveling around publicly in the capital and its environs. He and His disciples went out to a town called Ephraim, which was near the wilderness (see John 11:54). The identity and location of this village remains uncertain, though it was possibly 12 to 15 miles northeast of Jerusalem. Then, as Jesus began His final trip to the holy city, He did so knowing He would die on the cross as an atoning sacrifice for the lost (see Luke 9:51). The journey leading up to His divinely appointed end involved Him traveling from one town or village to the next and teaching the residents about the kingdom of God (see 13:22; 17:11; 18:31; 19:28, 41). The Greek of 9:51 literally says that Jesus "set His face" to go to the capital, which is an idiomatic way of indicating the Messiah's steadfast resolve to complete the mission of redemption His Father had given Him (Isa. 50:7). In short, the Son came to earth to give His life as a ransom for many, and nothing would deter Him from that end (see Matt. 20:28).

It was in the spring of A.D. 30, six days before the Passover was to begin, when the Messiah went back to Bethany (see John 12:1). This would be the last Jewish festival to occur before Jesus went to the cross. As our "Passover Lamb" (1 Cor. 5:7), Jesus' bore our sin on the cross so that through faith in Him we could experience God's declaration of pardon. In the days leading up to the sacred assembly, pilgrims from the rural areas around Jerusalem traveled to the capital to prepare themselves ritually (see John 11:55). In order to participate, the religious establishment required that worshipers ceremonially purify themselves. As they congregated in the temple courts, the pilgrims kept looking for Jesus and wondering whether He would come to observe Passover (see vs. 56). Meanwhile, the ruling council had publicly ordered that anyone who saw Jesus should report it at once to the authorities. In this way, the chief priests and Pharisees hoped to bring about Jesus' arrest (see vs. 57).

Discussion Questions

1. What was the circumstance involving Lazarus that deeply moved Jesus?
2. Why did Martha question Jesus' command to roll away the heavy stone from the entrance to the tomb?
3. Before restoring Lazarus to life, why did Jesus stop and pray?
4. What implications does the restoring of Lazarus to life have for us as believers?
5. How has the hope of eternal life changed the way you live in the here and now?

Contemporary Application

The raising of Lazarus called forth faith from Mary and Martha, and from many of the Jews who witnessed the miracle. Tragically, however, it angered the religious leaders and convinced them that Jesus had to be executed. When people consider Jesus today, some are so impressed that they give themselves fully to Him in faith. Others, however, do not take Him and His miracles seriously. They do not believe that He is the one and only source of eternal life.

Christians have a sure hope in the face of sickness and death, and people need to hear about our faith and hope. One of the best ways is to invite them to study the life of Jesus. He prayed that people would believe in Him because He restored Lazarus to life. When we invite people to consider the miracles that Jesus performed, we give them an opportunity to believe and be saved.

Like Mary and Martha, we can become sad and distraught when events don't turn out the way we'd hoped. But God works in mysterious ways. From the human point of view, all appeared to be lost when Lazarus died. But then Jesus reversed the situation by restoring Lazarus to life. This episode would only be eclipsed by Jesus' resurrection from the dead.

The Messiah's resurrection is a promise of our own resurrection and victory over sin, suffering, and death. Though our ultimate triumph will be realized when we one day join the Lord Jesus in heaven, we can also be victors here on earth. It's possible because the focus of our faith is on Jesus and we are remaining faithful to God's will.

A Day of Deliverance

Scripture

Background Scripture: *Exodus 12:1–14; Numbers 28:16–25; Mark 14:12–26*
Scripture Lesson: *Exodus 12:1–14*
Key Verse: "This is a day you are to commemorate; for the generations to come you shall celebrate it as a festival to the LORD—a lasting ordinance." *Exodus 12:14*
Scripture Lesson for Children: *Exodus 12:1–14*
Key Verse for Children: "This is a day you are to commemorate." *Exodus 12:14*

Lesson Aim

To never underestimate what God can do in our lives.

Lesson Setting

Time: 1446 B.C.
Place: Egypt

Lesson Outline

A Day of Deliverance

  I. The Preparations for the Passover: Exodus 12:1–11
    A. *The Lord's Statement: vs. 1*
    B. *The Selection of the Lamb: vss. 2–5*
    C. *The Slaughter of the Lamb: vss. 6–7*
    D. *The Eating of the Lamb: vss. 8–11*
  II. The Meaning of the Passover: Exodus 12:12–14
    A. *The Protection of the Israelites: vss. 12–13*
    B. *The Commemoration of the Event: vs. 14*

Introduction for Adults

Topic: *Free at Last!*

Care and compassion typified the lives of Moses and Aaron for their fellow Israelites. The brothers proved by their devotion to God and His chosen people that they were willing to sacrifice their personal desires and ambitions for the greater good. Such commitment is remembered and celebrated in Scripture.

Florence Nightingale (1820–1910) also exemplified a self-sacrificing mind-set. At age 17, she felt God calling her to serve Him. She found her place of service in nursing, which in the early 1800s was done mostly by untrained volunteers. During the Crimean War (1853–1856), Nightingale and 38 nurses, whom she trained, organized hospitals for 5,000 wounded British soldiers. She established the first real nurses' training, fought for sanitary hospitals in Britain, and helped make nursing the respectable profession it is today.

But Nightingale felt uncomfortable when Queen Victoria and Parliament honored her. She explained that she was doing God's work. "Christ is the author of our profession," Nightingale said of nursing. She later refused a national funeral and burial in Westminster Abbey when it was offered to her. She wanted only to be buried with her family in a rural churchyard, in a simple service.

Introduction for Youth

Topic: *Celebrating Deliverance*

Homeless, hungry refugees often fill our television screens. We watch them clamor and fight for food and clothing being thrown from trucks. While Moses, Aaron, and the Israelites were slaves in Egypt, they were a displaced and disparaged people who longed for a new beginning in their own homeland.

What kept Moses and Aaron going was their faith in God and courage to remain devoted to His people. Yes, the Israelites were trying to survive. Yet, despite their hardships, Moses and Aaron encouraged God's people to trust and obey Him. This included following the instructions He gave for the Passover.

Adolescents can relate to the struggles the Israelites experienced—losing a loved one, moving to a strange place, and so on. Saved teens also know that peers who do not share their faith in Christ sometimes treat them like outcasts. They should be encouraged to remain loyal to the Savior. They can do so knowing that He will be with them every step of the way.

Concepts for Children

Topic: *A Day of Remembrance*

1. God told Moses and Aaron how the Israelites were to observe the Passover.
2. The people were to kill a young lamb.
3. The people were to place the lamb's blood on their door frames.
4. God promised to spare only those houses marked by the blood.
5. Through faith in Jesus, we are saved from God's judgment.

Lesson Commentary

I. THE PREPARATIONS FOR THE PASSOVER: EXODUS 12:1–11

A. The Lord's Statement: vs. 1

The LORD said to Moses and Aaron in Egypt …

God revealed to Moses that He would harden Pharaoh's heart. Even though the Lord would perform several "signs and wonders" (Exod. 7:3) throughout Egypt, the nation's ruler would refuse to listen to Moses. But Pharaoh's stubbornness would only intensify the great "acts of judgment" (vs. 4) the Lord would use to bring His people out of Egypt. Furthermore, these miraculous deeds would prove to the Egyptians that the God of Israel was the sovereign Lord of the universe (see vs. 5). It's helpful to remember that Egypt was polytheistic, which means the Egyptians believed in many gods and goddesses. Even today, scholars are unsure about the total number of pagan deities the Egyptians venerated. Most lists contain somewhere in the neighborhood of 80 idols.

Because Pharaoh remained unrelenting in his refusal to let the chosen people leave Egypt, God launched a series of 10 plagues that would devastate the nation. Bible scholars have noted that the number 10 symbolizes completeness, which indicates the Lord's wide-ranging and thorough judgment. For several months, ending in March or April (corresponding to the Hebrew Passover celebration), one plague after another wreaked havoc on the Egyptians. In Egyptian religion, the chief deity was the sun god, Re. Next in line was the ruling pharaoh of Egypt, who was considered the son of Re. Hence, Pharaoh himself was reputedly a deity in his own right. Understanding the Egyptian belief system adds a whole new dimension to the Exodus account. It's as if a contest occurred between the true God (along with Moses) on the one side and all the false deities of Egypt (along with Pharaoh) on the other side.

In the first plague, the waters of the Nile River were turned to blood (see vss. 14–25). This calamity was a condemnation of Nilus, the sacred river god. The second plague involved a horde of frogs (see vss. 8:1–15), in which Heqet, the goddess of reproduction, was judged. In the third plague, a swarm of gnats invaded the land (see vss. 16–19). This episode was a denunciation of Seb, the god of the earth. The fourth plague brought an infestation of flies (see vss. 20–32), and signified the repudiation of Khephera, the sacred scarab. In the fifth plague, Egypt's livestock was wiped out (see vss. 9:1–7). The event was a condemnation of Apis and Hathor, the sacred bull and cow god.

The sixth plague led to an outbreak of boils on the nation's citizens and animals (see vss. 8–12) and was a rebuke of Sekhmet, the goddess with power over disease. In the seventh plague, hail pummeled Egypt (see vss. 13–25) and denoted a repudiation of Nut, the sky goddess. The eighth plague brought a swarm of locusts on the land and signified a judgment on Serapis (see vss.

10:1–20), the god protecting crops from locusts. In the ninth plague, darkness spread over Egypt (see vss. 21–29), signifying a condemnation of the sun god, Re. The tenth and final plague resulted in the death of the firstborn of the nation's people and animals (see vss. 11:1—12:30), which meant that Ptah, the god of life, had been denounced.

God accomplished at least three objectives by sending the 10 plagues on the Egyptians. First, He showed them that He is the Lord and the one true God. Second, He demonstrated His concern for the Israelites. Third, He proved Himself superior to the Egyptians' many false gods. When God spoke to Moses and Aaron (see vs. 12:1), He apparently never revealed to them how many plagues He intended to send upon the Egyptians. The brothers neither knew what the next plague would be nor which would be the one to break Pharaoh's will. Moses and Aaron simply obeyed. Moses was 80 years old at the time, and Aaron was 83 (see vs. 7:6). If age was any factor at all in their selection to be leaders, advanced age apparently was a positive factor. Specifically, their age indicated they had a degree of wisdom and experience. God could have chosen a young man to confront Pharaoh, but instead He chose two elderly men—Moses and Aaron.

B. The Selection of the Lamb: vss. 2–5

"This month is to be for you the first month, the first month of your year. Tell the whole community of Israel that on the tenth day of this month each man is to take a lamb for his family, one for each household. If any household is too small for a whole lamb, they must share one with their nearest neighbor, having taken into account the number of people there are. You are to determine the amount of lamb needed in accordance with what each person will eat. The animals you choose must be year-old males without defect, and you may take them from the sheep or the goats."

What God was about to do for His people would be momentous. So, when the Israelites counted months, the month in which the exodus from Egypt occurred was to be remembered first (see Exod. 12:2). After all, the Israelites' freedom from Egypt would be for them a new beginning as God's people. Therefore, even though the events that were about to occur would happen in the seventh month of the civil year (known as Abib, which straddled March and April in our modern calendar; see 13:4), God declared that the month of Abib should be recognized as the first month of the religious year.

God revealed that, while striking down the firstborn of Egypt, He would pass over the people of Israel. This act would lead to the Israelites' deliverance from bondage. For this reason, the celebration of Passover would become for the Israelites the most significant of holy days. The account of the Passover would be recited repeatedly to remind each new generation of the Lord's redemption of His people. God still wants us to recite to others the story of our salvation. The Father longs for us to tell our family and friends about His Son's crucifixion and resurrection. The Father yearns for us to explain how the Son's sacrifice for our sins exemplifies both the Father's love for all humanity and His desire that we have eternal life.

God told Moses and Aaron to let the entire covenant "community" (vs. 12:3) know that on the "tenth day" of this "first month" (vs. 2), they were to remember His act of deliverance by formally celebrating the occasion. God's instructions on how to celebrate the event were the only regulations He gave the Israelites while they were still being held as slaves in Egypt. To institute this day of commemoration, each Israelite household was to begin making preparations by selecting a lamb for roasting. If there were too few people in a household to eat a whole lamb, two or more households could share one (see vs. 4). The lamb the Israelite households were to select for roasting was a one-year-old male that had no physical defects (in other words, being free from any blemishes or diseases). Moreover, the animals could come from either "the sheep or the goats" (vs. 5).

C. The Slaughter of the Lamb: vss. 6–7

"Take care of them until the fourteenth day of the month, when all the people of the community of Israel must slaughter them at twilight. Then they are to take some of the blood and put it on the sides and tops of the doorframes of the houses where they eat the lambs."

The Lord, through Moses and Aaron, directed the Israelites to take special care of the animals selected for slaughter until twilight on the fourteenth day of Abib (see Exod. 12:6). At that time, the members of the covenant community were to apply the blood from the animals to the two side posts and the top of the doorframe of the houses where the participants consumed the "lambs" (vs. 7). The tenth plague would be unlike the other plagues in its scope and severity, during which God promised to protect His chosen people (see vss. 9:7, 26; 10:23). Due to the nature of the final calamity, each Israelite family had to prepare for and act on God's warning. By doing so, they would be demonstrating their faith in the Lord's provision for their lives.

D. The Eating of the Lamb: vss. 8–11

"That same night they are to eat the meat roasted over the fire, along with bitter herbs, and bread made without yeast. Do not eat the meat raw or cooked in water, but roast it over the fire—head, legs and inner parts. Do not leave any of it till morning; if some is left till morning, you must burn it. This is how you are to eat it: with your cloak tucked into your belt, your sandals on your feet and your staff in your hand. Eat it in haste; it is the LORD's Passover."

Exodus 12:8–11 states that on the night of the Passover, all the Israelite households were to roast the whole lamb with its head and legs intact. In addition to eating the lamb, the participants were to eat bitter herbs (to remind them of their years spent in oppression) and unleavened bread (to remind them of the hurriedness with which they would leave Egypt). The Lord said the whole meal was to be eaten hastily and with an air of expectancy. Therefore, their robes should be tucked into their belts, their sandals should be on, and their staffs should be in hand. If any meat remained after the meal, it was to be burned before daybreak.

Centuries later, the Passover that Jesus ate with His disciples followed a well-established Jewish pattern for celebrating this feast. During an opening prayer, the first of four cups was blessed and passed around. Each person at the table then took herbs and dipped them in salt water. Next, the host took one of three flat cakes of unleavened bread, broke it, and laid some of it aside. Typically, the youngest member of the group then asked, "What makes this night different from all others?" The host responded by recounting the events of the Passover. This was usually followed by the singing of Psalms 113 and 114 and by the filling and passing around of the second cup.

Before the actual meal was eaten, all the participants washed their hands. Thanksgiving to God was prayed, and more of the bread was broken apart. The host dipped bread in a sauce usually made of stewed fruit, and then distributed a portion to each person gathered at the table. Finally, the time for the meal arrived. Eating a roasted lamb was the high point of the evening. It was after Jesus and His disciples had eaten the Passover meal that He instituted the Lord's Supper. Jesus took the third cup, which was known as the "cup of blessing," and uttered a prayer of thanks to God. He then instructed each of His disciples to take the cup and share its contents among themselves. Then He took a flat cake of unleavened bread, broke it, and passed it around so that each of His disciples could eat a portion of it.

II. THE MEANING OF THE PASSOVER: EXODUS 12:12–14

A. The Protection of the Israelites: vss. 12–13

"On that same night I will pass through Egypt and strike down every firstborn—both men and animals—and I will bring judgment on all the gods of Egypt. I am the LORD. The blood will be a sign for you on the houses where you are; and when I see the blood, I will pass over you. No destructive plague will touch you when I strike Egypt."

Exodus 11:4–6 reveals that at about midnight, the Lord had sworn to go throughout the land, killing the firstborn sons of the Egyptians from the highest to the lowest social levels. He would also kill the firstborn offspring of the Egyptians' livestock. Because of the massive number of deaths that would occur, the Egyptians would mournfully wail through the night. Six of the previous nine plagues had been initiated with the use of Moses' or Aaron's staff. This final plague would fall on the Egyptians directly from God, without the intervention of Moses or Aaron. In the end, it would be clear to both the Egyptians and the Israelites that the hand of the Lord inflicted this judgment.

In contrast to the wailing of the Egyptians, God said there would be peaceful silence among the Israelites. The Egyptians' wailing and the Israelites' silence would mark the distinction between God's favor for those who worship Him and His judgment of those who worship pagan deities (see vs. 7). After the plague on the firstborn, the ruler's officials would bow before Moses, beg that he leave, and request that he lead the Israelites away from Egypt. Moses would honor their entreaty by delivering his people from slavery (see vs. 8). When this occurred, the Israelites were to ask their Egyptian neighbors for "articles of silver and gold" (vs. 2). The Egyptians, whom God had made "favorably disposed" (vs. 3) toward both Moses and the Israelites, would willingly hand over their valuables. After all, they would by then have suffered through 10 destructive plagues.

The preceding details are recapped in 12:12–13. Through Moses and Aaron, God once again informed the Israelites what He was about to do. By sending nine plagues, God had judged both Pharaoh and many of the pagan deities of Egypt. Now in one final calamity, He would execute "judgment" (vs. 12) on all Egypt's false "gods." The Lord asserted the right to do so, for He is the one true God, as well as the Creator and moral Governor of the universe. That night the Lord's holy presence would roam throughout Egypt, bringing about the deaths of the firstborn offspring of both humans and animals. Yet those who had obeyed God and had applied blood to their door frames would be spared.

B. The Commemoration of the Event: vs. 14

"This is a day you are to commemorate; for the generations to come you shall celebrate it as a festival to the LORD—a lasting ordinance."

The night of Passover was to be only the beginning of the Israelites' observance. God wanted His people to commemorate the event by celebrating a weeklong festival (see Exod. 12:14). On the first day of Passover, they were to remove all yeast from their houses (see vs. 15). Then, for the following seven days—representing the beginning of the exodus from Egypt—they were to eat bread that had been made without yeast. A "sacred assembly" (vs. 16)—that is, a time to worship God—would mark the beginning day and ending day of the festival. God's instructions are restated in verses 17–20, where the weeklong observance is called the Festival of "Unleavened Bread." God expected everyone within the covenant community to participate, and He even made an allowance for Gentile converts to observe the ritual with the Israelites.

After being told what God wanted him to say, Moses gathered the elders of Israel and conveyed to them God's instructions regarding the Passover (see vs. 21). Moses told them to apply the lamb's blood to their door frames with "a bunch of hyssop" (vs. 22). Moses also told the elders that once the Israelites had entered their houses near the end of the day, they were not to leave their homes until daybreak. As the Lord went throughout the land, He would notice the doors marked with blood. No one within those homes would be harmed. The "destroyer" (vs. 23), who would take the lives of Egypt's firstborn, was probably an angel of the Lord. Moses reminded the elders that the Passover observance was not to be a onetime event, but an annual celebration. Each generation of Israelites was to be taught both the reenactment and the meaning of the Passover (see vss. 24–27).

Following Moses' instructions, the Israelites worshiped the Lord, realizing that their deliverance was about to occur. Then they returned to their homes where they observed for the first time the Passover ritual (see vs. 28). At midnight, with the Israelites safe inside their homes, the Lord performed the most horrifying of the 10 plagues. All Egypt's firstborn sons, regardless of their social standing, died that very hour. Even the firstborn among the Egyptians' livestock perished (see vs. 29). In the middle of the night, Pharaoh and all other Egyptians were awakened. Perhaps the wailing of one household stirred a neighboring family, who joined in the wailing when they found that tragedy had also struck them. Whatever the case, the entire nation had begun to mourn its massive losses (see vs. 30). Previously, God had told Moses, "I know that the king of Egypt will not let you go unless a mighty hand compels him" (vs. 3:19). Now the Lord's awesome power had struck, causing death to touch every Egyptian family.

Discussion Questions

1. Why was each Israelite household to obtain a lamb?
2. What were the Israelites to do with the blood of the sacrificial lamb?
3. In the tenth plague, why did God choose to kill all the firstborn in Egypt?
4. What does the distinction God made between the Israelites and the Egyptians tell us about who He is?
5. In what way is the Lord Jesus our sacrificial lamb?

Contemporary Application

It's true that, whether by our own doing or by events beyond our control, we can get into some pretty messy situations. It's also true that God is able to deliver us, as He did the Israelites in Egypt, from any circumstance in which we find ourselves.

As we consider our potential to get into tough spots and God's power to rescue us, it's possible, however, for us to come to some mistaken conclusions about God's role in our lives. For one, we might come to think of God as our personal genie. Supposedly, whenever we're in a difficult situation, we can rub the lamp (in other words, say a prayer) and He'll appear, do whatever we ask of Him, and then He'll go back from where He came, leaving us to continue living as we please. Another false notion is that God will refuse to come to our aid when we need Him, because we assume we've been too bad.

Neither of these extremes is accurate. God's motive for His redeeming work in our lives, as in the lives of the Israelites in Egypt, is His unconditional love for us. It's a love that flows out of God's character—that is, out of who He is. Also, the Lord's goal for delivering us from our difficulty is to make Himself known to us, so that we might be drawn into relationship with Him. He will always work toward that end. To God, there seem to be few worthier goals than building relationships with His spiritual children.

A Day of Thanksgiving

Scripture

Background Scripture: *Leviticus 23:15–22; Numbers
28:26–31; Acts 2:1–36*
Scripture Lesson: *Leviticus 23:15–22*
Key Verse: "Count off fifty days up to the day after the
seventh Sabbath, and then present an offering of new
grain to the LORD." *Leviticus 23:16*
Scripture Lesson for Children: *Leviticus 23:15–22*
Key Verse for Children: "Present an offering of new
grain to the LORD." *Leviticus 23:16*

Lesson Aim

To offer joyful praise to God for the many ways He
blesses us.

Lesson Setting

Time: 1446 B.C.
Place: Mount Sinai

Lesson Outline

A Day of Thanksgiving

    I. Observing the Feast of Weeks: Leviticus 23:15–21

       A. *Bringing an Offering of Grain and Bread:
         vss. 15–17*

       B. *Bringing Additional Animal and Grain Offerings:
         vss. 18–21*

    II. Showing Generosity to the Indigent:
       Leviticus 23:22

Introduction for Adults

Topic: *A Bountiful Harvest*

Watching just 30 minutes of a nightly news broadcast is enough to convince most people that we live in uncertain times. There are reports about rogue leaders across the globe who have brought anguish and loss to many people. We also learn about floods, tornadoes, earthquakes, and wildfires that leave untold destruction and death in their wake.

What are we to do in a world filled with so much uncertainty? To whom should we turn for guidance and help? Leviticus 23:22 states that the Lord is our God. In Him we place our hope.

Thousands of years ago, the Israelites understood the preceding truth, and it was the reason why they could draw strength and encouragement from the Creator. When we rest our confidence in Him, we will also never be disappointed.

Introduction for Youth

Topic: *Joyful Praise and Thanksgiving*

There's a certain company in the United States that markets its product by claiming that it can keep battery-operated devices going and going, seemingly endlessly. This self-assured optimism is reflected throughout society in the West. It doesn't seem to matter whether we're talking about young people, middle-aged individuals, or those heading into retirement. People from each age group seem to have a durable confidence that they can do whatever they want, however they want, and whenever they want.

Leviticus 23:22 states that the Lord is our God. The implication is that we completely depend on Him for our existence. The Israelites, recognizing this truth, observed an annual harvest festival, in which they thanked God for His sustaining presence and provision.

Even as we move through 2016, people still are not the captains of their own destiny, though they like to think they are. Ultimately the course of our lives falls under the control of God. The Creator determines when we are born and when we will die. Even such things as the shape of our hands and the size of our feet are controlled by Him. Isn't it time we begin to acknowledge this in the way we live?

Concepts for Children

Topic: *A Grateful Heart*

1. Every year God's people planted seeds in the ground.
2. The people also raised animals, such as lambs, bulls, and rams.
3. At the end of the growing season, God's people gathered their crops.
4. The people offered praise to God for taking care of them.
5. God is pleased when we thank Him for taking care of us.

Lesson Commentary

I. OBSERVING THE FEAST OF WEEKS: LEVITICUS 23:15–21

A. Bringing an Offering of Grain and Bread: vss. 15–17

"From the day after the Sabbath, the day you brought the sheaf of the wave offering, count off seven full weeks. Count off fifty days up to the day after the seventh Sabbath, and then present an offering of new grain to the LORD. From wherever you live, bring two loaves made of two-tenths of an ephah of fine flour, baked with yeast, as a wave offering of firstfruits to the LORD.'"

The laws, purposes, and character of God are intriguingly portrayed in Leviticus. For instance, believers learn through a study of this book how God blessed and admonished those whom He had chosen to be His representatives to the rest of the world. Indeed, Leviticus has much to teach Jesus' followers today, especially as they seek to be God's people within society. In this book, readers discover that for the Lord it was not enough to deliver the Israelites out of the cruel hands of the Egyptians (as pivotal as this event was in the history of Israel). He also wanted them to thrive as His chosen people.

To be specific, the Israelites' newly obtained freedom did not mean that they could do whatever they wanted. Rather, God's will for them was to follow His sacred laws, to serve His divine purposes, and to be a reflection of His character to their pagan neighbors. God pledged to protect the Israelites as long as they remained faithful to Him. Also recorded in Leviticus are details about how the Israelites were to be the Lord's consecrated people. By obeying the decrees and regulations that God wanted them to observe, the Israelites would be prepared to flourish in the promised land.

As noted in lesson 2, the central themes developed in Leviticus are God's holy character and His desire for the holiness of His chosen people. Moses, in writing the book, sought to show the Israelites how they could exist in ritual and moral purity. Leviticus discloses that when the Israelites endeavored to maintain virtue and integrity in their daily conduct, the Lord could dwell in their midst and they could worship in His presence. The basis for doing so was explained in the various codes, decrees, and ordinances recorded in Leviticus. For example, chapters 1—7 concern the system of sacrifices; chapters 8—10 deal with the ordination of priests; chapters 11—16 relate the laws concerning what is clean and unclean; and chapters 17—27 deal with the mandates for holy living.

In chapter 16, Moses described in detail the procedures governing the Day of Atonement. Then, throughout the rest of the book, Moses provided further regulations on how God's people were to remain set apart to the Lord. These ordinances are known as the holiness code. Actually, chapter 17 serves as a bridge between the material concerning the atonement rituals and the manual on holiness. The rules in this portion deal with various issues related to making sacrifices and eating meat.

Many practices of the pagan inhabitants surrounding the Israelites were an abomination to God. So, in the material that makes up chapters 18—20, Moses transmitted rules to keep the Israelites a holy people—that is, distinctly different from the Canaanites. These edicts condemned such offenses as sexual immorality, social injustice, and idolatry. Since the priests played a prominent role in the life of Israel, even stricter regulations were assigned to them. As readers find in chapters 21—22, Moses outlined special rules for the Israelites, giving particular attention to what sacrifices God found acceptable.

A part of God's plan for His chosen people was that they should set aside certain dates in their annual calendar as special days. These had different purposes and kinds of observances, but they all were meant to deepen the people's devotion to the Lord and give them occasions for joy and celebration. Accordingly, in chapter 23, we read about the Israelites' weekly holy day, the sabbath, and about six of their annual religious festivals. All of these special days are described in more detail in other parts of the Bible.

Furthermore, some sacred festivals not mentioned in Leviticus 23 are described elsewhere in Scripture. But in this chapter, we have the fullest biblical account of the major feasts in terms of how they fit into the annual calendar. This information from the Lord about the holy assemblies was to be conveyed by Moses to the people (see vss. 1–2). As usual, he was God's mouthpiece. The chapter does not go into detail on the rituals associated with the appointed days. This shows that the information was not meant primarily for the priests, but for the Israelites. The essential facts would let the average farmer, homemaker, or merchant know when a special convocation was coming and what was expected of him or her at that time.

Moses was to announce to Israel God's prearranged gatherings. The underlying concept was one of a pilgrimage. This reflected the fact that the people would have to make a trip to the central sanctuary to participate in specific festivals. The Hebrew noun rendered "sacred" (vs. 2) denotes national gatherings intended for public worship. The first holy convocation Moses proclaimed was the "sabbath" (vs. 3). In Hebrew reckoning, the seventh day of each week was from Friday at sundown until Saturday at sundown. As noted in lesson 1, the noun translated "sabbath" refers to a day set aside for "rest." Wherever God's people lived, they dedicated this time to the Lord by refraining from labor.

What follows the sabbath injunction is a description of the annual festivals God consecrated for Himself. These feasts are listed in the order that they would fall in the Israelites' religious calendar. First we have the spring festivals: Passover, Unleavened Bread, and Weeks. It was God who appointed these sacred convocations and determined when they were to occur (see vs. 4). They were holy and were meant to be observed faithfully.

The first assembly on the calendar was to be the Passover, perhaps the most important feast to the Israelites. As noted in lesson 3, during this festival, the people would commemorate the final plague in Egypt, when the angel of death passed over the Israelites while killing the firstborn of Egypt (see Exod. 12:1–30). Passover was to begin on the evening of the fourteenth day of the first month (see Lev. 23:5). We know from other writings that the Israelites would kill a lamb and on that evening eat a special meal. This was designed to remind them of the meal their ancestors ate on the first Passover night, before leaving Egypt.

The second gathering, the Festival of Unleavened Bread, was to begin on the day following Passover and continue for seven days. During that time, the Israelites were not to eat their usual bread, which had yeast (leaven) in it to make it rise, but rather bread made without yeast (see vs. 6). This food would remind the Israelites of the unleavened bread their ancestors ate hurriedly the night before the Exodus. The Israelites were to gather for worship during the first and last days of this holy occasion. As on the sabbath, during these two days the people were not to work. They were, however, to make sacrifices at the altar (see vss. 7–8).

Once the Israelites were settled in Canaan and farming the land, they were to follow additional observances at the Festival of Unleavened Bread. Specifically, they were to bring a sheaf of grain—the first agricultural produce of their harvest—to the priests. In turn, they would lift up and wave these sheaves in the air, as if to say, "Lord, this grain is dedicated to you" (vss. 9–11). Probably the purpose for making this particular wave offering was to demonstrate the people's gratitude for the bounty God had given them.

The preceding offering was to be presented the "day after the Sabbath" (vs. 11). Some think the offering was to be made on the day after the sabbath that fell sometime during the weeklong feast. According to this view, the procedure was undertaken on a Sunday. Others, however, think the sabbath in this case refers to the first day of the feast, which was to be a designated time of rest. In this interpretation, the wave offering was to be conducted on the sixteenth of the month (see the reference in vs. 6 to the fifteenth day of the month).

In addition to bringing a sheaf of grain for a wave offering, a worshiper was to bring the materials for a burnt offering, a grain offering, and a drink offering (see vss. 12–13). For the burnt offering, a year-old lamb without defect was needed. For the grain offering, two-tenths of an ephah (or about four quarts) of flour mixed with oil was required. For the drink offering, a quarter of a hin (or about a quart) of wine was the expectation. All of these contributions the priest would sacrifice in the prescribed way to the Lord. It was only after these sacrifices had been made that the Israelites were allowed to eat of the new season's produce (see vs. 14). They were to give God the firstfruits of their harvest as a token to show that ultimately it all came from Him and all belonged to Him.

The next holy convocation the Israelites were to observe was the Festival of Weeks. According to verses 15–16, this sacred assembly was to be held 49 days from the day of the firstfruits wave offering, or according to the common interpretation, 50 days from the beginning of the Festival of Unleavened Bread. Since to the Israelites the number seven represented perfection and completion, the interval of 49 days (namely, seven times seven days) clearly had symbolic importance. In Israel, barley was harvested before wheat in the springtime. So it was probably a sheaf of barley that the Israelites would present as firstfruits for a wave offering during the Festival of Unleavened Bread.

Because of the directive in verse 15 to count off seven complete weeks, this holy convocation is called the Festival of Weeks. By the time of the New Testament, however, this feast had become known as "Pentecost," which means "fiftieth," referring to the time elapsed between Passover and Weeks (see Acts 2:1; 20:16; 1 Cor. 16:8). As with other major special gatherings, during the Festival of Weeks, the Israelites were to present additional offerings (see Lev. 23:16). The first of these was bread presented as a firstfruits wave offering. The bread was made out of grain obtained from the recent harvest. Also, the portion was to be twice the size as the grain offering presented at the Festival of Unleavened Bread, except that this time the bread was made with yeast (see vs. 17).

B. Bringing Additional Animal and Grain Offerings: vss. 18–21

"Present with this bread seven male lambs, each a year old and without defect, one young bull and two rams. They will be a burnt offering to the LORD, together with their grain offerings and drink offerings— an offering made by fire, an aroma pleasing to the LORD. Then sacrifice one male goat for a sin offering and two lambs, each a year old, for a fellowship offering. The priest is to wave the two lambs before the LORD as a wave offering, together with the bread of the firstfruits. They are a sacred offering to the LORD for the priest. On that same day you are to proclaim a sacred assembly and do no regular work. This is to be a lasting ordinance for the generations to come, wherever you live."

Accompanying the offering of bread were offerings of animals and wine (see Lev. 23:18–21). The worshiper was to present seven lambs (all the right gender, age, and quality), as well as a young bull and two rams, as a burnt offering. This burnt offering was to be accompanied by the appropriate grain and drink offerings as a soothing fragrance to God. Also, the worshiper was to present a male goat for a sin offering and two year-old lambs for a fellowship offering. The priest would wave the lambs and the bread before the Lord, and then keep them as his own portion. The Israelites were to do no ordinary work on this day, but were to assemble together as God's holy people. Regardless of where they lived, from one generation to the next, this sacred occasion was to be a day of joyous festivity and worship, with no one occupied in his or her own individual pursuits.

Centuries later, the spring festivals became connected with Christian tradition through the death of Jesus Christ and the descent of the Holy Spirit. For instance, Jesus' Last Supper with His disciples was a Passover meal in which He transformed parts of the mealtime ritual into the Christian practice of Communion. Jesus was arrested, crucified, and buried shortly before the Festival of Unleavened Bread began, and He was resurrected the day after the firstfruits were (presumably) offered at the Jerusalem temple. After Jesus' ascension to heaven, the early Christians were worshiping together during the Festival of Pentecost (Weeks). Suddenly, the Holy Spirit came upon them and they praised God in many languages. In this way, 3,000 people, including many festival pilgrims, became followers of the Messiah (see Acts 2:1–11, 41).

II. Showing Generosity to the Indigent: Leviticus 23:22

"When you reap the harvest of your land, do not reap to the very edges of your field or gather the gleanings of your harvest. Leave them for the poor and the alien. I am the LORD your God.'"

The Festival of Weeks would coincide with the end of the grain harvest. The prescribed offerings, consequently, were much larger than they were at the Festival of Unleavened Bread, which was celebrated at the beginning of the grain harvest. The Israelites now had more produce to present to the Lord. That fact explains why it was at this time the priests were permitted to keep a portion of the offerings for themselves. This was also an appropriate point at which to mention the importance of remembering the poor. Specifically, as the crops were harvested, instead of removing every last head of grain out of their fields, farmers were directed to leave some grain standing at the edges. Furthermore, they were not to pick up the grain that had fallen to the ground as the crops were reaped. In this way, the indigent and foreigners could pick up some of the leftover grain for themselves to keep off hunger (see vs. 22).

In Exodus 23:9, God directed His people to be kind and considerate to non-Israelites dwelling temporarily within their community. The Lord reminded the Israelites that they had once been sojourners in Egypt. Foreigners usually had no family nearby to protect them, especially when they were attacked. That is why God said they deserved protection and provision. In verses 10 and 11, the Israelites were also instructed to plow the fields and harvest crops for six years, but during the seventh year they were to let the land lie idle. God promised that the harvest of the sixth year would be sufficient to sustain them until they took in another harvest (see Lev. 25:20–22).

The Lord even displayed His concern for the wild animals He had created. God said the crops that grew unattended in the seventh year were to be left as food for poor people as well as for any animal in the field (see Exod. 23:11). A number of other Scripture passages indicate God's concern for the wildlife of His creation. The following are four representative texts that show how He makes special provisions for all earth's creatures: (1) "He makes grass grow for the cattle, … bringing forth food from the earth," (Ps. 104:14). (2) "The lions roar for their prey and seek their food from God" (vs. 21). (3) "Are not two sparrows sold for a penny? Yet not one of them will fall to the ground" (Matt. 10:29) in the absence of God's knowledge and permission. (4) "Consider the ravens: They do not sow or reap, they have no storeroom or barn; yet God feeds them" (Luke 12:24).

Clearly, God's provision extends to all His creatures, not just to human beings. Moreover, from the stipulations recorded in the Mosaic law, we can learn that not only are we to thank the Lord for what He has given us, but also we must share that blessing with those in need. God does not want us to ignore the destitute and spend every cent we earn on ourselves. Instead, while providing for our families, we should give a helping hand to the impoverished living among us.

Discussion Questions

1. Why were the Israelites to count seven full weeks to offer their sheaf of grain to the Lord?
2. In what sense was the odor of the burnt offering pleasing to God?
3. What emotions do you think accompanied the Israelites' observance of the harvest festival?
4. What does God's directive about showing generosity to the poor suggest our attitude should be toward them?
5. What are some specific ways God may want you to help others around you in need?

Contemporary Application

Praise is often stimulated by awe. The more we can explain and rationalize the facts we see around us, the less likely we are to praise the Creator for making them happen. If our response to an event is "That's no big deal," then obviously praise to the "Lord [our] God" (Lev. 23:22) is not likely to follow. However, when we see or hear something that causes us to exclaim, "How did the Redeemer of life do that?"—then praise is a natural response. We praise out of wonderment.

This week's lesson invites us to offer joyful praise to God for the many ways He blesses us. When we are astonished at the wonder of creation, we are more likely to praise God than when we attempt to explain it rationally. For example, to realize that a single tongue of a solar flare is more than 40 times the diameter of the earth causes amazement. And even rapidly counting nonstop, it would take us thousands of years to number the stars in just one galaxy. The universe over which God reigns contains untold numbers of galaxies.

We should praise the eternal Lord not only for His wonderful works but also for the way He sustains everything He made. Without God's sustaining hand, life would become intolerable. As the Israelites were reminded during their annual harvest festival, it would be impossible to find adequate food, water, or clothing (see vss. 15–21). Such information helps us to better appreciate the grandeur, diversity, and power of the world that God has made and our dependence on Him. He truly is worthy of our highest praise!

A Day of Reconciliation

Scripture

Background Scripture: *Leviticus 16; 23:26–32; Numbers 29:7–11; Hebrews 7:26–28; 9:24; 10:4–18*
Scripture Lesson: *Leviticus 16:11–19*
Key Verse: "He will make atonement for the Most Holy Place because of the uncleanness and rebellion of the Israelites, whatever their sins have been. He is to do the same for the Tent of Meeting, which is among them in the midst of their uncleanness." *Leviticus 16:16*
Scripture Lesson for Children: *Hebrews 10:4–6, 9–10, 15–18*
Key Verse for Children: "I will put my laws in their hearts, and I will write them on their minds." *Hebrews 10:16*

Lesson Aim

To affirm that Jesus made the supreme sacrifice for the forgiveness of our sins.

Lesson Setting

Time: 1446 B.C.
Place: Mount Sinai

Lesson Outline

A Day of Reconciliation

    I. The Purification Offering on Behalf of the Priests: Leviticus 16:11–14
       A. *Entering Behind the Curtain: vss. 11–12*
       B. *Ministering Behind the Veiled Curtain: vss. 13–14*
    II. The Purification Offering on Behalf of the People: Leviticus 16:15–19
       A. *Purifying the Most Holy Place: vss. 15–17*
       B. *Purifying the Altar for Burnt Offerings: vss. 18–19*

Introduction for Adults

Topic: *A Clean Slate*

In the Old Testament, every year the high priest made atonement for his sins and for those committed by his fellow Israelites (see Lev. 16:11–19). The ritual of forgiveness the high priest annually performed anticipated the redemptive work Jesus accomplished on the cross.

In our Christian life, we have a Savior who understands us and takes an active interest in our well-being. He knows the problems we face and the imperfect ways we struggle to resolve them. He experienced the same sorts of things we experience. Most important, He's here for us right now.

We have the immense responsibility to point the way to the Father's forgiveness. And as pardoned sinners, we never outgrow the need to give our testimony to others who want to know the way to salvation and forgiveness through faith in the Son.

Introduction for Youth

Topic: *Making Things Right*

At times, life was a struggle for God's people in the Old Testament. And amid challenging circumstances, they were prone to violate God's commands. Leviticus 16:11–19 details the rituals of atonement the Israelites were to perform each year in order for them to experience God's forgiveness.

Adolescents are not immune from feeling overwhelmed by struggles and succumbing to temptations. For times of turmoil, there are many crisis hotlines across the country that teens can call. When they have a problem, they can talk to someone who is sympathetic and understands their problem. Why is the counselor able to relate so well? Usually it's because the person answering the phone has been through the same problem as the caller or is familiar with others who have had similar problems.

Jesus is the teens' ultimate friend in the highest place of all—heaven. He's there right now to intercede on their behalf, offer them forgiveness when they sin, and give them hope. But at the same time, He's right here with the adolescents in your class, providing them with advice, encouragement, and support. This should give them the confidence they need to face their problems in His strength, with integrity.

Concepts for Children

Topic: *The Supreme Sacrifice*

1. A long time ago, God's people offered animals to Him.
2. Many years later, Jesus came to earth to offer Himself for us.
3. Jesus died on the cross so that God could forgive us.
4. Jesus invites us to trust in Him for salvation.
5. We can tell our friends that when they trust in Jesus, He forgives them.

Lesson Commentary

I. THE PURIFICATION OFFERING ON BEHALF OF THE PRIESTS: LEVITICUS 16:11–14

A. Entering Behind the Curtain: vss. 11–12

"Aaron shall bring the bull for his own sin offering to make atonement for himself and his household, and he is to slaughter the bull for his own sin offering. He is to take a censer full of burning coals from the altar before the LORD and two handfuls of finely ground fragrant incense and take them behind the curtain."

Leviticus 16:1 points back to an incident in which Aaron's two sons, Nadab and Abihu, offended the Lord by burning incense on a fire pan within the most holy place of the tabernacle, even though He had not directed them to do so (see vs. 10:1). Consequently, fire from God consumed them for their disobedience (see vs. 2). Evidently, the Lord wanted to prevent errors like that of Nadab and Abihu from reoccurring. Also, the focus of the ceremonial offerings previously had been on the sins of individual members of the community, such as the priests (chap. 8). But now the purpose of the sacrificial rituals detailed in chapter 16 was to make atonement for the entire nation of Israel.

As noted in lesson 2, Hebrew religion was highly concerned with ceremonial cleanness and uncleanness. When people became unclean, they could become clean again by following the proper ritual. But since there were so many laws about cleanness, it was inevitable that some people would become unclean without knowing it and consequently would pollute the central sanctuary. So, once a year on the Day of Atonement (later referred to as Yom Kippur), the high priest performed a special ritual to restore the tabernacle to cleanness (see vss. 16, 19). Aaron did not have free access to the most holy place of the tabernacle. He would die like his two sons if he stepped behind the veiled curtain when he was not authorized, for God's glorious presence hovered over the ark of the covenant (see vs. 2). The sanctity of this area was too great even for the high priest to enter without God's approval.

Before Aaron could perform his duties as high priest on the Day of Atonement, he first had to be cleansed. He was to begin his preparation by bringing a bull for a sin offering and a ram for a burnt offering into the sanctuary (see vs. 3). These animals were to be sacrificed to atone for the sins of Aaron and his family. Next, Aaron had to wash himself with water before he could dress in the sacred garments of the high priest. These clothes included undergarments, a tunic tied with a sash, and a turban. All these garments were made of linen, probably bleached white to represent purity (see vs. 4). Along with the bull and ram that Aaron was to bring for himself and his family, he also was to have two male goats and a ram. He was to take all these animals from the community to offer on behalf of the Israelites (see vs. 5). Additionally, these various animals were to be used for a sin offering and a burnt offering.

In verses 6–10, we have a preview of the rituals for the Day of Atonement that are described in more detail later. First, Aaron was to sacrifice the bull, which he would bring to the tabernacle, as a sin offering for himself and his family (see vs. 6). This sacrifice would atone for his sin, making him ceremonially clean and able to perform the rituals for the Day of Atonement. At this point, Aaron would be ready to present the two goats before God at the entrance to the tabernacle (see vs. 7). Aaron was to cast lots (sacred stones called the Urim and Thummim; see Exod. 28:30; Lev. 8:8) to determine which goat would be sacrificed as a sin offering and which would become Israel's scapegoat (or escape-goat).

The meaning of the Hebrew noun translated "scapegoat" (Lev. 16:8, 10, 26) remains uncertain. One view is that it describes the idea of entire removal. In this case, the term would refer to the manner in which the goat took away the Israelites' sins. A second option is that the noun denoted a desolate, isolated place to which the goat was sent (see vs. 22). A third possibility is that the noun should be translated "rocky precipice." In this case, the noun referred to a cliff from which the goat would be pushed to its death. Finally, in later Jewish writings, the noun was thought to be the name of a desert demon, who was the arch rival of the Lord (see 1 Enoch 8:1; 9:6).

Whatever is the correct translation, the point of the ritual remains the same. Aaron was to sacrifice the goat chosen by lot to become an offering, and in this way make atonement for the people's sins (see Lev. 16:9). Aaron was to send the other animal into the wilderness, symbolically bearing with it the nation's trespasses (see vs. 10). In God's judgment, one goat was not enough to atone for the sins of the people. From a New Testament perspective, both goats can be seen as pointing to the Messiah. He died as the ultimate sacrifice to atone for our sins. Furthermore, He was led outside the walls of Jerusalem, where on the cross He bore our iniquity (see Heb. 13:11–12).

Beginning in Leviticus 16:11, the Lord went into detail about the rituals in which Moses was to instruct Aaron. First, the high priest was to slaughter the bull to atone for his own sins and those of his household. The reason is that Aaron had to be right with God before the high priest could intercede on behalf of others. Next, Aaron was to take a censer (or incense container) with burning coals from the altar of burnt offering. He was to take the fire pan inside the tent to the incense altar, where he was to gather up two handfuls of finely ground, aromatic powder, which was made of several kinds of rare and expensive spices. Then he was to step behind the inner veiled curtain that covered the entrance to the most holy place (see vs. 12).

B. Ministering Behind the Curtain: vss. 13–14

"He is to put the incense on the fire before the LORD, and the smoke of the incense will conceal the atonement cover above the Testimony, so that he will not die. He is to take some of the bull's blood and with

his finger sprinkle it on the front of the atonement cover; then he shall sprinkle some of it with his finger seven times before the atonement cover."

Once Aaron had stepped behind the inner veiled curtain with the censer, he was to add the incense to the coals to create smoke. The purpose of the smoke was to completely obscure the presence of the Lord so that Aaron would not die from having seen God (see Lev. 16:13). As the smoke from the incense filled the most holy place, the priest was to sprinkle some of the bull's blood on the front of the ark's lid. He was also to sprinkle blood seven times in front of the lid (see vs. 14). This sprinkling reconsecrated the covenant box.

From at least the time Abel offered the firstborn from his flock to the Lord (see Gen. 4:4), people shed the blood of an animal as an act of sacrifice to God. Indeed, this ritual pervades the Old Testament, in which blood sacrifice was regarded as an atonement for sin. So, the sacrificial animal became a ransom for the transgressors. This ceremony, however, was not totally effective. True atonement could occur only through the shed blood of Jesus, who died on our behalf to cleanse us from sin (see John 1:29, 36; Heb. 9:25; 10:11).

In the Old Testament era, there were three orders in the hierarchy of priests: the high priests, priests, and Levites. Whereas the Levites were subordinate sanctuary officials who supervised the minor duties of the temple, the priests were associates of the high priests. Priests were to come from the tribe of Levi and had to be without any physical defect. They were organized into 24 divisions that served the sanctuary in rotation. Each of the divisions ministered for a week, beginning on the sabbath, except during the annual festivals, at which time all the priests served together. The ceremony of consecration of the priests was much like that for the high priest, but not as elaborate. The chief duties of the priests were to take care of the sanctuary vessels and to make the sacrifices at the altar. But the priests also taught the Mosaic law, watched over the physical health of the nation, and administered justice.

II. THE PURIFICATION OFFERING ON BEHALF OF THE PEOPLE: LEVITICUS 16:15–19

A. Purifying the Most Holy Place: vss. 15–17

"He shall then slaughter the goat for the sin offering for the people and take its blood behind the curtain and do with it as he did with the bull's blood: He shall sprinkle it on the atonement cover and in front of it. In this way he will make atonement for the Most Holy Place because of the uncleanness and rebellion of the Israelites, whatever their sins have been. He is to do the same for the Tent of Meeting, which is among them in the midst of their uncleanness. No one is to be in the Tent of Meeting from the time Aaron goes in to make atonement in the Most Holy Place until he comes out, having made atonement for himself, his household and the whole community of Israel."

Aaron was now ready to sacrifice the goat to atone for Israel's sins. As with the bull's blood, the high priest sprinkled some of the goat's blood on the ark's lid and in front of it (see Lev. 16:15). By then, Aaron would have cast lots and determined this goat as the substitute to be given to the Lord (see vs. 8). After sprinkling goat's blood in the most holy place, Aaron was to go out and do the same in the rest of the tabernacle. This was a portable, tent-like structure that had been established under Moses after the Exodus from Egypt. The central sanctuary was where God's people brought their offerings and where their priests led them in the worship of the one true God.

A thick curtain separated the most holy place from the holy place. The most prominent object in the sacred tent was the covenant box. It was a chest made out of acacia wood and overlaid with gold. On the lid were golden statues of two cherubim (winged angels) facing one another. As noted in lesson 1, inside the ark were two stone tablets on which were inscribed the Ten Commandments, a golden pot with manna in it, and Aaron's rod (see Heb. 9:4). The ark was like a throne for God, the Israelites' supreme Ruler (see Ps. 99:1). Accordingly, the covenant box was set in the inner sacred section of the tabernacle (see Exod. 40:3).

Being located in the midst of the Israelites, the tabernacle and its most holy place were considered to be made unclean by the Israelites' various trespasses (whether committed intentionally or accidentally; Lev. 16:16). The Hebrew noun translated "rebellion" denotes personal offenses or transgressions. The noun translated "sins" refers to individuals who missed the mark or way of God's perfect moral standard. The high priest's rituals of burning incense and sprinkling blood to purify the most holy place were to be performed in private. No one but Aaron was to be in the tabernacle while he made atonement for himself, his family, and all Israel (see vs. 17). God, of course, would be present and would witness the rituals. Centuries later, the Messiah felt alone when He hung on the cross for our sins—even to the extent that the Father forsook the Son during that awful episode at Calvary (see Matt. 27:46; Mark 15:34).

B. Purifying the Altar for Burnt Offerings: vss. 18–19

"Then he shall come out to the altar that is before the LORD and make atonement for it. He shall take some of the bull's blood and some of the goat's blood and put it on all the horns of the altar. He shall sprinkle some of the blood on it with his finger seven times to cleanse it and to consecrate it from the uncleanness of the Israelites."

After making atonement for the tabernacle, Aaron was to do the same for the "altar" (Lev. 16:18) that stood before the Lord. Some identify this as the golden altar of incense within the tabernacle (see Exod. 30:10; Lev. 4:7, 18). Others, however, think that it was the altar for burnt offerings outside the tabernacle, in the courtyard (see Lev. 1:3, 5; 4:24). In either case, Aaron was to sprinkle the altar's horns with the blood of the bull and the goat. He was to do this seven times in order to purify the altar from the sins of the Israelites (see vs. 16:19).

The next step in this ceremony was for Aaron to bring forward the scapegoat chosen by lot (see vs. 20). The high priest was to lay his hands on the goat's head and make a general confession of all the sins of the people. As noted earlier, Aaron would symbolically transfer the sins to the goat. Then a man would lead the goat into the wilderness, where he would release it. Symbolically, therefore, the Israelites' sins were removed from them (see vss. 21–22). Once the scapegoat had been sent off, Aaron was to go back into the sanctuary and change clothes. He was to take off the special linen garments that he had worn while in the most holy place. Then he was to bathe to clean himself from contamination. Finally, he was to dress in his regular priestly clothing and return to the courtyard (see vss. 23–24).

At the bronze altar, the high priest was to sacrifice burnt offerings to atone for himself and the people (see vs. 24). Included in this stage of the ritual was the burning of the fat on the altar (see vs. 25). As was the rule for the sacrifice of animals, the fat was a special portion of the offerings set aside for God. Meanwhile, the man who had taken the scapegoat into the desert had to wash his clothes and body in order to be admitted back into the Israelite camp (see vs. 26). By his association with the goat that bore the sins of the people, sin had tainted this person, and therefore he needed cleansing. In addition, those parts of the bull and goat that had not been burned as offerings were to be carried outside the Israelite camp and burned (see vs. 27). Like the person who led the scapegoat out of the encampment, the individual who burned the carcasses had to wash his garments and himself with water in order to be readmitted into the community (see vs. 28).

In Hebrews, we learn that the Day of Atonement rituals prefigured, or pointed to, Jesus' crucifixion. On the cross, our Lord achieved what the high priests attempted on Yom Kippur. While Aaron was a sinner who had to ritually purify himself before making atonement for others, Jesus is sinless and needed to offer no sacrifices for Himself (see Heb. 7:26–28). While Aaron had to repeat sacrifices regularly, Jesus' death secured for us an eternal redemption (see vss. 9:6–14, 25–28).

Aaron's rituals allowed him to enter the earthly sanctuary, but Jesus' death led Him into the heavenly sanctuary (see vs. 24). The repetition of Aaron's sacrifice was a reminder of the persistence of sin, but Jesus' sacrifice occurred once for all and it secured the permanent forgiveness of sin (see vss. 10:1–18). Finally, while only the high priest could enter the most holy place (and he only once a year), all believers may enter the presence of the Father at any time through faith in the Son (see vss. 19–22).

Our great High Priest is perfectly suited to meet our temporal and eternal needs. His ability to do so is based on four characteristics. First, Jesus is "holy" (vs. 7:26). Second, He is blameless, meaning that He is innocent and without evil. Third, He is pure, in the sense that He is undefiled. Fourth, He is set apart from sinners in that He is "exalted above the heavens." His sacrificial work on earth has been accomplished, and He now sits at the right hand of the throne of

God. When taken together, these four characteristics imply that Jesus possesses the morally spotless character of God. Whether in motives, thoughts, words, or acts, the Messiah is upright and pure. He is free from all forms of evil, and also loves all goodness and truth. Accordingly, He abhors every aspect of wickedness, ethical impurity, and duplicity.

Discussion Questions

1. Why was it necessary for Aaron to make atonement for himself?
2. What did Aaron do with the bull's blood?
3. Why was no one but Aaron permitted to enter the most holy place?
4. What is the basis of believers being cleansed from their sins?
5. How is it possible for Jesus to save us completely and forever?

Contemporary Application

In this week's lesson we learn that after Aaron made atonement for himself, he was to enter the most holy place of the tabernacle to make atonement for it. Next, he was to consecrate the rest of the central sanctuary and the incense altar. Then he was to send out a goat bearing the sins of the nation and make a sacrifice for the nation.

The Israelites' rituals of atonement point to Jesus' sacrificial death on the cross. Hebrews 10:20 explains that the access the Son inaugurated into the Father's presence was "new and living." The way was fresh in that it was based on the new covenant established by Jesus' sacrifice. And it was always present because it depended on the Son Himself, our eternally living Lord.

Not only do we have a spiritual sacrifice enabling us to enter the Father's presence, but we also have a great High Priest "over the house of God" (vs. 21). Scripture reveals that the Son of God became a human being so that He could purchase our salvation through His death on the cross. Nonetheless, He still reigned supreme over all God's people. The author of Hebrews made it clear that after the Son completed His work of salvation, He returned to heaven, where He now sits at the place of highest honor, namely, the right hand of God the Father (see vs. 1:3). From there the Son intercedes for us before the Father.

In light of what Jesus has done for us, Scripture urges us to be proactive in living for the Messiah. Because of our provisions from the Son and our position in Him, we should claim what He has promised to us. In essence, the writer of Hebrews said that Jesus' work of salvation should spur us into action. This includes holding firmly to our "hope" (vs. 10:23) in the Son. We can do so without doubt or hesitation, for God is resolutely faithful to His promises to us.

A Day to Recall

Scripture

Background Scripture: *Leviticus 23:33–43; Numbers 29:12–40; Deuteronomy 16:13–17; 1 Corinthians 15:20–29; Revelation 14:1–5*

Scripture Lesson: *Leviticus 23:33–43*

Key Verses: "Live in booths for seven days: All native-born Israelites are to live in booths so your descendants will know that I had the Israelites live in booths when I brought them out of Egypt. I am the LORD your God.'" *Leviticus 23:42–43*

Scripture Lesson for Children: *Leviticus 23:33–43*

Key Verse for Children: "'These are the LORD's appointed feasts, which you are to proclaim.'" *Leviticus 23:37*

Lesson Aim

To honor God by commemorating the ways in which He has provided for us.

Lesson Setting

Time: 1446 B.C.
Place: Mount Sinai

Lesson Outline

A Day to Recall

   I. A Solemn Occasion: Leviticus 23:33–38
     A. *The Sacred Assembly: vss. 33–36*
     B. *The Regular Daily Offerings: vss. 37–38*
   II. A Joyous Occasion: Leviticus 23:39–43
     A. *A Perpetual Statute: vss. 39–41*
     B. *A Reminder of God's Deliverance: vss. 42–43*

Introduction for Adults

Topic: *Our Heritage and Hope*

The Festival of Tabernacles was part of Israel's annual religious calendar. It was an occasion of joy in which God's people celebrated the ways He protected and provided for them.

The effort the Israelites made to commemorate God's personal involvement in their lives is instructive for us. This is a situation where ignorance is not bliss. Instead, taking the time to remember can become an opportunity for us to experience the "joy of the Lord" (Neh. 8:10).

For instance, on specific occasions throughout the year, we can set aside a day or portion of a day to individually give thanks to God. Even better are appointed times when entire church communities agree to express their gratitude to the Lord for His abundant provision in their lives.

For the Israelites, this included a look back on their 40 years of travel in the wilderness. For us, the effort may involve commemorating the particular ways we recall how God has provided for us. It can also become an opportunity for us to affirm our spiritual heritage and renew our hope.

Introduction for Youth

Topic: *Remembering What God Has Done*

Some of the religious festivals detailed in Leviticus 23 were somber occasions. One example would be the Day of Atonement. It was an opportunity for the Israelites to be purified from the stain of their sins.

In contrast, the Festival of Tabernacles was supposed to be a joyous, commemorative event. The sorrow associated with the Day of Atonement was to give way to a jubilant time of celebration. The Festival was intended to be a special occasion in which God's people recalled what He had done for them in the past.

Here we see the balance of God's Word. It brings us to confession and joy. Divine words of truth are always the right and best ones for us. When we neglect them, it's like disregarding food and drink for our bodies. The Bible helps us to overcome our sins, to rejoice, and to give joy to others (see Neh. 8:10).

Concepts for Children

Topic: *A Time to Remember*

1. God wanted the Israelites to know that He loved and cared for them.
2. The Israelites gave thanks to God by observing the Festival of Tabernacles.
3. This festival lasted a week and was filled with joy.
4. During this special time, the Israelites lived outside in shelters.
5. God also wants us to remember that He watches over us.

Lesson Commentary

I. A SOLEMN OCCASION: LEVITICUS 23:33–38

A. The Sacred Assembly: vss. 33–36

The LORD said to Moses, "Say to the Israelites: 'On the fifteenth day of the seventh month the LORD's Feast of Tabernacles begins, and it lasts for seven days. The first day is a sacred assembly; do no regular work. For seven days present offerings made to the LORD by fire, and on the eighth day hold a sacred assembly and present an offering made to the LORD by fire. It is the closing assembly; do no regular work.'"

Throughout Leviticus 23, we read that the Lord spoke directly to Moses (see vss. 1, 9, 23, 26, 33). As noted in lesson 11, Moses served as the Lord's authoritative spokesperson. Put another way, Moses was the human conduit of divine revelation at Mount Sinai. According to verse 44, Moses transmitted to the Israelites all the information about the sabbath and the annual festivals he had received from the Lord. In turn, these instructions were to be followed by generation after generation.

Moses not only accurately communicated God's directives but also faithfully carried out His commands. Perhaps this truth is one reason why, at Moses' death, Deuteronomy 34:5 referred to him as the "servant of the LORD." A case in point would be the setting up of the tabernacle, which is recounted in Exodus 40. Repeatedly, the narrative states that Moses painstakingly heeded God's instructions (see vss. 16, 19, 21, 23, 25, 27, 29, 32).

Beginning with Leviticus 23:23, another series of religious festivals is described as occurring in the seventh month of the year, namely, Tishri (or September–October). As noted in lesson 10, Abib (which straddled March and April in our modern calendar) was recognized as the first month of the religious year. In contrast, according to the secular calendar, Tishri was the first month of the year. (The Jewish people presently regard this day as their New Year, or Rosh Hashanah, which in Hebrew means "the beginning of the year.") With the grapes and olives picked and the autumn rains expected soon, it was at this point in the annual calendar that the agricultural cycle was considered to come to an end and begin again.

The first autumn festival the Israelites were to observe was also on the first of the month (see vs. 24). The Israelites were to mark this day with blasts of trumpets. Since calendars were not commonly available among the people, loud ram's horn blasts were used to signal important events. On this particular day, trumpets were blown throughout the land in order to assemble the people. They were not to work, but instead to gather for worship and present special gifts of food to God (see vs. 25). Resting and offering sacrifices would show their reverence for this day and for the Lord.

Nine days after the Festival of Trumpets came the Day of Atonement (see lesson 12 for a detailed description of the divine regulations connected with Yom

Kippur). At this time, the Israelites were again to assemble and present offerings to God (see vss. 26–27). The prescribed rituals of this annual event were intended to cleanse the priests and people of their sins. On this day the Israelites were supposed to "deny" themselves. This may refer to fasting (that is, denying oneself food) and perhaps other forms of showing humility. The people were also not to work on this day. The reason given is that at this time atonement (or purification) would be made for them (see vs. 28). Expressed differently, offerings were made to the Lord to cleanse the covenant community of their sins.

Ignoring either of God's commands—to deny oneself and to rest—would earn harsh punishment. Those who did not deny themselves would be "cut off" by the hand of God (see vs. 29). This may refer to death through direct judgment from God or perhaps through various judicial processes. Those who did not refrain from doing any work on this day would forfeit their lives (see vs. 30). It was to be a perpetual statute that future generations were to observe, regardless of where they lived (see vs. 31). These punishments show the seriousness with which God viewed heeding His commands, and so does the fact that He repeated them (see vs. 32).

As noted in last week's lesson, Christians view the Day of Atonement as pointing to the work of the Messiah when He sacrificed His own earthly life to pay the price for sins. Although the need for sacrifices and rituals to cleanse us of our sins is past, the call to humble ourselves remains. As Jesus declared in Matthew 16:24, those who aspired to be His followers had to "deny" themselves, bear their "cross," and submit to Him (see Matt. 10:38; Luke 14:27). Put differently, the Savior expects total commitment to Him.

Five days after the Day of Atonement, the Israelites were to begin observing the Festival of Tabernacles, which was a weeklong event (see Lev. 23:33–43; Exod. 23:16; 34:22; Num. 29:12–40; Deut. 16:13–17). The Hebrew noun rendered "Tabernacles" (Lev. 23:34) literally means a "hut" or "booth" and refers to a small, temporary shelter. On the first day of this holy convocation (also known as Booths or Ingathering), God's people were not to perform any routine work (see vs. 35). Instead, the entire covenant community was to gather together and dedicate this time to the Lord. By doing this, they would begin this sacred occasion not only with the proper attitude toward God but also as a united people.

Each day during the weeklong festival, the Israelites were to present a special food offering made by fire to God (see vs. 36). In this way, they would thank Him for His bountiful provisions (for instance, of grain and grape harvests; see Deut. 16:13). Then, on the eighth day, the people were to gather once more for solemn worship and to present another special food offering to the Creator on behalf of the nation. On this day of the final assembly, right after Tabernacles, the Israelites were to again refrain from performing their customary, daily tasks.

B. The Regular Daily Offerings: vss. 37–38

(*"These are the LORD's appointed feasts, which you are to proclaim as sacred assemblies for bringing offerings made to the LORD by fire—the burnt offerings and grain offerings, sacrifices and drink offerings required for each day. These offerings are in addition to those for the LORD's Sabbaths and in addition to your gifts and whatever you have vowed and all the freewill offerings you give to the LORD.'"*)

In Leviticus 23:37–38, Moses referred to all the divinely prearranged festivals when he distinguished between the offerings designated for specific holy convocations and other offerings that were normally made. The latter included those undertaken on the Lord's sabbath. Presenting one offering did not exempt a person from the obligation to fulfill other duties. These consisted of sabbath observances, personal gifts, offerings made to fulfill one's solemn promises to God, and a wide range of voluntary offerings made to the Lord (whether animal sacrifices, agricultural produce, or other objects).

As noted in lesson 2, the "burnt offerings" expressed total devotion and dedication to God, along with atoning for general sins. "Grain offerings" were made to convey one's gratitude to God for His provision and protection. "Sacrifices" denoted animals (such as bulls, goats, and rams) offered to the Lord. And "drink offerings" referred to libations (such as water, oil, and wine) presented to God.

II. A JOYOUS OCCASION: LEVITICUS 23:39–43

A. A Perpetual Statute: vss. 39–41

"'So beginning with the fifteenth day of the seventh month, after you have gathered the crops of the land, celebrate the festival to the LORD for seven days; the first day is a day of rest, and the eighth day also is a day of rest. On the first day you are to take choice fruit from the trees, and palm fronds, leafy branches and poplars, and rejoice before the LORD your God for seven days. Celebrate this as a festival to the LORD for seven days each year. This is to be a lasting ordinance for the generations to come; celebrate it in the seventh month.'"

Leviticus 23:39 reiterates that the Festival of Tabernacles was to commence on the "fifteenth day of the seventh month" (vs. 34). It was only after the Israelites had harvested the crops from their "land" (vs. 39) that the holy convocation could officially begin. The Hebrew verb rendered "celebrate" indicates that the annual weeklong festival was to be a joyous observance, with times of rest being observed on the first and eighth days, respectively. It would be a tangible reminder that God had chosen and forgiven them.

At the beginning of the sacred occasion, the Israelites were to take various kinds of branches and use them to construct temporary shelters for themselves. The building materials included foliage obtained from lush trees, such as palm branches, twigs, leafy limbs, and boughs. The whole endeavor was to be characterized by a glad or joyful disposition (see vs. 40). The Lord declared that this was to be a perpetual statute, one that the covenant community was to observe from one generation to the next (see vs. 41).

B.   A Reminder of God's Deliverance: vss. 42–43

"'Live in booths for seven days: All native-born Israelites are to live in booths so your descendants will know that I had the Israelites live in booths when I brought them out of Egypt. I am the LORD your God.'"

Leviticus 23:42 reiterates the Lord's command to every "native-born" Israelite living in the promised land. Once a year for an entire week, they were to dwell in temporary shelters. As the participants resided in tree-branch huts (rather than their permanent homes) for the duration of the festival, they would be reminded of what their ancestors experienced. In particular, after God liberated them from their enslavement in Egypt, they dwelt in lean-tos for 40 years while wandering in the wilderness (see vs. 43).

The declaration "I am the LORD your God" would remind the chosen people of the preamble to the Ten Commandments, in which their Redeemer summarized the gracious acts He had displayed toward them (see Exod. 20:2; Deut. 5:6). As noted in lesson 1, the Lord had rescued the Israelites from four centuries of servitude. The freedom God had obtained for His people was the necessary foundation for the inauguration of His covenant with them.

Like the other decrees recorded in the Mosaic law, the stipulations connected with the Festival of Tabernacles were a reflection of the Lord's personal relationship with the Israelites. The perpetual statutes were not to be substituted for or elevated above that relationship. Instead, the Creator intended these ordinances to help His people live in a way that reflected their dependency on and gratitude toward Him. After all, it was the Lord—and no other entity—who reigned supreme in the affairs of Israel and the nations.

Centuries later, after God's people had returned to Judah from exile in Babylon, the leaders of each family, along with the priests and Levites, assembled to meet with Ezra in Jerusalem. He helped them understand the Mosaic law better (see Neh. 8:13). They discovered that the Festival of Tabernacles was celebrated during the fall season five days after the Day of Atonement (see vs. 14). The leaders announced in Jerusalem and Judah that the people were to observe the sacred occasion. The latter involved going out to the hill country and obtaining a variety of branches—from cultivated and wild olive trees, myrtle trees (evergreen shrubs that gave off a pleasant fragrance), date palms, and other leafy trees—to construct temporary shelters for living outside. This was to be done in accordance with the law (see vs. 15).

The people complied with the directive. They went out, cut branches, and used them to build shelters in every possible location of the city—on the flat roofs of their houses, in the courtyards of their homes, in the outer and inner courtyards of God's temple, and in the plazas around the Water Gate and the Ephraim Gate (the latter being on the north side of the city and facing toward the territory of Ephraim; vs. 16). The people living in the surrounding villages also built temporary shelters. This sacred occasion had not been observed in quite this way and with this much joy since the time of Joshua. The people were once again giving thanks to God for His blessings with the same enthusiasm and zeal as the Israelites of Joshua's day had done (see vs. 17).

Understanding of biblical truth is dry without the joy that God produces. Likewise, feasting and joy are meaningless without the firm foundation of God's Word. That is why Ezra read from the Mosaic law each day throughout the entire seven-day period of celebration. On the eighth day, a solemn assembly took place in accordance with the law (see vs. 18). The purpose of the reading was not only to preserve the law but also to encourage every generation to revere and obey God's Word. This public reading led the Jews to renew their commitment to God's covenant and to instruct their children to do the same.

The Festival of Tabernacles, with its emphasis on God's people dwelling in temporary shelters, serves as a spiritual reminder that we live in an "earthly tent" (2 Cor. 5:1). This refers to our mortal bodies, which will meet their demise when we die. The sobering prospect of death did not discourage Paul, for he knew that another body awaited him, an everlasting one made by God. In 1 Corinthians 15:53, the apostle wrote about this new body believers would receive at the Savior's return. Paul's focus on his future glorified body kept him from becoming dismayed at the diminishing faculties of his earthly body. Also, knowing that his earthly body was meant to be only temporary helped him weather the persecution and tribulations inflicted upon him. Through Jesus' resurrection, someday the apostle's old, worn-down body would be replaced with a new, heavenly, and eternal body.

Paul's groaning did not stem from a complaining nature or from his desire to die. Rather it arose from his eager longing to take up residence in his heavenly home—that is, his resurrection body (see 2 Cor. 5:2). The apostle desired to be alive when Jesus returned and granted Paul his spiritual body. Yet he also realized that he would eventually be given a resurrection body, even if he died before the Lord's return. The apostle described the interim period between the death of the physical body and the reception of the spiritual body as a time of being "naked" (vs. 3). The period between death and the resurrection apparently is a time in which the Christian's soul, while absent of any sort of body, resides in Jesus' presence. Believers wait to be clothed with their resurrection bodies.

Although Paul expressed his hope that Jesus would return before the apostle experienced death, he still had a positive view of this time. He recognized that though his soul would be without a body, his soul would nonetheless be with the Savior (see Phil. 1:23), and that nothing, not even death, could separate Paul from Jesus' love (see Rom. 8:38–39). The apostle's confidence in obtaining a spiritual body must have been one of the factors that drew people who knew him to the Redeemer.

The same can be true for us. Regardless of whether people admit it, they are aware that life is relatively short and often filled with suffering. The Christian's hope of eternity is a promise of immortality in a place where there will be no more sin, death, or tears. Our hope is more than enough to give us confidence regarding our future, even in the midst of pain. Also, if we exemplify that hope and confidence, then others will be drawn to the Lord.

Discussion Questions

1. What was the intent of the Festival of Tabernacles?
2. Why did God want His people to refrain from doing any work?
3. Why was the festival to be a time of celebration?
4. What connection do you see between the law of God and celebration?
5. What are some ways you can joyously express your gratitude to God?

Contemporary Application

Leviticus 23 summarizes the commemorative events that occurred each year in Israel's religious calendar. These appointed times celebrated the various facets of God's relationship with His people. For instance, the Festival of Tabernacles recalled the temporary shelters the Israelites used when they left Egypt.

The holy convocation reminded God's people that He controlled the events of history and would watch over them through their earthly pilgrimage. The Festival of Tabernacles also reinforced to the Israelites the importance of remaining unwavering in their devotion to the Lord. Do your students have the same attitude about obeying God? When a strong commitment is absent, believers are more prone to violate His Word.

Missionaries tell stories about people who have never before heard the truths of God's Word, becoming amazed and overcome for the first time. They seek God's forgiveness for their sins and joyously welcome Jesus as their Savior. In contrast, there are people who have repeatedly heard the Bible read and taught, and yet remain spiritually unmoved. The Word of God becomes so familiar to them that it loses its initial forcefulness on their consciences.

We also face the problem of Bible ignorance and neglect. Public opinion polls show that among Christians, regular Bible reading is largely neglected. Yet we can be thankful that local Bible study groups flourish in many churches and communities.

In Matthew 5:6, Jesus said that those who hunger and thirst for righteousness would be spiritually satisfied. When we turn our attention to God as the Israelites did during the Festival of Tabernacles, and put Him first in our lives, we will listen to, study, obey, and teach His Word. Compared to the people of Moses' day, we are satiated with Bibles and Scripture study materials. So our judgment will be severe if we neglect these gifts and opportunities from the Lord.

A Vibrant Faith

Scripture

Background Scripture: *Mark 9:14-29*
Scripture Lesson: *Mark 9:14-29*
Key Verse: Immediately the boy's father exclaimed, "I do believe; help me overcome my unbelief!" *Mark 9:24*
Scripture Lesson for Children: *Mark 9:14-29*
Key Verse for Children: [Jesus said,] "Everything is possible for him who believes." *Mark 9:23*

Lesson Aim

To recognize how Jesus can help us overcome our moments of unbelief.

Lesson Setting

Time: A.D. *29*
Place: Somewhere near Caesarea Philippi

Lesson Outline

A Vibrant Faith
  I. The Dire Situation: Mark 9:14-19
      A. *The Savior's Question: vss. 14-16*
      B. *The Explanation Offered: vss. 17-18*
      C. *The Savior's Indignation: vs. 19*
  II. The Savior's Intervention: Mark 9:20-29
      A. *The Father's Desperation: vss. 20-24*
      B. *The Savior's Expulsion of the Demon: vss. 25-27*
      C. *The Savior's Clarification: vss. 28-29*

Introduction for Adults

Topic: *Doubt and Faith*

Mark 9:24 records the father of a demon-possessed boy exclaiming to Jesus, "I do believe; help me overcome my unbelief!" This distraught parent honestly acknowledged his need for more faith, knowing Jesus could help.

When Terry Waite was held captive in Beirut, Lebanon (from 1987–1991), after about a year he plunged into depression. Until then, he had been able to maintain a positive outlook, but when a splitting earache attacked him, he could not even pray or read his Bible. He thought his faith was just so much superstition.

Eventually, Terry and his faith survived. Often that is the case with us. It's not until we are challenged with the impossible that we realize the limitations of our faith. Each day gives us an opportunity to grow spiritually. The more we grow, the better we will be prepared to face the impossible with prayer and trust in God's love, wisdom, and power.

Introduction for Youth

Topic: *Yes, You Can!*

For the desperate father spotlighted in this week's lesson, his mountain was seeing his son being traumatized by a demon. Our mountains may be a broken family, a difficult class assignment, or a close friendship gone bust. For others, the mountains might be nicotine, alcohol, or other chemical addictions, or bulimia or anorexia. Whatever the case, such mountains can lead to despair, depression, and even suicide.

Christians believe God's intervention offers hope for removing these mountains. They also believe God offers many ways of deliverance. Christian love and friendship are vital means that God uses to move mountains.

Of course, faith in the Lord is crucial. Faith motivates our prayers. Faith assures us God cares and that He works to deliver us. People must see our faith in action. Faith is not a leap in the dark. Our faith rests on God's Word and Jesus' promises. That's why we encourage people to investigate the claims of Christ and to study His Word. Faith must be fed. Strong faith brings us the hope and relief we need.

Concepts for Children

Topic: *Jesus Helps a Child*

1. The presence of a large crowd led Jesus to ask what was going on.
2. Jesus' followers could not rid a boy of an evil spirit.
3. When the father brought his son to Jesus, the Savior got rid of the demon.
4. Jesus explained to His followers why they were not able to help the child.
5. Every day we need to depend on the Lord to do as He wants.

Lesson Commentary

I. THE DIRE SITUATION: MARK 9:14-19

A. The Savior's Question: vss. 14-16

When they came to the other disciples, they saw a large crowd around them and the teachers of the law arguing with them. As soon as all the people saw Jesus, they were overwhelmed with wonder and ran to greet him. "What are you arguing with them about?" he asked.

Mark 9:1 records Jesus' statement that some of those who were present with Him would not "taste death" before they saw the divine "kingdom" manifested with great "power." About six days later, Jesus split up His group, taking three of the disciples with Him up the side of a "high mountain" (vs. 2). The literary context seems to indicate that the ensuing event occurred in the vicinity of Caesarea Philippi (see 8:27). While Jesus was praying on the mountain, He was "transfigured" (Mark 9:2). The Greek verb used here means an essential change in form. Mark noted that Jesus' garments became radiantly white—indeed, far more than any launderer on earth could bleach them (vs. 3). Matthew 17:2 adds that Jesus' countenance shone with the brightness of the sun. The glow on Jesus' face was translucent, coming from within.

As if the Lord's transfiguration in glory was not enough, two former heroes of the faith—Moses and Elijah—appeared and began talking with Jesus (Mark 9:4). The subject of their conversation was Jesus' approaching death (see Luke 9:31). In all likelihood, these two men appeared because Moses (the foremost author of the Torah) represented the Law and Elijah (a premier spokesperson for God) represented the Prophets. Their appearance was a visual reminder that Jesus fulfilled the entire Old Testament revelation.

Peter and his peers were so terrified that Peter (speaking for all of them) seemed to be at a loss for words (Mark 9:6). Still, Peter was able to suggest building three temporary "shelters" (vs. 5) to prolong the experience, that is, one each for Jesus, Moses, and Elijah. Peter's wording shows he was thinking of Jesus as being on a par with the other two luminaries. Peter failed to recognize that Moses and Elijah were secondary figures compared to Jesus. Furthermore, though Peter's motive seemed laudable (at least on the surface), his timing was out of sync with that of God and the Old Testament messianic prophecies. In short, Peter was eager to experience Jesus' promised glory without the suffering Jesus had foretold.

While Peter was still speaking, a bright cloud (representing God's presence) enveloped the people on the mountaintop (vs. 7). In turn, the Father's voice saying, "This is my Son," affirmed Jesus' earthly ministry before His disciples. The Father commanded that the Son's teachings were to be taken to heart and heeded. The implication is that Jesus was not just another hero of the faith, but rather God's very Son. According to Matthew 17:6, the three disciples were terrified by hearing the voice of God and fell prostrate. With genuine sensitivity and compassion, Jesus came and gave the disciples a reassuring touch. He then invited them to get up and no longer be terrified (vs. 7).

Mark 9:8 clarifies that suddenly when the disciples looked up, Jesus alone was with them. Moses, Elijah, and the cloud were gone and the extraordinary experience was over. As Jesus and His three followers descended from the mountain, He directed them not to tell anyone about the incident, that is, not until after Jesus rose from the dead (vs. 9). One reason is that Peter, James, and John did not really understand the full import of what they had witnessed. They were especially perplexed, wondering what Jesus meant, when He talked about His upcoming resurrection (vs. 10).

When Jesus, Peter, James, and John rejoined the other nine disciples at the foot of the mountain, they encountered a large crowd. Also present were some scholars of the Mosaic law, who were questioning and arguing with the disciples (vs. 14). The religious elite in Jerusalem may have dispatched the scribes to spy on Jesus, whom they regarded as a fraud and troublemaker (see 3:1-6). Though the specifics of the dispute are not provided, at first it could have centered around some aspect of Jesus' teaching and preaching. By this time in His earthly ministry, He had gained quite a following, and His fame had spread to many regions. On this occasion, the crowd watched Jesus in awe as He drew near to them. In fact, the people were so excited that they rushed over to "greet" (9:15) Him.

It may be that Jesus' presence created within the throng an overwhelming sense of amazement. Another possibility is that, in the midst of a critical need demanding immediate attention, Jesus arrived at an appropriate time to help. Evidently, the scene was one of commotion, especially as Jesus' disciples wrangled with the religious experts. Undoubtedly, the presence of such a large and noisy crowd added to the sense of confusion and agitation. Jesus, desiring to ascertain what was going on, asked His disciples (who possibly were feeling embarrassed) about the issue prompting them to debate vehemently with the scribes (vs. 16). The answer was not long in coming.

B. The Explanation Offered: vss. 17-18

A man in the crowd answered, "Teacher, I brought you my son, who is possessed by a spirit that has robbed him of speech. Whenever it seizes him, it throws him to the ground. He foams at the mouth, gnashes his teeth and becomes rigid. I asked your disciples to drive out the spirit, but they could not."

By addressing Jesus as "Teacher" (Mark 9:17), the distressed parent gave Jesus the same level of respect as the religious experts who were arguing with His disciples. The father explained that he had a son who was demon-possessed. (See lesson 7 for more information about the nature of demons.) The evil spirit prevented the young person from speaking. In fact, the demon often seized control of the boy, caused him to spasm violently on the ground, foam at the mouth, involuntarily grind his teeth, become paralyzed, and possibly lose consciousness. Out of desperation, the parent brought his son to Jesus' disciples to see whether they could expel the malevolent entity, but the nine were unable to heal the boy (vs. 18).

It's reasonable to suppose that Jesus' disciples felt they could cast out the demon from the youth who displayed epileptic-like symptoms. After all, the Savior had given them authority to cast out evil spirits (3:15), and they had enjoyed some measure of success so far (6:13). In this situation, however, the nine failed in their repeated attempts. In turn, this led to a heated exchange with the experts in the Mosaic law. Understandably, the disciples were defensive because of their inability to work the miracle. They possibly used arguments to cover up their inadequacy. This prompted Jesus' critics to attack both His character and that of His followers and, by doing so, gave the scribes a pretext for rejecting Jesus as the Messiah.

C. The Savior's Indignation: vs. 19

"O unbelieving generation," Jesus replied, "how long shall I stay with you? How long shall I put up with you? Bring the boy to me."

It appears from Mark 9:17 that the parent whose son was demon-possessed pleaded with Jesus to perform a miracle. Previously, in Jesus' absence, the father presented his appeal to the disciples. Perhaps Jesus' followers had inadequate faith, and in turn their unbelief negatively affected the father's confidence in their ability to restore his tortured son to health.

Jesus' comment in verse 19 about an "unbelieving generation" is understood by some to be a reference either to all humankind or to the Jewish leaders and people of Jesus' day (see Deut. 32:5, 20; Isa. 65:2; Jer. 5:21-23; Phil. 2:15). Another possibility is that the Savior was specifically referring to the lack of faith in His disciples. In this case, we can sense Jesus' intense disappointment with His closest followers. Despite all He had taught them and authorized them to do, they had utterly failed to exorcise the demon.

The two questions the Savior asked are somewhat rhetorical. He wanted to know "how long" (Mark 9:19) it was necessary for Him to stay with His immature disciples and bear with the unpleasant circumstance involving them. Jesus' queries spotlight how much He longed to be with His heavenly Father. Also, Jesus' questions remind us that even His closest followers were plagued by spiritual dullness throughout much of the Savior's earthly ministry. We can be thankful that, in the midst of such disappointment, Jesus never gave up on His disciples. He remained faithful to them, even when they struggled with doubt, unbelief, and incompetence. Moreover, Jesus patiently taught and nurtured them in their faith. Such commitment is evident in the Savior's command to have the boy brought to Him.

II. THE SAVIOR'S INTERVENTION: MARK 9:20-29

A. The Father's Desperation: vss. 20-24

So they brought him. When the spirit saw Jesus, it immediately threw the boy into a convulsion. He fell to the ground and rolled around, foaming at the mouth. Jesus asked the boy's father, "How long has he been like this?" "From childhood," he answered. "It has often thrown him into fire or water to kill him. But if you can do anything, take pity on us and help us." "'If you can'?" said Jesus. "Everything is possible for him who believes." Immediately the boy's father exclaimed, "I do believe; help me overcome my unbelief!"

It may have taken several strong adults to lift up the convulsing young person and bring him to Jesus (Mark 9:20). Perhaps a scene of panic erupted among the crowd as the evil spirit, upon seeing Jesus, at once threw the youth into a violent spasm similar to those of epilepsy. We can only imagine how horrified the father must have felt as he stood by, powerless, while his tormented son was forced by the demon to the ground in a contorted and tortured shape. Then, as the young person writhed in anguish, he began "foaming at the mouth." His wretched condition mirrored the description his father had given earlier.

Despite the circumstance, Jesus remained calm and fully in control. When He asked the father of the demon-possessed boy the length of time he had endured this oppressive situation, the parent stated that it was since his son was very small (vs. 21). It's not hard to imagine the depth of emotion and fear welling up inside the father, who loved his son deeply and felt unable to do anything constructive for him. In what way should such a parent respond, especially as he watched the evil spirit take control of the young person, hurl him into a raging fire or pools of water, and try to kill him in the process? It's amazing that the youth was still alive, given all he had been through (vs. 22).

We can imagine that when the father left home, he strongly believed Jesus could expel the demon from the boy. But now that the Savior's own handpicked followers—who ministered on His behalf—had failed to free the youth from the demon's tortuous grip, the father's confidence was shattered. He pleaded with Jesus to have mercy on the boy and help him. It's almost as if the father was saying, "Please do something—*anything*—if you can!" The father had a small amount of faith mixed with a huge dose of doubt, and Jesus instantly picked up on this.

The father wasn't sure that anyone—even Jesus—could overcome this seemingly insurmountable problem. The Savior, however, knew otherwise. The issue wasn't "if," as in whether Jesus could actually expel the demon from the tormented boy. Rather, it was whether his father was willing to believe Jesus' statement of assurance without any presence of doubt. This explains Jesus' declaration in verse 23. To those who had faith, God could bring about all sorts of unimaginable miracles. Jesus wanted to excise the "if you can" thought from the distressed and desperate parent before the malevolent spirit was exorcised from his child. (See lesson 9 for a description of biblical faith.)

In verse 24, the father's intense desperation and feelings of helplessness are unmistakable. He had a measure of faith, but his doubt had placed limits on what he thought the Lord of life could do. To the father's credit, he acknowledged that he was struggling with feelings of uncertainty and asked the Savior to help him overcome his "unbelief." As we learn, Jesus did just that. This demonstrates that the spiritual well-being of those to whom Jesus ministered was just as important to Him as their physical condition.

B. The Savior's Expulsion of the Demon: vss. 25-27

When Jesus saw that a crowd was running to the scene, he rebuked the evil spirit. "You deaf and mute spirit," he said, "I command you, come out of him and never enter him again." The spirit shrieked, convulsed him violently and came out. The boy looked so much like a corpse that many said, "He's dead." But Jesus took him by the hand and lifted him to his feet, and he stood up.

Undoubtedly, the father's pleas for help and the child's violent convulsions were attention-grabbing. In addition to the large crowd already present, more people were hurrying to see what was causing the commotion. Soon there would be an uncontrollable throng, especially if Jesus didn't act quickly. So, He censured the malevolent spirit. Then the Son of God commanded the demon—who had produced deafness and muteness in the young person—to leave the boy immediately and "never enter him again" (Mark 9:25). In Bible times, popular exorcists traveled the countryside, trying to cast out demons with various magical incantations. Sometimes they even added local herbal medicines. Jesus demonstrated His superiority and authority by expelling the demon with a simple command.

The wickedness of the demon in the youth is emphasized by the horrendous way in which the evil entity left the boy. Before departing, the demon screamed and forced the youth to thrash about "violently" (vs. 26). For a brief moment, the boy lay so motionless (perhaps due to extreme exhaustion) that the crowd assumed he had perished. The throng, however, was incorrect. When Jesus stepped forward and took the youth by the hand, it was clear to the onlookers that the boy was now quite alive. The Savior helped raise him up so he could stand on his feet (vs. 27). For the first time in his relatively brief existence, the boy was at peace both physically and spiritually. Where the disciples had failed, Jesus succeeded in fully healing the young man. This display of God's life-giving power—which in a few months would raise Jesus up from the dead—astonished the crowd (see Luke 9:43).

C. The Savior's Clarification: vss. 28-29

After Jesus had gone indoors, his disciples asked him privately, "Why couldn't we drive it out?" He replied, "This kind can come out only by prayer."

After Jesus cast out the demon, He and His disciples left the area and went "indoors" (Mark 9:28). Then, in the seclusion of the private residence, the Twelve asked Jesus why they had failed to expel the evil spirit from the boy. In response, the Savior revealed that it was only by means of "prayer" (vs. 29) that this sort of cruel and powerful entity could be driven out. Some ancient Greek manuscripts mention fasting, along with prayer, as a requirement for expelling the demon. In the parallel account in Matthew 17:21, there is also textual evidence for the inclusion of "fasting" in Jesus' answer to His disciples. While some still seek to retain the requirement of fasting in these two passages, many modern translations leave it out, based on the oldest and most reliable textual evidence.

In Matthew 12:45, Jesus indicated there are differences among the demons. Also, in Ephesians 6:12, Paul referred to a hierarchy of fiendish spiritual forces. Jesus' reminder about the necessity of prayer most likely means His followers had assumed that the power to heal resided within them, not in God. This is a reminder that our biggest spiritual failures are due to our weak faith and often result in less frequent prayer.

Discussion Questions

1. When Jesus descended from the mountain, what did He see?
2. What explanation was offered by the father of the demon-possessed boy?
3. What reason did Jesus give for the disciples' failure to expel the demon?
4. What role does faith have in our efforts to minister to others?
5. What are some specific ways we can minister to people?

Contemporary Application

The father of a demon-possessed boy felt desperate. First, he went to some of Jesus' disciples to see what they could do. But when their efforts failed, the parent pleaded with Jesus for help. He responded by expelling the evil spirit.

According to Christian tradition, most of Jesus' first followers died as martyrs for Him. Peter is said to have been crucified upside-down in Rome, while Paul was beheaded—the same fate James suffered. Luke was hanged in Greece, and Philip was hanged in Phrygia. Matthew was murdered by the sword in Ethiopia, while Bartholomew was flayed alive. Andrew died on a cross, and Thomas was run through with a spear in India.

Many of these believers were the same disciples whose faith wavered even more than that of the father of a demon-possessed boy. Nonetheless, Jesus never gave up on His followers. He proved time after time that if they put their faith in Him, He would not let them down. Those disciples are not the only ones who have gained such trust in Jesus. Throughout the past two millennia, Jesus has helped countless millions like the students in your class to overcome their moments of doubt. Be sure to encourage the class with the truth that Jesus is always present to empower them to live by their abiding faith in Him.

An Authentic Faith

Scripture

Background Scripture: *Mark 10:17-31*

Scripture Lesson: *Mark 10:17-31*

Key Verse: Jesus looked at him and loved him. "One thing you lack," he said. "Go, sell everything you have and give to the poor, and you will have treasure in heaven. Then come, follow me." *Mark 10:21*

Scripture Lesson for Children: *Mark 10:17-27*

Key Verse for Children: [Jesus said,] "All things are possible with God." *Mark 10:27*

Lesson Aim

To stress the importance of giving Jesus first place in our lives.

Lesson Setting

Time: A.D. *30*

Place: Judea and Perea

Lesson Outline

An Authentic Faith

   I. Jesus and the Rich Man: Mark 10:17-22

      A. *The Rich Man's Question: vs. 17*

      B. *The Lord's Answer: vss. 18-19*

      C. *The Rich Man's True Need: vss. 20-22*

  II. Jesus and His Disciples: Mark 10:23-31

      A. *The Lord's Explanation: vss. 23-25*

      B. *The Lord's Declaration: vss. 26-27*

      C. *The Lord's Promise: vss. 28-31*

Introduction for Adults

Topic: *The Gain in Giving*

Have you ever listened to famous people list their priorities in television interviews? Some will say their careers, families, or friends. Occasionally, someone will mention God, but that is rare. Whatever people may say, we can discover their priorities by what they do.

Even Christians may say that God comes first, but an examination of how they spend their time and money may reveal that some other things outrank God. How easy it is to slip into putting our careers first, or our financial security, or our health. It seems hard to find time to worship God and witness for Him.

The rich young ruler in this week's lesson thought he had his priorities straight, especially because he kept most of God's commandments. But Jesus knew that law-keeping was not enough, for money was the official's idol, and Jesus had taught, "You cannot serve both God and Money" (Matt. 6:24).

Introduction for Youth

Topic: *True Treasure Costs*

When one young person robs another young person to take an electronic device, we know that materialism controls the first individual. Adolescents have been attacked for a pair of athletic shoes. And teens from various economic backgrounds wear expensive designer clothes in an effort to validate themselves.

Wherever we look, we see the unmistakable presence of materialism. So we can appreciate why Jesus told the rich young man to sell everything he owned. Jesus was emphatic about this because He knew how susceptible all of us are to the lure of having lots of money, clothes, electronic devices, and other possessions.

Teens may try to imitate the lifestyle of the rich, but they are destined to be disappointed, for no matter how much they acquire, it can never satisfy their spiritual needs. It's much better in the present life and for eternity to give Jesus control of everything. He not only takes care of us, but He also gives us an inner joy that money cannot buy.

Concepts for Children

Topic: *A Rich Man Refuses to Follow*

1. A rich man asked Jesus what someone had to do to get to heaven.
2. The rich man thought he was a really good person.
3. The rich man loved his money and possessions more than following Jesus.
4. God has the power to save us.
5. The Father wants us to trust in the Son for salvation.

Lesson Commentary

I. JESUS AND THE RICH MAN: MARK 10:17-22

A. The Rich Man's Question: vs. 17

As Jesus started on his way, a man ran up to him and fell on his knees before him. "Good teacher," he asked, "what must I do to inherit eternal life?"

The episode recorded in Mark 10:17-31 occurred in the winter of A.D. 30. Though Jesus was in Judea at this time, He was heading with unshakable resolve to Jerusalem (see Luke 9:51; 13:22; 17:11; 18:31; 19:28). As the Savior did so, someone came running up to Him and fell before Him in a position of worship. When we look at the details of the various Gospel accounts, we discover that the man was not only rich, but also a leader and young in age (that is, probably less than 40 years old; see Matt. 19:16, 20, 22; Mark 10:17, 22; Luke 18:18, 23). Add to this his record of law-keeping, and we can see that he was quite a noteworthy individual.

The descriptions found in the Synoptic Gospels could have fit one of the local Jewish council or court representatives. They acted under the authority of the Roman government and exercised judicial as well as administrative responsibilities. Such observations notwithstanding, the distinguished person lacked assurance of "eternal life" (Mark 10:17). Perhaps based on rumors he heard about Jesus, the inquirer sought out the itinerant preacher from Nazareth for the answer to his quest.

Evidently, the young man whom Jesus encountered on His way to Jerusalem expected to be given a task he could accomplish to win favor with God. From this observation it is clear the ruler thought in terms of earning salvation through the scrupulous observance of rules. Likewise, the aristocrat seemed unaware of the truth that eternal life can only be received as the Father's gift from the Son. We might paraphrase the official's query as, "What is missing?" He had been raised to heed the Mosaic law, but he still felt unfulfilled. There was a spiritual void within him.

B. The Lord's Answer: vss. 18-19

"Why do you call me good?" Jesus answered. "No one is good—except God alone. You know the commandments: 'Do not murder, do not commit adultery, do not steal, do not give false testimony, do not defraud, honor your father and mother.'"

In his initial greeting, the young man effusively referred to Jesus as "good teacher" (Mark 10:17). The Greek adjective translated "good" denotes what is upright or honorable. In this context, the noun rendered "teacher" refers to distinguished rabbis who instructed others in truths about God, His commandments, and His expectations for humankind (see also a similar comment made in last week's lesson). To point the aristocrat's thinking in the proper direction,

227

Jesus asked why the wealthy ruler considered Jesus to be "good" (vs. 18) within His essential nature.

Next, the Savior declared that no person is impeccably good. Indeed, only God is infinitely holy and so He alone could be called "good" (vs. 18). Jesus' point was that true virtue is not found in sinful people or the deeds they perform. Rather, there is only one source of supreme goodness—namely, God. It would be incorrect to conclude that Jesus was denying His own moral perfection (see 2 Cor. 5:21; Heb. 4:15; 7:26; 1 Pet. 1:19; 2:22). Behind His statement is the awareness of His unity with the Father and the Spirit (see John 10:30). Also, Jesus wanted the young man to seriously consider the implications of calling the Savior "good" (Mark 10:18) before frivolously using the term.

Jesus next said that if the aspiring leader truly prized the life God gave, he should obey the "commandments" (vs. 19; see Deut. 30:15-20). The term used here renders a Greek noun that refers to precepts, injunctions, and edicts of God, particularly those recorded in the Old Testament. It would be incorrect, however, to conclude from Jesus' statement that He thought heeding the Mosaic law could earn eternal life, for this can only be received as a gift through faith. Rather, Jesus' strategy was to help His inquirer recognize his inability to obtain eternal life through good works. Jesus could have done the ruler's thinking for him by telling him that salvation can never be merited by what one does. Instead, Jesus worked with the aristocrat on his current level of understanding and led him to confront the truth on his own terms and in his own way.

According to Matthew 19:18, the man asked which commandments he should keep. Jesus' response in Mark 10:19 focused on those Ten Commandments that primarily concerned one's relationship with other people. The Messiah cited prohibitions against murder, adultery, stealing, perjury, defrauding (which is akin to coveting), and dishonoring parents. He also stressed the importance of people loving others as much as themselves (Matt. 19:19).

C. The Rich Man's True Need: vss. 20-22

"Teacher," he declared, "all these I have kept since I was a boy." Jesus looked at him and loved him. "One thing you lack," he said. "Go, sell everything you have and give to the poor, and you will have treasure in heaven. Then come, follow me." At this the man's face fell. He went away sad, because he had great wealth.

The young man claimed to have wholeheartedly observed all the commandments Jesus mentioned since his childhood (Mark 10:20). Most likely, this points back to the inquirer's *bar mitzvah* (literally, "son of the commandment") at the age of thirteen when all Jewish youths assumed personal responsibility for heeding the Mosaic law. Evidently, the aspiring leader thought Jesus needed to give him a longer list so he could set about observing those directives too.

Obviously, the official had not yet grasped the fact that keeping the law can never save anyone. It can only disclose our sin and the need we have for a Savior (see Rom. 7:7-12; Gal. 3:24). Also, for the ruler, obedience to the law was a matter of external compliance. He did not realize that inner conformity was also imperative and that it is impossible for people to fully achieve this by themselves.

According to Mark 10:21, Jesus looked at the aristocrat intently and felt love for him. The Greek verb rendered "loved" denotes the unselfish, unconditional compassion of the Messiah. It seeks to reach out to others in need, even when the object seems unworthy of being loved (see John 3:16 and the commentary in lesson 13 of Quarter 4). The editorial note in Mark 10:21 shows how Jesus' love for all people was individualized in this situation. Out of compassion, the Savior told the young man something he did not want to hear—namely, to sell all he had and give the money to the destitute. Jesus assured the official he would have riches in "heaven." By doing this, he would show that earthly wealth no longer prevented him from exclusively following the Lord.

The Greek verb rendered "lack" (vs. 21) pointed to an area of the inquirer's spiritual life that was deficient. Jesus drew attention to this when, according to Matthew 19:21, He addressed the leader's desire to be "perfect" (see 5:48). The latter renders an adjective that also can be translated "mature" or "full grown." In this context, it refers to the complete absence of deficiency in any area of one's spiritual life. Regrettably, this was not the case with the rich young ruler, for he was unduly attached to his material possessions.

Jesus had touched the inquirer's heart, and the official was devastated. The idiomatic expression that his "face fell" (Mark 10:22) translates a Greek verb that metaphorically can refer to the sky being covered with dark clouds. The verb rendered "sad" denotes the presence of grief, distress, or anguish. In the case of the aristocrat, he became gloomy and went away dejected, for he did not want to part with his earthly riches for the treasures of heaven. Jesus never specifically stated the one item or attribute the young man lacked. Nonetheless, as soon as Jesus instructed the ruler to sell whatever he owned, the one shortcoming took control of his heart and dictated his response. He chose his possessions over eternal life.

Jesus' directive to sell everything pointed to the commandments He did not mention, namely, those requiring that God be first. From this we see the official was an idolater for whom material wealth was a god. It is worth stressing that the directive to sell one's possessions is not a command God dictates to everyone. Yet, we all must be willing to relinquish whatever distracts us from following Jesus. Ultimately, of course, giving to the poor will not save anyone. In this ruler's case, however, his possessions were a barrier between him and God. Some may need to surrender in a similar way, especially if greed is a problem for them. Others who give their lives to the Lord will need to do something else. Jesus' call to commitment is individualized.

II. JESUS AND HIS DISCIPLES: MARK 10:23-31

A. The Lord's Explanation: vss. 23-25

Jesus looked around and said to his disciples, "How hard it is for the rich to enter the kingdom of God!" The disciples were amazed at his words. But Jesus said again, "Children, how hard it is to enter the kingdom of God! It is easier for a camel to go through the eye of a needle than for a rich man to enter the kingdom of God."

After the wealthy official left, Jesus focused His attention on His disciples. He said it was difficult for the wealthy to enter the divine kingdom (and for that reason submit to God's rule; Mark 10:23). The Savior's remark caused the Twelve to be "amazed" (vs. 24). The latter translates a Greek verb that also can be rendered "astonished" or "perplexed." Their shocked response shows they had accepted the common thinking of that day regarding the presence of wealth as an ironclad indication of God's special favor (see Prov. 10:22). Jesus, of course, rejected this mistaken notion.

The Savior was even more direct when He declared again that it was extremely difficult to get into God's kingdom. This was true for all people, not just the rich. In fact, it was impossible. Jesus clarified His assertion by noting that it was easier for a camel to pass through a needle's eye (perhaps the smallest opening imaginable for Palestine's residents) than for those who amassed lots of possessions to make the passage into heaven (Mark 10:25). In New Testament times, camels were the largest and most common beasts of burden in Palestine.

According to one tradition, Jesus' word picture referred to a low gate in the wall of Jerusalem. This gate, which was for those who arrived after the main gates had been shut for the night, was called "the eye of the needle." People could get through easily, but camels could crawl through only with great difficulty—on their knees—and only if their cargo was unloaded. According to this tradition, Jesus' point was that the wealthy could enter the kingdom only if they got down on their knees (in other words, humbled themselves) and unloaded their possessions. In some ways this tradition may seem attractive, but there is no reliable evidence that there ever was a gate called "the eye of the needle." It seems more consistent with Jesus' style of teaching and His use of humor and exaggeration to conclude He meant a literal camel and a literal needle. He was talking about an impossibility, not a difficulty. Only God can save a human being.

B. The Lord's Declaration: vss. 26-27

The disciples were even more amazed, and said to each other, "Who then can be saved?" Jesus looked at them and said, "With man this is impossible, but not with God; all things are possible with God."

Jesus' provocative statement was designed to elicit a response from His followers, and it did. In fact, the disciples were even more "amazed" (Mark 10:26). This word translates a Greek verb that can be loosely rendered "struck with astonishment" or "feeling overwhelmed." Jesus' followers were so shocked that they wondered how anyone could be "saved." This renders a verb that, in this context, refers to deliverance from the penalties of divine judgment. Evidently, the Twelve agreed with the religious leaders, who taught that those who had many material possessions were most favored by God. If, therefore, the rich could not enter heaven, how could the poor ever hope to do so?

Now Jesus gave the answer he had anticipated after making his provocative statement. Entering heaven is impossible for people to merit, but all things are possible for God to do in His grace (vs. 27; see also the commentary in last week's lesson on 9:23). Put another way, while no one (not even the wealthy) can earn eternal life through the scrupulous observance of the law, the Father gives salvation freely to those who believe in the Son. Admittedly, while our sinfulness makes it impossible for any of us to become regenerate on our own, the rich have temptations to sin unique to them. Yet, God can achieve the impossible; He can change any human heart.

C. The Lord's Promise: vss. 28-31

Peter said to him, "We have left everything to follow you!" "I tell you the truth," Jesus replied, "no one who has left home or brothers or sisters or mother or father or children or fields for me and the gospel will fail to receive a hundred times as much in this present age (homes, brothers, sisters, mothers, children and fields—and with them, persecutions) and in the age to come, eternal life. But many who are first will be last, and the last first."

Apparently, the Twelve were still operating on the basis of payment and reward. Peter, at least, reflected this mind-set when he reminded the Savior (perhaps with an attitude of smugness) that the entire group had abandoned everything in order to become His disciples (Mark 10:28). Evidently, Peter and the rest of the Twelve thought they deserved more recognition than others for the sacrifices they had made to accompany Jesus. Thankfully, the Messiah decided not to debate how genuinely unselfish the Twelve had been up to this point. Instead, Jesus affirmed their commitment, imperfect though it was.

"Truth" renders the Greek adverb *amen*, which is Hebrew in origin and points to the dependability and certitude of a statement. In this case, verse 29 says the Father would not overlook any sacrifice His spiritual children made for the sake of His Son and the "gospel." The latter renders a Greek noun that refers to the good news of the kingdom, particularly that salvation is freely offered to those who trust in the Messiah for eternal life. Jesus specifically mentioned His followers giving up all sorts of financial claims and inheritance rights in connection with their families (including their parents and siblings) and ancestral estates (including their homes and fields).

The Messiah reassured His disciples that in the "present age" (vs. 30), He would shower them with innumerable spiritual blessings, especially "eternal life." Their generous reward also included becoming part of the worldwide body of Christ, along with its numerous members (including spiritual brothers, sisters, mothers, fathers, children, congregations, and so on) and the possibility of being maltreated for one's faith. Though believers may suffer for their devotion to the Messiah, they were assured that the kingdom of heaven belonged to them (see Matt. 5:10).

Jesus concluded His teaching on this subject with a declaration that in the future kingdom, the status and prestige savored by the elite would be upended. The profound irony is that many who are now regarded as being the greatest would one day be regarded as the least important. Oppositely, those who appear to be the least important now would one day be the greatest (Mark 10:31; see Matt. 20:16; Luke 13:30). Unlike the religious teachers, Jesus knew that the rich, far from being shining examples of piety, are often the worst of sinners. In contrast, many of the poor and despised are in fact the most faithful servants of God. When the Lord established full and final justice, realities, not appearances, would form the basis of judgment.

Discussion Questions

1. What was the rich man looking for in his encounter with Jesus?
2. What did the official say to justify his personal sense of righteousness?
3. What were the commandments the man had tried to keep?
4. Why is it more important to obey God than to do things that make us feel good?
5. How can we maintain the right priorities with our material possessions?

Contemporary Application

This week's lesson makes it clear that it is not enough to mentally acknowledge that Jesus died for our sins. We must also have a deepening trust in His sacrifice and a growing awareness that He saves us from eternal separation from God and eternal bondage to sin. All of our so-called good deeds are worth nothing toward our salvation. Jesus paid it all, for only He is qualified to do so. That's why we must trust in Him—and only Him—for eternal life.

Jesus calls us to be like the good soil, receiving His seed—the Gospel—joyfully and with total commitment. We are to listen to God's Word when it comes to us, not only when we first hear the Gospel, but also every time thereafter. We should have the same attitude as the believer who stated in Psalm 119:105 that God's Word was like a "lamp" to one's "feet" and a "light" for one's "path."

It is sometimes difficult to discern God's truth in the midst of a world that often justifies immorality and other sin as socially acceptable. In fact, we find the attitude of "everybody's doing it" all around us. Therefore, as Christians, we need to continuously commit ourselves to being increasingly responsive to the Bible—from the call of salvation onward. The Lord's bountiful goodness and blessings come to us when we hear and obey His Word.

A Struggling Faith

Scripture

Background Scripture: *Mark 14:26-31, 66-72*
Scripture Lesson: *Mark 14:26-31, 66-72*
Key Verse: "I tell you the truth," Jesus answered [Peter], "today—yes, tonight—before the rooster crows twice you yourself will disown me three times." *Mark 14:30*
Scripture Lesson for Children: *Mark 14:26-31, 66-72*
Key Verse for Children: Jesus answered [Peter], "today—yes, tonight—before the rooster crows twice you yourself will disown me three times." *Mark 14:30*

Lesson Aim

To recognize that despite our failures, God forgives us.

Lesson Setting

Time: A.D. *30*
Place: Mount of Olives and Jerusalem

Lesson Outline

A Struggling Faith

   I. Jesus' Prediction of Peter's Denial: Mark 14:26-31
      A. *Leaving the Upper Room: vs. 26*
      B. *Walking to Gethsemane: vss. 27-31*
  II. Peter's Renunciation of Jesus: Mark 14:66-72
      A. *Peter's Three Denials: vss. 66-71*
      B. *Peter's Deep Remorse: vs. 72*

Introduction for Adults
Topic: *Failure and Restoration*

Someone has compared the Christian life to the ocean's surging waves. Waves rise and fall, but they move steadfastly toward the shore. Believers face successes and failures, but they know the Father plans to bring them to maturity in union with the Son.

Surprisingly, the Bible does not hide Peter's failures or those of other heroes like Abraham and David. Readers connect with failures because they see themselves in the accounts.

Of course, God's grace, mercy, and forgiveness loom over these failures to give us hope. We cling to the hope of doing better tomorrow than we did today. Peter's experience compels us to not quit. It tells us that, if we stumble, we can get up again. We can defeat sin. We can please the Lord and live wholeheartedly for Him.

Introduction for Youth
Topic: *Another Chance*

Anyone who has failed his or her first driver's test appreciates another opportunity to pass. How many of us would be driving if we had not been given a second or third chance?

As Christians, we face innumerable hurdles more difficult than passing a driver's test. Moral and spiritual hurdles threaten to trip us at every turn, especially if we are not careful. How important it is to get the proper training in godly living, so we do not stumble and fall.

That's why it's so crucial to cultivate basic spiritual disciplines—fellowship with other Christians, Bible study and prayer, worship and witness. If we do not prepare ourselves spiritually, no matter how many chances we get, we'll fall flat on our faces.

Peter's experience warns us against complacency. It also instructs us to guard against things that don't seem very important. Even a simple question like, "Are you a Christian?" can be the means of either denying or confessing our faith in Jesus.

Concepts for Children
Topic: *Being Forgiven*

1. Jesus said His followers would reject Him.
2. Peter said he would never reject Jesus.
3. In a moment of fear, Peter rejected Jesus.
4. Later, Jesus forgave Peter.
5. Even when we sin, Jesus can forgive us.

Lesson Commentary

I. JESUS' PREDICTION OF PETER'S DENIAL: MARK 14:26-31

A. Leaving the Upper Room: vs. 26

When they had sung a hymn, they went out to the Mount of Olives.

As noted in lessons 10 and 11 from the December quarter, the Festival of Unleavened Bread commemorated the Israelites' exodus from Egypt and their release from Egyptian bondage (see Exod. 12:1-14; Lev. 23:5-8). Days of the week were calculated between sunrise and sunset. So, according to custom, the Passover lamb was killed on Thursday, and eaten that evening after sundown, which marked the beginning of Friday (Mark 14:12). Apparently at this time, Jesus and His disciples were staying in Bethany (see 11:1, 12), but the Passover meal had to be eaten within Jerusalem's area. Therefore, the disciples asked Jesus where they should go to prepare the meal (14:12).

In response, Jesus sent two disciples (namely, Peter and John; see Luke 22:8) on an errand with specific instructions regarding what they would find and what they should say (Mark 14:13-15). Everything occurred exactly as Jesus said it would (vs. 16). Most likely, the meal was hosted in a large, furnished, upstairs room of a Jewish home with a flat roof. The disciples' preparations could have included roasting the lamb, setting out unleavened bread and wine, and securing the other items required for the usual Passover meal. Once everything was ready, Jesus and His disciples went from Bethany to Jerusalem to observe the feast.

During the meal, Jesus addressed two important matters with the Twelve (vs. 17). The first issue regarded His betrayal, while the second concerned the new meaning of the bread and wine they ate and drank at this feast. In the first century A.D., diners reclined on couches for special meals. As Jesus and His disciples ate, He announced that one of them would betray Him (vs. 18). Understandably, His followers were distressed by what He declared (vs. 19). Jesus noted that the traitor would dip his hand with Jesus in the bowl (vs. 20). He was describing taking a piece of unleavened bread, or a piece of meat wrapped in bread, and dipping it in a sauce of stewed fruit. In that culture, to share a meal with someone and then betray that person was the worst kind of disloyalty.

Each of the Twelve, being heart-stricken by Jesus' assertion, literally asked, "It is not I, is it?" (vs. 19). But the disciples, as a group, received no reassurance from Jesus. Matthew 26:25 reports that Jesus pointed to Judas as the betrayer. Evidently, the other disciples did not suspect Judas' guilt, even when he left the meal early (see John 13:28-30). Despite the predicted dire turn of events, it fulfilled God's sovereign purpose in the plan of salvation (Mark 14:21; see Ps. 22; Isa. 53). Nonetheless, as a free moral agent, Judas bore full responsibility for his action. The interjection rendered "woe" (Mark 14:21) denotes deepest pity for a person whose destiny is so horrible to contemplate that nonexistence would be far better.

Next, Jesus addressed the new meaning of the bread and wine. The bread Jesus blessed and broke was the unleavened cakes prescribed for the Passover feast (vs. 22). The cup contained a mixture of one-third wine and two-thirds water (vs. 23). Before offering the bread and the wine to His disciples, the Son gave thanks to the Father. As Jesus passed the pieces of bread and the cup of wine around to His disciples, He said the items were, respectively, His "body" (vs. 22) and "blood" (vs. 24). In all likelihood, the disciples understood these two elements to be figurative, not literal, representations of the one who was physically present with them. On the cross, Jesus' body would be sacrificed and His blood would be shed to atone for the sins of all people.

The old covenant was based on the system of sacrifices and ceremonies that reminded people of their need for salvation. The new covenant was based on Jesus' sacrificial death. In His crucifixion, Jesus fulfilled all that was symbolized in the old covenant and provided a complete means of forgiveness. God alone established the terms of the new "covenant" arrangement (see Heb. 8:6-13). Fallen humanity could only accept or reject, not alter, the covenant's terms. Jesus told His disciples He would not drink with them again during the present church age. The next time He drank with them would be after the inauguration of God's kingdom (Mark 14:25). This is probably a reference to the future, final form of the kingdom (see Rev. 20:4-6).

At the conclusion of the Passover meal, it was customary to sing the second half of the Hallel Psalms (Pss. 113—118). Mark 14:26 indicates that Jesus and His disciples followed this practice as they left the upper room and headed east to the Mount of Olives (or Olivet). This is a two-mile-long ridge running north to south across the Kidron Valley from Jerusalem. On the eastern side of the ridge is the village of Bethany, home of Mary, Martha, and Lazarus. And beyond Bethany is the arid Wilderness of Judea and the lonely road to Jericho. For centuries extensive olive groves had grown in the rich limestone soil of the ridge, giving it its name.

The slopes rise 200 feet higher than the city itself, so even today a person can stand on the Mount of Olives for a panoramic view of Jerusalem. Jesus had such a view on the day of His triumphal entry, when He stopped on the Mount and wept over the city (Luke 19:41-44). The Gospels say Jesus and His disciples went to the Mount of Olives often (Luke 22:39; John 18:1). Matthew says that it was here that Jesus explained to His disciples the future and the end of the age (Matt. 24:3), a highly significant place to do so in light of what Zechariah 14:1-5 says about the return of the Lord. Both Jews and Muslims see the Mount of Olives as the place of final judgment in the last days, so there are large Jewish and Muslim cemeteries on the slopes today.

B. Walking to Gethsemane: vss. 27-31

"You will all fall away," Jesus told them, "for it is written: "'I will strike the shepherd, and the sheep will be scattered.' But after I have risen, I will go ahead of you into Galilee." Peter declared, "Even if all fall away, I will not." "I tell you the truth," Jesus answered, "today—yes, tonight—before the rooster crows twice you yourself will disown me three times." But Peter insisted emphatically, "Even if I have to die with you, I will never disown you." And all the others said the same.

In Jesus' day, there was a place called Gethsemane (which literally means "oil press") on the western slopes of Olivet (Mark 14:32). There was likely an oil mill, a large grinding stone turned by two people, that crushed the olives so their oil could be collected for baking and frying. The use of the Greek word translated "place" indicates that it was an enclosed piece of ground. It probably was not a "garden" of flowers and trees, but a privately owned olive grove that Jesus and His disciples had permission to enter and use.

As the group made their way to Gethsemane, Jesus revealed that all His disciples would be spiritually tripped up and forsake Him (vs. 27). The Savior quoted Zechariah 13:7, which foretold the striking of the messianic "shepherd" and the scattering of His panic-stricken "sheep." The latter occurred when Jesus' disciples became terrified at His arrest and fled from the scene (see Mark 14:50). This grim outcome, along with Jesus' crucifixion and burial, would be followed by His resurrection from the dead and going ahead of His disciples into Galilee (vs. 28; see Matt. 28:10, 16; Mark 16:7).

It seems Peter had been uneasy over Jesus' declaration that one of the Twelve would betray Him. Then, when Jesus predicted that all of them would prove to be cowards, Peter had had enough. Perhaps it was Jesus' choice of an illustration from Zechariah 13:7 that really upset Peter. He may have felt insulted, having been compared with scattering sheep. In any case, Peter presumed to teach the Savior. Perhaps with bravado, Peter asserted that even if the other Twelve should spiritually stumble and abandon Jesus, Peter would never do so (Mark 14:29). Jesus responded by disclosing that before a rooster crowed twice that evening, Peter would deny Jesus "three times" (vs. 30).

Peter was so self-assured that he vehemently insisted that even the prospect of death would not prevent him from remaining loyal to Jesus. Not to be outdone, the rest of His disciples also voiced their unwavering allegiance to the Savior (vs. 31). Jesus, however, knew that human resolve was inadequate without the strength the Spirit provided. On their own, Jesus' disciples would not be able to withstand the pressure to desert Him.

II. PETER'S RENUNCIATION OF JESUS: MARK 14:66-72

A. Peter's Three Denials: vss. 66-71

While Peter was below in the courtyard, one of the servant girls of the high priest came by. When she saw Peter warming himself, she looked closely at him. "You also were with that Nazarene, Jesus," she said.

But he denied it. "I don't know or understand what you're talking about," he said, and went out into the entryway. When the servant girl saw him there, she said again to those standing around, "This fellow is one of them." Again he denied it. After a little while, those standing near said to Peter, "Surely you are one of them, for you are a Galilean." He began to call down curses on himself, and he swore to them, "I don't know this man you're talking about."

Jesus, knowing that within hours He would be crucified, relocated to Gethsemane to pray (Mark 14:32). He also urged His disciples to pray, though they struggled to remain awake. As Jesus prayed, He asked the Father to keep Him from suffering, but submitted to God's will over His own desire (vss. 33-36). Meanwhile, Judas Iscariot led a crowd into the grove to arrest Jesus. Peter reacted by striking the high priest's servant with a sword. Jesus ordered His disciples to refrain from violence, and healed the man Peter had struck (vss. 39-52).

When Jesus appeared before the Sanhedrin, He was inside one of the rooms located on an upper floor of Caiaphas' palace overlooking the courtyard. Meanwhile, Peter remained below in the open atrium (14:66). On this cool springtime evening, he stayed near a fire to keep himself warm. Just then, one of the high priest's female slaves (possibly the doorkeeper mentioned in John 18:16) looked directly at Peter and announced (possibly with a trace of disdain) that he was a follower of the Nazarene named Jesus (Mark 14:67). Evidently, the girl had seen Jesus and Peter together. Caught off guard, Peter claimed he neither knew nor understood what the girl was asserting. Perhaps at this point, Peter looked upon his actions as innocent self-preservation. After all, what was the sense of being arrested? That would do nothing to help Jesus.

Having denied the Savior, Peter got up and, seeking to remain inconspicuous, withdrew to an entryway that faced a street (vs. 68). Several Greek manuscripts add that just then a rooster crowed. When the female slave saw Peter standing in the vestibule, she began to repeat to those nearby that Peter was one of Jesus' disciples (vs. 69). As before, Peter again emphatically denied any association with Jesus (vs. 70). A short time later, some bystanders who heard Peter talking also accused him of being one of Jesus' disciples, for Peter spoke with a distinctive Galilean accent (see Matt. 26:73). Once more, he insisted that he did not even know the person being interrogated and condemned by the Sanhedrin. Also, either Peter cursed Jesus (a sacrilegious act) or Peter invoked a curse on himself. Presumably, God would punish Peter if he were lying (Mark 14:71).

B. Peter's Deep Remorse: vs. 72

Immediately the rooster crowed the second time. Then Peter remembered the word Jesus had spoken to him: "Before the rooster crows twice you will disown me three times." And he broke down and wept.

Right after Peter's third denial, a rooster crowed a second time. According to Luke 22:61, it was at that moment when Jesus turned and looked directly at Peter. As the two exchanged gazes, Peter recalled Jesus' prediction. Peter realized he had done the very thing he had ardently pledged not to do. He demonstrated by his repudiation of Jesus that the disciple's devotion to the Savior was shallow. It was then that Peter rushed out of the courtyard and began to weep uncontrollably (Mark 14:72).

Restoration began in the heart of Peter when he was crushed by his own denial. Finally, he saw himself as he really was, not as he thought he was. It was not until after Jesus' resurrection, when He appeared to some of His disciples along the shore of the Sea of Galilee, that He reinstated Peter (see John 21). As the group ate an early morning meal consisting of bread and fish, Jesus confronted Peter. He had denied the Lord three times, and Jesus asked Peter three times whether he loved the Savior. On each occasion, Peter affirmed his love for and commitment to Jesus.

Specialists debate about the significance of the use of two different Greek words for "love" in verses 15 and 17. Some think a distinction in meaning is intended, while others feel the variations in wording are only for stylistic reasons. The Savior's commands to Peter also contain subtle distinctions. In verses 15 and 17, Jesus directed Peter to feed (or pasture) His flock. But in verse 16, Jesus told Peter to take care of (or shepherd) His flock. Peter was to do more than spiritually feed God's people. Peter was also to watch over them, just as a shepherd would stand guard over the vulnerable sheep (see 1 Pet. 5:2-4).

Through this exchange, Jesus signaled that He had forgiven Peter and was reinstating him as one of the apostles whom Jesus had commissioned to evangelize the lost. In the Savior's meeting with Peter, Jesus also foretold how Peter would die. That he would stretch out his hands and be led where he did not want to go seemed to indicate death by crucifixion. We know from biblical accounts that Peter traveled through Judea, to Antioch, and possibly to Corinth (Acts 9:32; 1 Cor. 1:12; Gal. 2:11). Furthermore, Paul noted that Peter took his wife with him on his missionary travels (1 Cor. 9:5). Eventually, it is believed that Peter, like Paul, traveled to Rome (1 Pet. 5:13).

Tradition says that, while Peter was in Rome, he was persuaded by the church there to leave the city and avoid death during Nero's persecution (about A.D. 67–68). As Peter was departing through the city gate, he had a vision of the Messiah coming into the city. When Peter asked Jesus where He was heading, He said He was going to be crucified again. According to an early church leader named Jerome, Peter then returned to Rome, was incarcerated in the Mamertine prison, and was crucified. Peter told those crucifying him to do so with him positioned upside down. The apostle reasoned that he was unworthy to die in the same manner as his Lord.

It is instructive to compare and contrast Judas and Peter. Jesus, after choosing Judas as a follower, gave him the job as treasurer for the group (see John 12:6; 13:29), possibly because of his ability as a businessperson. But due to his greed, the fiduciary inclination of Judas helped lead to his downfall. Though Judas was associated with the Messiah, heard His teaching, and witnessed His works, Judas did not have an abiding spiritual union with the Son. Rather than bearing fruit, the life of Judas ended in destruction. Jesus also chose Peter to be one of His disciples. Jesus taught him the same truths and gave him the same sorts of opportunities to witness that He had given Judas. Peter did not begin his life as a disciple with great success, but after some pruning (such as his denial of the Son and later reinstatement), Peter bore much fruit. He found the key to a productive life in vital union with the Savior (see John 15:1-17).

Discussion Questions

1. Why would the Twelve abandon Jesus on the night before His crucifixion?
2. How would you have felt if you were Peter and heard Jesus predict Peter's denial of Him?
3. Why did Peter's strategy in the courtyard fail?
4. Why did Peter invoke a curse upon himself?
5. What are some ways believers can strengthen their relationship with Jesus?

Contemporary Application

When Jesus was led away to the house of the high priest, Peter followed and waited in the courtyard. But when others in the courtyard recognized Peter as the one who had been with Jesus, Peter denied the Savior three times.

The eye contact Peter made with Jesus, and the rooster's crowing, jarred Peter into recognizing what he had done. Jesus' prediction came flooding back into Peter's mind. He was so overcome with grief that he left the courtyard and wept bitterly. His denial of the Savior was tragic. But Peter's immediate repentance made it possible for him to later reaffirm his loyalty to Jesus.

At times, like Peter, we may feel as if our relationship with Jesus needs to be strengthened. There will be high points, such as when Jesus proves Himself faithful by answering our prayers. But there will also be low points, such as when we fail Him by committing some sin. In the low times, we should remember that, like Peter, God's grace can help us to recover and once again follow the Lord.

It is imperative that we remember the preceding truths, especially when life sometimes seems to be a series of setbacks and failures. The lure of sin can catch us off guard and cause us to stumble. But no matter what we have done or failed to do, there is always hope until we give up hope. Ultimately, it is God's unconditional forgiveness that enables us to once again faithfully follow Him.

A Resurrection Faith

Scripture

Background Scripture: *Mark 16:1-8*

Scripture Lesson: *Mark 16:1-8*

Key Verse: "Don't be alarmed," [the young man] said. "You are looking for Jesus the Nazarene, who was crucified. He has risen! He is not here. See the place where they laid him." *Mark 16:6*

Scripture Lesson for Children: *Mark 16:1-8*

Key Verse for Children: "You are looking for Jesus the Nazarene, who was crucified. He has risen!" *Mark 16:6*

Lesson Aim

To affirm the reality of Jesus' resurrection and express saving faith in Him.

Lesson Setting

Time: A.D. *30*

Place: Jerusalem

Lesson Outline

A Resurrection Faith

   I. The Empty Tomb: Mark 16:1-3
      A. Bringing Aromatic Spices: vss. 1-2
      B. Discovering the Repositioned Stone: vss. 3-4
  II. The Resurrected Lord: Mark 16:5-8
      A. Encountering the Angel: vs. 5
      B. Learning Jesus Had Risen: vss. 6-7
      C. Running from the Tomb: vs. 8

Introduction for Adults

Topic: *Alive from the Dead*

The first time a death in the family confronts us, we realize as never before its terrible finality. This is the end. Until then, we think we are immortal. We fail to grasp the fact of our mortality. But, as Paul revealed, the mortal must be clothed with immortality (1 Cor. 15:53).

The account of Jesus' death and resurrection reminds us that "death has been swallowed up in victory" (vs. 54). Jesus experienced death for all of us so our sins might be forgiven. He was raised for our justification. His resurrection proves His victory over sin and death.

Death is final only in the sense that it terminates our mortality. It is not the end, but the beginning. Jesus' empty tomb guarantees that all who believe shall be saved and enjoy eternal life.

Introduction for Youth

Topic: *Alarmed and Amazed*

Is faith a leap in the dark, as some have argued? Or is our faith based on solid, unshakable evidence? The account of Jesus' death and resurrection reminds us that our faith is historically valid and logically acceptable. Our faith in the risen Lord inspires courage and boldness to witness to others.

At the same time, we have to admit the scary side of commitment to Jesus. We do our friends no favors if we pretend there are no risks in taking a step of faith. The risk is not that our faith might prove to be invalid, but that our faith might require some courageous acts.

The classic definition of faith is believing what we can't see (Heb. 11:1). The unknown and the unseen may frighten us. But when the reality of Jesus' love and power grips us, we can take our first baby steps of faith and keep growing from there.

Concepts for Children

Topic: *Alive!*

1. After Jesus died, several women went to the tomb where Jesus' body had been laid.
2. The women saw that the stone covering the tomb's entrance had been rolled away.
3. An angel told the women Jesus had risen from the dead.
4. The women were so frightened that they ran away from the tomb.
5. God wants us to believe the truth about Jesus' resurrection.

Lesson Commentary

I. THE EMPTY TOMB: MARK 16:1-3

A. Bringing Aromatic Spices: vss. 1-2

When the Sabbath was over, Mary Magdalene, Mary the mother of James, and Salome bought spices so that they might go to anoint Jesus' body. Very early on the first day of the week, just after sunrise, they were on their way to the tomb.

After Jesus' arrest, He had two trials—one Jewish and one Roman. Each of these trials had three parts. The Jewish trial began with a preliminary hearing before Annas, a former high priest (John 18:12-14, 19-23). Next, the Sanhedrin tried Jesus in the quarters of the current high priest, Caiaphas (Mark 14:53-65). This trial ended with an official condemnation of Jesus at daybreak (15:1). The Jews took Jesus to the Roman governor of Judea, Pontius Pilate, who questioned Him (15:2-5). Then Pilate sent Jesus to be examined by Herod, the ruler of Jesus' home territory (Luke 23:6-12). Finally, Pilate gave a judgment against the Son of God (Mark 15:6-15).

Verse 15 says Pilate had Jesus "flogged" before delivering Him up to the Roman soldiers to be "crucified." The Roman practice of flogging was a horrible punishment, and many victims died from it. The flog was a whip made out of leather strips embedded with chips of bone or metal. When captives were beaten across the back with a flog, their flesh was left in shreds. Sometimes, even their bones or internal organs would be exposed. After Jesus' flogging, the soldiers led Him away to be crucified. The latter was a form of execution the Romans adopted for rebels and lesser criminals.

First, the executioners used iron nails to pin the convict's wrists to the horizontal beam of the cross. Then, they lifted this beam and attached it to another beam placed upright in the ground. Next, the soldiers nailed the convict's feet or ankles together to the vertical beam, with his knees bent to one side. Above his head, they erected a sign stating the crime for which he was being executed. Crucifixion was one of the cruelest and most degrading methods of punishment ever contrived. Many victims lingered for two or three days before dying of exhaustion, exposure, or their wounds.

In Jesus' situation, after the soldiers tortured and mocked Him, they led Him a short distance north and just outside Jerusalem to a place called Golgotha (vss. 16-20). It was customary for the condemned man to carry the horizontal beam of his own cross. Jesus, however, was weak due to the flogging and the strain He had been under during the preceding days. He only managed to carry His beam a short distance. Then the soldiers forced a bystander named Simon to carry the beam the rest of the way. He was a native of Cyrene, a major city in northern Africa. He may have been a Jew who had come to Jerusalem for the Passover (vs. 21).

Once the group had reached the execution site, the soldiers crucified Jesus. It was nine in the morning, and the charge against Jesus was His claim to be the Jews' messianic king. Meanwhile, the soldiers gambled to see which of them would keep Jesus' clothes (vss. 22-26). Mark records three negative reactions to Jesus' crucifixion. The first came from bystanders in the crowd. They mocked Him with His own prophecy of resurrection. The second disparaging exchange came from the religious leaders. They said nothing directly to Jesus, but among themselves exchanged smug assurances that they had gotten the best of Him. The third instance of ridicule came from the two outlaws who were crucified with Jesus (vss. 27-32). At first, the pair insulted Jesus, though later one of them had a change of heart (see Luke 23:40-43).

After three hours had passed, when the sun was at its highest, a mysterious darkness fell over the area. Much like the plague of darkness that occurred before the first Passover (Exod. 10:21-23), this darkness symbolized God's curse and lasted until three o'clock that afternoon. Near the end of the period of darkness, Jesus cried out (Mark 15:33-34). He was experiencing the agony of separation from the Father. This was the torment the Son had anticipated in Gethsemane. Jesus' cry (recorded in its original Aramaic) quoted the first line of Psalm 22, a prophetic ode fulfilled in many ways during that day. Some of Jesus' hearers imagined He was summoning Elijah to save Him. Their motive for offering Jesus a drink may have been to extend His life in case Elijah would come (Mark 15:35-36).

Jesus, having maintained consciousness until the end, breathed His last. The splitting of the Jerusalem temple curtain, which occurred at the moment of Jesus' death, had an important symbolic meaning. This veil stood between the holy place and the most holy place to guard the entrance to the presence of God. By splitting this veil, God showed that the way into His presence had been opened through the sacrificial death of His Son (vss. 37-38; see Heb. 10:19-22). While most observers of the crucifixion ridiculed Jesus, a few others responded differently. One was a Roman officer who had been assigned guard duty at the cross. He must have been used to violence and suffering, but something about Jesus' death moved the soldier. This Gentile warrior concluded that Jesus was the "Son of God" (Mark 15:39). As such, Jesus was the divine, messianic king.

Another devout response to Jesus' death came from a small group of women who watched at a distance (vss. 40-41). They had given assistance to Jesus during His earthly ministry, and now they kept a vigil as He completed His mission of redemption for sinners. Mark mentioned three of the women: (1) Mary Magdalene, a woman Jesus had liberated from demons (see Mark 16:9; Luke 8:2); (2) Mary the mother of James and Joseph; and (3) Salome, who also may have been the mother of Zebedee's sons (James and John; see Matt. 27:56) and Jesus' aunt (see John 19:25). Some of these women became the first witnesses of Jesus' resurrection.

The Romans commonly left a body on a cross to rot away as a sign of disrespect to the dead criminal and as a warning to others. But Jewish law required corpses to be buried before the Sabbath, which was no more than three hours away. This is one reason why Joseph of Arimathea hurried to provide his own nearby tomb as a burial place for Jesus. Joseph was a member of the Sanhedrin. In addition to being wealthy and influential, he was also a person of courage, for he put himself at risk by asking Pilate for Jesus' body. This act amounted to a public confession of faith in Jesus.

Pilate was surprised to learn Jesus had died within six hours of being crucified, since victims often lingered for days. The centurion mentioned earlier confirmed Joseph's report that Jesus was dead (Mark 15:39-45). Along with fellow Sanhedrin member Nicodemus (John 19:38-40), Joseph removed Jesus' body from the cross. At the tomb, the two men hastily prepared Jesus' body for burial. Probably, they washed the body and wrapped it in linen, sprinkling spices between the folds of cloth. When they left, soldiers sealed the tomb with a large circular stone (vs. 46).

Verse 47 states that "Mary Magdalene and Mary the mother of Joseph" observed where Jesus' body had been placed. As an act of love and devotion, the two women intended to complete the anointing of His body later. Admittedly, these were difficult hours for Jesus' followers. Nonetheless, they were necessary. Had Jesus not died, there would be no provision for our redemption. Also, His burial, which several people witnessed, was necessary proof confirming Jesus' death and resurrection.

Indeed, as Mark 16 reveals, Jesus' rising from the dead was the grand, confirming act of His atoning sacrifice at Calvary. He was buried late on Friday afternoon. After sunset on Saturday, when the Sabbath had ended, the Jewish shops reopened. It was then that the same three women who had witnessed Jesus' death purchased some aromatic oils for anointing His body. According to verse 1, the women were "Mary Magdalene, Mary the mother of James, and Salome." By the time the three made their purchase, it was too late for them to do the anointing. So, at first light on Sunday (possibly around 5:30 A.M.), the women headed to the burial site (vs. 2).

B. Discovering the Repositioned Stone: vss. 3-4

And they asked each other, "Who will roll the stone away from the entrance of the tomb?" But when they looked up, they saw that the stone, which was very large, had been rolled away.

As the three women walked to the tomb where Jesus was buried, they discussed the fact that the burial site was closed off. As noted earlier, this was done with a large disk-shaped stone fitted into a groove hewn in the bedrock at the entrance. The channel slanted down, so the stone easily rolled in front of the opening, but was extremely hard to dislodge (Mark 16:3-4). Matthew 27:62-66 adds that the tomb was marked with an official seal of the Roman government to ensure that no one opened it. Also, a soldier was posted to guard the body and protect it from being stolen. The three women may not have been aware of all this before they went to the burial site. However, if they were, their visit to the grave was not just an act of devotion, but also one of considerable bravery.

II. THE RESURRECTED LORD: MARK 16:5-8

A. Encountering the Angel: vs. 5

As they entered the tomb, they saw a young man dressed in a white robe sitting on the right side, and they were alarmed.

Matthew 28:2 indicates that at some point, most likely before the women's arrival at the tomb, an earthquake occurred. Then an angel of the Lord descended from heaven, rolled back the stone from the entrance to the gravesite, and sat upon it. The angel did not remove the stone to enable Jesus to leave the tomb. Instead, the angel did so to permit others to enter the sepulcher and see for themselves that Jesus' body was gone.

In the case of the three women, not only did they see that the stone had been removed from the entrance, but also they saw an angelic figure dressed in a white robe and seated on the right side of where Jesus' body had been placed (Mark 16:5). According to Matthew 28:3, the face of the heavenly emissary beamed with the brightness of lightning and his clothes were brilliant like snow. When he first arrived at the tomb, his awesome presence caused the guards to tremble with fear and faint (vs. 4). Then, when the three women arrived at the burial site, they too were "alarmed" (Mark 16:5).

B. Learning Jesus Had Risen: vss. 6-7

"Don't be alarmed," he said. "You are looking for Jesus the Nazarene, who was crucified. He has risen! He is not here. See the place where they laid him. But go, tell his disciples and Peter, 'He is going ahead of you into Galilee. There you will see him, just as he told you.'"

The Lord's angel had four facts he wanted the three women to know. First, both he and the women were referring to the same individual—namely, "Jesus the Nazarene" (Mark 16:6; see 1:24; 10:47; 14:67). Second, He had been "crucified" (16:6) and so He really had been dead. Third, Jesus was no longer dead, for He had been resurrected. Fourth, because Jesus had broken the grip of death, He was not in the sepulcher. Matthew 28:6 adds that Jesus' resurrection occurred just as He had foretold (see Mark 8:31; 9:9, 31; 10:34). As proof that Jesus was truly alive, the angel invited the women to examine the spot where Jesus' body had been placed (16:6).

After the women had taken some time to examine the empty tomb, the angel told them to deliver an important message to the rest of Jesus' disciples. The women were to tell the others that their Shepherd, who had overcome death as the Lamb of God (see John 1:29, 36; Rev. 5:6), was "going ahead" (Mark 16:7) of

His spiritual flock into Galilee (see 14:27-28). This region in northern Palestine played a prominent role in Jesus' earthly ministry. The angel specifically wanted Peter to know about Jesus' resurrection. At this time, Peter probably no longer felt he could have a place of leadership among the rest of Jesus' disciples. From the angel's message, though, Peter would understand that Jesus had forgiven and restored him to faithful service (also see the corresponding commentary in last week's lesson).

C. Running from the Tomb: vs. 8

Trembling and bewildered, the women went out and fled from the tomb. They said nothing to anyone, because they were afraid.

Mark 16:8 states that the three women were "trembling" with fear and overcome with bewilderment. After they exited the tomb, they "fled" from the scene. Due to alarm, they did not say anything about what they had seen, that is, until they reached the other disciples. It was then that the women declared the amazing news of Jesus' resurrection (see Matt. 28:8; Luke 24:9).

Today, we would not consider the witness offered by these three women to be uncommon. But for first-century writings, it was highly unusual to describe women as reliable observers to the empty tomb and spokespersons announcing that Jesus had risen from the dead. Also, the testimony of women and slaves was inadmissible in Jewish courts, so that what women had to say was often considered of no value. At first, even the male disciples were skeptical of the women's testimony (see Luke 24:11). But the truth of their assertions was soon verified.

By comparing the earliest and most reliable manuscripts, many specialists have concluded that Mark 16:8 is the last line that has survived in the second Synoptic Gospel. Numerous copies of Mark, though, contain a mosaic of additional shorter and longer endings (as reflected in the KJV). These differ from the rest of the Gospels in literary style, vocabulary, and (some say) theology. Possibly early in the second century A.D., Christians spliced together excerpts from the other three Gospels. Perhaps the author originally had another ending that has been lost. Or perhaps Mark intended for his Gospel to end abruptly on the note of surprise and amazement that greeted the fact of Jesus' resurrection. After all, the Savior's conquering death not only ends one account, but also begins another. The history of the church, which includes us, proceeds directly from the victory Jesus won over the grave.

It was on the basis of Jesus' resurrection that He had the power and authority to commission His disciples for evangelistic outreach. Matthew 28:16-20 reveals that just as Jesus had commanded, the eleven disciples traveled north from Jerusalem to Galilee to meet with Him. These disciples were originally from Galilee, and (as noted earlier) Jesus had spent much of His earthly ministry there. So it was fitting for the risen Lord to meet His followers in Galilee at a certain "mountain" (vs. 16) that remains unidentified. When the disciples saw

Jesus, their response was mixed (vs. 17). Some "worshiped" Him, which means they recognized Jesus to be the risen Lord and paid Him homage as the Son of God. Others, however, were uncertain either about whether Jesus truly had risen from the dead or about whether the person they were meeting was actually Jesus.

At the mountain, Jesus declared that the Father had given Him all authority in heaven and earth (vs. 18). Having been completely faithful in His mission on earth, Jesus had proved His right to have such authority. This was the basis for the commission He was about to give. Jesus appointed His disciples to serve Him as His ambassadors, to "go and make disciples of all nations" (vs. 19). His followers must have been surprised at such a commission. Generally, Jews believed Gentiles were outside the favor of God, or that if Gentiles were to receive God's favor, they first had to become Jews. But here was Jesus telling His followers to disperse into the world and make disciples of people from all over. God had thrown His arms wide to graciously receive all people who love and believe in His Son.

Discussion Questions

1. How did the three women show their devotion to Jesus?
2. How would you have responded to the angel in the tomb?
3. Why were the women frightened at the news of Jesus' resurrection?
4. How would you describe the power of God exhibited at Jesus' resurrection?
5. Why is the truth of Jesus' resurrection important for us to remember?

Contemporary Application

People today find it no easier to believe in Jesus' resurrection than did the disciples when they first heard the news. In our experience, people who are dead do not come back to life. So perhaps we should not be surprised when our non-Christian friends view the resurrection message as interesting but not at all convincing.

As Christians we need to recognize the importance of affirming that Jesus' resurrection actually took place. But how do we do it? We do so by cultivating a personal relationship with the risen Lord in our daily life. When we pursue a personal relationship with our Savior, we show that we truly believe He is alive, having been raised from the dead.

What naturally results from this is a desire on our part to express our faith, especially by sharing the Gospel message with others. In fact, the Gospel will burn in our hearts, and sharing the good news about Jesus' resurrection will not be a burdensome obligation to us, but rather a joyful privilege. Expression may take the form of evangelism, but it also may take the form of song or prayer. There are many ways we can express our faith in Christ's resurrection, but whatever way we do it, we show our trust and hope in the resurrected Lord.

A Remarkable Trust

Scripture

Background Scripture: *Luke 7:1-10*
Scripture Lesson: *Luke 7:1-10*
Key Verse: When Jesus heard this, he was amazed at him, and turning to the crowd following him, he said, "I tell you, I have not found such great faith even in Israel." *Luke 7:9*
Scripture Lesson for Children: *Luke 7:1-10*
Key Verse for Children: "But say the word, and my servant will be healed." *Luke 7:7*

Lesson Aim

To recognize that Jesus has the ability to meet our every need.

Lesson Setting

Time: A.D. *28*
Place: Capernaum

Lesson Outline

A Remarkable Trust

  I. The Centurion's Request: Luke 7:1-5
     A. *The Savior's Arrival at Capernaum: vs. 1*
     B. *The Centurion's Advocates: vss. 2-5*
  II. The Centurion's Humility: Luke 7:6-10
     A. *An Acknowledgment of Unworthiness: vss. 6-8*
     B. *An Expression of Amazement: vss. 9-10*

Introduction for Adults

Topic: *Restored to Health*

The account of Jesus healing the centurion's dying slave reminds us that life is filled with hardships, many of which are unexpected and unavoidable. It's in these tough, overwhelming circumstances that Christian faith swings into action. We find that Jesus is loving, wise, powerful, and trustworthy. How exciting it is to discover that, even in life's darkest moments, the Lord is there to watch over and provide for us.

Christians sometimes say, "Oh, that wouldn't matter to Jesus." Or, "It's too trivial to pray about." But we soon learn that nothing is inconsequential to the Savior. He invites us to experience the great privilege of praying to Him about everything, not just major crises. In fact, we grow the most spiritually when we place all of our needs in His hands.

This week's study of how Jesus intervened in the life of a Roman army officer and his bondservant will bring us fresh insight concerning the ability He has to meet our needs. We will learn that nothing is impossible for Him to do for us.

Introduction for Youth

Topic: *Remarkable Faith*

The teenager and his father returned to the car after fishing for a couple of hours, only to discover that the car keys were nowhere to be found. They searched everywhere and finally the father said, "Let's pray and ask the Lord to help us find those keys." So the two did just that, and in a matter of minutes the keys turned up.

Was this a minor miracle? Regardless of our response, the lesson is clear. Our faith in Jesus covers all areas of our lives. Faith is not confined to the church building, the Sunday worship services, or the youth meeting. Rather, Jesus wants us to trust Him in every circumstance of life.

Like the centurion whose bondservant lay close to death, Jesus encountered people at the point of their greatest needs. He used these incidents to teach His disciples to trust Him more. These were also opportunities for the crowds to hear His teaching and receive His healing touch. By studying the way Jesus ministered to others, we are encouraged to depend on Him more in our trying situations.

Concepts for Children

Topic: *Help Will Come*

1. Jesus finished speaking to some people.
2. Jesus went to a city called Capernaum.
3. Jesus heard that a soldier's close friend was dying.
4. Jesus healed the soldier's friend.
5. Jesus wants us to trust Him to help us.

Lesson Commentary

I. THE CENTURION'S REQUEST: LUKE 7:1-5

A. The Savior's Arrival at Capernaum: vs. 1

When Jesus had finished saying all this in the hearing of the people, he entered Capernaum.

Luke 6:17-49, which records an extended message Jesus delivered at a "level place" (vs. 17) or plateau, forms the immediate context of the information in 7:1. At this time, Jesus was at the northwest corner of the Sea of Galilee near Capernaum. Like the Sermon on the Mount recorded in Matthew 5—7, the discourse found in Luke 6:17-49 begins with the Beatitudes and ends with the lesson on the builders. A key emphasis of Jesus' message was the importance of displaying unconditional love toward others, even one's enemies. The Savior also cautioned against unjustly condemning others and encouraged His disciples to forgive those who wronged them. Toward the end of Jesus' discourse, He told three parables about logs, trees, and houses to teach His followers about avoiding hypocrisy, about bearing good fruit, and about obeying His teaching.

Matthew 7:28-29, which forms the epilogue to the Sermon on the Mount, reveals that Jesus' audience was favorably impressed with His teachings. In fact, when He had finished preaching, the crowds were astounded and perhaps somewhat perplexed. Here was someone who had not received the formal religious training that other leaders of His day had obtained. Yet, despite Jesus' lack of proper credentials, He taught with distinctive power and persuasiveness. The legal experts of the day typically would cite other scholars to support their statements. But when Jesus taught, He spoke as the Son of God. This meant His authority, which was divine, not only exceeded that of the legalists of His day, but also that of Moses, the renowned lawgiver.

At the end of Jesus' sermon, which He delivered to a large crowd, He left that locale (Luke 7:1). The crowd included His disciples, along with numerous people from various regions of Judea, Jerusalem, and as far north as the seacoasts of Tyre and Sidon (7:17). Not only had the crowds listened to Jesus' teaching, but He also healed many of their diseases and cured those suffering from unclean spirits (vs. 21). As a result, Jesus' popularity grew considerably in a relatively short period of time, with many people from all over Palestine and its surrounding regions following Him (see Matt. 4:23-25).

Luke 7:1 states that Jesus made His way to Capernaum. This city, which was the home of some of Jesus' disciples, served as the Lord's headquarters during a large portion of His public ministry. It was a fishing village built on the northwest shore of the Sea of Galilee. Capernaum hosted a Roman garrison that maintained peace in the region. Major highways crisscrossed at Capernaum, making it militarily strategic. Because of its fishing and trading industries, the city was something of a melting pot of Greek, Roman, and Jewish cultures. Visitors to the site today can see the remains of an early Christian church believed to have been constructed on the site of Peter's home.

B. The Centurion's Advocates: vss. 2-5

There a centurion's servant, whom his master valued highly, was sick and about to die. The centurion heard of Jesus and sent some elders of the Jews to him, asking him to come and heal his servant. When they came to Jesus, they pleaded earnestly with him, "This man deserves to have you do this, because he loves our nation and has built our synagogue."

The presence of a detachment of Roman troops at Capernaum was intended to maintain law and order in the area. This army unit (possibly in the service of Herod Antipas) was commanded by a "centurion" (Luke 7:2). In the provinces of the empire—including Palestine—the Roman army was organized into legions. A legion was made up of six thousand men. Each legion was divided into ten cohorts; each cohort had three maniples; and each maniple had two centuries. As the name implies, a century had about 100 soldiers and was led by a centurion. All the centurions mentioned in the New Testament are represented in a favorable light (see also the corresponding information in lesson 7 of the September quarter).

The non-commissioned officer had a male slave, whom he greatly esteemed and who had demonstrated his considerable worth on a number of occasions. In Jesus' day, slavery was prevalent throughout the Roman Empire. In fact, during the early Christian period, one out of every two people in the empire was a slave. The majority of slaves were laborers performing such duties as cooking, cleaning, and farming. A minority served as tutors, physicians, artisans, and managers of households. More skilled and better-educated slaves generally enjoyed superior food, clothing, and shelter, which was not provided to their unskilled and uneducated counterparts.

Under Roman law, slaves were not considered legal persons. They could be bought and sold like animals. Additionally, slaves were not allowed to represent themselves in court, inherit property, or select a mate. Nevertheless, the law protected them against mistreatment by their masters. There were two basic situations in which slaves could obtain freedom: either their masters could emancipate them or they could purchase their freedom with funds they accumulated over time. Now and then, an owner might grant freedom to all the slave members of a household. On other occasions, a freed slave might be forced to leave family members behind.

The Greek adverb rendered "sick" (vs. 2) is more idiomatically translated "to be in a bad state" or "ill." In the case of the centurion's slave, he was bedridden and "paralyzed" (Matt. 8:6). He not only experienced intense anguish, but also was at the point of death (Luke 7:2). The soldier was unable to help his beloved bondservant. But the news about Jesus and His ability to heal gave the centurion hope. He believed Jesus could cure the officer's dying slave. So, when the centurion found out Jesus was in Capernaum, he sent some Jewish "elders" (vs. 3) as his emissaries to Jesus. Perhaps the centurion did not feel it was appropriate for him, as a Gentile, to make his request directly to such an admired Jewish teacher as Jesus. So the officer dispatched the local religious or civil leaders to ask Jesus to come to the centurion's home and heal his slave.

Once the elders found Jesus, they began to implore Him "earnestly" (vs. 4). The intermediaries explained that the centurion, while not a full convert to Judaism, was a God-fearing Gentile who loved the people of Judea, admired their culture, respected their worship, and sponsored the construction of the local "synagogue" (vs. 5) in Capernaum. This could mean he personally paid for the building costs. Or it could be that the soldier used his influence to solicit Roman funds for the construction of the Jewish meeting place. In either case, the elders considered the soldier to be a worthy individual who deserved to receive help from Jesus.

Wherever ten Jewish families lived, they formed a synagogue (literally "congregation" or "assembly"). Sacrifices could be made only at the Jerusalem temple. But from the time of the exile, teaching of the Mosaic law and engaging in corporate worship took place in synagogues situated wherever Jews had been scattered throughout the world. After a recitation of the *Shema* ("Hear, O Israel; the LORD our God, the LORD is One"; see Deut. 6:4), prayers, Scripture readings, and teaching followed. Because there was no professional clergy (since rabbis held secular trades to earn their living), the synagogue leader could invite anyone to teach. Typically, seven members of the congregation would stand to read Scripture. The designated teacher would then sit down to teach.

In antiquity, a variety of diseases plagued individuals, including malaria, smallpox, boils, water-borne infections (such as cholera and typhoid fever), and environmental afflictions (such as sandy fever). In these prescientific societies, priest-physicians shouldered the care of the sick and the dying. They used a combination of practical and superstitious methods to treat the afflicted. For instance, in Egypt, fiber splints might be advocated for treating fractures, but then magic incantations would be utilized to reduce a severe fever. In Babylonia, practitioners might use an empirical approach to deal with common eye problems, but then attribute other ailments to demonic activity. In Jesus' day, ill individuals selected eclectically from whatever was available. These sources included a number of healing cults and their shrines, along with various seeminlgly magical potions, spells, amulets, and sacred inscriptions.

Scripture presents the Lord as the divine healer (Exod. 23:25; Deut. 32:39; Ps. 41:3-4). God used the Old Testament prophets, as His representatives, to predict sickness and death. This was true of Nathan (2 Sam. 12:14), Ahijah (1 Kings 14:4-6), Elijah (2 Kings 1:4), and Elisha (5:27; 8:10). The prophets also intervened to bring about the healing of the son of the Zarephath widow (1 Kings

17:19-23), the son of the Shunammite (2 Kings 4:18-37), Naaman (5:3-14), and Hezekiah (20:1-7). Moreover, Jesus expressed a deep concern for the sick, disabled, and oppressed (Luke 4:18). He was firmly convinced that God's will for humankind included health, wholeness, and salvation (John 3:17; 10:10). In the early church, Jesus' disciples continued His healing ministry (Acts 2:43; 3:2-8; 5:12; 8:7; 9:40; 14:8-10; 28:8). It was their desire that their fellow believers would enjoy both good health and spiritual fitness (3 John 2). They affirmed that health and healing ultimately came from God.

II. THE CENTURION'S HUMILITY: LUKE 7:6-10

A. An Acknowledgment of Unworthiness: vss. 6-8

So Jesus went with them. He was not far from the house when the centurion sent friends to say to him: "Lord, don't trouble yourself, for I do not deserve to have you come under my roof. That is why I did not even consider myself worthy to come to you. But say the word, and my servant will be healed. For I myself am a man under authority, with soldiers under me. I tell this one, 'Go,' and he goes; and that one, 'Come,' and he comes. I say to my servant, 'Do this,' and he does it."

Jesus was convinced by what He heard from the Jewish elders. In turn, He accompanied them to the home of the centurion. Unexpectedly, the soldier, after first asking Jesus to come to him (Luke 7:3), next asked Jesus not to come (vs. 6). The Savior was not far from the centurion's home when he dispatched a group of his "friends." When they reached Jesus, they addressed Him respectfully as "Lord" (the Gentile equivalent of "teacher" or "rabbi") and said He need not bother personally showing up at the soldier's house. The reason was that, despite what others may have thought, he did not consider himself sufficiently "worthy" (vs. 7) for such an esteemed religious leader to enter his home. Likewise, the army officer did not deem himself virtuous or pious enough for Jesus to come to him.

Strict Jews of the day would have agreed with the centurion. They believed Jews became ceremonially unclean when they entered the home of a Gentile (see Acts 10:28 and the corresponding commentary in lesson 7 of the September quarter). The irony is that this ritually impure Gentile proved to have more faith than his more scrupulous Jewish peers (see Luke 7:9). Nonetheless, the centurion would not make any presumptions and risk offending Jesus. Instead, he simply asked Jesus to issue the command for the slave to be cured. The officer believed that when this happened, his bondservant would be "healed" (vs. 7). As a soldier in charge of others, he leveraged his understanding of how the chain of command worked. For instance, he could use his "authority" (vs. 8) to direct subordinates to come and go whenever it was necessary. The centurion could also command one of his slaves to do this or that, and the order was quickly performed.

B. An Expression of Amazement: vss. 9-10

When Jesus heard this, he was amazed at him, and turning to the crowd following him, he said, "I tell you, I have not found such great faith even in Israel." Then the men who had been sent returned to the house and found the servant well.

While the centurion acknowledged that he had some authority in physical realms, he believed Jesus had power in the spiritual realm that was not limited by distance, time, or even maladies. As noted concerning Luke 7:7, the soldier believed that if Jesus would "say the word," the chain of command would go into action and the dying slave would be cured. The army officer's grasp of the spiritual dynamic both pleased and "amazed" (vs. 9) Jesus. Perhaps to emphasize His point, He turned to face the throng accompanying Him. Then Jesus noted that the faith and humility displayed by the Gentile soldier were exemplary. In fact, Jesus exclaimed He had not seen "faith" this great or profound throughout the nation of "Israel." Undoubtedly, Jesus' declaration would have shocked many of His Jewish listeners.

There were also times when Jesus was just as astounded by the unbelief of His Jewish peers (see Mark 6:6). Perhaps this is why Matthew 8:11-12 records Jesus' statement that at the end-time messianic banquet, many people would come from the "east" and the "west" to dine with the patriarchs "Abraham, Isaac and Jacob." In contrast, the religious elite, who assumed they would automatically enter the "kingdom of heaven," would experience the horror of eternal separation from God and unimaginable anguish in hell (see Luke 13:28-29).

In Jesus' day, the concept of "kingdom" was rooted in the Old Testament. The term most often referred to the reign or royal authority of a king. Jewish people prayed daily for the coming of God's reign. When they prayed for His kingdom, they did not doubt that God presently reigned over His creation. Yet they longed for the day when God would rule unchallenged and all peoples would acknowledge Him. Most Jews, therefore, associated this kingdom with the coming of a Jewish ruler who would lead his people to victory over their enemies (see John 6:15; Acts 1:6).

The biblical concept of God's kingdom embraces all who walk in fellowship with Him and do His will. It is governed by God's laws, which are summed up in our duty to love God supremely and to love others as ourselves. And this kingdom, which was announced by the prophets and introduced by Jesus, will one day displace all the kingdoms of this world, following Jesus' return. We can draw several principles about the afterlife from Jesus' teaching. How we live in this life affects our status in the afterlife. One's eternal destiny is fixed at death. The righteous go to a place of blessing and comfort. The unrighteous go to hell, a place of torment. There is conscious awareness in the afterlife.

In the present circumstance, Jesus was amazed by the centurion's faith that his slave would be "healed" (Luke 7:9). As a result, when the officer's subordinates arrived at his home, they discovered that the bondservant had been fully restored to health (vs. 10). In addition to healing the centurion's slave, Jesus performed many other miracles during His earthly ministry, some of which are not recorded in the Gospels. His miracles were extraordinary expressions of God's power. Toward the end of the Fourth Gospel, John made it clear why he wrote his treatise. He could have described many other miracles that he witnessed but which are not contained in his account of Jesus' public ministry. What the apostle did write, however, was sufficient to convince any reader that Jesus is the Messiah and the Son of God, and that by believing in Him they might have eternal life (20:30-31).

Discussion Questions

1. Why did the centurion ask Jesus for help?
2. Why did the Jewish elders think the soldier deserved Jesus' help?
3. Why did the army officer think he was unworthy of Jesus' help?
4. Why is it appropriate for us to turn to Jesus in a crisis?
5. What are some ways Jesus has displayed His power in your life?

Contemporary Application

We have all faced severe crises in our lives. These might involve the loss of a job, the death of a loved one, or the onslaught of a frightening disease. Regardless of the nature of these trials, it is virtually impossible for us to avoid them. And they have a way of pushing us to the limits of our faith.

Whatever the nature of our most pressing needs, Jesus offers to meet them. The question we face is whether we, like the centurion with a dying bondservant, have the courage to believe that Jesus can help us. In other words, it's not a matter of what Jesus can do, but rather of our willingness to trust Him every step of the way.

Our popular culture, of course, ridicules the idea that Jesus can make a difference in our trauma-filled lives. In fact, when believers talk about the power of the Redeemer to meet their needs, the lost often do not take them seriously. Our job is not to win over the skeptics by the sheer force of our intellectual arguments. Rather, we should encourage them to investigate for themselves the teachings, claims, and deeds of Jesus.

When people are honest enough to consider the facts objectively, many times they will change their minds about Jesus. The Spirit can move them to come to Jesus in faith, receive His forgiveness, and feed on His Word. Perhaps God might use us to invite people to take a fresh look at Jesus. We need not fear, for Jesus is here to help!

A Reversal of Shame

Scripture

Background Scripture: *Luke 7:36-50*

Scripture Lesson: *Luke 7:36-50*

Key Verse: "I tell you, her many sins have been forgiven—for she loved much. But he who has been forgiven little loves little." *Luke 7:47*

Scripture Lesson for Children: *Luke 7:36-50*

Key Verse for Children: "I tell you, her many sins have been forgiven." *Luke 7:47*

Lesson Aim

To learn that our burden of sins needs Jesus' forgiveness.

Lesson Setting

Time: A.D. *28*
Place: Galilee

Lesson Outline

A Reversal of Shame

   I. The Woman's Act of Kindness: Luke 7:36-38

      A. *The Invitation: vs. 36*

      B. *The Anointing: vss. 37-38*

  II. The Savior's Endorsement of the Act: Luke 7:39-50

      A. *The Indignation: vs. 39*

      B. *The Parable: vss. 40-43*

      C. *The Explanation: vss. 44-47*

      D. *The Declaration of Forgiveness: vss. 48-50*

Introduction for Adults

Topic: *Forgiven!*

Like the immoral woman who made her way to Simon's house, none of us is immune from disobeying the Lord. Spiritual waywardness is something all believers struggle with at some point in their journey of faith (see 1 John 1:8-10).

Even when we go through the painful process of repentance, we must never forget that Jesus shows mercy and graciously bestows blessings upon us because it pleases Him to do so, not because we deserve it. Many people, believers and unbelievers alike, act as if Jesus is somehow obligated to grant any and all requests made of Him. But since sin placed all humanity under a death sentence, it would be unwise indeed to demand that a just and holy God give us what we deserve.

This week's study involving the Pharisee, his guests, and the immoral woman can become an opportunity for your students to seek Jesus' forgiveness for transgressions in their lives. When they do, they will discover that He is eager to lavish them with His mercy and grace.

Introduction for Youth

Topic: *Pardoned!*

As a child, Sheila regularly attended church with her parents. Her father was the pastor. Only occasionally, when visiting another church, did Sheila have the opportunity to sit next to her dad.

In those times, Sheila often did what some of you may have done in church. She got tired! She would yawn. If she began to lean toward her father, what would he do? He would raise his arm. To do what? To shake Sheila back into an alert state? No, he offered her grace. Her dad raised his arm so his daughter could cuddle against his side and rest comfortably.

Like the immoral woman who unexpectedly showed up at Simon's home, when we come to Jesus, sometimes not in the best of shape, He never pushes us away. He does not seek to shake us up. He receives us as we are. He offers His forgiveness and love—that is, if we will lean on Him.

Concepts for Children

Topic: *Forgiven!*

1. A religious leader named Simon invited Jesus to dinner.
2. A woman poured expensive perfume on Jesus' feet.
3. Simon was annoyed because he thought the woman's action was wasteful.
4. Jesus said the woman showed great faith and He forgave her sins.
5. When we believe in Jesus, He also forgives us.

Lesson Commentary

I. THE WOMAN'S ACT OF KINDNESS: LUKE 7:36-38

A. The Invitation: vs. 36

Now one of the Pharisees invited Jesus to have dinner with him, so he went to the Pharisee's house and reclined at the table.

In all four Gospels, there is an account of a woman anointing Jesus. Most likely, the same episode is narrated in Matthew 26:6-13, Mark 14:3-9, and John 12:1-8. It took place at Bethany in A.D. 30 during the last week of Jesus' earthly ministry. Previously, Jesus had been going through towns and villages, telling the good news about God's kingdom. Along with the Twelve, a number of women accompanied Him from time to time (Luke 8:1-3). At Bethany, the setting was the Jewish Passover. This yearly festival of national redemption came to symbolize Jesus as the believers' Passover Lamb who died in their place to secure their redemption from sin (see Exod. 12:3-6; 12:21; Mark 14:12; 1 Cor. 5:7; 1 Pet. 1:19).

Most likely, the account recorded in Luke 7:36-50 is a different event, one that occurred in A.D. 28 somewhere in Galilee. This assessment is based on the significant disparities between what the third Synoptic Gospel reported and what is found in Matthew, Mark, and John. In particular, Luke 7:36 states that a Pharisee, possibly a synagogue official, named Simon (see vs. 40) asked Jesus to eat a meal with him. It may have been the Sabbath, perhaps around midday after a synagogue service. In turn, Jesus accepted the invitation by accompanying the religious leader to his home and sitting down to eat at the "table" (evidently as the guest of honor). As noted in lesson 3, special meals were not eaten while sitting in upright chairs at a table. Instead, people would recline on their left elbows on the cushioned floor, with their head being closest to the low table and their feet being the farthest away.

In the first century A.D., the Jewish social spectrum was wide and diverse. The upper class consisted of the priestly and lay aristocracies and the scribes. The priestly nobility included the high priest, any retired high priests, and the chief priests who administered temple affairs. The middle class consisted of Jews of pure descent, among whom were found the ordinary priests (who served in the temple), the Levites (who served as temple musicians and servants), merchants, artisans, and farmers. The lower classes embraced all Jews who were not of pure descent as well as Jewish slaves, Jews with a slight blemish (proselytes), Jews with a grave blemish (eunuchs), and Jews who worked in despised trades. Gentile slaves and Samaritans held the lowest rank in this social order.

Jewish men ranked higher than women in all forms of public life. Even within the home, the man was master, and boys ranked higher than girls. For example, only boys received formal schooling. Except for those of nobility, Jewish women took no part in public life. They were to stay home and perform domestic chores. However, where economic necessity dictated, wives helped their husbands with their work. Rules of propriety forbade a man to look at a married woman or to greet her. Also, it was disgraceful for a scholar to speak to a woman in the street. While rural women had a little more freedom, they did not speak to men they did not know.

The priests were descendants of Levi through Aaron. They oversaw the offering of sacrifices at the temple and operated as mediators between God and His people in making atonement for their sins. The Levites assisted the priests by preparing sacrifices, ministering in music at worship gatherings, ensuring the upkeep of the temple, and serving as doorkeepers. The scribes were the keepers and registers of public documents. They studied and interpreted the Mosaic law to people, were considered the highest form of teacher, and were primarily Pharisees.

There were about 6,000 Pharisees in the time of Jesus. As noted in lesson 4 from the December quarter, they would be classed as a conservative, ritualistic party and were more popular with the people because of their anti-foreign attitude and high regard for the Scriptures. In the Sanhedrin (the supreme religious court of justice in that day), the Pharisees held a majority. They believed the oral law with its many interpretations and traditions to be just as binding as the Old Testament. They went to great lengths to perform all the prescribed religious duties and to keep themselves separated from everything they considered unclean. Hypocrisy was their most notorious and persistent sin. The Pharisees believed in a future state and the resurrection of the dead. They also kept the messianic hope alive, though their concept of the Messiah tended to be erroneous.

The Sadducees were the priestly party and were smaller in number than the Pharisees. They were mostly from wealthy, influential priestly families. The Sadducees were the rationalists of the day, only believing what they thought was reasonable. They denied the authority of the oral law, the resurrection, future punishment, and future rewards. It is a paradox that these same unbelieving priests were the ones who ministered in the temple and offered the sacrifices. Yet, as a class, they did not personally believe in the value or necessity of those sacrifices.

As noted in lesson 2, the Jews in Jesus' day felt that a person's lot in life was a measure of God's approval. If a person was wealthy, it was regarded as a sign that God was on his or her side. Oppositely, if a person lived in poverty, it was assumed that person had sinned and was suffering God's judgment. Jews also measured people by their role in society. The people most respected were the religious leaders (such as the Pharisees and the priests) and the ruling classes. Affluent laypersons and the working middle class were respected, but they were a little lower in the social order and tended to look up to the Pharisees and other religious leaders.

B. The Anointing: vss. 37-38

When a woman who had lived a sinful life in that town learned that Jesus was eating at the Pharisee's house, she brought an alabaster jar of perfume, and as she stood behind him at his feet weeping, she began to wet his feet with her tears. Then she wiped them with her hair, kissed them and poured perfume on them.

Jesus' critics accused Him of being a "friend of tax collectors and 'sinners'" (Luke 7:34). By this the religious elite especially meant those whom they deemed were impious. Because these transgressors failed to observe the Mosaic law as scrupulously as the Pharisees and scribes, they were often treated as social outcasts. This would have been the case with the woman mentioned in verse 37, who had a reputation for living in a "sinful" or immoral manner. Despite the stigma she bore, when she found out Jesus had arrived and was dining at Simon's home, the woman showed up at the meal. She was carrying a long-necked "alabaster" flask filled with perfumed oil. Because of the product's rarity and expense (perhaps worth as much as the wages a day laborer earned in one year), only the wealthy could afford to buy and use it to anoint their esteemed guests.

As Jesus reclined at the table with the rest of the guests, the unnamed woman, while crying audibly, stood behind the Savior's feet. Undoubtedly, to the shock and amazement of the host (see vs. 39) and guests, the sobbing woman used her "tears" (vs. 38) to bathe Jesus' feet (which would have been soiled from walking on dusty roads). Next, since the woman had no towel, she used her "hair" to dry off Jesus' feet. Then, as the woman repeatedly kissed Jesus' feet, she broke the seal on the flask and drenched Jesus' feet with the perfumed oil. In His day, slaves usually took care of the guests' feet. So the woman's actions were a sign of humility and reverence. In Jewish culture, most women would not disgrace themselves by unbinding their hair in public. But the woman did not allow this social convention to stop her from showing devotion to the Messiah. The sacrificial aspect of the woman's action is evident by the expense of the "perfume" she used to anoint Jesus.

II. THE SAVIOR'S ENDORSEMENT OF THE ACT: LUKE 7:39-50

A. The Indignation: vs. 39

When the Pharisee who had invited him saw this, he said to himself, "If this man were a prophet, he would know who is touching him and what kind of woman she is—that she is a sinner."

Jesus regarded the intruder as someone whose life He had touched. But Simon considered the woman only as a local, notorious "sinner" (Luke 7:39; possibly an adulteress or prostitute). The objectionable display unfolding before Simon convinced him that despite Jesus' claims, He was not really a "prophet." Otherwise, Simon reasoned, Jesus would have recognized He was permitting an immoral woman to touch Him and make Him ceremonially unclean. Supposedly, a true spokesperson for God would never permit this to happen.

B. The Parable: vss. 40-43

Jesus answered him, "Simon, I have something to tell you." "Tell me, teacher," he said. "Two men owed money to a certain moneylender. One owed him five hundred denarii, and the other fifty. Neither of them had the money to pay him back, so he canceled the debts of both. Now which of them will love him more?" Simon replied, "I suppose the one who had the bigger debt canceled." "You have judged correctly," Jesus said.

Despite Simon's skepticism, Jesus demonstrated His prophetic powers in a surpassing manner. Rather than show He knew the woman's heart, Jesus proved He was aware of Simon's thoughts. Jesus did so by stating He had something to share, to which the host grudgingly gave his permission (Luke 7:40). What follows is a parable about two debtors who owed larger and smaller sums of money to a creditor. The amounts were 500 and 50 "denarii" (vs. 41), respectively, for which the financier charged a fixed interest rate. In Jesus' day, a denarius was a Roman silver or copper coin worth about a day's wages for a common laborer.

Notwithstanding the huge differences in the size of their loans (about two years' wages for one versus two months' wages for the other), neither debtor could repay the amount he owed. So, in an incredible display of kindness, the creditor literally "forgave" or "pardoned" their loans (vs. 42). Jesus asked Simon which of the two debtors "loved" the creditor to a greater extent. The Pharisee guessed that it would be the person who owed more and did not have to pay anything back. In turn, Jesus approved of this answer by noting that Simon was correct in his assessment (vs. 43).

Here we see that Jesus used parables as a favorite teaching technique. The parables were effective because they appealed to the entire person, touching the emotions, challenging the mind, and igniting the imagination. The Gospels of Matthew, Mark, and Luke record 40 parables told by Jesus. They are short stories and sayings drawn from familiar events of daily life (such as lending money). But Jesus used these stories to communicate spiritual truths that may have been unfamiliar to His audience.

Jesus would start by commenting on something in the physical world and then compare it to something in the spiritual world. Jesus' parables usually emphasized one primary concept that could be applied in a variety of ways. Not all the details of a parable necessarily had significance. (This serves as a caution against reading too much into a parable.) The parables motivated interested listeners (such as the disciples) to find out more about what was being taught. At the same time, the parables hid the truth from disinterested listeners (such as proud religious leaders).

C. The Explanation: vss. 44-47

Then he turned toward the woman and said to Simon, "Do you see this woman? I came into your house. You did not give me any water for my feet, but she wet my feet with her tears and wiped them with her hair. You did not give me a kiss, but this woman, from the time I entered, has not stopped kissing my feet. You did not put oil on my head, but she has poured perfume on my feet. Therefore, I tell you, her many sins have been forgiven—for she loved much. But he who has been forgiven little loves little."

Jesus added an observation His host most likely did not want to hear. Perhaps for emphasis, Jesus shifted His attention to the woman and asked Simon to notice her. Then, in keeping with the parable Jesus had told, He compared how the woman and the Pharisee treated Him. For instance, after Jesus entered Simon's residence, he snubbed his guest by withholding any water for Jesus to clean His feet. In contrast, the woman used her tears to wash Jesus' feet, and she dried them with her hair (Luke 7:44). Also, Simon, in a discourteous violation of etiquette, did not greet Jesus with a customary "kiss" (vs. 45) on the cheek. Yet, since Jesus had arrived, the woman continued to kiss the Savior's feet.

Moreover, Simon did not even anoint Jesus' head with cheap olive oil. Meanwhile, the woman covered Jesus' feet with a costly aromatic oil (vs. 46). Jesus acknowledged that, on the one hand, the woman's transgressions against the Mosaic law were numerous. On the other hand, Jesus had "forgiven" (vss. 47) all of her trespasses. For this reason, she was filled with gratitude and love for being pardoned. Oppositely, someone such as Simon, who regarded himself as being exceptionally pious, was convinced he did not need to have that many infractions remitted (if any at all). Accordingly, the Pharisee only expressed affection in a miserly, grudging way.

D. The Declaration of Forgiveness: vss. 48-50

Then Jesus said to her, "Your sins are forgiven." The other guests began to say among themselves, "Who is this who even forgives sins?" Jesus said to the woman, "Your faith has saved you; go in peace."

Jesus assured the woman, who was still standing by, that despite the immoral acts she had committed, the Savior had pardoned her (Luke 7:48). Then Jesus kindly sent her away (vs. 50). When Jesus declared the woman no longer to be guilty of wrongdoing, it caused quite a stir among the others reclining at the table with Simon and Jesus. After all, they understood that only God could forgive sinners (vs. 49). Jesus was well aware of the consternation being expressed by the others present. Yet that did not stop Him from telling the woman her faith in Him had delivered her from God's wrath. Also, though the woman entered Simon's house feeling distressed because of her iniquities, she departed with the joy and inner tranquility of knowing she had been unconditionally forgiven (see Rom. 5:1).

Scripture teaches that God alone has the authority to forgive sins (see Isa. 43:25; 44:22). After all, it is ultimately against Him that people commit sin (see Ps. 51:4). Because the religious leaders rejected Jesus' claim to be God, they charged Him with blasphemy. The religious leaders, then, did not deny that God had the power to forgive people and save them. What bothered them so much in Jesus' message is the radical idea that God loves and saves "sinners" as they are, without their first having to follow the Mosaic law, "clean up their act," and therefore be deserving of His love and mercy.

Jesus offered Himself to several different groups of people. The barriers that separated them from Him and one another meant nothing to Jesus. He wanted to break down those barriers. Moreover, the standards by which some saw themselves as superior meant little to Him. Some received Him with joy, at least for a while. Some stayed with Him in the long term. And some ultimately helped murder the Son of God. In nearly two millennia, nothing much has changed. Our communities and even our churches are full of these same types of people today, all of whom desperately need Jesus' love, forgiveness, and healing power.

Discussion Questions

1. Why did the woman risk showing up at the religious leader's home?
2. What was the purpose of the parable Jesus told his host?
3. How did the Pharisee and woman contrast in the way they treated Jesus?
4. In what significant ways has God recently forgiven you?
5. Why is it appropriate for believers to show gratitude to God for saving them?

Contemporary Application

"All have sinned" (Rom. 3:23). This applied to the Pharisee, the immoral woman who showed up at his home, and it applies to us. Just because one person has committed a qualitatively different kind of sin than another doesn't change the fact that we all stand in need of mercy from a holy and just God. Thankfully, He grants us all the mercy and forgiveness we could ever need, but on one condition: that, in a spirit of repentance, we admit our transgressions (1 John 1:9).

There is a huge difference, of course, between finding sin in our lives by self-examination and being confronted about sin in our lives by others. The result may be similar, but the process reflects our spiritual maturity. Children are under the scrutiny of adults. They need adults to confront them when they do wrong. As we move into adulthood, however, the expectation is that we will examine ourselves and correct our own attitudes and actions. Sadly, that is not always the case.

As you consider your own life, what burdens of sin-induced guilt and shame do you find yourself carrying around in your own heart? Right now, Jesus sees past your outer circumstances to the heart of the matter, and He longs to set you free from the burden of your sin. At this moment, He extends forgiveness—complete, unconditional, all-out forgiveness—no matter how horrible the word, deed, attitude, or thought. Why not take this time to respond in prayer to Jesus' offer of forgiveness?

A Sound Mind

DEVOTIONAL READING

Philippians 2:1-11

DAILY BIBLE READINGS

Monday April 11
Isaiah 61:1-7 Completeness in God

Tuesday April 12
Jeremiah 31:21, 31-35 Renewed Relationship

Wednesday April 13
Psalm 119:41-48 Steadfast Love

Thursday April 14
1 Corinthians 9:19-27 Disciplined Freedom

Friday April 15
Romans 8:1-11 Freedom in the Spirit

Saturday April 16
Philippians 2:1-11 Christian Freedom

Sunday April 17
Luke 8:26-36 A Sound Mind

Scripture

Background Scripture: *Luke 8:26-39*
Scripture Lesson: *Luke 8:26-36*
Key Verse: People went out to see what had happened. When they came to Jesus, they found the man from whom the demons had gone out, sitting at Jesus' feet, dressed and in his right mind. *Luke 8:35*
Scripture Lesson for Children: *Luke 8:26-36*
Key Verse for Children: Those who had seen it told the people how the demon-possessed man had been cured. *Luke 8:36*

Lesson Aim

To gain confidence in Jesus' power and take our spiritual and physical needs to Him.

Lesson Setting

Time: A.D. 29
Place: The region of the Gerasenes

Lesson Outline

A Sound Mind

I.   Meeting a Demon-Possessed Man: Luke 8:26-29
     A. *The Encounter: vss. 26-27*
     B. *The Confrontation: vss. 28-29*

II. Restoring a Demon-Possessed Man: Luke 8:30-36
     A. *Identifying the Demons: vs. 30*
     B. *Targeting a Herd of Pigs: vss. 31-33*
     C. *Reacting to the Miracle: vss. 34-36*

Introduction for Adults

Topic: *S.O.S., Jesus!*

Jesus meets us at every level to provide hope for healing. In this week's lesson, we learn about a man who was tormented by a legion of demons. Luke's account does not give all the details of the victim's life. Even so, the critical issue is that Jesus met the man in his desperate condition and freed him from his anguish.

In the grip of fear, we can learn how to take important steps of faith. Sometimes we get the answers while praying and meditating on Scripture. On other occasions, it's through worshiping and preaching. Often our faith is bolstered by the encouragement we receive from fellow Christians.

Whatever the circumstances, we can cry out to Jesus when we feel as if we are going under. We may not find immediate relief, but we should continue to believe, for we know He is there, He cares for us, and He will not forsake us.

Introduction for Youth

Topic: *Demons, Go Away!*

As a teenager, Mike was an accomplished golfer. He also liked to play for money. One summer he went to youth camp. There he studied the Bible and met other Christian teens like himself.

Mike soon became uncomfortable with the idea of focusing so much on money, so he resolved to change his ways. But Mike was afraid he would lose some of his golf buddies. Mike prayed to the Lord for power to stick to his decision. The Lord gave Mike courage to tell his friends that he would no longer be so preoccupied with money. Much to his amazement, Mike's friends did not ridicule or reject him. One of them even asked to know more about the Savior.

Jesus is stronger than our bad habits. Not only was He able to expel a multitude of unclean spirits from a tormented man (the focus of this week's lesson), but Jesus also can give us the power to change. When we trust in the Savior and pray for courage to make the right choices, He honors our faith.

Concepts for Children

Topic: *Healed!*

1. Jesus met a man who was controlled by an evil spirit.
2. The evil spirit was mean to the man.
3. The evil spirit would not leave the man alone.
4. Jesus freed the man from the evil spirit.
5. Jesus cares for us, and He wants to keep us safe.

Lesson Commentary

I. MEETING A DEMON-POSSESSED MAN: LUKE 8:26-29

A. The Encounter: vss. 26-27

They sailed to the region of the Gerasenes, which is across the lake from Galilee. When Jesus stepped ashore, he was met by a demon-possessed man from the town. For a long time this man had not worn clothes or lived in a house, but had lived in the tombs.

Luke 8:1 indicates that while Jesus traveled with His disciples through various towns and villages of Galilee, He announced the "good news" of the divine kingdom. As noted in lesson 5, God's kingdom refers to His rule over His creation, especially through the Son. This kingdom is heavenly (2 Tim. 4:18), unshakable (Heb. 12:28), and eternal (2 Pet. 1:11). Moreover, it is characterized by supernatural power (1 Cor. 4:20), promise (Jas. 2:5), glory (1 Thess. 2:12), and the "renewal of all things" (Matt. 19:28).

In addition to the Twelve, several women accompanied Jesus. These were individuals He had set free from "evil spirits" (Luke 8:2) and cured of various maladies. Out of a sense of gratitude, they used their personal resources to help fund Jesus' earthly ministry (vs. 3). They became convinced that He was the incarnate Son of God. The preceding observation is brought into sharp relief in the episode where Jesus calmed a storm on the Sea of Galilee (vss. 22-25). He decided He and His disciples were to cross from one side of this freshwater lake to another. Ordinarily, this would be about a two-hour trip, but on this occasion it must have taken longer. Perhaps after a long day of ministry, Jesus was exhausted. Most likely, He curled up to sleep beneath the platform on which the fishermen would kneel to work with their nets. This would explain why the sudden storm did not disturb Him.

In Jesus' day, fishermen like His disciples made a good living on the Sea of Galilee. Shoals just offshore were a fisherman's paradise. Hundreds of fishing boats trawled the lake. In fact, Galileans ate little meat besides fish. It came very salted, for there was no other way of preserving the fish. Fishermen used various kinds of spears, nets, hooks, and lines in the work (see Job 41:7; Isa. 19:8; Matt. 13:47-48; Mark 1:16; Luke 5:2). Their day, however, did not end with a return to shore. Mending and washing nets, preserving fish, maintaining boats and supplies, training and supervising crews, and negotiating with merchants and others in the shipping industry made for long, tiring hours.

Because of the location of the Sea of Galilee in a basin with mountains on each side, sudden and violent storms often come up without warning. This one, however, must have been especially fierce to terrify the experienced fishermen among the disciples. Jesus, in contrast, remained asleep during the ordeal. After the disciples struggled on their own for a while, they woke Jesus and asked whether He cared that the boat was ready to capsize and drown them. This was more of an accusation than a question. Jesus' disciples mainly doubted His compassion, not His knowledge or power.

When Jesus woke up, He commanded the storm to cease. Here we see a demonstration of the Savior's complete power and deity, for only God the Creator can calm wind and sea. Next, Jesus turned His attention to the disciples' weak faith. Their questions emphasize that their fear was unreasonable. Evidently, the disciples ignored these questions, focusing instead on what Jesus had done to the weather. His followers were no longer afraid of the storm. Now they felt unnerved in Jesus' presence. He who was able to heal the sick and cast out demons was also able to rule over the elements. Apparently, Jesus was even more authoritative than His disciples had anticipated.

When Jesus and His followers reached the other side of the lake, they landed their boat in an area called the "Gerasenes" (vs. 26). The actual name of the region remains debated, with some Greek manuscripts reading either "Gadarenes," "Gergesenes," or "Gerasenes." The territory was mainly inhabited by Gentiles, which would explain the presence of a herd of pigs in the area (see vs. 32). Excavators working at a place called Kursi on the Sea of Galilee's eastern shore have suggested this as the site of the event. There is a slope near the water that could have been the place of the pig stampede (see vs. 33). Also, not far off are some cavern tombs that show signs of human habitation (see vs. 27). The site includes the ruins of an early Christian church building and a memorial to the swine miracle (see vs. 35).

On the shore, a man from the nearby city, who was controlled by a demon (vs. 27) or unclean spirit (Mark 5:2), came up to Jesus. (Matt. 8:28 mentions two men whom Jesus encountered.) In addition to being exceedingly violent, the man neither wore "clothes" nor dwelt in a "house" (Luke 8:27). Instead, he inhabited the "tombs," making the cemetery a dangerous place for other local residents to visit. Also, a Jew would become ritually unclean due to contact with the dead (see Num. 19:11, 14, 16). Under the influence of demons, this man had been terrorizing anyone who made the mistake of coming near. But the demons did not terrorize Jesus. In fact, He threw terror into them, for they recognized His divine authority.

B. The Confrontation: vss. 28-29

When he saw Jesus, he cried out and fell at his feet, shouting at the top of his voice, "What do you want with me, Jesus, Son of the Most High God? I beg you, don't torture me!" For Jesus had commanded the evil spirit to come out of the man. Many times it had seized him, and though he was chained hand and foot and kept under guard, he had broken his chains and had been driven by the demon into solitary places.

Popular culture tends to dismiss demons as nothing but a myth or fantasy. Scripture, however, presents demons as real beings involved in historical events. We know from God's Word that demons are fallen angels who joined with Satan in rebellion against the Lord. While the Bible does not discuss the origin of evil spirits, the New Testament does speak about the fall and later imprisonment of a group of angels (2 Pet. 2:4; Jude 6). Many think the demons' rebellion occurred sometime before God created the world. Then, after God brought the human race into existence, Satan and his followers contaminated people with wickedness (Gen. 3; Matt. 25:41; Rev. 12:9).

The New Testament makes a number of references to demoniacs—that is, people under the influence of one or more unclean spirits. The demonization the New Testament describes is distinct from various forms of physical and mental illness people may suffer. Jesus made it clear that demons possessed enormous diabolical power. The Gospels not only describe Jesus' casting out demons from their victims, but also relate Jesus' direct speech to the evil entities. Furthermore, when Jesus was in the presence of a demon-possessed person, the unclean spirits often acknowledged who He was and cowered at His authority. Manifestations of demon possession included extraordinary strength, multiple personalities, and physical and mental afflictions. The latter could involve muteness, deafness, blindness, seizures, crippling, and symptoms of mental illness. It was not always possible to distinguish between the personality of the host and the influence of the demons within him or her.

In the current account, when the demons spotted Jesus, they forced their host to shriek and fall prostrate at Jesus' feet. Then, screaming in a loud "voice" (Luke 8:28), the unclean spirits literally asked Jesus, "What to me and to you?" This idiomatic expression indicates the presence of hostility between the demons and Jesus. They resisted any attempt on His part to interfere with their control of their host and wanted Jesus to leave them alone. In referring to Him as "Jesus," the evil spirits drew attention to His supreme mission of delivering people from their sin (see Matt. 1:21; Luke 1:31). Also, by calling Jesus the "Son of the Most High God" (Luke 8:28), the demons acknowledged that He is fully divine and reigns supreme over all entities in the universe (see Gen. 14:18-22; Ps. 78:35; Phil. 2:9-11). Despite Jesus' exalted status, He became a human being so He could make the Father known to humankind (see John 1:14, 18).

Moreover, the demons invoked God's name, thinking this would enable them to exercise power over Jesus. Through their host, the unclean spirits implored Jesus not to torment them (Luke 8:28). Matthew 8:29 adds "before the appointed time." Their question appears to show that Satan and his demonic cohorts were aware that at the end of the age, they would face God's judgment. The demons oppressing their host (both physically and mentally) hoped to escape premature judgment at the hands of the Son. In the present encounter, Jesus had begun to order the unclean spirits to leave the man (Luke 8:29). Often, his tormentors would take control of him and so overpower him that he would break the shackles others placed on his hands and feet. And once freed from these restraints, the demons would force their host to uninhabited places. Mark 5:4-5 adds that no one could subdue the demon-possessed man, even as he wandered howling among the graveyards and through the hills and lacerated himself with stones.

II. RESTORING A DEMON-POSSESSED MAN: LUKE 8:30-36

A. Identifying the Demons: vs. 30

Jesus asked him, "What is your name?" "Legion," he replied, because many demons had gone into him.

Next, Jesus asked the unclean spirits to identify themselves. Through their host they said, "Legion" (Luke 8:30). The reason is that many "demons" inhabited the man. In ancient times, Roman legions of between 5,000 and 6,000 soldiers marched along the King's Highway that ran from the Gulf of Aqaba north to Syria, through the Decapolis. This was near the lakeside cemetery where the man lived. In a similar way, perhaps hundreds or even thousands of unclean spirits took up residence in the body of their host. With so many of them inhabiting the man, it is no wonder he was in terrible distress. His actions were so mournful and self-destructive that they inspired fear in all who came near him. Under the influence of the multitude of demons, the man possessed almost superhuman strength.

B. Targeting a Herd of Pigs: vss. 31-33

And they begged him repeatedly not to order them to go into the Abyss. A large herd of pigs was feeding there on the hillside. The demons begged Jesus to let them go into them, and he gave them permission. When the demons came out of the man, they went into the pigs, and the herd rushed down the steep bank into the lake and was drowned.

Luke 8:31 reveals that the demons implored Jesus not to command them to depart into the "Abyss." The term renders a Greek noun that denotes a well-like bottomless pit. At the end of the age, this underground chasm will become the place of confinement for Satan, unclean spirits, and the Antichrist (see Rev. 9:2; 11:7; 17:8). In Jesus' day, people visualized the earth as being a flat, disk-shaped landmass that was completely surrounded by water. Pillars upheld the ground, while mountains located on the distant horizon supported the sky. The sky itself was thought to be a solid dome or tent-like structure on which the celestial bodies (namely, the sun, moon, and stars) were engraved and moved in tracks.

In this ancient three-tiered view of the universe, rain, hail, and snow from an immense body of water located above the overarching sky fell to earth through openings. God's temple was located in the upper heavens, which in turn rested atop the sky (or lower heavens). The temple in Jerusalem was regarded as the earthbound counterpart to the divine abode. A series of graves led to the netherworld (*sheol*), which was located beneath the earth, while mighty Leviathan skulked in the depths of the seas.

Luke 8:32 states that in the present encounter, a "herd of pigs was feeding" on a nearby "hillside." So, suggesting an alternate course, the "demons" pleaded with Jesus to allow them to enter these animals. In turn, the Savior gave His consent. Then, after the unclean spirits left their host, they took up residence in the "pigs" (vs. 33). The demons then forced the entire "herd" to plunge head-long down a precipitous slope leading into the sea, where the animals (which were poor swimmers) "drowned." According to Mark 5:13, there were about 2,000 pigs in the herd.

It is understandable for readers to wonder why the unclean spirits would ask permission to go into the swine, why Jesus would give His permission, and why the demons would bring about the death of so many animals. In response, it is helpful to remember that to Jews, pigs were ritually unclean animals (see Lev. 11:7; Deut. 14:8). But the eastern shore of the Sea of Galilee was populated by Gentiles, who routinely kept pigs and sold them in their marketplaces. Also, it is possible the demons craved physical bodies to inhabit. Moreover, Jesus may have determined that the loss of so many animals was less egregious than a human being—who was created in God's image (see Gen. 1:26-27; 9:6; 1 Cor. 11:7; Jas. 3:9)—to continue experiencing torment. Finally, through this sober-ing outcome, Jesus could have sought to demonstrate to the bystanders the devastating, destructive reality of the unseen demons.

C. Reacting to the Miracle: vss. 34-36

When those tending the pigs saw what had happened, they ran off and reported this in the town and countryside, and the people went out to see what had happened. When they came to Jesus, they found the man from whom the demons had gone out, sitting at Jesus' feet, dressed and in his right mind; and they were afraid. Those who had seen it told the people how the demon-possessed man had been cured.

The pigs' caretakers saw what had taken place. In turn, they hurried off to the nearby city and its environs, where they related what Jesus had done (Luke 8:34). Upon hearing the news, the inhabitants went to the spot where the incident had occurred. They verified that the entire herd had drowned. Furthermore, when they reached Jesus, they discovered that the man who had been afflicted by so many demons was now freed from them. Whereas before he acted in a violent, deranged way, now he was rational, behaving sensibly, and sitting at the Savior's feet as one of His disciples (vs. 35). One would expect the people of that region to have honored Jesus because of the changes in the former demonic. Instead, Jesus frightened the populace, evidently because of the supernatural powers He demonstrated in delivering the man from the horde of unclean spirits (vs. 36).

The throng failed to understand that Jesus' power, though staggering, was characterized by goodness, not evil. Consequently, the local residents, perhaps filled with superstition, approached Jesus and begged Him to leave their ter-ritory (vs. 37). His reputation probably had not yet penetrated the Gentile territories east of the Sea of Galilee. There would have been no predisposition either to love or hate Jesus. The townspeople's rejection of Him arose strictly because of this incident. Some people likely were disturbed because Jesus' presence contributed to an economic catastrophe for them. Others may have disliked Jews and wanted this seemingly strange person gone from their country.

In response, Jesus and His disciples began to enter their boat and leave the area (possibly to return to Capernaum). At first, the cured man implored Jesus to let him depart with the Savior (vs. 38). But He declined the man's request. Instead, Jesus told the healed demoniac to return to his home and tell people what God had done for him. This the grateful man did. He even traveled throughout the region to let others know how Jesus had set him free from his former life of anguish under the control of so many demons (vs. 39). As people living in the Decapolis heard the man's testimony, they marveled at how Jesus transformed his life (Mark 5:20). The Decapolis was a cluster of Greek towns (originally 10 in number) mainly located in a large area east of the Jordan River.

Discussion Questions

1. What was the nature of the man's desperate situation?
2. Why do you think Jesus allowed the demons to enter the herd of pigs?
3. How do you think the man felt once the demons were gone?
4. In what ways have you seen Jesus demonstrate His healing power?
5. How can Jesus free believers from oppressive spiritual forces?

Contemporary Application

In the episode involving the demon-possessed man, physical needs mirrored deeper spiritual needs. Every person needs the deliverance and forgiveness only Jesus can provide. Those who have never placed saving faith in Him as the only sacrifice sufficient to satisfy the righteous demands of God are as helpless as the man Jesus encountered in the region of the Gerasenes. Unsaved people need to be rescued from the terrible effects of sin.

Christian men and women stand in need of situational deliverance and forgiveness. Although the eternal issue of salvation has been dealt with, physical disease and personal sins are still realities of life. Believers need to look to the Lord for help in time of sickness and for forgiveness of the transgressions that damage fellowship with the heavenly Father. We can be confident that Jesus has the power and desire to address our spiritual and physical needs in the way that is best for us.

People can provide what amounts to little more than an adhesive bandage for our physical and psychological afflictions. As physicians, they can try to treat our physical ailments—sometimes successfully for a while, sometimes not. As counselors, they can try to treat our psychological problems—again, sometimes successfully for a while, and sometimes not. But none of them can deal with any of our problems completely and permanently. They simply do not have that kind of healing power. Only Jesus does, for He is the healing God.

A Family Reunion

Scripture

Background Scripture: *Luke 15:11-32*
Scripture Lesson: *Luke 15:11-24*
Key Verse: "'This son of mine was dead and is alive
again; he was lost and is found.' So they began to
celebrate." *Luke 15:24*
Scripture Lesson for Children: *Luke 15:11-24*
Key Verse for Children: "'This son of mine was dead
and is alive again; he was lost and is found.' So they
began to celebrate." *Luke 15:24*

Lesson Aim

To rejoice with God in the salvation of the lost.

Lesson Setting

Time: A.D. *30*
Place: On the way to Jerusalem

Lesson Outline

A Family Reunion
   I. Living Recklessly: Luke 15:11-16
      A. *The Son's Demand: vss. 11-12*
      B. *The Squandered Inheritance: vss. 13-16*
  II. Experiencing Unconditional Forgiveness:
      Luke 15:17-24
      A. *A Pivotal Decision: vss. 17-19*
      B. *A Joyous Reunion: vss. 20-24*

Introduction for Adults

Topic: *Back Home Again*

Many adult education classes do an expert job of celebrating special occasions. We have celebrations that follow the calendar from New Year's Day to Christmas, and the times of fellowship are special to God's people.

But what should we do when a fellow believer spiritually stumbles? We might gossip about what happened, take pleasure in the fact that we are not in this tragic circumstance, or react with anger, accusation, or despair. We might resort to prayer because we feel helpless to do anything else. But seldom do we work to reconcile the fallen believer to the faith community.

Sadly, we are even more hesitant to celebrate the spiritual restoration of a wayward believer. Imagine how wonderful it would be if we publicly acknowledged when grievances have been settled, hard feelings softened, transgressions forgiven, broken families healed, and sinners brought back to God. Perhaps one Sunday a year we could testify to God's goodness in each of these areas. This is the sort of thing that happened at the end of the parable Jesus told concerning the lost son, which is this week's lesson focus.

Introduction for Youth

Topic: *Welcome Home!*

The speaker at a youth rally read Jesus' parable about the lost son. Afterward, a group of adolescents rushed to the front and asked him where he had found the story. They were astonished to learn that Jesus originally told this parable and that it could be found in the Bible.

The parable caught the attention of these young people because it revealed something about God they had never heard before. They found it hard to believe that the father in the story would run out and welcome home his rebellious son rather than scold and discipline the youth.

Teens long to hear that God wants them to come to Him just as they are. Yet they fear that Christians will judge and ignore them because of their shortcomings. We can put them at ease by sharing that all of us are sinners in need of God's mercy and grace. The Good News is that He is waiting to welcome us into His family. Perhaps we can let others know!

Concepts for Children

Topic: *Lost and Found*

1. Jesus told a story about a young man who left home and got into a lot of trouble.
2. When the young person returned, his father welcomed and forgave him.
3. We hurt ourselves when we disobey God's Word.
4. God is ready and wants to forgive us when we return to Him.
5. We can tell our friends about God's love and forgiveness.

Lesson Commentary

I. LIVING RECKLESSLY: LUKE 15:11-16

A. The Son's Demand: vss. 11-12

Jesus continued: "There was a man who had two sons. The younger one said to his father, 'Father, give me my share of the estate.' So he divided his property between them."

By now, Jesus was heading with unshakable resolve toward Jerusalem (see Luke 9:51; 13:22; 17:11; 18:31). Throughout the years of Jesus' earthly ministry, He attracted the outcasts of society, including "tax collectors and sinners" (5:30; 7:34; 15:1). The Jewish tax collectors usually gathered much more than what was reasonable. Also, they were despised by their own people as collaborators with the occupying Roman forces. (One of Jesus' disciples, Matthew, was a tax collector; see Matt. 9:9; 10:3.) "Sinners" (Luke 15:1) referred to immoral people or those who followed occupations that the religious leaders claimed violated God's law. The transgressors included criminals, prostitutes, and other people with bad reputations.

The Pharisees and scribes took the Mosaic law seriously and followed strict disciplines designed to promote holiness. In an earlier day, they may have represented the virtuous lifestyle God wanted His people to follow. But by the first century A.D., the elitists had exchanged a sincere love of God for sterile legalism. As they became increasingly caught up in rule-keeping, the Pharisees and scribes removed themselves from those who could not achieve their excessive standards or conform to their burdensome rituals. In self-righteous indignation, the religious leaders allowed their hearts to become calloused toward others.

Tragically, the religious tradition of the day offered the outcasts of society nothing but harsh judgment. In contrast, they sensed Jesus' love, and found hope in His teachings about repentance and forgiveness. Though Jesus did not condone their sins, He welcomed them into His Father's kingdom when they repented and followed Him. Not surprisingly, the Pharisees and scribes complained that Jesus associated with individuals they considered despicable (vs. 2). The elitists were convinced that being around disreputable people made one spiritually unclean. In this way of thinking, Jesus could not be from God, for He didn't remain pure in His associations. So the religious leaders rejected Him.

Jesus, however, was not constrained by the distorted views of the elitists. He knew He could mingle with sinners and remain morally pure. In fact, He sought to change their lives by saving them from their iniquities. Of course, the Pharisees and scribes neither grasped nor accepted what Jesus was doing. So, rather than praise God for His mercy to these outcasts, the religious leaders criticized Jesus for being loving and accepting. They saw no need to repent themselves, and they couldn't accept the truth that God would allow returning sinners into His kingdom.

It's helpful to recall that over the course of Jesus' earthly ministry, the elitists grew increasingly opposed to Him. They envied His popularity, resented His challenges to their traditions, and hated His exposure of their hypocrisy. Undoubtedly, the Pharisees and scribes wondered whether Jesus had political aspirations and worried how His increasing influence would affect their control over the people. The religious leaders allowed their petty concerns to blind them to the truth that Jesus was their Messiah.

Jesus refused to ignore the latest charge made by the religious leaders—namely, that He welcomed sinners. In a series of three parables, the Savior contrasted the attitude of the Pharisees and scribes with that of God toward the lost. The elitists taught that God would welcome a remorseful sinner. But these parables teach that God also *seeks out* transgressors. In the parable of the lost sheep (vss. 3-7), Jesus noted that the Lord and His angels rejoice when the wayward repent and come to Him in faith. In the parable of the lost coin (vss. 8-10), Jesus contrasted the exclusiveness of the Pharisees and scribes with the unconditional love of God. And in the parable of the lost son (vss. 11-32), Jesus gave a striking illustration of God's compassion for rebellious human beings.

In the first story, the shepherd demonstrates genuine concern by making personal contact, rather than by sending someone else to look for the sheep. The shepherd was willing to inconvenience himself to rescue the one lost animal, by descending into a difficult situation, until the missing creature was reclaimed. This is also true with regard to how our heavenly Father rescued us. In addition, the summons to rejoice is similar to the joy of the eternal Shepherd when one who is lost is brought into His fold.

In the second story, Jesus used the episode of a woman who lost a coin to get the religious leaders to think about two questions. First, did they seek those who were lost from God with the same intensity as the woman in the story who searched for her missing coin? Second, did the elitists share the joy of heaven when a transgressor repented and came into a personal relationship with the Creator? Regrettably, while God's angels rejoiced over the salvation of the lost, the Pharisees and scribes complained and found fault with Jesus' methods.

In the third story, Jesus drew attention to a father of high social standing who had two sons (vs. 11). Jesus noted that the younger son (possibly no older than 18) demanded his inheritance immediately so he could live independently on his own terms. In ancient times, the firstborn son was entitled to two-thirds of his father's property, and normally that did not occur until the father either died or was too old to manage the property (Deut. 21:17). Although fathers sometimes chose to divide up their inheritance early and retire from managing their estates, the sons were never expected to initiate such a division.

Consequently, for the younger son to demand his inheritance early showed his arrogant disregard for his father's authority as the head of the family. In effect, the son was saying, "Father, I wish you were dead so I could have my share of your money now!" Jesus' parable suggests that the younger son would receive one-third of the estate. Both the younger son's outrageous demand and the father's granting of it were contrary to the social customs of the day. In fact, to make such a demand amounted to rebellion, for obedience to and respect for one's parents were emphasized in ancient Jewish culture. The father had the right to refuse his son's request, but he didn't (Luke 15:12). Because the father gave in, Jesus' audience may have concluded that the father was a fool. They would discover, however, that the father dealt with his son in a wise and loving manner.

Jesus' audience would have intuitively understood He was using this story to teach about the insurrection of sinners against God. In the current parable, the wealthy parent represented the Father in heaven. The younger son embodied the Gentiles and sinners, especially those who recognized their need for God's forgiveness. The older son epitomized the elitists, who though claiming to remain true to their religious heritage, wallowed in a toxic cesspool of self-righteousness (see vss. 25-32). Amazingly, the Pharisees and scribes, despite their vaulted claims, failed to see their need for repentance and forgiveness.

B. The Squandered Inheritance: vss. 13-16

"Not long after that, the younger son got together all he had, set off for a distant country and there squandered his wealth in wild living. After he had spent everything, there was a severe famine in that whole country, and he began to be in need. So he went and hired himself out to a citizen of that country, who sent him to his fields to feed pigs. He longed to fill his stomach with the pods that the pigs were eating, but no one gave him anything."

The impulsive and headstrong young man, after selling off his portion of the family inheritance for money, did not waste any time in asserting his independence. After only a few days, he packed whatever he owned and relocated to a foreign "country" (Luke 15:13). This decision was prompted by a desire to get as far away as possible from his father's attentive gaze. In that distant place somewhere outside of Palestine, the young man fell in with a wild bunch of people. It did not take long for his reckless, immoral lifestyle to deplete and wipe out his financial resources. We don't need to have the details about what he did, for we can easily imagine that his inheritance was wasted virtually overnight.

Gambling, drinking, and carousing were well-practiced activities throughout the Roman Empire, less among Jews than among Gentiles. Perhaps there were some in Jesus' audience who could identify with the young man's moral downfall. If so, Jesus' parable resonated with them. Jesus did not specify how long the young man continued in his debased ways, but the impression is that he quickly became destitute. Compounding his difficulty was the onslaught of an intense shortage of food (whether due to drought or pestilence) that spread throughout the entire region (vs. 14). It did not take long for the young man's circumstance to grow acute. Because he had nothing left, he began to starve.

To deal with the problem, the young man found a job feeding pigs (vs. 15). As noted in last week's lesson, Jewish law labeled pigs as ritually unclean animals (see Lev. 11:7; Deut. 14:8). Soon, the young man wished he could be eating some "pods" (and its sweet, pulpy seeds; Luke 15:16) produced by the carob tree, which he gave to the swine. But no one took pity on him, not even those who once befriended him when he was flush with cash. One could hardly picture a more degrading situation. The young man vividly exemplified moral and spiritual lostness, as well as bankruptcy and hunger. But perhaps some in Jesus' audience felt the young man had gotten what he deserved, especially since his sins were many. For instance, he had dishonored his father, squandered his inheritance, and hired himself out to a pig farmer.

II. EXPERIENCING UNCONDITIONAL FORGIVENESS: LUKE 15:17-24

A. A Pivotal Decision: vss. 17-19

"When he came to his senses, he said, 'How many of my father's hired men have food to spare, and here I am starving to death! I will set out and go back to my father and say to him: Father, I have sinned against heaven and against you. I am no longer worthy to be called your son; make me like one of your hired men.'"

Possibly to the amazement of some in Jesus' audience, the parable took an unexpected turn. The wayward youth's dire straits forced him to take inventory of his situation. On the one hand, his father's servants back at home ate as much food as they wanted. On the other hand, the father's distraught son was dying of hunger (Luke 15:17). As a result, he recognized the error of his ways, repented of his sin, and decided to return to his father. What a radical change in attitude! The young man had started out being arrogant, greedy, and selfish. He also thought his money could buy him happiness and friends in a foreign land. But then he found himself abandoned, starving, and alone. He wisely decided to discard his debased lifestyle.

It wasn't easy for the young man to recognize the extreme error of his ways. He had to admit he was completely wrong about how to find true happiness. He also had to acknowledge that immorality had ruined him, rather than satisfied him. And he had to affirm that his greed was iniquitous. True repentance means a change of mind that leads to a change of life. This is what happened to the once insubordinate youth. He gave up the debauchery he previously had cherished and confessed that he had transgressed against God and his father (vs. 18). Then the young man, being convinced of his own unworthiness, rehearsed his confession. He was willing to forego his place as a son in the family and accept a job as a temporary day laborer, if only his father would welcome him back (vs. 19).

Perhaps some of Jesus' listeners were just as amazed by the son's return as they were by his departure and sinful life. Was he truly repentant for the monstrous transgressions he had committed? Was he simply acting out of desperation because he was starving? Of course, we can't presume to know the once-intransigent youth's motives when he repented. Yet it's clear that God used the young man's awful circumstances to get him to think uprightly once again.

B. A Joyous Reunion: vss. 20-24

"So he got up and went to his father. But while he was still a long way off, his father saw him and was filled with compassion for him; he ran to his son, threw his arms around him and kissed him. The son said to him, 'Father, I have sinned against heaven and against you. I am no longer worthy to be called your son.' But the father said to his servants, 'Quick! Bring the best robe and put it on him. Put a ring on his finger and sandals on his feet. Bring the fattened calf and kill it. Let's have a feast and celebrate. For this son of mine was dead and is alive again; he was lost and is found.' So they began to celebrate."

It's unnecessary for us to pinpoint the young man's exact motives. Yes, he was starving. But his decision to return home seems to go deeper than his desire to satisfy his hunger. He genuinely recognized how terribly he had sinned, and he was humble enough to rejoin his family and confess his wrongdoing. Given the fact that the father could have rejected his son for his rebellious lifestyle, the young man took an enormous risk by throwing himself at his father's mercy. It was one thing for the son to wake up and go home, but quite another for his father to welcome him back with open arms and affection (Luke 15:20).

While the youth was still a long way off, his father saw him coming. Perhaps the parent, longing for his son to return, frequently interrupted what he was doing to gaze at the horizon. Long ago, with his heart aching, he watched his son disappear down the road. But the father always hoped that one day he would see his son coming back to the estate. When it finally happened, the father could not restrain his feelings. Being filled with deep-seated love, he hurried to reach his son, hug him, and kiss him. In ancient Palestinian culture, persons with status and seniority would not degrade and humiliate themselves by running. Yet the father's affection for his son compelled him to break the rules.

We can only imagine how difficult it was for the son—who returned feeling chastened by his previous folly—to look past his father's effusive display of affection and repeat the memorized repentance speech (vs. 21). Evidently, the father interrupted his son's admission of guilt, choosing instead to summon the household slaves. He directed them to quickly locate the finest "robe" (vs. 22; signifying honor and favor) and place the long, flowing garment on the son. The young man was also to get a signet "ring" (denoting royal status and authority) for his finger and "sandals" (befitting a cherished family member) for his bare feet. Moreover, the father ordered his bondservants to prepare a prized, grain-fed "calf" (vs. 23) to be served at a lavish, festive banquet.

Why all the fuss? The father explained that his son, who was as good as "dead" (vs. 24), had now returned to life, at least in a moral and spiritual sense. So the young man's homecoming was reason enough to begin eating and celebrating.

Though Jesus did not use the word *grace* in this parable, it showcases the meaning of the term as it is used elsewhere in the New Testament (for example, see Eph. 2:5, 8; Rom. 3:24). Grace means God giving us what we do not deserve. Admittedly, this is the opposite of how the world thinks. Nonetheless, by God's unmerited favor, He acquits transgressors (see Rom. 4:5).

It's important for us not to miss the contrast between the response of the father and that of the older brother. The father unconditionally forgave because he was filled with love. The eldest son, however, refused to forgive because he was bitter about the alleged injustice he felt had occurred. His resentment indicated that he was just as lost to the father's love as his younger brother had been (vss. 25-31). Jesus noted that when the older brother complained about the feast for his formerly rebellious brother, the father restated the explanation he gave to the slaves (vss. 24, 32). Here we find a key point Jesus wanted to make. The religious leaders failed to understand that the Father desires to save sinners. Despite their spiritually lost condition, they can be redeemed through faith in the Son. This is the Good News worth sharing with others!

Discussion Questions

1. Why did the religious leaders criticize and oppose Jesus?
2. Why did the father's youngest son demand his share of the inheritance?
3. Why was the father's response to his son's return so amazing?
4. What caused you to turn to God in repentance and seek His forgiveness?
5. What can we do to be as grace-oriented as God is toward the lost?

Contemporary Application

We often hear about human catastrophes that compare with the tragedy Jesus described. So, Jesus' parable of the lost son is extremely relevant. However, we do not often hear about people whom the Lord has freed from sin. This would include accounts of adolescents and adults who have experienced God's love, mercy, and forgiveness and are eager to tell believers about it. Is this because our churches are not doing all they can to reach out to the lost with the message of salvation? Is it due to the fact that some Christians find it hard to welcome those who need Jesus the most?

As we've seen from Jesus' parable of the lost son, it's much easier to judge the wayward than it is to love and accept them unconditionally. It's also less risky to act righteous than it is to be merciful. Perhaps this is because we put a higher priority on our own welfare than on that of the lost. Or maybe we have fallen into the self-righteous trap of the Pharisees. Whatever the reason, this week's lesson reminds us that the mission of the church is to tell the lost about the Father's love and mercy through faith in the Son. There's no other goal of greater eternal value than that!

A Decision to Forgive

Scripture

Background Scripture: *Luke 17:1-10*
Scripture Lesson: *Luke 17:1-10*
Key Verse: "Watch yourselves. If your brother sins, rebuke him, and if he repents, forgive him." *Luke 17:3*
Scripture Lesson for Children: *Luke 17:1-10*
Key Verse for Children: "If your brother sins, rebuke him, and if he repents, forgive him." *Luke 17:3*

Lesson Aim

To be equitable and responsible in our ministry to others.

Lesson Setting

Time: A.D. *30*
Place: On the way to Jerusalem

Lesson Outline

A Decision to Forgive
   I. Living Equitably: Luke 17:1-4
      A. Being a Positive Influence on Others: vss. 1-2
      B. Dealing with Sin Prudently: vss. 3-4
  II. Living Responsibly: Luke 17:5-10
      A. Potent Faith: vss. 5-6
      B. Dutiful Service: vss. 7-10

Introduction for Adults

Topic: *Being Like Jesus*

In 1859, the poet Emily Dickinson wrote, "Success is counted sweetest by those who never succeed." She had in mind individuals who believe success in life for them is just around the corner. Presumably, it's the result of getting a different job or having the right kinds of things or winning a lottery jackpot.

From this week's lesson we learn that people who pursue what the world calls *success* will never really succeed. After all, there is always more of whatever they crave just beyond their reach.

Jesus wants His followers to be successful. Yet, He redefines for us what real success entails. To Him, being last is being first. Also, faith-inspired greatness is giving oneself in humble service to others, as He did for us. Here we find that to reach the pinnacle of greatness, we need to climb down, not up.

Introduction for Youth

Topic: *Ministering to Others*

Jesus defined greatness in terms of humbly serving others. Consider the example of Alice. Though she has been blind from birth, every day she walks from her apartment to the nearby train station, takes the train to the city, holds down an important job, and spends several hours each week ministering in her local church. To look at Alice, one would think she is totally helpless. But in more than 40 years of blindness, she has learned how to take care of herself and serve others with remarkable ingenuity and courage.

Alice has moved from helplessness to boldness. She models kingdom greatness by being a powerful witness in her church and community. Her commitment to Jesus stands out in her life, her demeanor, and her values. Instead of whimpering and complaining, she looks to the Lord for strength to serve others.

Alice shines as an example of what it means to be great at any age. And her life illustrates the kind of courage we all need—even as young people. God calls every one of us to live by faith.

Concepts for Children

Topic: *Depend on Jesus*

1. Jesus warned against encouraging other people to sin.
2. Jesus wants us to forgive those who have been mean to us.
3. Jesus wants us to depend on Him in whatever we do.
4. Jesus wants us to be thoughtful of other people and their needs.
5. With Jesus' help, we can control how we act.

Lesson Commentary

I. LIVING EQUITABLY: LUKE 17:1-4

A. Being a Positive Influence on Others: vss. 1-2

Jesus said to his disciples: "Things that cause people to sin are bound to come, but woe to that person through whom they come. It would be better for him to be thrown into the sea with a millstone tied around his neck than for him to cause one of these little ones to sin.

As noted in last week's lesson, Jesus was resolutely journeying with His disciples toward Jerusalem (see Luke 17:11; 18:31). Along the way, Jesus sought to prepare them for the time when He would no longer be with them. He especially wanted them to understand and apply basic truths they needed to know. In this case, He drew their attention to common human experience, in which all sorts of enticements to transgress seemed inevitable (especially due to the tendency for people to act immorally). In some contexts, the Greek noun translated "cause . . . to sin" (17:1) referred to a bait or trap that snared an animal. In other contexts, the noun denoted a stone or other object in a pathway that caused travelers to stumble and fall. Metaphorically, the noun conveyed the idea of misleading others to compromise their faith and spiritually fall away.

Jesus used the Greek interjection rendered "woe" to draw attention to the sorrow that awaited those (like the religious leaders) who tripped up His followers. The Savior declared that it would be more advantageous for the offenders to experience a premature death than to live long enough to lure and entrap believers in wrongdoing (vs. 2). Jesus vividly illustrated His point by referring to people allowing a "millstone" weighing hundreds of pounds to be placed around their "neck" and then being cast into a large body of water, where they eventually would drown. In Jesus' day, a mill consisting of two extremely heavy stones was used to pulverize grain (such as wheat) into flour. A laborer would pour grain through a hole in the upper, rubbing stone (which was either flat or convex). Then a donkey tethered to a wooden handle (on the stone's outer edge) would turn the object. In this way, the kernels were ground against the rough base stone (which had either a flat or concave surface).

The Greek adjective translated "little ones" could refer broadly to any of Jesus' disciples, whom the offenders regarded as being insignificant or unimportant. An examination of Matthew 18:6-7 and Mark 9:42 suggests the adjective could also have a narrower connotation. In this case, it would denote impressionable children, whom adults led astray (whether intentionally or unintentionally) and in the process undermined the faith of the young persons. From these passages we learn that a person's character is evident in the way that individual treats those of little consequence in the eyes of the world. Although here Jesus was talking about children, His point applied to all who were powerless, vulnerable, or spiritually immature. Matthew 18:1-4 adds that those who come to God with the humble, unpretentious faith of little children will be the greatest in the divine kingdom. While the age of the young person is not mentioned, the Greek noun used in this passage often denoted a very small child.

B. Dealing with Sin Prudently: vss. 3-4

"So watch yourselves. If your brother sins, rebuke him, and if he repents, forgive him. If he sins against you seven times in a day, and seven times comes back to you and says, 'I repent,' forgive him."

It is unclear whether the imperative "watch yourselves" (Luke 17:3) points back to verse 2 or looks ahead to verse 4. If the former case, Jesus was warning about the disastrous consequence of enticing another believer to sin. Or, if Jesus had verse 4 in mind, He was exhorting His disciples to be careful in the way they handled circumstances in which their fellow believers committed misdeeds. The Greek verb rendered "sins" (vs. 3) metaphorically pictures missing the mark of something that is being sought. Depending on the context, the verb could signify either rebellious conduct or negligent actions. In either situation, the inappropriate behavior resulted in guilt.

Jesus told His disciples that when one of His followers transgressed against them (whether deliberately or accidentally), the faith community was neither to ignore the circumstance nor become hardened against the offender. Instead, those who were wronged were to censure the believer who sinned. Some people use verse 3 to justify the harsh ways they deal with those who fall into trespasses. But the purpose of the "rebuke" was to lead the wayward believer to repentance. The underlying Greek verb conveys the idea of experiencing a change of heart (involving both one's thoughts and feelings). The outcome is that one abandons iniquitous conduct for behavior that is characterized by virtue and integrity.

Once the offended party expressed strong disapproval over another believer's misdeeds, the persons in the right were to "forgive" the remorseful individual. In the Greek text, Jesus used the imperative form of the verb to indicate that His aggrieved disciples were morally obligated to let the matter go. Admittedly, human nature seems more inclined toward judging than forgiving. Nonetheless, when a believer repented, those who were wronged needed to jettison all feelings of resentment.

In the first century A.D., the rabbis taught that a perfect person would forgive three times. Here Jesus more than doubled the conventional admonition. Yet, He did not intend that number to be taken literally. Jesus was not telling His disciples to keep records so they could cut off people after forgiving them "seven times" (vs. 4) in one day. Christlike forgiveness was to be unlimited. The unconditional forgiveness believers have in union with the Son was motivation for doing so (see Eph. 4:32; Col. 3:13). Making allowance for the faults of others and being willing to overlook an offense were the means by which believers clothed themselves with Christian virtues (see Eph. 4:22-24; Col. 3:12).

Matthew 18:21-22 records an exchange between Jesus and Peter, who asked how many times he should forgive a fellow believer who had mistreated him. Jesus stated that forgiveness should be extended an inexhaustible number of times. Of course, there could be occasions when we may object, "I can't forgive him for what he did to me," or "I'll never forget the pain she caused me—so don't tell me to forgive!" Letting go of wrongs and hurts isn't easy. In fact, it's impossible when we try to do it on our own. Forgiveness is possible only when we ask the Lord to do the forgiving through us.

In Galatians 6:1, Paul urged balancing every admonishment with the attitude of tenderness. The apostle had in mind situations in which believers are "caught in a sin." The idea behind this phrase is not that others have found out someone's sinning, but rather that the sinner has allowed himself or herself to be trapped or enticed by sin. Once the person's sinning has become public knowledge, Paul said those who were spiritual should help restore the transgressor. The idea is that other Christians should support and guide the struggling believer as he or she recovers from the sinning.

Restoration of church members who have sinned can mean different things depending on factors in the situation. Here are some possible steps in restoration: (1) The restorers help those sinning recognize the gravity of their sin, come to a point of true repentance, and confess their sins privately and (if necessary) publicly. (2) The restorers help those who sinned accept God's forgiveness once the ones who sinned have genuinely repented. (3) The restorers help the repentant sinners plan strategies to deal with the effects of their sin and to change their behavior. (4) The restorers help the reformed sinners move back into full participation in church life and service.

This process of restoration requires sensitivity on the part of the restorers. Its purpose is to draw sinners toward spiritual healing, not to make them feel bad. Therefore, restoration must be done gently, not sternly or vindictively. Unless restoration is performed carefully, those who sinned can rebel and fall into worse sin. This process can also harbor dangers for the restorers. Putting them in a position of moral authority may tempt them to feel superior. That's why Paul warned restorers to watch themselves to avoid the risk of becoming proud, and so falling into sin themselves. We all have cause for humility.

II. LIVING RESPONSIBLY: LUKE 17:5-10

A. Potent Faith: vss. 5-6

The apostles said to the Lord, "Increase our faith!" He replied, "If you have faith as small as a mustard seed, you can say to this mulberry tree, 'Be uprooted and planted in the sea,' and it will obey you.

We can imagine Jesus' "apostles" (Luke 17:5) feeling overwhelmed by the seemingly impossible admonition to forgive. Recognizing their weakness in this area prompted them to ask Jesus to "increase" their "faith." On the one hand, His followers already trusted in Him. On the other hand, they sensed that their belief in Him could be strengthened and its depth made greater. Hebrews 11:1 reveals that saving faith is a present and continuing reality. It is the confident assurance that gives substance to what we "hope for." Faith is also the evidence for the believers' conviction of the certainty of "what [they] do not see."

It was the faith of the Old Testament saints that made them pleasing to God. Their trust in the Lord was well-founded, for He is the Creator and Ruler of the universe (see Ps. 146:6). Jesus' followers perceive with the mind that the temporal ages were set in order by God's spoken "command" (Heb. 11:3). Biblical faith also enables Christians to recognize and accept the truth that what is seen was made out of what cannot be seen. Despite all appearances to the contrary, God gave existence to the cosmos. Believers have nothing but the Word of God to explain how life first began, and they affirm what it has revealed to them.

Jesus, in response to His disciples' request concerning faith, did not offer a quick-fix solution. Instead, He told them to make effective use of the "faith" (Luke 17:6) they already had, even if it seemed to be no larger than a "mustard seed." Though the mustard seed was tiny (the smallest seed that farmers in Palestine knew about), it produced a large shrub. The cultivated black mustard, which was commonplace in Palestine, could grow to a height of over 10 feet. In a region with a dry climate and few trees of any size, such large plants received a lot of attention.

Jesus disclosed that small, vital amounts of faith were enough to accomplish seemingly insurmountable feats. For example, He stated that even if the "faith" (vs. 6) of His followers seemed tiny, it was still anchored to their all-powerful, ever-living Savior. With rhetorical flair, He had the disciples imagine a circumstance in which they commanded a "mulberry tree" to pull itself up by its roots and replant itself in the ocean. In turn, the tree would do as it was told. Hebrews 11:1 clarifies that this kind of faith makes what seems undoable a fact, not by the force of human will, but by a settled conviction that the Creator is performing the action.

The black mulberry tree, which could grow to a height of over 30 feet, has long been known for its deep, strong, and widespread roots. It was said that because of its roots, it could stand for six centuries, and nothing could dislodge it. So, in Jesus' day, to "move a mulberry tree" became an expression that meant doing something humanly impossible. Yet, even what people could not accomplish in their own limited strength could occur through faith in God. Ephesians 3:20 indicates that His ability to meet the needs of His people far exceeds any request they could make in prayer or even imagine requesting.

B. Dutiful Service: vss. 7-10

"Suppose one of you had a servant plowing or looking after the sheep. Would he say to the servant when he comes in from the field, 'Come along now and sit down to eat'? Would he not rather say, 'Prepare

my supper, get yourself ready and wait on me while I eat and drink; after that you may eat and drink'? Would he thank the servant because he did what he was told to do? So you also, when you have done everything you were told to do, should say, 'We are unworthy servants; we have only done our duty.'"

In Luke 17:7-10, Jesus used a parable to summarize His statements about basic Christian duties. He asked His followers to envision a master pampering his slave. Presumably, the disciples would have laughed at the thought. After all, in the first century A.D., bondservants were considered living tools, that is, implements owned by the master. This meant that slaves did their fieldwork (whether tilling the soil for planting crops or tending a flock of sheep) without expecting to receive any special praise or commendation in return, and none was given. Moreover, the slaves first attended to their master's needs (such as providing him with food and drink). Then, after the master was satisfied, the bondservants would be permitted to eat and drink. This was the established and followed protocol.

Christians are to be like servants who willingly do their tasks. This does not mean gritting their teeth and forcing themselves to perform good deeds to earn God's appreciation. In fact, no amount of pious works could be enough to merit His approval. The world says people are successful when they are in control. Jesus taught that His disciples were successful when they surrendered to His will. The implication is that He wants humble followers, not power brokers. Here we see that the mark of Christlikeness is genuine humility, not hubris. This does not mean believers are to say coyly, "I'm just a humble Christian, who's not worth too much." Then, all the while they hope someone will contradict them and remark how fantastic, talented, and wonderful they are. Likewise, believers are not to use humility as an excuse for refusing to do their best.

In Ephesians 6:5-9 and Colossians 3:22-24, Paul provided instructions for slaves and masters who were believers. The apostle advised slaves not only to obey their masters, but also to have the right attitude—as though their labor was for the Lord. Along with rewards for those who obeyed Jesus were punishments for those who rebelled against Him. Furthermore, Paul commanded masters to be humane in their treatment of slaves, remembering that they, too, had a heavenly Master. These same principles can be applied to Christians today who labor in the workforce. How supervisors and subordinates serve one another can bring great honor to God.

The many wars the Roman Empire engaged in produced enormous numbers of slaves from around the world. Owners wielded absolute power over their slaves, and many of them treated their forced labor inhumanely. Naturally, a number of slave revolts occurred that prompted the Roman authorities to enact even stricter laws. Quite often, runaway slaves were executed. During Paul's day, slaves in general received a more merciful treatment than those who suffered during the first decades of the Roman Empire. In fact, slaves often occupied important positions in wealthy families, in government, and as tutors. In many cases, they lived better than the poor. Paul neither expressed his approval nor disapproval of this pervasive institution. Instead, he first sought to change the people within the system, probably hoping the system would eventually be changed as well (see also the commentary in lesson 5 regarding the issue of slavery in the first century A.D.).

Discussion Questions

1. What is so terrible about causing other believers to stumble spiritually?
2. How well does your church deal with members involved in serious sin? How can you help?
3. What relationship is there between trusting in Jesus and being effective in ministry?
4. What does it mean to be a humble servant in God's kingdom?
5. Besides Jesus, who else do you think is a model of humble servanthood?

Contemporary Application

Jesus warned about the consequences of enticing believers to sin. He also taught His disciples to forgive those who repent of their wrongdoing. Then, when the disciples asked Him to increase their faith, He said those with even a small amount of faith could accomplish great things. He also encouraged His disciples to humbly perform their duties.

Perhaps we are most vulnerable when we think we don't need other people. And possibly that's why Jesus envisioned a fellowship of believers together fighting the battle against sin, rather than either fighting against or exploiting one another. He talked about our being individually responsible, but He also called us to be responsible for one another.

Being equitable and responsible in our ministry to others starts by entrusting our lives to Jesus. In turn, He empowers us to evaluate how much time we spend feeding our hearts and minds on the truths of the Gospel. Confession and repentance are demanded. In places where we fall short, we must acknowledge the error of our ways. We should also seek the help of others to keep us on the road to godly living. As we rejoice and praise the Lord together, we allow the words of the Savior to penetrate our hearts and minds.

Another key element is our readiness to obey Jesus. This, in turn, can lead us down unexpected paths. At first this might seem scary to us. But then we come to see that the sovereign Ruler of the universe knows what is best for us. We learn through life experiences to wait on His timing when it comes to enjoying the blessings of faith. Some of these come in this life, but most are received in eternity. Regardless of how many options lay before us, it is always Jesus' will that we act in harmony with His Word.

An Attitude of Gratitude

Scripture

Background Scripture: *Luke 17:11-19*
Scripture Lesson: *Luke 17:11-19*
Key Verse: One of them, when he saw he was healed, came back, praising God in a loud voice. *Luke 17:15*
Scripture Lesson for Children: *Luke 17:11-19*
Key Verse for Children: [The healed man] threw himself at Jesus' feet and thanked him—and he was a Samaritan. *Luke 17:16*

Lesson Aim

To understand that Jesus is uniquely able to help the afflicted.

Lesson Setting

Time: A.D. *30*
Place: On the way to Jerusalem

Lesson Outline

An Attitude of Gratitude

I. Being Cured of Leprosy: Luke 17:11-14
    A. *A Request to Be Healed: vss. 11-13*
    B. *An Experience of Cleansing: vs. 14*
II. Expressing Gratitude: Luke 17:15-19
    A. *Displaying Thanks: vss. 15-16*
    B. *Receiving Commendation: vss. 17-19*

Introduction for Adults

Topic: *Having the Right Attitude*

We should be thankful that Jesus heals us, as sinners, to spiritual wholeness, for otherwise none of us would be saved. Yet, once we become Christians and settle down among the nice people in church, we often forget that Jesus wants to touch the lives of all people with His reconciling power.

Sometimes those whom Jesus calls embarrass us, and we feel uncomfortable in their presence. We don't approve of the way they look and the things they do. Would we ever sit down to dinner with people who are social outcasts, like the ten lepers Jesus graciously healed (the focus of this week's lesson)?

The church's hardest task is to expand its vision to unlikely candidates for salvation and fellowship. Once our lives get cleaned up, we don't want to get dirty again. But if we refuse to reach sinners like Jesus did, then the church becomes a holier-than-thou club. It fails to fulfill its divine mission.

Introduction for Youth

Topic: *Gratitude*

All children reach the stage when they realize they cannot fix everything on their own. They need their parents to bandage the scrape, clean up the spill, or ease them through painful trials. As children grow up, suddenly it's humiliating for them to think they cannot help themselves. They may pretend that there is nothing wrong or that they don't need anyone's help. Regrettably, they refuse to reach out.

As we move through the twenty-first century, there still remain physical and spiritual ailments that even the marvels of modern science cannot remedy. Thankfully, Jesus, the divine healer, is able to do what medicine cannot. Just as He miraculously intervened in the lives of ten lepers (the focus of this week's lesson), so too He alone is uniquely able to help the afflicted today.

Concepts for Children

Topic: *Thank You!*

1. Jesus and His followers were walking to Jerusalem.
2. Ten men with a skin disease asked Jesus for help.
3. Jesus healed the ten men.
4. Only one of the men, a person from another country, was thankful.
5. Jesus is pleased when we thank Him for helping us.

Lesson Commentary

I. BEING CURED OF LEPROSY: LUKE 17:11-14

A. A Request to Be Healed: vss. 11-13

Now on his way to Jerusalem, Jesus traveled along the border between Samaria and Galilee. As he was going into a village, ten men who had leprosy met him. They stood at a distance and called out in a loud voice, "Jesus, Master, have pity on us!"

In last week's lesson, we examined Jesus' teachings in Luke 17:1-10 about sin, forgiveness, faith, and duty. This week, we turn our attention to verses 11-19 and the encounter Jesus had with ten lepers. The third Synoptic Gospel portrays Jesus as the divine Redeemer, whose mission included seeking and saving the "lost" (19:10). Accordingly, Jesus is depicted as both the Jewish Messiah and the Savior for all the people of the world. So far this quarter in our study through selectively chosen portions of Luke, we have encountered the Gospel's emphasis on the truth that redemption is not solely the possession of one group of people. It is open to individuals of all races and all human conditions. Put differently, the salvation Jesus won through His sacrificial death at Calvary is sufficiently broad to include all persons.

Because of Jesus' redemptive mission, it was divinely necessary for Him to begin the pilgrimage that would lead to Jerusalem and the cross. Luke's account of Jesus' trek to the holy city first takes in His ministry in Judea (9:51—13:21), and then His activities in and around Perea (13:22—19:27). In Jesus' day, Judea primarily denoted the southern part of Palestine, though on occasion the name was used to refer to its western environs. Perea was the land to the east of the Jordan River (hence, the alternate name of the Transjordan). To the north of Judea lay Samaria, a region roughly extending from Antipatris in the south to Jezreel in the north. The bulk of Samaria's economy was tied to agriculture (due to its fertile farmlands) and trade (especially occurring along major international routes). North of Samaria lay Galilee, a rustic, scenic, and mountainous region extending approximately 30 miles from east to west and 60 miles from north to south. The economy was diverse (ranging from farming to fishing) and the inhabitants were renowned for their political autonomy.

During this final phase of Jesus' earthly ministry, He had several goals He sought to complete. He wanted to challenge the religious elite, especially their erroneous views about God and the nature of His relationship to humankind. Jesus also sought to prepare His disciples for His crucifixion, resurrection, and ascension to "heaven" (9:51). Moreover, due to the fact that the power brokers in Jerusalem rejected Jesus as their Messiah (see 13:34-35), He endeavored to invite the outcasts of society to trust in Him for eternal life (including swindlers, crooks, adulterers, tax collectors, and lepers; see 18:11). By Jesus' own example, He demonstrated to His disciples what it meant to follow Him, even if it included anguish and rejection. One common thread between people of the first century A.D. and people living today is their need for a Savior. Men and women are bruised and battered by life's disappointments, and so were people in Jesus' day. People today must face the awfulness of their own sin, just as people did in the first century. And people today can find strength and hope through faith in the Redeemer, just as did His earliest disciples.

The preceding observations are illustrated by Jesus' encounter with ten lepers. According to 17:11, Jesus was passing through the area between Samaria and Galilee. This was not a haphazard decision on His part. Instead, Jesus was intentional to arrive at the border of these two regions and minister there, even for a relatively short time. On one occasion, Jesus and His disciples were on the outskirts of a small town when ten men with "leprosy" (vs. 12) spotted the visitors. Because of this dreaded skin disease, the group endured an isolated existence as social outcasts. The ten men maintained a certain distance from the Savior. Yet they were still close enough to be heard shouting their plea for the itinerant rabbi from Nazareth literally to have "mercy" (see vs. 13) on them. This was a request to be healed, not a demand for alms or other forms of charity. In referring to Jesus as "Master," the lepers affirmed that He not only was a distinguished teacher but also a person of high status.

B. An Experience of Cleansing: vs. 14

When he saw them, he said, "Go, show yourselves to the priests." And as they went, they were cleansed.

In contrast to the religious elitists in Jerusalem, Jesus was not put off by the ten lepers who implored Him to show them compassion. The Redeemer directed these social outcasts to present themselves to the local "priests" (Luke 17:14) to verify they had been healed. The lepers' willingness to do so was a demonstration of their faith (see vs. 19). After all, Jesus did not perform any flamboyant ritual, such as waving His hands over the lepers and invoking God's name (see 2 Kings 5:11). Instead, the ten lepers simply took Jesus at His word. And as they went along, they were cured of their disease (Luke 17:14). The Greek text literally says they were "cleansed," which implies that their physical restoration also resulted in the removal of their ceremonial contamination or impurity.

"Leprosy" is a term used in Scripture to describe several types of infectious and incurable skin diseases, not just the ailment we identify today by this name (Hansen's disease). Symptoms included ringworm, lesions, and psoriasis, as well as damage to one's eyes, limbs, and nerves. Leviticus 13:1-46 describes how the Israelite priests were to inspect swellings, rashes, and sores on people to see whether the anomalies were signs of a serious affliction. If the hair covering the affected body parts turned white, or if raw flesh appeared, the person was branded as unclean and sent outside the community.

White skin, one symptom of these skin diseases, is mentioned several times in Scripture as covering the afflicted person, but not disabling him or her (see

Exod. 4:6; Num. 12:10). For instance, Naaman seems to have been able to exercise the functions of a general in the Aramean (or Syrian) army, so that his was probably not a disabling or contagious skin disease (see 2 Kings 5:1). Verse 27 implies that his skin was "white as snow," since this is the color Elisha's servant, Gehazi, turned when he was stricken with "Naaman's leprosy." Leviticus 14:1-32 prescribed a ceremony of purification for those cured of skin diseases. It is interesting, when considering Naaman, that part of the purification included sprinkling water on the diseased person seven times.

II. EXPRESSING GRATITUDE: LUKE 17:15-19

A. Displaying Thanks: vss. 15-16

One of them, when he saw he was healed, came back, praising God in a loud voice. He threw himself at Jesus' feet and thanked him—and he was a Samaritan.

Perhaps it did not take long for one of the ten lepers to realize that he had been completely cured from his skin disease. It remains unclear, though, whether the man ever reached a priest to verify he had been "healed" (Luke 17:15). If the former leper cut his trip short, it was due to his joy over being freed from his dreaded ailment. So, out of a sense of intense gratitude, he turned back to find Jesus. As the appreciative man walked along, he could hardly contain his excitement. Indeed, he enthusiastically shouted out praises to God. Undoubtedly, the spectacle caught the attention of passersby.

In Jesus' day, some rabbis taught that leprosy was a punishment for sin. To them, the ailment was the visible sign of inward corruption. Moreover, the Jews feared leprosy, not only because it was disfiguring, but also because lepers were treated as untouchables. As noted earlier, lepers lived in communities outside the city gates and were not allowed contact with others. Religious law also declared that a person became unclean (that is, ceremonially polluted) by touching a leper. The possibility of ritual defilement, though, did not prevent Jesus from letting the former leper prostrate himself at the Savior's feet and repeatedly thank Him for what He had done (vs. 16). In short, Jesus was moved by kindness at the sight of suffering and willingly removed its cause.

Luke noted that the person expressing intense gratitude to Jesus was a "Samaritan." As noted earlier, Palestine in Jesus' day consisted of three major provinces. Galilee was to the north, Samaria occupied the central highlands, and Judea was to the south. Many Jews would not enter Samaria because they believed they would be defiled if they had any contact with the region's inhabitants. The mutual hatred between these two people groups can be traced back several hundred years before the advent of the Messiah. For instance, in 722 B.C., the Assyrian Empire defeated the northern kingdom of Israel and deported most of the Israelites to other parts of their realm. The Israelites who remained intermarried with foreigners. Out of these marriages came a religion that mixed the worship of the Lord with that of pagan deities. Later, in 539 B.C., when the Jews returned to Jerusalem from Babylonian captivity, they encountered Samaritans who were hostile to them and their religion. By the first century A.D., the Jews had cultivated and nurtured a deep animosity for the people who lived in Samaria.

John 4:20 draws attention to a longstanding dispute that existed in Jesus' day between Jews and Samaritans. The Jews recognized that God had instructed Solomon to build a temple in Jerusalem. They could go there to offer sacrifices and to worship Him. Meanwhile, the Samaritans argued that worship of God should be performed at Mount Gerizim, where they claimed many blessed events occurred. The Samaritans taught that Abraham proved his faithfulness and obedience to God when the patriarch offered his son, Isaac, on Mount Gerizim. The Samaritans also taught that Abraham and Melchizedek met on this mountain. More importantly, the Samaritans believed the Lord commanded Moses to build an altar on Mount Gerizim for God's people to worship Him. Since the Samaritans regarded only the Pentateuch (the first five books of Moses) as sacred, they naturally dismissed the Jewish belief that the center of worship should be at the temple in Jerusalem. In contrast, the Jews claimed that the Samaritans distorted the Scriptures. This controversy over the proper place to worship God only added to the enmity between the Jews and Samaritans.

B. Receiving Commendation: vss. 17-19

Jesus asked, "Were not all ten cleansed? Where are the other nine? Was no one found to return and give praise to God except this foreigner?" Then he said to him, "Rise and go; your faith has made you well."

As the former leper lay facedown at Jesus' feet, the Savior rhetorically asked whether ten men had been healed of their disease. The answer, of course, is that the entire group had been "cleansed" (Luke 17:14). That being the case, Jesus asked His disciples concerning the whereabouts of the other nine benefactors of God's grace. Jesus observed that aside from the Samaritan, whom Jesus referred to as a pagan "foreigner" (vs. 18), none of the other men made any effort to come back and offer "praise to God." Evidently, at least some of the remaining nine were Jews. Based on Jesus' remarks it appears they took the healing for granted. Yet their lack of appreciation did not prevent Jesus from telling the cured Samaritan to stand up and be on his way. Verse 19 literally says the Samaritan's "faith" had "saved" him. The tense of the underlying Greek verb indicates that he had been permanently rescued from his predicament. The implication is that as a result of his trust in the Son, the former leper's physical healing accompanied his spiritual deliverance from sin.

Three years earlier, in A.D. 27, Jesus' rejection at Nazareth prompted Him to make comparable and disparaging remarks about His peers. During a Sabbath synagogue service, after Jesus finished reading Isaiah 61:1-2, He rolled up the scroll, handed it back to the attendant, and sat down. (In ancient times, worshipers sat on wooden benches extending across from the platform.) The mood was tense, especially as everyone in the gathering stared intently at Jesus (Luke 4:20). His earthly ministry involved Him presenting Himself to the Jews as the Messiah. Verses 14-30 serve as a summary of the Savior's entire ministry. Early on, He was a very popular preacher due to His miracles and His teaching. But from the time Jesus presented Himself as the Messiah, there was a deep point of division among the people who heard Him.

Boldly and without hesitation, Jesus told His audience that Isaiah's prophecy had been fulfilled (vs. 21). Jesus' claim couldn't have been clearer. He was the long-awaited Messiah. He implied that He would bring the good news of salvation to pass, but in a way that the people would not yet be able to grasp. This, of course, was an astounding claim to make. Some of the listeners were impressed, but others were not so sure. At first, some of those in the synagogue spoke well of Jesus. In fact, they were amazed by the gracious words that had fallen from His lips. This prompted them to wonder how Jesus' messianic claims could possibly be true. After all, wasn't He the son of Joseph, a local carpenter of the town (vs. 22)?

Jesus had grown up in Nazareth and was familiar with the people who lived there. He knew they found it hard to believe that a humble carpenter's son would be such a central figure in God's plan. He acknowledged that they would want to see dramatic evidence of His power. The maxim "Physician, heal yourself!" (vs. 23) stressed the people's demand that Jesus repeat the type of miraculous work He had performed in Capernaum (see Mark 1:21-27). It was not enough for them to believe what He had claimed in the synagogue. The requests of the people for signs often contained a tone of mockery. Jesus realized this and responded by declaring that a prophet is usually not accepted by the people "in his hometown" (Luke 4:24). Because the residents of Nazareth couldn't imagine God raising up one of their own to be a prophet, Jesus would not show them God's power (Matt. 13:58). From this we see that doubt can limit what God does in people's lives.

Jesus drove home His point by reminding the skeptical worshipers that because God's chosen people doubted, they had missed blessings Gentiles then received. Jesus cited an incident in the time of Elijah when a three-year drought brought severe famine to the land. Though there were many widows in Israel, God sent Elijah to a widow of Zarephath, that is, a foreigner in the land of Sidon (1 Kings 17:8-16; Luke 4:25-26). (Zarephath was a Phoenician coastal city located between Tyre and Sidon.) Jesus also mentioned Elisha the prophet, who healed Naaman, a Syrian, rather than the many lepers in Israel who needed help (2 Kings 5:1-14; Luke 4:27). The Savior's point was that God bypassed all the widows and lepers in Israel, yet showed grace to two Gentiles. The Lord's concern for Gentiles and outcasts is one of the main emphases of Luke's Gospel.

Jesus was talking about a period of widespread unfaithfulness to God. During this time, judgment came on Israel in the form of various calamities (such as drought and famine). The only people to receive healing were Gentiles. Jesus warned His hearers not to be unfaithful like their ancestors by rejecting His message. Here we see that God reveals His love and mercy according to His divine wisdom. His ultimate revelation of Himself was in His Son, the Lord Jesus (see Heb. 1:1-2). Therefore, the Nazarenes risked God's judgment if they turned their backs on Jesus and His claim to be their Messiah. Also, they were foolish if they continued to put their trust in their religious and national heritages.

Discussion Questions

1. Why do you think Jesus decided to pass between Samaria and Galilee?
2. Why did the ten lepers cry out to Jesus for help?
3. What role did the healed leper's faith serve in his cure?
4. If you had been the healed leper, how do you think you would have expressed your gratitude?
5. Like Jesus, what risks do believers sometimes face when they reach out to persons in need?

Contemporary Application

In this week's lesson, physical needs mirrored deeper spiritual needs. For instance, in the case of the ten men with leprosy, their ailment was a result of the fallen condition of all creation. In fact, their physical condition reflected their spiritual helplessness.

Every person needs the deliverance and forgiveness only the Lord Jesus can provide. Those who have never placed their trust in the Messiah for salvation are as helpless as the ten lepers who came to Jesus for assistance. Unsaved men and women need to be rescued from the terrible effects of sin, just as those afflicted by a dreaded skin disease needed deliverance and healing.

Christian men and women stand in need of situational deliverance and forgiveness. Even though the eternal issue of salvation has been dealt with, physical disease and personal sins are still realities of life. Believers need to look to the Lord for help in time of sickness and for forgiveness of the transgressions that damage fellowship with the heavenly Father. In light of these truths, how can we not go to our loving Savior for help and hope?

A Humble Disposition

Scripture

Background Scripture: *Luke 18:9-14*
Scripture Lesson: *Luke 18:9-14*
Key Verse: "The tax collector stood at a distance.
He would not even look up to heaven, but beat his
breast and said, 'God, have mercy on me, a sinner.'"
Luke 18:13
Scripture Lesson for Children: *Luke 18:9-14*
Key Verse for Children: "Everyone who exalts himself
will be humbled, and he who humbles himself will be
exalted." *Luke 18:14*

Lesson Aim

To remain humble before God and in the way we relate
to people.

Lesson Setting

Time: A.D. *30*
Place: On the way to Jerusalem

Lesson Outline

A Humble Disposition

I.   The Setting: Luke 18:9-10
   A. *Broaching the Issue: vs. 9*
   B. *Introducing the Two Men: vs. 10*
II. The Contrast: Luke 18:11-14
   A. *The Pharisee: vss. 11-12*
   B. *The Tax Collector: vss. 13-14*

Introduction for Adults

Topic: *Valuing Humility*

"If you can do it, it ain't bragging." "Nobody's going to toot your own horn for you." "Tell me why you're the best person for the job." And so the litany of cliches go.

Sure, there are times when we need to put our best foot forward. And we might want to do some "horn tooting" at a job interview or at a review for a salary raise. But what about all the other times, when the right action is to be humble?

Believers have wrestled with humility since Bible times. Jesus told a parable about a Pharisee and a tax collector who both came to the Jerusalem temple to worship (Luke 18:9-14). For the Pharisee, that meant recounting his many acts of righteousness and thanking God for helping him to be better than others. For the tax collector, worship meant acknowledging his own sinfulness and praying for God's forgiveness. God wants us, like the tax collector, to humble ourselves before Him and acknowledge our need for mercy.

Introduction for Youth

Topic: *God Favors the Humble*

Insecure adolescents are prone to idolize conceited athletes, actors, and other popular individuals in society. And attention-starved teens look to their well-liked peers for the affirmation they so desperately feel they need. In the process, young people can fall into the trap of thinking that getting ahead means boasting about oneself and talking down about others.

This week's lesson challenges the preceding, impoverished mind-set. We discover that the humble tax collector, not the conceited Pharisee, was on the right track. Being humble does not mean saved teens turn into powerless doormats. Instead, humility actually gives adolescents in the church the strength they need to withstand peer pressure to be arrogant. They learn from Jesus' parable that those practicing humility and respect will do God's work with His attitude.

Concepts for Children

Topic: *Jesus Tells a Story*

1. Jesus told a story about putting God and others first.
2. In this story, there was a religious leader and a tax collector.
3. The religious leader was proud.
4. The tax collector was sorry because he had sinned.
5. When we tell God we're sorry for sinning, He forgives us.

Lesson Commentary

I. THE SETTING: LUKE 18:9-10

A. Broaching the Issue: vs. 9

To some who were confident of their own righteousness and looked down on everybody else, Jesus told this parable.

As Jesus moved toward Jerusalem and the climax of His ministry, He prepared His disciples for the time when He would no longer be with them. In Luke 17:20-37, Jesus countered the Pharisees' misconception about the Messiah by asserting that the kingdom of God was internal and spiritual. Also, since He, the King, was in their midst, the kingdom was (in a sense) already present. Jesus also told His disciples that His second coming would occur suddenly, bringing judgment.

In light of the afflictions and hardships of life, along with the certainty of approaching judgment, Jesus used a parable to encourage His disciples to pray persistently, no matter how gloomy the circumstances might be (18:1). Simply put, praying is talking to God. The act of praying does not change what God has purposed to do for us. Instead, it is the means by which He accomplishes His will. Also, talking to God is not a contrived method of getting us excited about what we have asked to be done. Instead, prayer creates within us a reverent attitude concerning the will of God. Moreover, prayer is not so much getting God to do our will as it is demonstrating that we are as concerned as He is that His will be done (Matt. 6:10).

To stress the importance of constant prayer, Jesus told a parable. He noted that in a certain city there was a wicked judge. He did not worship God and he held people in contempt (Luke 18:2). The judge portrayed in Jesus' story is like the kind appointed by Herod or the Romans. These magistrates were motivated only by what benefitted them. Since they heard cases that did not go to the religious courts, they often sold their services to the highest bidder. Jesus did not intend this corrupt official to represent God, but rather to stand in contrast to Him. If such a judge, who didn't care about others, would respond to persistent pleas, how much more would God, who is not only just but also merciful and loving, do so more readily?

Jesus said that a widow lived in the same city. In Bible times, many in society viewed widowhood with reproach. So a widow without legal protection was often vulnerable to neglect or exploitation. If a woman's husband died when her children were adolescents, they were considered orphans. Sadly, it was far too common for greedy creditors and unscrupulous agents to defraud a destitute widow and her children of whatever property they owned.

There were three primary ways a widow could provide for the financial needs of herself and her children. First, she could return to her parents' house.

Second, she could remarry, especially if she was young or wealthy. And third, she could remain unmarried and obtain some kind of employment. The last prospect was rather bleak, for it was difficult in Jesus' day for a widow to find suitable work that would meet the economic needs of her family.

The helpless widow in Jesus' parable repeatedly came to the wicked judge. The widow appealed to him for justice against someone who had harmed her (vs. 3). Expressed differently, the widow wanted to receive fair treatment in a court of law. At first, the hardhearted magistrate was unmoved by the widow's appeals, but eventually he relented. He did not change his mind because he saw it as his duty to God and the community. Rather, the judge gave in because the widow's persistent complaint would wear him out (vss. 4-5). He determined that it was better for him to yield to her demands than ignore her and tarnish his reputation.

Despite the odds against the widow, she kept going back to the only one who could help her. That is why she illustrates persistence in prayer. She had a specific need and she never stopped pleading her case. Jesus' disciples could easily make the connection between the helpless widow and themselves. They might have been tempted to quit, for they did not have financial resources or religious or political power. Only their persistence in prayer would see them through.

Accordingly, Jesus urged His disciples to learn a lesson from the evil judge in the parable (vs. 6). In the end, even this wicked man rendered a just decision. If godless judges (such as this one) responded to constant pressure, how much more would our great and loving God respond to us? Jesus' point was that the Lord would hear the cries of believers (His "chosen ones"; vs. 7) for help. He would not put them off. Rather, He would give justice to them, especially because they pleaded with Him "day and night." God's intervention included moderating the amount and duration of persecution, along with giving believers the strength to endure.

Jesus was emphatic in stating that God would grant justice expeditiously (vs. 8). The idea was that regardless of whether it was now or in eternity, God would vindicate the cause of the righteous. The problem, then, was not with God, but rather with His spiritual children. They often lacked the faith and devotion (as seen in perseverance in prayer) that the Lord wanted to see. Jesus' comment about finding "faith" when He returned suggests that, at His second coming, the enthusiasm of the upright would wane because of persecution. Only perseverance (for example, in prayer) would stem such spiritual decline.

Persistence tends to be the most unpopular concept regarding the practice of prayer. Whatever our misgivings about going before the all-knowing, all-powerful God with the same petitions over and over, persistence is scriptural. God does not become more willing to answer because of our perseverance. Rather, we may become more capable of receiving God's answer to our request. Also, perseverance can distinguish in our minds deep-seated desire from fleeting whim. Moreover, talking to God about the deepest desires of our hearts can prepare our souls to more fully appreciate the answers He gives to our requests.

Jesus directed His second parable to those guilty of being extremely arrogant. They were convinced of their own "righteousness" (vs. 9), while at the same time, they treated other people with contempt. Metaphorically speaking, those who were self-assured regarded everyone else as being despicable. In the New Testament, the Greek word translated "righteousness" comes from a root term that means "straightness" and refers to that which is in accordance with established moral norms. In a legal sense, righteousness means to be vindicated or treated as just.

B. Introducing the Two Men: vs. 10

"Two men went up to the temple to pray, one a Pharisee and the other a tax collector."

In Jesus' second parable, two men made their way up to the Jerusalem temple (which sat on a hill) to "pray" (Luke 18:10). But each came from entirely different backgrounds. As noted in lesson 6, the Pharisees comprised a religious and political party in Palestine. They were known for insisting that the law of God be observed (according to the interpretation of the scribes). Also, the Pharisees were famed for their observance of the laws of tithing, fasting, and ritual purity. The Pharisees collected and preserved the Talmud and the Mishnah, which were two immense products of oral tradition and Old Testament commentary. By reputation, Pharisees were legalistic and fanatically devoted to rabbinical tradition. Some even refused to eat with non-Pharisees for fear of being contaminated by food not rendered ritually clean.

As noted in lesson 8, tax collectors were agents or contract workers who collected tariffs and tolls in designated areas. In order to make a profit, they would charge several times more than what the Roman government required. The desire for personal gain would invariably lead to the inflation of tolls and customs. Each person involved in the collection process would pocket some of the excess money being charged. The Jews held their fellow citizens who were tax collectors in disdain because they served as agents of the despised Roman government. Also, everyone could see how the tax collectors became rich at the expense of their own people. Furthermore, Jewish tax collectors were considered ceremonially impure, for they had frequent contact with Gentiles.

II. *The Contrast: Luke 18:11-14*

A. The Pharisee: vss. 11-12

"The Pharisee stood up and prayed about himself: 'God, I thank you that I am not like other men—robbers, evildoers, adulterers—or even like this tax collector. I fast twice a week and give a tenth of all I get.'"

Jesus told this parable with a specific audience in mind—namely, those who were spiritually smug and compulsive about their pious behavior. Although

Luke does not say, it is reasonable to surmise that Jesus' listeners included many religious leaders. The Gospels describe numerous confrontations Jesus had with the spiritual elitists of His day over their arrogance. This parable cuts to the heart of what makes for effective prayer. Though first-century Jews could pray anywhere, some considered petitions offered in the Jerusalem temple to carry more weight with God than entreaties made elsewhere (see 2 Chron. 7:15-16).

Moreover, the self-righteous put great stock in works they believed earned them credit with God. They imagined that the more pious they were, the more God would listen to them. It's no wonder, then, that the Pharisee in Jesus' parable showed contempt for the tax collector in the temple precincts. The Greek phrase rendered "about himself" (Luke 18:11) indicates that the Pharisee was his own ethical point of reference and that his statements were made out loud. This ensured that others (including the tax collector) would take note of his sterling lifestyle. In essence, the religious leader was not praying sincerely. Rather, he was putting on a show in order to gain the applause of people.

In ancient Jewish culture, it was common for worshipers to stand while they prayed (see Matt. 6:5; Mark 11:25). Evidently, the religious leader positioned himself in a prominent place (such as the inner court of the temple) to make his declarations. Also, being filled with self-confidence and arrogance, he wasted no time in announcing to God how great he was, especially in contrast to the dishonest tax collector. Today, these two individuals might be comparable to a renowned bishop within a denomination versus a notorious drug dealer in the community.

The Pharisee bragged that he never cheated anyone, wasn't guilty of wickedness, and didn't commit adultery. Instead, the legalist fasted twice a week and gave God a tenth of his income (Luke 18:12). In Jesus' day, scrupulous Pharisees fasted on Mondays and Thursdays. Those were market days, when the city would be full of people who would see the religious leaders' whitened faces and disheveled clothes. The Pharisee failed to understand that even his human goodness fell far short of God's perfect moral standard (see Rom. 3:23 and the commentary in lesson 7 of the June quarter). It was only by renouncing his own righteousness and receiving by faith the righteousness Jesus offered freely and unconditionally that the religious leader could enjoy God's favor and forgiveness.

B. The Tax Collector: vss. 13-14

"But the tax collector stood at a distance. He would not even look up to heaven, but beat his breast and said, 'God, have mercy on me, a sinner.' I tell you that this man, rather than the other, went home justified before God. For everyone who exalts himself will be humbled, and he who humbles himself will be exalted."

In the eyes of the people, tax collectors were on the lowest rung of the religious ladder. In this case, it seems the tax collector had hit an emotional and spiritual bottom. Perhaps he felt overwhelmed by deep conviction and remorse for a life consumed by greed. Unlike the haughty Pharisee, the tax collector stood some distance away (perhaps in the Court of the Gentiles, the outermost section of the temple) and did not even dare lift his eyes to heaven as he prayed. We can imagine that the tax collector did not want to make a public scene, knowing that others in the temple would be only too eager to scorn him. It was as if the tax collector remained outside in the church parking lot, while the Pharisee stood in the middle of the sanctuary so all the attendees could see and hear him trumpet his piety.

The tax collector was filled with abject sorrow for his sin, and he repeatedly beat his chest over his spiritual and ethical shortcomings. The only thing he could think of doing was to ask God for "mercy" (Luke 18:13), even though he was a "sinner." The Greek verb rendered "have mercy" literally means "to be propitiated." The implication is that the tax collector was asking God to turn away from His wrath for the man's numerous transgressions. The Father, in love, could do this because of the atoning sacrifice His Son, Jesus Christ, would make on the cross. Because Jesus is the offering for our sin, God's wrath is appeased and the punishment for our transgressions has been satisfied (see Rom. 3:24-26; 1 John 2:2).

Jesus stated that when the two men went home, it was the tax collector, not the Pharisee, whom God "justified" (Luke 18:14). In the New Testament, the Greek word translated "justified" signified a court setting, with a judge announcing an individual to be "not guilty." Luke, a Gentile, may have been particularly struck by the grace demonstrated through the Son. He brought salvation not merely for Jews but also for Gentiles (see 2:32; 3:6; 4:25-27; 7:9; 24:47). Jesus offered hope to the poor (see 1:53; 2:7; 6:20; 7:22) as well as the rich. Jesus befriended tax collectors and other social outcasts (see 3:12; 5:27-32; 7:34, 37-50; 19:2-10; 23:43) along with the righteous and respectable.

Most likely, the elitists listening to Jesus' parable identified with the Pharisee and may have expected the story to end with God giving the religious leader favor and honor. So imagine how shocked some must have felt when Jesus explained that if we put ourselves above others, God would use the circumstances of life to bring us down. In contrast, if we humble ourselves, God would honor us. The path, then, to true identity is not building ourselves up and tearing other people down. Instead, it is being honest about ourselves and becoming humble like Jesus. There is no risk in admitting our sins to God, for He already knows about them. And when we go to Him in repentance and faith, we experience His forgiveness and restoration. Conversely, if we try to build ourselves up by looking down on others who are less fortunate or gifted than us, we will reap loneliness and resentment from others and disdain from God.

In Greek thought, humility was a negative trait that suggested weakness and a lack of worth or dignity. Jesus, however, made it a cornerstone of Christian character (see Matt. 18:4; 23:12; Luke 18:14). The biblical concept of humility knows nothing of putting oneself down (see Col. 2:18, 23). Scriptural humility involves an absence of arrogance rooted in the understanding that all we are and have we owe to God. Humility focuses on others rather than self. A humble person praises and lifts others up without any regard for self-exaltation (see Phil. 2:3-4), just as John the Baptizer gladly elevated Jesus' ministry over his own (see John 3:30). The ultimate example of humility is the Savior Himself (see Matt. 11:29; Mark 10:45; John 13:1-17; Phil. 2:5-8). God the Son was willing to become one of us, subject to the human condition with its weaknesses and failings. Without Jesus' willingness to be born as a human being, live as a servant, and die like a criminal, salvation would have been impossible.

Discussion Questions

1. Why did the Pharisee regard the tax collector with contempt?
2. What could the Pharisee have learned from the tax collector?
3. What aspects of Jesus' parable would have shocked His audience?
4. Why do you think some people are self-assured about their presumed devotion to God?
5. What are some ways you can grow in humility?

Contemporary Application

Luke 18:9-14 records a parable in which Jesus contrasted an arrogant Pharisee with a contrite tax collector. The latter person showed a humble attitude that pleased God. In contrast, the religious elitist conveyed a smug attitude that displeased the Lord.

In the world, aggression is seen as strength, while humility connotes weakness. Occasionally, a prominent leader with a servant attitude is honored. But for all of them, there are hundreds of arrogant celebrities who count ego and pride as virtues. Few among them would be willing to relate to others with humility.

This week's lesson urges us to remain humble before God and in the way we relate to people. The apt metaphor of being clothed with humility means seeing ourselves as God does and respecting others by relating to them without pretense. As Helen Keller said, "There is no king who has not had a slave among his ancestors, and no slave who has not had a king among his."

While these observations apply to all believers, it is especially imperative for Christian leaders to take them to heart. After all, they are the role models for other believers. This truth necessitates that Christians who supervise others must lead by example, as our Lord did. He did not direct His followers to do anything He personally had not done or was unwilling to do. He lived as a humble servant, died for the unrighteous, and loved the unlovely without limits.

A Receptive Heart

Scripture

Background Scripture: *Mark 10:13-16; Luke 18:15-17*
Scripture Lesson: *Mark 10:13-16; Luke 18:15-17*
Key Verse: [Jesus said,] "I tell you the truth, anyone who will not receive the kingdom of God like a little child will never enter it." *Luke 18:17*
Scripture Lesson for Children: *Mark 10:16;*
Luke 18:15-17
Key Verse for Children: [Jesus said,] "Let the little children come to me, and do not hinder them."
Mark 10:14

Lesson Aim

To appreciate that all people, including children, are welcome in God's kingdom.

Lesson Setting

Time: A.D. 30
Place: On the way to Jerusalem

Lesson Outline

A Receptive Heart
  I. Trying to Stop the Children: Mark 10:13;
     Luke 18:15
  II. Letting the Children Come: Mark 10:14;
      Luke 18:16
  III. Nurturing a Childlike Faith: Mark 10:15-16;
       Luke 18:17

Introduction for Adults

Topic: *Children Have a Place*

Evidently, Jesus' disciples thought children weren't important enough to receive Jesus' attention. Likewise, today some Christians think ministry to children is unimportant.

Before his death in 2009, well-known columnist William Safire quipped that Richard Stans was the most saluted man in the United States. Safire pointed out that millions of schoolchildren place their right hands over their hearts to pledge allegiance to the flag, and to the republic for Richard Stans. Safire also claimed that many youngsters start the famous pledge by saying, "I pledge a legion to the flag," while others begin with, "I led the pigeons to the flag." The words "one nation, indivisible" sometimes are corrupted into "one naked individual" or "one nation in a dirigible" or "one nation and a vegetable."

While we may smile at these childish misunderstandings of the words to the Pledge of Allegiance, we should note that many of our children have just as poor an understanding of what God's Word says. When we adopt the deplorable attitude displayed by Jesus' disciples, we end up failing to teach our children well, in age-appropriate ways. When that happens, we must heed the warning that the generation that forgets the truths of Scripture will spiritually perish.

Introduction for Youth

Topic: *Children Are Valued*

If you wear glasses, you know how frustrating it is to drop them and have the frame snap right at the bridge holding the two lenses together. Glue might work for a while, but most people realize that glue is not a solution to the problem. The bridge is too vulnerable to stress.

The lives of teenagers can be as fragile as glasses frames. Many fractures occur, and some lives are damaged and even ruined. These teens need more than glue to hold together pieces of their lives. They need the inherent, integrating power of Jesus' love, wisdom, and guidance.

When adolescents in our churches come to us with questions and concerns, let us not be like Jesus' disciples. They thought devoting energy and attention to young people was a waste of time. Thankfully, Jesus thought differently, and as His faithful followers, so should we.

Concepts for Children

Topic: *You're Welcome Here!*

1. Some parents brought their children to Jesus.
2. Jesus' followers tried to stop the parents.
3. Jesus told His followers to let the children come to Him.
4. Jesus prayed for the children who came to Him.
5. Jesus also cares about us and deeply loves us.

Lesson Commentary

I. TRYING TO STOP THE CHILDREN: MARK 10:13; LUKE 18:15

Mark 10:13 People were bringing little children to Jesus to have him touch them, but the disciples rebuked them. . . . Luke 18:15 People were also bringing babies to Jesus to have him touch them. When the disciples saw this, they rebuked them.

The three Synoptic Gospels record the episode in which parents brought their young family members to Jesus so that He might place His hands on them, pray for them, and impart a blessing to them. The parents did so because they held Jesus in high regard. Matthew 19:13 and Mark 10:13 use the same Greek noun rendered "little children." These would have been boys and girls who had not yet reached the age of adolescence. Luke 18:15 uses a different noun, which is translated "babies," but also could be rendered "infants." Despite the sincere and reasonable intentions of the family members, Jesus' disciples reprimanded the adults (Matt. 19:13; Mark 10:13; Luke 18:15).

A comparison of the three Synoptic Gospels indicates that prior to the episode involving Jesus' ministering to infants and young children, He dealt with the issue of divorce and remarriage. Even in the first century A.D., whether married couples stayed together impacted the well-being of the entire family, including their children. After teaching in Galilee (Matt. 19:1), Jesus traveled south and then east through Judea, crossed the Jordan River, and began ministering in Perea (Mark 10:1). Though Jesus spent some time in Perea, He kept His focus on Jerusalem and the crucifixion that awaited Him there.

The Savior continued to be a popular figure among the people, for large crowds came to Him. Although Jesus recently had been focusing His attention on His disciples (9:30-31), He nonetheless made an effort to teach the spiritually needy throng that was gathering around Him. While Jesus was speaking, some Pharisees came to Him and asked whether it was proper for a man to divorce his wife (10:2). On the surface, it appeared as if they genuinely wanted to know what the Savior taught. However, their motives were evil, for they tried to catch Jesus off guard and use His words against Him.

The religious leaders' question was ambiguous, for Deuteronomy 24:1-4 clearly stated that the lawfulness of a divorce depended on the circumstances. Also, the Pharisees may have wanted to entangle Jesus in the debate concerning Herod Antipas and his unlawful marriage. If the Jewish authorities could trap Jesus into making an unguarded remark, they might have been able to convince Herod to arrest Jesus. Herod had earlier married Herodias, the wife of Herod's brother, Philip. (Herodias happened to be Herod's niece as well as his sister-in-law.) John the Baptizer rightly declared that this action was immoral, since the Mosaic law barred a man from marrying the wife of his living brother (see Lev. 18:16; 20:21). In order to please Herodias, Herod arrested John and put him in prison (Mark 6:17-18).

The issue of divorce was far from being settled in Jesus' day. The religious leaders in Palestine generally agreed that the Mosaic law permitted divorce. However, the Pharisees and scribes debated how Deuteronomy 24:1 should be interpreted. The followers of the Jewish rabbi, Shammai, argued that the phrase translated "something indecent" referred to some sort of impurity in the wife. They said her uncleanness resulted from gross moral lapses, such as adultery. So a husband could divorce his wife only if she had flagrantly violated the law. The followers of the Jewish rabbi, Hillel, argued that the phrase "who becomes displeasing to him" permitted divorce for anything the wife did that upset or shamed her husband, regardless of whether the affront was real or imagined. So, for example, a husband could divorce his wife if she burned his dinner, failed to bear his children, or appeared unattractive to him.

Rather than become embroiled in this debate, Jesus asked the Pharisees what the Mosaic law had to say about the issue (Mark 10:3). In turn, they referred to Deuteronomy 24:1-4, noting that Moses permitted a husband to write out divorce papers before sending away his wife (Mark 10:4). The "certificate" of dismissal the Pharisees mentioned highly favored the Jewish husband. In fact, while a husband could divorce his wife, under Jewish law, a wife could not divorce her husband. Women did not marry but, like property, were given in marriage (see Luke 20:34-35). Nonetheless, the husband's divorce papers had to meet certain legal requirements. This included being written on lasting materials with ink that would not fade. Also, once the divorce was granted, it remained permanent. Though a wife could not divorce her husband, she had the right to go to court and try to force him to divorce her if she regarded his occupation as being distasteful or if he had certain diseases.

Jesus responded to the Pharisees' inquiry by explaining that Moses permitted divorce because of the hardness of the people's hearts (Mark 10:5). In other words, since the Israelites were just as ungodly as other people, Moses knew some Israelites would inevitably divorce their spouses. So Moses regulated divorce to minimize the hardships it caused and prevent the worst abuses from happening. The lawgiver was wise in doing this, because in ancient times women (along with their children) had little legal protection. Jesus, however, noted that divorce was not God's original intent (vss. 6-8). Jesus quoted Genesis 1:27 and 2:24 to stress that God created the genders and ordained the union of a man and a woman in marriage. This union was both physical and spiritual in nature. So marriage was not a mere legal contract that could be easily dissolved, but an intertwining of two people.

God intended marriage to be a living example of interdependence and harmony between a man and a woman (as well as their children). As the couple united in marriage, they began to share their time, emotions, goals, and resources. Also, in their relationship, they built a bond of trust, loyalty, and faithfulness. So the relationship was not something that could easily be dissolved (Mark 10:9). In making this statement, Jesus took a more restrictive view on the matter of divorce than either side in the Jewish debate. He said the concession Moses made to the moral weakness of married couples originated with the Sinai covenant, not God's creation order. So, unlike marriage, God did not institute divorce. Instead, God regarded divorce as a sign that one or both spouses had fallen short of His intended ideal.

When Jesus and His disciples were alone, they asked Him more pointedly about what He had told the Pharisees (vs. 10). He said that those who divorced their spouses and then remarried committed adultery (vss. 11-12). Jesus may have been saying that even after a divorce, the original marriage was in some sense still in effect. As before, Jesus was taking a more extreme position on the issue than other religious teachers of His time. Jesus also went beyond other teachers of His day by intimating the equality of the man and the woman in marriage. In contrast with Jewish law, Jesus taught that neither the husband nor the wife could divorce without consequences and called on both to honor their marriage commitment (which also impacted their children). Evidently, Jesus' comments looked beyond Jewish society to the prevailing Greco-Roman culture, where wives were permitted to divorce their husbands.

In Matthew 19:9, Jesus named one acceptable reason for a person to divorce his or her spouse—namely, promiscuity on the part of the wayward husband or wife. The Greek noun rendered "sexual immorality" may encompass a variety of licentious behaviors, such as adultery, homosexual acts, and incest. Some also think Paul, in 1 Corinthians 7:15, mentioned another acceptable reason for divorce. The apostle was discussing incidents in which one marriage partner was a believer and the other was not. The verse seems to suggest that if an unbelieving spouse abandoned his or her mate (along with their children), the believing spouse was permitted to obtain a divorce and remarry.

II. LETTING THE CHILDREN COME: MARK 10:14; LUKE 18:16

Mark 10:14 When Jesus saw this, he was indignant. He said to them, "Let the little children come to me, and do not hinder them, for the kingdom of God belongs to such as these." . . . Luke 18:16 But Jesus called the children to him and said, "Let the little children come to me, and do not hinder them, for the kingdom of God belongs to such as these."

It was noted earlier that Jesus' disciples tried to stop the parents who brought their children to Jesus so He could bless them (Matt. 19:13; Mark 10:13; Luke 18:15). Perhaps the disciples wanted to shield Jesus from interruption and fatigue. Also, His followers may have been thinking the children were not important enough to deserve Jesus' attention. In first-century Palestinian culture, older people were revered (especially distinguished elders, rabbis, and scribes). Although the Jews did, of course, love their children, often adults considered children to be of lesser value than adults. Some might even consider daughters a disadvantage. Along with the dismissive attitude displayed by Jesus' disciples, the religious leaders called on Jesus to silence children who praised Him as He rode into Jerusalem (see Matt. 21:15–16).

Mark 10:14 reveals that Jesus became upset at the actions of His disciples. The Greek verb rendered "indignant" denotes the presence of annoyance or irritation over an injustice. In this case, Jesus discerned that His disciples had treated the parents and their children harshly and unfairly. Luke 18:16 indicates that Jesus sidestepped the disciples' affront by summoning the "children" to His side. Perhaps as they approached Him, the parents felt a sense of relief and gratitude. In contrast, Jesus' disciples possibly were embarrassed when they heard Him say it was acceptable for the infants, toddlers, and older "children" to be by His side. The Savior explained that the "kingdom of God" was populated by people who were like the little ones standing next to Him. By this Jesus meant His heavenly Father welcomed those who approached Him with childlike trust. The latter even included the powerless and vulnerable, whom society often regarded as being inconsequential (see also a similar comment made in lesson 9).

In Matthew 19:14, the phrase rendered "kingdom of heaven" appears, rather than "kingdom of God" (Mark 10:14; Luke 18:16). The most likely reason for this difference is that Matthew's Gospel, which was originally written for a predominately Jewish audience, substituted "heaven" for "God" out of respect for the sacredness of the divine name. The implication is that the "kingdom of God" and the "kingdom of heaven" do not refer to two different realms (for example, one that is earthly and temporal versus another that is heavenly and eternal). In all three Synoptic Gospels, the rule of the Father (especially as seen in the abiding presence of the Son) is understood to encompass the past, the present, and the future. So, even though God resides in heaven and reigns from there, His rule extends over the entire universe, including everyone and everything on earth.

III. NURTURING A CHILDLIKE FAITH: MARK 10:15-16; LUKE 18:17

Mark 10:15-16 "I tell you the truth, anyone who will not receive the kingdom of God like a little child will never enter it." And he took the children in his arms, put his hands on them and blessed them. . . . Luke 18:17 "I tell you the truth, anyone who will not receive the kingdom of God like a little child will never enter it."

Jesus' opening statement in Mark 10:15 and Luke 18:17 is literally translated, "Amen, I say to you." As noted in lesson 2, the Greek adverb rendered "amen" comes from a Hebrew term that means "so be it." In Jewish worship during the Old Testament era, participants would say *amen* as a way to affirm or agree with a speaker (see 1 Chron. 16:36; Neh. 5:13; 8:6). Jesus used the term to emphasize the truthfulness and certitude of His statements. It is almost as if He were declaring, "Rest assured, what I am about to say is absolutely valid and to be taken seriously."

In the present circumstance, Jesus revealed that in order to enter God's king-dom, people had to do so "like a little child" (Mark 10:15; Luke 18:17). Just as boys and girls are dependent on their parents, so also believers must rely on the Father in heaven for their eternal well-being. The Savior's emphasis included believers having a humble attitude, receptive heart, and trusting spirit. After making this statement, Jesus welcomed with open arms the children standing next to Him. Then, as He placed His hands on each of them, He invoked a blessing (Mark 10:16). Unlike Jesus' wary, overprotective disciples, He did not hesitate to associate with young children and their parents. He knew this was a worthwhile investment of His time.

The reason for the preceding attitude is that the Son's redemptive mission included making the Father known and accessible to humankind. In this case, those who put their faith in the Messiah received the right, or legal entitlement, to become God's children (John 1:12). Belief in the Son made the recipients' freedom, capacity, and capability to undergo this change of status a reality. This was a situation in which believing sinners were adopted into God's family and received all the corresponding rights and privileges that went along with it (see Rom. 8:14-17; Gal. 4:4-6). Additionally, the Father delivered them from the power of darkness and transferred them to the kingdom of His beloved Son (see Col. 1:13).

The false teachers John was combating in the Fourth Gospel maintained he-retical notions about how one became united with God. To refute counterfeit declarations that it was a human-centered, self-initiated process, the apostle declared that those who become God's children are not spiritually reborn in this way (see Jesus' comments in 3:3, 5, 7-8). Specifically, regeneration is not a matter of "natural descent" (1:13) from human parents. Likewise, it is not the outworking of fleshly human desires, regardless of whether such are charac-terized by virtue or vice. Furthermore, the new birth did not result from any human volition whatsoever.

John was not insinuating that the flesh in its unfallen state was inherently wicked. Rather, the apostle revealed that the new birth was the result of God's gracious action. He sovereignly brought it about (see 2 Cor. 5:17; Gal. 6:15; Titus 3:5) when people put their faith in the Son for eternal life (see Eph. 1:13; 2:8-9). The recreation of the fallen human nature signified a new start for believing sinners. They were transformed in their volition, emotions, and actions (see Rom. 12:1-2). Despite the assertions of heretics, this inner renewal was not the result of people, apart from the Spirit, willing themselves to change by acquiring knowledge. The new birth was entirely the work of the triune God and became a reality when people received the Son by faith for salvation.

In Titus 3:4, Paul explained the nature of Jesus' transforming work within His spiritual children. The incarnation of the Son, whom Paul described as both Savior and God, was a revelation of the Father's kindness and love. This same thought was expressed earlier in 2:11. In view of human selfishness, Jesus' saving work seemed inexplicable. Accordingly, in 3:4, Paul emphasized that the divine plan of redemption was not motivated by any virtuous deeds believers performed. Instead, the Father's mercy made salvation possible. Apart from the Son, even our best actions have been tainted by the self-centered perspective described in verse 3.

Moreover, the Father dealt with the guilt incurred by human sin through "the washing of rebirth" (vs. 5) and "renewal by the Holy Spirit." These two phrases point to the same event, with each one describing a slightly different aspect of the salvation experience. Like two sides of the same coin, they cannot be separated. The Son's death made it possible for the Spirit to regenerate believers, and the outpouring of the Spirit was the culmination of Jesus' earthly ministry.

Discussion Questions

1. What feelings do you think the parents had as they brought their children to Jesus?
2. How do you think the parents felt when Jesus' disciples rebuked them?
3. Why was Jesus eager to bless the children?
4. What does it mean to be a child of God?
5. How can believers encourage those who want to know more about Jesus?

Contemporary Application

When some parents brought their babies and other children to Jesus, His disciples censured the parents. Evidently, the disciples thought Jesus was too important to waste His time on blessing little ones. But Jesus directed the Twelve to permit the children to come to Him. He explained that every person is important in the heavenly kingdom.

Jesus willingly spent time with people of all ages because He understood that we are sinful and separated from God. Despite this sobering truth, the Lord longs to live in loving relationship with us. How then can sinful people and a holy God be reconciled? The Father's answer is the Son—the one who came as God in human form.

In His full humanness, Jesus faced and triumphed over temptation, never giving in to it. Because of this, He was eligible to give His life for the sinful. His pure sacrifice satisfied God's requirements for dealing justly with sin. Moreover, since Jesus is fully God, when He had successfully met every obstacle to His mission, He exercised His authority over sin and death, setting believers free from the ultimate destruction of these powers.

When we trust in the Son, we are reconciled to the Father (see Rom. 5:10-11; 2 Cor. 5:18-21). In turn, we are freed to approach the Lord with eagerness and sincerity. We also have the wonderful privilege of encouraging others—including children—to do the same (see Heb. 4:16).

A Joyous Response

Scripture

Background Scripture: *Luke 19:1-10*
Scripture Lesson: *Luke 19:1-10*
Key Verse: "The Son of Man came to seek and to save what was lost." *Luke 19:10*
Scripture Lesson for Children: *Luke 19:1-10*
Key Verse for Children: "[Jesus] came to seek and to save what was lost." *Luke 19:10*

Lesson Aim

To learn that Jesus takes the initiative in saving the lost.

Lesson Setting

Time: A.D. 30
Place: Jericho

Lesson Outline

A Joyous Response

   I. Seeking to Meet Jesus: Luke 19:1-4
      A. Passing through Jericho: vs. 1
      B. Encountering Zacchaeus: vss. 2-4
  II. Receiving Jesus' Affirmation: Luke 19:5-10
      A. The Request: vss. 5-6
      B. The Restitution: vss. 7-8
      C. The Announcement: vss. 9-10

Introduction for Adults

Topic: *Finding a New Direction*

How can believers communicate the message of salvation to the lost? Admittedly it's difficult, for many individuals seem to have no interest in their eternal future. Heaven and hell are too remote for them to worry about, and the unsaved don't think about God in personal terms.

This doesn't mean the lost are unredeemable. In fact, Luke's account of Zacchaeus (a wealthy tax collector) teaches otherwise. Perhaps no one in Jericho, where he lived, could have guessed that he was so interested in spiritual matters. Thankfully, Jesus was willing to go to him, share the good news of the kingdom, and see Zacchaeus become spiritually transformed.

How can we find and reclaim the lost? It takes prayer, love, and kindness. It also takes befriending them and winning their trust and respect. When we do these things, they will see that Jesus truly cares for them. Hopefully they will also be much more interested in putting their faith in Jesus.

Introduction for Youth

Topic: *Getting Back on Track*

Imagine being at a gathering where free tickets to a music or sporting event were being given away as the prize. That's a situation where we'd welcome being singled out. There are other times, however, when we've done something foolish and would prefer hiding in the crowd. Such a response is part of our psychological makeup.

When it comes to God, two similar responses are possible for youth (as well as for the rest of us). They can either step out of the crowd and welcome Him, or try to escape by fading into the mix of people. What character quality determines how young people will respond to the Gospel? It's their willingness to be honest with themselves and the Lord.

In Luke's account about Zacchaeus (the focus of this week's lesson), we learn that many people in Jericho were following Jesus, but only one person seemed honest enough to admit his need for new life. Zacchaeus was fed up with his old, sinful ways and rejoiced when Jesus summoned him from the crowd to give him a fresh start. Jesus can do the same thing for adolescents if they will let Him.

Concepts for Children

Topic: *Jesus Visited Zacchaeus*

1. Jesus and His followers came to a city called Jericho.
2. Jesus met a man named Zacchaeus who was selfish with his money.
3. Zacchaeus promised to share his money.
4. Jesus accepts us just as we are.
5. Jesus has the power to change our lives.

Lesson Commentary

I. SEEKING TO MEET JESUS: LUKE 19:1-4

A. Passing through Jericho: vs. 1

Jesus entered Jericho and was passing through.

As noted in previous weeks, Jesus spent the months before His crucifixion in Perea. Except for His return to restore Lazarus to life (see John 11:17-44), Jesus remained out of the Jerusalem area during this time until His triumphal entry. Luke 18:31-34 provides a useful literary and theological context to the Savior's encounter with Zacchaeus and the emphasis in 19:10 on Jesus' redemptive mission to "seek and save" those who were spiritually "lost." As Jesus and His disciples traveled toward Jerusalem, He stopped to warn them about what would happen to Him in the city. According to Luke, this was the third such warning Jesus gave His disciples regarding His crucifixion (see also 9:22, 43-45).

We can only imagine the solemnity of the moment as Jesus gathered the Twelve around Him (18:31). Next, Jesus detailed the harsh treatment that awaited Him, such as mocking, insults, and flogging (vs. 32). In some instances, the scourge used for the mocking was enough to cause death. Jesus did not specifically mention the cruel and horrible crucifixion, but He did imply it by describing all the events that typically led up to it. For the first time, Jesus also identified His executioners as Gentiles and foretold His resurrection on the third day. In making these declarations, Jesus sought to prepare His followers for the worst, assure them that all the upcoming events followed the Old Testament prophecies regarding the Messiah, and affirm them that He would triumph over the grave (vs. 33).

A growing sense of alarm was welling up in Jesus' disciples. They heard Jesus' words, but they did not comprehend their meaning until after the events had occurred (vs. 34). The Twelve could not imagine such horrible events happening to Jesus. Perhaps they thought this was another of Jesus' paradoxical sayings, which they would later understand. Or Luke may be saying that the meaning of Jesus' words was concealed from His disciples in the same way that His identity was veiled from the disciples on the road to Emmaus (see 24:16). Furthermore, it is difficult to know exactly how the Twelve perceived Jesus as the Messiah and how that impacted their grasp of unfolding events. Acts 1:6 indicates Jesus' followers were caught up in the popular idea that the Messiah would throw off foreign rule and establish a Jewish kingdom.

Consequently, the notion of a suffering Redeemer was foreign to the disciples, as it was to most Jews of that day. They reveled in the prophecies from the Psalms, Daniel, and elsewhere that foretold a conquering Messiah-Monarch. They overlooked those oracles (especially from Isaiah) that also spoke about the Redeemer as a suffering Servant. For this reason, when Jesus spoke about

His crucifixion, the Twelve could not comprehend such a concept and perhaps instead looked for some hidden meaning in Jesus' words. It was not until after His crucifixion and resurrection were complete that the disciples looked back and fully realized that Jesus had foretold everything that would happen. Interestingly, the chief priests and Pharisees recognized Jesus' claim that He would rise again and requested that a guard be posted at His tomb (see Matt. 27:62-66). But the events took His disciples by surprise.

The fact remains that everything Jesus foretold in Luke 18:31-33 came true. This highlights the reliability and accuracy of God's Word. Jesus' statements also remind us of the unity that exists between the Old and New Testaments. It's true that there are many differences in these two portions of Scripture. Nevertheless, they are harmonious in what they reveal about the Messiah. The fact that so many prophecies concerning Jesus were literally fulfilled gives us greater appreciation for God's plan of redemption through His Son. God spoke through the prophets about His Son's coming and His suffering so we might have sufficient evidence to place our faith in Him. There's no other satisfactory explanation for the fulfillment of these prophecies, which were made centuries before Jesus was born.

As Jesus continued on His way to Jerusalem, He passed through Jericho (Luke 19:1). Jericho is one of the oldest inhabited cities in the world and the first city the Israelites conquered under Joshua's command. It's located in a wide plain of the lower Jordan River Valley at the foot of the Judean mountains. Jericho is about eight miles northwest of the spot where the Jordan flows into the Dead Sea and about five miles west of the Jordan. The combination of rich soil, water from seasonal rains, and constant sunshine made Jericho an attractive place for settlement. Jesus passed through Jericho on several occasions. Near there John baptized Jesus in the Jordan River (Matt. 3:13-17). Then, on the adjacent mountain range, Jesus was tempted (4:1-11). His parable of the good Samaritan has the road from Jerusalem to Jericho as its setting (Luke 10:30-37). Also, while coming near Jericho, Jesus met and healed a blind beggar (18:35-43).

B. Encountering Zacchaeus: vss. 2-4

A man was there by the name of Zacchaeus; he was a chief tax collector and was wealthy. He wanted to see who Jesus was, but being a short man he could not, because of the crowd. So he ran ahead and climbed a sycamore-fig tree to see him, since Jesus was coming that way.

After Jesus entered Jericho, He met a rich and influential tax collector named Zacchaeus (Luke 19:2). Even though his name literally meant "pure" or "innocent," most likely he acquired his wealth through fraudulent means. Because Jericho was on a major trade route and was a center for commerce, there were plenty of opportunities to become rich. It could be that Zacchaeus was walking along the main thoroughfare or heading toward his customs station when he heard the commotion of the crowd. It remains unclear why Zacchaeus wanted to catch a glimpse of Jesus (vs. 3).

Despite the tax collector's efforts, his short stature (perhaps being no more than five feet tall) prevented him from looking over the heads of the entourage following the Savior. Also, it is likely that no one would let a despised tax collector move to the front for a better view. So Zacchaeus decided to climb up a sycamore-fig tree beside the road (vs. 4). These trees typically had low-hanging branches and were easy to climb. Undoubtedly, Zacchaeus intended to remain hidden in the tree. After all, a person with his wealth and influence would not want to be spotted up in a tree. Nonetheless, his encounter with the Savior that day would prove to be a life-changing experience for Zacchaeus.

Because of the opportunity to become wealthy, tax collectors paid the Romans for the opportunity to collect polls and tariffs. Tax collectors (in Latin, their name was *publicani*) were usually Romans. But, as in the case of Zacchaeus, some of them were Jewish. Under the Roman system, all males over the age of 14 and all females over 12 were subject to a poll tax. There was also a land tax, as well as several indirect taxes on imports and exports, and even taxes on common items such as salt. Farmers who tried to move their goods outside of their own territory were hit with road tolls that ate up most of their profits. Many transported goods, including slaves, were also subject to taxation.

In keeping with the observations made in lessons 8 and 11, the Jews of the day hated their fellow citizens who collected taxes for the Romans. Besides representing the Roman domination of their land, these tax collectors typically gouged the people and kept the surplus. Those who wanted the job of organizing other tax collectors had to bid for it. The person with the highest offer was able to pocket substantial commissions. As a "chief tax collector," Zacchaeus most likely employed and supervised local Jews to do the actual task of levying fees and charges. These individuals would probably know the ways the local people tried to avoid taxation. In rabbinical writings of the day, tax collectors were characterized as robbers. Also, since tax collectors worked on the Sabbath and had frequent contact with Gentiles, the religious elite regarded tax collectors as being ritually unclean.

II. RECEIVING JESUS' AFFIRMATION: LUKE 19:5-10

A. The Request: vss. 5-6

When Jesus reached the spot, he looked up and said to him, "Zacchaeus, come down immediately. I must stay at your house today." So he came down at once and welcomed him gladly.

Imagine the astonishment Zacchaeus must have felt when Jesus passed by, spotted the tax collector, and made eye contact with him. With Zacchaeus being up above eye level in the tree, he probably would not have been seen by anyone else. But Jesus already knew about Zacchaeus and reached out to him. His heart must have started to race when Jesus called him by name and summoned him down from the sycamore-fig tree where he was perched (Luke 19:5). Jesus literally said it was "necessary" for Him to lodge that night in the home of Zacchaeus. Jesus' words implied His acceptance and forgiveness of Zacchaeus were unconditional.

The request must have come as a surprise to a person accustomed to the scorn of his fellow Jews. Also, consider how flabbergasted the crowds were when they heard that a popular and highly regarded Jewish teacher wanted to socialize with someone they considered to be a cheater and turncoat. Perhaps Jesus wanted others to know that all people—even a loathed tax gatherer such as Zacchaeus—needed to hear the good news of the kingdom. After all, Jesus had come to redeem people just like him. It's unclear why Zacchaeus was thrilled to accept Jesus' request (vs. 6). Despite possible embarrassment on the tax collector's part, he quickly climbed down the tree and received Jesus as his guest into his home. This episode is a wonderful illustration of what it means to open our hearts to the Savior.

B. The Restitution: vss. 7-8

All the people saw this and began to mutter, "He has gone to be the guest of a 'sinner.'" But Zacchaeus stood up and said to the Lord, "Look, Lord! Here and now I give half of my possessions to the poor, and if I have cheated anybody out of anything, I will pay back four times the amount."

The crowd was displeased with Jesus' choice of whom to honor with His fellowship, and they displayed their annoyance by complaining to one another (Luke 19:7). In the people's opinion, Zacchaeus had violated the Mosaic law and so was unworthy to be in Jesus' presence. The throng, however, failed to realize that Jesus came to save the lost (Matt. 18:11). Certainly Zacchaeus—along with everyone else in the crowd—fit that description (Prov. 20:9). Even today, those who, like Jesus, befriend "outsiders" risk being the target of hostility.

Judging from the reaction of the crowd to Jesus' decision, Zacchaeus must have been an extraordinarily dishonest tax collector. Though he was a notorious transgressor, he seemed desperate to see Jesus. Otherwise, why would such a wealthy, influential man as Zacchaeus risk the undignified action of climbing up a tree? Those blinded by pride could not see how God had prepared the heart of Zacchaeus to meet the perfect, sinless Messiah. So, even though the throngs were correct about Zacchaeus' notorious past, they failed to appreciate the grace-oriented nature of Jesus' redemptive mission.

Zacchaeus had wronged many people, and the law required full restitution plus one-fifth more in circumstances in which money was acquired by fraud (see Lev. 5:16; 6:5; Num. 5:6-7). But Zacchaeus went far beyond what the law mandated. Perhaps later that day, during a meal hosted by Zacchaeus in honor of Jesus, the tax gatherer stood up in front of his guests and said he would give half his wealth to the destitute. Also, if he had overcharged people on their taxes, he would give them back four times as much (Luke 19:8). The law required a four-fold restitution only when an animal was stolen and killed (see Exod. 22:1; 2 Sam. 12:6). If the animal was found alive, only two-fold restitution was required (see Exod. 22:4). Evidently, Zacchaeus judged his own crime severely, perhaps acknowledging that he was as guilty as the lowest common robber. So, in contrast to the religious elite, Zacchaeus truly repented of his sins.

C. The Announcement: vss. 9-10

Jesus said to him, "Today salvation has come to this house, because this man, too, is a son of Abraham. For the Son of Man came to seek and to save what was lost."

Jesus took note of the decision Zacchaeus made. The Savior declared that this repentant tax collector had shown by his generosity to the poor and desire to make restitution that he was genuinely saved. He was a true descendant of Abraham and child of the promise (Luke 19:9). Scripture reveals that Abraham is the spiritual ancestor of all who trust in the Lord for redemption (see Rom. 4:1-3 and the commentary in lesson 7 of the June quarter). Jesus earlier declared that it was difficult for those awash in riches to be redeemed. But the salvation of Zacchaeus shows that it's not impossible (see Luke 18:24-27). Ironically, the tax collector stood in sharp contrast to the rich young ruler (vss. 18-23).

The residents of Jericho had criticized Jesus for associating with Zacchaeus, whom they also slandered and rejected. However, in 19:10, the Savior declared He had come to earth to "seek" (like a shepherd) and "save" (or rescue) those who were "lost." In referring to Himself as the "Son of Man," Jesus drew attention to His unique, authoritative status as the suffering Servant and Messiah (see Dan. 7:13-14; Isa. 52:13—53:12). Luke 19:10 is a fitting summary of why Jesus came to earth. In brief, Jesus' mission wasn't to please Himself, but rather to redeem sinners from divine judgment (see Mark 10:45).

Like Zacchaeus, Paul was also grateful that Jesus showed Paul unconditional mercy. In 1 Timothy 1, the apostle noted that the Lord considered him faithful and appointed him to His service. Not only did the Lord enable the apostle to serve Him, but also He poured out His grace on Paul by forgiving his past. Faithfulness, not Paul's abilities or knowledge, was the apostle's primary qualification for the ministry that resulted from God's grace (vs. 12). Before his conversion, Paul opposed Jesus' followers. Paul's opposition caused him to use hateful language against the Messiah, even as Paul hunted down Jesus' followers to put them in jail. The Greek noun Paul used for "violent" (vs. 13) describes an arrogant individual who inflicted pain for the delight of seeing another person suffer. The intent was to bring humiliation as well as injury. Paul used the strongest words possible to describe his malicious spirit before conversion.

Despite his wicked behavior, Paul received mercy from the Lord (vs. 14). Paul's comment that he had acted ignorantly in unbelief was not intended to excuse his actions or lessen his guilt. Paul had been sincere in believing that he was serving God when he persecuted the church. But even though Paul had been zealous for God, he still needed the mercy and grace that were poured out on him. The resulting faith in Paul's life proved that God's work of grace was successful in changing him. As Paul reflected back on his own life, he verbalized a doctrinal truth that was both trustworthy and deserving of full acceptance. In short, Jesus the Messiah came into the world to provide redemption for sinners. This is the heart of the Gospel message (see Rom. 1:16-17 and the commentary in lesson 4 of the June quarter).

Paul's confession can give us hope as we think of loved ones and friends who seem far from surrendering their lives to the Lord. Because Jesus saved infamous persons such Zacchaeus and Paul, no one can be regarded as too tarnished by wrongdoing to receive His grace. We should not regard others as hopeless, but continue to pray for their salvation. Treacherous people who genuinely repent often become unstoppable soldiers in the advancement of God's kingdom. The grace poured out on the lives of Zacchaeus and Paul served as a pattern for all who would trust in Jesus and receive salvation.

Discussion Questions

1. Why would Zacchaeus be despised by his Jewish peers?
2. Why did Jesus risk offending the crowd by associating with Zacchaeus?
3. How had Zacchaeus shown himself to be a true descendant of Abraham?
4. Why is changed behavior a good indicator of a genuine profession of faith?
5. What motivates you, like Zacchaeus, to be a committed follower of Jesus?

Contemporary Application

We marvel that Jesus—with all that was on His mind—took particular interest in a hated tax collector named Zacchaeus. In the eyes of the people, there was no justifiable reason for Jesus to associate with such a person. But Jesus recognized the spiritual need of Zacchaeus and in love reached out to him with the truth. In turn, this led to the tax collector's salvation.

This week's lesson reminds us that all sorts of people—whether rich or poor, popular or despised—need to hear the Gospel. They also need to know that it's only through faith in Jesus that they can be saved. God has called us, as believers, to share this Good News with them. Yes, the task is difficult. And there may be times when we run the risk of being misunderstood and criticized by others. Nevertheless, our divine mission remains. The Lord wants us to introduce the lost to Jesus so they can have eternal life.

We will never regret making such a commitment. Our joy in serving the Lord will be renewed and our ability to effectively witness for Him will be enhanced. With repentance, of course, comes the responsibility to commit our lives to Jesus while being faithful to His commands. Like Zacchaeus, we too are called to follow Him. And like Zacchaeus, we can obey and serve the Messiah faithfully.

A Time of Reckoning

Scripture

Background Scripture: *Genesis 1:1—2:3; Zephaniah 1:2—2:4*
Scripture Lesson: *Zephaniah 1:4-6, 14-16; 2:3*
Key Verse: "Seek the LORD, all you humble of the land, you who do what he commands. Seek righteousness, seek humility; perhaps you will be sheltered on the day of the LORD's anger." *Zephaniah 2:3*
Scripture Lesson for Children: *Genesis 1:1-13*
Key Verse for Children: In the beginning God created the heavens and the earth. *Genesis 1:1*

Lesson Aim

To give God first place in our lives.

Lesson Setting

Time: Near the beginning of King Josiah's reforms 621 B.C.
Place: Judah and Jerusalem

Lesson Outline

A Time of Reckoning

    I. A Time of Judgment: Zephaniah 1:4-6, 14-16
        A. *Removing Pagan Worship: vs. 4*
        B. *Cutting Off Idolaters: vss. 5-6*
        C. *Experiencing Distress: vss. 14-16*
   II. A Plea to Seek the Lord: Zephaniah 2:3

Introduction for Adults

Topic: *Seeking the Lord*

Complacency tells us to postpone checking the oil in our cars and to ignore regulating our blood pressure and cholesterol. Complacency also asserts that God isn't concerned about our eternal future. So why should we be concerned about a divine judgment that supposedly won't ever happen?

Scripture, however, tells us that there is a day of reckoning coming. At the end of time, all of us will have to give an account to God for our actions. Only those who have trusted in Jesus for salvation will be delivered from unending punishment. From this we see that God is to be neither ignored nor underestimated.

Zephaniah's prophecies reveal that the people of Judah and Jerusalem trifled with God and lost. In a sense, they suffered the consequences of their spiritual complacency. May we learn from their mistakes and avoid making them ourselves.

Introduction for Youth

Topic: *Desiring God*

Sports writers coined the word *upset* to describe the outcome of a game in which the "weaker" team defeats the "stronger" team. Upsets happen because one group of athletes succumbs to pride and views the opponent too casually.

A prophet named Zephaniah predicted an upset (of sorts) for Jerusalem and its inhabitants. He noted that the elite and powerful lived in luxury and failed to worship the Lord. Zephaniah also declared that God would overturn the fortunes of His wayward people.

We should never minimize God's active presence in our lives. He is aware of everything we think, do, and say. When the light of His Word shines into our souls, we should repent and seek forgiveness through His Son.

Concepts for Children

Topic: *Creation Started*

1. God is real and He exists.
2. God created the entire universe.
3. God created all the plants and animals.
4. God also created us.
5. When we obey God's Word, we are happiest.

Lesson Commentary

I. A TIME OF JUDGMENT: ZEPHANIAH 1:4-6, 14-16

A. Removing Pagan Worship: vs. 4

"I will stretch out my hand against Judah and against all who live in Jerusalem. I will cut off from this place every remnant of Baal, the names of the pagan and the idolatrous priests."

The prophets Nahum, Zephaniah, Habakkuk, and (possibly) Obadiah ministered in a period that ranged from approximately 663 B.C. until about 586 B.C. The northern kingdom of Israel had already fallen to the Assyrians, who posed a continual threat to Judah until the Assyrians fell to the Babylonians in 612 B.C. During the reigns of Manasseh and Amon, idolatry and wickedness prevailed in Judah. Then, when Josiah came to the throne (640–609 B.C.), he brought reformation to the nation by destroying idols and honoring God's Word. After the king's untimely death, Judah quickly returned to its evil practices. Zephaniah and Habakkuk spoke out against the oppression in Judah and prophesied that Babylon would be the one to punish the nation.

In 605 B.C., the Babylonians defeated Egypt at Carchemish and became the most dominant force in the ancient Near East, replacing Assyria as the area's superpower. After that victory, Nebuchadnezzar came through Judah and took some of the nobility to Babylon. Daniel and his friends—Shadrach, Meshach, and Abednego—were among that group. Next, in 598 B.C., Nebuchadnezzar returned to Jerusalem because Jehoiakim had aligned Judah with Egypt. Nebuchadnezzar took the foolish ruler of Judah in shackles to Babylon, along with several items from the temple. Finally, in 586 B.C. the formidable warrior-monarch of Babylon destroyed Jerusalem and took many of the remaining Judahites into captivity.

Zephaniah (whose name means "the Lord hides, protects, or treasures") began his book by telling his readers that he received his prophetic message from the Lord during the reign of King Josiah (1:1). In turn, Zephaniah proclaimed the oracle to the people of Judah. He traced his lineage back four generations to godly King Hezekiah. That would make Zephaniah a distant relative of King Josiah and the royal princes whom the prophet denounced (see 1:8; 3:3). As a person of considerable social standing, Zephaniah was no stranger to the temptations that lured royalty. Most likely, he wrote his book before the well-intentioned reforms King Josiah initiated. Those short-lived changes, however, did not nullify Zephaniah's message of God's discipline and judgment of His people. Despite the impending calamity, the people could rest assured that God remained in control. He would prove it by one day overthrowing the idolatrous Gentile nations and reestablishing Israel in her homeland.

Zephaniah began his message with a dire, universal warning. God would gather up and utterly "sweep away" (1:2) whatever was found on the planet, whether humans or animals, birds or fish (vs. 3). In effect, God would negate what He created at the dawn of time (see Gen. 1:20-28). He would do so because the wicked were guilty of making idolatrous images out of earth's creatures (see Rom. 1:23 and the commentary in lesson 4). Not even humanity would escape the Creator's hand of judgment. Many of the Judahites had become complacent, thinking God would not interfere in their lives (see Zeph. 1:12). The prophet's opening words were meant to get the attention of those who had become comfortable with their immoral conduct. If God would completely remove everything on the earth because of sin's curse, how could Judah's aristocracy expect to escape? Nothing would be left untouched.

The phrase "face of the earth" (1:2) was also used to describe the flood that inundated the world during the time of Noah (Gen. 6:7; 7:4). In Zephaniah, the phrase indicates another horrific, wide-ranging judgment that would again affect all of creation. Yet, in light of God's promise to Noah (see Gen. 8:21-22), how could He again legitimately send such devastation upon the earth? Perhaps Zephaniah viewed this time of wrath as a part of the judgment that would end this present world and bring in the new heavens and earth (see 2 Pet. 3:3-13; Rev. 21:1).

In Zephaniah 1:4, God's spokesperson moved from a broad declaration of divine wrath to a specific warning of judgment against Judah and Jerusalem (which, ironically, means "city of peace"). The idiomatic expression of God stretching out His "hand" brings to mind the various afflictions He brought upon Egypt in order to free His people from their oppressors (see Exod. 3:20; 6:6; 7:4-5; 9:15). In a dramatic reversal of fortunes, the Lord would perform a special work of punishment against Judah's wayward inhabitants. Even the identity of the pagan priests would be removed from human memory. Those who worshiped Baal, the Canaanite deity of rain and fertility, were singled out as objects of God's wrath. Josiah attempted to destroy Baal worship, along with its apostate religious leaders (see 2 Chron. 34:4-5), but some idolatry still remained. The coming judgment would finally abolish this uncleanness from the promised land. God's personal intervention would play a decisive role in guaranteeing the outcome (see Isa. 5:25; 9:12).

B. Cutting Off Idolaters: vss. 5-6

"Those who bow down on the roofs to worship the starry host, those who bow down and swear by the LORD *and who also swear by Molech, those who turn back from following the* LORD *and neither seek the* LORD *nor inquire of him."*

Another group of idolaters venerated the sun, moon, stars, and planets from the flat rooftops of their homes (Zeph. 1:5). This locale provided a good view of the heavenly objects, as well as a place to burn incense upon makeshift altars (see Jer. 8:2; 19:13; 32:29). Josiah acted against this practice, but failed to eliminate it (see 2 Kings 23:5).

Furthermore, idolaters not only claimed to be loyal to the Lord, but also took oaths in the name of some entity specialists find difficult to identify. The ambiguity is reflected in the various ways the ending of Zephaniah 1:5 is rendered. Some think the Hebrew text refers to swearing allegiance to "Molech," a deity worshiped by the Ammonites. The rituals involved in the worship of Molech included sacrificing babies in the flaming lap of a stone idol. These abominable acts would ignite God's anger. Others think the verse points to the veneration of "Milcom," which many identify with Molech. Still others render the ending as "their king," which could be a reference to an ungodly monarch or the pagan deity he revered. In any case, God's people were guilty of combining their worship of the Lord with the veneration of foreign gods and goddesses.

Verse 6 reveals the Judahites also turned away from following the Creator. In particular, they refused to go to Him for help and seek His guidance, especially in times when their need was acute. Zephaniah possibly includes those who at first heeded the reformations under King Josiah, but later departed from serving the Lord. Others, however, remained indifferent to God from the beginning and were still living in complete disregard of their spiritual need for Him.

C. Experiencing Distress: vss. 14-16

"The great day of the LORD is near—near and coming quickly. Listen! The cry on the day of the LORD will be bitter, the shouting of the warrior there. That day will be a day of wrath, a day of distress and anguish, a day of trouble and ruin, a day of darkness and gloom, a day of clouds and blackness, a day of trumpet and battle cry against the fortified cities and against the corner towers."

The faithless, idolatrous Judahites were commanded to "be silent" (Zeph. 1:7; signaling reverence and respect) because the "day of the LORD" was close at hand (see Hab. 2:20; Zech. 2:13). The preceding expression was popular among Old Testament prophets to indicate God's entering human history to decisively judge sin. It refers to a time when God would pour out His wrath upon the nations and His chosen people. It was also a time of universal restoration connected with the Messiah's return. The day of the Lord ends with universal peace and the Creator ruling over the nations (see Isa. 11; Zech. 14).

The prophet described the judgments of that day as a "sacrifice" (Zeph. 1:8). But this time the people of Judah would be the offering and the dreaded Babylonians would be the "consecrated" priests performing the ritual (see Isa. 13:3; Jer. 46:10; Ezek. 39:17). Not even the officials of Judah's royal court and the members of the monarch's family—all of whom observed pagan rituals and were enamored with foreign customs—would be spared. Instead of promoting God's ways, these leaders championed idolatrous, abhorrent behavior.

"All who avoid stepping on the threshold" (Zeph. 1:9) may refer to a pagan superstition that began when the Philistine god, Dagon, fell into pieces on the entryway of its shrine (see 1 Sam. 5:4-5). Zephaniah 1:9 indicates that God's anger was directed against those who avoided the doorstep of the houses they had raided (by using oppressive, deceptive means). Evidently, these robbers thought it was sacrilegious to step across a "threshold," for they feared the action would offend the deities amassed there to guard the home they occupied.

Verse 10 says that when the day of judgment arrived, shrieks would arise from the "Fish Gate" (see 2 Chron. 33:14; Neh. 3:3; 12:39). This was located on the north side of the Jerusalem wall near the Temple Mount. Nebuchadnezzar, the Babylonian king, and his bloodthirsty army broke through the city walls at this spot. The "New Quarter" (Zeph. 1:10) may have been a more recent addition to the city built for the affluent living northwest of the temple (see 2 Kings 22:14; 2 Chron. 34:22; Neh. 11:9). The deafening sound coming from the "hills" (Zeph. 1:10) represents the progress of the Babylonians as they overran key positions within Jerusalem. The elevated areas were Zion, Moriah, and Ophel. The "crash" was the noise of walls crumbling and buildings collapsing as the conquerors relentlessly advanced.

Verse 11 directs the readers' attention to the "market district." This was a bowl-shaped basin in the lower part of the city's southern sector (perhaps comparable in appearance to a mortar used for pulverizing grain). Here "merchants" or "traders" (literally, "people of Canaan") gathered to barter and sell their merchandise. Even this area would feel the pounding, crushing force of God's judgment as the Babylonians razed everything in their path. The searching with lanterns suggests a thorough probe of every dim crevice in the city so no one would escape judgment (vs. 12; see Amos 9:2-4). When the Babylonians arrived, they seized people from their homes, as well as from the sewers and tombs where they hid.

Just as Zephaniah foretold, not even those who smugly thought God was indifferent to their iniquity would escape judgment (see Isa. 32:9; Ezek. 30:9; Amos 6:1). The phrase "wine left on its dregs" (Zeph. 1:12) was a common expression of the day to refer to apathy and callousness. At the end of the fermentation process, the liquid was poured from vessel to vessel to separate the wine from its bitter dregs. If this was not done, the wine became acidic and undrinkable. Like wine left on its dregs, those wallowing in sin become bitter and useless.

Verse 13 discloses that the inhabitants of Judah and Jerusalem would witness the Babylonians pillage their "wealth," tear down their "houses," and uproot their "vineyards." Just as foretold elsewhere in the Old Testament (see Lev. 26:32-33; Deut. 28:30, 39; Amos 5:11; Mic. 6:15), God's people would see all they had worked for confiscated and destroyed. God's people were to take note, for their own excruciating day would soon arrive. These calamities foreshadowed the final time of distress that would overtake the world, known as the "day of the LORD" (Zeph. 1:14). This judgment was called "great" because of its impact upon the whole earth.

Like many Old Testament prophecies, the "day of the LORD" had an immediate and a future fulfillment. Ultimately, the time of horrendous distress would mark the Messiah's return. In Zephaniah's day, this oracle had its first fulfillment when the Babylonians ransacked Judah and demolished Jerusalem. In verses 15 and 16, Zephaniah gave a vivid description of the terror produced by the approaching judgment. The first four terms ("distress," "anguish," "trouble," and "ruin") describe the dreadful nature of that day when everyone would weep and wail. The last four words ("darkness," "gloom," "clouds," and "blackness") detail that day's ominous conditions. The Babylonians would burn Judah's "fortified cities" (vs. 16) and fill Jerusalem's lofty "towers" with the stench of death.

II. A Plea to Seek the Lord: Zephaniah 2:3

Seek the LORD, all you humble of the land, you who do what he commands. Seek righteousness, seek humility; perhaps you will be sheltered on the day of the LORD's anger.

Zephaniah 1:17 disclosed that the suffering of God's people would be profound. Bewilderment and despair would so "blind" them that they would stagger (see Deut. 28:29). They would also reel from the affliction that had come upon them because of their sins. The blood of the dead would cover the streets like worthless dirt. Also, putrefying bodies would be piled up everywhere and fertilize the ground like "filth" (Zeph. 1:17). No amount of material wealth (especially riches obtained by fraudulent means) would deliver Judah's inhabitants from this catastrophe. Not even the aristocrats could bribe their way out of undergoing the agony produced by God's "wrath" (vs. 18).

After all, the entire nation of Judah was disgraced by their iniquities. Collectively, they were like straw or stubble that God's fiery anger would incinerate. The latter judgment anticipated a future day in which God allowed the whole earth and all who lived on it to be wiped out. Yet, before the time of horror finally arrived, there was something God's people could do to escape or delay the frightful outcome. They could gather together as a "shameful nation" (2:1), humbly acknowledge their sin, and plead with the Lord to turn away from His judgment. There was no time to spare. They had to repent before the Creator's "fierce anger" (vs. 2) overtook them like a violent storm blowing away "chaff." In Bible times, farmers would toss harvested grain into the air to separate the kernels from the husks covering the grain. While the kernels fell to the ground, the wind would blow away the worthless husks.

In verse 3, Zephaniah pleaded with Judah's citizens who were truly "humble" to "seek" God's favor. They were to abandon their iniquity, idolatry, and injustice and heed the Lord's ordinances and decrees. Also, God's spokesperson directed His people to pursue "righteousness." The latter translates a Hebrew noun that refers to the practice of honesty and integrity. "Humility" refers to a meek and submissive disposition. The implication is that the upright could not pretend to repent. Their return to the Lord had to be shown through genuine attitudes and sincere actions.

.If this happened, then perhaps the righteous remnant somehow would be "sheltered" (vs. 3) when the time came for God to display His "anger." "Sheltered" renders a Hebrew verb that literally means to be "concealed" or "hidden." It denotes being protected or kept safe in a time of great turmoil. Turning to the Lord was the only hope for the godly (see Jer. 26:3; Amos 5:15). But even then, doing so might be too late to prevent disaster from overtaking Judah and Jerusalem.

As we look around our world today, we might wonder why God does not judge the wickedness and violence that are so rampant. Yet, just as with Judah, our gracious God always gives everyone ample opportunity to abandon their sin before they experience His wrath. His desire is that no one would perish (see 1 Tim. 2:4; 2 Pet. 3:9). Nonetheless, for those who resist their opportunity to cry out to God for deliverance, His discipline proves to be swift and sure.

Discussion Questions

1. Why would God bring judgment on Judah?
2. Why did God's people refuse to follow Him?
3. What sorts of events were associated with the day of the Lord?
4. Why is it important for believers to center their lives on God?
5. In what ways can believers pursue righteousness?

Contemporary Application

Zephaniah began his prophecy with a vision of impending judgment on Judah and Jerusalem. Because of the wickedness of its rulers and inhabitants, the promised land would be reduced to rubble.

All of us want to be free from danger, anxiety, and despair. Left to ourselves, however, we might try to obtain safety, peace, and hope in the wrong places. For example, we might seek to protect ourselves from financial problems by stockpiling lots of money. We might attempt to shore up our sagging feelings through having fun with our family and friends. Finally, we might try to alleviate our lack of confidence by trying to succeed in our jobs.

The longer we remain self-satisfied, the less we will trust God. We also run the risk of becoming more insecure. We might try to compensate for this by trying to impress others with our accomplishments or by indulging in self-congratulatory thoughts. We know, though, from this week's lesson that these efforts accomplish nothing of eternal value.

We recognize from the lives of God's people that when we doubt the Lord, it leads to insecurity. We do not trust Him as much as we should when we look to the things of the world, rather than Him, for peace of mind and protection. Our confidence is misplaced when we rely on our wealth, family and friends, or jobs instead of God to meet our needs.

A Depraved Lifestyle

DEVOTIONAL READING

Deuteronomy 8:11-18

DAILY BIBLE READINGS

Monday June 6
Deuteronomy 4:9-14
Remember God's Commands

Tuesday June 7
Proverbs 16:1-9 Godly
Planning

Wednesday June 8
Ezekiel 33:27-33 Ungodly
Planning

Thursday June 9
Matthew 11:25-30 Promised
Rest

Friday June 10
1 Peter 5:1-6 Humble
Planning

Saturday June 11
1 Peter 5:7-11 Faithful
Planning

Sunday June 12
Zephaniah 3:1-8
Consequences of Disobedience

Scripture

Background Scripture: *Genesis 1:1—2:3; Zephaniah 3:1-8*
Scripture Lesson: *Zephaniah 3:1-8*
Key Verse: "Wait for me," declares the LORD, "for the day I will stand up to testify." *Zephaniah 3:8*
Scripture Lesson for Children: *Genesis 1:14-23*
Key Verses for Children: God said, "Let there be lights in the expanse of the sky." . . . And it was so. *Genesis 1:14-15*

Lesson Aim

To note that the harsh consequences of sin can move us to seek the Lord.

Lesson Setting

Time: Near the beginning of King Josiah's reforms 621 B.C.
Place: Judah and Jerusalem

Lesson Outline

A Depraved Lifestyle

I. The Wretchedness of God's People:
Zephaniah 3:1-5
    A. *A Rebellious City: vs. 1*
    B. *Unprincipled Leaders: vss. 2-4*
    C. *God's Integrity: vs. 5*

II. The Lord's Purifying Judgment: Zephaniah 3:6-8
    A. *Devastation of Nations: vs. 6*
    B. *Eagerness to Sin: vs. 7*
    C. *Assurance of Vindication: vs. 8*

Introduction for Adults

Topic: *Maintaining Hope!*

Most, if not all, of your students are probably Christians. No doubt most of them have experienced God's love. And yet, despite the many ways God has shown His love to us, we all have areas in our lives where we stubbornly insist on doing what we want to do rather than what God expects us to do. Zephaniah 3:7 reveals that this was also true for the residents of Jerusalem.

Although your students are adults, in some ways they may act like self-centered and spoiled little children. Remind your students that God views us in the same way parents view their young children. Just as we expect our children to develop into mature adults, so God wants us to mature as Christians.

Of course, as we grow in the Lord, we will make many childish mistakes and even rebel occasionally, as Jerusalem's habitants did (see vss. 1-5). One important truth is that though we often act selfishly and behave stubbornly, God continues to love and nurture us (see vs. 7). It's the presence of His compassion that gives us hope in the midst of despairing circumstances.

Introduction for Youth

Topic: *Despair and Hope*

Zephaniah 3:1-4 lists the sins the people of Jerusalem committed. For the upright, it was easy to lose hope and begin to despair. Yet, God encouraged them to "wait" (vs. 8) patiently for Him to one day bring justice to pass.

A high school student lost his older brother in a car accident. For three years the adolescent struggled to find hope in the midst of this tragedy. During that time, he could not talk about it. Meanwhile, after the accident, some other students who were not Christians came to faith because of the witness the deceased brother had maintained on campus when he was alive. They found that the only way to deal with the tragedy was to commit themselves to Jesus.

The world-famous explorer and missionary, Wilfred T. Grenfell, left us with some sound advice when we think about despair and hope. He wrote, "The faith that Christ asks for is not to understand Him, but to follow Him. By that and that alone can we convert the tragedy of human life—full of disappointments, disillusionments, and with death ever looming ahead—into the most glorious field of honor, worthy of the dignity of a [child] of God."

Concepts for Children

Topic: *Creation Continues*

1. God created the heavens and the earth because He loves us.
2. Before God created anything, He said what He would make.
3. God said what He had created was good.
4. God showered His goodness on everything He created.
5. We can thank God for His goodness to us.

Lesson Commentary

I. THE WRETCHEDNESS OF GOD'S PEOPLE: ZEPHANIAH 3:1-5

A. A Rebellious City: vs. 1

Woe to the city of oppressors, rebellious and defiled!

Zephaniah 2:1-3 focused on God's judgment of Judah and Jerusalem. Having described the ominous day of reckoning, God's spokesperson turned his focus to the nations located around Judah. The Philistines (vss. 4-7), Moabites and Ammonites (vss. 8-11), Cushites (vs. 12), and Assyrians (vss. 13-15) would also experience God's wrath at the hand of the invading Babylonian army. The neighboring nation of Philistia, long a thorn in the side of Israel, would be completely destroyed by Nebuchadnezzar and his army. The four cities mentioned in verse 4 represent the whole area inhabited by the Philistines. The timing of the attack on Ashdod and Ekron, "at midday," shows the unexpected nature of the assault. That was usually an interval when everyone rested from the heat of the day. It was not a likely occasion for an invasion.

The Hebrew adjective rendered "Kerethite" (vs. 5) probably indicates that at least a part of the Philistines, if not all, had emigrated from the island of Crete. The Lord warned that their once densely populated land would be abandoned and turned into a desolate pasture for shepherds, with the ruins of their homes turned into folds for the sheep. In the end, the land of Philistia would belong to the remnant of Judah (vs. 7). When they returned from captivity in Babylon, these Jews would occupy the territory of their former, longtime adversary. There the Lord, like a shepherd, would "care for them" and "restore their fortunes." So, despite the impending judgment, there was hope for Judah's future.

For an extended period, the Moabites and Ammonites heaped insults upon Israel and caused problems for the nation's inhabitants whenever the adversaries found an opportunity (vs. 8; see also Num. 22—24; 1 Sam. 11:1-5). After the fall of Israel and the demise of Judah, Moab and Ammon reproached God's people all the more and attempted to profit by seizing land from them. In response to their behavior, Zephaniah announced that Moab and Ammon, too, would feel the wrath of God. The fierceness of His anger with these two nations would result in destruction similar to that of Sodom and Gomorrah, which were often used as biblical symbols of total devastation (Zeph. 2:9). The present-day ruins of ancient towns in these regions show the accuracy of Zephaniah's prophecy that the area would become a desolate and permanent wasteland. The remnant of God's people eventually plundered the riches of Moab and Ammon and occupied their land. Zephaniah identified pride as the cause that led these adversaries to taunt and mock God's people (vs. 10).

Despite the grim nature of Zephaniah's judgment oracles, God's ultimate aim was not to destroy sinful nations. Instead, it was to show the futility of trusting in pagan deities and cause people to turn to the Creator in faith (vs. 11). The false gods and goddesses were ruined when the nations that depended on them were defeated, for idols had no existence apart from the minds of their worshipers. The intended result of God's judgment was that nations everywhere would serve Him. In the view of some, this oracle is ultimately fulfilled in the spread of the Gospel (see Mark 16:15, 20; Acts 1:8). Others see the prophecy as a reference to the Messiah's second coming. At that time, all the nations would acknowledge the Son as their Lord (see Isa. 2:2; Mich. 4:1).

Zephaniah's next target was the Cushites, who lived south of Egypt and are often identified as the Ethiopians (Zeph. 2:12). Without providing many details, the Lord simply declared through His spokesperson that they would "be slain by my sword." Ezekiel prophesied that God would put His sword in the hand of the king of Babylon when he came against Egypt (see Ezek. 30:24-25). Cush eventually fell by the sword of Nebuchadnezzar as he led the Babylonians against them.

Assyria's demise, described by the prophet Nahum, is recounted by Zephaniah in 2:13-15. At that time, Assyria was a mighty empire—and Nineveh, its capital city, was an impenetrable fortress that boasted of a fabulous irrigation system. Yet, despite all this, Assyria would be destroyed and Nineveh would be left "utterly desolate and dry as the desert" (vs. 13). Zephaniah's prediction that Nineveh would become a place for "flocks and herds" (vs. 14) was literally fulfilled. Even today, sheep still graze on the spot where the renowned city once stood.

No one, apart from the Lord, could have imagined that such a powerful and prosperous city as Nineveh would be reduced to rubble in such a short time. Its leaders certainly could not discern that destruction was in their future. The city boasted of its self-sufficiency by proclaiming, "I am, and there is none besides me" (vs. 15). Only God could legitimately make that claim, and He did not overlook Nineveh's challenge to His authority. The city soon became an object of contempt, while the Lord remained self-sustaining and worthy of all praise and adoration.

After pronouncing judgment on the surrounding nations, Zephaniah returned his focus to Judah and particularly to Jerusalem. The context of 3:1-5 makes it clear that this unnamed city was none other than Jerusalem. By not directly naming the city, Zephaniah indicated with rhetorical skill that Jerusalem was on the same moral footing as the pagan Ninevites. Specifically, Jerusalem was filled with those guilty of oppression—that is, committing hostile, violent acts against the innocent. The tyrants were responsible for disregarding the rights of the weak, such as the poor, orphans, widows, and foreigners. Showing love to others was a fundamental aspect of the Mosaic law that the people of Jerusalem chose to disobey.

Moreover, a "rebellious" (vs. 1) spirit characterized Jerusalem's inhabitants. Put differently, the city's residents were contentious and obstinate in their hearts. Although the citizens possessed God's revealed Word, they repudiated its authority. Likewise, the people boldly refused to perform what the Lord clearly instructed them to do. Just as tragic was Jerusalem's "defiled" condition. The latter meant the city and its people were morally stained and spiritually unclean. This was due to their association with the worship of Baal, the stars, and Molech (see 1:4-5). Despite all Jerusalem's obsession with performing religious ceremonies, it was desecrated and about to be handed over to judgment because of its ethical filthiness. All three descriptive terms in 3:1 (namely, "oppressors," "rebellious," and "defiled") point to Israel's breaking of its covenant with God.

B. Unprincipled Leaders: vss. 2-4

She obeys no one, she accepts no correction. She does not trust in the LORD, she does not draw near to her God. Her officials are roaring lions, her rulers are evening wolves, who leave nothing for the morning. Her prophets are arrogant; they are treacherous men. Her priests profane the sanctuary and do violence to the law.

God sent many prophets to Judah and Jerusalem. Yet, despite His repeated efforts, the nation, its leaders (both civil and religious), and its citizens resisted all exhortations to repentance (see Jer. 7:13, 25; 11:7; 25:3; 26:5; 29:19; 32:33; 35:14-15; 44:4). The first part of Zephaniah 3:2 is literally rendered "does not hear a voice." This idiomatic expression means Jerusalem spurned heeding God's instruction. "Correction" translates a Hebrew noun that refers to chastisement and reprimands coming from God. The term indicates that the people refused to abandon their wicked ways.

"Trust" renders a Hebrew verb that denotes placing one's confidence in the Creator. Rather than depend on the true and living God, the inhabitants of Jerusalem relied on the pagan nations around them. Moreover, instead of drawing near to the Lord in heartfelt worship and gratitude, His people moved deeper into idolatry and wickedness. God gave Jerusalem a favored position, but the city squandered its opportunity (see Rom. 3, 9, and 11, along with the commentary in lessons 6, 11, and 12, respectively).

Next, Zephaniah described the iniquities of Jerusalem's unprincipled leaders. Though he named several groups, the prophet carefully avoided saying anything that would implicate King Josiah, who initiated genuine attempts at spiritual reform. Zephaniah depicted the princes as fierce "lions" and the magistrates as ravenous "wolves." In the evening, the aristocrats preyed on the helpless. Metaphorically speaking, the wicked rich so thoroughly devoured the flesh of their victims that by morning there was nothing left on their bones (vs. 3). Rather than act in fairness and impartiality like judges, these leaders satiated their greed at the expense of those they were called to serve. Also, instead of protecting the defenseless like shepherds, the power brokers exploited them. God saw these perversions of justice and acted to stop all abuses of power.

Zephaniah characterized the prophets of his day as "arrogant" (vs. 4). The term renders a Hebrew verb that denotes someone who is reckless, audacious, and unscrupulous. This description would be true of the dishonest prophets, who misled God's people into a false sense of security when disaster was closing in upon them (see Jer. 23:32). The noun rendered "treacherous" (Zeph. 3:4) denotes spokespersons known for their deceitful words and duplicitous behavior. We know there were several good prophets at that time, such as Jeremiah and Nahum. But many other prophets were unfaithful to their calling.

The priests were just as despicable in their conduct. They were supposed to demonstrate God's holiness and accurately interpret His law (see Lev. 10:10-11). Instead, the priests' wicked example and careless reading of Scripture caused many to stumble. For instance, they desecrated what was sacred in the temple and spurned the distinction detailed in the Mosaic law between what was ritually clean and unclean (see Ezek. 22:26). Through the priests' abuse and distortions of the Torah, they encouraged the city's rebellious ways.

C. God's Integrity: vs. 5

The LORD within her is righteous; he does no wrong. Morning by morning he dispenses his justice, and every new day he does not fail, yet the unrighteous know no shame.

Zephaniah 3:5 clearly marks the city as Jerusalem, for no other urban area could boast of having the living God dwelling in the midst of its temple. While the princes, judges, prophets, and priests were derelict in their duty, their divine Ruler acted uprightly and with integrity. Whereas Judah's leaders were characterized by wickedness, the Lord remained impeccable in His conduct (see Deut. 32:4; Job 34:10; Ps. 92:15). God did not go into hiding because of all the sin occurring in Jerusalem. Instead, He stayed to expose the evil and set Himself up as the perfect moral standard.

From one morning to the next, the Creator administered "justice" (Zeph. 3:5). (Morning was the normal time to do so in that era.) And, with each "new day," He succeeded in bringing equity to pass. Some suggest God's righteousness was expressed through the daily temple ceremony (see Exod. 30:7; 2 Chron. 13:11). Others view Zephaniah 3:5 as a general reference to the continuous manifestation of the Lord's rule in His treatment of Judah and the surrounding nations. Despite God's holy presence, the seared consciences of the aristocrats and the masses they controlled caused them to remain brazen.

II. THE LORD'S PURIFYING JUDGMENT: ZEPHANIAH 3:6-8

A. Devastation of Nations: vs. 6

"I have cut off nations; their strongholds are demolished. I have left their streets deserted, with no one passing through. Their cities are destroyed; no one will be left—no one at all."

God reminded His people how He had wiped out entire nations (Zeph. 3:6; see 1:3-4, 13; 2:4, 9, 13, 15). This included flattening the walls and leveling the corner towers of their fortified cities. Nothing was left but heaps of rubble in their once-bustling thoroughfares. There has been much speculation about the identity of these nations and cities, particularly since the northern 10 tribes had already been taken captive by Assyria. Perhaps it was meant as a general reference to those who had fallen to the wrath of God, including the northern kingdom of Israel.

Why did God suddenly begin talking through Zephaniah to emphasize His devastation of other countries? The Lord's judgment of these other nations was meant to be a warning to the people of Judah. They should have observed how the Creator had punished the sin of these lands and how the idols were powerless to protect those who venerated the pagan deities. Regrettably, the covenant community missed the message and kept on serving lifeless idols.

B. Eagerness to Sin: vs. 7

"I said to the city, 'Surely you will fear me and accept correction!' Then her dwelling would not be cut off, nor all my punishments come upon her. But they were still eager to act corruptly in all they did."

In light of all God had done to judge sins in the surrounding nations, He expected His people to repent and obey Him (Zeph. 3:7). The Lord's purpose in judging transgressions was to create a godly reverence (rather than a cringing dread) within His people and motivate them to submit to His hand of discipline. In turn, He would not have to carry out His sentence of destruction on Jerusalem.

If the inhabitants humbly returned to the Creator, He would refrain from demolishing their homes and bringing even more severe calamities upon the owners because of their wrongdoing. Yet, not only did the people persist in their immorality, but also they were enthusiastic to carry out their wickedness. The Hebrew text of verse 7 literally says they "got up early," which emphasizes the earnest and defiant nature of the people's actions. Despite seeing God's judgment on other nations and knowing the severe penalty for their atrocities, the covenant community neither repented nor sought mercy from the Lord.

C. Assurance of Vindication: vs. 8

"Therefore wait for me," declares the LORD, "for the day I will stand up to testify. I have decided to assemble the nations, to gather the kingdoms and to pour out my wrath on them—all my fierce anger. The whole world will be consumed by the fire of my jealous anger."

After the disappointing response described in Zephaniah 3:7, one might anticipate verse 8 to begin with a declaration of God's intention to punish Judah. The incorrect impression is that the prophet's oracles were entirely characterized by doom and gloom. Yet, as with 2:3, we find a note of mercy and grace in 3:8. The Lord, through His spokesperson, instructed Judah (especially the godly remnant) to wait patiently for a time when He would act decisively to vindicate and deliver them.

Some versions of the Hebrew text literally read, "when I arise for plunder." The emphasis is on God bringing judgment on the nations. Other versions (based on the Septuagint) read, "when I arise as a witness." In this case, a courtroom scene is depicted in which the Creator testifies against earth's rulers. Both options stress that the Lord was just to gather the kingdoms of the earth together and pour out His wrath upon all of them at one time. Rather than simply warn Jerusalem about what the Babylonians would do to it, God told the city to wait expectantly for a day when He would pronounce a guilty verdict on the entire earth. This would become the legal basis for God to "pour out" (like a libation) His righteous indignation—that is, His burning "anger"—on the nations. Then the entire planet would be "consumed" by His fiery, zealous "anger" (see 1:18).

Discussion Questions

1. In what ways was Jerusalem a corrupt, rebellious city?
2. Why did Jerusalem refuse to heed the Lord?
3. How had God remained just in His treatment of His people?
4. Why does God ask believers to wait patiently for Him to vindicate them?
5. How can believers resist the temptation to take justice into their own hands?

Contemporary Application

Zephaniah warned of calamity coming to Jerusalem because of its acts of oppression and rebellion (see 3:1-5). The prophet's oracle about the harsh consequences of sin was intended to move God's people to seek Him. Some people think this means all one has to do is recite a pious-sounding prayer and that is the end of it. More accurately, seeking the Lord is a process in which believers individually and collectively turn their hearts to Him in unwavering devotion. It means they go out into the world and make His presence known through their words and deeds.

Seeking the Lord means we dedicate every aspect of our lives to His service. When we do so, we figuratively hand God a blank sheet to fill in, with our name signed at the bottom. We orient our minds and hearts to His will. We effectively say *no* to our sinful ways and *yes* to His holy desires. At times we might not feel inclined to seek the Lord as much as we ought. It is in those moments that we should pray to God for a willing mind and heart.

Seeking the Lord entails running away from all forms of sin in our lives (see vss. 6-8). This is what repentance is all about. It implies that we are altering our way of looking at life. We are taking God's point of view rather than our own. Repenting of sin can be difficult. After all, we are rejecting unwholesome activities we may enjoy (see Heb. 11:25). It is good to remember that God condemns many of the things the world praises. Likewise, many of the things He approves of, the world rejects. Ultimately, our standard for living must be the Lord and His Word, not the misguided edicts of fallen humanity.

A Promise of Restoration

Scripture

Background Scripture: *Genesis 1:1—2:3;*
Zephaniah 3:9-20
Scripture Lesson: *Zephaniah 3:9-14, 20*
Key Verse: Sing, O Daughter of Zion; shout aloud,
O Israel! Be glad and rejoice with all your heart, O
Daughter of Jerusalem! *Zephaniah 3:14*
Scripture Lesson for Children: *Genesis 1:24—2:3*
Key Verse for Children: By the seventh day God had
finished the work he had been doing; so on the
seventh day he rested from all his work. *Genesis 2:2*

Lesson Aim

To turn to God for comfort, restoration, and renewal in
times of difficulty.

Lesson Setting

Time: Near the beginning of King Josiah's reforms 621 B.C.
Place: Judah and Jerusalem

Lesson Outline

A Promise of Restoration
  I. The Humble Remnant: Zephaniah 3:9-13
     A. *Uniting God's People: vss. 9-10*
     B. *Cleansing God's People: vss. 11-13*
  II. The Reestablished Remnant: Zephaniah 3:14, 20
     A. *A Summons to Rejoice: vs. 14*
     B. *A Promise of Restoration: vs. 20*

Introduction for Adults

Topic: *Taking Comfort in Renewal*

Different things represent comfort to people. Some perceive a soft chair, an expensive sports car, warm and sunny weather, or delicious food as something that can make them comfortable. Others think they would feel more contented if they had better health, minimal stress, or a large savings account. Nevertheless, adults are rarely satisfied with the circumstances that surround them. There is always something about which they can complain.

For the people of Zephaniah's day, their level of comfort had much to do with what they had experienced. The same is true of us. That's why we need to understand that God's comfort may not come in ways we want. However, that does not mean God is trying to make our lives miserable.

People tend to be comfortable when they receive the things they want. That's why it is hard for them to thank God for difficult times. It is even more challenging for them to see the ways God seeks to comfort, restore, and renew them, for He may choose to do so in ways they don't expect. Regardless, let your students know that His approach is always best.

Introduction for Youth

Topic: *Finding Joy in Restoration*

What do you do with a broken-down car that needs repairs and paint? You look beyond the wreck and envision a sparkling new paint job and a motor that purrs sweetly down the road. You give that car all the sweat you can muster because you have high hopes for it.

Perhaps if we were writing Zephaniah's oracles today, rather than comparing God to a protective shepherd, we would compare Him to a sensitive, careful, hardworking, and loving mechanic. That's because we bestow the same kind of love on our cars that shepherds do on their sheep.

The main point is that God can bring about restoration and renewal in the lives of youth, especially if they submit to His will. He has wonderful plans for them that they can't even imagine. Metaphorically speaking, God can take their dings and dents, and all the misfirings of their cylinders, and make a beautiful vehicle out of their lives. Through faith in His Son, they can make a fresh start down the road to hope!

Concepts for Children

Topic: *Creation Completed*

1. God created people to be like Him.
2. God created the man and woman to take care of the earth.
3. God's creation of people was the high point of what He had done.
4. God said everything He had created was very good.
5. We can thank God for giving us life.

Lesson Commentary

I. THE HUMBLE REMNANT: ZEPHANIAH 3:9-13

A. Uniting God's People: vss. 9-10

"Then will I purify the lips of the peoples, that all of them may call on the name of the LORD and serve him shoulder to shoulder. From beyond the rivers of Cush my worshipers, my scattered people, will bring me offerings."

In last week's lesson, we learned that the idolatry, immorality, and injustice of the people living during the time of Zephaniah were fueled by deception and duplicity. This was especially true of the false prophets, who misled the people with unfounded declarations of peace and prosperity. In this way, they misrepresented the Lord. Instead of preaching false security, they should have been warning the people to repent. Such outright lies eventually helped to bring about the downfall of Judah and Jerusalem.

In Zephaniah 3:8, God's spokesperson described a catastrophic judgment on the scale of what had happened in Noah's day. Next, Zephaniah discussed the results of God's action. The prophet pictured the global outpouring of the Lord's anger producing a massive revival in which people from all countries called out to the Lord (vs. 9). His defeat of the gathered nations would result in a time of peace when all humanity spurned their veneration of pagan deities, gave the Creator heartfelt praise, and joined one another to serve Him.

Some regard the Hebrew phrase rendered "purify the lips" (vs. 9) as referring to a "purified language." In turn, it is suggested this denotes an untainted Hebrew dialect to be spoken by the remnant of Israel in the last days (perhaps signifying a reversal of the confused speech occurring at Babel; see Gen. 11:1-9). Although this is a possible inference of Zephaniah 3:9, it does not fit the context of calling "on the name of the LORD" mentioned later in the passage. The latter denotes an inner spiritual cleansing, as well as a sincere and somber seeking of God in heartfelt worship and service (see Isa. 6:5-7). It usually comes in response to a critical need, especially as people recognize their sinfulness and the necessity of depending on the Creator (see Gen. 4:26; 12:8; 13:4; 21:33). God responds favorably to all who call upon Him in such a manner (see Ps. 145:18; Joel 2:32; Acts 2:21).

Zephaniah 3:10 has been understood in a variety of ways. Some think the verse concerns the Gentiles escorting God's people, the Jews, back to the promised land as their "offering" to the Lord. Others interpret the verse to mean that after judgment, God would bring His people back from the remotest areas of the earth, even as far south as Cush (Nubia, once called Ethiopia, in the upper region of the Nile River). Still others see this verse referring in part to the return of the Jews to their homeland after the Babylonian captivity, and in part to Gentiles (regardless of their ethnic background) coming to the Father through faith in the Son, the Lord Jesus (see John 11:51-52).

Micah 4:1-3 (along with Isaiah 2:1-4) describes a future time of righteousness, justice, and peace in which redeemed Jerusalem would be a city of God for all the nations. Also, the temple mount would become the center of widespread devotion to the Lord. In the ancient world, pagan shrines were often located at the tops of mountains or other high places, because of the idea that they were entrances to heaven. In similar fashion, the Israelites built their temple on a Judean hilltop.

Admittedly, other mountains—even ones nearby—were taller. Yet, Micah 4:1 declared that the temple mount in Jerusalem would be raised higher than other hills. By this, the prophet meant that the city's sacred elevation would become the most important one, for it would be the place where peoples of the world would come to offer worship to the one true God. According to Revelation 15:3-4, in that day all nations would assemble and revere the Creator, whose ways were upright and true.

God chose the family of Abraham, Isaac, and Jacob as His covenant people. In one sense, the Israelites were exclusively the Creator's possession. Yet, here and there in the Old Testament (including Zeph. 3:9), we find hints that a time was coming when individuals from many of the world's people groups would follow the Lord. In this vein, Micah 4:2 described a time when "many nations" would eagerly praise God at the Jerusalem temple and would obey His law.

When people from across the globe honored the Creator, life on earth would be incredibly different and better (vss. 3-4). Specifically, God would establish just relations between nations. People would give up their violent ways by converting weapons into tools and abandoning the arts of warfare. They would have a sense of security, enjoying life on their own property without fear. The era when people would worship the Lord had not yet begun in the lifetimes of Zephaniah and Micah. Other nations still venerated pagan deities. So what were the people of Judah to do as they expectantly waited for the promised era of widespread submission to their God (Zeph. 3:8)? The upright remnant was to remain true to the Lord forever (Mic. 4:5).

B. Cleansing God's People: vss. 11-13

"On that day you will not be put to shame for all the wrongs you have done to me, because I will remove from this city those who rejoice in their pride. Never again will you be haughty on my holy hill. But I will leave within you the meek and humble, who trust in the name of the LORD. The remnant of Israel will do no wrong; they will speak no lies, nor will deceit be found in their mouths. They will eat and lie down and no one will make them afraid."

Zephaniah 3:11-13 describes a future restoration of Israel. On that day, the upright remnant would not experience the "shame" connected with their former acts of insurrection. Instead, they would be filled with gratitude over God removing their guilt far from them and healing the crippling effects of their sin. Also, all those who proudly refused to repent would be taken away. No one would arrogantly assert his or her self-dependence again on God's "holy hill," that is, Jerusalem.

Verse 12 literally says that after God's judgments were finished, only the "needy and poor" people would be left in the promised land. It may be that their impoverished circumstance pointed to a modest and reverent spiritual disposition (see Matt. 5:3-5; Luke 6:20). This group is further identified as those who sought refuge "in the name of the LORD" (Zeph. 3:12), rather than in themselves. God's spokesperson regarded hubris as a chief cause of Judah's sin and God's anger against the nation, including Jerusalem. Once God finished His refining, purifying work with His chosen people, conceited, self-serving power brokers would no longer be found in the promised land.

The Hebrew phrase translated "remnant of Israel" (vs. 13) denoted a faithful minority who survived a judgment or catastrophe (see also the corresponding observations in lesson 12). Zephaniah's oracle revealed that after the Babylonian captivity, the remnant of the Jewish nation that returned to the promised land never again resorted to idolatry. But the scope of the passage seems to go beyond that time, pointing to a day when all forms of injustice would be totally purged from the chosen people. Instead of lying, they would tell the truth. Also, rather than deceive others, they would treat people honestly. Like sheep, the remnant would calmly graze and then "lie down" contentedly. Their Shepherd would make sure there were no predators to threaten them. With no one left to harm God's people, they would be able to enjoy a time of prosperity and uninterrupted peace (see Jer. 30:10; 46:27; Ezek. 34:28; 39:26; Mic. 4:4).

Psalm 23 is an uplifting reminder of the preceding truths. It states that because God cared, David (the author of the poem) never lacked what he needed (vs. 1). The Lord consistently provided the necessities of food and water. Also, the Shepherd led His own into a calm, unstressed situation (vs. 2). The Hebrew phrase translated "paths of righteousness" (vs. 3) indicates that the Creator guided His people into lifestyles and settings that would honor Him. He did so for the "sake" of His "name," which means to spotlight the integrity and glory of His being. Even when David found himself in the darkest "valley" (vs. 4), he knew his Shepherd was well equipped to protect the poet from life-threatening dangers. Moreover, God had been like a gracious and caring host to David (vs. 5). Certainly, that led the poet to look forward to a lifelong residency in the sanctuary of the Lord. Indeed, David knew the Creator's love would be with him then and that he would be in God's sacred presence in eternity (vs. 6).

In John 10:27, Jesus stated that His true followers heard and heeded Him in much the same way as sheep follow the voice of their shepherd. In fact, the true test of love for the Son was a willingness to keep His commands (see 14:15; 15:10). Those who obeyed Him were the genuine recipients of the eternal life

He offered. Because He is the resurrection and the life (see 11:25), His disciples would never perish or be lost, but enjoy unending fellowship with the triune God in heaven. Also, their eternal future was secure in the good Shepherd, who promised that no one could seize them from Him (10:28).

II. THE REESTABLISHED REMNANT: ZEPHANIAH 3:14, 20

A. A Summons to Rejoice: vs. 14

Sing, O Daughter of Zion; shout aloud, O Israel! Be glad and rejoice with all your heart, O Daughter of Jerusalem!

In light of the coming glory for Israel, Zephaniah 3:14 exhorted the chosen people (referred to as the "daughter of Zion," "Israel," and the "daughter of Jerusalem," respectively) to "sing," "shout aloud," and wholeheartedly "rejoice." Zion is first mentioned in 2 Samuel 5:7 as a Jebusite fortress on a hill. After being captured by David, this fortress was called the City of David. Here Israel's king brought the ark of the covenant, thereby making the hill a sacred site (6:10-12). Moreover, in the religious tradition of Israel, Zion came to represent safety and protection. Specifically, Zion was the place where the ever-present Creator and Ruler of the universe defended the righteous by vanquishing their foes (see Pss. 9:11-14; 20:2; 48:1-3, 12-13; 76:1-3).

In the future day that Zephaniah had envisioned, the Judahites were to celebrate the glory promised for their nation as though it were a present reality. God's spokesperson did not merely look forward to this festive day or simply tell the city and the nation about a joy that belonged to future generations. Instead, the prophet encouraged his contemporaries to join in the celebration, for God would one day restore Israel. Despite the judgment that was headed for them, they were to revel in the coming era of unparalleled blessing.

Earlier in Zephaniah 3, the Lord expressed His hope that Judah would repent so He would not have to send His judgment upon it (see vs. 7). But in verse 15, God's spokesperson looked forward to a time when the Creator would remove the nation's punishment and turn away its enemies. The implication is that He would also acquit the chosen people of all the guilt associated with their previous transgressions (see Isa. 40:2; Rom. 8:1, 33-34; and the commentary in lesson 10). Moreover, with the Lord in its midst, the nation would enjoy tremendous security, free from the fear of impending calamity.

The emphasis of Zephaniah 3 is upon the safety the people would experience in the days described in verse 15. The long wars and captivities would be over. There would be no more need for fear or for letting their "hands hang limp" (vs. 16) in paralyzing despair. After all, the Lord would be with the people as a conquering warrior and triumphant hero (vs. 17; see Isa. 9:6-7; 40:10-11). The Lord pledged to do much more than just rescue His people from impending disaster. Their invincible champion would celebrate and delight in His relationship with the upright remnant. Also, He would no longer chastise them as He did in the past, but in a quiet expression of love, He would renew them both physically and spiritually.

B. A Promise of Restoration: vs. 20

"At that time I will gather you; at that time I will bring you home. I will give you honor and praise among all the peoples of the earth when I restore your fortunes before your very eyes," says the Lord.

In Zephaniah 3:17, the prophet disclosed that one day God would rejoice and actually sing over His people. While God must punish sin, it is equally true that He cheers for those who humbly turn from their iniquities to follow Him. As a loving, heavenly Father, He takes great delight in each one of His children. Though the Hebrew text of verse 18 is somewhat obscure, it seems to indicate that God, in a display of His compassion for His people, would enable them to celebrate their sacred festivals once again. The years of captivity would bring the exiles sorrow and shame, especially as they felt weighed down with a yearning to observe their solemn assemblies. But a glorious day was coming in which their sadness would be removed.

Furthermore, the Creator disclosed that a time was coming when the upright remnant would be a source of blessing, rather than a disgrace, to the world. According to verse 19, included among the nations gathered for destruction would be those who had oppressed Israel and were hostile to God. Then, after abolishing the remnant's enemies, Israel's eternal Shepherd would assemble His flock from the lands in which they had been dispersed and return them to their ancestral home (see Isa. 11:12; Ezek. 28:25; 34:13; Amos 9:14). Moreover, instead of the world despising the former exiles, individuals from across the globe would esteem and speak highly of God's people.

A corresponding prophecy can be found in Micah 4:6-8. God characterized His people as "the lame," "the exiles," "those I have brought to grief," and "those driven away." Clearly, the people of Judah had been (or would be) suffering. Yet the Lord promised to make them into "a remnant" and "a strong nation." The people would be mighty because they would have an all-powerful Ruler: God. Judah's human monarchs had gotten the nation into a lot of trouble as a result of violating the stipulations of the covenant. But Judah's heavenly King would rule perfectly from Mount Zion. Indeed, after a time of considerable anguish for His people, the Creator would restore dominion and kingship to Jerusalem.

Zephaniah 3:20 ends the prophet's oracle with a further emphasis on God's pledge to gather together His scattered people and return them to the promised land. The Shepherd of Israel wanted the upright remnant to understand that He would bring to pass what may have seemed impossible to them. In that future day, "honor" would replace dishonor, and "praise" would supplant ridicule. When the Creator again made His people prosperous, everyone throughout the world would realize it and bless the name of the Lord. Some think this passage found its initial fulfillment 70 years after the Babylonian captivity, when the Israelites were permitted to return to Jerusalem. Other interpreters also see a future realization of Zephaniah's prophecy, when the Lord Jesus returns to the earth to establish His kingdom.

In any case, God's faithful people have great temporal and eternal rewards awaiting them. Paul recognized this truth, and in Romans 11:33-36, he expressed praise to God for His wonderful plan of redemption involving His chosen people. The apostle noted that God's riches were great, and there was no limit to the profoundness of His wisdom and knowledge. No human being, Paul observed, could really fathom God's eternal ways. Likewise, no one could offer Him any advice or demand from Him what He unconditionally offered by grace. The apostle disclosed that everything came from the Creator. Similarly, all things existed through Him and for His honor. For this reason, only He deserved unending glory.

Discussion Questions

1. In what sense would the people of the world one day seek God?
2. Why should we seek God, rather than turn away from Him?
3. What was the destiny of those who were proud and boastful?
4. Why would the upright remnant sing and shout for joy?
5. What should be our response to God's admonitions and promises?

Contemporary Application

Zephaniah emphasized the promise of God to deliver His people in their times of difficulty. God's compassion and care for them undergirded His commitment to fulfill His pledge one day to restore them to their homeland.

The Lord is also able to help us in our times of difficulty, and His unfailing love is the basis for this promise. The mystery of God's love is that He accepts and meets us at the point of our deepest need. When we trust God's promises, we experience His comfort and blessings in our lives.

It would be incorrect to think that when God comforts, restores, and renews us, all our troubles go away. Being consoled may mean we receive strength to endure our trials and hope to face a potentially troubled future. The greater the difficulty we face, the more God reaches out to us in love to give us solace. Even in the darkest moments of our lives He is always present to give us strength and hope to endure.

God has never failed in His promise to uphold us. We should not only acknowledge this truth but also thank the Lord for the ways He has restored and renewed us during difficult times in the past. Unlike flowers, which are a temporary delight in our eyes, God's love and care are everlasting. Let us express our gratitude to God for being like a shepherd in His consolation to us, especially when life is rough.

A Path to Destruction

Scripture

Background Scripture: *Psalm 8; Romans 1:18-32*
Scripture Lesson: *Romans 1:18-23, 28-32*
Key Verse: Since the creation of the world God's invisible qualities—his eternal power and divine nature—have been clearly seen, being understood from what has been made, so that men are without excuse. *Romans 1:20*
Scripture Lesson for Children: *Psalm 8*
Key Verse for Children: O LORD, our Lord, how majestic is your name in all the earth! *Psalm 8:1*

Lesson Aim

To confidently share the Good News with the lost.

Lesson Setting

Time: About A.D. 57
Place: Corinth

Lesson Outline

A Path to Destruction

I. The Rejection of God: Romans 1:18-23
   A. *Divine Wrath: vs. 18*
   B. *Awareness of God: vss. 19-20*
   C. *Idolatrous Impulses: vss. 21-23*

II. The Dire Consequences: Romans 1:28-32
   A. *A Depraved Mind: vs. 28*
   B. *A Morally Corrupt Existence: vss. 29-32*

Introduction for Adults

Topic: *The Lifeline of the Gospel*

In Romans 1, Paul declared that people have rejected the Creator. Even worse, they prompt others to spurn the Lord and His will for their lives.

Against this sordid backdrop, Paul declared that the good news about Jesus did not embarrass the apostle, for the Gospel represented the power of God at work in saving everyone who believes (vs. 16). Sadly, we find many people in our culture who reject the importance of getting right with God by embracing the Gospel. It's true that, according to the polls, a lot of people claim to be "religious." Nevertheless, many in the West take little notice of God. Perhaps there is no fear of facing a holy God because the idea of sin has virtually been abolished.

The Gospel, which Paul proclaimed, won't make the evening news on television. It won't even garner interest in social media outlets. So it's the responsibility of believers to carry the Good News far and wide so all may hear it and have the opportunity to be saved. Perhaps God in His grace might use our proclamation of the Gospel to prompt some who hear it to get right with Him.

Introduction for Youth

Topic: *Good News for All*

A customer bought two batteries, took them home, and inserted them into his flashlight. Yet nothing happened. He then returned the batteries to the store and received two new ones. He eventually discovered, however, that his problem was not with the batteries but rather with the way he had inserted them.

The same sort of thing happens when we carve out our own plans for pleasing God. As Romans 1 reveals, we trick ourselves into thinking that, regardless of what we do, God is pleased most of the time. This reasoning reflects the mind-set of a college student who said God would accept him because he did what was right 99 percent of the time. This is flawed thinking, for as James 2:10 says, the person who keeps all of the laws except one is as guilty as the person who has broken all of God's laws.

Who, then, has the power to obey the Father? Apart from the Son, no one has this ability. But the Good News is that through faith in Him, not only are we declared righteous, but also we receive power to obey God. With Jesus at our side, we can live in a way that genuinely pleases God.

Concepts for Children

Topic: *An Amazing Creation*

1. There is no name more wonderful than that of God, who made us.
2. God is pleased when we take time to praise Him for giving us life.
3. Even though God is very great, He still cares for us.
4. God loves us so much that He gives us important things to do.
5. We can show our love for God by doing what He wants.

Lesson Commentary

I. THE REJECTION OF GOD: ROMANS 1:18-23

A. Divine Wrath: vs. 18

The wrath of God is being revealed from heaven against all the godlessness and wickedness of men who suppress the truth by their wickedness.

Paul wrote Romans toward the end of his third missionary journey. It was shortly before his visit to Jerusalem to deliver a monetary gift from the Gentile congregations (Acts 24:17; Rom. 15:25). Internal indications suggest that at this time Paul was in Corinth since he refers to Phoebe, a member of the church at Cenchreae (the port of Corinth; Rom. 16:1-2), Gaius (Paul's host; Rom. 16:23; 1 Cor. 1:14), and Erastus (Corinth's financial officer; Acts 19:22; 2 Tim. 4:20). So Paul wrote Romans during his three months in Greece (Acts 20:2-3).

In 1:1, Paul referred to himself as Jesus' bondservant, summoned by God to be an "apostle" to herald the good news of salvation from God. The Greek noun rendered "apostle" literally refers to a messenger, envoy, or ambassador. Paul carried out his evangelistic duties by God's grace (vs. 5). The goal was to bring Gentiles to obedience through their faith in the Messiah (vs. 6). The Lord intended His Gospel for all people, including those in Rome. Through the work of the Spirit, they joined the ranks of God's holy people (vs. 7).

Paul's message had its origin in the Hebrew Scriptures and had been the subject of the prophets' interest (vs. 2). In fact, the Good News is set forth throughout the Old Testament in illustration and type. The Son is the person unveiled in the Gospel, which emphasizes both His full humanity and absolute deity (vs. 3). His resurrection transferred Him from His condition of humiliation to a new phase of lordship and glory. His entrance into post-resurrection glory was perfectly compatible with the sinlessness of His humanity and the result of the Spirit's limitless power (vs. 4).

An examination of Romans indicates why Paul wrote this letter. Because Phoebe—a fellow Christian and the likely carrier of the letter—was going from Corinth to Rome, Paul was presented with a good opportunity to write (16:1-2). He was interested in the church at Rome, and for many years had wanted to visit it (1:13). He also wanted to proclaim the Gospel and impart a spiritual benefit to his fellow believers in Rome (vss. 11, 15). Further, Paul planned to do missionary work in Spain, and so wanted to visit the Christians in Rome for financial support (15:24, 28). The apostle wanted to present a full statement of his theological understanding of the Gospel and so help to defend his ministry from his opponents' false insinuations.

Paul's confidence in heralding the Gospel in Rome arose from his sense of indebtedness to all people, regardless of their race, social status, or mental ability (1:14). The capital was the great prize to be won, and Paul anticipated his visit with eagerness. He was ready to go (vs. 15). In this regard, Paul felt no embarrassment or remorse when he proclaimed the Gospel. In fact, he was overjoyed to do so. Admittedly, it had no special appeal to the haughty. Also, the Good News could not boast of a great antiquity in Rome, like the pagan religions of that city. Nevertheless, the heralding of the Gospel unleashed God's supernatural power (vs. 16). Specifically, God worked through the efforts of missionaries such as Paul to deliver the lost from eternal ruin. Through their faith in the Messiah, they were rescued from the tyranny of the devil, the mastery of the sin-principle, and the state of spiritual death.

Salvation never occurs apart from faith in the Son. (See lesson 9 of the March quarter for a description of biblical faith.) Also, deliverance includes everything the Father does for us in the Son. In particular, the Father forgives our sins and grants us eternal life. We face the prospect of enjoying His presence forever. Moreover, salvation is the possession of Jews and Gentiles, equally. Neither has any priority on the claims of the Gospel. Of course, since Jews were the heirs of the promises of Abraham and the people from whom the Messiah came, it was appropriate that the Gospel should have been preached first to them. Paul followed this order on several occasions. In general, the Jews rejected the message of salvation through a crucified Messiah, and then Paul turned to the Gentiles.

The Gospel disclosed the "righteousness" (vs. 17) that came from the Father (especially in connection with the Son's atoning sacrifice; see 3:22, 25-26) and was the starting point for the believers' spiritual transformation (or sanctification). As noted in lesson 11 from the March quarter, the Greek noun translated "righteousness" comes from a root word that means "straightness." It refers to what is in accordance with established moral norms. In the language of the law court, righteousness means to be vindicated or acquitted of wrongdoing. God's character is the definition and source of what it means to be just. So the legal status of people is defined in terms of God's holiness. Because He alone provides righteousness, human efforts cannot produce or obtain it.

In verse 17, Paul was not talking about a divine attribute—namely, God's justice. Rather, the apostle was referring to an upright moral standing of which the Lord is the author and which provides an answer to the sinful condition of people. They must appropriate God's offer of forgiveness by faith. It is the experience of all who trust in the Son. Moreover, a right standing with the Father comes by faith and appeals to faith from beginning to end. "The righteous will live by his faith" is a quotation from Habakkuk 2:4. The prophet's words confirmed the apostle's point that divine acquittal (along with the changed life it initiates) is the result of entrusting one's existence to the Creator.

Since Paul's primary focus in Romans was salvation through faith in the Son, the apostle pointed to human sin and the subsequent need for redemption. The one who does not sense a problem (sin) will not seek a solution (salvation). Paul explained that God, who reigned from heaven, made known His "wrath" (vs. 18) against all forms of wickedness. Manifestations of His righteous judgment in the present anticipated the final day of reckoning. The lost used profane thoughts (especially about God) and debased behavior (especially between people) in an attempt to hold down the "truth" about God's eternal existence and sovereign rule. All such efforts were futile, for the Creator would never permit anyone to restrain the knowledge of His character and the reality of His invisible qualities from being disclosed in creation.

B. Awareness of God: vss. 19-20

Since what may be known about God is plain to them, because God has made it plain to them. For since the creation of the world God's invisible qualities—his eternal power and divine nature—have been clearly seen, being understood from what has been made, so that men are without excuse.

In Romans 1:19-20, Paul declared that God has made the truth of His existence obvious to humankind. God, who is "spirit" (John 4:24), is invisible (Col. 1:15; 1 Tim. 1:17; Heb. 11:27). Though the physical eye cannot see Him, His existence is reflected in what He has made. The apostle explained that since God brought the universe into existence, He has made His "invisible attributes" (Rom. 1:20) plainly evident. Those attributes included God's "eternal power" and His "divine nature." Indeed, since the dawn of time, people have an instinctive awareness—which is reinforced by observing creation—that there is a supreme being. So they cannot justify their decision to reject the Creator and refuse to submit to His will.

In light of what Paul said, it's worth briefly considering what happens to those who have not heard the Gospel. Specifically, would God condemn people for not accepting a message they never received? The apostle declared that God has revealed His essential nature to all people, regardless of their exposure (or lack of exposure) to the Gospel. Before people tried to squash God's truth, they could see His power in the natural order. They could also discern His invisible qualities, including His holiness—and the absence of holiness in themselves. Before suppressing the truth, every person could sense his or her "disconnectedness" from the Creator of the universe, and their consequent need for reconciliation.

In rare cases, this inner need for redemption has driven people to acknowledge their sinfulness and to seek reconciliation with God. Hebrews 11:6 indicates that believing in God's existence is a starting point. For all who seek Him (Acts 17:27), God will prove Himself a rewarder. Acts 10 and 11 provide a case study of someone who sought the Father sincerely and to whom He revealed Himself redemptively in the Son (see the corresponding commentary in lessons 7 and 8 of the September quarter). In most instances, however, the inner need for salvation is repressed or ignored, and people seek out substitutes for God. They have sunk so deep that only God's special revelation—the Bible—can pull them out. For these who are lost, we must continue to proclaim the Gospel.

C. Idolatrous Impulses: vss. 21-23

For although they knew God, they neither glorified him as God nor gave thanks to him, but their think-ing became futile and their foolish hearts were darkened. Although they claimed to be wise, they became fools and exchanged the glory of the immortal God for images made to look like mortal man and birds and animals and reptiles.

Paul's controlling thought is that the lost venerated and served what God cre-ated rather than Him (Rom. 1:25). For instance, by seeing the intricate design of the universe, people—who bear God's image—could innately understand certain aspects of His nature. Yet instead of extolling God for His power, they looked for idolatrous substitutes. Also, in their foolishness, fallen humanity refused to express gratitude to the Creator (vs. 21). In turn, their ability to reason became pointless and useless. Likewise, their inner self (with its volition and emotions) grew spiritually calloused and senseless. When people turn from God's truth, their ability to perceive reality becomes impaired and confused.

The elitists of Paul's day insisted they were ingenious and prudent. Yet, in God's assessment, they were morally deficient, regardless of their mental prow-ess and educational attainments (vs. 22). After all, these individuals turned away from God and His eternal splendor to create their own deities patterned after various creatures (vs. 23; see Deut. 4:15-18; Ps. 106:20; Jer. 2:11). Notice something of a descending hierarchy: humans, birds, animals, and reptiles. The aristocrats went from bad to worse, creating gods and goddesses after increas-ingly weaker creatures. Their enslavement to idols led to their alienation from the one, true, and living God.

II. *The Dire Consequences: Romans 1:28-32*

A. A Depraved Mind: vs. 28

Furthermore, since they did not think it worthwhile to retain the knowledge of God, he gave them over to a depraved mind, to do what ought not to be done.

Because of idolatry, God deliberately abandoned the Gentiles to their depravity (Rom. 1:24). So instead of attempting to restrain their wickedness, God simply allowed their vile behavior to run its course. Specifically, the Creator removed His influence and permitted fallen humanity's willful rejection to produce its natural and inevitable consequences, which in this case were deadly. To what fate did God, in an act of judgment, surrender the Gentiles? Verse 24 indicates it was sexual impurity.

Paul was writing from Corinth, the location of Aphrodite's temple. At the time he penned Romans, this shrine housed hundreds of temple prostitutes who were used sexually as an act of worship to pagan deities. These degrading acts were believed to provoke the gods into doing similar acts, which resulted in increased crops and larger families. Such religious prostitution was common in Roman culture. In this way, the unsaved traded the truth about God's existence and rule for a "lie" (vs. 25), particularly when it involved idol worship. As noted earlier, through their attitudes and actions, people revered created things rather than the all-powerful Lord. As a counterweight to humankind's perverted acts, Paul burst forth in praise to God and sealed the exclamation with an "amen."

In verse 26, we read for the second time that God intentionally abandoned humankind, but in this case it was to degrading passions. Yet, unlike the immorality committed by the cultic prostitutes, these sexual sins were private. Individuals perverted God's gift of physical intimacy in the context of marriage by shamelessly engaging in homosexual acts. Men and women exchanged "natural relations" (between men and women) with "unnatural" relations (men with men and women with women). Indeed, Paul literally said those of the same gender "burned with intense desire" (see vs. 27) for one another.

As a result of such indecent behavior, people received the divinely sanctioned "penalty"—namely, the scourge of wallowing in their perversion. Homosexual practice is consistently condemned in Scripture (see Lev. 18:22; 20:13; 1 Cor. 6:9,; 1 Tim. 1:9-10). The only intimate, physical relationship recognized as God-honoring is a heterosexual one within the context of marriage (see Gen. 2:21-24; Matt. 19:4-6; and the commentary for lesson 6 of the December quarter). While the latter is a gift from God, sexual intercourse outside of, or prior to, marriage is a sin against oneself and God. As Christians, we must be careful to guard this area of our lives. God requires sexual purity of those who would follow Him.

In Romans 1:28, we read for the third time that God actively abandoned people, but in this case it was to a morally reprehensible way of thinking. People not only refused to acknowledge the Creator's existence, but also to submit to His will. Expressed differently, the reprobates put God's sensible boundaries out of their thoughts, and He responded by surrendering them to a warped view of reality. Out of this mind-set arose all kinds of evil deeds. From this we can see that the intent of one's mind always precedes the sinful act (see Mark 7:20-23).

B. A Morally Corrupt Existence: vss. 29-32

They have become filled with every kind of wickedness, evil, greed and depravity. They are full of envy, murder, strife, deceit and malice. They are gossips, slanderers, God-haters, insolent, arrogant and boastful; they invent ways of doing evil; they disobey their parents; they are senseless, faithless, heartless, ruthless. Although they know God's righteous decree that those who do such things deserve death, they not only continue to do these very things but also approve of those who practice them.

Romans 1:29-30 lists the indecent behaviors condemned in verse 28. Paul categorized the conduct of the morally degenerate into four clusters of active sin: wickedness (the opposite of righteousness), evil (the profound absence of empathy, shame, and goodness), greed (the relentless urge to acquire more than one needs), and depravity (a constant bent toward immorality). These four basic kinds of deliberate, odious behavior in turn express themselves in specific ways.

Those whom God abandoned are full of envy, murder, strife, deceit, and malice. They are gossips, slanderers, God-haters; they are insolent, arrogant, and boastful; they invent ways of doing evil; they disobey their parents; they are senseless, faithless, heartless, and ruthless (vss. 29-31). The despicable conduct of these individuals was not due to ignorance of God's commands (vs. 32). Rather, they sinned despite their limited awareness of God, making them all the more culpable. Even worse, they applauded these reprehensible practices among others. Perhaps seeing their peers do these debased activities filled the instigators with a sense of self-justification. In any case, they received what they deserved—namely, death or eternal separation from God.

Discussion Questions

1. In what ways do the unsaved try to suppress the truth of God's existence?
2. Why is it foolish for people to pretend that God does not exist?
3. What are some contemporary examples of idolatry?
4. How can believers safeguard what goes into their minds?
5. What eventually happens to people who refuse to worship and serve God?

Contemporary Application

In Romans 1, Paul detailed the ways in which people have rejected God and the result of doing so. Even though people have an innate awareness of God's existence, they refuse to submit to His will. The consequence is that their minds are depraved and they engage in morally corrupt behavior.

The preceding observations do not negate the truth that people can be highly innovative and accomplished. Indeed, powerful ideas have spawned a chain of events that have affected the world. In the end, though, no philosophy can match the saving power of the Gospel, for neither of them deals with our basic need to find forgiveness and righteousness from God.

Paul knew a lot about religion in his time, and he debated with some of the best Greek and Jewish minds of his day. The apostle never flinched when it came to staking out the claim that the Gospel was God's power to change people and give them eternal life. Paul made it clear that he was not just offering a new idea. In fact, he preached a person, Jesus of Nazareth, whom the authorities had executed and whom God had raised from the dead. Only this message can offer eternal hope and peace to the lost. When we believe in Jesus, God forgives us.

The truth is that Jesus Christ, God's anointed Son, is alive and in heaven. We do not need to make any apologies for believing in Him. Rather, like Paul, we should be eager to tell the Good News with confidence.

An Intentional Ignorance

Scripture

Background Scripture: *Psalm 104; Romans 2:14-29*
Scripture Lesson: *Romans 2:17-29*
Key Verse: It is not those who hear the law who are righteous in God's sight, but it is those who obey the law who will be declared righteous. *Romans 2:13*
Scripture Lesson for Children: *Psalm 104:1-9, 24-25*
Key Verse for Children: O LORD my God, you are very great. *Psalm 104:1*

Lesson Aim

To refuse to blame God or others for our own misdeeds.

Lesson Setting

Time: About A.D. 57
Place: Corinth

Lesson Outline

An Intentional Ignorance

   I. Breaking the Mosaic Law: Romans 2:17-24
      A. Ethnicity Asserted: vs. 17
      B. Privileges Enjoyed: vss. 18-20
      C. Transgressions Committed: vss. 21-24
  II. Recognizing the Significance of Circumcision: Romans 2:25-29
      A. The Value of Circumcision: vss. 25-27
      B. The True Children of God: vss. 28-29

Introduction for Adults

Topic: *Matching Words with Actions*

Grandpa tried to help his grandson put together a new toy. "I know how to do this," the boy said, rejecting his grandfather's assistance. Perhaps initially we might think such an attitude represents childish pride. But then it's sobering to realize that this way of thinking is evident in many of us as adults.

"I don't need your help" means we feel self-sufficient. When we have such an attitude, it's humiliating to admit that we need help. Perhaps this is the greatest stumbling block that keeps many people from coming to faith in the Son. After all, who wants to admit sin and guilt? And who wants to say that God judges all people?

The Gospel cuts to the heart of the issue—our stubborn pride and willful independence from God. As Paul argued in Romans 2:17-29, until we understand and accept the consequences of our sin, we will not be prepared to come to the Creator on His terms. It's only when we admit our need that we will be ready to receive the Father's gift of salvation through faith in the Son.

Introduction for Youth

Topic: *Walk the Talk*

Children grow up expecting each other to play fairly. Perhaps that's why arguments and fights erupt when someone cheats. And even as they get older, adolescents expect justice to be built into the social system under which they live.

How interesting it is, then, when Christians declare that God is just and punishes rule breakers. "That isn't fair," some teens might say. Where did they get their ideas of justice? And how does it mesh with the truth of the Gospel?

When we accept God's justice, as revealed in Romans 2:17-29, we become the recipients of His love and grace. We are saying to God that we come to Him on His terms, not ours. We admit that we have no excuses for our sin and no solution to our dilemma. We also acknowledge that the Creator alone is able to forgive us because Jesus died for us. Now that's good news worth sharing!

Concepts for Children

Topic: *Giving Praise*

1. God, in His great wisdom, created all things.
2. All creation depends on God for life and food.
3. We should respond to these truths by singing praises to God.
4. We can also thank God for what He has done for us.
5. We should tell others about our wonderful God.

Lesson Commentary

I. BREAKING THE MOSAIC LAW: ROMANS 2:17-24

A. Ethnicity Asserted: vs. 17

Now you, if you call yourself a Jew; if you rely on the law and brag about your relationship to God.

In the latter half of Romans 1, Paul discussed human depravity as it was manifested in pagan culture. The apostle argued that the unsaved were completely destitute of those qualities that characterized God's righteousness. Then, in the first part of chapter 2, Paul noted that not all people indulged in the idolatry and immorality of the pagan masses. Yet even these moralists were depraved and stood guilty as sinners before God. We can imagine some of Paul's religious peers affirming his condemnation of Gentile wickedness, while being unaware of their own failure to honor God. Perhaps the apostle encountered this attitude when he preached in the synagogues during his missionary trips. His words were deliberately shocking, intended to knock the spiritually arrogant off their self-constructed pedestals (in a manner of speaking).

Paul noted that while those people may have been skilled excuse makers, none of them had any adequate defense before the divine law court (vs. 1). In this regard, God's judgment was based on infallible truth (vs. 2). This means the Creator used an objective and impartial moral standard by which the hearts of all people were measured. That benchmark was nothing less than God's flawless character. Appearances counted for nothing. Since even Paul's religious peers were guilty of doing what they condemned in others, they would not escape God's punishment (vs. 3). Though the Creator, in His mercy, did not always judge sin immediately (vs. 4), a day of reckoning was still coming. Scripture indicates there is a future time when God's patience will be exhausted.

Paul said the legalists, through self-deception, stubbornness, and impenitence, were inviting divine retribution upon themselves (vs. 5). Their sinful actions and attitudes were building up a reservoir of wrath from heaven that would one day break forth like a dam under tremendous pressure. The apostle revealed that God would judge people according to what they did during their earthly sojourn (see 1 Cor. 3:10-15). Paul quoted Old Testament Scripture to that effect (Rom. 2:6; see Ps. 62:12; Prov. 24:12). A person's habitual actions indicated the state of his or her heart.

For instance, those who regularly engaged in good works showed their hearts had been regenerated (Rom. 2:7). They understood that the glory, honor, and immortality they sought could only be found in union with the Savior. Those who habitually engaged in evil deeds demonstrated their alienation from the Creator (vs. 8). These individuals were not God-seeking but self-seeking, and rejected the truth about their sinful condition. Paul was not saying good works could save a person. After all, the apostle stated later in his letter that no one could be acquitted by observing the law (see Rom. 3:20; Eph. 2:8-9; Titus 3:5). Good works did not result in salvation. They simply attested to the eternal life a person had already received by faith.

Paul's declarations applied to all people—both Jews and Gentiles (Rom. 2:9-10). No one was exempt. All who continued to do evil (indicating their unsaved state) would suffer God's wrath. Meanwhile, all who continued to do good (as evidence of their regenerate hearts) would receive glory, honor, and peace through the Son. "First for the Jew" (vs. 10) simply means that historically God had dealt with Israel first and then the rest of the world. God's just recompense was without regard to ethnic background (vs. 11). The Creator's judgment was based upon how people responded to the revelation they were given. In the Mosaic law, the Jews were blessed with a special revelation of God's ethical boundaries. Though the Gentiles did not have a written code of conduct, God enabled them to distinguish between moral right and wrong. Their awareness took the form of an internal law, or what we know as conscience.

Those who sinned apart from the law were Gentiles (vs. 12). Since they were not the recipients of the law, God's assessment of them could not be based on the written code Moses wrote. Also, because God evaluated people according to the moral light they had received, His judgment of the Gentiles was based upon the law He had written upon their hearts (vss. 14-15). Those who sinned under the law were Jews (vs. 12). So, the Creator assessed them according to that legal code. They heard and understood the law and were expected to heed it. Of course, since none of Paul's religious peers had succeeded in keeping the whole law, all were ultimately condemned. Reciting the Mosaic law was a regular part of synagogue worship, so the Jews consistently heard it (vs. 13). Becoming righteous, however, did not happen by hearing the legal code. Instead, salvation came by faith and was consistently evidenced by virtuous acts.

Verses 14 and 15 are parenthetical, positioned between verses 13 and 16. In Paul's day, many of his Jewish peers disdained Gentiles because they did not have the Mosaic law. But the apostle pointed out that there were Gentiles who acted in ways affirmed in the law, indicating that its basic requirements were written on their hearts. This statement does not mean the Gentiles fulfilled every aspect of the law. Rather, it refers to what they did, based upon the natural impulse of their hearts, that agreed with the essence of the legal code. God gave every person an innate sense of right and wrong. Though this intuitive knowledge was often suppressed, it still remained, and so the Creator held everyone responsible for their actions.

The Father would judge all humanity (both Jews and Gentiles), the Son would be the agent of His judgment, and His assessment would focus on the secrets of people's hearts (vs. 16). Sometimes people do good things that are actually rooted in selfish intentions. Other times they may appear guilty of a wrongdoing when there was no bad intention. Sometimes people internalize blame for the iniquities others committed. Regardless of the situation, the Lord would act accordingly. On the momentous day, all that was hidden would be revealed. There would be no second-guessing when it came to motives. God's judgment would be impartial, perfect, and absolutely equitable.

In verse 17, Paul directed his attention to his self-righteous peers. They prided themselves on being descendants of the tribe of Judah and claimed the promises God made to them in the Abrahamic covenant. They also depended upon and found solace in the Mosaic law, as well as publicly asserted that they enjoyed a special relationship with the Lord (see 3:1-2; 9:4-5). Paul could speak candidly in this way to his religious counterparts, for he once had been a law-keeping, self-justified Jew. This included being one of the "Hebrews," one of the "Israelites," and one of "Abraham's descendants" (2 Cor. 11:22). Also, Paul was "circumcised on the eighth day" (Phil. 3:5), and as a Pharisee, excelled at keeping the law. Moreover, Paul studied under Gamaliel, the top Jewish rabbi of the day (Acts 22:3).

B. Privileges Enjoyed: vss. 18-20

If you know his will and approve of what is superior because you are instructed by the law; if you are convinced that you are a guide for the blind, a light for those who are in the dark, an instructor of the foolish, a teacher of infants, because you have in the law the embodiment of knowledge and truth.

Paul affirmed that there were a number of distinctives that gave the Jews a sense of superiority over Gentiles. In addition to the Jews' devotion to the Mosaic law (Rom. 2:17), some elitists claimed to understand God's will. Because of their presumed ability to ascertain what was morally worthwhile (based on their meticulous study of the Torah; vs. 18), the legalists confidently tried to escort the spiritually "blind" (vs. 19) to the truth and lead those who stumbled about in moral darkness. The apostle's peers took it upon themselves to admonish and correct others lacking good judgment, as well as to impart knowledge and skills to the immature. The elitists contended they could do all this because they had mastered the sum of what God revealed and taught in the law (vs. 20).

Paul described each of the preceding distinctives with a present tense verb, indicating the habitual, ongoing nature of the elitists' sense of superiority. Also, in their discourse, the legalists commonly used such labels as the "blind" (vs. 19), the "foolish" (vs. 20), and "infants"—along with references to "dogs" and "swine." The apostle's main point was that his unrepentant peers were just as guilty before God as pagan Gentiles. Paul even demonstrated that the assets claimed by the legalists had become liabilities due to their hypocrisy. Though the specialists made grand professions and boasted about their high standing with God, there was a contradiction between their assertions and their conduct. Though they extolled the law, their hearts were far from the Creator, who originally gave the legal code to Moses. Furthermore, while they observed the externals of their religion, there was little—if any—inward righteousness.

C. Transgressions Committed: vss. 21-24

You, then, who teach others, do you not teach yourself? You who preach against stealing, do you steal? You who say that people should not commit adultery, do you commit adultery? You who abhor idols, do you rob temples? You who brag about the law, do you dishonor God by breaking the law? As it is written: "God's name is blasphemed among the Gentiles because of you."

In Romans 2:21-24, Paul asked a series of concise, rhetorical questions with the intent of compelling his religious peers to recognize their own hypocrisy. These queries related to disregarding the truth of Scripture, especially in terms of stealing, committing adultery, robbing temples, and breaking the law. All these acts were violations of the Ten Commandments (see Exod. 20:4-5, 14-15; Deut. 5:8-9, 18-19). Though the elitists taught Gentiles not to engage in such despicable and ignominious conduct, the legalists were guilty of doing the same, though perhaps in more subtle ways.

Stealing may have taken the form of dishonest business practices. Signs of adultery may have been literal, or a matter of the heart. Though Paul's religious peers found idols repugnant, they would readily plunder Gentile shrines to make a profit, evidently by selling the items they stole (especially objects made from precious metals; see Deut. 7:25-26). Moreover, they not only dishonored God but also, by their behavior, encouraged pagans to revile His holy name.

Throughout Romans 2, Paul was using a common style of communication in ancient times called the diatribe. His pointed questions to an imagined dialogue partner were not primarily meant to attack but to instruct and admonish. In the present case, the apostle employed this literary technique to help his peers see their duplicity and (hopefully) repent. Paul met the elitists on their own ground. Indeed, his condemnation of their pretense was based on their own Scriptures (that is, the Old Testament).

For instance, in verse 24, Paul quoted from the Septuagint version of Isaiah 52:5 to declare that God's enemies used the hypocrisy of His people as a pretext to slander Him (see also Ezek. 36:21-23). Unlike today, in the ancient world, a name was not a mere label. A name was considered as equivalent to whomever or whatever bore it. So knowing a person's name amounted to recognizing that individual's essence or being. Accordingly, God's name pointed to Him as the Creator and Ruler of the universe. It was ironic that the iniquity committed by some of the apostle's peers impelled pagans to defame the Lord.

II. RECOGNIZING THE SIGNIFICANCE OF CIRCUMCISION: ROMANS 2:25-29

A. The Value of Circumcision: vss. 25-27

Circumcision has value if you observe the law, but if you break the law, you have become as though you had not been circumcised. If those who are not circumcised keep the law's requirements, will they not be regarded as though they were circumcised? The one who is not circumcised physically and yet obeys the law will condemn you who, even though you have the written code and circumcision, are a lawbreaker.

In Romans 2:25-27, Paul used the rite of circumcision to illustrate his point that some of his religious counterparts were guilty of violating the Mosaic law. For centuries, circumcision represented an oath affirming the agreement between God and His chosen people. Also, the cutting of circumcision reflected the literal meaning of the Hebrew phrase rendered "to make a covenant," which is "to cut a covenant." In essence, circumcision implied, "If I remain untrue to the covenant, may I be cut off like my foreskin."

Among the Jews living at the time of Paul, circumcision was considered a guarantee of God's favor and blessing. Legalists also tended to think that only the circumcised would have a place in the life to come. This is why, as noted in lesson 10 of the September quarter, some elitists taught that non-Jews had to be "circumcised" (Acts 15:1), as well as obey the other laws of Moses, in order to be saved. Paul countered that it was wrong to make this religious rite conditional to salvation (see Rom. 3:29-30), for it was no longer the sign of the covenant for Jews and Gentiles who put their faith in the Messiah (see Eph. 2:8-9; Gal. 2:15-16).

Against this backdrop, Paul pointed out that when his religious peers violated the law, their "circumcision" (Rom. 2:25) ceased to have any real or lasting benefit. Even worse, the transgressors were no better off in avoiding God's wrath than individuals who had never been "circumcised." The Greek of this verse is much more forceful than our English translations would suggest. It virtually says, "If you are a lawbreaker, your circumcision has become nothing more than a foreskin." Paul's point, of course, was that in overstepping the law, the elitists had become just like an impious Gentile. It was as if the legalists had the sign of the covenant for no reason.

Paul said the opposite was also true (vs. 26). When Gentiles (presumably believers) conscientiously heeded the stipulations found in the Mosaic law, they would be considered among the "circumcised" (that is, members of God's covenant people). Gentiles became like circumcised Jews in that they were devoted to the law of God written upon their hearts—something their circumcised counterparts had been called to do, but in reality had constantly failed to achieve. Continuing this line of argumentation, Paul said that the Gentiles who had never been "circumcised" (vs. 27)—if they fulfilled the purpose of the "written code"—brought condemnation upon the legalists who trespassed it. Put another way, if a non-Jew should outdo a Jew in demonstrating personal integrity, it would show the latter person to be under divine censure, for that individual actually had the higher moral standard (namely, the Mosaic law).

B. The True Children of God: vss. 28-29

A man is not a Jew if he is only one outwardly, nor is circumcision merely outward and physical. No, a man is a Jew if he is one inwardly; and circumcision is circumcision of the heart, by the Spirit, not by the written code. Such a man's praise is not from men, but from God.

In Romans 2:28-29, Paul drove home his main point: It's not the external rite of "circumcision" that matters, but instead the inner transformation of the human heart, brought about by the Spirit (see 2 Cor. 3:6; Phil. 3:3). In Paul's thinking, being a "Jew" (Rom. 2:28) was not so much a matter of undergoing physical "circumcision" (in addition to observing a litany of dietary regulations and celebrating numerous feast days). Instead, it was a matter of having a circumcised "heart" (vs. 29; see Deut. 30:6; Jer. 4:4; 9:25-26). When the inner person (including one's thoughts, desires, and endeavors) was characterized by virtue and commitment to God, the underlying intent of the law was fulfilled.

Many legalists in Paul's day went through the motions of being circumcised and rendered external obedience to the tenets of their religion, but they were not right with God (see Ps. 119:70; Isa. 29:13; Ezek. 33:31). In contrast, there were Gentiles (such as the Roman centurion, Cornelius; see Acts 10:1–2) who recoiled from doing wrong and were devout in serving God. The apostle closed his argument by saying that the Creator, not one's peers, commended an individual's upright lifestyle (Rom. 2:29). Ultimately, the recognition offered by one's peers was fleeting, whereas God's affirmation (especially that given at the end of the age to the redeemed) would last for eternity.

Discussion Questions

1. How had Paul's religious peers bragged about their relationship with God?
2. How had the legalists dishonored the Creator?
3. Under what circumstance would circumcision have any value?
4. How can believers keep their lives free from hypocrisy?
5. Why should receiving praise from God be of utmost importance to us?

Contemporary Application

This week's lesson spotlights the issue of personal sin in our lives and whether we will accept God's just judgment of it. Initially, the truth of God's justice may seem reasonable to us. But a fear of the negative consequences of our actions can prompt us to shirk taking responsibility for what we have done.

Against this sobering backdrop, we can see that Jesus is unlike any person who ever lived. He did not try to hold others accountable for His behavior. Rather, He took full responsibility for His actions. He went even further by willingly accepting the punishment for the sins of humanity. While the rest of the world was busy blaming God and others for their misdeeds, Jesus voluntarily made the sacrifice necessary to save them.

The noble example of our Lord should encourage us to stop blaming Him and others for the things we have done wrong. If we have been unfair or unkind to someone, we should freely admit it. If we have broken a promise we made, we should acknowledge our failure. Regardless of the situation, we should make every effort not to blame God or others for our mistakes.

A Slave to Sin

Scripture

Background Scripture: *Psalm 136:1-9, 26; Romans 3:9-20*
Scripture Lesson: *Romans 3:9-20*
Key Verse: No one will be declared righteous in [God's] sight by observing the law; rather, through the law we become conscious of sin. *Romans 3:20*
Scripture Lesson for Children: *Psalm 136:1-9, 26*
Key Verse for Children: Give thanks to the LORD, for he is good. His love endures forever. *Psalm 136:1*

Lesson Aim

To stress that any sin is an affront to God.

Lesson Setting

Time: About A.D. 57
Place: Corinth

Lesson Outline

A Slave to Sin

I. Universal Iniquity: Romans 3:9-18
   A. All Under Sin: vs. 9
   B. All Have Turned Away: vss. 10-18

II. Universal Culpability: Romans 3:19-20
   A. All Are Held Accountable: vs. 19
   B. No One Is Declared Righteous: vs. 20

Introduction for Adults

Topic: *Human Indifference*

Paul demonstrated in Romans 3:9-20 that none are declared righteous in God's sight and that He holds everyone accountable for their misdeeds. Admittedly, even saved adults don't like to admit they are sinful creatures. They would prefer to hide from their transgressions and pretend their wrongs don't exist, or that someone or something else is to blame.

When we fail to acknowledge our iniquities, it comes at the expense of broken relationships with others that have lasting effects. Most importantly, our calloused indifference to sin is an affront to the Creator and damages our relationship with Him.

In this week's lesson, we discover that God wants honesty from us. This includes recognizing our guilt and acknowledging our need for the forgiveness the Father offers through faith in the Son. When we admit our sin and accept God's provision of acquittal, it strengthens our relationship with Him. And when our relationship is right with the Creator, human relationships have a chance of being restored to their proper place.

Introduction for Youth

Topic: *Tangled Up*

In Romans 3:9-20, Paul demonstrated through airtight logic that all of us have turned away from our Creator. Even worse, apart from faith in the Son, none of us can escape the judgment the Father will bring on people for the sins they have committed.

For Christian youth, the rationale to sin might be the "everybody's doing it" immorality of popular culture. It could be a peer who goes out of her or his way to make life feel miserable for believers. It might be a teacher who lampoons anyone who has Christian faith.

Regardless of the challenging situation, God calls saved adolescents to make a decision to be courageous and not retreat in unbelief and disobedience. They need to know that the Lord is always there to help them resist the temptation to sin and avoid its harmful consequences. When they choose to follow His will, they will be eternally blessed.

Concepts for Children

Topic: *How Can I Say Thanks?*

1. We can thank God for His love.
2. We can thank God for creating the world.
3. We can thank God for giving us a place to live.
4. We can thank God for giving us food to eat and clothes to wear.
5. God is pleased when we give Him thanks.

Lesson Commentary

I. UNIVERSAL INIQUITY: ROMANS 3:9-18

A. All Under Sin: vs. 9

What shall we conclude then? Are we any better? Not at all! We have already made the charge that Jews and Gentiles alike are all under sin.

In the first three chapters of Romans, we are in a heavenly courtroom, and the entire human race is on trial. The Judge is almighty God, whose infallible character makes Him alone qualified to weigh all the evidence, hear every testimony, and act with absolute justice. The charge is that people have consistently broken His laws. When the data is impartially examined, no one is found to be innocent of wrongdoing. Consequently, people cannot claim that their religious heritage and painstaking adherence to rules and rituals make them immune from God's judgment.

It is against the preceding backdrop that Paul made his points in 2:17-29, in which he deflated the ego of his morally tainted Jewish peers. They not only disobeyed the Mosaic law, but also rejected the Messiah. The question naturally arises whether there was any distinctive "advantage" (3:1) to being a Jew over a Gentile. In addition, what usefulness or practicality, if any, did the rite of "circumcision" have? Paul responded to these queries by declaring that God's chosen people enjoyed a number of spiritual benefits (vs. 2). Foremost among several noteworthy blessings was that the Creator "entrusted" Jews with His oracles (see 9:4-5 and the commentary appearing in lesson 11). Paul was referring to the entire Old Testament, including its messianic promises of salvation.

Even today, Christians can agree with Paul that the covenant community enjoyed a wonderful privilege. Also, with the advantage came a huge responsibility. Yet, tragically, some within Judah proved unfaithful to their divine stewardship. Indeed, they failed to live up to God's ethical standards. The fact that the Jews of Paul's day were the recipients of God's Word raised the important issue of faith in His oracles (Rom. 3:3). More specifically, the apostle addressed the concern as to whether the refusal of some Jews to believe invalidated or abolished God's commitment to be faithful to His promises. Paul's emphatic response was literally, "May it never be!" (vs. 4). The Creator is portrayed in Scripture as remaining loyal to His Word (see Deut. 7:9; 1 Cor. 1:9; Rom. 9:11-24; Heb. 10:23; along with the commentary appearing in lesson 12).

The Bible has much to say about God's unwavering commitment. For instance, faithfulness is one of God's attributes (Deut. 7:9; 32:4). The Creator is a covenant-making God, and He will always be steadfast in upholding His pledges (Gen. 6:18; 9:9-17; Exod. 2:24; 2 Sam. 7:11-16). The Lord is a promise-making God, and He will always fulfill what He has vowed to do on behalf of His chosen people (1 Kings 8:56), including the salvation of Israel (Rom. 11:25-27). God's fidelity endures throughout all generations (Ps. 100:5). Finally, God remains faithful even when human beings are disloyal to Him (2 Tim. 2:13).

In Romans 3:4, Paul declared that regardless of the situation, God would be proven "true," even if everyone were shown to be liars. The context of this verse makes the apostle's meaning clear. He was emphasizing God's integrity in the face of infidelity among some of Paul's Jewish peers. They were not alone in this regard. Ecclesiastes 7:20 reveals that no one could claim to always be good, continuously do what is best, and never commit any sin (see 1 Kings 8:46; Prov. 20:9). It is only when people recognize their moral bankruptcy before the Father that they can avail themselves of the Son's eternal riches.

Paul supported his argument in Romans 3:4 by quoting from the Septuagint version of Psalm 51:4. The backdrop was David's plea for mercy, in which he acknowledged his sin with Bathesheba and petitioned God for cleansing. Paul stressed that in the heavenly law court, the Creator's testimony would forever be proven true. Likewise, even when people tried to judge God, He would win His case every time. When the Lord punished sin, it demonstrated His faithfulness to His righteous character. Because the Creator was infinitely holy, He would never disregard iniquity, and when He judged, His decisions were impeccable. On the one hand, it is a comfort to know that God always fulfills His promise. On the other hand, it is a challenge to recognize that we can count on God to discipline us when we sin.

As noted in last week's lesson, Paul used a literary technique called the diatribe in which he introduced and answered rhetorical questions to an imaginary dialogue partner. This is evident in Romans 3:5, in which the apostle anticipated another possible objection to his argument. Supposedly, the transgressions committed by Jews (as well as Gentiles) had the favorable outcome of providing the evidence for God's upright character. So, from a merely human perspective (albeit one that is imperfect), wasn't it unfair for the Creator to punish His chosen people (along with Gentiles) when their misdeeds confirmed His indictment against them? After all, His glory and grace shone all the more brightly as a result of sinners luxuriating in their wickedness.

Once more, Paul was quick to renounce any supposition that God was guilty of wrongdoing by judging evildoers, regardless of their ethnic and religious heritage (vs. 6). Without question, the presence of evil in the world was the result of human disobedience. Also, God's glory did not need a backdrop, especially one provided by human sin. The Creator's integrity and reliability were the apostle's unassailable premise. It ensured the Lord was absolutely qualified to "judge" every entity throughout the universe (see Gen. 18:25; Job 8:3). In doing so, no conflict of interest ever arose.

Paul next addressed the question of how God could remain blameless in condemning a sinner—whether a Jew or Gentile—when that transgressor's lack of integrity magnified the truthfulness and glory of the Creator (Rom. 3:7). Put another way, since evil apparently benefitted God, how could He rightly judge criminals for their odious acts? According to this twisted logic, God should commend, not censure, the wicked for doing Him a favor. Paul brought up this issue because his opponents tried to denigrate him and malign the Gospel he proclaimed. They impugned the apostle's integrity by alleging he promoted the idea that people should participate in "evil" (vs. 8) to magnify the Creator's goodness. In essence, the end justified the means.

Paul refused to respond to such an absurd accusation. He considered it sufficient to note that God's denouncement of the apostle's adversaries was warranted. He had already demonstrated that unsaved Gentiles were under God's condemnation. In verse 9, Paul asked whether it was appropriate to conclude that unregenerate Jews enjoyed any spiritual advantage when it came to salvation. Expressed differently, did the status as God's chosen people exempt them from His judgment, especially when they violated the stipulations of the Mosaic covenant? The apostle emphatically stated that none of his religious peers could claim any superior moral standing with the Creator. Paul added that all human beings—whether Jew or Gentile—were enslaved to the merciless taskmaster called "sin" and likewise were condemned for their iniquities. Consequently, they deserved to be expelled from God's holy presence.

B. All Have Turned Away: vss. 10-18

As it is written: "There is no one righteous, not even one; there is no one who understands, no one who seeks God. All have turned away, they have together become worthless; there is no one who does good, not even one." "Their throats are open graves; their tongues practice deceit." "The poison of vipers is on their lips." "Their mouths are full of cursing and bitterness." "Their feet are swift to shed blood; ruin and misery mark their ways, and the way of peace they do not know." "There is no fear of God before their eyes."

In Romans 3:1-8, Paul argued that God would remain faithful to His covenant promises to His chosen people, even though many of them wavered in their commitment to Him. Then, in verse 9, the apostle declared that all people—both Jews and Gentiles—were guilty of sinning and languished under the sentence of death before God. Next, in verses 10 through 18, Paul emphasized the universality of humanity's sin. In doing so, he wanted his readers to recognize the importance of this theological truth.

Paul quoted or paraphrased a series of Old Testament passages (primarily taken from the Septuagint) to prove his charge (see Pss. 5:9; 10:7; 14:1-3; 36:1; 53:1-3; 140:3; Isa. 59:7–8). Threading these verses together—like pearls on a string—was a common mode of argumentation in ancient times. In this way, Paul demonstrated that no one is righteous (Rom. 3:10); no one understands or seeks God (vs. 11); all have turned away (vs. 12a); no one does good (vs. 12b); they are deceitful (vs. 13); their hearts are full of cursing and bitterness (vs. 14); they are quick to shed blood (vs. 15); ruin and misery mark their ways (vs. 16); they do not know the way of peace (vs. 17); and they have no fear of God (vs. 18). These characteristics can be seen, in varying degrees, in every person who has ever lived. Before trusting in the Savior, we were rightly called God's "enemies" (5:10).

In Romans, Paul quoted, alluded to, or paraphrased numerous Old Testament passages. This is quite typical of how the rest of the New Testament uses the Old Testament. Sometimes a New Testament writer gave the general sense of the Old Testament passage without intending to quote it. Other times a New Testament writer combined two or more Old Testament passages together. Still other times the New Testament writer directly quoted from the Old Testament. Of course, all of this was done under the inspiration of the Holy Spirit (2 Tim. 3:16). God supernaturally directed the entire process (2 Pet. 1:21).

Notice in Romans 3 that Paul mentioned specific parts of the human body. He did this to point to the totality of sin's infection in the people—including the throat, tongue, and lips (vs. 13), the mouth (vs. 14), the feet (vs. 15), and the eyes (vs. 18). In short, the whole person is spiritually infected; no part of human nature remains untainted by sin. By using such imagery, Paul set forth what some theologians have called moral depravity. This does not mean that every person is as bad as they can possibly be. Rather, it means that every aspect of the human being has been plagued by iniquity.

Paul's point in verse 18 is especially important. The inability of Jews and Gentiles to reverence the Creator was a particularly serious offense, for the "fear" of the Lord is the mark of a godly person (see Ps. 111:10; Prov. 1:7; 9:10; Eccl. 12:13). If anyone worshiped and served God, it should have been His chosen people, but on the whole they failed to do so. Instead, like their Gentile counterparts, many of Paul's Jewish peers were characterized by arrogance and folly. When we lose focus on who we are in union with the Son, hubris and imprudence can easily slip into our lives. Also, if we've lost that sense of wonder over the depth of God's grace for us despite our sin, it is clearly time for self-examination (see Ps. 139:23-24).

II. UNIVERSAL CULPABILITY: ROMANS 3:19-20

A. All Are Held Accountable: vs. 19

Now we know that whatever the law says, it says to those who are under the law, so that every mouth may be silenced and the whole world held accountable to God.

Paul's letter to the Romans is both the deepest and most important of his various epistles. A number of Bible scholars agree that Romans has had more influence on the development of Christian theology and the growth of the church during the last two millennia than any other New Testament book. Many believe that Romans presents the most systematic and comprehensive exposition of the Gospel than any other portion of the New Testament. Indeed, we need only consider some of the important roles Romans has played throughout the history of the church to realize its vast and continuing impact.

For instance, as Augustine struggled in the garden at Milan with his own sinfulness and lack of belief, he heard someone say to him, "Take up and read! Take up and read!" And it was Romans that he eventually picked up and studied, bringing about in him a personal change that would also transform the face of the early church. As Martin Luther brooded over the theological beliefs and religious practices of his peers, it was his examination of Romans that enabled him to discover the truth of justification by faith. Subsequently, the Protestant Reformation was born. At Aldersgate Street, John Wesley listened carefully to a reading of Luther's preface to Romans and Wesley's heart was "strangely warmed," igniting in him a fire that would eventually spread a revival of faith across several continents.

The cogency of Paul's theological reasoning is on display in 3:19. The apostle affirmed that whatever the Mosaic law declared, it especially applied to God's chosen people, who lived under its authority. The idea is that the Jews were obligated to obey and heed the Old Testament. The Torah was not just a list of rules and a catalog of rituals. More importantly, it was divine instruction on how to live in a godly manner. The covenant community was subject to the Old Testament's legal authority because it originated from the Creator. Paul revealed that the purpose of the law was to stop people from making excuses for their sinful behavior, to demonstrate that everyone was guilty of transgression, and to show that the whole world existed under God's condemnation. The Torah effectively unveiled God's righteous and holy standards. It also convincingly disclosed humanity's inability to measure up to His decrees. No one was in a position to argue sin away, for the law invalidated all rationalizations.

B. No One Is Declared Righteous: vs. 20

Therefore no one will be declared righteous in his sight by observing the law; rather, through the law we become conscious of sin.

On one level, sin is any form of lawlessness or trespass against God's will (see 1 John 3:4). This includes failing to do what His law requires or doing what it forbids, whether in thought, word, or deed (see Matt. 5:22; Rom. 1:32; 1 John 3:15). On another level, sin is a state of alienation from God. The Lord originally created humankind without sin. Adam and Eve were morally upright and inclined to do good. But sin entered human life when our first human parents violated God's direct command (see Gen. 3:6-7; Rom. 5:12).

In Romans 3:20, Paul drove home his point about the universality of sin by alluding to Psalm 143:2. He noted that the Mosaic law was never provided as a means of attaining righteousness or of being pronounced innocent before God (see Acts 13:39; Gal. 2:16; 3:11). Rather, as noted earlier, the Torah was given to make people aware of their wrongdoing. It was through the decrees, ordinances, and rituals recorded in the Old Testament that human beings became conscious of their iniquity and saw their need for a solution to their sin problem. In this light, the Torah was an instrument of condemnation, not justification. The law, written on the hearts of all, shone the spotlight on our desperate need for a Savior.

We might compare the law to a mirror that reflects the perfect righteousness of the Lord and a person's own sinfulness and shortcomings. While the Torah does not cause people to transgress, it frames their actions as iniquity by revealing God's evaluation of what they have done (see Rom. 7:7). The law not only makes people aware of their errors, but also it steers them away from sin and toward the Savior (see Gal. 3:19-24). In this regard, the Torah is like a map. While it does not mark out the road to the Creator, it does show people the landscape of a God-pleasing life once they are traveling on the road. Moreover, the law may restrain evil. The Torah cannot change the wicked bent of the human heart. Nonetheless, the law can somewhat inhibit anarchy by its threats of judgment, especially when those warnings are reinforced by civil codes that administer punishment for confirmed transgressions (see Deut. 13:6-11; 19:16-21; Rom. 13:3-4).

Discussion Questions

1. What does it mean to exist under the power of sin?
2. How did Paul substantiate the point he made in Romans 3:9?
3. What are some ways people transgress God's Word with their speech?
4. How does the Mosaic law make us aware of our iniquity?
5. From what has the Lord delivered us?

Contemporary Application

Paul emphasized that both Jews and Gentiles alike are guilty and condemned before God (Rom. 3:9-18). The apostle also stressed that God designed the Mosaic law so that through it people would see their shortcomings. Rather than brag about righteousness, they would silently stand accountable before Him. In fact, the law shows us that no one can be righteous before God by doing good deeds (vss. 19-20).

The existence of sin is the backdrop against which these statements are made. Sin creates an infinite gulf between God and us. It is a gulf we have created and over which we are unable to build a bridge ourselves. Since God created us in His image and made us to be in unending fellowship with Him, He is angry when sin blinds us to that image and breaks that fellowship.

Often we either desperately try to remove the stain of sin within us through our own efforts and fail miserably; or we do not care how sin has tainted our souls. In either case, we cannot avoid this fact—each sin leaves a hideous blot on our soul that only the blood of Jesus can wash away. Also, unless our souls are cleansed of sin, we cannot have fellowship with God.

A Sacrifice of Atonement

Scripture

Background Scripture: *Psalm 148; Romans 3:21-31*

Scripture Lesson: *Romans 3:21-31*

Key Verses: There is no difference, for all have sinned and fall short of the glory of God, and are justified freely by his grace through the redemption that came by Christ Jesus. *Romans 3:22-24*

Scripture Lesson for Children: *Psalm 148:1-10, 13*

Key Verse for Children: Praise the name of the LORD, for his name alone is exalted; his splendor is above the earth and the heavens. *Psalm 148:13*

Lesson Aim

To affirm that sinners are declared righteous through faith in the Son.

Lesson Setting

Time: About A.D. 57

Place: Corinth

Lesson Outline

A Sacrifice of Atonement

  I. Righteousness Disclosed in the Son: Romans 3:21-26
      A. *Righteousness for All Who Believe: vss. 21-22*
      B. *God's Free Gift of Grace: vss. 23-24*
      C. *Acquittal through Jesus' Sacrificial Death: vss. 25-26*
  II. Righteousness Received by Faith: Romans 3:27-31
      A. *Faith, Not Works: vss. 27-28*
      B. *For Both Jews and Gentiles: vss. 29-31*

Introduction for Adults

Topic: *Admitting Our Need*

In this week's lesson, we learn that the Father sent His Son to earth to provide redemption for the lost. The cross makes it possible for the Father to offer believing sinners forgiveness and the opportunity to be declared righteous in His sight. This means we are acquitted for our iniquities.

Frederick Whitfield's old hymn "I Saw the Cross of Jesus" expresses what we all should remember about ourselves and our sin: "I love the cross of Jesus, it tells me what I am—a vile and guilty creature, saved only through the Lamb."

Let your students know that the Father presented the Son as an atoning sacrifice to take the punishment for our sins and to satisfy His anger against us. Jesus did what we could not do, and He offers us what we otherwise could not have. When we believe that Jesus shed His blood, sacrificing His life for us, we are made right with God (see Rom. 3:25).

Introduction for Youth

Topic: *Grace for All*

When we think about King David's notorious sins of adultery and murder, we may be surprised to learn that he wrote songs about this terrible time in his life. Even more astounding is that, through the marvels of God's grace and mercy, David found forgiveness, and this prompted him to rejoice in the Lord.

David's experience stands as a strong corrective to adolescents who think that God could not possibly forgive them for all the awful things they have done. Tragically, many teens are caught in the deadly snare of thinking they are beyond redemption.

It's true that believing sinners can do nothing to be accepted by God, especially since everyone falls short of His "glory" (Rom. 3:23). Yet, as Paul declared, there is hope. Specifically, when those who are lost trust in the Son, the Father forgives them (vs. 24).

Concepts for Children

Topic: *A Symphony of Praise*

1. God lives in heaven.
2. God created the sun, moon, planets, and stars.
3. God created the birds, animals, and fish on the earth.
4. Angels are joyful when they praise God.
5. We can be happy, too, when we praise God.

Lesson Commentary

I. RIGHTEOUSNESS DISCLOSED IN THE SON: ROMANS 3:21-26

A. Righteousness for All Who Believe: vss. 21-22

But now a righteousness from God, apart from law, has been made known, to which the Law and the Prophets testify. This righteousness from God comes through faith in Jesus Christ to all who believe. There is no difference.

In Romans 1:18—3:20, Paul argued that all people are sinners by nature and by practice. All of us have a spiritual malady called sin. Regardless of how hard we try to cure ourselves, we remain depraved. At the bar of divine justice, three witnesses testify against humankind. The creation presses charges against pagan Gentiles for having rejected the light of nature. The conscience accuses the moralists (whether Gentiles or Jews) for having broken the ethical precepts God has written on the tablet of the human heart. And Scripture witnesses against scrupulous Jews for having violated the Mosaic law. The evidence against the entire human race is undeniable and condemning.

Having established that all humanity exists under the sentence of God's judgment, Paul next discussed how people could get right with the Lord. Specifically, they had to trust in the Messiah for salvation. In 3:20, Paul said no one could be declared righteous by observing the law. Indeed, no one enjoyed God's pardon by meticulously heeding the directives recorded in the Pentateuch (the first five books of Moses), the historical writings, the wisdom literature, the Psalms, and the prophetic books. As noted in last week's lesson, rather than acquit the lost, the law shone the spotlight on their sin and disclosed their need for a Redeemer.

The Greek phrase translated "but now" (vs. 21) indicates not only a decisive shift in Paul's argument, but also points to a new phase in God's plan of redemption. The one who is absolutely holy and just provided a way to reconcile sinners to Himself. Even though a right standing with God occurred apart from the decrees and institutions established in the Torah (including being circumcised, observing food ordinances, and attending sacred convocations), the entire Old Testament (that is, the "Law" and the "Prophets") affirmed the truth disclosed in the Gospel (see Matt. 5:17; 22:40; Luke 24:27). In particular, the Father offers forgiveness through faith in His Son. Regardless of one's gender, ethnicity, or socio-economic status, all who trust in the Messiah are saved (Rom. 3:22; see 1 Cor. 12:13; Gal. 3:28; Col. 3:11).

In emphasizing the importance of the believers' faith (along with the Savior's faithfulness in providing redemption for the lost), Paul revealed that our acquittal could never be earned or merited. The apostle made a similar point in Ephesians 2:8-9, namely, that the provision of redemption was by the Father's grace through repentant sinners believing in the Son. Some mistakenly think the act of trusting is a good work that earns one a place in heaven. Rather, faith is merely a response of the broken heart to the Father's saving work in His Son. In essence, the believer is saying, "I'm depending entirely on Jesus to deliver me from God's wrath."

The Creator receives all the praise for this incredible gift of salvation. Because of Jesus' sacrificial death at Calvary, God enabled the lost to turn away from their sin and humbly believe in Jesus. Also, as verse 10 indicates, the Father enables repentant sinners, by His Spirit, to live for Him as His obedient bond-servants. So, when the redeemed do the will of the Father, they demonstrate to the world that they are His work of art. Put another way, believers are those whom the Father has recreated in union with the Son so they might do all He planned for them long ago.

B. God's Free Gift of Grace: vss. 23-24

For all have sinned and fall short of the glory of God, and are justified freely by his grace through the redemption that came by Christ Jesus.

Paul explained that everyone has "sinned" (Rom. 3:23), which means both Jews and Gentiles are guilty of violating God's will. Even the apostle's religious peers were just as guilty as pagan Gentiles and deserving of God's condemnation. More sobering was Paul's indictment that all human beings fall short of God's glory. The Greek verb translated "fall short" is in the present tense, which indicates continuing action.

The idea is that regardless of how long and hard people try, they perpetually fail to attain God's infinitely perfect moral standard. The Greek noun rendered "glory" not only refers to God's magnificent and sublime presence, but also to the outward manifestation of His attributes, including His goodness, righteousness, and holiness. The implication is that humanity's transgressions subvert the reality of people being created in God's glorious image (see Gen. 1:26-27; 9:6; 1 Cor. 11:7; Jas. 3:9). Their iniquities also alienate them from the Lord and exclude them from enjoying His loving, sustaining grace in their lives.

Humanity's problem of not measuring up compelled God to provide a solution, one that is found in justification (vs. 24). Like two sides of a coin, the Greek verb translated "justified" has two complementary meanings. On one side of the coin, the term denotes a person being pronounced not guilty before the Creator. On the other side, the verb means that same individual is declared to be in a right relationship with God (see also the corresponding comments made in lesson 4). Justification is a wonderful event that happens at the moment of conversion. It begins a lifelong process of transformation called sanctification (or growth in holiness) in which the believer becomes more like the Son (see also lesson 9 for additional information).

Though many of Paul's religious peers tried to earn a right standing with God by performing a litany of pious deeds, the apostle indicated that God's pardon was offered "freely" (vs. 24) as a "gift," because of His "grace," or unmerited favor. The truth is that we couldn't possibly do enough good works, and do them well enough, to earn God's mercy and love. One day we will see the depths of personal sin from which God saved us, and we will be stunned into silence. No matter how deep our disobedience and arrogance has taken us, God's grace is deeper still.

God's grace is one of His key attributes. For instance, Exodus 34:6 reveals that the Lord is both "compassionate" and "gracious," as well as extremely patient, overflowing in steadfast "love," and unrelenting in His "faithfulness." God's redemption of His people from Egypt and His establishment of them in Canaan were superlative examples of His grace. He rescued them despite their disloyalty and iniquity (Deut. 7:7-8; 9:5-6). The Son is the supreme revelation of the Father's grace. Jesus not only appropriated divine grace, but also incarnated it (Luke 2:40; John 1:14). Moreover, Jesus died on the cross and rose from the dead so that the lost, by faith, might partake of God's grace (Titus 2:11).

The Creator is able to free the lost from the penalty of sin because of what Jesus did at Calvary. Specifically, His sacrificial death is the means by which salvation is accomplished for all who repent and believe. The Greek noun translated "redemption" (Rom. 3:24) carries overtones of a "ransom payment." The term is adapted from the slave market. We were formerly in bondage to sin, but Jesus delivered us from that evil taskmaster so we might become Jesus' faithful servants (see 6:6-7, 14, 16-22 and the commentary in lesson 9).

C. Acquittal through Jesus' Sacrificial Death: vss. 25-26

God presented him as a sacrifice of atonement, through faith in his blood. He did this to demonstrate his justice, because in his forbearance he had left the sins committed beforehand unpunished—he did it to demonstrate his justice at the present time, so as to be just and the one who justifies those who have faith in Jesus.

Paul presented several key theological ideas connected with the justification of believers. For instance, the phrase "sacrifice of atonement" (Rom. 3:25) renders a Greek noun that some associate with the mercy seat. This lid (made out of pure gold) covered the ark of the covenant located behind the veil within the most holy place of the Jerusalem temple (see Exod. 25:17, 22; Heb. 9:4). Once a year, on the Day of Atonement (later referred to as Yom Kippur), the high priest sprinkled blood (obtained from animal sacrifices) on the mercy seat to make satisfaction for his sins, along with those committed by the rest of the covenant community (see Lev. 16:11-19, 34, and the commentary in lesson 12 from the December quarter).

The Greek noun in Romans 3:25 is more literally translated as "propitiation." This word communicates the idea that the Son's redemptive work on the cross turned away the Father's justifiable wrath against sinners. Jesus' sacrifice also provided "expiation," or the removal of personal guilt. Paul was making a parallel between the animal sacrifices offered in the temple and Jesus' death on the cross. The lost appropriated the saving benefits of what Jesus accomplished by trusting in Him. As noted previously, eternal life is not something that can be earned, but only received by depending on the one who is "Faithful and True" (Rev. 19:11).

In Romans 3:25 and 26, Paul referred to the demonstration of God's "justice" or "righteousness." Before the advent of the Son, the Father suspended (literally, "passed over") the full punishment for humanity's sins (see Acts 14:16; 17:30). The animal sacrifices offered in the temple symbolically atoned for the transgressions committed by the chosen people. Nonetheless, these offerings were a temporary and imperfect shadow of Jesus' saving work on the cross (see Heb. 10:1-4). To be sure, the Creator's "forbearance" (Rom. 3:25) did not last indefinitely. So, when the new era of salvation arrived, the Son voluntarily went to the cross. This enabled the Father, who demanded justice, to make provision for it (vs. 26). By dealing with humanity's sin once and for all in such a visible way, the Creator maintained the integrity of His character, while at the same time He showed mercy in vindicating transgressors.

II. RIGHTEOUSNESS RECEIVED BY FAITH: ROMANS 3:27-31

A. Faith, Not Works: vss. 27-28

Where, then, is boasting? It is excluded. On what principle? On that of observing the law? No, but on that of faith. For we maintain that a man is justified by faith apart from observing the law.

To drive home his point, Paul asked some incisive questions to an imagined dialogue partner (reflecting the diatribe style of communication). He began by wondering what place was left for bragging (Rom. 3:27). In short, God completely shut out any opportunity for people to gloat over their accomplishments. The apostle next literally asked, "by what sort of law," that is, on the basis of what standard, norm, system, or code (see 7:21, 23).

We can imagine Paul's religious peers drawing attention to their heeding the ordinances of the Mosaic covenant. But the apostle countered that the believers' acquittal was literally due to the "law of faith" (3:27). Since a considerable number of Jews in that day were driven by legalistic impulses (whether overt or subtle in nature), Paul used a play on words to refer to the "law" metaphorically. He wanted his religious peers (along with all people) to understand that trusting in the Messiah, not observing the Torah (nor any other pious activity), was the reason for God pardoning and accepting the lost (vs. 28).

B. For Both Jews and Gentiles: vss. 29-31

Is God the God of Jews only? Is he not the God of Gentiles too? Yes, of Gentiles too, since there is only one God, who will justify the circumcised by faith and the uncircumcised through that same faith. Do we, then, nullify the law by this faith? Not at all! Rather, we uphold the law.

In light of Paul's argument, some Torah-observant Jews may have wondered about their relationship with the Creator, especially in comparison to the Gentiles. While the apostle affirmed that the chosen people enjoyed a number of spiritual advantages (see Rom. 3:1-2; 9:4-5), it would have been incorrect for them to conclude that the Lord was only *their* God. He also belonged to the Gentiles (3:29). Indeed, all humanity owed its existence to the Creator (see Acts 17:24-28 and the commentary in lesson 12 of the September quarter). In previous history, the Gentiles had been involved in the worship of pagan deities. By contrast, the members of the covenant community prided themselves in their worship of the one, true, and living God. Nonetheless, as Paul demonstrated, both Jews and Gentiles were condemned sinners in need of deliverance from eternal punishment.

In Romans 3:30, Paul affirmed that there is "only one God." The phrase refers to the Jewish confession known as the *Shema*, which is recorded in Deuteronomy 6:4. The implication is that the Creator acquitted both Jews and Gentiles in exactly the same way—namely, as a result of their faith in the Savior. Paul's religious peers might wonder whether his emphasis on "faith" (vs. 31) overturned the need for the law. The apostle emphatically denied such a conclusion, especially because he regarded the Mosaic legal code to be "holy, righteous and good" (7:12). Paul declared that faith in the Son did not abolish the importance of the law, but instead confirmed its validity. The law was fulfilled when it led people to see their sinfulness, turn to the Savior in faith, and conform their lives to the moral norms taught in the law.

Paul built his case for faith-righteousness on Abraham and David—two of the most respected figures in the Old Testament. Abraham would be particularly important as an example, for the Jews of Paul's day thought they had a privileged relationship with God by virtue of their physical relationship with Abraham as his descendants. If Paul could show that Abraham was declared righteous, by faith rather than works, then the false presumptions of the apostle's religious peers would collapse. He began with the rhetorical question, "What then shall we say?" (4:1). His concern was to address what Abraham discovered on the issue of justification by faith.

Many of Paul's peers believed Abraham was a perfect example of a person justified by works. Jews in the first century A.D. also believed that Abraham had so much righteousness in terms of good works that he had a surplus of merit. Allegedly, it was available to all the patriarch's descendants. The apostle fully agreed that Abraham was a virtuous individual and that, as such, he had something to boast about before people—but not before God (vs. 2). In verse 3, Paul substantiated his point by referring to Genesis 15:6. Because Abraham believed God's promise concerning Isaac, God credited righteousness to the patriarch's account. So, Abraham's life was a suitable illustration of Paul's point—namely, that faith, not works, was the basis for an upright relationship with God.

Paul noted that workers' wages were not given to them as a gift, but rather were paid because it was owed to them (Rom. 4:4). So, if works could attain salvation, then it could not be called the gift of God. Conversely, for the person who did not work but rather placed faith in God, that person's trust was credited as righteousness (vs. 5). Abraham was an illustration of the second type of person. Paul further illustrated his point from the life of David (vss. 6-8). The apostle quoted David's words in Psalm 32:1-2, showing the blessedness of one whose account has been credited with God's righteousness. The latter was appropriated through faith, apart from works. Because of God's grace, such a person's sins were covered, and the Lord would never hold that individual's wrongdoing against him or her.

Once again, Paul asked whether justification by faith was only for the Jews (the circumcised) or also for the Gentiles (the uncircumcised; Rom. 4:9). As before, the apostle appealed to Abraham. Paul's basic argument was that the patriarch was not acquitted as a result of faith plus circumcision. Likewise, Abraham was not pardoned as a result of faith plus keeping the Mosaic law. Instead, he was declared righteous by faith alone (vss. 10-11). Accordingly, Paul said that all of Abraham's offspring—both saved Jews and Gentiles—received righteousness (justification) by faith and according to God's grace (vs. 16).

Discussion Questions

1. Why do we need God's righteousness?
2. Why is God's righteousness received apart from keeping the Mosaic law?
3. What does it mean for us to be declared righteous by God's grace?
4. Why would God forgive us when we have rebelled against Him?
5. How can God remain blameless and at the same time pardon us?

Contemporary Application

If God were only just, humanity would not have a chance. Our situation is clear: we have sinned before a holy God (Rom. 3:23). The only equitable response from God is our death. At the same time, if God were solely loving, we would all be gathered to His presence without a glance at the sinfulness of our hearts.

Yet it is not one or the other, for God is neither solely just nor exclusively loving; He is both. He loves us and wants us to join Him in His eternal kingdom. But He first had to establish a way for our sin to be annulled. That was what the Father accomplished through the Son's atoning sacrifice on the cross (vs. 25).

Figuratively, God has sent us an invitation marked RSVP (*Répondez s'il vous plaît*)—French for "Please reply." Although our Lord waits patiently for our favorable response, He has set a limit on how long He will wait. At some point He must say, "Enough!" and the doors of heaven will swing shut. Before it's too late, we must say *yes* by faith to His invitation and join His great banquet.

A Renewed Hope

Scripture

Background Scripture: *Romans 5:1-11*
Scripture Lesson: *Romans 5:1-11*
Key Verse: Hope does not disappoint us, because God has poured out his love into our hearts by the Holy Spirit, whom he has given us. *Romans 5:5*
Scripture Lesson for Children: *Romans 5:1-11*
Key Verse for Children: We rejoice in the hope of the glory of God. *Romans 5:2*

Lesson Aim

To emphasize that our hope in the Son gives us the courage to go through trials.

Lesson Setting

Time: About A.D. 57
Place: Corinth

Lesson Outline

A Renewed Hope

  I. The Essence of Hope: Romans 5:1-5
    A. *Peace with God: vss. 1-2*
    B. *Growth through Suffering: vss. 3-5*
  II. The Provision of Reconciliation: Romans 5:6-11
    A. *Salvation for the Ungodly: vss. 6-8*
    B. *Reconciliation for God's Enemies: vss. 9-11*

Introduction for Adults

Topic: *Hope for All*

The first rule of advertising is to describe the benefits of the goods being sold. This is based on the awareness that, before making a purchase, people want to know how their life will be better for using certain products and services. Perhaps that's why, when we watch those 30-second dramas being enacted on television commercials, we're told that using the right item will make us successful.

We know, of course, that such promises are inflated. This is far different than God's pledges to us. For instance, the Father has promised that when we trust in the Son, we reap several eternal benefits. These include peace, grace, and the abiding presence of the Spirit (see Rom. 5:1-5). We don't have to make any purchases or perform a noble deed. In fact, there is nothing we can do on our own to enjoy the vast riches of God's love. We must simply put our faith in Jesus for salvation and forgiveness.

Introduction for Youth

Topic: *Got Hope?*

Once in a while we read about someone stepping forward to pay another person's debt or fine. But nowadays we never hear about people volunteering to take the place of a convicted criminal on death row.

During World War II, however, a Polish pastor offered to take the place of a man the Germans had decided to execute. The Germans took his offer and shot him instead. He died in the condemned man's place as his substitute. Now that was a profound kind of love!

God's love for us is even more profound. When we were utterly helpless to save ourselves, God sent His Son to rescue us from our plight. And even though we were guilty of rebelling against God, He still allowed Jesus to die in our place on the cross, so great is God's love for us (Rom. 5:6-8). Such love should fill us with joy, hope, and compassion for others.

Concepts for Children

Topic: *We Have Hope*

1. The Bible teaches us to believe in Jesus.
2. When we believe in Jesus, God gives us peace.
3. Believing in Jesus gives us hope.
4. The Holy Spirit is always with us to help us live for Jesus.
5. Because Jesus loves us so much, we should follow Him.

Lesson Commentary

I. THE ESSENCE OF HOPE: ROMANS 5:1-5

A. Peace with God: vss. 1-2

Therefore, since we have been justified through faith, we have peace with God through our Lord Jesus Christ, through whom we have gained access by faith into this grace in which we now stand. And we rejoice in the hope of the glory of God.

In last week's lesson, we learned about the Father's provision of righteousness through faith in the Son (Rom. 3:21-31). Paul argued that long before the advent of the Messiah, Abraham and David were justified by faith (4:1-8). The apostle clarified that faith was also the basis for the covenant between God and His chosen people (vss. 9-15). Indeed, God's promise of grace extended to all Jews and Gentiles whose faith in the Creator was like that found in Abraham. Though he was exceedingly old and Sarah was past childbearing, Abraham still believed God's promise that he would have a son through Sarah. Because of the patriarch's unwavering trust in God's ability to do what seemed impossible, God credited righteousness to Abraham (vss. 16-22).

Paul noted that the words "it was credited" (vs. 23) to Abraham were not just written for the benefit of the patriarch, but for all who believed in God (vs. 24). Paul closed his argument by reflecting on the central role of the risen Savior in our justification (vs. 25). He was delivered over to death on account of our sins, and He was raised to life to make us right with the Creator (see Isa. 53:4-6). Jesus, as the spotless Lamb of God, paid the redemptive price for our sins (see John 1:29, 36; 1 Cor. 5:7; 1 Pet 1:19). Just as Abraham, our spiritual ancestor (Rom. 4:11-12, 16), was pleasing in God's sight on the basis of faith, not pious deeds, so too are we. Also, just as Abraham was declared righteous due to his trust in the Lord, likewise so are we. The Creator, who is able to do whatever He promises (vs. 21), does not hesitate to give us eternal life when we believe in the Messiah (see John 1:12-13; 20:31).

In many respects, Romans 5 is a point of transition for Paul's entire letter. In the first four chapters, he explained how repentant sinners were acquitted in God's sight. Then, beginning in chapter 5, the apostle discussed how believers were to live as God's redeemed and forgiven children. On the one hand, we learn that Jesus delivered us from punishment. On the other hand, we discover that He also saved us to a full and abundant life (see John 10:10). It compares to being released from death row in a maximum-security prison and being invited to move into a governor's mansion.

For Paul, justification was not only an event that put believers in a right position with God. Justification also had practical, lifelong implications for believers. First among these benefits was the enduring "peace" (Rom. 5:1) they experienced with the Father as a result of the Son's atoning death at Calvary.

Because of sin, people were estranged from God and were objects of His wrath (see 1:18—3:20). Yet, because of Jesus' sacrifice on the cross (3:24-26), not only did believers avoid receiving the wrath they deserved, but also they enjoyed a state of peace with God (see John 14:27; Eph. 2:14-15). They expected fury, but received grace. Formerly they were God's enemies, and now they were His friends (see Col. 1:21-22).

A second benefit that resulted from justification was the believers' ongoing, direct "access" (Rom. 5:2) to God's "throne of grace" (Heb. 4:16). At one time, because of sin, they were barred from coming into the Creator's sacred presence. Now, as a consequence of the new life believers received, they had full and unrestricted "access" (Rom. 5:2). The underlying Greek noun means "privilege of approach," which was available through faith in Jesus. In usages outside the New Testament, the term sometimes pictured individuals being ushered into the royal court of a monarch. Scripture teaches that the Son opened the door for believers into the Father's holy presence. The noun could also indicate a safe harbor or haven for ships. This likewise fits the biblical concept of believers finding refuge with the Father through their union with the Son.

Verse 2 points to a corresponding blessing—namely, God's provision of "grace," on which His children took their "stand." Because believers were cleared of guilt, they lived in the sphere of God's undeserved kindness. It was also in this realm that they enjoyed "every spiritual blessing" (Eph. 1:3) in union with the Son. The gift of grace was the basis for believers exulting in the "hope" (Rom. 5:2) of experiencing the Creator's "glory," from which they previously fell short (3:23). In particular, divine grace enabled believers to be "conformed" (8:29) to the "image" of the Son (1 Cor. 15:49; 2 Cor. 3:18; Phil. 3:21; 1 John 3:2) and anticipate dwelling forever in glorified, resurrection bodies with the triune God (see Isa. 60:1; 62:2; Rom. 8:17-18, 21, 30; Rev. 21:3, 22-26).

B. Growth through Suffering: vss. 3-5

Not only so, but we also rejoice in our sufferings, because we know that suffering produces perseverance; perseverance, character; and character, hope. And hope does not disappoint us, because God has poured out his love into our hearts by the Holy Spirit, whom he has given us.

Paul did not want his readers to conclude that their being at "peace with God" (Rom. 5:1) would result in tranquility for them during the course of daily living. Rather, they would encounter "sufferings" (vs. 3), in which the underlying Greek noun could also be rendered "afflictions," "distresses," or "pressures." These are broad words that encompass all kinds of situations that could go wrong. Some people had financial pressures; some had health afflictions; some had job-related distresses; and others struggled with broken relationships.

Whatever the difficult circumstance, believers could have joy in the midst of it. Also, in union with the Son, they had the power to choose how they responded to their conditions, no matter how burdensome the situation felt.

It's clarifying to note that believers rejoiced "in" (vs. 3) their sufferings, not "because of" them. This was an important distinction. Paul was not exhorting believers to be superficially happy when life seemed overwhelming. Instead, he was encouraging Christians to make their troubling situations the object of their joyful confidence, especially when they recognized the beneficial outcomes God produced from their hardships.

Verses 3 and 4 record a series of interconnected outcomes: suffering fostered perseverance (steadfast endurance under pressure); perseverance led to tested and proven character; and character produced hope (a confident expectation about the future). (Progressions such as this, called concatenation, were a common literary device used in ancient times.) So, believers could maintain a jubilant attitude in the midst of afflictions because they knew God was always at work for their eternal good and would vindicate their unwavering commitment to Him (see 8:28). Instead of being meaningless and frustrating, distressing circumstances could bear Christlike fruit, including perseverance, character, and hope.

Paul affirmed that the believers' "hope" (5:5) would not lead to disappointment. The underlying Greek verb refers to bringing shame, dishonor, or disgrace on someone. The idea is that the believers' confident expectation in the Creator (along with His covenant promises) would result in everlasting splendor, not embarrassment, for Him and His children (see Pss. 22:5; 25:3, 20). God's unconditional love for believers was the basis for their inner fortitude and joyful anticipation of future glory.

The idiomatic expression rendered "poured out . . . into our hearts" (Rom. 5:5) depicted the Spirit inundating the innermost being of Christians with the Father's tender mercy (see Isa. 32:15; Ezek. 39:29; Joel 2:28; Zech. 12:10). The Spirit, who indwelt all believers (see Rom. 8:9, 11; 1 Cor. 6:19; 2 Tim. 1:14), was also the agent who expressed God's love in and through the believers' hearts. Such inexhaustible compassion enhanced their hope, for its provision did not hinge on circumstances. Even when life threw God's children a punch, His grace continued to flow through their hearts to heal their bruises.

Of the 53 times the Greek word for hope appears in the New Testament, nearly one-fourth of those occurrences (13) are found in Romans. Throughout the letter, Paul made several observations about hope: Abraham believed in "hope" (4:18); we are saved in this "hope" (8:24); we can be joyful in "hope" (12:12); through the endurance and encouragement that come from the Scriptures, we can have "hope" (15:4); the Lord is a God of "hope" (vs. 13); and the power of the Holy Spirit enables us to "overflow with hope" (vs. 13). Furthermore, Paul often linked hope together with faith and love (or charity), making hope one of the central virtues of the Christian life (see 1 Cor. 13:13; Col. 1:5; 1 Thess. 1:3; 5:8).

II. THE PROVISION OF RECONCILIATION: ROMANS 5:6-11

A. Salvation for the Ungodly: vss. 6-8

You see, at just the right time, when we were still powerless, Christ died for the ungodly. Very rarely will anyone die for a righteous man, though for a good man someone might possibly dare to die. But God demonstrates his own love for us in this: While we were still sinners, Christ died for us.

Previously, in Romans 3:21-31, Paul explained that the Son's atoning sacrifice at Calvary was the historical, objective basis for the Father acquitting repentant sinners. Then, in 5:6, the apostle pointed back to Jesus' crucifixion as the foremost example of God's love for the lost. Before, in 3:23, Paul declared that everyone was guilty of sinning and failed to live up to God's perfect moral standard. Now, in 5:6, the apostle indicated that at one time all believers were "powerless" (morally weak and helpless) and "ungodly" (irreverent evildoers).

Ephesians 2:1-3 is even more explicit about the deplorable condition of the unsaved. Because of their "transgressions" and "sins," the lost were spiritually "dead." They not only adhered to the wicked "ways" of pagan society, but also obeyed Satan, who ruled over a demonic cohort. Moreover, all people followed the cravings, desires, and thoughts of their sinful state (literally, "flesh"). In short, before coming to faith in the Son, both Jewish and Gentile believers literally had been "children of wrath" (vs. 3). This Semitic expression suggests that all the unsaved were people characterized by and destined for God's judgment.

Despite all this, the Father did not hesitate in permitting His Son to go to the cross (Rom. 5:6). This was not a haphazard decision, but one God initiated at the perfect "time" in salvation history. For centuries the Mosaic law had been in operation—provoking and exposing sin, along with showing people their need to be reconciled with God. But now the occasion had come for the Messiah to be born, at just the right moment in God's plan of redemption (see Gal. 4:4). Furthermore, Jesus became our representative and substitute on the cross. We deserved to die for our sins, but He took our place and was offered on our behalf. What an amazing act of love the Savior performed!

Paul admitted that people seldom, if ever, gave up their lives for the upright. Occasionally, there might be someone heroic enough to die for an exemplary benefactor or a noble cause (Rom. 5:7). Of course, as the apostle revealed, no one was sufficiently virtuous to merit God's favor. Even so, the Creator was forthright in providing incontestable proof of His love for "sinners" (vs. 8). He did so by sending His Son to the cross. Put another way, the sinless Son of God literally died for the "sons of disobedience" (Eph. 2:2), that is, people characterized by insurrection and alienated from the Creator. The contrast between the one who laid down His life and those for whom He died is stark. Such an act of self-sacrifice could only be motivated by unfathomable love. Just as remarkable, this compassion was publicly displayed at Calvary (see Rom. 3:25-26).

In Hebrews 12:1-3, the Christian life is depicted as a footrace and Jesus is portrayed as the champion runner of the ages. As we struggle in our race, we can know that He has already been there and has shown that the race can be won. Just as we are to keep our eyes fixed on Jesus, so He kept His eyes fixed on the joy of completing the mission the Father had given to Him. Also, just as we are to persevere in the race marked out for us, so Jesus "endured the cross, scorning its shame." The cross brought great suffering and disgrace, but Jesus kept in mind that the glory of enduring the crucifixion would be much greater.

B. Reconciliation for God's Enemies: vss. 9-11

Since we have now been justified by his blood, how much more shall we be saved from God's wrath through him! For if, when we were God's enemies, we were reconciled to him through the death of his Son, how much more, having been reconciled, shall we be saved through his life! Not only is this so, but we also rejoice in God through our Lord Jesus Christ, through whom we have now received reconciliation.

Romans 5:9-11 continues to build on Paul's teaching concerning justification by faith. We learn that Jesus' shed blood is the basis for repentant sinners being declared righteous. As disclosed in 3:25, Jesus' sacrificial death must be appropriated by "faith." Paul reasoned that since this greater point was true, the lesser one was just as valid (being a less difficult endeavor to achieve)—namely, that through the believers' union with the Son, they would be rescued from experiencing the Father's eternal punishment (5:9; see Rom. 1:18; 12:19; 1 Thess. 1:10). Expressed differently, since believers have been made positionally right with God, they would certainly not be abandoned to await a verdict of condemnation (see John 5:24).

In Romans 5:10, Paul again argued from a greater to a lesser truth. On the one hand, the Father "reconciled" His "enemies" (His hostile opponents) to Himself as a result of His Son's "death." Reconciliation refers to bringing two alienated parties into harmony. It is the establishment of peace in a relationship once marked by separation and hostility. Jesus' atoning sacrifice is the basis of a restored fellowship between the Father and His children (see 2 Cor. 5:20-21). With God having accomplished the more arduous task, there was no doubt that at the end of the age, He would deliver believers from the "second death" (Rev. 20:14) because of their union with the One who lives and who literally held the "keys of death and of Hades" (1:18).

Paul's point was that since the Creator no longer looked on believers as His "enemies" (Rom. 5:10), the basis of their salvation was complete, having been obtained by the Messiah. The reference to Jesus' "life" went beyond His earthly sojourn to His postresurrection existence in heaven. An example of Jesus' present ministry to believers was the way He lived to make intercession for them from God's sacred throne (see Heb. 7:25). The Son literally was their "advocate with the Father" (1 John 2:1). In summary, the believers' acquittal was brought about through Jesus' crucifixion. Also, their sanctification and glorification were made possible through His resurrection life (see Rom. 8:29-30).

In 5:11, Paul explained that not only did believers have future provision in union with the Messiah, but also they exulted in the present moment because of what the Father achieved on their behalf through the Son. To reiterate, the Creator, by sending Jesus, made peace with repentant sinners. Consequently, instead of being God's enemies, they were now His friends. Their peace with God was not a truce. The latter was passive. It was cease and desist. Peace, however, was active. God wanted believers to be mindful of the activity of His peace in their lives whenever they were anxious (Phil. 4:6-7), afraid, or discouraged (John 14:27). Their peace with God impacted their peace with each other, and peace became one of the guiding rules of conduct in their relationships (Rom. 12:18; 1 Thess. 5:13).

Discussion Questions

1. What is the basis for our peace with God?
2. How is it possible for us to rejoice in the midst of afflictions?
3. Why does our hope in God never prove to be a disappointment?
4. In what sense is the Spirit a gift from the Father to us?
5. What did God do to make us His friends?

Contemporary Application

As we get older, we come to realize that life is filled with both joys and disappointments. We tend to become weary when there are more losses than gains, and more failures than successes. In that situation, we can begin to feel as if life is hopeless. The Good News is that, despite life's hardships, we have "hope" (Rom. 5:2) in Christ. He is the anchor of our soul and the foundation of our faith. When we trust in Him, He can fill our hearts with peace and our minds with hope that go beyond human understanding.

The preceding truths emphasize how important it is for us to remain united to the Son by faith. As long as we remain in touch with Jesus and the new life He offers, we will produce a lot of spiritual fruit. For instance, we will be godly individuals and witnesses for the Lord. Tragedy results, however, when we allow our spiritual communion with Jesus to weaken. We are not as fruitful as we ought to be and our testimony to others is severely damaged.

Some believers might be uncomfortable with the idea of finding hope in the new life the Father offers in the Son. After all, they become used to doing things on their own and in their own way. This is a terrible policy to adopt, however, when it comes to the spiritual life. If we rely only on ourselves, it is impossible for us to overcome sinful habits and resist the forbidden cravings of our sinful nature. Ultimately, only by remaining in the Son will we have the assurance of victory over the things of the world.

A New Life

Scripture

Background Scripture: *Romans 6*
Scripture Lesson: *Romans 6:1-4, 12-14, 17-23*
Key Verse: We were therefore buried with him through baptism into death in order that, just as Christ was raised from the dead through the glory of the Father, we too may live a new life. *Romans 6:4*
Scripture Lesson for Children: *Romans 6:1-4, 12-14, 20-23*
Key Verse for Children: Just as Christ was raised from the dead through the glory of the Father, we too may live a new life. *Romans 6:4*

Lesson Aim

To highlight that our union with the Son frees us from sin so we can obey the Father.

Lesson Setting

Time: About A.D. 57
Place: Corinth

Lesson Outline

A New Life

I. Replacing Death with Life: Romans 6:1-4, 12-14
   A. *Death to Sin: vss. 1-4*
   B. *Alive to God: vss. 12-14*

II. Exchanging Sin for Holiness: Romans 6:17-23
   A. *Freedom from Sin: vss. 17-18*
   B. *Free to Be Holy: vss. 19-23*

Introduction for Adults

Topic: *A Renewed Life*

One of the common testimonies of people whose heart ailments have been treated with bypass surgery is that they have found new life. Instead of feeling weak, tired, and short of breath, they now have energy to do things they could not do before.

Jesus' resurrection does the same sort of thing for us in the spiritual realm. At one time we were "dead in . . . transgressions and sins" (Eph. 2:1). But when we trusted in Jesus for salvation, we passed from death to life (vs. 5). This is possible because we have been united with Jesus' death, burial, and resurrection (Rom. 6:1-4).

If we think of our old, sinful life as dead and buried, we have a powerful motive to resist sin. We now have the option of consciously choosing to treat the temptations and desires of the old nature as being dead. This is possible because of the wonderful new life we have in Jesus.

Introduction for Youth

Topic: *Choose Life*

One day a teenager returned to his job after having been to a Christian summer camp. While away, he had made a commitment to God that he would quit a certain habit he knew was not good for him. After his return, his peers saw the difference in his behavior, and he became afraid that they would ridicule him. But when the adolescent explained his conversion experience, one of his friends simply said, "More power to you!"

It's easy for us to think of power in terms of athletes with large muscles or automobiles with big engines. In the spiritual realm, however, it is something quite different. It's the ability to say *no* to sin and *yes* to God and His will. The reason is clear. We have been spiritually united with Jesus in His death, burial, and resurrection (Rom. 6:1-4). He gives us the ability, through the Spirit, to obey Scripture and in this way honor the Lord.

Concepts for Children

Topic: *Living a New Life*

1. Jesus died on the cross.
2. Jesus also rose from the dead.
3. When we trust in Jesus, we can live in a new way.
4. For instance, Jesus helps us to stop sinning.
5. Jesus also helps us to do what is right.

Lesson Commentary

I. REPLACING DEATH WITH LIFE: ROMANS 6:1-4, 12-14

A. Death to Sin: vss. 1-4

What shall we say, then? Shall we go on sinning so that grace may increase? By no means! We died to sin; how can we live in it any longer? Or don't you know that all of us who were baptized into Christ Jesus were baptized into his death? We were therefore buried with him through baptism into death in order that, just as Christ was raised from the dead through the glory of the Father, we too may live a new life.

In Romans 5:12-21, Paul drew a parallel between Adam and Jesus. At the dawn of history, Adam rebelled against the Creator by deliberately violating His specific command. As a result, the entire human race became alienated from God. Whereas Adam's transgression brought condemnation to all humanity, Jesus' atoning sacrifice brought forgiveness and new life to all who trusted in Him. The Mosaic law was added so that an awareness of sin and acts of trespass might increase. Also, where sin increased, grace increased considerably more. Similarly, the more people became aware of their hopeless condition and their capacity to sin, the greater the opportunity for God's grace to do its work of justification.

Apparently, Paul's detractors reasoned that since God's grace increased when sin was prevalent, people should deliberately plant their lives in the soil of iniquity so His undeserved kindness could blossom even more (6:1). The apostle used a rhetorical question-and-answer technique to challenge and reject the validity of this premise. Also, throughout this chapter, Paul personified sin as a despotic power terrorizing it victims. The apostle noted that through faith in the Messiah, believers became dead to sin and its chokehold. In light of this reality, it was unthinkable for them to adopt an immoral lifestyle.

The Greek verb translated "died" (vs. 2) is in a tense indicating that believers spiritually expired at a specific point in the past—that is, when they got saved. Theologically speaking, when a person trusted in Jesus, he or she perished to sin at that moment. In this context, death implied separation. For instance, spiritual death was separation from God, whereas physical death was the separation of the soul from the body. Accordingly, dying to sin involved being separated from its controlling power and influence. The Father's grace, offered in the Son, made this new reality possible.

Paul elaborated that Christians were "baptized into" (vs. 3), or united with, the Messiah in His "death." This also included being joined with Jesus in His burial and resurrection. The apostle stated that the Father's glorious power "raised" (vs. 4) the Son "from the dead." Previously, in 1:4, Paul disclosed that Jesus was resurrected by the Holy Spirit's power and shown to be the "Son of God." Now, as a result of Christians being united with Jesus in His death, burial, and resurrection, they too were raised literally to "newness of life" (see 6:4).

Also, it was in this regenerate state that the Creator wanted them to abide and walk.

Scholars debate whether verses 3 and 4 refer to water baptism or spiritual baptism. If the emphasis is on water baptism (see 1 Cor. 1:13-17; 15:29), it would seem to teach that this rite is necessary for salvation. Other passages of Scripture, though, offer a different perspective (see Acts 2:38; 10:44-48; 16:29-33; 1 Pet. 3:21). For instance, as Paul taught in Romans 1 through 5, salvation hinges solely on the lost believing in the Son. In light of this, some maintain that water baptism dramatizes the work of salvation in a person's heart, and it is the basis for them concluding that spiritual baptism is the emphasis in 6:3-4. The idea is that when the lost trust in the Son, the Spirit joins them to the body of Christ (see 1 Cor. 12:13; Gal. 3:27). Regardless of which view is preferred, Paul's basic point about sin remains the same. Because of the believers' union with Jesus in His death, burial, and resurrection, they have died to sin's power and have been raised to "new life" (Rom. 6:4).

B. Alive to God: vss. 12-14

Therefore do not let sin reign in your mortal body so that you obey its evil desires. Do not offer the parts of your body to sin, as instruments of wickedness, but rather offer yourselves to God, as those who have been brought from death to life; and offer the parts of your body to him as instruments of righteousness. For sin shall not be your master, because you are not under law, but under grace.

Paul continued to build his case by providing more details on the relationship between Jesus' resurrection and the destruction of sin's power in the believer's life. The apostle emphasized that since believers were united with Jesus in a death resembling His, they would also be joined with Him in a resurrection resembling His (Rom. 6:5). On one level, Paul was referring to the believers' future bodily resurrection. On another level, the apostle had in mind the believers' present spiritual union with Jesus (see Eph. 2:6; Col. 2:12; 3:1). This emphasis is made clear in Romans 6:6, where Paul argued that the believers' death and resurrection with Jesus was to be understood as their dying to sin and experiencing newness of life in submission to God.

In verse 6, Paul said the believers' "old self" (literally "old man") was crucified with Jesus. The apostle was referring to everything the lost were, when in union with Adam before trusting in Jesus for salvation (see 5:12, 17, 19). Specifically, before their conversion, the unregenerate were enslaved to sin (see 3:9), irreverent (see 5:6), and God's enemies (see vs. 10). In short, the "old self" (6:6) pointed to an individual's fallen state under the old regime before being born again (see Eph. 4:22; Col. 3:9). As a result of the believers' union with the Son, their entire person was spiritually nailed to the cross. Furthermore, this broke the rule sin exercised over repentant sinners. Paul depicted sin as an evil taskmaster whose reign was brought to nothing, with the outcome that believers would no longer remain under sin's dominion.

In Romans 6:6, Paul literally made reference to the "body of sin." It would be incorrect to conclude from this phrase that the human body was intrinsically evil. The apostle was simply referring to the entirety of a human being as dominated by rebellion. After the believers' conversion and their entering the era of the new covenant, the brutal control of sin in their lives was abolished. Verse 7 reiterates that because sin was made impotent, it ceased having any legal right to exercise its authority unchallenged in the lives of the believers. By God's grace, they could now choose to live as His freed people.

In verses 8 through 11, Paul further developed what it means to be dead to sin and alive to God. The apostle affirmed that because of the believers' union with Jesus in His death and resurrection, they were raised to a new quality of life (vs. 8). The latter was a present reality that would be fully realized at Jesus' second advent. When the lost put their faith in the Son, they began to share in His resurrection life. Since Jesus conquered the grave, He would never die again (see Acts 2:24). Also, because Jesus was forever removed from death's sphere of influence, it no longer had any dominion over Him (Rom. 6:9).

On the one hand, Jesus died to sin once and for all time (see Heb. 7:27; 9:12; 10:10). On the other hand, the Son now perpetually lived to bring glory to the Father (Rom. 6:10). There were profound implications to the objective, historical reality of Jesus' resurrection. First, believers were joined by faith with Him. Second, on the basis of this truth, they were to continually regard themselves as dead to the controlling power of sin. Expressed differently, they were to give no more response to the lure of sin than a deceased individual could provide. Third, the new birth Christians experienced in union with the Son was the basis for the Spirit enabling them to bring glory to the Father (vs. 11).

In verses 12 through 14, Paul shifted his attention to the practical application of what he had just said. Specifically, believers were to conform their behavior to the reality of their new birth. The apostle portrayed sin as a slave driver who exercised dominion over the "mortal body." Paul exhorted believers not to permit this type of control to continue over their thoughts, emotions, and actions. After all, the power of this tyrannical master had been shattered as a result of the believers' union with Jesus. When they yielded to sin, they also surrendered to the depraved passions it spawned. These impulses were usually manifest in and through one's physical body. The Good News is that Jesus provided all that His followers needed to resist their sinful enticements. In sum, their union with the Messiah was the basis for their victory.

Believers were not to relinquish any part of their bodies to sin, which it often used like weapons for despicable ends. Instead, they were to present every aspect of their lives in service to the Creator for upright purposes (vs. 13). Put another way, rather than be vassals of evil, Jesus' followers were to be bondservants who sought to please and glorify God. Doing so was in keeping with the fact that He had spiritually regenerated believers and placed them under the dominion of His "grace" (vs. 14), rather than the Mosaic "law." As noted previously, God instituted the law centuries earlier so that the awareness of trespasses might increase (see Rom. 5:20; 1 Cor. 15:56). Now, in connection with God's undeserved kindness, believers had the freedom to live according to a higher principle—namely, one rooted in the resurrection life of the Messiah and the new era of salvation He inaugurated.

II. Exchanging Sin for Holiness: Romans 6:17-23

A. Freedom from Sin: vss. 17-18

But thanks be to God that, though you used to be slaves to sin, you wholeheartedly obeyed the form of teaching to which you were entrusted. You have been set free from sin and have become slaves to righteousness.

Paul sensed that his detractors might allege they could throw off all moral restraint and act autonomously. In response, the apostle tersely renounced the idea that God's grace sanctioned believers to indulge in sin with impunity (Rom. 6:15). After all, they had exchanged sin as their master for righteousness (or behavior approved by God). The apostle revealed that people were "slaves" (vs. 16) to whomever they served—whether it be to "sin," which resulted in "death" (that is, eternal separation from God), or "obedience," which resulted in "righteousness" (see John 8:34-36).

Paul acknowledged that prior to their conversion, his readers had been enslaved to "sin" (Rom. 6:17). Yet, the apostle expressed thanks to the Creator for bringing about their spiritual rebirth. Through the proclamation of the Gospel, the believers in Rome had been "entrusted" with apostolic "teaching." In turn, they not only enthusiastically received these truths, but also heeded them. Paul's readers were not just rendering external, ritual obedience, but demonstrated an inner, unequivocal commitment to follow the Savior's commands and serve His followers (see Rom. 1:5-6; 15:18; 16:26; 1 Cor. 9:21; Gal. 6:2; Jas. 2:8).

Now that Paul's readers (along with all Christians) were unshackled from "sin" (Rom. 6:18), they had become enslaved to "righteousness" (meaning they submitted to God's holy standards). Others could see that these adherents of the new "covenant" (Jer. 31:33) had God's "law" placed deep within them and His instructions written on their "hearts." Paul rejected any notion of a compromising, neutral position for believers, especially since the two respective options were quite different from each other (see Matt. 6:24). One type of bondage was ruthless and led to eternal separation from the Creator. The other form of servitude was kind and benevolent, resulting in uprightness and reconciliation with God. One required involuntary subjection, whereas the other involved willing bondservants who obeyed because they were motivated by God's love.

B. Free to Be Holy: vss. 19-23

I put this in human terms because you are weak in your natural selves. Just as you used to offer the parts of your body in slavery to impurity and to ever-increasing wickedness, so now offer them in slav-

ery to righteousness leading to holiness. When you were slaves to sin, you were free from the control of righteousness. What benefit did you reap at that time from the things you are now ashamed of? Those things result in death! But now that you have been set free from sin and have become slaves to God, the benefit you reap leads to holiness, and the result is eternal life. For the wages of sin is death, but the gift of God is eternal life in Christ Jesus our Lord.

In the closing verses of Romans 6, Paul expressed regret for speaking in somewhat inadequate everyday language (vs. 19). He recognized the shortcoming of describing a personal relationship with a gracious God in terms of enslavement (see also the commentary in lessons 5 and 9 of the March quarter). Yet the apostle discerned his readers were limited in their capacity—whether it was to overcome the sinful nature or to understand a complex theological subject. For that reason, Paul affirmed the value of using the analogy of slavery.

Admittedly, believers were not in cruel bondage to God as unbelievers were enslaved to sin. Still, the concept of slavery was appropriate in that it reflected what people truly served, either sin or righteousness. So Paul sought to draw a strong contrast between the lifestyles of unbelievers and those of Christians. To emphasize his point, the apostle reiterated what he had said in verses 16 and 17. At one time, his readers (along with all believers) surrendered every aspect of their lives to moral filth. They also offered themselves to "wickedness" (vs. 19), with the result that they compulsively engaged in one evil act after another.

Now that Paul's readers were born again, they were to present themselves as slaves who sought to please God by living uprightly. The outcome literally was their "sanctification." As noted in lesson 7, the underlying Greek noun refers to a progressive growth in moral purity. At the moment of salvation, Christians became holy in a legal sense, for they were declared righteous in God's eyes. That event was called justification. Then, throughout their lives, the Spirit worked to bring the believers' moral condition into conformity with their legal status. He helped to make them actually holy. This process was called sanctification.

By way of analogy, if justification was the root of the believers' salvation, then sanctification was the fruit. Or, if justification symbolized the pool in which Christians swam, sanctification represented their effort to do so in the Spirit's power. On one level, sanctification was a settled truth that God produced (see 1 Cor. 1:2; 6:11; 1 Thess. 5:23; Heb. 2:11). On another level, believers were to submit to the Creator's will to become increasingly holy (see Phil. 2:12-13; 1 Thess. 4:3). Being dedicated entirely to God had implications for their conduct. For instance, they were to keep away from all forms of iniquity, injustice, and immorality.

When God declared repentant sinners to be righteous, His intent was not only to save them from His wrath, but also to make it possible for them to live in a way that brought Him honor. As Paul explained in Galatians 2:20, because of the believers' union with the Savior, their old sinful state was "crucified," and they now shared in Jesus' resurrection power. This did not mean their old nature was completely eradicated. But it did mean that by continuing to trust in the Messiah, they could limit the power of sin and even experience victory over it (see 1 John 5:4-5). So, rather than lead to increased iniquity, the believers' union with the Son gave them the ability to live in a holy manner.

In Romans 6:20, Paul once more indicated that slavery to sin and to righteousness were mutually exclusive options. One could not operate in both domains (vss. 13, 16). How much better it was, then, to be enslaved to God and committed to His upright moral standards (vss. 20-22). After all, bondage to sin marred one's earthly sojourn with disgrace and resulted in death. In contrast, believers were forgiven by God and committed to do what was right. The final outcome was "eternal life" with the Creator. "Wages" (vs. 23) translates a Greek noun that refers to the money paid for the services a laborer or soldier performed. With respect to "sin," the compensation it disbursed was eternal separation from God in a place of great suffering (see Luke 16:24-25). In contrast, the Father offered "eternal life" (Rom. 3:23) as His abundant "gift" to those who were united to the Son by faith and operated in the power of the Spirit.

Discussion Questions

1. What does it mean to be a slave to sin?
2. What does it mean for believers to have died to sin?
3. What can believers do to overcome sin in their lives?
4. What does it mean to be a slave to righteousness?
5. What are some ways holiness is evident in the lives of believers?

Contemporary Application

In my youth, children often played a game called "Cops and Robbers." We used our fingers as guns, and if someone "shot" you, you had to stay on the ground and pretend you were dead. For some children this was not easy. They would get up again and start playing, even though they had been "shot." Then would come the argument, "I shot you—you are supposed to stay dead. You can't get back up and start playing again. You have to stay on the ground."

This account helps us to appreciate the import of Jesus' resurrection. Instead of remaining in the grave, He left the tomb. The Gospels reveal Jesus' disciples were shocked by the news, even though Jesus told them He would rise from the dead. Perhaps Satan was shocked the most. He thought he had the victory when Jesus died. But when Jesus rose again, that took away the devil's power. Just like the kids in my old neighborhood who argued, "I shot you—you are supposed to stay dead," Satan, I imagine, had a similar response.

Tragically, some believers today do not understand that they do not have to "stay on the ground" (in a manner of speaking). As Paul reveals in Romans 6, believers have new life in union with the Messiah. They do not have to be controlled by their old self. They have been rescued from a life of old habits and negative behaviors to a new life that pleases God.

A Safe Place

Scripture

Background Scripture: *Romans 8:28-39*
Scripture Lesson: *Romans 8:28-39*
Key Verse: If God is for us, who can be against us?
Romans 8:31
Scripture Lesson for Children: *Romans 8:28-39*
Key Verse for Children: [Nothing] will be able to
separate us from the love of God that is in Christ Jesus
our Lord. *Romans 8:39*

Lesson Aim

To claim the hope of future glory in light of Jesus'
enduring love.

Lesson Setting

Time: About A.D. 57
Place: Corinth

Lesson Outline

A Safe Place
  I. God's Glorification of Believers: Romans 8:28-30
      A. *The Divinely Intended Outcome: vs. 28*
      B. *The Divinely Intended Process: vss. 29-30*
  II. God's Vindication of Believers: Romans 8:31-39
      A. *The Provision of the Son: vss. 31-32*
      B. *The Acquittal of Believers: vss. 33-34*
      C. *The Enduring Love of God: vss. 35-39*

Introduction for Adults

Topic: *Safe Indeed*

The legless beggar pulled herself along a crowded city street. Who cared for her? The once prosperous businessman had suffered a stroke and could no longer speak. Who cared about him?

We cannot avoid people who seem devoid of hope. The Gospel does not promise a life free of pain and disappointment. But Jesus does promise that when we look beyond present pain, we can find future heavenly glory. As Paul declared in Romans 8:28-39, we who are Christians know that our eternal future is safe with God. We also know heavenly glory awaits us.

Moreover, we know that since the Father gave us His Son, He will provide all we need to live in a godly manner in union with Jesus. The Lord cares supremely, even when we feel cast off and forsaken. We understand that, no matter what life brings, nothing will ever cut us off from the Father's love for us in union with the Son.

Introduction for Youth

Topic: *We Can Conquer!*

As the Gospel was being presented to a woman, she explained she had tried her best to please God. Then she added, "But I'm afraid God will never accept me." The Christian talking with her said, "I agree with you. He never will."

A look of astonishment came over the woman's face, for she had not expected such a response. The believer then explained, "No, He never will, but God has accepted His Son, and if you join yourself to Him through faith, you will find God's favor!"

Many young people have been deceived into thinking they must somehow earn acceptance in the eyes of God. The Bible, however, tells us that there is nothing in us, nor in what we do, that can in any way merit God's love and favor (see Rom. 3:28). Our salvation is rooted in the Father's unconditional acceptance of us because of His Son's sacrificial death at Calvary (8:32). Indeed, nothing in all creation can separate us from the Father's eternal love for us (vss. 38-39).

Concepts for Children

Topic: *Surrounded by Love*

1. God loves us very much.
2. God's love is like a blanket that surrounds us.
3. God, in His love, protects us.
4. Our loving God comforts us.
5. God's love for us helps us to do what is right.

Lesson Commentary

I. GOD'S GLORIFICATION OF BELIEVERS: ROMANS 8:28-30

A. The Divinely Intended Outcome: vs. 28

And we know that in all things God works for the good of those who love him, who have been called according to his purpose.

In Romans 7:1-12, Paul described how sin (personified) used the Mosaic law to arouse the desire for iniquity within people. When believers trusted in the Son, their relationship to the law was severed. In turn, this undercut a major way sin exercised its authority unchallenged in their lives. In verses 13-25, the apostle described what life dominated by the sinful nature looked like. He affirmed how easy it was for people to succumb to sin's control. He also revealed that it was only through faith in the Son that true spiritual freedom was possible.

In chapter 8, Paul detailed how God's grace delivered believers from the wretched state of existence the apostle lamented in 7:24. He explained that because Jesus was able to rescue those who once were slaves to sin, there was no condemnation for them in union with Him (8:1). Through the Son's sacrificial death on the cross, the Father pardoned repentant sinners. Moreover, the Spirit released believers from the consequences of the law of sin and death. Paul used the Greek noun rendered "law" twice in verse 2 to describe distinctive controlling powers. Specifically, the apostle referred to the controlling power of the Spirit, who freed believers from the controlling power of sin and death.

In chapter 8, Paul emphasized the Spirit because His role was pivotal to the believers' new life. For instance, the Spirit regenerated the lost at salvation (see Titus 3:5). Also, the Spirit acted as a controlling power in the lives of the regenerate so they could overcome sin (Rom. 8:2). Whereas the law was holy and pointed people to God's perfect moral standard, sin rendered the law powerless by using it to provoke disobedience (see 7:5, 11-12). So, attaining righteousness by keeping the law was impossible. What the law could not do (provide acquittal for humanity), the Father did through the offering of His Son as payment for sin (8:3). By one act of obedience, Jesus condemned sin (to crucify the old self) and made provision for righteousness (to empower the new self).

When a person became a Christian, an amazing exchange occurred. The new believer's sinfulness was transferred to the Son on the cross and His perfect righteousness was transferred to the new Christian. Through this exchange, the requirements of the law were met in full. Jesus' righteousness in the believer enabled that person to consistently live according to the Spirit, rather than according to the sinful state (vs. 4). When Paul used the Greek term literally rendered "flesh," he meant a condition, natural to people, in which the Creator and the spiritual realm were disregarded.

Verses 5 through 17 describe the sharp contrasts that existed between the sinful and redeemed states of existence. For instance, the sinful state was focused on gratifying the cravings of the flesh. The redeemed state endeavored to accomplish the will of the Spirit. The sinful mind led to death. The redeemed mind led to life in union with the Son. The sinful mind was hostile to God, for it refused to submit to His Word. The redeemed mind was motivated by love for God to obey His Word. The sinful mind was enslaved to fear. The redeemed mind was a bondservant of righteousness. Those who did not have the Spirit also did not belong to the Son. The Spirit confirmed to believers that they were God's children. Those who lived according to the sinful state experienced unending separation from God. Those who lived according to the Spirit enjoyed unending communion with God.

In verse 18, Paul affirmed that the suffering believers endured would be outweighed by the glory to be revealed in them. The believers' affliction was always temporary, but their glory in union with the Son would never end (see 2 Cor. 4:17). When Paul wrote about the present age and the glory yet to come, he borrowed concepts that were familiar to the Jews of his time. In this regard, Jewish thinking included two eras: (1) the present, corrupt age, which was completely given over to sin, decay, and death; and (2) a new, restored world that would follow a day of judgment.

Paul revealed that currently every aspect of creation was subjected to God's curse (Rom. 8:20). Adam had been assigned to a position of authority over creation as God's representative (see Gen. 1:26-30; 2:8, 15). So, when God's judgment came against humanity in the garden of Eden, all creation was adversely affected (see 3:17). Yet a time was coming when creation would be free from the influences of sin, Satan, and physical deterioration (Rom. 8:21). What awaited creation also lay ahead for Jesus' followers (vss. 22-25). Their confident expectation was that at His return, He would finally deliver them from an existence dominated by sin and characterized by decay and death.

Paul disclosed that prior to Jesus' second advent, believers were not left to wait alone, enduring their afflictions without a comforter. The Spirit helped them in their weaknesses and frailties (vs. 26). Though believers might be at a loss concerning what to pray for, the Spirit unceasingly pleaded their case before the Father. Also, the Spirit did so with groanings that could not be expressed in words. The Father, who continually searched the hearts of His children, also had perfect and complete knowledge of the Spirit's "mind" (vs. 27). So, the Spirit's utterances did not need to be conveyed using human language, especially since the Father was intimately familiar with the Spirit's heart.

Next, Paul revealed that the Creator brought an eternally beneficial outcome in each and every circumstance His children experienced. That "good" (vs. 28) result was in accordance with God's redemptive plan, which included summoning and enabling the lost to trust in the Messiah, along with becoming Jesus' coheirs in His future kingdom (see vs. 17). The Father's will also included believers loving Him wholeheartedly and showing kindness to others (see Lev. 19:18; 1 Cor. 2:9; 8:3; Eph. 6:24). Yes, many difficult circumstances arose in the lives of Christians. Yet, while these hardships could feel overwhelming, God used them to bring about Christlike fruit in His children.

B. The Divinely Intended Process: vss. 29-30

For those God foreknew he also predestined to be conformed to the likeness of his Son, that he might be the firstborn among many brothers. And those he predestined, he also called; those he called, he also justified; those he justified, he also glorified.

Romans 8:28-30 focuses on God's glorification of believers. Whereas verse 28 concerns the divinely intended outcome, verses 29-30 deal with the underlying process of the believers' call to salvation. In particular, those whom the Father lovingly chose in eternity past, He also determined in advance to become spiritually like the Son (see Eph. 1:4; 2 Thess. 2:13; 1 Pet. 1:20). The divine intent was that Jesus would be exalted as the "firstborn" (Rom. 8:29; or "preeminent one") among the redeemed (see Col. 1:15, 18), whom the Spirit was conforming to the Son's "image" (see 1 Cor. 15:49; 2 Cor. 3:18; Phil. 3:21; 1 John 3:2).

Moreover, these are the same individuals whom the Father regenerated (in their response to the proclamation of the Gospel), declared to be not guilty (as a result of their trust in the Savior), and "glorified" (ultimately through their resurrection from the dead; Rom. 8:30). Each of the main verbs in verses 29 and 30 are in a Greek tense denoting a past action that remained true in the present. The Creator was the active agent in bringing about the full and final redemption of believers. Also, even though that outcome would not occur until the Son's future return, the Father regarded it as an already accomplished fact that impacted the daily lives of believers.

There are at least two distinct views of what predestination means when it is discussed in Scripture. One option is that the Father gives all people enough grace to have faith. This remains true, even though many reject His undeserved kindness. In this way, the Father predestines some for redemption in the sense that He knows beforehand those who will decide to believe the truth of their own independent choosing. A second option is that people are so debased by sin that they are unable on their own to respond to the offer of salvation made available in the Son. According to this view, those who believe have the ability to do so only because the Father previously selected them for redemption. Put another way, He gives them grace, and this enables them to believe the truth.

Regardless of which option is preferred, Ephesians 1:11-12 discloses that the Father's eternal plan for His children did not occur by accident. Instead, He brought it about through the atoning sacrifice of His Son at Calvary. In fact, the Father's grand design was to bring everything together—whether in heaven or on earth—under the Son's authority. The Father also planned that believing Jews and Gentiles would receive an eternal inheritance.

II. GOD'S VINDICATION OF BELIEVERS: ROMANS 8:31-39

A. The Provision of the Son: vss. 31-32

What, then, shall we say in response to this? If God is for us, who can be against us? He who did not spare his own Son, but gave him up for us all—how will he not also, along with him, graciously give us all things?

After Paul said God had marked out wonderful plans for those who followed His purposes (Rom. 8:28-30), the apostle concluded (through the use of a series of rhetorical questions) that believers had several reasons to live as God's redeemed people with confidence. Specifically, no one could successfully thwart believers from receiving their eternal inheritance, for the Creator was on their side (vs. 31). Through their faith in Him, Christians were protected by His power to receive salvation on the last day (see 1 Pet. 1:5). Of course, God did not support self-serving agendas, especially those contrary to His will.

Paul declared that the Father would not withhold from His children anything necessary for their redemption. After all, like Abraham—who, when divinely directed, did not spare Isaac (see Gen. 22:16)—the Father offered His greatest gift—His own Son—when Jesus died on the cross for humanity's sins (see Isa. 53:6, 12; John 3:16; Rom. 5:6-8). This greater truth being so, the lesser truth was equally valid—namely, that God would bestow on believers whatever He knew to be essential to accomplish His eternal plans for them. The latter was brought to fruition as a result of what Jesus accomplished at Calvary on behalf of the lost.

Although God was on the side of His children, it remained an open question as to whether they were always and consistently on His side. In order for them to be victorious in their Christian walk, they first had to surrender their aspirations to the Lord. Put differently, to align themselves on God's side, their desires and ambitions had to bow to His plan. Also, by the Father sacrificing His Son for the lost, God showed that He desired the very best for believers. They could be sure, even when circumstances seemed out of control or unbearable, that God was working out His ultimate good in the lives of Jesus' devoted followers.

B. The Acquittal of Believers: vss. 33-34

Who will bring any charge against those whom God has chosen? It is God who justifies. Who is he that condemns? Christ Jesus, who died—more than that, who was raised to life—is at the right hand of God and is also interceding for us.

Believers could serve God with confidence, for He would not permit any adversary to impugn His children. After all, He had chosen them and declared them to be righteous (Rom. 8:33; see Isa. 50:8-9). Even today, it would be unthinkable for people to be arrested for a crime if others have already turned themselves in to the authorities. Similarly, Jesus paid the penalty for His disciples' sins.

Furthermore, no one could render a guilty verdict against believers, since Jesus died, rose again, and now interceded on their behalf in the place of honor at God's "right hand" (Rom. 8:34; see Ps. 110:1; Matt. 26:64; Acts 2:33-34; 5:31; 7:55-56; Eph. 1:20; Col. 3:1; Heb. 1:3, 13; 8:1; 10:12; 12:2; 1 Pet. 3:22). In His death and resurrection, Jesus assumed the blame for His followers' transgressions. He was like a defense attorney who declared, "I take responsibility for these crimes and shoulder the consequences. So, no sentence can be given to my clients" (see Heb. 4:14-16; 7:25; 1 John 2:1-2).

Since the Father exonerated repentant, believing sinners, He left no grounds for would-be accusers to assail His children. Even Satan could not do so, though he would like to (see Rev. 12:10). In the heavenly court of divine justice, Christians were already vindicated (see vs. 11). Admittedly, in the secular realm, it would be unheard of for a defense attorney to willingly bear the punishment of a client. Yet that is what Jesus did for the lost. He made it impossible for those who trusted in Him to be held liable for their iniquities. Even though Jesus led a life totally free from sin (see Heb. 7:26; 1 Pet. 2:22), He became an offering for humanity's misdeeds (see 2 Cor. 5:21). At Calvary, He took the place of the lost as their substitute and bore the judgment they deserved.

C. The Enduring Love of God: vss. 35-39

Who shall separate us from the love of Christ? Shall trouble or hardship or persecution or famine or nakedness or danger or sword? As it is written: "For your sake we face death all day long; we are considered as sheep to be slaughtered." No, in all these things we are more than conquerors through him who loved us. For I am convinced that neither death nor life, neither angels nor demons, neither the present nor the future, nor any powers, neither height nor depth, nor anything else in all creation, will be able to separate us from the love of God that is in Christ Jesus our Lord.

Paul asked whether there was any entity that could isolate believers from the unconditional, self-sacrificing "love" (Rom. 8:35) Jesus had for them. Paul mentioned seven afflictions—all of which he personally experienced (see 1 Cor. 4:10-13; 2 Cor. 6:4-5; 11:22-27). None of these possibilities—not trouble ("pressure," "distress"), hardship ("being pressed in"), persecution, famine, nakedness, danger, or the sword—could separate Christians from their Savior's compassion for and commitment to them (Rom. 8:35). Paul quoted from Psalm 44:22 to emphasize that the redeemed, while in the world, would face adversity—perhaps even martyrdom (Rom. 8:36; see Acts 14:22; Phil. 1:29; 2 Tim. 3:12). In all such difficulties, believers were more than triumphant through their union with the Messiah (Rom. 8:37). Believers not only won their battles, but in the end, they enjoyed Jesus' abiding presence.

Paul exulted in the fact that nothing could sever believers from the Father's covenantal love for them in union with the Son (vss. 38-39). The apostle provided a series of items to illustrate his point. Most of these are in pairs—the extremes of existence (death, life), spiritual armies (angels, demons), time (present, future), and space (height, depth). None of these potentialities—at either extreme—could drive a wedge between the Creator and His children.

Indeed, the apostle declared with certitude that it was impossible for the redeemed to be cut off from God's mercy and pardon.

The examples Paul gave in verses 38 and 39 indicate spiritual temptations as much as physical enticements. This is the reason why the apostle included "angels" as a possible opponent to God's love. Some suggest Paul was consistent with a prevalent Jewish understanding of angels in the first century A.D.— namely, that angels are evil. Others say these angels should be understood as good, suggesting that no such angel would seek to come between God's love and believers. In contrast, "demons" are wicked spirits and would be happy to separate believers from God's love.

Moreover, time could not separate believers from God's love—whether present time with its temptations and sufferings, or future time with its unpredictability. Neither could "powers," which probably refers to spiritual forces engaged in warfare against believers (see Eph. 6:12). "Height" (Rom. 8:39) denoted a star at its peak, when allegedly it was most influential. "Depth" referred to the star at its lowest point, waiting to regain control. In short, the stars (personified) could never hurt God's children and certainly were unable to separate them from His love, for it was real, substantial, and would last forever.

Discussion Questions

1. How has God turned around difficult events in your life for good?
2. In what sense is God on the side of believers?
3. Why is it inappropriate for believers to take God's love for granted?
4. Why has Jesus chosen to love repentant sinners?
5. Why can nothing separate believers from God's love?

Contemporary Application

"Cast all your cares on God; that anchor holds," wrote the English poet Alfred, Lord Tennyson. When personal hardships seem unbearable, God is there to steady us because He cares for us. As Paul disclosed in Romans 8:28-39, He can bring eternal good out of our afflictions. And His unfailing love is the basis for our hope of future glory.

Ultimately, God is the source of every mercy. His consolation is evident when we are lonely, under stress, or fatigued. He helps us deal with financial problems, family tensions, and difficulties at work. Indeed, there is no trial we may experience where God's consolation is not available.

If we were to list all the times God has comforted us, the list would be practically endless. In fact, it is hard to imagine all the ways God has shown us His mercy and love. There are numerous examples throughout the Bible of how God has comforted His people, and these accounts can encourage us as well as those around us who are hurting.

A Gift of Mercy

Scripture

Background Scripture: *Romans 9:6-29*
Scripture Lesson: *Romans 9:6-18*
Key Verse: God has mercy on whom he wants to have mercy, and he hardens whom he wants to harden. *Romans 9:18*
Scripture Lesson for Children: *Romans 9:6-18*
Key Verse for Children: It is not the natural children who are God's children, but it is the children of the promise. *Romans 9:8*

Lesson Aim

To recognize that God remains faithful to His covenant promises.

Lesson Setting

Time: About A.D. 57
Place: Corinth

Lesson Outline

A Gift of Mercy

  I. God's Promise and Choice: Romans 9:6-13
    A. *God's Promise: vss. 6-9*
    B. *God's Choice: vss. 10-13*
  II. God's Justice and Mercy: Romans 9:14-18
    A. *God's Justice: vss. 14-15*
    B. *God's Mercy: vss. 16-18*

Introduction for Adults

Topic: *God's Pledge*

Promises are the great stuff of life. We make promises when we get married. Our children exact promises from us. And we obtain promises from our employers. God's covenantal promises to His chosen people were so astonishing that we find it hard to relate to them. God pledged to give them the Mosaic law and a homeland. Best of all, they had the promise of the Messiah (see Rom. 9:1-5).

Perhaps these promises sound too much like the pledges politicians make during their election campaigns. After all, pledges are only as good as the one who makes them. Indeed, nothing is worse than a broken promise!

Nonetheless, Paul taught that God always remains faithful to His pledges (vs. 6). For this reason, we can be refreshed and encouraged by God's covenantal promises to us. We live in hope because we believe in the total reliability and trustworthiness of God. And like Paul, the Lord can enable us to leave a legacy of faith to those who follow after us.

Introduction for Youth

Topic: *Divine Promises*

We love to ask children, "What do you want to be when you grow up?" Later on, when they finish high school, we may ask, "What are your career goals?" That's when youth begin to wrestle with their dreams. Sometimes it takes years for them to figure out what they want to do with their lives.

Since we build our lives on God's will and His special promises to us in Scripture, it's good to remind ourselves of the truth Paul declared in Romans 9:6. Specifically, none of God's salvation promises will ever fail. This is a wonderful truth that saved adolescents need to hear, especially in moments of discouragement.

Believing teens also need the reminder that they are God's children forever and have the assurance of His unfailing love for them. So they can be sure that God's desire for their success as Christians far outweighs their doubts. Let them know that obedience to God right now will lead to greater opportunities to serve Him in the future.

Concepts for Children

Topic: *A Promise Kept*

1. The Bible is full of God's promises.
2. God promised to send Jesus as our Savior.
3. Sadly, some people do not believe in Jesus.
4. God wants us to put our faith in Jesus.
5. God wants us to tell others about Jesus.

Lesson Commentary

I. GOD'S PROMISE AND CHOICE: ROMANS 9:6-13

A. God's Promise: vss. 6-9

It is not as though God's word had failed. For not all who are descended from Israel are Israel. Nor because they are his descendants are they all Abraham's children. On the contrary, "It is through Isaac that your offspring will be reckoned." In other words, it is not the natural children who are God's children, but it is the children of the promise who are regarded as Abraham's offspring. For this was how the promise was stated: "At the appointed time I will return, and Sarah will have a son."

In Romans 1 through 3, Paul spoke about the responsibilities of Jews and Gentiles in light of the knowledge God had provided for each of them. Then, in chapters 9 through 11, the apostle picked up this discussion and described the roles that each group would play in God's plan of salvation. The Israelites had gloried in the fact that they were God's chosen people (see Deut. 7:6; 14:2; 1 Kings 3:8). But they had largely forsaken the Lord, and subsequently He gave believing Gentiles a significant role in His plan (see Eph. 2:11-13; 1 Pet. 2:9-10).

Did the preceding truths mean that the Creator had abandoned the Jews in favor of the Gentiles? Paul addressed this important question in Romans 9 by describing God's unwavering commitment to His covenant promises involving the Jews. The apostle began by affirming that his heart was filled with deep, continual grief over Israel's rejection of the Messiah (see 9:2). Paul also declared that in addition to his conscience, the Son and the Spirit confirmed the truthfulness of the apostle's intense sorrow (9:1). Perhaps Paul brought up the issue of his conscience because some of his religious peers thought he was indifferent to the plight of his fellow Jews after he became a Christian.

The apostle wanted to remove any doubt concerning the depth of his love for his Jewish brothers and sisters (vs. 3). Paul often experienced their stubbornness firsthand. Whenever the apostle went on a missionary journey, he consistently went to the Jewish synagogues first to preach the Gospel, and time after time he was rebuffed by Jewish unbelief (see Acts 18:6). Paul's distress over Israel was so great that, in a manner reminiscent of Moses (see Exod. 32:30-32), the apostle literally said he could wish himself "accursed" (see Rom. 9:3) from the Savior. Put differently, the apostle would have been willing to suffer eternal separation from Jesus if it resulted in Israel's turning to Him for salvation. This sentiment reflected the genuine desire of Paul's heart for his own ethnic group.

In verses 4 and 5, the apostle listed a number of privileges that belonged to Israel as God's chosen nation. For example, Paul stated that God had adopted the Israelites as His children. Though this concept is not used of the nation in the Old Testament, it is definitely present (see Exod. 4:22; Deut. 32:6; Isa. 63:16; 64:8; Jer. 31:9; Hos. 11:1; Mal. 2:10). The Israelites also witnessed God's "glory" (Rom. 9:4) in the tabernacle and temple. His majestic splendor was evidence of His sacred presence among His people (see Exod. 16:7, 10; 29:43; 40:34; 1 Kings 8:11; Ps. 63:2; Ezek. 43:4). Another privilege was that the Israelites were the recipients of God's "covenants" (Rom. 9:4). These included those God made with Abraham (see Gen. 15:9-21; 17), Moses (see Exod. 19—24), and David (see 2 Sam. 7:5-16; Eph. 2:12).

Furthermore, the Israelites were the beneficiaries of God's "law" (Rom. 9:4) revealed on Mount Sinai (see Exod. 19—20; Deut. 5). Many Jews who lived during Paul's day revered the law (see Rom. 2:17). In addition, they valued the rituals their priests performed within the temple (especially involving the sacrificial system). This was a great privilege in view of the fact that God manifested His presence in the sanctuary. Moreover, the Jews were heirs of God's redemptive "promises" (Rom. 9:4), especially those made to Abraham, the ancestor of the Jews (see Gen. 12:1-2; 15:4-6, 18-21). Paul also noted Israel's intimate connection with the "patriarchs" (Rom. 9:5), Abraham, Isaac, and Jacob. Through them God pledged not only to bless Israel, but also the entire world (see Gen. 18:18; 22:17-18; 26:3-4; 28:13-14; 35:11-12).

All the preceding privileges specifically applied to God's chosen people. Paul, as a Jew, was acutely aware of the role each of these blessings played throughout history in Israel's relationship with the Creator. Most importantly, from the Jews was traced the physical lineage of the Messiah, whom Paul described as "God over all" (Rom. 9:5). This verse is one of the apostle's strongest affirmations of the deity of the Messiah (see Phil. 2:6; Col. 1:15, 19; 2:9; Titus 2:13). Ethnic Israel could not boast about its affiliation with the Savior in the same way that it could draw attention to its relationship with the patriarchs. The nation's connection to the patriarchs was one involving physical descent, whereas a genuine union with the Redeemer was a spiritual matter.

The preceding truth was pivotal in discerning the ongoing relationship of the chosen people with God. The fact that many of them in Paul's day had rejected the Son did not mean the Father had "failed" (Rom. 9:6) to fulfill His covenant promises or somehow stumbled in bringing about His plan for the salvation of Israel (see 11:25-29). After all, as the apostle explained, the true "Israel of God" (Gal. 6:16) was not the same as the biological descendants of Jacob. Those who had genuine faith in the Creator, as Abraham did, comprised the righteous remnant (see Rom. 4:11-12). Also, a person was an authentic Jew only if he or she was one inwardly—that is, one whose heart the Spirit had circumcised (see 2:28-29).

In the Old Testament, there were always unbelievers and believers within Israel. To illustrate this point, Paul offered three specific examples: Isaac and Ishmael (9:7-9), Jacob and Esau (vss. 10-13), and Pharaoh (vss. 14-18). In the first illustration, Paul cited Genesis 21:12 to emphasize that the line of promise would come through Isaac (Rom. 9:7). Ishmael had been born to Abraham's concubine, Hagar (see Gen. 16). In addition, the six sons of Keturah were also among Abraham's descendants (see 25:1-4). Nonetheless, in terms of the divine promise, these individuals were not counted as Abraham's offspring.

Despite the prevailing view that Israel's physical descendants would automatically inherit eternal life (see Matt. 3:9; John 8:39), Paul literally said it was not the "children of the flesh" (see Rom. 9:8) who were necessarily God's heirs. Instead, it was the "children of the promise" who were regarded as Abraham's descendants. In short, the members of the covenant community involved God's sovereign choice. Looking back to Genesis 18:10 and 14, Paul cited the Lord's words to Abraham that within a year, Sarah, Abraham's wife, would have a son (Rom. 9:9). In turn, Isaac would be the one through whom the line of promise would come.

B. God's Choice: vss. 10-13

Not only that, but Rebekah's children had one and the same father, our father Isaac. Yet, before the twins were born or had done anything good or bad—in order that God's purpose in election might stand: not by works but by him who calls—she was told, "The older will serve the younger." Just as it is written: "Jacob I loved, but Esau I hated."

Paul moved on to his next illustration, based on the second generation of Jewish ancestry, namely, Jacob and Esau, the twin sons of Isaac and Rebekah (Rom. 9:10). In this historical episode, God made His choice regarding the promised line even before the twins were born and they had done anything characterized by virtue or vice (vs. 11). One view is that God looked into the future, saw Jacob's eventual willingness to obey, and chose him on that basis. A second view is that God's choice of Jacob over Esau was not due to the deeds either offspring performed throughout their lifetimes. Instead, God simply made an autonomous decision in accordance with His redemptive "purpose." His choice involved not only the promised line, but also that the descendants of Esau (the Edomites) would serve the descendants of Jacob (the Israelites; vs. 12; see Gen. 25:23; 2 Sam. 8:14; 1 Kings 22:47).

In Romans 9:13, Paul quoted Malachi 1:2-3, which reveals that God "loved" Jacob, but "hated" Esau. The passage refers specifically to the nations arising from these two individuals. In ancient times, the word "hate" was often used figuratively to refer to preference. So, in the current context, with respect to the promised line, "hate" carries the meaning, "Jacob I chose, but Esau I rejected." Furthermore, Paul was not depicting God as being a capricious and loathing deity. The Creator's disposition was not petulant, but influenced by His covenantal promises.

The fact that God did not emotionally "hate" Esau is clear from the fact that the Lord bestowed many temporal blessings on Esau, his family, and his descendants. Against the backdrop of God's covenantal promises, one could say that the word *hated* here carries the meaning "loved less" (see Gen. 29:31, 33; Deut. 21:15). "Hatred," in the sense of "loving less," was illustrated by what Jesus said in Matthew 10:37 and Luke 14:26. Jesus was not using the word *hate* in an absolute sense, but in connection with a higher choice.

II. GOD'S JUSTICE AND MERCY: ROMANS 9:14-18

A. God's Justice: vss. 14-15

What then shall we say? Is God unjust? Not at all! For he says to Moses, "I will have mercy on whom I have mercy, and I will have compassion on whom I have compassion."

Paul knew that his detractors, after reading his words about God's sovereignty, might accuse him of teaching that the Lord was guilty of injustice (Rom. 9:14). Expressed differently, wasn't it unfair for the Creator to arbitrarily select Isaac over Ishmael? In response, Paul emphatically denied such a warped assertion (see Gen. 18:25; Deut. 32:4; 2 Chron. 19:7; Ezra 9:15; Neh. 9:33; Dan. 4:37; 9:14). Then, in Romans 9:15, the apostle explained why by quoting from Exodus 33:19. In that passage, Moses learned it was God's sole prerogative to show "mercy" and "compassion" on whomever He chose. The context of the verse was Israel's idolatrous worship of the golden calf at Mount Sinai. If God had acted solely according to His justice, He could have eradicated the Israelites for their sin. Instead, He summoned Moses to return to Mount Sinai, where he once again received the Ten Commandments.

B. God's Mercy: vss. 16-18

It does not, therefore, depend on man's desire or effort, but on God's mercy. For the Scripture says to Pharaoh: "I raised you up for this very purpose, that I might display my power in you and that my name might be proclaimed in all the earth." Therefore God has mercy on whom he wants to have mercy, and he hardens whom he wants to harden.

In Romans 9:14-15, Paul argued that God had the supreme authority to do as He pleased with His creation. This included being gracious to whomever He desired. Because of the depth of human rebellion, the Lord was not obligated to show undeserved kindness to anyone. Paul said God's actions (such as the bestowal of mercy) did not depend on anyone's intentions or endeavors. The Creator's decisions rested only on His sovereign choice (vs. 16).

In Paul's third illustration, he moved from Moses (the leader of the Israelites) to Pharaoh (the leader of the Egyptians). Specifically, verse 17 contains a quote from Exodus 9:16. It reveals that God brought Pharaoh onto the stage of human history for the "purpose" of displaying God's saving "power" and declaring His holy "name" (or character) throughout the world. The Egyptians believed in many deities. Even Pharaoh was considered a god. But through the 10 plagues, the Lord demonstrated His absolute power over all the idols of Egypt, including the country's ruler. When all the other nations heard about this, they were in awe at the God of Israel (see Exod. 15:14-16; Josh. 2:9-11; 9:9).

Once more, in Romans 9:18, Paul deduced that God was merciful to whomever He wished. Likewise, it was His uncontested right to increase the callousness of those who refused to heed His will. It may be that Pharaoh hardened his own heart a number of times before God hardened it (see Exod. 7:13-14, 22; 8:15, 19, 32; 9:12, 35; 10:27; 11:10). If so, the implication is that God sovereignly confirmed what was already taking place in Pharaoh's heart. Egypt's ruler was still responsible for his actions, even though God reinforced Pharaoh's obstinate moral state in order to deliver Israel.

Paul again anticipated a question that might surface among his detractors. If God increased the stubborn disposition of people's hearts, how could He justifiably hold them responsible for their iniquities? Supposedly, if God's will was irresistible, then any accusation of wrongdoing appeared to be misplaced (Rom. 9:19). Paul responded by rebuking the arrogant attitude motivating such insinuations (vs. 20). The apostle did not condemn honest inquiry. Rather, he reprimanded those who sought to escape personal responsibility by insisting the Creator was the wellspring for their sin. This type of blame-shifting was common among people who refused to acknowledge their trespasses.

Paul illustrated his point by drawing an analogy between God and a potter (vs. 21). The apostle, citing Isaiah 29:16 and 45:9, argued that the potter had the right to make out of one lump of clay some pottery for honorable purposes and some for ordinary use (see Jer. 18:6). Then, in Romans 9:22-23, Paul spoke about God's intentions for two different peoples—the "objects of his wrath" and the "objects of his mercy." The recipients of God's anger were the unsaved (see 1:18). These would suffer eternal judgment. Yet, despite their sin and horrible destiny, God had patiently endured their antagonism toward Him (see 3:25).

The Creator could have immediately wiped evildoers off the face of the earth. But He did not do so because, as is clear from 2:3-4, the purpose of God's patience and mercy was to bring about repentance. God tolerated those who were wicked for the sake of those among them who would eventually be saved (see 1 Tim. 2:4; 2 Pet. 3:9). Nevertheless, a time was coming when God's patience would run out and judgment would come.

The other group of people were the recipients of God's "mercy" (9:23). He chose these individuals to reveal to the world His abundant "glory." Indeed, He chose the redeemed in advance to share in His majestic splendor, beginning with them receiving His gift of salvation. Paul declared that the objects of God's grace included believing Jews and Gentiles (vs. 24). To drive home this point, the apostle quoted from Hosea 2:23 and 1:10 (see Rom. 9:25-26). Under divine direction, Hosea gave his children symbolic names: Lo-Ammi, which means "not my people," and Lo-Ruhamah, which means "not loved."

In context, the names pointed to God's abandonment of sinful Israel to captivity and exile (see Hosea 1:2-9). Yet the verses being quoted also pointed to God's plan to restore the Israelites. Paul applied Hosea 2:23 and 1:10 to the Gentiles (see 1 Pet. 2:10). Specifically, God took a group of individuals who were not His chosen people—the Gentiles—and brought them into a familial relationship with Him. Whereas the Gentiles were not originally part of the righteous remnant, now by divine grace, they were called children of the "living God" (Rom. 9:26). If the Creator could abandon and restore Israel, then certainly He could also bring saved Gentiles into His protective fold.

Paul revealed that God's sovereign calling always included a contingent of believing Jews. Even though the Israelites had rebelled, there were a few that remained faithful. Since God preserved only a remnant in Old Testament times, this raised an important issue for Paul's Jewish peers who read Romans. They had no reason to draw any automatic security from their heritage, for only the faith community would survive God's judgment. In verses 27-29, Paul substantiated his point by quoting from Isaiah 10:22-23 and 1:9. God had a loyal remnant during the exile, and He also had a believing contingent during Paul's day (see Rom. 11:5). Had a remnant not survived, Israel would have been obliterated like Sodom and Gomorrah. But God's covenantal love held His punishment in check. So Israel retained a significant role in His sovereign plan of salvation.

Discussion Questions

1. Why is it incorrect to think that God's covenant promises have failed?
2. How was God's sovereign choice evident in the lives of the patriarchs?
3. What was God's purpose in choosing Jacob over Esau?
4. In what ways has God been merciful to you?
5. How might believers convince the lost that God treats all people fairly?

Contemporary Application

Like Paul, we may struggle with the reality that some put their faith in Jesus, while others reject Him. Even when God's ways remain a mystery to us, we reject the notion that "God's word" (Rom. 9:6) has somehow "failed." Instead, we affirm that He always remains faithful to His covenant promises.

There are times when God says *no* to our plans. It would be incorrect, however, to assume that God doesn't want us to serve Him. Rather, He wants us to do something else for Him. At other times, God says *yes* to plans for us we did not anticipate. In every circumstance, we should accept the part God has for us in His eternal plan and not try to go beyond it. We do this by taking full advantage of the present opportunities God gives us to serve Him.

Jesus assures us that His love will always be with us. This remains true, even when some of our noble dreams crumble. Such circumstances remind us to live by faith, not by sight. In fact, the entire Christian life is based on eternal truths, which we cannot see. That is the essence of our faith (Heb. 11:1). As Paul explained in Romans 9, we did nothing to deserve God's blessings, whether past, present, or future. So, our foremost response is to praise and thank the Father for giving us eternal life with Him through faith in His Son.

A Display of Kindness

Scripture

Background Scripture: *Romans 11:11-36*

Scripture Lesson: *Romans 11:11-24*

Key Verse: Consider therefore the kindness and sternness of God: sternness to those who fell, but kindness to you, provided that you continue in his kindness. Otherwise, you also will be cut off. *Romans 11:22*

Scripture Lesson for Children: *Romans 11:11-24*

Key Verse for Children: Consider therefore the kindness . . . of God . . . to you. *Romans 11:22*

Lesson Aim

To understand that God's plan of salvation includes believing Jews and Gentiles.

Lesson Setting

Time: About A.D. 57

Place: Corinth

Lesson Outline

A Display of Kindness

   I. An Explanation of God's Plan of Salvation: Romans 11:11-16

      A. *Inclusion of Believing Gentiles: vss. 11-12*

      B. *Inclusion of Believing Jews: vss. 13-16*

  II.A Warning to Gentile Christians: Romans 11:17-24

      A. *Being Reverent, Not Arrogant: vss. 17-21*

      B. *Appreciating God's Kindness: vss. 22-24*

Introduction for Adults

Topic: *Letting Others Know*

A Christian magazine once asked 12 theologians from different denominations to describe the Gospel in about 350 words. They all said much the same thing, but they said it with a lot of big words and long sentences. How could the average person possibly understand what the "experts" had to say?

Our peers want simple and direct answers to life's biggest question—how can people be saved and go to heaven? Sometimes the question is expressed indirectly—how can people find meaning in life? Or, how can people get out of the mess they have made of their lives?

Whatever the actual words, we know the lost are looking for a clear and meaningful answer. That's why we should be as straightforward as Paul when he gave the heart of the Gospel. In Romans 11, he declared that Jesus is offered freely to everyone without distinction. In turn, the lost experience God's eternal blessings when they put their faith in the Son.

Introduction for Youth

Topic: *Including Others*

Some Christians in the church at Rome began to think that God favored them more than He favored others. Paul dealt with this sinful attitude by teaching that the Father offered His grace without distinction to everyone who trusted in the Son. That is why all sorts of people need to know the good news about Him.

It is commonly believed that if we invite people to church, they will hear the Gospel. In some cases, the lost are saved as a result of attending church. But often, when we ask people how they came to faith in Christ, they give a wide variety of answers that don't involve initially going to a worship service. It's amazing how many ways God uses to bring people to Himself.

This observation should encourage us to keep learning as much as we can about how people actually come to faith in Christ. As we grow in our understanding, we will not be content to assume that an invitation to church is the only way to bring about the conversion of the lost. Therefore, our task as proclaimers of the Good News is to first find a connecting idea somewhere in a friend's life story. Then, with patient love and prayer, we can introduce him or her to Jesus and the salvation He offers.

Concepts for Children

Topic: *Everyone Needs to Know*

1. Paul knew some people did not believe in Jesus.
2. Paul did not stop telling others about Jesus.
3. Paul said everyone needs to know about Jesus.
4. Paul said Jesus helps us tell others about Him.
5. Jesus wants us to tell others about the joy we have found in Him.

Lesson Commentary

I. An Explanation of God's Plan of Salvation: Romans 11:11-16

A. Inclusion of Believing Gentiles: vss. 11-12

Again I ask: Did they stumble so as to fall beyond recovery? Not at all! Rather, because of their transgression, salvation has come to the Gentiles to make Israel envious. But if their transgression means riches for the world, and their loss means riches for the Gentiles, how much greater riches will their fullness bring!

Romans 9—11 deliberates the issue of ethnic Israel as God's chosen people within His redemptive program. Despite the privileges and promises God had bestowed, many of Paul's Jewish peers spurned the truth about the Messiah (9:1-5). Nonetheless, there still existed an upright remnant of saved Jews and Gentiles who had experienced the new birth (vss. 6-29). The paradox was that many of the religious elite in the first century A.D. remained disobedient, while many repentant Gentiles flooded into God's kingdom (9:30—10:21).

Perhaps some antagonists claimed Paul's emphasis on God's grace to the Gentiles meant He had turned His back on ethnic Israel. In response, the apostle emphatically rebuffed any notion of the Creator abandoning His own people (11:1). Then Paul provided two specific proofs to back up his assertion. The first was related to his own Jewish identity and pedigree (see 2 Cor. 11:22; Phil. 3:4–5). He also had once been an ardent persecutor of the church. If God could save Paul, then certainly God could save any Jew (see Acts 9:1-19; 1 Tim. 1:15-16). At one time, Paul had tried to ingratiate himself with God by keeping the law. But upon conversion, Paul received by faith the forgiveness Jesus obtained for the lost at Calvary. The apostle hoped that all his Jewish peers would discover the "knowledge of the truth" (1 Tim. 2:4).

Paul reiterated that God would never forsake ethnic Israel, whom He had chosen from the beginning (Rom. 11:2; see 1 Sam. 12:22; Ps. 94:14). Of course, the Creator knew before He established His covenant with the Israelites that many would spurn Him. Even so, God would not repudiate them, for He continued to be faithful to His salvation promises, none of which He would allow to fail (see Rom. 9:6; 11:29). As noted in lesson 3, even in the Old Testament era, during times of great apostasy, there was always a group that remained devoted to God. This remnant was the kernel of the nation that continued to exist, even up to the time of Jesus' advent (see Luke 1:5-6; 2:25, 36-37).

Paul illustrated the preceding truths by drawing attention to the ministry of Elijah (Rom. 11:2). The prophet was despondent over his hostile encounter with a wicked queen named Jezebel. In the midst of Elijah's depression, he pleaded with God for help. The prophet assumed he was the only faithful Israelite, and all the others were trying to murder him (Rom. 11:3; see 1 Kings 19:10, 14). In response, God told Elijah he was incorrect. Even though there was rampant apostasy in Israel, the Lord still had a group of 7,000 faithful Israelites (Rom. 11:4; see 1 Kings 19:18). The fact that a remnant existed was sufficient evidence of God's sovereignty at work.

Paul noted that just as there was a cohort of godly Israelites in Elijah's day, so there was a faithful remnant in the apostle's own day, despite extensive Jewish unbelief (Rom. 11:5). Paul's checkered past notwithstanding, he was one among numerous Jews who had trusted in the Son. The Father chose them for salvation because of His unmerited favor. Also, since God's "grace" (vs. 6) was the basis for their redemption, neither they nor anyone else could claim that their pious human efforts acquitted them. The Creator did not have to save anyone from His end-time wrath, whether Jew or Gentile. So, it was due to His undeserved kindness that He chose to maintain a remnant.

In verses 7 through 10, Paul dealt with the fact that many within ethnic Israel remained unsaved. On the one hand, they sought God's favor by meticulously heeding the Mosaic law. On the other hand, their inability to do so, regardless of how doggedly they tried, meant they were unable to gain reconciliation with the Creator (see 9:32; 10:3). Instead, it was only a smaller number whom God had chosen—that is, an Israel within Israel—who enjoyed a right relationship with Him. Tragically, the rest became obdurate (11:7).

To illustrate his point, Paul quoted from Deuteronomy 29:4 and Isaiah 29:10. These verses indicate that Israel's hardening resulted from spiritual drowsiness, judicial blindness, and deafness to God's will (Rom. 11:8). In sum, the legalists became impervious to spiritual truth. Also, this ossified disposition continued from Isaiah's time to Paul's day (see John 12:39-40). Next, in Romans 11:9-10, Paul cited Psalm 69:22-23 to demonstrate the results of God's active hardening of His people's hearts. Because the Israelites did not respond to God's truth in repentance, their eyes were blinded and their backs were bent under the heavy weight of their own guilt and punishment.

Paul anticipated some of his detractors alleging that if, as he claimed, Israel spiritually staggered, they would never be able to get up again. The apostle forcefully rejected such a notion (Rom. 11:11). Then he pointed to two divine purposes for Israel's temporary stumbling. For one, the nation's trespass provided an opportunity for God to offer "salvation" to the Gentiles (through the proclamation of the Gospel). For another, the Gentiles' faith in the Messiah served to provoke Paul's Jewish peers to jealousy (see Acts 13:44-48; 14:1-3; 18:4-7; 19:8-10; 28:23-29).

Paul was convinced that Israel's unbelief and spiritual poverty were temporary. One day, God's people would repent and be restored to Him. The apostle reasoned that the world had been spiritually enriched because so many Gentiles put their faith in Jesus. This being the case, even greater eternal blessings would be enjoyed when a full complement of Israelites trusted in the Savior and were fully reinstated to their rightful place as God's chosen people (Rom. 11:12).

B. Inclusion of Believing Jews: vss. 13-16

I am talking to you Gentiles. Inasmuch as I am the apostle to the Gentiles, I make much of my ministry in the hope that I may somehow arouse my own people to envy and save some of them. For if their rejection is the reconciliation of the world, what will their acceptance be but life from the dead? If the part of the dough offered as firstfruits is holy, then the whole batch is holy; if the root is holy, so are the branches.

In Romans 11:13, Paul directed his comments to the non-Jewish readers of his epistle. He acknowledged that he was called by the Savior to be an evangelist to the Gentiles (see Acts 9:15; 22:21; Rom. 1:5; 16:26; Gal. 1:16; 2:7, 9; 1 Tim. 2:7). Why did the apostle draw attention to his missionary work among non-Jews? It was to evoke jealousy among his fellow Jews so they would turn to the Messiah (Rom. 11:14). Those within ethnic Israel who placed their faith in the Son would then become a part of the upright remnant God chose and preserved by His grace.

In verse 15, Paul noted that ethnic Israel's refusal to accept the Messiah resulted in the Father's reconciling mercy being extended to the Gentiles. The apostle also envisioned a future day when the Jews' reception of the Savior would be like bringing the dead back to life. Specialists disagree concerning the precise meaning of this verse. At least three views have been suggested: (1) Some think it is referring to an extensive spiritual awakening in the world. (2) Others claim the verse is referring to the future resurrection from the dead when redemption would be complete. (3) Still others maintain the verse is referring to the conversion of the Jews as a joyful and glorious event that would result in great blessing for the world.

In any case, Paul was convinced that ethnic Israel's spiritual callousness was temporary (see vs. 11). The apostle also believed that God would fulfill His covenant promises to His chosen people (see 9:6), including the restoration of a remnant of saved Jews. To substantiate his point, Paul used two analogies—the firstfruits of harvested grain and an olive tree with cut and grafted branches (11:16). The apostle's first illustration was based on God's instructions to Israel in Numbers 15:17-21.

Specifically, the first portion of bread the people baked (out of finely ground flour from newly reaped grain) was to be presented as a sacred offering to the Lord. This "firstfruits" (Rom. 11:16) offering was believed to consecrate the whole batch. In Paul's analogy, the "firstfruits" were the patriarchs (namely, Abraham, Isaac, and Jacob), and the "whole batch" referred to the Jewish descendants (see 9:5; 11:28). In the second illustration, the "root" (11:16) of the olive tree also symbolized the patriarchs, while the "branches" denoted Jewish descendants. Metaphorically speaking, the patriarchs (the root) consecrated ethnic Israel (the branches). In short, God would be true to His covenant promises to the patriarchs, which included a spiritual future for His chosen people.

413

II. A WARNING TO GENTILE CHRISTIANS: ROMANS 11:17-24

A. Being Reverent, Not Arrogant: vss. 17-21

If some of the branches have been broken off, and you, though a wild olive shoot, have been grafted in among the others and now share in the nourishing sap from the olive root, do not boast over those branches. If you do, consider this: You do not support the root, but the root supports you. You will say then, "Branches were broken off so that I could be grafted in." Granted. But they were broken off because of unbelief, and you stand by faith. Do not be arrogant, but be afraid. For if God did not spare the natural branches, he will not spare you either.

The church at Rome was predominantly made up of Gentile Christians. Yet there was also a sizable minority of Jewish believers. Among Paul's readers, the Gentile Christians assumed a demeanor of moral superiority over their saved Jewish peers. This arrogant disposition was sustained by the incorrect supposition that God had abandoned ethnic Israel and transferred all the covenant promises to the predominately Gentile church.

Paul sought to dispel the notion that God no longer cared about ethnic Israel. So in Romans 11:17-21, the apostle again compared the relationship of the Jews and the Gentiles to an olive tree. In this context, the "tree" represented the people of God, which included all true believers. In Paul's day, some in Israel ("branches") were put aside ("broken off" the olive tree). The apostle meant that they had rejected God and His revelation, and so, like branches hewn off a tree, they were temporarily removed.

Next, Paul said the Gentiles—though a "wild olive shoot" (vs. 17)—were grafted into the olive tree. Currently, believing Gentiles shared in the spiritual nourishment ("sap") that formerly belonged only to the Jews. However, this was no reason for the Gentiles to boast. Since they were like a "wild olive shoot" that had been grafted in a cultivated olive tree, they were indebted to Israel, not the reverse (vs. 18; see John 4:22). Therefore, the Gentile believers should have remained humble and grateful for what God had done for them.

Paul told his Gentile readers that the "root" (Abraham) supported them, not the other way around (Rom. 11:18). In the apostle's analogy, the tree was the source of nourishment and life. Without the tree, the individual branches would wither and dry up. Earlier, Paul taught that Abraham was the spiritual progenitor of all who believed (see 4:11-12). So, because saved Gentiles (as wild branches) were grafted into the cultivated olive tree (the people of God), they were linked to Abraham (the root). They became recipients of blessings originally promised to the patriarch in the Abrahamic covenant (see Gen. 12:1-3).

Paul was aware that a contingent of his Gentile readers gloated over the fact that some of the original "branches" (Rom. 11:19; or Jews) were removed from the olive tree so that other wild "branches" (non-Jews) had a chance to be "grafted in." Also, Paul agreed that God put aside some Jews because of their "unbelief" (vs. 20). In contrast, the Father's mercy was the only reason formerly pagan Gentiles repented of their sins, put their trust in the Son, and joined the people of God (see Eph. 2:11-13; 1 Pet. 2:9-10).

Paul warned his Gentile readers not to become smug over this wonderful outcome. Instead, they were to display a proper reverence for God and His undeserved kindness (see 1 Cor. 10:12). The apostle explained that if God, in His righteousness, temporarily set aside ethnic Israel (the "natural branches"; Rom. 11:21) due to unbelief, He could certainly put aside the Gentiles, especially if they persistently sinned by bragging. This was a sobering thought. "Be cautious," Paul seemed to be saying. "You may become guilty of the same transgression the Israelites once committed—namely, becoming inflated with pride over a privileged position."

B. Appreciating God's Kindness: vss. 22-24

Consider therefore the kindness and sternness of God: sternness to those who fell, but kindness to you, provided that you continue in his kindness. Otherwise, you also will be cut off. And if they do not persist in unbelief, they will be grafted in, for God is able to graft them in again. After all, if you were cut out of an olive tree that is wild by nature, and contrary to nature were grafted into a cultivated olive tree, how much more readily will these, the natural branches, be grafted into their own olive tree!

Paul urged his readers to bear in mind how God could be both kind and severe (Rom. 11:22). On the one hand, He was stern to those who spiritually stumbled (unbelieving Jews). On the other hand, God was merciful to those who exercised faith (saved Gentiles). The preceding observations reflected how the Creator operated on a broader scale. He treated all those who trusted and obeyed Him with grace (both Jew and Gentile). Oppositely, He treated those who rejected and disobeyed Him with discipline (whether Jew or Gentile; see John 15:2, 6).

The implication is that Paul's Gentile readers were to take heed. Otherwise, they may have found themselves on the receiving end of God's rod of correction. In contrast, the apostle's Jewish peers could find themselves on the receiving end of the Father's undeserved favor, particularly if they placed their faith in the Son and obeyed Him. Also, if they repented of their unbelief, they again would be grafted back into the upright remnant, for God had the supreme power and authority to do so (Rom. 11:23). After all, God was able to take Gentiles, like a branch from a wild "olive tree" (vs. 24; unsaved humanity), and join them to the "cultivated olive tree" (the people of God), even though this may have clashed with the normal way trees and shrubs were raised. Likewise, God could just as easily take the Israelites (the "natural branches") and graft them back into the spiritual stock to which they belonged ("their own olive tree").

Paul disclosed that Israel's stumbling was a "mystery" (vs. 25). The apostle did not mean a baffling oracle that was difficult to comprehend. Instead, the apostle referred to a truth that was previously unknown, but had now been revealed and publicly proclaimed (see 1 Cor. 2:7; Eph. 1:9; 3:2-10; Col. 1:26-27). Specifically, in the Creator's supreme plan, He desired for people from all nations to become a part of His eternal family.

In achieving the preceding goal, God allowed Israel to be set aside and experience a hardened heart. This would continue until the full complement of the Gentiles was saved. From this we see that God has a certain number of Gentiles and Jews among the redeemed. It is clarifying to note two facts about Israel's "hardening" (Rom. 11:25). First, it was only partial. This means there always existed a remnant of Jews whose hearts had not become calloused. Second, this hardening was temporary. It would end when God's sovereignly chosen number of Gentiles had been saved and brought into God's family.

Paul said that following this interim, "all Israel" (vs. 26) would be "saved" by trusting in the Messiah. Specialists have suggested three possible ways of understanding this verse: (1) The phrase could be referring to the majority of Jews living in the final generation. (2) "All Israel" could denote the total number of God's elect Jews from every generation. (3) The phrase could indicate the total number of God's elect—both Jew and Gentile—from all generations. In any event, Paul blended passages from Isaiah 59:20-21 and 27:9 to state that at the second advent, Israel would return to the Father (see Jer. 31:33-34). Then the Son would remove every trace of wickedness from Jacob's descendants, pardon their iniquities, and vanquish their foes.

Discussion Questions

1. Why was ethnic Israel's spiritual stumbling not permanent?
2. Why did Paul seek to provoke unsaved Jews to jealousy?
3. Why was Paul so confident that God remained faithful to His chosen people?
4. Why should believers appreciate how God has spiritually blessed them?
5. How have you been spiritually nourished from the root of God's people?

Contemporary Application

Some of Paul's Gentile believers began to think they were more privileged than their saved Jewish peers. In Romans 11, the apostle clarified that God's plan of salvation equally included both believing Jews and Gentiles. Neither group, then, was to feel excluded from the body of Christ. Instead, Jesus wanted them to work together to spread the Gospel by word and deed.

The most basic command of Christianity is to go and tell the good news about Jesus. This should not be surprising, for He has left us with a clear mandate not to keep quiet about our faith. Instead, He wants us to live and speak in such a way that others will want to become His disciples (see Matt. 28:19-20).

Sadly, many in our day tend to look for God in the wrong ways. Some feel they have to live in a certain location or be near some well-known Christian personality in order to experience God's fullest blessing. This week's Scripture text, however, indicates that God offers His grace freely, regardless of who we are in terms of our ethnicity, culture, or status in society.

A Call to Love

Scripture

Background Scripture: *Romans 12:1-2; 13:8-14*

Scripture Lesson: *Romans 12:1-2; 13:8-14*

Key Verse: Let no debt remain outstanding, except the continuing debt to love one another, for he who loves his fellowman has fulfilled the law. *Romans 13:8*

Scripture Lesson for Children: *Romans 12:1-2, 9-21; 13:8-10*

Key Verse for Children: Love one another. *Romans 13:8*

Lesson Aim

To demonstrate by our compassion for others that we are Jesus' devoted followers.

Lesson Setting

Time: About A.D. 57
Place: Corinth

Lesson Outline

A Call to Love

 I. What It Means to Be Jesus' Followers: Romans 12:1-2
   A. *Living Sacrifices: vs. 1*
   B. *Experiencing Transformation: vs. 2*
 II. How We Demonstrate Our Devotion to Jesus: Romans 13:8-14
   A. *Showing Compassion: vss. 8-10*
   B. *Living Virtuously: vss. 11-14*

Introduction for Adults

Topic: *A Transformed Life*

What separates Christianity from other world religions? In those systems, people try to live in a holy way by doing pious deeds. However, as Romans 12:1 discloses, apart from the mercy of the true and living God, and faith in His Son, all these other religions are vain attempts to self-justify people's moral behavior.

As this week's lesson shows, the Creator does not desire change to come to your students through their own self-sacrificing efforts. Rather, the Lord desires true transformation that can only take place from the empowerment of the Spirit (vs. 2). In turn, He enables them to offer themselves completely as "living sacrifices" (vs. 1) to the Father. Moreover, their "worship" is not confined to what they do in church. What they undertake each day with their lives is their act of "worship" to God.

Introduction for Youth

Topic: *Living the Gospel*

From our earliest years in school we encounter individuals who delight in demeaning Christian values. If, for example, we refuse to fight, we are ridiculed as wimps. If we don't try to get even for some wrong done to us, we are said to be cowards. And if we refuse to participate in sin, we are scorned. In light of the above, it's not hard to understand why the temptation to sin is so great.

Romans 12:1-2 summons us to a radically different way of life. It is one characterized by thinking that has been transformed by the Spirit. In turn, how we feel and the way we act become increasingly more Christlike. Then as the Son, by the Spirit, begins living His life in and through us, we will develop an attitude of resistance to all the unsavory values of the world, especially those that pressure us to accept and live by unwholesome standards.

Concepts for Children

Topic: *Love One Another*

1. Jesus wants to change the way we think and act.
2. When we obey God's Word, we show that we love Jesus.
3. Jesus wants us to love each other.
4. We show love by being kind to others.
5. We also show love by helping others.

Lesson Commentary

I. WHAT IT MEANS TO BE JESUS' FOLLOWERS: ROMANS 12:1-2

A. Living Sacrifices: vs. 1

Therefore, I urge you, brothers, in view of God's mercy, to offer your bodies as living sacrifices, holy and pleasing to God—this is your spiritual act of worship.

In Romans 1 through 11, Paul focused on such important theological issues as sin, justification, and sanctification. He also discussed God's past, present, and future dealings with Israel. Upon this doctrinal foundation, the apostle spent the next five chapters building the superstructure of the Christian life. Here we see that ethics without solid doctrinal content are nothing more than empty moralizing. Indeed, apart from the believer's vital union with the Son, godly behavior would be impossible.

Paul began by stressing the importance of obedient service to God. Previously, the apostle talked about God's forbearance and compassion in providing salvation to those who believe. In light of God's manifold kindness, Paul exhorted believers to present their "bodies" (12:1) as a "living" sacrifice to the Lord. The focus here was on Christian service involving one's entire regenerated person. Because of the new birth (see 6:11, 13; 8:13), believers could minister to others as God's consecrated bondservants in ways that were characterized by moral purity. Such a thoughtful and sensible approach met with the Creator's approval.

As noted in lessons 2, 11, and 12 of the December quarter, sacrifices constituted a key part of all major religious festivals in ancient Israel. While there were different kinds, there were only four basic types or classes of sacrifices: the burnt offering (Lev. 1), the grain offering (chap. 2), the peace (or fellowship) offering (chap. 3), and the sin offerings (chaps. 4—5, 7). A special sacrifice was presented on the Day of Atonement (chap. 16). Leviticus reveals several basic facts about these sacrifices. They were made to God alone and so required the choicest animals and produce. Also, they were God's provision for humanity's approach to Him.

The act of offering sacrifices was an aspect of religion that Israel shared in common with other nations in the ancient Near East. Yet, unlike most pagan nations, Israel's sacrifices were usually performed by the worshiper and the priest together, not just the priest alone. They were limited in their value, especially since only God, not the blood of bulls and goats, brought about the sinners' pardon. Animal offerings represented a substitution. Often, the death of an animal was regarded as taking the place of the worshiper who brought the sacrifice. Ultimately, though, Jesus alone was qualified to serve as the perfect substitute for sin that deserved death.

In a spiritual sense, Jesus' followers were to offer themselves as believer-priests in loyal service to God (see 1 Pet. 2:5, 9; Rev. 1:6; 5:10; 20:6). After all, the body was the vehicle through which they did all things, whether good or bad.

When Jesus' followers dedicated themselves to the Lord, they surrendered unconditionally to His purpose. In Old Testament times, an animal designated for sacrifice was forced against its will to take part in the ceremony being conducted. In contrast, believers were enthusiastic participants when they devoted themselves to God. The priests of ancient Israel worshiped God by performing various rites and rituals. Those who were born again worshiped the Creator by devoting their lives in unpretentious service to Him. The effective stewardship of their time and talents, when motivated by Christlike love, were spiritual offerings that God accepted (see Heb. 13:16).

B. Experiencing Transformation: vs. 2

Do not conform any longer to the pattern of this world, but be transformed by the renewing of your mind. Then you will be able to test and approve what God's will is—his good, pleasing and perfect will.

Prior to the new birth, Jesus' followers allowed their thoughts, emotions, and behavior to be shaped—whether consciously or subconsciously—by the moral standards of pagan society (Rom. 12:2). In turn, the world's thinking was patterned after evil and ruled by the powers of darkness (see Gal. 1:4; Eph. 2:2). Anyone who chose to befriend the world became God's enemy (see Jas. 4:4). Consequently, believers were to avoid degenerate ways of thinking at all costs. Instead, they were to let the Spirit radically change their preferences and priorities and in this way renovate their entire approach to life so that their lives conformed to the likeness of Jesus.

Paul reasoned that the mind was the control center of one's ideas, attitudes, and desires (see Eph. 4:22-23). As Christians renounced the ways of the world (literally, "this age"; see Rom. 12:2), their minds were "transformed." This metamorphosis was not a onetime event, but a daily, ongoing process. As the Spirit remodeled the thinking of believers, they were better able to discern and recognize the Father's plan for them. There was nothing malevolent or self-serving about His intent for His children. Rather, the Creator's purposes were always beneficial, eternally satisfying, and impeccable. As Christians submitted to God's "perfect will," they matured as believers and led spiritually productive lives.

Minds shaped by Satan's evil system were characterized by haughtiness. So believers who failed to set aside the degenerate beliefs and actions of pagan society would probably demonstrate arrogance. In contrast, the mind shaped by the Spirit was characterized by humility. Because of the conflicts between saved Jews and Gentiles in the church at Rome, Paul exhorted his readers not to have an egotistic opinion of themselves or their importance within the body of Christ. Instead, they were to form an honest and objective estimate of their abilities in accordance with the amount of "faith" (vs. 3) God had provided for them. Here Paul showed the distinction between inflated self-esteem and healthy self-esteem. Exaggerated self-esteem could lead to arrogance. Oppositely, believers with appropriate self-esteem had an accurate perspective of their potential and limitations.

Dedicated, transformed Christians exhibited their regenerate lives through the effective use of spiritual gifts within the body of Christ. The human body was made up of many parts, and each of them had its own function (vs. 4). Similarly, the church had many members with different roles. Nonetheless, they were all united in Him as well to one another (vs. 5). Each member contributed in a different way to the common good of the whole body. Even though there was a diversity of functions within the body, they exhibited unity in purpose—namely, to survive and thrive together (see 1 Cor. 12:12-31). "Different gifts" (Rom. 12:6) refers to various special abilities the Spirit bestowed on believers to accomplish God's will (see 1 Cor. 12:4). Every Christian had at least one spiritual gift. In accordance with the grace the Lord had given them, they were to use their abilities to strengthen the body of Christ (see 14:26).

The special abilities named in Romans 12:6-8 are a representative list of the gifts the Spirit gave to believers (see 1 Cor. 12:8-10; 1 Pet. 4:10-11). For instance, those with the gift of prophesying were to communicate God's revealed truth to believers for their edification (Rom. 12:6). This and the other special abilities Paul mentioned were to be exercised in accordance with the measure of faith the Lord provided. Some had the gift of serving—that is, the ability to meet the needs of others in unique ways. Teaching refers to the ability to communicate biblical truth in a clear and relevant manner (vs. 7). Those gifted as encouragers were to provide reassurance or exhortation as needed (vs. 8). God enabled some believers to contribute significantly to those in need, and they were to do so generously. Others had a special ability to lead and govern the body of Christ, and they were to do so with devotion and enthusiasm. Finally, Christians with the gift of mercy were to be warmhearted and considerate, especially as they showed God's kindness to the disheartened.

The transformed pattern of Christian living Paul described in verses 9 through 21 was directly opposite to what the world (ruled by Satan) practiced. At the core of a Spirit-transformed and Spirit-empowered mind-set was self-giving, self-sacrificing "love." The word translates a Greek term that referred to the unwavering compassion God had for His children. This love denoted the reverence and submission believers had for God and the high esteem they displayed for their fellow human beings, especially other believers. While this word is not found in classical Greek at all, it is the most common word for love in the New Testament. It is perhaps the characteristic term of Christianity.

II. HOW WE DEMONSTRATE OUR DEVOTION TO JESUS: ROMANS 13:8-14

A. Showing Compassion: vss. 8-10

Let no debt remain outstanding, except the continuing debt to love one another, for he who loves his fellow-man has fulfilled the law. The commandments, "Do not commit adultery," "Do not murder," "Do not steal," "Do not covet," and whatever other commandment there may be, are summed up in this one rule: "Love your neighbor as yourself." Love does no harm to its neighbor. Therefore love is the fulfillment of the law.

In Romans 13:1-7, Paul taught that all the world's governments had been and always would be established by God's sovereign authority. So the apostle urged Christians to submit to governmental authority. After all, if Jesus' followers rebelled against their governmental authority, they were also rebelling against God. Perhaps Paul was responding to Christians who refused to submit to local governments by claiming loyalty only to Jesus. If so, the apostle rebuked such persons by claiming that if they were living as God's regenerate children, they had no reason to fear the governing authorities.

In verse 8, Paul stressed that Christians are duty bound to show "love" to all people. This reflects Jesus' teaching in Mark 12:29-31. He said the greatest commandment is to love God unconditionally and to love others as we love ourselves. Some Christians think Romans 13:8 prohibits all financial debt. Others maintain the verse leaves room for reasonable debt, such as an affordable home mortgage or car loan. In any case, we shouldn't stay in debt indefinitely. When believers pay off their debts in a timely fashion, they honor the Father and enhance the Son's reputation among the unsaved. The obligation to love others, however, can never be fully satisfied. There are always opportunities for Christians to help others in need (see Gal. 6:10). In fact, to refuse to assist the disadvantaged would be a denial of God's love for us (see 1 John 3:16-18). We ought to pay the debt of love even to those who do not love us. Of course, we must rely on the Spirit for the strength to be kind to those who are mean and coldhearted (see Gal. 5:22).

To unconditionally love others fulfills the requirements of Mosaic law. Romans 13:9 lists four of the Ten Commandments that appear in Exodus 20:1-17 and Deuteronomy 5:6-21, and these four all concern relationships with other people. The Lord forbids His children from committing adultery, murdering, stealing, and coveting the possessions of others. Paul could have mentioned numerous additional directives. This was unnecessary, though, for the command in Leviticus 19:18 sums up every conceivable law: "Love your neighbor as yourself." This mandate acknowledges a self-evident truth—namely, that we instinctively love ourselves. When we make every effort to treat others with the sensitivity and compassion of Jesus, we do what is prescribed in the law, for love is the essence of the law (Rom. 13:10).

When worldly people are mistreated, they usually desire vengeance. They may spend months or even years planning their revenge. During this period of stewing and plotting, bitterness eats away inside of them. If they succeed in their schemes, they are often astounded at the emptiness they feel. They expected a sense of vindication, and yet their heartache remains and, in most cases, has gotten even worse. In contrast, when the Savior's love rules in a believer's heart, that person will never desire another person's harm. Godly compassion for others leads to a fulfillment of all that the Mosaic legal code demands. As Christians, we should show the love of God in all of our relationships, even the difficult ones. By the power of the Spirit, we are able to wait for God's perfect justice. Just as Jesus loved us and gave His life for our eternal benefit, we also should reach out to others in a caring manner (see 1 John 4:7-11).

B. Living Virtuously: vss. 11-14

And do this, understanding the present time. The hour has come for you to wake up from your slumber, because our salvation is nearer now than when we first believed. The night is nearly over; the day is almost here. So let us put aside the deeds of darkness and put on the armor of light. Let us behave decently, as in the daytime, not in orgies and drunkenness, not in sexual immorality and debauchery, not in dissension and jealousy. Rather, clothe yourselves with the Lord Jesus Christ, and do not think about how to gratify the desires of the sinful nature.

As we have seen, Paul urged his readers to demonstrate Jesus' love in all their relationships. Since His return was near, His followers were to be consistently compassionate and kind to others (Rom. 13:11). So, instead of becoming spiritually lazy, they were to awaken from their lethargy and renew their commitment to serve the Lord. After all, the day of salvation was nearer now than when they had first put their faith in the Son. Love was their motivation, or their efforts would be nothing more than wasted time. Paul was not implying that his readers still needed to be converted, for in his letter he was addressing Christians. Rather, the apostle was referring to the final stage of salvation: glorification. While the Greek noun translated "salvation" is commonly used to refer to an initial conversion to faith in Jesus, it also denotes a spiritual process involving several steps. Among these are justification, sanctification, and glorification (see 8:20-21, 23, 30, and the commentary in lesson 10).

Paul referred to this present evil age as "night" (13:12) and to the time of Jesus' return as "day." Admittedly, no one knows the day or hour of the Son's second advent except the Father (see Mark 13:32). The duration might be long or short, but Jesus' return is certain to take place. With each passing moment, the consummation of His kingdom draws nearer. In light of this truth, Paul urged his readers to stop behaving like people who lived in spiritual "darkness" (Rom. 13:12). No longer were they to act as they did before they were saved. Instead, believers were (figuratively speaking) to clothe themselves with the weapons of "light." These were used to wage war against the spiritual forces of evil and unbelief (see Eph. 6:10-17; 1 Thess. 5:8).

As those who walked in the light of Jesus' redemptive presence, believers were to be characterized by virtue and honor. Paul provided three pairs of items defining activities the Christians were to shun. The first pair, "orgies and drunkenness" (Rom. 13:13), speaks of unbridled revelry. The second, "sexual immorality and debauchery," indicates carnal license. The third, "dissension and jealousy," deals with contention between individuals. When the believers at Rome trusted in Jesus for salvation, He renewed their minds and hearts through the work of the Spirit (see 12:1-2). Believers were to be as near to the Savior as the clothes they wore. Also, they were to purify themselves from even the thought of doing evil deeds (13:14).

By keeping Jesus first in their lives, Paul's readers could devote their full energy to serving and pleasing the Son. No longer would they try to satisfy the desires of their sinful state (literally, the "flesh"; see vs. 14). Instead, their actions would reflect the love and compassion of the Messiah abiding within them. Clearly, the life of those who followed the Lord was not to be characterized by selfish indulgence. Moreover, Jesus' followers were to put to death the inclinations of their old "nature" and allow the desires of their reborn inner selves to grow and flourish. Through the power of the Spirit, they could live for the Creator and act in ways that were virtuous.

Discussion Questions

    1. What is the world's way of thinking and acting?
    2. How should believers, when renewed by the Spirit, think and act?
    3. How has the Spirit transformed your preferences and priorities?
    4. In what ways does Christlike love fulfill the Mosaic law?
    5. What motivation did Paul give believers for living responsibly?

Contemporary Application

In the natural world, "blending in" can make a difference between life and death. Animals camouflage themselves to keep from being eaten, while other organisms hide themselves within the patterns of their environment to give them an advantage against clueless prey. Life for these creatures is all about staying hidden.

Sadly, Christians may try to "blend in" as well as animals and insects do. While it may be difficult to tell the difference between Christians and non-Christians by just looking at them, it should be possible to tell them apart by observing their lives. Paul called on believers at Rome to be so different from the world around them that they would no longer blend in to its corrupting pattern of behavior, but instead be transformed into new people who would serve Jesus instead of themselves and show compassion and kindness to others.

To live in a caring, empathetic way, Christians should reject pride and deceit and welcome all believers, regardless of their social status. Christians should always strive to live peacefully with everyone, but at times the actions and attitudes of others may make it impossible to maintain harmonious relations. Nevertheless, when concord is broken, a Christian should not be the cause of the failure. Peace could also result from believers showing love to their enemies, rather than seeking revenge against them.

INDEX OF PRINTED SCRIPTURE TEXTS

Below is a list of the printed Scripture texts for 2015–2016. They are arranged in the order in which they appear in the Bible, followed by the page number in this lesson book.